CW00518440

1 MONTH OF
FREE
READING

at

www.ForgottenBooks.com

By purchasing this book you are eligible for one month membership to ForgottenBooks.com, giving you unlimited access to our entire collection of over 1,000,000 titles via our web site and mobile apps.

To claim your free month visit:

www.forgottenbooks.com/free894654

* Offer is valid for 45 days from date of purchase. Terms and conditions apply.

ISBN 978-0-266-82268-4
PIBN 10894654

This book is a reproduction of an important historical work. Forgotten Books uses
state-of-the-art technology to digitally reconstruct the work, preserving the original format
whilst repairing imperfections present in the aged copy. In rare cases, an imperfection in
the original, such as a blemish or missing page, may be replicated in our edition. We do,
however, repair the vast majority of imperfections successfully; any imperfections that
remain are intentionally left to preserve the state of such historical works.

Forgotten Books is a registered trademark of FB &c Ltd.
Copyright © 2018 FB &c Ltd.
FB &c Ltd, Dalton House, 60 Windsor Avenue, London, SW19 2RR.
Company number 08720141. Registered in England and Wales.

For support please visit www.forgottenbooks.com

THIRTIETH ANNUAL REPORT

OF THE

FRUIT-GROWERS' ASSOCIATION

OF

ONTARIO.

1898

(PUBLISHED BY THE ONTARIO DEPARTMENT OF AGRICULTURE, TORONTO.)

PRINTED BY ORDER OF

THE LEGISLATIVE ASSEMBLY OF ONTARIO.

TORONTO.
WARWICK BRO'S & RUTTER, PRINTERS &c., 68 AND 70 FRONT ST. WEST.
1899.

CONTENTS

THIRTIETH ANNUAL REPORT

OF THE

FRUIT GROWERS' ASSOCIATION OF ONTARIO.

1898.

To the Honorable John Dryden, Minister of Agriculture :

SIR,—I have the honor to submit for your approval the Thirtieth Annual Report of the Fruit Growers' Association of Ontario. The discussions therein contained are upon matters of great importance to the Fruit Growers of our Province, such as the best export markets and the best and most economical methods of transportation.

I am, Sir,

Your obedient servant,

L. WOOLVERTON,
Secretary.

GRIMSBY, January, 1899.

1 F.G.

FRUIT GROWERS' ASSOCIATION OF ONTARIO.

OFFICERS FOR 1899.

President,—W. E. WELLINGTON, Toronto.
Vice-President.—W. M. ORR, Fruitland.

Directors.

District No. 1 .... W. A. WHITNEY, Iroquois.
     "   2 .... R. B. WHYTE, Ottawa.
     ·· 3 .... GEO. NICOL, Cataraqui.
     ·· 4 .... W. BOULTER, Picton.
        5 .... THOS. BEALL, Lindsay.
        6 .... E. C. BEMAN, Newcastle.
     ·· 7 .... M. PETTIT, Winona.
     ·· 8 .... A. M. SMITH, St. Catharines.
        9 .... J. S. SCARFF, Woodstock.
       10 .... J. I. GRAHAM, Vandeleur.
     ·· 11 .... T. H. RACE, Mitchell.
     ·· 12 .... ALEX. McNEILL, Walkerville.
     ·· 13 .... G. C. CASTON, Craighurst.

Auditors.—A. H. PETTIT, Grimsby ; GEO. E. FISHER, Freeman.

FRUIT GROWERS' ASSOCIATION OF ONTARIO.

The annual meeting was held in Court House, St. Catharines, on December 1st and 2nd, 1898.

The President, Mr. W. E. Wellington, took the chair, after which the following committees were duly appointed :

Fruit Exhibit : Messrs. A. H. Pettit, A. M. Smith and Edward Morris.

Resolutions : Messrs. M. Burrell and Thos. Beall.

New Fruits : Profs. H. L. Hutt, W. T. Macoun, the President and the Secretary.

Nominations : Messrs. Alex. McNeill and T. H. Race (by the President), and Messrs. Murray Pettit, R. B. Whyte and G. C. Oaston (by the Association).

FRAUDS IN FRUITS AT FAIRS.

By A. M. Smith, St. Catharines.

It has always been the mission and aim of this Association to advance the interests of fruit growing and to encourage any object or project calculated to benefit the fruit grower; and the work that it has done in the past gives ample evidence that its mission has not been in vain. When we compare fruit growing of to-day with what it was forty years ago in this Canada of ours, and see what rapid advancement it has made, and realize that it has largely been accomplished by the efforts of this Association in introducing varieties adapted to our country, and new methods of cultivation, fertilization and combatting insect enemies and diseases affecting fruit, and devising better methods of packing, transporting and marketing, we can but wonder it has done so much ; indeed we almost wonder if it can do any more, until we take up the programme before us to-day and see on it such questions as " How can we prevent fraudulent packing ? " " How can we punish the dishonest packer ? " and the subject assigned to me : " Frauds in Fruits at Fairs." All this suggests that there is a moral side to this business that has not been sufficiently cultivated, and which needs attention. I believe it is just as much the duty of this Association to introduce good *morals* among fruit growers and assist in their cultivation as it is to develop good *fruit*, and it is as much their duty to point out and warn the public of the evils of fraud and deception in packing, marketing and exhibiting fruit and trying to prevent it as it is to warn the public of the danger from insect pests and fungoid diseases and how to exterminate them. If we could devise some effectual means of exterminating these evils we would confer a greater good upon the public at large as well as on fruit growers, than we have by any act in the past. I shall not attempt to answer the questions regarding dishonest packing, but would simply remark that a man who would show fruit at a fair as his own that his neighbor grew, would be able, perhaps, to throw some light on the question if so disposed, or at least be well acquainted with the business.

Although the Fruit Growers' Association of Ontario does not give prizes at horticultural exhibitions and fairs, it always takes a deep interest in them, believing if they are rightly conducted they are a great means of educating the people in fruit growing and they have taken great pains in formulating and publishing tables giving the relative value of fruits for the guidance of judges at fairs ; and they have often recommended to directors of fairs suitable persons to act as judges, and it is with chagrin they see anything on

[3]

the part of either directors, judges, or exhibitors that indicates unfairness to any one, or fraud in any individual for the sake of gain. But that there is fraud, if not perjury, at many, if not all of our fairs in connection with fruit exhibits, I think no one who is familiar with fruit exhibits will deny. There is a certain class of exhibitors whom you might term professionals, who grow very little, if any, fruit themselves, but who buy, beg or *borrow*—to use a mild expression—all the best samples the country affords, and go from one fair to another showing them as their own production, and raking in the prizes— sometimes they go singly, and sometimes they club together and divide the spoils. I have even heard of their getting themselves put on as judges when, from some cause the appointed judge was absent, and judging fruit they were interested in themselves. I think it is one of the rules of all Agricultural Societies that the grain, vegetables and fruit must be grown by the exhibitor, and he must swear or certify to that effect when making his entries. Now, if a neighbor of mine shows fruit grown on my trees, no matter how he comes by it, and signs a certificate that it is his own growing, what would you call it ? I know many men do this who would not like to be called dishonest or guilty of fraud, and they argue that they are not defrauding the Society, as they would have to pay the prizes to someone in any case ; but they do not stop to think they are defrauding their neighbor and obtaining money under false pretences. I fear that, in many cases, directors wink at this kind of work and think it helps the show to get out these fine displays. I think they make a mistake even in this regard, for this practice has become so prevalent that many honest fruit growers will not bring out their fruit to compete against these professional prize takers, and thus many of our best fruits are kept back from exhibition. If directors of fairs are going to allow this sort of thing, let them amend their rules so as not to make men swear falsely and encourage them in dishonesty. I have noticed, with pain, that many of our young men are getting into this business. They are naturally anxious to attend fairs, and here is an opening to pay their way, have a good time and make a little money out of it besides, so they fall into the temptation.

I do not know what means to recommend to exterminate this evil, but I think this Association should at least enter its protest against such a state of affairs, and the officers of all agricultural societies should so amend and enforce their rules that these frauds may be suppressed.

Mr. BURRELL, (St. Catharines) : I always understood it was a rule at fairs that visitors should exhibit what they grow themselves. I understand, however, that at Toronto Fair you have not to sign a declaration of that kind. It is very hard to refuse a neighbor who comes in for some specimens as he is making up a variety. It is difficult when there is a rule that exhibitors must sign a declaration that the fruit is their own growing.

Mr. SMITH : Of course there are certain collections open to the general public ; but if there is not such a rule as that, and you do not have to sign a document of that kind, I would like to know it.

THE PRESIDENT : Being a Director, and also Chairman of the Fruit Committee of the Toronto Fair, I would say that the rules and regulations are that all exhibits must be the *bona fide* produce of or grown by the exhibitor. We do not go the length of asking every man to make a declaration to that effect, but if we are shown on complaint of an exhibitor, or anyone in fact, that fruit so exhibited at the Exhibition was not grown by the exhibitor, that fruit would be ruled out and not be passed upon. It is just the same way in the naming of varieties. The rule is very strict in that respect, and it lies in the hands of the judges to throw out any exhibit, no matter how meritorious it may be, if there is one wrongly named plate in the collection, for instance. It seems sometimes a little hard. The idea is to have all fruit exhibited true to name, because we wish as far as it is possible to make the exhibition an educator in the fruit interests, and we think that centered there in Toronto where the large exhibits are made everything should be correct ; and the judges who are present in the room know that I have always, hard as the case made be, insisted that the rule be strictly adhered to in that regard. Of course if it were thought necessary, or in the interest of the fruit growers, that a declaration should accompany every exhibit we would take measures to carry that out.

Mr. ORR, (Fruitland) : I think the object of giving awards for fruit exhibits is to encourage growers to grow the very best fruit that they can grow. As far as Toronto Fair is concerned, I think the fruit exhibited should be strictly the produce of the party exhibiting. Probably that does not apply to counties, at the Toronto and London Fairs where we have people from all parts of the world, many from neighboring States, I think we ought to have the very best possible exhibit irrespective of who is the grower. Whether it would be desirable to have another class for exhibits of that kind I don't know, but I don't think we should hamper having the very best possible exhibit gathered from where you will, where so many people see the exhibit and see the products of our country.

Mr. BURRELL : I think Mr. Orr's objection is well taken. I only spoke because I think that if there is a stipulation of that kind, whether it is expressed in the way of requiring a declaration on the part of the exhibitor or not, it should be made more emphatic, because if a man is going to show what he does not grow when there is a rule against it, then he may just as well perjure himself right out by making a declaration, and that will keep any man who feels a little dubious about doing it ; but I would have it right open or else have him sign a declaration. and I would make it clear. The thing should be stated either one way or the other. I think Mr. Orr's views are correct as far as Toronto is concerned.

THE PRESIDENT : I may point out that it does not prevent us from having an exhibit that will really show what can be done in Canada no matter where the fruit is grown, because there is a class at present open to Societies. It is a class we have been trying to encourage of late years. That of course enables them to gather the best specimens of fruit in their district, and consequently in that exhibit you have the best the land produces, while in the other class where there is individual competition you have what I think is only fair, the actual growth by the exhibitor. Of course I am your representative there, and if this meeting wishes that that clause should be done away with I could take means to have it done, but with the open classes that there are at present I don't think it would be advisable.

Mr. BURRELL : The only open classes now are for Societies ?

THE PRESIDENT : That is all.

Mr. BURRELL : That has only led to two Societies, Oakville and Burlington, exhibiting, and that is over an immense range of fruits that no one man is likely to touch ; and it is in the small selections where this thing is done. I think it should be thrown open— either no declaration at all wanted, or a declaration wanted, so as to leave no half way. Have no clause at all, or else have a clause expressly stating, and have a man sign it when he makes his entry.

A. MCNEILL, (Walkerville) : Would that it were possible to get back to the good old classic times when they used to compete for the glory of the thing. I would like to see the rules framed so as to throw more on the honor of the person exhibiting, and that less stress should be placed on the money question. It is not desirable even for the purpose of securing a good exhibit of fruit that this class of men should be encouraged.

We as Canadians have a reputation which I think without undue modesty we can claim, of being honest, and as far as the regulations can be framed to put down that kind of thing and secure honesty in that respect the better. I think the Toronto people have done well in putting a premium upon the exhibits of fruit from Horticultural Societies, and more stress should be laid upon that. Horticultural Societies should look to the educational value of these collections, and look upon it as part of their legitimate work to make the exhibits and to make them educative. Less stress should be laid upon the money side and more upon the credit of having a good exhibit for the individuals and the societies and the country in they which live.

Mr. ORR : When we get rich and can do as they did in the classic land, where the members of Parliament served without money, and it was all honor, and they could afford to live for honor, all right ; but I am satisfied it would very seriously interfere with our exhibits at the fairs if the prizes were done away with. I know men that go out in their orchard, and up and down the country gathering fruits that no society would do, and I know these men get together splendid exhibits that are a credit to our country, and I do think it would be well to have a class just for that kind of thing.

Mr. A. M. SMITH : You will often see men going through the country begging or borrowing or buying fruit—an: they have the excuse, that they are gathering for certain societies—that there is a class, as there is in Toronto, open to the general public or any association or society. They go through the country and gather up this selection of fruit, and a very close observer will often find some of that fruit on a plate of private individuals, shown as their own producing. I know what I am taking about, because I have seen some of my own fruit shown in that way, that I had taken pains to fix so that I could identify it.

Mr. CASTON (Craighurst) : Mr. Smith's paper was aimed at what may be called the professional exhibitor, and we have a number of them. At the Industrial this fall one of the experimenters told me that a party there wanted to purchase the best selection of the fruit and offered him a pretty good figure for it, and he asked me what I thought about it, and I said "The best thing is to sit on him and sit on him heavy too." He was one of these professionals. They follow up the fairs as long as they last during the fall. It is a money business with them. If, as Mr. McNeill suggested, we do away with the money prizes and have people exhibit for the honor of the thing in the shape of medals or diplomas, there would not be that inducement to these professionals, as there would be no money in it for them. On the other hand, as Mr. Orr' suggests, we would not have as many exhibitors if the money prizes were withdrawn. It is rather a troublesome question to deal with, and I hardly know how we are going to get at that class to stamp them out.

Mr. ROBT. THOMPSON (St. Catharines) : I don't think we can stamp them out. As far as making a declaration is concerned, the rules of all societies at present are that any person, any other exhibitor, can make a protest against one of these professional men. How often is it done? When it is done, in 99 cases out of a 100 these professionals will take that declaration and swear that the article is their own growth and produced on their own place. If this declaration were made compulsory when they are making the entry, Mr. Burrell would have some good fruit and of course he would exhibit as his own. The professional will do the same thing. They have done it in the past and will do it in the future. I am sorry we cannot confine it to the growers, but with my experience of fairs I know that it is impossible to do it, and, as Mr. Orr says, it would work detrimental to our fruit exhibit. I believe that all the large exhibits should be thrown open and that clause done away with, because I am satisfied it will never be observed.

Mr. BURRELL : I am inclined to think those ideas are right as far as the Provincial show goes. I believe we can shut out all those men in the different localities, because they are known and it is known what they grow, but at Toronto you will never shut down on them altogether, and I would say either push it so as to make it very stringent or else let it go. I would ask Mr. Smith his views on ringing grapes. Everyone in Toronto who is a judge of grapes must know that the majority of the prizes in Toronto go to the grapes that are ringed. We all know the process. Is that to be upheld? Lots of the prizes this year were to be given for grapes that any man knows had been ringed. That is certainly a very unfair thing to the man that shows the grape in its natural state.

THE PRESIDENT : If the meeting feel that that should be looked after it would be a very easy matter to stop it by giving the judges power and authority to throw out all ringed grapes, which would soon bring that to an end. It is simply a question now whether you think they should be thrown out.

Mr. BURRELL : Many men do not ring their graspes because they do not think it is a fair way of competing, and at the same time they know they will not get the prize unless they do ring them. Eyerybody should understand that they will be allowed to ring them. One judge told a competitor who was complaining that he did not get a prize, ". You ought to ring them."

Mr. Caston : Do you think that the judges can always determine ?

Mr. Burrell : I do not say you always can. but there are many cases where there is absolutely no doubt about it.

Mr. Caston : I should think it would be very difficult for a judge to decide.

Mr. Burrell : Sometimes it is very difficult, but it is sometimes very easy.

Mr. Huggard (Whitby) : If we were to adopt the system Mr. Burrell advocates, the best in fruits would not be exhibited at all. That is, giving none of the prizes to grapes that were ringed. It would apply equally to all manner of cattle, and horses, and stock ; the better you feed it and the better you doctor it up, it would make it win a prize all the sooner. I don't see any reason why, if a man goes to the trouble to ring his grape vines and produce a few clusters of extra good grapes, it would not be equivalent to another man who would pick most of the pears off his pear tree and bring in a few choice ones of very extra ones. You would have to prevent the one just as much as the other. My notion is to let everybody bring the best that they can possibly produce ; but have a specific rule and see that it is carried out, that in the case of any one begging, borrowing, or stealing fruit that is not his own, the prizes should be withheld. The majority of the exhibitors send in their exhibits for the money value that is in the prize. Our township people go there for the purpose of getting money out of the exhibitions, and if they are awarded the prize and don't get it, no matter how trifling it is, you will hear a great deal of squealing against the association or society. I think the best way that an association can do is to encourage growing grapes of the largest possible kind, whether ringed or otherwise, and the best of every kind of fruit that we are capable of producing, and if a rule which is severe enough now is applied to these professionals who collect fruit through the districts and exhibit it as their own, they will soon drop out.

R. B. Whyte (Ottawa) : It seems to be a question whether the ringed grapes are the best. I think it is generally understood that they are bad in flavor, and would never be bought by anybody in competition with other grapes ; therefore ringed grapes should be prohibited. They are large and watery and of poor flavour. In our Horticultural Society we had a little trouble with exhibitors by requiring every member in making his entry to sign a declaration that all articles exhibited by him were of his own growth. We have not had a bit of trouble this year. I cannot see any object in having an exhibition at all if it is not the production of the individual grower. I do not think we can take a better way of having a small exhibition than by allowing people to go about and collect what they do not grow. There are some fruit men along the St. Lawrence that gather up wherever they can. Our Horticultural Committee are trying to stop that, but the fact in the past has been that the local fruit growers did not gather in competition because they had no chance with those men that gather wherever they can. It deterred so many people from exhibiting that it had the effect of making a smaller exhibition than we otherwise would have.

A. H. Pettit (Grimsby) : I think every exhibitor in a local show should sign a certificate that his fruits are his own product. I think it is very unfair to individual growers who want to make an exhibit of their own products at the fair to come in competition with those who come from all over the country ; but I do think it is quite necessary to have in our exhibitions, particularly in Toronto, a sort of go-as-you-please class, where a man can collect the products of the whole country if he wants to and show them ; but I would put that exhibit in this way, that everything should be very correctly named. We don't want a lot of fruits in this class exhibited to the public given fictitious or other incorrect names. Why ? Because that is exhibited as an educator of the people ; it is there for that purpose ; it is to show the resources of our country and the variety of fruit we can successfully cultivate, and I think it is a good thing to have it, for the reason that you get a big exhibit of this great Dominion of ours at that exhibition, and I think that is what we want, but the individual who is showing his own product wants to be protected by this form of declaration that they are his own product. As to the grape question, I have been a judge on several occasions, and I say that if you passed a rule that ringed grapes are to be ruled out, there should be a very plain card placed on every one of those plates, and the judge should write on that card in plain language that they are ringed grapes ; for if the public passing by the tables and seeing the work that you have left behind you, all the finest plates upon the table ruled out, want to know what is the matter ? They will tell you at once you do not understand your business. The plates look a great deal better than those you have given the prizes to. Now, here you are educating the people. Let us do it properly if you are going to do it ; let ringed grapes be plainly marked so that people can see why judges rule them out. In an exhibition to show what we can produce in this country I don't know that you should rule out ringed grapes any more than you would an animal that was overly fat. You see lots of animals shown at these exhibitions that we know are too fat for breeding purposes, and your ringed grapes come the same way—they are a little too large in size to have that quality and flavor that is so desirable. If we look at the exhibitions as an educational institution, let us encourage them along the educational lines as much as we can, and give a go-as-you-please class for Societies, requiring that every fruit in it be correctly named. Then if we protect the individual grower that has to come in competition with this class of exhibitors I think you will come pretty nearly to the right thing.

M. PETTIT (Winona) ; I have judged grapes for the last fifteen or twenty years, and I defy any man to say in every instance whether grapes have been ringed or not. If a vine has been ringed very early the grape will appear very bloated and the flavor insipid, but if you ring it later on you will increase the size and color and no judge can tell whether it has been ringed or not, there are so many degrees of it, depending on the time and the season at which the vine has been ringed. The prize list says " the best." My experience in judging and working with other judges is that those very large overgrown grapes do not always get the prize. For my own part I very often go for throwing them out where there are better flavored and nice even grapes in the same class, and I have just made it stand that way. It works all right. We show people fine fruit, and if the judges do their duty they go there and show the people what good fruit is, and the kind of fruit that should be put upon the market and upon the tables should be well colored, well flavored fruit. (Applause.)

Mr. BURRELL : I do not think it is quite fair to argue, as Mr. Huggard and Mr. Pettit did, that ringing was a sort of natural process. I don't care whether grapes are ringed or not in Toronto Fair as long as everybody is allowed to exhibit them ; but the ringing of grapes is not an normal process like the thinning of fruit, or the fattening of cattle. If I were to use a comparison I would say, suppose an animal eats a bushel of grain and gets very fat, but it is going to die in twenty minutes, it would not be fair to exhibit it. It is not an normal or healthy process.

Mr. McNEILL : Nor a commercial process.

Mr. BURRELL : No. If they admit ringing, all right, but let everybody ring, because otherwise it is competing on an unfair basis.

The PRESIDENT : Unless you wish to take some definite action on the matter, which I should judge from the discussion could hardly be done, we will have to close the question here. Judges will have to take this matter into consideration, as they always do.

IS FRUIT GROWING CONDUCTIVE TO MORALITY ?

BY F. G. H. PATTISON, GRIMSBY.

In introducing his paper the writer said : Before reading this paper, I would like to say I do not wish it to be taken too seriously. It has been my misfortune sometimes, notably at Kingston, to have my serious papers taken in a jocular strain. I don't wish that to be taken in an opposite way—that a paper that is intended to be taken in a slightly jocular strain should be regarded from a too serious standpoint. It is peculiarly fortunate to the interest of this paper that I am about to read that Mr. Smith has already directed your attention to frauds in fruit at fairs. In this short paper, it is my object to throw what I think is a new light upon the temptations and the difficulties surrounding the business of fruit growing, and one which the general public, and also fruit growers themselves, have entirely ignored up to the present time. My proposition is this : That there is an inherent original sin in fruit itself, which exposes those who plant it in the nursery, those who grow it in the orchard, and those who sell it on the market, to peculiar trials and temptations. On looking back to the earlier stages of the human race, we are told in the story of the Garden of Eden how the Devil, in the guise of a serpent, entered into, not a cabbage, nor a potato, but an apple ; and since then, apparently, not only apples but all other fruits, although pleasant to the eye, and seductive to the palate, have retained that primeval devilishness. If this be *not* the case, how do we account for many well-known facts relating to the fruit business ? For example, the way in which the large apples, peaches, strawberries, etc , find their way to the top of the basket, and the small, wormy, and bruised ones to the bottom. The outside public say that the growers put them there. I know this to be erroneous, because the growers have told me that they do not, and I will undertake to say that if one of the outside public were to ask any fruit grower in the whole Province if he put the large ones at the top and the little ones at the bottom of a basket or barrel, he would reject the idea with scorn. But the public say that the large apples, etc., *do* come to the top and the small etc., to the bottom. Are we then to consider the public as liars ? By no means. This seemingly inconsistent state of affairs had long puzzled me, until I was led to make the following experiment. I collected a basket of fruit and put it by itself in the fruit house, carefully placing the small and poor specimens at the top, and the large fine ones at the bottom. It was then left by itself for two or three days, without being watched or interfered with. At the expiration of that time, upon examination, the large ones were all at the top and the little ones at the bottom. This experiment has been repeated several times, with a similar result. It is true that certain scoffers have suggested the children as the authors of this strange metamorphosis, failing them that it was owing to rats. But to both of these objections I think " rats " is the proper reply. I am forced, then, to the following conclusion, viz : That if fruit in a basket or other package be left to itself and remain quiescent for a considerable period, that the big ones will work themselves to the top, and the small, wormy ones to the bottom. Now to prevent this requires great watchfulness and care on the part of the grower, added to high moral principle, and the purchaser little knows what a struggle has been gone through, what a moral victory gained, when he remarks, on examination of a basket of fruit he has purchased from the store, " Why, I have actually got a basket that is good all through ! " But this same character follows the fruit into the hands of the commission men and retail dealers. How else do we account for the marvelous discrepancies between the actual sales and the growers' returns therefrom, of which great complaints are being continually made ? No doubt the commission men are an honourable body, but, unless the moral qualities of people handling fruit are unusually strong, the innate devilishness of the fruit itself overcome them. For to the commission man the fruit-devil whispers : " That was a splendid sale you made, but you need not return the full amount to the grower. Ten per cent. is but a beggarly amount to receive for a sale like that, owing to *your* energy and business capacity, besides he will be satisfied with much less." And too often this fruit-devil is listened to, the commissionman falls, and the grower suffers.

Look at the number of "wet," " slack " and ".wasty "returns that come back from the old country. Think you that there is no fruit-devil at work there ? I am afraid that the English commissionman too often, like his Canadian *confrere*, does not exhibit sufficient moral fibre to withstand his temptations. Even in the nursery row fruit trees exhibit their evil propensity, for which some blame the nurserymen, who are in the main a fine body of men of more lofty principle, who would scorn of themselves to do anything wrong, and yet, varieties first-class when planted, turn out but third class at bearing time, ironclads fail to resist the slightest frost, and prodigious bearers decline to bear anything. Plenty of other instances might be brought forward in support of my discovery; but why take up more of your time ? The more you study the matter, the more you will see the truth of my discovery, and the more apparent it will be that high moral principle is the first requisite for the fruit business ; and it is much to the credit of the noble body of men now engaged in the business that matters are not worse than they are, that occasionally the fruit at the bottom of a basket is not much worse than at the top, and that sometimes there are no wormy or bruised apples at the bottom of a barrel.

What, then, should be done to remedy this state of affairs ? Firstly, gentlemen, let us be thankful that this discovery has been made ; now that we know the real cause we can take measures for its prevention and cure. Secondly, a board should be appointed by the Government, selected from our highest and most moral citizens, to award certificates of moral character to anyone about to engage in handling fruit or fruit stock. Thirdly, no one should be allowed to engage in growing or selling fruit or fruit stock without such a certificate Fourthly, the writer should be president of the board at a handsome salary. Fifthly, no fruit package should be left alone for any considerable period. By the adoption of these measures we can, in time, attain to perfect honesty ; and, instead of its being a matter of surprise for a private purchaser to receive an honest basket of fruit, it will be the most ordinary, every-day occurrence.

OBSERVATIONS ON RUSSIAN FRUITS AT THE CENTRAL EXPERIMENTAL FARM, 1898.

By W. T. Macoun, Horticulturist, Central Experimental Farm, Ottawa.

It is a great pleasure for me to be with you this morning. It is the first time that I have had the pleasure of attending a meeting of the Ontario Fruit Growers' Association. Knowing as I do full well the high esteem in which you held Mr. Craig, the late Horticulturist of the Farm, I feel that without your sympathy and co operation the work that I may do there will not be such as if I felt you were all my friends.

Before giving my observations on Russian fruits for 1898, let me relate the history of these fruits as grown at the Central Experimental Farm, Ottawa.

A large number of Russian fruits have now been tested for ten years at the Central Experimental Farm. In the year 1888 there were planted in the orchards 133 supposed varieties of apples, twenty-eight of pears, eight of plums, and thirty-eight of cherries. Since that time others have been added at intervals, and notwithstanding those that have been winter-killed, there are now about 160 supposed varieties of apples in the orchard, eighteen of pears, twenty-eight of cherries, and seven of plums. A few of the apple trees planted in 1888 fruited in 1890. The trees did well and made vigorous growth up to the year 1892, when blight appeared in the pear orchard and continued to spread throughout the summer and autumn, notwithstanding all efforts to hold it in check. All the Russian varieties of pears were affected, twenty-five trees being killed to the ground. The apples were also affected that year, though not so seriously. In 1893 the disease appeared earlier in the season and committed great ravages, both among the apples and the pears. Many apple trees were reduced to stubs, while the pears were still more badly injured than in 1892. This left these orchards in a very dilapidated condition. Some trees had died altogether, others were reduced to stumps, and again others which had large diseased limbs sawn off, had lost their symmetry. The trees were not so much affected in 1894 and 1895, but owing to the severity of the winter of 1895-6 a large number were root killed ; the last of the pear trees originally planted going at that time. Further injury from root-killing occured in the winter of 1896-7. During the past two seasons, most of the apples and pears which have been replaced, made good growth, and some of the apple trees which were badly affected by blight are regaining symmetrical proportions. Out of about 288 apple trees planted in 1888, there are now 149 trees living, 139 having died, of which 104 died in the spring of 1896, twenty-seven in the spring of 1897, and eight this year.

The cherries did well at first, beginning to fruit in 1890. In 1895 a very fine crop was produced, but during the following winter nearly all of the trees were root-killed. This was owing, in a large measure, to their being grafted on tender stocks. Since that time they have been propagated to some extent on Bird Cherry (*Prunus pennsylvanica*) stock. Some trees propagated on this stock in 1891 continue to do well. An exception to the almost general winter-killing of the cherries in 1895 6 was the Koslov Morello, sent out by the Ontario Fruit Growers' Association in 1890. Out of twenty-four trees only five died from the effects of that winter. These cherries are, however, on their own roots. The Russian plums planted in 1888 have all been winter-killed with the exception of two trees, Early Red and Voronesh No. 102, although these two trees are not very healthy. Other varieties have been planted of late years and some of these are still doing fairly well.

Russian Fruits, 1898 : Last winter was not a hard one on trees and there were scarcely any losses. Most of the trees in the Russian apple orchard, which were old enough, produced a good crop of fruit this year. Owing to the extremely hot, dry weather the summer apples—to which class nearly all the Russian varieties belong—dropped very badly. The trees on the whole made fair growth. No blight was noticed. About fifty varieties among those planted in 1898 and 1890 look thrifty, but some of these are evidently synonyms, which would reduce this somewhat.

Of the varieties which fruited this year, the following seem to be the most promising: Livland Raspberry, (Melonen). There seems to be no difference between these apples as grown at the Experimental Farm. Tree, upright, fairly vigorous ; fruit, medium size, roundish, conical ; skin, pale yellow, well splashed and washed with bright red ; flesh, white, tinged with pink near skin, firm, crisp, juicy, sub-acid, pleasant flavor ; good quality. Ripe, August 3rd.

Switzer : The Switzer grown at the Experimental Farm does not color so highly as that grown by Mr. R. W. Shepherd of Como, Que. Tree, moderately upright, fairly vigorous ; fruit, medium size, oblate ; skin, pale green, almost white, firm, crisp, juicy, sub acid ; good flavor with a high aroma ; very good quality. Ripe, August 10th.

Pointed Pipka (Summer Arabka, Broad Cheek, Throne, 135 M. Budd): All the trees under these names seem to be of the same variety. Tree spreading vigorous, fruit above medium size, oblong, conical, ribbed ; skin, pale yellow, well splashed and streaked with purplish-red ; flesh, white, rather coarse, juicy, mild sub acid, pleasant flavor, good quality.

Romna (Hibernal, Aport, 244 Beadle, Longfield 56 M.—not Longfield as generally grown—Silken Leaf): These are all apparently the same apple, as grown at the Experimental Farm. Tree, vigorous, spreading ; fruit, above medium size, sometimes large, oblate, conical ; skin, greenish-yellow, streaked and splashed with purplish-red ; flesh, yellow, tender, melting, juicy, acid ; quality, medium. Ripe last week in September. This is more valuable as a cooking apple than as a dessert fruit. It is one of the most vigorous trees that we have, but not more so than McMahan White, which, in my opinion, is a better apple.

Plikanoff : Tree, planted 1893, vigorous, spreading. Fruited for the first time this year, Fruit, large, roundish, slightly conical ; skin, yellow, well washed with bright red and splashed with a darker shade ; flesh, yellowish, tinged with red, rather coarse, fairly juicy, sub acid, good flavor ; good quality. Season, probably October.

Repka Winter : Tree, upright, fairly vigorous : fruit, above medium size, oblate, flat-tened ; skin, yellowish-green lightly streaked and splashed with purplish-red ; flesh, white, crisp, fairly juicy, mild sub-acid ; quality, medium. Will probably keep until February.

Antonovka Though sometimes favourably mentioned, this will, on account of its lack of color—it being a yellow apple—probably not be a profitable variety.

Winter Arabka : Did not fruit here this year. It is considered one of the best of the Russian varieties, and is a winter apple.

The Switzer and Pointed Pipka are the only two varieties fruiting this year which can compare with dessert apples of their season in the best apple districts of Ontario.

Other varieties favorably spoken of by those who have tested the Russian varieties in Canada are :—Stettin Red, Gipsy Girl, Titovka, Flat Aport, Amtmann, Boradovki, Belin, and St. Peters.

In the year 1890 a Russian seedling orchard was planted comprising about 3,000 trees grown from seed imported from E. Goegginger, Riga, Russia. The seed from which these were grown was supposed to be taken from apples grown North of Riga. Of these there are now 1,016 remaining, the rest having been killed either by blight or winter. These began to fruit last year, and this year about sixty trees bore fruit. None of these apples are sufficiently promising to be worthy of special mention, but a few of them are as good as the majority of the Russian varieties. These will be further tested at Ottawa, and scions sent to the farms at Brandon and Indian Head, to determine whether they are hardy there or not. The rest of the trees which fruited this year will be cut out.

PEARS : The Russian pears, planted since 1895, have done well and have not been much affected by blight since that time. Only one variety, the Baba, fruited in the pear orchard this year, but two others, Gliva Kurskays and Sapieganka—which have borne heavy crops annually in the Director's experimental garden for some years—were again loaded this year. The Russian pears yet tested at Ottawa are in season but a very short period when they get soft and mealy. If used at the proper time, they are fairly good to eat raw and are very nice when preserved, but are not worth planting where other varieties will succeed.

PLUMS : The Europeans plums have not done well in the orchard at the Experimental Farm. The situation is very exposed and the trees have suffered severely. This year four Russian varieties fruited, namely, White Nicholas, Early Red, Voronesh (blue) and Yellow Voronesh. All of these but Voronesh (blue) are of good quality. The Yellow Voronesh is almost as large as Yellow Egg and of somewhat the same shape, is juicy, sweet, and of good flavor ; cling stone ; good quality. Ripe, August 22nd. Two of the hardiest of the European class of plums yet tested are the Glass Seedling and Richard Trotter.

CHERRIES : Of the cherries planted in the orchard from 1888 to 1895, the following varieties have survived—Strauss, Minnesota Ostheim, Ostheim, Cerise d'Ostheim, No. 207, Koslov Morello, Heart-shaped Weichsel, Orel 24, Orel 27, Riga 18, Shadow Amarelle, No. 206, Orel 25, Griotte du Nord, Spate Amarelle, Brusseler Braun, June Amarelle, Lutovka, Amarelle Hative. Most of the trees of those varieties which were planted in 1888 do not look as if they would live much longer. These trees are on tender stocks. Trees of a number of varieties in a nursery row, propagated on *Prunus pennsylvanica* in 1891, are very healthy and produced a heavy crop of fruit this year, as did also most of the other cherry trees which were old enough to bear. The best of the European and Russian cherries ripened in the following order this year : Amarelle Hative, June 26th ; June Amarelle, July 2nd ; Shadow Amarelle, July 3rd ; Heart-shaped Weichsel, July 8th ; Griotte du Nord, July 8th ; Orel, July 25th ; Cerise d'Ostheim, July 12th ; Brusseler Braun, July 25th ; Koslov Morello, July 26th. These cherries gave a continuous succession of fruit for about five weeks. The apparent gap between July 12th and July 25th is filled up by the Ostheim, the fruit of which ripened rather unevenly this year.

The Koslov bush Morello cherries, received from the Ontario Fruit Growers' Association in 1890, deserve special mention. These little, bush-like trees, after eight years' growth, now average only about 5 feet 6 feet in height. There are 21 trees yet living out of the original planting. Of these, 15 produced fruit this year, nearly all of which appear to be different. This is the first year that they have fruited to any extent, although planted for eight years. Most of the trees produced fruit of inferior quality, some being bitter, and others very acid. Two of the most promising, on account of their hardiness and lateness in ripening, are the following Koslov Morello (R. 6, T. 29). Tree, bushy, height, 5 feet 6 inches. Heavy crop ; fruit large, long, heart-shaped, slightly flattened, firm ; stalk, very long, slender ; suture, rather indistinct ; skin, deep red ; flesh, deep red, juicy, very acid ; pit, large, long. Ripe, July 20th. Would probably make a good preserving cherry.

Koslov Morello (R. 6, T. 27) : Tree, bushy, height 6 feet 6 inches. Fair crop ; fruit, large, heart-shaped, rather deep red, firm ; stalk, long, stout ; suture, distinct ; flesh, bright red, very acid ; pit, large, oval, flat. Ripe, July 26th.

The observations made this year, and the opinions drawn, are unbiased, and should another year's experience change my views on the varieties mentioned I shall be glad to express them.

The SECRETARY : I am very glad to know what Prof. Macoun says as to the Koslov Morello cherry. I have five or six of those trees in bearing in the orchard, and I have been very favourably impressed with the cherry. As he says, there is a great difference in them. They are all grown as seedlings. Mr. Niemetz of Russia sent out 50 trees of that cherry to me in the year 1889 ; of which those sent to the Experimental Farm were a portion. He stated that the best way of propagating them was by the pit, and he thought they would begin bearing about five years from the seed. They have done so with me, although it is only the last two years that they have borne freely. As Mr. Macoun says, they are only bushes, and I think they ought to be grown as bushes and not as trees. I have mine about three feet apart in the row. I did not intend when I planted them to leave them so near together, but it has just proved to me that they might be grown in rows as we grow berry bushes, and cultivated as we do our berry crop, and that an acre would produce a tremendous yield of fruit. By picking the pits of the best fruit and planting them I believe we might continually improve on the quality and make a very profitable thing of growing that cherry for the market. It is very late, the latest cherry that I think I had in my orchard. Mr. Niemetz said that it was grown very largely by peasants in Russia, and he thought it might be very valuable indeed for the northern sections of Canada on account of its hardiness, and I also believe it would be valuable for the southern sections. It is figured and described in our Fruit Experiment Station Report of Ontario for 1897.

Mr. MACOUN : The Russian cherries have a flavor of their own, and this flavor is brought out distinctly when they are preserved. In the Ottawa local markets these cherries are sought after by the people there more than any others they can get. They always ask for these Russian cherries.

Mr. HUGGARD : You mentioned the Raba pear, considering it a hardy tree and a good fruit.

Mr. MACOUN : The tree that we have so far as I know fruited for the first time the year. The tree is apparently quite hardy. I think it was planted in the spring of 1896. The fruit is large ; it reminded me of the Bartlett ; to see it at a distance you would almost take it for a Bartlett pear. The quality is medium. If you take it at the proper time it is not bad at all ; it is not high flavored.

Mr. HUGGARD : I set out three of them in 1896, and one of the trees had fruit on this year which was inferior to the Keiffer pear.

Mr. ORR : How does the blight show on these trees, and have the ordinary varieties grown in Canada blighted as badly as the Russian varieties ?

Mr. MACOUN : No, the standard varieties have not blighted as badly as the Russian, although they have blighted considerably. It begins in the tips of the branches and runs in a very short time down the main stem. The practice Mr. Craig followed was to saw off the limb as soon as the blight appeared.

Mr. WHYTE : Mr. Brodie is here as a delegate from the Quebec Horticultural Society, and has had some experience in this line. We shall be glad to hear from him.

Mr. BRODIE : My experience in cherries has been similar to Mr. Macoun's, and I would like to recommend one variety, the Griotte d' Ostheim. The fruit is hardly compared with the Early Richmond, while the Early Richmond could not resist t ͞ early frosts in the spring. The Griotte d' Ostheim had a very hardy crop. I put it on the hardy list of the fifteen varieties of cherries I had fruiting. My cherry crop this year, both of Russian and our own varieties, started to ripen about the 21st of June, and I had them right on in August, so that made a pretty long cherry season. With reference to the Russian apples, there are two varieties I suggest to be placed on the list ; one we call Golden White, a fall apple, in quality very much like the Northern Spy and about as large, more conical in shape, fine, bright red color, and sells well on the local market. Another variety is the Regal. The *Mercanos* are very much like the Canada Red, only more conical in shape, a little larger than the Ben Davis, and quality very good. I think it is the only really good Russian apple that I have fruited so far. The rest of them are only comparatively fall apples. As to Russian pears, my experience is where you can grow the Flemish Beauty like we can in Montreal it is not encouraging to go into Russian pears, but there were two varieties of Russians I thought might be well worth a trial. Say *Casa bianca*, that I got from the late Charles Gibb, which was entirely different from the one I got from Prof. Budd of Ames College, Iowa. My situation there is a little more favorable to pear culture than the Experimental Farm at Ottawa. I am not sure how it would be for hardiness.

Mr. CASTON : I have been growing some Russian pears, and I think they are a very valuable acquisition. I think they would succeed over a large section of Ontario. With regard to Russian apples, it was the late Chas. Gibb and Prof. Budd who gathered most of those that were grown in a latitude 600 miles north of the City of Ottawa, and they were grown as dwarfs, and the snow was very deep and they got protection in that way. Seventy miles north of Toronto some of them have failed and were tender, but having them propagated on a hardy root and growing as a dwarf in localities where the snow remained deep they would succeed very far north. One of the troubles about those Russian fruits is that I don't think we will find any good winter apples among them— nothing e. g. that comes up to our Northern Spy. They seem to be mostly all early apples. For the most part they are hardy,—clean skinned and good bearers, and I believe they would be valuable for grafting on. I think with Mr. Macoun that a number are of the same variety with different names. I think it would be a good thing if they could be Americanized. Those Russian names are jaw breakers. Mr. Gibb made an attempt and published a pamphlet entitled "Nomenclature of the Russian Fruits," and he endeavored to straighten it up a little, but it is a good deal of a tangle yet. I have two varieties, one called the Hare Pipka, but they are close akin to the Alexander and the Wolf River. I believe the Russian apples and cherries would be very valuable in extending fruit culture farther north through this country. Most of them are hardy, and the Russian cherries for canning can scarcely be equalled—and that is mainly what cherries are grown for. They bear when they are young and they seem exceedingly healthy. They do not seem to be so liable to the black knot as a good many of the old varieties.

Mr. ARMSTRONG, (Queenstown) : I would like to ask what protection those trees that were winter-killed at Ottawa had during the winter.

Mr. MACOUN : That winter there was a great scarity of snow at the Experimental Farm ; they had no protection from snow covering. They simply had a clover cover crop, which has been adopted at the Experimental Farm for some years. That year however the clover was killed, and it had not near the same protection that it would other winters on that account, there were more trees killed than would otherwise be the case. That was the winter of 1895-96

Mr. WHYTE : That winter there were many apple trees killed. It was the most disastrous winter in the Ottawa district on account of there being no snow to cover the roots.

PEACH BORER.

By Martin Burrell, St. Catharines.

I have not had very much experience with the Peach Bark Beetle. As far as the Peach Borer goes I have done a little experimental work in the last year or two, and as we all know it is one of the worst insects we have to fight, especially on a sandy soil. Probably most of you know a great deal about its life history. What we call the borer is not the bark beetle, as most of the wood boring insects are, but is the larva of a moth a good deal like a wasp. The female moth is $\frac{3}{4}$ of an inch long, and is bigger than the male. The front wings are dark blue, and the hind wings quite transparent, and you can always know it from the shape of the body, which is a darkish blue with one large orange band around the abdominal segments. You cannot mistake it for any other insect. The male is very much smaller and inconspicuous. The wings are transparent, and there are some slight little marks about the body, but it is much smaller and less showy insect than the female. In this latitude I found that the moth never emerged before July 15th or 20th. It was thought at one time that the moth began to emerge very early in spring and commence laying, and it is rather an important point, as you can see, because in hunting out these borers, whether you put on a wash to prevent them laying the eggs, or put on papers, or whatever practice is adopted, it is necessary to know what is the best time to go to work. It was formerly thought that they came out very early, and it was necessary, in order to prevent them laying, to put on washes very early. As a matter of fact in New York State they do not come out until about July 15th, as Mr. Slingerman tells me at Cornell, and here I have never observed one out before July 20th. This is important for the reason that you are always safe if you can clear them out before that time, for you will destroy the crop for that year—that is you will prevent the moths emerging. If you use any wash to prevent the moths laying the eggs, the greatest difficulty is to find a wash that will remain on the tree the whole season, because the moths start emerging about the 20th July and keep on from that time until the 20th of October emerging and laying. There is only one brood a year. For instance, in the case of the moth that lays the eggs July 20th, the larva hatches and gets three-quarter grown by the late fall. It then passes the winter in the tree below the ground dormant, and the next spring starts working, and then turns into a chrysalis fairly early, about June, and remains about a month in the pupa stage. Those that come out in September do not hatch out until about the following September. The whole process is just about one year. That period of time extends very much longer than some people thought, and it is all the more necessary if you are going to have a wash to prevent the moth laying its eggs to cover the whole of that period from early in July to early in October. There are very few washes that will stay on the tree during that time intact, and if we go to the expense of two washes it makes the matter very much more cumbersome. Mr. Smith, of New Jersey, told me that he found 600 eggs in one moth, and Mr Slingerland has found 300 by examining them with the microscope very carefully. They have found as many as 28 laid on one tree. I have taken out 14 borers on one tree, and of course the tree was nearly gone. The danger is worst on the smooth trees, because the tree of course is only about two inches through. If a half-grown borer is there it can almost girdle it. Every man should examine peach trees before he plants them, because there is many a time you get a borer in a nursery row. I have often taken them out of the trees I had from the nursery, and taken them out before I planted them. Those of us who hunt them regularly generally hunt them out with a knife or a wire, and any time during the year; but the best time to do it would be once in the early spring before the larvæ matured, and the next late in the fall. I believe we get very much better results if we practice the application of some washes. A year ago last spring I tried three different kinds of paper—tar paper, bunches of wrapping paper, and ordinary newspaper, and also heaping up air-slacked lime around the trees and Bordeaux mixture, with half the amount of lime and half the amount of copper ; the wash of Prof. Saunders, that is, a saturated solution of soda ; and I also tried hydraulic cement and skimmed milk mixed together, and hydraulic cement and water ; also the wash they used up in Mr. McNeill's district of ashes and lime. After hunting the trees, I put all these washes on before July 15th, and then observed the condition of the washes and of the wrapping in different periods during the season to see how long they lasted and the effect they had, and we came to the conclusion that as far as wrappings went, the cheapest and most satisfactory one was the ordinary newspaper wrapping, that is, just taking one ordinary newspaper to a tree and wrapping it up the tree, unwinding it when the tree begins to swell, so that you will not girdle your tree. We do not get any borers unless the moth gets past the newspaper. It is an effectual stop, and will stay on for more than two months. Of course it will not cover the whole period. None of the washes stayed on during the whole season with the exception of the two cement washes. Prof. Smith, of New Jersey, told me about both of them. The cement and water was just mixed up into a good thick paste and put on with a whitewash brush about twelve inches from the foot of the tree. About the middle of August the cement was just about as good as if it was put on in July. By the end of August that one had very considerably cracked. Skim milk and cement seem to make it more adhesive, and in September that wash was as good as it was when put on in July. It is easily put on, and especially on the young trees where the bark was not rough it was perfectly successful. I only found two borers on the trees after putting the cement and skim milk on, and they were in little spots, rough places where the cement had failed to cover. I would strongly advise everybody to try that particular wash—just the hydraulic cement and skimmed milk mixed up into thick paste and put on before that date.

E. MORDEN (Niagara Falls) : What about earthing up in the late summer ?

Mr. BURRELL : I would earth up earlier than that—just after I hunted. If I were putting on a wash I would examine my trees during May or June, and then I would put the earth after I examined early, and then the moths would have to lay above that point where the earth was. I would do it before July.

Mr. ARMSTRONG : As an old peach grower, the wash indicated by Mr. Burrell, particularly that one described as hydraulic cement mixture, has a tendency to harden the new bark and hinder the sap coming up, especially in the young trees. I would not recommend it, and the coal tar has another effect which is very injurious to the growing trees, especially the young trees. I find the best wash I can get is simply the soft soap wash. It not only protects the trees from the insects but it assists in cleaning and clearing the bark.

Mr. BURRELL : I cannot say I have observed any injury in that way. I took note of all the washes I applied, and the Bordeaux and this lime and ashes and the cement were all about in the same condition ; that is, they were smoother and shinier and in better shape. I put cement on two years running, not a very thick coat, and noticed to see if it would hurt. The peach trees were four years old. I saw no particular injury.

The PRESIDENT : Mr. Armstrong, you said you found coal tar was injurious to the tree. In what way ? What is your experience ?

Mr. ARMSTRONG : I have found that during the growing season the coal tar hardens the bark. I got it in St. Catharines fifteen or sixteen years ago, and I discarded it after a trial or two. I have found under the bark, instead of being thrifty and green and sappy it had a tendency to darken and stiffen the bark.

Mr. BURRELL : The cement is more or less porous ; the tar would not be as porous.

The PRESIDENT : Was it a light coating, or was it put on pretty heavy ?

Mr. ARMSTRONG : It was in July I think I put it on. I put it on lightly with a whitewash brush.

Mr. ORR : I have been using a mixture of lime and hardwood ashes. Last year, after careful searching, we found six borers out of 400 acres ; this year we found five. The trees were in almost perfect condition.

Mr. PATTISON (Grimsby): I have been in the habit of using a composition of ordinary washing soda and soft soap which acted fairly well. It has the fault of not staying on as long as one might wish, but for a considerable period it acts very well.

Mr. BURRELL: What soil is yours, Mr. Orr?

Mr. ORR: Sandy.

Mr. BURRELL: Were you ever troubled much with borers before?

Mr. ORR: This is a young orchard. In the old orchard we were very badly troubled with them.

Mr. BURRELL: The satisfactory report may be because there were not very many borers about.

Mr. ORR: We mixed it with skim milk. Besides that, slacking the lime with hot water makes it more adhesive.

Mr. GREGORY (St. Catharines): Would you recommend laying bare the roots?

Mr. ORR: No; we get the collar entirely clean and then whitewash the limbs right down to the roots.

O. M. HONSBURGER: The old adage "An ounce of prevention is worth a pound of cure," is a good one. I would like to ask Mr. Burrell what mode he would adopt in finding borers in young trees?

Mr. BURRELL: You can only get at them by picking them out with a knife.

GREETINGS FROM SISTER SOCIETIES.

The PRESIDENT: We have to-day a representative from the Quebec Horticultural Society, and I am sure every one in this room will hear him with the greatest of pleasure. We can always learn from those engaged in horticulture from other districts, and we take it very kindly that the Quebec Society has thought fit to send us a delegate, and I may say that in return, at the meeting of the Board last evening, representatives were appointed to attend the meeting of the Quebec Horticultural Society, and also horticultural societies in the States and at other points. I will now call upon Mr. Brodie, representing the Quebec Horticultural Society.

Mr. BRODIE: I have great pleasure in meeting you here this afternoon, and I greatly regret that my confrere, Mr. Shepherd, did not come along with me, as he is a much better speaker than I am. The first Horticultural Society in Quebec was started at Abbottsford, the home of the late Charles Gibb. Abbottsford in Scotland is connected with the name of Sir Walter Scott; here, in Canada, Abbottsford will always be connected with a name just as dear to us, that of Charles Gibb. (Applause.) Our Society comprises French Canadians as well as English speaking people, and it would do you good to see how well we get on together. There is no rivalry; everything is carried on, although sometimes there is a little delay in translation and so on; still we get on very harmoniously. I find that being able to speak both languages is a real blessing, so if you delegates come down to Quebec I hope you will not be disappointed if you hear a little of our discussions in the French language. We have had a great deal of difficulty in contending with severe winters. The winter of 1895-96 was most disastrous to us in our fruit work. Whole sections of plum orchards in the L'Islet and Kamarouska were destroyed with the exception of a few trees, and in my own orchard near Montreal I lost between 50 and 60 valuable trees. I noticed coming up here how clean you have your orchards. Well, we have to let the grass grow to be a protection to our orchards. Another reason why I like to have a good coating of grass under my trees in an autumn like this is that the apples ripen up very rapidly, and I had about 300 barrels of windfalls. We had a very wet October. If we had to pick up these windfalls out of the mud we would have realized a pretty small price for them, while for those we did gather I got from $1.70 to $1.90 a barrel in the Quebec market. That is one reason why I

2 F. G.

think what would suit your country up here would not suit ours at all down in the St. Lawrence Valley. Perhaps one reason is we have a greater rainfall down there; we are not subject to such great drouths as you have here. I believe in manure, and if we cannot get manure, we get wood ashes or fertilizer. I am fortunate in being able to get manure hauled on my place for ten cents a load. I can put a whole cartload on each tree, and in that way am able to grow fairly good apples. The secret of all is to spray the trees. I was surprised at the Ottawa Exhibition to see so many apples from the Ontario districts spotted and stung with codling moth. Had it been in the Province of Quebec, where we are not kings in horticulture like you are up here, I would not have been so surprised, but I found out from those exhibitors there they did not believe in spraying. Well, if they had only been at my orchard this year I think they would have gone home convinced, for my neighbor's trees had hardly a decent apple on, and they shook off the few they had, while I had 1500 barrels out of my orchard. I hope those who come to Montreal will not be disappointed, because we cannot get a gathering like you have here of representative horticulturists, but we will do the best we can to make it pleasant for you. (Applause.)

Mr. CARPENTER : [As a Horticultural Society we are progressing rapidly. Two years ago we started with seventeen members, and now we have seventy four. We have been spraying more extensively in our section this year, and somehow we don't seem to see much difference between those that are sprayed and those that are not sprayed. My own crop would be about half culls. Others show very good results from spraying.

C. W. BUNTING being called on said : I am one of the officers of the Niagara Fruit Growers' Association. Our President and Secretary are unavoidably absent to-day, but on behalf of that Association I have great pleasure in welcoming to this peninsula the Ontario Fruit Growers' Association, and I trust your visit in this place will be productive of pleasant and profitable results to all the members who have made it convenient to attend ; and I am sure I but echo the sentiments of the Fruit Growers of this section in welcoming you here.

Mr. MORDEN : We have in Niagara Falls a system of spraying on a gigantic scale nowhere else seen on the face of the earth—we have the Falls of Niagara. The fruit growers emulate that system in spraying, but I cannot report very much in that direction, though I am satisfied that the future fruit grower will do more spraying. We are getting on fairly successful. We have had a good membership and no doubt some good has come from our Society there. When you go to the Falls in the summer I hope you will come out and see us, and we will take you all through our fruit plantations, and let you look at this beautiful fruit. (Pointing to the display of fruit on the table, amid applause.)

The PRESIDENT read a letter from Mr. Walter Ross directed to Mr. Boulter, our Director in Prince Edward County, from one of our valued societies, in which he speaks most highly of the satisfaction given by the Canadian Horticulturist, and the good success of their work at Picton.

EXPORT OF FRUIT PULP.

Mr. C. C. James, Deputy Minister of Agriculture for Ontario, then read to the meeting a series of letters on the export of fruit pulp, from Mr. Harrison Watson, Curator of the Canadian Section of the Imperial Institute. These letters have already been published and distributed and need not be reprinted here. Copies may be had by applying to the Department at Toronto. A lengthy discussion took place of which the following may be given here :

Prof. ROBERTSON : I had the pleasure last summer of seeing Mr. Harrison Watson and several large importers of fruit pulp in Britain. I found there is a demand usually for raspberry pulp and apricot pulp only. The others are a very small trade and anuncertain demand. The very top prices are about £40 per ton, rarely £42, usually from £18 to £26. Now, these prices would nett in Canada not more than 5 cents per pound for the raw fruit at the very best, down to almost nothing when the pulp sells for £18 a ton ; so if the fresh fruit can be sold at all at anything like the common prices then it would not pay to turn it into pulp for export. But sometimes there is a surplus of fresh fruit that is unsalable either from very small size or poor quality, and that might make a fair quantity of pulp ; but at £40 per ton the 8½ cents per pound there would not nett more than five cents per pound for the green fruit after taking off the cost of the package, the cost of the fruit, the commission and allowing 10% for shrinkage for the evaporation of the fruit during the preserving process. When it gets down to £20 per ton, the cost of the package, freight, commission and shrinkage reduces the account sales into a cipher for the man who ships ; so that in the normal conditions of the market there is not a cent a pound for our green fruit, and in the abnormal conditions which have existed the last few years it would not be five cents a pound for the raspberries and the apricots. If any of the fruit growers are anxious to try this business and will furnish the pulp, our Department will take charge of the shipment of such pulp and see that they are put in the best markets of England, and give full returns for the fruit before the trial is made. I am not hopeful that any large trade will grow up for that stuff from Canada, since we have such a good market now for those two classes of fruit which are wanted in the form of fruit pulp.

MR .BOULTER (Picton) : At £40 per ton it would not realize quite as much as Prof. Robertson stated, that is, taking out ordinary charges. However, later on I will be able to ship pulp, and if any members of the Association have large plantations of raspberries that are any way convenient to Toronto it could be got very cheaply. I intend to give this a thorough test the coming season. My theory is that unless a grower can get at least four or five cents a pound for his raspberries in their natural state there is not a great deal of money in it ; and unless it could nett that to the grower—which we have always failed to do in our county—I would not advise a person going into it unless he were skilled in putting it up. It costs considerable to get it up. It is a good idea that that invitation came, because for the last two years raspberries have been a drug in Ontario, and they have not been selling as they should have, for what reason I do not know. There is a variety of raspberry that might be cultivated for pulp—the Shaffer. It is an enormous bearer, much better producer than the Cuthbert, but inferior in quality, and it will not do for our business in Canada in what is called preserving, being too soft and going to pulp. Cuthberts will stand up under the cooking necessary to be done. Possibly as they could be grown for one to two cents a quart less than Cuthberts, and a success might be made of them. I have sent some of them over to see if they would do as well as the Cuthberts have. In the prices quoted, you must remember that a ton is a long ton, not 2000 pounds, but 2240, which cuts quite a hole in the amount you expect to receive. My own opinion at present would be that there is nothing in the pulp business except for raspberries. Do not attempt anything else. Do not attempt strawberries. This pulp is an experiment yet, but I intend to send over quite a lot next year if the crops are good.

COMMITTEE. Messrs. W. Boulter, of Picton, A. McNeill, of Walkerville, and Rev. W. J. Andrews, of Grimsby, were appointed a committee to investigate the subject and make arrangements for some trial shipments.

Canners and others interested are requested to correspond with this committee.

PROSPECTS FOR EXPORT OF TENDER FRUIT.

PROF. J. W. ROBERTSON, Commissioner of Agriculture, said : Mr. President and Gentlemen : Before I say much for the prospects for an export demand for tender fruits I would like to make a few observations on the present status of the business of growing tender fruits in Canada. In thinking over why many people went into fruit growing, one is soon led to the conclusion that the general fall in the prices of cereals a while ago made many give up grain farming, in which they had had experience, and for which they had natural fitness, and go into fruit growing, without either the special knowledge or personal aptitude for making a success of that business. Great areas of Canada are devoted to fruit growing for that reason. When the ordinary operations of farming did not pay well, there was general discussion as to whether fruit growing would not pay better. There was a great deal of information of the most indefinite kind diffused over the Province in regard to the benefits and advantages and profits of fruit growing, and the consequent agitation led a great many men into that business. That was a good thing for agriculture and a good thing for those men, because for a while the fruit growing business paid very well—much better than the land which was devoted to it had paid the occupiers through ordinary farm work.

GLUTTED MARKETS. That leads one in looking over the fruit growing business, particularly in Ontario, to examine into the kind of fruit that these people have been growing and why they grow the kinds they do grow. Most of the men have planted the kinds that can be grown easiest, with least risk, and that yield largely without regard to whether there would be a permanent or large enough demand for that class of fruit. In addition to growing the kinds that I have alluded to, they have grown a great many kinds, and still grow them just because they have some *interesting* characteristics, and because the cuts of them look well in some nice book or catalogue. Just go over a fruit farm and find the kinds that are growing and why they are being grown, and while my statements are rather unpalatable, they are quite true in regard to most farms where fruit growing is carried on. That has led to this state of things in Canada, that the Canadian fruit growers are growing more tender fruits than their home markets take care of. I do not say that they are growing more tender fruits than the people of Canada can and would readily consume if they got the kinds they want in the condition they like them, because we import more tender fruit from California than would fill the pockets of a great many Ontario fruit growers with all the profits they could expect from their business The markets are glutted not because the Canadian appetite is satisfied with Canadian fruit, but because Canadian fruits have not been of the sort or put up in the way that the Canadian consumer wants ; and if not suitable for the Canadian, how much less for the ten times more fastidious Englishman ? I want to have you think of that before I speak of the prospects for an export trade in tender fruits.

If one grows a great many varieties of any sort of fruit, his only chance to make any money is by having what I will call a particular personal market. The grower can go direct to the home eater and meet his needs But if a man has to put his products on an open market of this country or Britain, or the general market, then he must not have a whole promiscuous assortment of fruit, but he must have a few definite varieties that they like. Otherwise he cannot make it pay. In promiscuous growing he does not grow any variety on a large enough scale to have his expenses low enough, and he does not have enough quantity of any one kind to attract attention in a good market. Confirmation of my judgment on this subject from the bulletin just published by Prof. Bailey of Cornell University that came to my hands even after I had my subject thought out for this meeting. He makes this very clear in his bulletin, that the kind of fruit-growing which a man may follow with profit, for the personal market where he supplies the fruit to the homes in his locality, is quite different from the kind of fruit-growing a man may follow who puts his fruit on the open general market.

That being so, if we have in Canada now considerably more tender fruits than our own markets will take care of, can we find an outlet abroad at profitable prices for these varieties of fruit ? That is the problem ; and I will tell you a little of our experience. A man who follows fruit-growing for his home market will find customers who pay special prices for special quality, but the man who grows fruit for a general market can get only the current prices for ordinary good quality. The two markets are quite different in regard to returns the grower may get. More than that ; the man who grows fruit for the home market may carry on the work on a small fruit farm, put a good deal of expenditure into the carrying on of his business, and get paid for that by the specially high prices that people will pay for just the particular things they want; whereas if a man throws his stuff on the general open market he has to take the price which the man who grows fruit on a large scale with the least possible expense is willing to take. If we are to have an export trade for the finer fruits we will have to confine ourselves to a few staples in the fruit foods and get these produced of the best quality and at the lowest cost to ourselves.

DEMAND. That brings me to the inquiry, "Is there any demand in Great Britain ?" which I take to be the market for which we are catering, when we speak of an export demand. Of pears, Britain usually imports about a million dollars' worth a year; sometimes more, sometimes less; of plums about a million and a quarter dollars' worth a year; and of grapes about two and a quarter million dollars worth a year from various countries. I have not mentioned apples because they do not come under the heading of tender fruits. The British market does consume an enormous quantity of tender fruits. The market is only opened for them. It is not by any means developed and supplied. In the past the price of pears has been so high that the demand has not been one-tenth of what it may be and will be if Canadians put their pears on the British market as abundantly as they put their apples on the British market. There is a tremendous demand and market there for high-grade pears, because pears enter into the food of the people, through cooking and in many ways. That is an important consideration when you try to estimate the capacity of the market. On the contrary, grapes are always and only a dessert fruit—not a food fruit; and for them the demand is consequently limited, and also more fastidious, because in a dessert fruit people want something particularly pleasing to their eye and palate. They cannot mask the flavor by cooking or in any other way.

SOME ESSENTIALS TO SUCCESS. Then can an export trade in tender fruits be made a success of from Canada? I suppose twenty times a month men write me problems "Will it pay me to do so-and-so?" Anyone who has done work of investigation can say, whether a certain principle is applicable or not, or whether a certain statement is true in regard to it coinciding with principles; but no man can say of a business proposal, "That will be successful," or, "That will not be successful." Success depends on the personality of the man and not on the nature of the business. I do not know whether exporting tender fruits can be made a success except as I learn the kind of men who take it up. There are principles and there are reasons, and as far as a man understands those and applies them he can make it a success; but the success depends on the person and not on the opportunity, because the opportunity may have existed for twenty years, but so far the person has not risen to make success out of the opportunity. It may have been for want of information, it may have been for want of transportation conveniences, it may have been for want of cold storage in the ships; still that is the state of things to-day. Can they be altered from this time on?

QUALITIES WHICH DETERMINE VALUE. The person who undertakes the shipping of fruit to Britain must know the conditions that the British consumer and importer impose on him. I have learned by experience that the British consumer and importer does not care a snap of his fingers for the fancy names of the specially esteemed kinds of fruit. He does not care a brown bawbee if it has been cracked up by every specialist in the country. Soundness is the first consideration, then keeping qualities, then nice appearance in regard to color, size and shape, and lastly he looks for as nice flavor as you can give him. The latter is not a matter of the first importance at first in the commerce of this business. Soundness, keeping qualities, appearance, and then flavor, is the order. Too often the fruit-grower reverses that order and says, "Oh, but such a kind of fruit is the most delicious and high-flavored." It may be, and may pay to grow for the personal, particular market of the man who is going to pay a high price for special intrinsic quality; but the British market will pay just the common price in the order of those qualities. I want to repeat that over and over again; it is the secret of the whole situation, soundness and keeping qualities after the fruits are there, then nice appearance, and then a flavor as good as you can get.

When trial shipments were made by the Department of Agriculture at Ottawa in 1898, we found those things that we had learned in 1897 were still further emphasized. In 1897 the Department took charge of 7,141 packages of tender fruits and sent them to Great Britain. In 1898 the Department took charge of 3,815 packages of tender fruits. We sent in 1897 about 3½ times more than in 1898. The less quantity was not because the Department was less willing to take the fruits and test them in the British market, but because for various reasons, mainly climatic, the shippers in the Grimsby district were not able this year to provide as much fruit as they expected, or as the Department wanted to carry on its trial shipments. The fruits shipped were practically the promiscuous gatherings from various farms. That was unfortunate. The arrangement with the shippers was that the Department guaranteed a certain price at the shipping point, and if there was a revenue above that, that also went to the shippers. The kind of package that was used was a comparatively small package, measuring inside 22 inches by 11¼ by from 4 to 6 inches deep according to the size of the fruit. The packages were light; they were open for ventilation and for cooling the fruit; and they had an attractive appearance, and also the good quality of being reasonably cheap, costing about six cents apiece. They held all the way from 24 to 30 lbs. of fruit according to the size of the individual fruits. Each separate fruit was wrapped in tissue paper, and the packages were filled from the side so as to cause the least surface to be faced.

RIPENESS. The condition of ripeness desired when the fruit was picked was that the pears should be of full size and quite green and firm. The California pears that go to England are sold particularly well because the receivers there say they can keep them for two weeks after they get them. Observe!—soundness, keeping quality. Anybody in Canada knows that a Bartlett is a joy to eat compared with a tough old tasteless pear from California—(laughter)—still, the pears from California would fetch nine shillings a case whereas our best would fetch only six shillings because the California pears would keep, and the man who bought them did not fear losing them next morning. The same was true in regard to the condition in which it was desired to have peaches picked; but it is exceedingly difficult in practice to tell when a peach is at the right stage of ripeness. I do not know any means of determining that, and I have not found any fruit-grower who can. I went through the orchards in Grimsby and elsewhere and I found they told by the appearance of the peaches and then by "the feel" of them. They were quite often disappointed that way. A peach will ripen a great deal in half a day if the weather is hot; and it is practically useless to pick peaches at the same condition of ripeness as can be observed in the picking of pears.

After the fruit was packed in the cases it was cooled down in the cold storage room at Grimsby to between a temperature of 36° and 40° Fahr. The cold storage could be easily held at these temperatures, and as the packages were small the fruit was cooled to the core to about 38° Fahr. at the time it was put in the railway car. The Railway Company furnished refrigerator cars. They went forward to Montreal without loss of time, and the fruit was delivered on the steamships in very good condition, with this exception to that remark : that quantities of the tomatoes and some of the peaches were considerably too ripe before they were put into the cold storage at Grimsby. A low temperature does not seem to have the same power to arrest the ripening of tomatoes as it does to retard the ripening of pears. I had pears put into cold storage at Ottawa ; and two months after they were put in they were perfectly sound, firm and hard. Tomatoes put in under the same condition became too ripe in ten days' time at a temperature of 36° and 38° Fahr.

PEARS. The quantity of pears sent over was 2,208 cases. The cases were not weighed, but were estimated to hold about one basket and a quarter, and they held from 26 pounds to 28 pounds—I think I found one weighing 30 pounds of fruit, which was quite exceptional. Taking the prices at which the several lots were sold and averaging them these pears realized on the average 73.6 cents per case at Grimsby after the freight charges and all expenses were taken off. The shippers would realize 67 cents for that quantity of pears after allowing for the cost of the package. Now I think that is a very good price. I do not know whether you fruit growers would be satisfied or not with that price for pears— (Voices, " Yes, yes ")—but that was a fair price, and includes two shipments when the

British market was said to be dull and glutted for pears. Now, all pears are not alike in the British market ; the buyers won't pay the same price for all pears ; and the nett returns at Grimsby showed a much greater difference than the selling prices in Great Britain, because you have the very same freight charges, and the very same insurance and other charges to take off the low-priced pears in England, as off the high-priced pears. The first shipment of pears that went over realized all the way from one dollar a case at Grimsby to forty six (46) cents a case at Grimsby ; that is, one portion of the same shipment, fetched a dollar and the other portion forty-two (42) cents. I took the average of all the highest prices at which the pears in each shipment were sold, and then the average of all the lowest prices. In the second shipment they netted from sixty-three (63) to fifty-five (55) cents per case ; the third shipment from ninety-six (96) to seventy-six (76) cents per case at Grimsby. The smaller sized pears fetched the lower prices I have mentioned. This year, these pears were not creditable to Canada. I am not imputing any blame to the shippers at Grimsby beyond saying that the pears this year were small, and not creditable to Canada as showing what we can do usually. The weather was unfavorable during part of the season, even to the extent that some shippers were not able to send pears at all after the first shipment. If we could send forward the best quality of Bartlett pears we would have an enormous market, I am sure, because the people like them so well there is an almost unlimited demand under ordinary conditions at the prices I have mentioned The very best prices that were gotten for any considerable quantity were six shillings and threepence (6s. 3d.) a case in England for these small cases. That would nett at Grimsby one dollar and twelve cents ($1.12) cents a case containing from 26 to 30 lbs. The difference in price between the varieties was hardly noticeable. In one case the Duchess fetched from four shillings and sixpence (4s. 6d.) to four shillings (4s.) ; and in another case the Keiffers fetched from four shillings (4s.) to three shillings and sixpence (3s. 6d.).

The English market likes not a monster pear, but a large pear, or rather a large medium size ; about 70 pears to the case weighing 28 pounds were a fine size. They would weigh about three to the pound. Those would be pears of first-rate size.

PEACHES. I want to deal next with the matter of peaches. We sent altogether 324 cases of peaches. For one small shipment we realized one dollar and fifty cents ($1.50) a case nett at Grimsby, and for a great many other shipments we realized 32½ cents less than nothing at Grimsby. That was a loss of the total expense of carrying them to England, because they sold for nothing there, in fact were condemned by the health inspectors. They were carried in the same refrigerator car, in the same part of the ship, and at the same temperature as our pears which fetched those prices I have mentioned. Those were mainly the Bartlett and other tender pears. It was not that the cold storage was not sufficient ; it was that the Crawford peaches sent from Canada had not the qualities in them to let them be in good keeping condition in the English climate 20 days after they left Grimsby by any system of cold storage we have yet devised. A few peaches each time were excellent, and a few peaches each time were rotten, and a number of peaches each time were pithy, dry and tasteless. There comes the difficulty of making a commercial success of shipping peaches. If they are picked just the least little bit too green they have almost no flavor and are not mellow when they come out of the cold storage. If they are just right they stay right ; but if they are a little too ripe they go to soft rottenness on the other side the day after they come out of cold storage. In some cases where the peaches were sold for good prices the purchasers brought them back next day and demanded their money back saying they would get the health officer to condemn the peaches unless they were settled with at once. There is the difficulty : unless you have some means of determining just when the peaches are sufficiently ripe, and not too ripe, you would have so many losses that they would take away all the profit from those that were in good condition.

Mr. BURRELL: Did you see anything of the African peaches, the Cape peach, because I was told by friends in England that they had arrived in very good condition and realized splendid prices.

Prof. ROBERTSON : The Californian peaches also arrived in good condition and realized good prices. I did not see the African peaches myself. They come in after our spring is about begun, but the Californian peaches arrived in some cases in excellent condition, because they have toughness of flesh, and the shippers seem to have a better means of getting a large quantity in the right condition of ripeness.

TOMATOES. Of tomatoes we sent 428 cases. Most of them, I think, were a little too ripe at Grimsby. One or two of the latter shipments I saw in Montreal were also too ripe in appearance. Here is the difficulty with tomatoes, that they keep on ripening slowly at low temperatures. When the tomatoes were taken from the cold storage in England, they often looked fairly well, but they simply collapsed in two days in most cases. Tomatoes that go into England from outside markets do not go in cold storage ; they go on the decks of the ships, where the ventilation is thorough. They are allowed to ripen gradually, and they do ripen very well during the period of ten days ; but longer than that makes it exceedingly difficult to have them delivered safely. If they were picked green, then cooled at once and gradually warmed to 50, or 60, Fahr. before they were exposed to the air in England, they might fetch a good price, but the price they would fetch would hardly tempt anyone to lay himself out to grow tomatoes in Canada for the English market. A few cases realized thirty-seven (37) cents at Grimsby, a few thirty six (36) cents, and nearly all the rest were failures to the extent of realizing nothing and causing loss to the extent of the freight paid on them. They went in the same cold storage chambers as the pears that we landed in first-rate condition and at the temperature that the Californian shippers keep their fruit at viz., from 38 to 40 degrees, on the way across.

QUINCES. Fourteen cases of quinces realized fifty-nine (59) cents, but I do not know that we have exact information enough in regard to quinces to give any information as to whether they may be carried safely as a rule or not. Some of the 149 cases were landed in good condition and some were not. That seemed to be owing to the condition of the quinces when they were put in the cases at Grimsby.

APPLES. Of apples in those small packages, 254 cases were sent. They realized forty cents at Grimsby, but the reports all said, " Do not send any more apples in such small cases ; larger sized cases will pay you very much better. " Apples of tender sorts, that cannot be sent at all without cold storage, have been sent to England in the very best of condition through cold storage, and they realized very fair prices. Mr. Brodie of Montreal was telling me this morning of some apples he shipped from Montreal in cold storage that netted him fair prices this year.

Apples like the Duchess, that could not at all be sent to England hitherto, can be sent in excellent condition in cold storage if they are properly packed ; but a discussion of that will come under the head of Transatlantic Transportation.

Mr. BRODIE : This shipment of mine was sent direct to London. It was 20 days from Montreal to London. That was a long voyage to remain in cold storage.

Prof. ROBERTSON : What did they realize at Montreal ?

Mr. BRODIE : About $2.25 a barrel ; but the dock charges were something tremendous; also cartage 15 shillings on 30 barrels of apples from the London dock to Covent Garden Market—about 12-½ cents a barrel. For 2½ cents we can get apples carted from one end of the city to the other in Montreal.

Prof. ROBERTSON : I think anyone who has large experience in consigning small shipments to England will agree with Mr. Boulter, that the English commission merchant has wonderful facility and thoroughness in devising new items of expenses that he can add to account sales and in making a long, long list of charges.

GRAPES. I have a few observations to offer on the trial shipments of Grapes. There were 441 cases forwarded. Twenty packages that were sent to Glasgow realized seventy (70) cents at Grimsby for about 18 pounds to the case ; twenty-five packages realized (41) cents per case, sixty-two packages realized nineteen cents (19) cents per case; but the other grapes did not fetch anything at all worth mentioning.

Mr. PATTISON : With the grapes that were successful, was it a matter of varieties or of condition that they arrived in ?

Prof. ROBERTSON : It was a question of the market they happened to strike   The grapes that were sent to Bristol were landed in first-class condition ; there was no fault to find, but simply the people did not like the flavor and would not pay a price.   Grapes from other countries were so low in price that they would not take any risks with the new thing.

EXTRACTS FROM LETTERS.

Pears.   In the matter of pears, the first extract I have to mention is from a letter Oct. 18, by an agent of the Department in Great Britain, who writing about the California pears, says :

"Pears—(and these went by way of Montreal from California by our cool route)—sold from 7s. to 9s. 6d. per case of from 18 to 20 pounds of fruit ; and plums sold from 6s. 6d. to 12s. per case of from 18 to 20 pounds of fruit. The fruit was all in fine condition, having been picked green ; in fact some pears will not be ripe for some weeks, but they sell well for keeping stock."

Seven shillings to nine shillings and sixpence because they had keeping qualities ; the keeping qualities are what they pay for in England in the meantime. That fruit was landed from the ship's cold storage at from 38 to 40 degrees. The next short extract I have in regard to pears is in a letter also from Mr. Grindley, of Oct. 22, in regard to the shipment of fruit in one of the steamships :

"I am glad to say it is turning out in regard to condition much better than the first three con- signments. Pears very good, Peaches in very fair condition, some cases still too ripe. Tomatoes sound and still green."

Those were the tomatoes that two days after they were sold collapsed and would not keep after they came out of cold storage.

Then there is a letter of Oct. 4 from the firm of Elder, Dempster & Co., the steam- ship owners, and also the men who sold the fruit. They have developed an enormous trade for the distribution of fruit in England. They say :

"Pears have made what we consider a good return, and the shipments received since have been in better condition than the first, and we show considerably better results by these." Mr. O. W. Van Duzer's pears very fine, and should advise shipping large quantities to this market.

I happened to see two of these lots of pears that were selected,—about the size and shape and quality to throw on the open market. The next quotation I want to make is from Elder, Dempster & Co., speaking of pears again :

"Packing of pears satisfactory, but we should like them a little greener than they have been. Tomatoes absolutely useless, and we should prefer that this packer sent no more to this market."

MR. McNEILL : May I enquire whether that Canadian packer had any experience locally in shipping tomatoes ?

Prof. ROBERTSON : I suppose that this man had, because all seem to grow tomatoes and ship them to the local markets in Canada. We find that tomatoes will do very well carried in a ventilated space but do not seem to keep well in cold storage. The toma- toes that we put to the test in Ottawa seem to have gone in the same way. This is from Thomas Russell, a fruit merchant in Glasgow, to whom a shipment was sent :

"The pears sold well, especially as at the time of their arrival our market was in a manner glutted with French pears which were being sold very cheap."

I have this further to say before I leave the pear subject : That you will see from the reports even from the last observation, that the pears from Canada this year did not strike any special catch market. On three different occasions the report was, "The market is rather glutted and dull from large arrivals from the continent."

Mr. PATTISON : Can you tell us anything as to the varieties of pears ?

Prof. Robertson : They do not give us any statements of preference for any particular variety. The reports are for soundness, keeping quality and appearance, and then for variety or flavor after that.

A Delegate : Do you know if there were any Kieffers sent ?

Prof. Robertson : Yes, in the last shipment, and they were sold at from 4s. to 3s. 6d. per case of about 28 pounds ; that would bring from 59 to 47 cents nett at Grimsby, and that was at the time when the price was lowest in England.

Mr. Smith : Are we to understand there is no preference for any variety of pear ?

Prof. Robertson : The Kieffers were sold for within twelve cents a case as much as the Duchess. So far as our testing of the English market goes, the price paid is according to the soundness, the keeping quality and the appearance, and then the flavor is considered. California pears were sold at much higher prices than even our Bartletts, because they had keeping qualities. The flavor and other eating qualities must be fair.

The Secretary : Last year one shipper who received a case of Kieffer pears in Great Britain said that he did not care to buy a second box.

Mr. Brodie : Do they use that Kieffer pear for table decoration or for use ? (Laughter.)

Prof. Robertson : I am unable to say that. Some kinds must be used for table decoration, but that is not the kind that should be sent. While soundness and keeping qualities and appearance are things wanted now, in the course of a few years they will begin to discriminate, and if we have given them good pears with fair keeping qualities all along we will have the first place in the market. In the meantime their money is paid only for the fruit having soundness and keeping qualities ; so let us get our fruit there in that condition, and of the best flavor and flesh we can. We will then have the preference in the market in the long run when the keener competition comes.

Peaches. The following are a few extracts from letters in regard to Peaches :

"Peaches turned out six over ripe in eleven cases and 40 cases are now in Elder, Dempster & Co.'s back yard completely rotten."

These went in cold storage at from 36 to 38 degrees. The second says :

"Peaches already shipped have the appearance of having been chilled, besides, on being exposed to warm temperature, they gather moisture which hastens decay—some of the paper wrappings being quite wet."

That is, from being very cold, moisture from the English atmosphere was condensed on them ; and that hastened their decay. The next quotation on that matter is in a letter from Elder, Dempster & Co., of 4th October. They say :

"Peaches.—We would advise you to stop shipments of these as they will cost senders more money than they will realize. Your Mr. Grindley has seen these goods, and, we understand, he is advising you to stop shipments of them."

Then on October 24 the same firm writes :

"Peaches realized much better prices than we anticipated, but since selling these by auction we have received numerous complaints with enquiries for money to be returned. They arrived here in a condition which we are unable to put into words, namely : Dry. They being absolutely useless for dessert fruit. We should advise this packer not to ship any more of these in cold storage, and if you can pack in smaller packages, containing about two dozen peaches, wrapped in wool, and picked green, so that they can ripen on the voyage, we are sure you should make a good market here."

That would seem to indicate that they would like trial shipments, not in cold storage but in ventilated space. The peaches I put in cold storage kept all right, but those that we put in green became dry and almost quite tasteless. The difficulty is to get the peaches just at the right condition of ripeness for shipment.

Plums. Then there is a remark about Plums :

"Plums were in very bad condition, they being picked when a little too ripe. Apples in good condition, but packages are too small to pay for voyage."

Grapes. The quotations I have next are about Grapes.

From Mr. Grindley, Oct. 7 :

"I have cabled and written to you several times regarding the unsatisfactory condition in which the peaches and tomatoes are reaching here, and should advise the stoppage altogether of consignments of both peaches and tomatoes, and I might also add grapes, for although they arrive in fair condition, there is no demand for them owing to the flavor."

Then on October 18 :

"I noticed in Bristol one large fruit dealer was selling our grapes (card in window) as 'Choice California.' They told me nobody wanted 'Canadian Grapes,' but they sold some as Californians."

I am giving you the facts without being able to account for all the mysteries of English commerce and of the English palate. The varieties shipped were mostly Rogers Red, Rogers Black, Lindley and Niagara ; and I think only a few Concords. I think the bulk of them were Rogers Red and Rogers Black. I think the grapes this year were representative of the best grapes in the Niagara Peninsula at the time the shipments were made.

Mr. GREGORY : Have you a statement of what the grapes sold for per pound ?

Prof. ROBERTSON : Most of them fetched no price at all ; they were nearly all given away. The four shipments from Mr. Linus Woolverton illustrate the rest. In the first shipment of grapes there were sent ten cases which netted twenty-three (23 9) cents a case at Grimsby ; that would be about sixty (60) cents over there. The next netted 19¼ at Grimsby ; the next lot were a complete loss ; and also the fourth a complete loss, leaving the freight and other expenses to be paid on the last two shipments, in addition to the loss of the fruit and the packages.

Mr. GREGORY : Was that in the same market ?

Prof. ROBERTSON : The same market. After the first two shipments, they would not buy them. There was not any complaint as to the condition of the grapes. They were not mildewed or soft or out of condition by falling off the stems.

The next extract in regard to grapes is from Glasgow, in which the salesman says :

" Grapes--The demand for these were very slow on account of the peculiar flavor which they have and which is not relished as yet by our countrymen."

In these cases the grapes were Wilder, Agawam, Lindley and Niagara. They were sold all the way from five shillings and eightpence per case, the highest—(that is, $1.36 per case over there)—down to eightpence per case (that is 16 cents per case over there). There were a few Wilder grapes sold for four shillings and eightpence—(that is $1.12 over there). That would realize about 72 cents at Grimsby. Nine cases of Agawams were sold for three shillings and eightpence ; Lindleys for two shillings and one shilling and threepence. Twenty-eight other cases of Lindleys were sold for four shillings and fourpence. Niagara grapes were sold for from two shillings down to eightpence per case. Thirteen boxes of Red Rogers were sold for four shillings and eightpence, and seven boxes of Black Rogers were sold for five shillings and eightpence. These were all sold in Glasgow. The grapes which were sent to Bristol in the last two shipments were simply given away.

Tomatoes. Another extract from Elder, Dempster & Co.'s letter :

" As we have previously told you the grapes and tomatoes are useless to us, and we are bound to c aim from you any money which may be due for freight on them."

The next letter is from Mr. Grindley, the agent of the Department, dated November 10, in which he says :

" I examined tomatoes from Canary Islands packed in peat dust, and brou ht here as deck-loads, and they were in perfect condition."

That is where England gets most of its tomatoes from abroad. Then from the fruit salesman October 4.

" We are not satisfied by your putting these goods in cold storage, as the low temperature is detri - mental to the shipment, especially for peaches and tomatoes."

"Tomatoes—These have deteriorated considerably, as have peaches, owing to their being in cold storage, and we have had continual complaint from our customers of them. When they have been placed on show they melt into water, and 24 hours after being bought they are in a useless condition, and we have been compelled in many cases to return the money that was made at sale."

Then from Glasgow there comes the report :

"Tomatoes—There was no great demand for these on account of the cold weather, and the plentifu supply of local grown fruit."

Now, Mr. Chairman, I have come to the end of the extracts, and also to the end of my remarks, except these few things I have to say in conclusion. I think the prospect for a profitable trade in the exportation of Canadian pears is very good. We have the conditions for producing abundantly this class of fruit which the British public are both able and willing to pay good prices for.

A DELEGATE : How would quinces be ?

PROF. ROBERTSON : So far we find them sometimes being sold well and sometimes being given away.

MR. PATTISON : Is there any prospect of putting plums on that market in good shape ?

PROF. ROBERTSON : I think little prospect of making them pay well, because of the suitability of their own climate for growing them in most years. I think we might have a "snap market" occasionally.

A DELEGATE : What is the method of cold storage ?

PROF. ROBERTSON : Mechanical refrigeration by the use of ammonia to a temperature of 36 to 40 Fahr.

PROF. MILLS : Do California apples, tomatoes, plums and peaches reach there in good shape ?

PROF. ROBERTSON : Their main trade has been in pears, and they were at it four or five years before they made a success of it. This year they have added peaches. They had failures for two years, the shippers were said to have lost $200,000 in one year. After they had learned to pack and carry pears successfully they have gone into the peach business, and apparently are making a success of that.

PROF. MILLS : Have they done anything with tomatoes and grapes ?

PROF. ROBERTSON : I think not with tomatoes. They have with grapes ; their grapes have thick skins and tough flesh.

A DELEGATE : Did you send any Sultana plums ?

PROF. ROBERTSON : No, and as far as I could learn on the spot from talking with merchants, the English grown plum is usually sufficient for their own needs at fair prices, and we have not any chance of getting a demand for our plums at a profit.

With regard to peaches it does not seem to me that we can expect a profitable trade in exporting peaches from Canada to Great Britain by means of cold storage, nor can we expect a profitable trade at all in sending over Crawford peaches from Canada to England. The fruit is so tender that unless picked at a particular hour of the day, when its development is just right, there would be a risk of loss so great that no commercial man would take up the venture on a large scale.

With regard to tomatoes the position is still doubtful, but the increased production in the south of England and the Canary Islands is putting the price down there so low that counting our extra expense and our extra risk I am not hopeful we will have a trade in tomatoes. Even if they could be carried safely it is doubtful if we could make it pay as against these other competitors.

I do not think we need look for trade of large volume in grapes.

A DELEGATE : Could you give us the month in which the peaches were shipped.

PROF. ROBERTSON : I think the first shipment of fruit went out on the 7th September.

A DELEGATE : Do you know if any Smock peaches were shipped ?

THE SECRETARY : There were a few.

PROF. ROBERTSON : An effort was made through Mr. Woolverton's own enterprise in sending thirty cases of grapes to one of the jam-makers, and he reported that they were entirely useless for his purposes.

In the case of the more tender sorts of apples I think a very large trade can be developed, and only developed by shipping them in cold storage.

GENERAL CONCLUSIONS.

My conclusions so far as they can be stated with any satisfaction to myself with some sense of the responsibility under which I say them, is that Canadians may have a continuously growing trade in the exportation of pears ; that there is a possibility of getting a trade that may leave a living profit from shipping tomatoes ; that there is no likelihood of making a success of sending over Crawford peaches ; and that the demand for Canadian grapes does not exist, and it is a question to be considered whether it would pay us to send about one carload a week of our best sorts to further try to create a demand or not. Other tender fruits such as raspberries and currants and things of that kind could only, I think, be sent across profitably in the form of pulp, and that may or may not be profitable just as there is a scarcity or a large crop of these small fruits in Great Britain for the year. If the crop there is large the price goes so low that there will be no profit in sending them over from here.

THE SECRETARY : Why could not Crawford peaches be sent in pulp ?

PROF. ROBERTSON : The price of all fruit pulp, except rasberry pulp, is from £18 to £22 per ton. I asked if they could take anything but raspberry pulp, and they said other things would have to create a demand for themselves. At £22 per ton, after taking off the costs of preparing the cost of packages, transportation and commissions, I do not think there would be enough left for the fruit to induce our people to provide it.

MR GREGORY : What is the charge per ton for transportation and for freight for grapes and pears ?

PROF. ROBERTSON : The freights from Grimsby to Montreal are 33 cents per hundred pounds. The freight on the ship is by measurement, usually about twenty shillings per forty cubic feet in cold storage. The total expenses for transportation this year comes to 34 cents per case.

MR. GREGORY : Per case of 28 pound?

PROF. ROBERTSON : Yes ; that was the whole expense—transportation and dock dues and everything on the other side excepting the item of commission, which was only three per cent. on these shipments.

MR. PRESIDENT : Now, I am sure that the time the Professor has taken up has been well spent indeed, and before we take up the next subject, which we might take up jointly with this the privilege will be given of asking the Professor any question you wish to ask.

MR. CASTON (Craighurst): There is more profit in the growing of early apples than in any other crop if you can get a maket for them, but they come in at a time when it was very hot. I would like to ask in regard to the ventilation of the barrel. There seems to be a difference of opinion as to how they should be shipped on board the car.

The PRESIDENT : That will come up under the head of transportation.

Mr. CASTON—Then I will confine myself at present to asking the Professor this question: Does he find the tender variety of apples deteriorate very fast on the other side ? That is what the commission men tell us ; they are trying to discourage the shipment of apples in cold storage.

Prof. ROBERTSON : The reports I have are that when apples are taken out of cold storage in warm-weather mo sture forms on them, and that causes them to deteriorate. Without cold storage they cannot be sent at all. A Montreal shipper shipped Duchess without cold storage and they were a complete loss.

Rev. W. WYE SMITH : Would the Professor tell us whether the Canadian manufac-turers have any good prospects for canned fruits in the Old Country ?

Prof. ROBERTSON : I saw a good many samples of Canadian canned fruits in Britain. I spoke of them as favorably as I could at the Board of Trade, when I met merchants, and I examined some cans in the hands of merchants there, who said they were pleased with them. I think that is a growing trade. Just how profitable it is I do not know. There is no chance at all of Canada putting up sweet preserves or jams and sending these from Canada to compete with those made in Britain. The cost of the sugar and the cost of the glass and the tin packages are so much greater here than there we are out of that trade.

Mr. BRODIE : I might mention one matter in connection with shipping apples in cold storage. The moment they are taken off the trees and put in a barrel they should be put in cold storage immediately, because if they are left even a couple of days the ripening process goes on and they will be a total loss to the shipper.

TRANSPORTATION.

The PRESIDENT : As the questions seem to come in the line of transportation I think it would be well to take that subject up now; and as you have had so much to do, Prof. Robertson, in the transportation of fruit, I would ask you to open the dis-cussion, and then Mr. Caston and others who are desirous of speaking on that subject will be gladly heard.

Prof. ROBERTSON : What I have to say on this subject will be rather suggestive than didactic. The more quickly an apple ripens the more quickly it rots. Ripening of apples goes on only when the fruit is held at a high enough temperature. If the temperature be put down low the ripening process practically stops. Now, unless some external means are taken to reduce the temperature, the ripening process goes on, and the ripening itself produces heat, and therefore makes the ripening go on still faster. I did not know one of the main uses of cold storage until I learned this morning from the paper read in the convention that the cause of the ever-increasing heat in apples was traceable to the actual presence of the devil in the fruit. (Laughter). Then I began to see that the devil himself, accustomed to a warm place, could not go on working in a very cold room. The reduction of temperature would certainly destroy the works of the devil, and that is said to be the highest use of human talent. Apples in ripening do create heat, and there must be a chance for letting the heat that is generated escape, and also a means of stopping the production of heat.

The early ripening apples should be cooled down below 50° just as soon as possible after they are taken off the trees; and then they should be cooled down as low as 40° as soon as may be after that. By that means even the very earliest ripening sorts could be landed in Great Britain in first rate condition. Now, if they are put in barrels at even 60° Fahr. and headed up close they will get up to 70° Fahr. in the centre of the barrel in a short time. If they are put in the hold of the ship, the whole place gets above 70° Fahr. in a short time, and then the apples all arrive as "wets" and "slacks." In 1897 a lot of over 500 barrels was sent, and the half that went in cold storage sold for 18s. a barrel and the half that went not in cold storage went for 8s. a barrel at the same time. There is no way of carrying these tender apples across except in cold storage.

Our large apple trade, saying nothing of the tender and early-ripening and early-decaying sorts, is not in a good way ; it is not on a good basis. I think I am quite within the mark in saying that 60 per cent. of the apples that go to Great Britain fetch less than two-thirds the price they could fetch if they were properly graded and properly and safely carried across the sea. Now, the grading and the packing and the carriage should not cost any more when done properly than in the haphazard way that has been allowed in the past. Just a word in regard to grading. It will pay any man who grows apples to feed all the small, mis shapen and in any way blemished apples to his pigs, and not to try to sell them in barrels—particularly if for the British market. Half a barrel of good apples well selected, well assorted and safely carried will fetch more money than half a barrel of good apples plus half a barrel of poor apples; and the expense of carrying the poor apples has to be charged against the price of the good apples. To protect ourselves—we will have to get some way of rousing the growers to a realization that they must not allow any man to pack their apples unless he does so in the best possible way. If the growers allow the other practice to prevail they are simply cutting off the best market, because the British public won't pay the price for mixed apples that they will pay for graded app'es.

The English merchant sells on commission, and he says, " Send in barrels," because he can sell more in barrels than in boxes; and the commercial man of to-day does not take any trouble if he can help it. Now, I would send apples across in bushel boxes and let the commission man fume for a while. A while ago they said, " You can't send any eggs here except in large cases." Now they all say our Canadian egg cases are the best on the market. Retail merchants tell me, " We can sell a small box of apples when we could not sell a barrel." It would pay a locality to have a cold storage into which the apples would go for three days before they are shipped. The steamship owners, without any contribution from the Government, have engaged this autumn to put in what they call ventilated cool storage in the ships; and apples will go better this way than in cold storage. It is provided by a duct to carry fresh cold air to the hold where the apples are. There is a cowl on top to catch the wind. Another duct leads from the top of hold to allow the warm air to escape. That makes a nice cool draught through the hold and allows the heat to escape. I think the apples should be cooled at the starting point, then carried in cool cars and in ventilated places on the steamships.

DR. MILLS : Would your recommendations apply to all varieties of apples ?

Prof. ROBERTSON : All apples that are moved in hot weather. If every apple is cooled down before it is shipped it simply gives it so much better keeping quality when it gets to England.

A DELEGATE : What line of steamers is it that is going to put in these ventilators ?

Prof. ROBERTSON : The Allans to Glasgow and London; Elder Dempster & Co. to Bristol; Thomsons to London ;|the Donaldsons to Glasgow, the Dominion Line to Liver. pool, and others. There are several big lines out of Montreal arranging to have them for the carriage of apples. Without them apples and cheese were being carried in such bad condition that the trade was being imperilled. I think if the Fruit Growers' Association of Ontario and the Fruit Growers of Canada do not take hold of this transportation pro. blem and bring about better methods and facilities, they may as well go out of the busi. ness. The fruit-growing has been done very well, but there has been so much loss and damage and dissatisfaction from the spoiling of fruit on the way to the markets, both for our home and foreign markets, that the matter must be taken hold of and corrected. It would pay every fruit locality to have a special cold storage building and a special agent. to look after the transportation.

Mr. BOULTER : The cattle men have spent a great deal of money and did succeed in impressing the Government with the necessity of having a man in Montreal to see that those cattle were properly shipped at Montreal on those vessels. Now, has the Fruit Growers' Association any more interest than they have ? And I want to ask, has any. one been appointed by the Government to look after the storing of fruit in the vessels and see that it is properly put on ?

Prof. ROBERTSON : We have a special cold storage Inspector in Montreal, who looks after the cold storage on the ships, because the Government contributes part of the ex. pense. I think the Government would not be willing to interfere—" Interfere " with a capital " I "—unless the trade ask them to; but if the fruit-growers ask to have a man at Montreal and St. John, N. B., to look after the proper storing of fruit, in the steamships I think the asking would likely be the receiving. (Hear, hear.)

Mr. BOULTER : I am sure something of that kind should be done. On the 8th or 10th an article appeared that our High Commissioner, Lord Strathcona, was in hopes of being able to get our evaporated apples in the British navy as ship stores. Now he has just arrived in Canada, and I think if he was waited upon by a deputation, something perhaps might be done. If that could be done there is an inexhaustible demand for our evaporated apples. We could thus use the immense quantity of apples that are not fit to ship to the Old Country. I think it is very important that some definite action should be taken by this Association to look after that while Lord Strathcona is in Canada.

A. H. PETTIT : I would like to ask what is the prospect of capacity in cold storage on board our steamships : A great many want to know if there is space enough for them to ship ?

Prof. ROBERTSON : I am not able to answer the question just yet, because negotiations are pending for a enlargement of the cold storage in the ships that now have it and the putting of it in the new steamships that are coming out. During this last season the cold storage chambers were more than filled from about the end of August. The applications for room in them were greater than the capacity of the cold storage from about the first week of September onwards ; and the steamship companies are now offering to put in larger cold storage apartments on certain conditions, but the negotiations are not yet carried to a conclusion. The probability is there will be enough cold storage accomodation next year for all the tender fruits that are ready to go, and a better ventilated cool storage space for some variety of apples that are half way between the very tender ones and the fall ones.

Mr. GREGORY : Is there any prospect of a more speedy transit of fruit across the Atlantic being obtained in the near future ?

Prof. ROBERTSON : The ships that are fitted with cold storage now are what they call nine and ten day boats from Montreal.

Mr. GREGORY : I notice the time you gave in your report was seventeen to twenty-one days. It seems to me that is longer than necessary from the time of its receipt on the ships till its arrival in the Old Country.

Mr. BRODIE : My experience is in shipping to Britain that when the market is glutted there are many slacks and wets, but when the market is firm the prices are good. I notice there are a great many commission men over here from the Old Country buying apples. Montreal is a great fruit centre. I think the best plan will be to have them come here and buy apples in Montreal. They cannot do without Canadian apples. American apples have no keeping properties, except Newtown Pippins, which bring better prices than some of our Canadian apples, but Canadian apples lead in price. I was speaking to one of our shippers in Montreal, and he told me there were more men from the other side buying apples than ever before, and he expected in the near future to see them all come over here to buy (Hear, hear).

Mr. CASTON : We have such a big country ourselves, we have a very large market within our own Dominion if we can land the apples there in a proper state. Great complaints come from Winnipeg and the Northwest about Ontario fruit arriving in such terribly bad condition, and the immense quantity of California fruit used there to the exclusion of ours. That is a very bad state of things. We require to study up the question of transportation within our own Dominion as well as across the ocean. I would like to ask the Secretary a question about the ventilated barrel There is a difference of opinion as to whether the fruit goes best in a refrigerator car, in a close barrel, or in a ventilated barrel. Some here have used the ventilated barrel, the Secretary among others, and I would like to know what his experience is in that respect. It is nearly always hot weather when the early fruit is packed, and if it is put in a close car I do not see how you can expect it to get to the Northwest or any distance in good shape. The temperature of a good refrigerator car with three or four tons of ice is about 45 deg., but it would carry fairly well in that. The question is, would it be well to have a ventilated package even in the refrigerator car, or have an ordinary close barrel? This is an important question, because there is a country from the head waters of the Ottawa to the Rocky mountains with a large mining as well as agricultural population, and in that stretch of country they will never be able to produce any of our fruits; and the farmers in the Northwest want our apples for cooking purposes at harvest time. (A voice: "That is right"). The transportation problem is in the way. The charges are too high. If we begin with the Duchess and follow that with our fall apples and lay them down so that the farmers could buy them, there is an immense outlet for our apples that is going to increase and grow. They grow No. 1 wheat and bring it down to compete with us, and we can retaliate with an article that they cannot grow. It is largely a question of transportation I think nearly everyone is aware that there is a great reduction coming in force in the year 1898 in the freight charges to the Northwest of 33 per cent.

Mr. BOULTER: It is not in force yet.

Mr. CASTON: That reduction in freight with quick transit facilities ought to give us a great outlet for our fruits. I think the same thing would be true about grapes up there, but transportation charges are so high as to put them out of the reach of the ordinary consumer. I think the fruit growers ought to take some action to see that there are proper intervals for re-icing those cars. I have known a man losing $100 on a car because the Railway Company would not undertake to re-ice the car. If these things are all in good order I do not see why our tender fruit should not be laid down in our own Dominion at a reasonable price to the consumer.

The SECRETARY: I think it is quite settled that the ventilated package is the only package for cold storage transportation. I have found that in my experimental shipments, and I have this summer sent some Astracans and Duchess across in a ventilated package with perfect success. This small package of Red Astracans has sold as high as five shillings for a case which only holds about a basket and a third, so you see that was exceedingly satisfactory. With regard to the ventilated barrel, I have used about 1,500 of the Kerr Patent Ventilated Barrel. I was very glad after the last was shipped, because the reports from England were that the ordinary tight barrel was the best, but that was not in cold storage. I believe for ordinary conditions the tight barrel is the best, but for cold storage I am satisfied you must have the ventilated package.

Mr. BOULTER: Last year 1 was in hopes that some of our own fruit was working its way into Winnipeg. The bulk of all the fruit in Winnipeg is from Missouri and Oregon, and complaint was made to me by one of the largest dealers that they could not get good early apples from Ontario. They want the apples out there in August, because they are commencing to work then. There is an unlimited demand for our early apples, but there are two very important items against them—first, the C.P.R. do not seem to understand it would be a great benefit for the people of Ontario to get apples into that country—it costs near $2.00 to get a barrel of apples to Calgary; then in the shipping of them they claim that they are not properly packed, and perhaps they are justified in the complaint. Why are not the apples properly shipped? The trouble is the C.P.R. discriminates. Sometimes I have had the same rates by rail as I have had lake and rail. If we could ship our apples there in a refrigerator car and get them all rail it would be very helpful. Last year I sent good Northern Spys to Rossland, and you would be surprised at the fine remarks I got as to them. A party I heard from came from Peterboro, and he said he had not seen a Northern Spy for the last six years in Calgary. It is a shame we cannot supply that country with our own Ontario apples. There is going to be a wonderful demand for our fruits in British Columbia. But we talk these things over and get very nervous and excited about them, and the thing collpases, there is nothing done; we appoint a committee, but what is everybody's business is nobody's. Let a little money be spent by some practical business men in seeing that arrangements are made to get these goods out there.

Dr. SAUNDERS: I would just like to say somewhat in extenuation of the position of the railway and express companies, that during the last year the express company reduced its rates from British Columbia to all points in the Northwest from $4 to $2.25. It was a big drop, and I believe the railway has also made some reduction in that direction, and I have no doubt the same rates, if they have not already been obtained, could be obtained in Ontario. That was a point I was going to bring out to-night, and I did not want to anticipate.

The PRESIDENT: I would like very much to hear from the representatives of the steamship lines, and if they are present we will take time to hear them, with pleasure. (Hear, hear.) Is Mr. J. D. Hunter present? Is there a representative of the Reford Company present? (Hear, hear.) It is evident they are not in the building, and it is very unfortunate they should leave the building just at a time when their subject is under discussion.

Mr. M. PETTIT: Unless the question of better transportation facilities in apples to Great Britain is discussed again I think we should not let these drop without taking some action. (Hear, hear.) Prof. Robertson has told us that if we ask for an Inspector, or whatever he may be called, to look after the better shipping facilities at the shipping ports, that we will likely get it. Well, I think we should appoint one or more delegates from this Association, and have our Secretary correspond with the Quebec Horticultural Society, and also the Nova Scotia Society, and have a delegation go to the Federal Government and urge strongly upon them the importance of having something done in this way. There is no question but there are hundreds and thousands of barrels of apples that are shipped across the ocean that are ruined on shipboard by being put in the wrong place, and if better facilities were brought about in this way it would be one of the greatest works that this Association has ever accomplished.

Mr. McNEILL: I quite agree with that view of it if it is a motion.

The PRESIDENT: You simply anticipated me in this matter. Acting on the hint that Prof. Robertson gave us I immediately named a committee to take action in the matter. It is one that I think is very important, and to save time I would appoint the Secretary, Mr. A. H. Pettit, and the Vice-President, Mr. Orr, as a committee to memorialize the Government and if necessary to act as a delegation to the Government and if possible to get them to appoint a man to see after the safe storage on ships and proper ventilation of holds.

Mr. M. PETTIT: It is right so far as it goes, but I think we should authorize our Secretary to urge upon the other societies the importance of joining with us in asking that this be done; it would strengthen us very much.

The PRESIDENT: I will ask you to appoint this Committee, and I will ask you to draw up a resolution to pass this evening giving them proper instructions. Will that be satisfactory? ("All right.")

The President read a letter from the Allan Steamship Company regarding cold storage, addressed to Mr. Hunter, and also a letter from the Reford Company to the Secretary of the Association.

The PRESIDENT: As a representative of the steamship companies are not here I do not see that we can do anything further. Meeting adjourned at 5.50 till 8 p.m.

ADDRESS OF WELCOME.

The Mayor of the City, Mr. GILLELAND, said: It affords me a great deal of pleasure to meet so large and influential a body of men as compose the Fruit Growers' Association of Ontario, and to extend to you on behalf of the citizens of St. Catharines a cordial and hearty welcome. The industry represented by this Association is one that in the last few years has been making very rapid progress. It is not so very many years since it was a rare thing to find upon farms, even in the most favored localities for fruit growing, any fruit of any great variety. Of course we had the old standard apple, and in this section we wish we had more of it this year as we are a little short. But of late years it would be almost impossible to find a farm but has plenty of fruit growing upon it. While I would not be favourable to putting a farm entirely in fruit, it is important to have fruit. The methods adopted have been very much improved of late years. We see here in the corridors machines for spraying fruit and bringing it to its greatest perfection. We think it is very fitting that this Association should meet in the old Niagara district—a district that has been noted for raising fruit and good fruits for so long a time. We who live in the County of Lincoln think we have the choice locality for fruit, although there are other localities heard from, and that favorably. When it was decided to hold your meeting here we were very pleased to hear you had done so. We knew full well the benefits to be derived from meetings of the Association to those engaged in this locality in the business who might not have had opportunities of any Association meetings previously. We knew it would be interesting to hear the topics discussed by those who were so competent to deal with them. I can only say we are glad to have you with us. I trust your Association will continue to make such favorable progress as you have in the past. I am told by a member of the Association that not a great while ago your meetings were comparatively small, but of late years they have been growing so much in interest that the Association has been gradually growing larger. I will only repeat my hope that you will enjoy the meeting here, that you will find it pleasant and agreeable, and I can assure you that anything that can be done by the members of the Council of the city and by the inhabitants generally to make your visit pleasant and agreeable will be done, and I trust that you will never have cause to regret having fixed your place of meeting in the city of St. Catharines. We welcome you, hope you will have a good time, and will be glad to have you repeat your visit at any future occasion. (Applause.)

The PRESIDENT: I am sure on behalf of the Fruit Growers' Association that very few words from me are necessary in reply to your address, because if you will look into the countenances of the officers and directors of this Association you will see that they are pleased already with their visit to this city. We are convinced, too, by the intelligent audience before us that the efforts of the Association are appreciated. A few years ago the work of this society was on very different lines from what it is in the present day. Then fruit growing was profitable without labor, I may say—that is, the labor that is now expended upon the industry. At the present time the efforts of the society have been directed not only to the prevention of the ruination of our orchards by disease, fungi and insects, but to meeting the problem of over-production of our local markets and towards finding other markets for our products. That always is a very important matter, and one of deepest interest to everyone engaged in the fruit-growing industry, because having invested their means in the growing of fruit, they naturally wish to follow the occupation out on those lines. It is not an easy matter to change from a fruit grower to a grain grower. It is very much easier for a grain grower to go into the fruit business. Having trees coming into bearing, and having fruit maturing each year, there must be an outlet for that if they are to continue in the business, and to go out of it would mean a heavy loss in capital and time. I am happy to say that the efforts of the fruit growers in that direction are bringing about happy results. We have received the greatest consideration from not only the local Government but the Dominion Government in that line. They have responded to our requests most nobly in every way where we have brought our troubles under their notice, and we are happy to say that with their efforts we believe we are now working on the lines which will bring us safely over the troubles I have indicated. But as far as St. Catherines is concerned, and the county of Lincoln, and indeed the whole Niagara Peninsula, everyone recognizes that in no part of this continent is there a more desirable situation for this industry, taking it from every point of view. It has flourished in the past, and while for a few years the outlook was rather poor, I believe we have a bright future before us. We certainly feel grateful to the city of St. Catharines and yourself and the Council for the hearty manner in which they have welcomed us. We are trying to do good. We labor in this institution without pay or favor, and labor for the common good ; and the greatest gratification and the best pay that we can have as members of the Association is to know that our efforts shall be crowned with success.

THE PRESIDENT'S ANNUAL ADDRESS.

By W. E. Wellington, Toronto.

It is always a source of gratification, when the head of a corporation can meet his Board of Directors, with a satisfactory balance sheet. The President's address is then one of a congratulatory nature, and the work is necessarily much lighter than when he has a long list of losses to explain in justification of his management. While we are not working for, or looking forward to dividends, in the Ontario Fruit Growers' Association, we are all much interested in the success of our Society, both from a financial point of view, and the accomplishment of the work that we give our time and thought to.

I am proud to say that I am able to congratulate the officers and members of the Ontario Fruit Growers' Association, on a successful year's work. Financially, I think the Society now stands higher than ever before in its history, and I believe the work of the Association is of the greatest benefit to the fruit growers of Canada.

Our monthly journal, under the able and industrious efforts of our Secretary and editor, is constantly improving, and is highly thought of, not only in Canada, but in many parts of the neighboring republic. While I do not think we have yet reached that point of excellence and superiority we should be ambitious to attain, we certainly are improving, and if we continue to improve in the next few years, at the same rate as the past year, we may look forward to soon publishing a journal that will take high rank with the best horticultural journals in America.

A few facts and figures will speak more eloquently than any words I can command. Last year, we reported $3,325.17 paid in fees, and this year we are able to report $4,147.13 paid in fees. The number of paid members in 1897 was 3315, while for 1898 we have 4,151 paid members, and in addition 375 members still unpaid, and this we look with confidence to receiving within a very short period of time.

The total receipts in 1896 have reached the magnificent sum of $6,585.94, and after paying all expenses, we are able to report a balance in hand of $784.96. This I think will be very gratifying to every member of the Association, and with this balance in hand, I would strongly recommend that for the incoming year efforts should be made to increase the size of the Journal, and also to increase again the subscription list. In fact, I believe if the size of the Journal is increased, and made at least one-third larger than at present, there would be little difficulty in securing additional members enough to carry on the work profitably, and also increase the benefits to every member of the Society in a practical way.

I wish particularly to draw attention to the numerous photogravures which illustrate the "Canadian Horticulturist", and which I think very materially increases its attractiveness. This is a decided improvement on the old style colored plate illustrations, and I think we can well afford to continue on these lines in the future.

Turning from the financial success of the Society, I would call your attention to the practical work of the Association, which I believe has been correspondingly successful.

The local horticultural societies are an interesting feature of our work, and are looked upon with great favor by the Department of Agriculture. These affiliated societies, are far more successful in their operations than the old agricultural societies, which benefited only a few professional prize-winners. Our plan is that every member should receive an equal benefit, either in literature or in plants. The number of Societies reported last year was 27. Now we have 36. In addition to this, there is the prospect of several more uniting with us during the present month. The Fruit Growers' Association has agreed to send a lecturer once a year, to each of these societies This will keep them in touch with us, and us with them, besides carrying out one of the most important conditions of the Agriculture and Arts Act.

I would call the attention of my hearers to the article on page 438 of the November number of the "Canadian Horticulturist" which describes the meeting of the Orange ville Horticultural Society. This is only a sample of the meetings held by the different societies with which we are affiliated, and will carry a very good idea of the interesting work that is being done. The enthusiasm which is awakened at some of these local meetings, is most gratifying, and encourages me to suggest that the work in that direction should be considerably extended the coming year.

Another work which may well be placed to the credit of the Ontario Fruit Growers' Association mainly, is the efforts to stamp out that terrible pest, the San José Scale. As you well know, a delegation from this Association was sent to Ottawa, to confer with the Minister of Agriculture regarding the importation of American stock, which has been so largely infested with this pest. On behalf of myself and colleagues who visited Ottawa, I wish to publicly thank the Hon. Sydney Fisher, for the courteous manner in which he received the delegation, and also for the prompt way in which he responded to our wishes. We found the Hon. Mr. Fisher had become fully alive to the importance of our mission, and his subsequent prompt action, shows that in him we have a man, who has thoroughly at heart the interests of the fruit growers of Canada.

The Local Legislature has in every way seconded the efforts of the Dominion Government in stamping out the San José Scale. I believe they have followed the work with vigor and energy, and are now able to show a comparatively clean sheet, and thus avoid the danger which threatened our fruit growers, of having their fruit excluded from the best foreign markets. Now, while Germany has excluded California fruit, there is no bar to that from Canada. We can now reasonably hope, that with the measures that have been adopted, the dreaded pest of the San José Scale will be kept in subjection in Canada, and we can only hope that at an early day, our neighbors across the line, who have now become very thoroughly awakened to the danger to fruit-growing in that country, will be able, by their efforts, to stamp out the pest, and that commercial relations may soon safely be resumed between the two countries.

Another important department of work, which has been largely brought about through the agency of our Association, is the Fruit Experimental work. I need not go into details of this work, because you are probably as familiar with it as I am. The reports printed by the Government are very full, and will give every member the fullest details as to the work of the different Stations. I think this work will prove of the greatest possible benefit to the Fruit Growers of Canada.

Not only have Stations been established in the well known fruit-growing districts of the Province, but the Board of Control have established Stations in the more exposed districts of Canada, where fruit-growing has never been successfully carried on.

At the last meeting of the Board of Control the Hon. Minister of Agriculture for Ontario, suggested that the Government Farm in Algoma might be used for experimental work, and it was decided to accept the offer, and plantings of the hardiest varieties of trees known to the Board will be sent to Algoma in the spring, and thoroughly tested. An experimental station will also be started at St. Joseph Island in Algoma, which is confidently hoped will be of estimable value to the settlers in northern districts.

At our southern stations efforts are being made to test nut culture for profit ; also new varieties of fruits, that otherwise might be lost to notice, and which, if of merit, we hope to bring into prominence.

In connection with the work of the Board of Control, a descriptive work on fruits of Ontario is being compiled by the secretary. Photographs of the different fruits are taken from year to year, as they can be obtained, and accurate descriptions written, so that at no distant date, we hope to present a work to the public, that will be reliable and of the greatest possible value to the fruit growers of this Province. We are also making the attempt this year to prepare a catalogue of fruits adapted to all parts of our Province.

Another important feature of the work of the Association is the plant distribution. Not only are the plants and trees distributed, of value to the subscribers, but sent as they are, to all parts of the Province—in fact, to all parts of the Dominion of Canada—it submits the different varieties to a test that will show their adaptability to the section in which they are planted. To give you an idea of the work that this distribution entails, and the interest with which the members of the Association regard it, I give you a list of the plants and trees distributed for 1898. They were :—430 Paeonias ; 1,582 Crimson Rambler Rose ; 292 Gault Raspberry ; 171 Victoria Black Currant; 1,151 Wickson Plum

Still another important feature of our work, is the encouragement which has been given to the export of fruit in cold storage to Great Britain. Especially has this been beneficial to fruit growers, in giving them practical knowledge as to the proper way in which to pack and prepare tender fruit for shipment in cold storage to Great Britain. Plans were formed by this Association, and submitted to the Minister of Agriculture, which have been carried out by him, and which are likely to prove of the most vital importance to the fruit growers of our country. Our own markets were beginning to be so over-stocked, that remunerative prices were no longer received for our produce, and our fruit growers were becoming discouraged, and were beginning to feel that they would have to give up the business.

Now, after two years of experiment, we have demonstrated clearly, that our pears can be exported to Great Britain, with the greatest success, and also bring to the grower the old prices which made fruit growing so profitable an industry in the past. Also that tender apples, such as Astrachan and Duchess, can be exported with success, and bring long prices in the British markets. Tomatoes also, with proper carriage, and if picked in a green state, can be safely exported, and will pay handsomely. I believe too, that in the near future, we shall find a profitable market for peaches, especially if varities are grown that are not so soft as the Early Crawford.

The experiments of two years, have on the whole, been attended with very gratifying results, and as we gain experience we shall soon be able, I feel certain, to land our best, and even some of our most tender fruits, in the British market, where prices will be realized that will be encouraging and profitable to our fruit growers. This work of the Society is of inestimable value to the fruit grower generally.

I might go more fully into facts and figures, but do not consider it necessary, after the article that appeared in the August number of the *Horticulturist*, on page 303. This article alone, with its accompanying illustrations, is worth many many times the expense attending the membership of this Society.

I might still further enlarge my address by referring to the crops of the different fruits in Canada and the United States, but this I think is needless because all such information is furnished in our magazine and other horticultural journals published on this continent.

We all know that for the past two years the apple crop has been rather light in most sections as compared with 1896, when the crop of apples from Canada and the United States was 69,879,000 barrels, which decreased in 1897 to 41,536,000, while this year the total crop is only 27,681,000 barrels. Nova Scotia this year is fortunate in having a crop of superb quality and fair proportions—the famous Annapolis Valley yielding 75 per cent. of the full crop, or three times the number of barrels produced last year. The quality is fine, and dealers are readily paying $2 per barrel.

The Ontario crop is decidedly short, Western Ontario having the best, but the heavy fruit belt from Buffalo around the head of Lake Ontario has a light crop, and the surplus for export will be comparatively small.

It is interesting to note that the number of apple trees planted in Ontario over fifteen years of age is 6,221,000, and under that age the number is 3,459,000. Probably, in round numbers, 10,000,000 of apple trees are growing in the Province of Ontario.

The apple crop in Europe being short, prices there will probably average higher than for many years past. I think on the whole the outlook for the fruit grower is encouraging.

I have as briefly as possibly gone over the main points of the work of this Association, and I trust that the members will agree with me that the year's work has been very satisfactory, not only financially, but that the practical work of the Association is such as to give it the confidence of the fruit grower ; and I believe I am safe in stating that in no other way can as much be obtained for one dollar as by becoming a member of this Association and subscribing to the *Canadian Horticulturist*, issued by the Fruit Growers' Association of Ontario.

I have now completed my second year of the presidency, and resign the work to the hands of the incoming president and officers, with every confidence that the good work will continue and that each year progress will be reported.

I wish to thank the officers and also the members of the Association for the help they have given in reaching the present gratifying position which the Fruit Growers' Association of Ontario holds.

MANITOBA AND THE NORTHWEST TERRITORIES AS MARKETS FOR ONTARIO AND BRITISH COLUMBIA FRUIT.

BY DR. WM. SAUNDERS, DIRECTOR EXPERIMENTAL FARMS, OTTAWA.

In view of the fact that Ontario is increasing so rapidly in the volume of fruit which it produces annually, it becomes of the greatest importance that we should look around for new markets, and that we should take advantage of every opportunity afforded us of increasing our sales in every direction. Although we now produce large quantities of fruit, we grow but a tithe of what we could grow provided we could find sufficiently large markets for our surplus. This subject has been given me, I presume, for the reason that travelling as I do across the Dominion every year, and sometimes twice a year, I have opportunities of becoming fairly familiar with the country and its products.

EXTENT OF COUNTRY.—I shall first call your attention to the extent of this country. Manitoba extends 320 miles along the C. P. R., and has its two additional southern lines running parallel ; it has also a line running north in the Dauphin Lake territory. A very important point in connection with the demand in any country for fruit is the number of villages, towns and cities to be supplied. Winnipeg now has a population of 40,000, Brandon 6,000, Portage la Prairie 4,500, and besides these larger towns there are many small places with a population varying from 200 to 1,000 or more in each. In addition there is a large population of farmers scattered through the country, and most of them, owing to the good crops which have been grown there for some years past, are very well to do, and as far as I know the people there are exceedingly fond of fruit and willing to pay almost any reasonable price for a good article. The cheaper it is, however, the larger the consumption will naturally be. Passing on to the Territories, we have a further stretch of settled country for 200 miles beyond the Manitoba boundary until we reach what is known as the Moosejaw district, where the general settlement of the country practically ends. Beyond that, for another 400 miles, until you reach the foot-hills of the Rocky Mountains the country, is more or less arid, and while agriculture is quite possible where irrigation can be practised the greater part of the country is bare of any attempts at cultivation, and is mostly used for ranching, bands of cattle and horses being kept at different points. As you approach within fifty miles of the Rocky mountains, you reach the town of Calgary, another important centre of population with about 4,500 people. It is also a railway centre, having a line running north for 200 miles to Edmonton, passing through many villages and small towns on the way to the terminus, and another line running south to Fort McLeod, which connects with the Crow's Nest Pass Railway at that point, and carries supplies to the population in the mining districts. So you see, taking those sections of the Territories together with the eastern part, Regina with its population of 2,200, Qu'Appelle with about 1,000, and Broadview 800, and a number of other small places along the main line, together with the branch line running from Regina to Prince Albert 250 miles, you have a stretch of country which although as yet sparsely populated is filling up with a fair amount of rapidity, many thousands of new settlers coming in every year, some from Europe and some from the United States. Throughout this whole region there is a growing demand for fruit which will admit of a consumption far exceeding anything we have at present any idea of, provided we can get the surplus stock which can be easily produced in Ontario landed there so as to be sold at reasonable rates. Talking with a gentleman from Prince Albert some time ago on this subject of fruit, he said, "Why, we have been so accustomed to pay about fifteen cents a pound for fruit that now it has got down to eight and ten cents a pound it seems to be a comparatively cheap article of diet, and we are making use of it very freely."

FRUIT GROWING IN THE NORTH-WEST COUNTRY.— I shall next call your attention to another aspect of the subject, and consider what these people living in this district, extending for a thousand miles from east to west, and 350 from north to south, are able to do for themselves in the way of growing fruit. The cultivation of strawberries has been tried at a great many different points in this part of our country, and it has not been attended with much success. Strawberry vines are hardy, but in the autumn, about the time when the young runners begin to root, the ground in the North-West is usually so dry that for an inch or two the soil becomes almost like ashes, and the winds are so frequent that the vines are rarely still, and the runners are blown about from point to point and never stay long enough in one place to send out roots, and for that reason there is seldom much success in propagating the strawberry. Where irrigation can be practised that difficulty can be overcome. Under such circumstances plots of strawberries may be grown with a fair measure of success as far as multiplication of the plants are concerned. But there is another difficulty to contend with. In the springtime it often happens that heavy frosts occur in the morning and a hot sun shines during the day. This occurs usually in April and sometimes in the early part of May, after the strawberries are in flower, and you know the effect of severe frost on strawberry blossoms—it destroys them completely, and so lessens the crop that strawberry growing cannot be relied on anywhere as a profitable industry, and this fruit is chiefly grown by amateurs. Raspberries are cultivated more successfully, and some fairly good crops are grown in some parts of Southern Manitoba, and also in the neighborhood of Winnipeg, but there is not a sufficient supply to give the general public what they want in this line. Black cap raspberries are less hardy, and blackberries are usually too tender. Red and white currants can be grown very successfully all over Manitoba and the Territories, provided there are no severe spring frosts to injure the crop after the blossoms open; in that case they can be depended on as a fairly reliable crop. The same may be said of black currants, all the varieties of which are hardy and succeed well, and, barring the effect of frosts, where they get a favorable season the crops are usually good.

Among the large fruit no success in a general way has attended the efforts to grow apples, pears, such plums as we grow in the east, or grapes. At the Experimental Farm at Brandon—and similar experiments have been carried on 200 miles further west at the Experimental Farm at Indian Head—we have tested over 200 varieties of Russian apples of the hardiest sorts that can be found. We have also tested all the hardy varieties of pears, plums and cherries, and have also tried a large number of small fruits. None of the larger fruits have succeeded, although we have been working on this line at Brandon and Indian Head for more than ten years. We have sent thousands of apple trees to these farms but have never yet succeeded in producing an apple. Hence, as you see, we have not had much encouragement thus far. Near Morden in Manitoba, which is in the Red River Valley and south of Winnipeg, at an altitude very much the same as that of Winnipeg, that is about 700 feet, or nearly 500 feet lower than the experimental farm at Brandon, there is one farmer who has an exceptionally sheltered spot who has grown fair crops of crab apples on a few trees, and he has also produced a few larger apples of several Russian varieties. This is considered quite a feat in that country, and is chronicled in the newspapers, and specimens are photographed and made much of, showing that it is a feat not often or very easily accomplished. I visited this plantation several years ago. It is owned by Mr. Stevenson, who is an enthusiast in this work. There have also been a few crab apples produced in the neighbor-hood of Winnipeg, and a few more in Southern Manitoba, and that is about the extent to which these fruits have been grown in that country thus far. I visited Edmonton, 200 miles north of Calgary, several years ago, and almost the first person I met when he knew who I was and where I came from said, " Oh, you must go and see Mrs. So and-So's garden; she has got a Tetofsky apple on a tree, and you must see that before you go." So I went over to see this prodigy, and there happened to be an American friend travelling with me with a camera, so I asked him to come along and take a photograph of this wonderful fruit. When we got there we found that the apple was not a Tetofsky apple at all, but a Whitney Crab. (Laughter.) As there was but one specimen on the lower part of the tree, and it was pretty well covered with foliage and the lady was much disappointed when it was pronounced to be a crab, we left the place without taking a photograph of this fruit. Altitude in the Northwest country often makes more difference and stands more in the way of success in the growing of trees and shrubs than latitude ; hence in going west, as you rise higher and higher the difficulties increase. At Brandon, where the altitude is 450 feet greater than it is at Winnipeg, we have had no such success as that I referred to as having been had by Mr. Stevenson near Morden. The only variety of fruit that can be called an apple which we have yet produced at Brandon is the berried crab *Pyrus baccata*, a small crab which grows wild in the northern part of Siberia. This fruit, which is about as large as a cherry and with a stem almost as long. would scarcely be recognized in this country as an apple—yet it is valuable for making jelly, for most of you no doubt know that jelly comes chiefly from the core, seeds and under the skin of the apple, and as these little apples are nearly all core, seeds and skin they make more jelly per pound than the larger apples would, and it is just as good. We are, however, trying some experiments at Ottawa which I hope may result in increasing the size of this apple. The *Pyrus baccata* has been crossed with such apples as Tetofsky, Duchess, Yellow Transparent, Fameuse and Ribston Pippin and quite a number of other varieties, includ- ing some of the hardier Russian forms, and we have now growing at Ottawa 750 of these young cross-bred trees, each one of which is a distinct variety, and we are hoping, by mul- tiplying the chances in this way, to produce something good eventually, and trust that in a few years we shall be able to thus improve this small, wild Siberian crab and increase its size so as to make it a tolerably useful apple to the people in the Northwest country. We do not expect to produce such varieties as will be competitors to any extent with the fruit that Ontario could ship there, but if we could grow an apple equal to the Transcendant crab and produce it in abundance it would be worth hundreds of thousands of dollars to that country. In many districts remote from railways the people seldom taste fruit at all, and to be able to grow fruit as palatable as the Transcendant crab would be something to be proud of. Householders would rejoice in such a production to an extent which these of you who are privileged to be surrounded by beautiful fruits can scarcely under- stand. Besides, the growing of such apples in that country would not only add largely to the comforts of the householder, but would give the climate of the country an addi- tional recommendation As you go further westward the altitude increases, and by the time you reach Calgary you have attained an elevation of 3,388. If so little can be done at Brandon at a height of 1,150 feet, but little success can be expected in the higher altitudes. In Manitoba in the river valleys, in the lower altitudes, the wild plum is common and usually fruits well, but the quality of the fruit is very variable. A large proportion of the trees produce inferior fruit. Some of them, however, have fruit which is very acceptable to the people, and it varies in color as the wild plum does in the east, from yellow to red. The trees are generally hardy, and they will not only grow in the river valleys, but when transplanted to higher altitudes most of them will grow and bear well. The Sand Cherry, *Prunus pumila*, is also found throughout most of that section of the Dominion, growing in many localities as far north as Prince Albert, where the fruit is produced in considerable abundance. The fruit of this shrub varies also, like the wild plum, very much in its quality and character. Some bushes produce cherries that are quite a good size. I have seen them nearly as large as the English Morello ; then again you find them but little more than a skin stretched over the stone, with no pulp at all worth speaking of, and not only astringent but bitter. By selecting the best of these varieties of Sand Cherry, as has been done at Brandon, and growing seedlings from them and propagating these by layers and distributing them among the people, we are doing a work which is much appreciated. Should the experiments now being tried on the *Pyrus Baccata* prove successful, and the further work of producing good varieties from the wild plum and the Sand Cherry by careful selection meet with good results, we have along these three lines of work some promise of useful fruits for this western country in the near future.

SOME NATIVE FRUITS.—In some districts wild strawberries are found, but not to any extent—the wild raspberry is much commoner. The fruit of the wild black currant is also common, and is used very generally, though it is rather strong in flavor. The Saskatoon berry is another favorite fruit in that country, and in plentiful years it is collected in large quantities and dried. The fruit is very much like what we know in the east as the Shad bush or June berry, and reminds one somewhat of the Blueberry in its flavor, and is a very good berry, especially if you are fruit hungry and cannot get anything else of that sort to eat. The Pin Cherry, *Prunus Pennsylvanica*, which grows in the east also has a very small fruit, yet it is regarded there with favor by many people, who gather it and make jams and jellies from the little pulp there is over the stone ; and by gathering plenty of the fruit one can succeed in getting a reasonable amount of jelly. These smaller fruits, with the wild plum, the Sand Cherry, and further east down towards Rat Portage the Blueberry, make rather a meagre bill of fare. Hence there is a very large demand for good fruit, most of which Ontario and British Columbia could supply, but up to the present time about eighty per cent. of it has been supplied by the United States, some of it coming from California, some from Oregon and Washington, and some from the Western States of Illinois, Michigan and Minnesota. It seems scarcely creditable to the enterprise of our fruit growers that four-fifths of all the fruit that is at present used over this whole stretch of country, populated at present probably by nearly 250,000 people, is sent in from the United States. Here is a market that Ontario should do something to capture.

FRUIT GROWING IN BRITISH COLUMBIA.—Let us see what British Columbia is doing, and what she can probably supply. Crossing the Rocky Mountains at a height about 5,000 or 6,000 feet you descend on the other side into what is known as the Columbia Valley, where the first crossing of the Columbia River occurs. In this valley, from Golden to Donald, which is at an altitude of about 2,530 feet, and much sheltered by high mountains, some experiments are being carried on in fruit growing, and although they have not been conducted long enough to demonstrate much, still there seems to be fair prospects of success with some of the hardier fruits in that valley. The Columbia River flows north at the first crossing, and makes a great bend above the base of the Selkirk range of mountains, and then flows south, so that after crossing the Selkirks, which form the second range of mountains at about the same altitude as that at which the Rockies are crossed, you descend into another valley where the Columbia is crossed the second time, and there the altitude is less. At that second crossing, at Revelstoke, it is only 1,475 feet—about 300 feet higher than we have at Brandon—and much more sheltered. There the climate is milder, and along that river valley from Revelstoke down to Rossland there have been within the last three or four years some very successful efforts made in the way of growing small fruits, and there are a few old-timers who have been there a number of years who have had apples and other trees which have been producing of late fairly good crops of fruit. Hence that may be taken as the beginning of the fruit growing district, or the eastern extremity of the fruit growing districts of British Columbia. After the third range of mountains known as the Gold range, is crossed, which is not nearly as high as either the Rockies or Selkirks, you strike another series of valleys at a point which you will find on the railway guide marked as Sycamous, a station which is 1,300 feet above the sea level, and stands at the head of what is called the Spulmacheen valley which extends south about 30 miles, and south of that lies the Okanagan valley, which most of you have heard of as a fruit growing district, where Lord Aberdeen has a large ranch, and has a 200 acre apple orchard which is coming into bearing very nicely. There is quite a large number of apples produced in that valley, but they get prices such as you would not dream of getting here. I travelled through that district in August last and visited Lord

Aberdeen's ranch at Coldstream, which is in the upper part of the Okanagan Valley, and another orchard which he has near the town of Kelowna, situated about the middle of the valley. At Kelowna the manager told me he had sold all his apples to a firm in that town at three cents a pound. All he had to do was to pick them and take them in in boxes, not packed in any way, and they undertook to pack them and ship them to the mining districts, and were doing fairly well with them, buying them at that figure. At the other ranch the manager said he was not willing to take such a low price, that he was doing better by shipping them direct to the mining districts. $1.80 a bushel would be considered a pretty good price for apples in this neighborhood, but there it was not regarded as anything extraordinary. Such prices are mainly due to the difficulties of getting fruit in from the outside on account of the great distance from the points of pro-duction and the expense of transportation. In the Okanagan valley there are large numbers of varieties of apples grown, and they do very well, and bear abundantly. There are also a number of pears produced, such as the Bartlett, Flemish Beauty, Anjou, and other good sorts, and these also bear well. Plums bear abundantly and cherries also have good crops, but the season is not long enough there for the ripening of grapes. The season is too short also in the Coast climate of British Columbia to permit of grapes ripening well ; so that as far as grapes are concerned Ontario has no competitor in this western country as far as the Dominion is concerned. California is the only country which can compete with you in that particular. I was surprised on going through the Okanagan valley last year to find in several places quite a number of peach trees in bearing. I had heard of peach trees down there doing wonderfully well, but had never before seen any trees with fruit on them, and as this was my third visit to the valley I began to think that possibly they never bore; but this year there was a considerable quantity of peaches of good quality, some of which I had the pleasure of testing on the trees, which sold in the orchards at five cents a pound, and must have netted their owners very good returns.

FRUIT IN THE COAST CLIMATE.—Starting from the terminus of the Canadian Pacific Railway at Vancouver, and coming east again, we have between Vancouver and the Coast range of mountains—which is the last range you cross in going to the Pacific Ocean—about 100 miles of territory in which there are a large number of valleys where the land is rich and the country sheltered by mountains, and the climate is very much like the climate of England. Here apples, pears, plums and cherries can be grown in the greatest abundance. Plums I have never seen grow so abundantly anywhere as in that region, and the apple trees also bear very heavily. Throughout this whole territorry a great deal of enterprise has been shown of late years in fruit growing, and orchards are being planted in every direction. During the past year, 1898, the weather has been warmer than usual, and at Agassiz, where the Experimental Farm is located for that Province, which is 70 miles east of Vancouver, we have succeeded in ripening quite a number of varieties of grapes, including the Delaware, Agawam, Brighton, and a number of other sorts, some of which have not ripened on that farm in any season before. The experience of this year shows, however, that in favorable years a limited quantity of grapes, such as people can eat, may be grown, but they are not thoroughly ripened or such as you would call fully ripe in this section of the country; they are, however, quite eatable and are in demand there. The quantity of such fruit available, nevertheless, even in a favorable season, is quite insufficient to supply the home market, and the crop is too unreliable to induce extensive planting. British Columbia, however, may be expected to be a formidable competitor of Ontario in the production of plums, apples, pears and cherries, and every year as the new orchards come into bearing—and they are coming into bearing very rapidly—the quantity of fruit produced will be increased very much. In point of distance, taking Winnipeg as the great distributing centre, which it is, Ontario has an advantage, for while Vancouver is 1,464 miles from Winnipeg, Ottawa is only about 1,300, and Toronto would be somewhat nearer. For Calgary, however, and Regina, and the lines running north, British Columbia is nearer, and would have some advantage in supplying those districts. The fruit growers in British Columbia have been very much handicapped by the heavy rates which have been charged in past years for transportation. Four years ago six cents a pound was charged to carry fruits by express from Vancouver to Winnipeg, subsequently it was reduced to five cents, and the year before last it come down to four cents ; but as fruits began to be produced in considerable quantities and the surplus had to be shipped somewhere the growers could not afford to pay four cents per pound to send plums to Winnipeg —it made the price too high to permit of the consumption becoming very large—so they organized and formed an Association, and made arrangements with the railway for cheaper rates by freight, and sent a man through with each carload of fruit, who landed a certain number of boxes at Calgary, other lots at Regina and other points, taking the remainder of the car through to Winnipeg. They had the privilege of thus unloading as they went along, all at the same rate. This reduced the cost of transportation to something less than two cents, but it delayed the distribution of fruit very much, and by the time the car had reached Winnipeg with all the delays incident to the journey, the fruit which was left was usually in bad order. In the meantime the express company found they would have to do something in the way of reducing rates, if they were to secure any part of this business, so this year negotiations were opened between the Association of Fruit Growers of the Fraser Valley and the Dominion Express Company, and the Company very generously brought the rate down to $2.25 from Vancouver or any point in British Columbia to Winnipeg or any. point in the Northwest. This great reduction has given a wonderful impetus to fruit growing in that Province, and has given the growers courage, so that they are trying to make the best of their opportunities and are doing remarkably well. In connection with their shipping association they have meetings to discuss the best kinds of packages, and instead of shipping their fruit in clumsy rough boxes as they used to do two or three years ago, they are using the California packages now, those small light boxes with four baskets in a box, and all their plums are sent to market in that way. They are also paying more attention to the selection of their fruit, which is a matter of great moment if a profitable business is to be done. In that Association every grower must put his name on every box of fruit he ships, so that the careless packing is easily traced to its source, and the man gets such a rubbing down from the secretary who looks after the affairs of the Association that he is very apt to mend his ways in a short time ; hence a much better condition now exists than formerly. Fruit reaches the consumer in about three days from the time of shipment by this arrangement with the express company and usually in good condition.

AN OPENING FOR ONTARIO FRUIT.—Ontario could secure a large part of this trade with Winnipeg and the west for apples and pears, also a considerable part of the trade in plums and cherries as far west as Regina, and as far as the grape trade is concerned, as I have already remarked, the whole of that is open to Ontario growers. Here is a market for our own fruits where the tastes of the people do not require to be educated to appreciate the flavor, for instance, of our grapes. Indeed, many of the people having been brought up in the east will prefer,— and I have been surprised at this—the Ontario grown grapes to the California grapes, which to my mind are very much better than those of Ontario ; but having acquired a fondness for the musky flavor found in many of our grapes they will give the preference even at the same price to Ontario fruit. At present, Ontario fruit has not a very high reputation in Winnipeg, largely it is said, for the reason that in the past it has been very carelessly shipped. To put a lot of baskets of grapes in a freight car and have them bumped and thumped against other freight cars for four or five days on the way to Winnipeg, generally shakes the baskets of this fruit to such an extent that a large part of the grapes are reduced almost to a condition of pulp. When bruised in that way, they soon get mildewed, and in a closed car, unless the car is iced, the chances of getting fruit of that character to Winnipeg in good condition in such packages as you use to send them to Toronto is not very great. Indeed, there must be a very thorough reformation in that particular, and the interests at stake will warrant the taking of any reasonable pains to bring success, and I do not think that any form of package yet devised is better adapted for this purpose than that used by the British Columbia fruit growers, which is the California package. In this there are four baskets, each holding about 6 pounds, the whole package weighing about 25 pounds, a weight which is easily handled. I have no doubt that arrangements could be made by Ontario fruit growers with the express company whereby they would get at least as good rates as are given to

British Columbia people, and by this route fruit could be delivered in three days from time of shipping to any part of that country on the main line as far as Regina, and Ontario grapes if well put up and carefully handled should stand that length of time in transportion and reach their destination in perfect order. A word to the wise, it is said, is sufficient. I hope that some Ontario fruit growers, although they may have made unsuccessful attempts in the past, will use their best efforts towards capturing some fair share of this market. It will not do to run away with the idea that any sort of fruit will suit the Winnipeg people. In talking recently with the largest fruit merchant there, he said: "If you have at any time the opportunity of talking to the large fruit growers in Ontaria, impress upon their minds the fact that nothing is too good for Winnipeg, and that it won't pay them to ship inferior fruit." He said "It is disagreeable for us to handle it, we have so many complaints, and it gives no profit whatever to the shipper, because so much of it has to be rejected" A demand for Ontario fruit once established in the Northwest country would be an ever-increasing one as the population multiplies, and would in a short time, I am sure, get to be a trade quite well worth looking after. Through the kindness of the manager of the Macpherson Fruit Company at Winnipeg I have been furnished with some particulars as to the quantity of fruit handled by that one firm during the past year, from that source. Mr. Scott tells me that they have handled of British Columbia plums this season about 10,000 cases of about 20 pounds each, besides small experimental shipments of 200 cases of strawberries and 25 cases of cherries. Many of the earlier shipments of plums he says, came in bad order, but the later shipments were all right. In regard to Ontario fruit, he said, "We have not had good results yet from plums or peaches, and we are inclined to think that it is a difficult matter to ship these two varieties of fruits to this point at a profit." He says it takes some time in a comparatively small market like that to dispose of a car load of fruit, and in the meantime the perishable varieties depreciate very rapidly. Grapes, however, he says, tomatoes and pears in baskets, or packed in boxes as the California pears are sent in, come in perfect condition, and if shipped in good refrigerator cars well iced, there would be no difficulty in carrying any quantity from Ontario to that market.

I might also speak of the demand further east, and nearer home, where there is another town of importance, Rat Portage, with 4,000 to 5,000 people, and some other smaller places between that and the fruit-growing districts of Ontario, which can scarcely be said to extend much further west than Pembroke. Beyond that you may say that fruit-growing is largely experimental, and the quantity of fruit produced is entirely insufficient for supplying the needs of the people. The residents in the west are hungry for fruit, and continually wondering why it is that with such vast quantities of fruit in Ontario, much of which is said to be sold at unremunerative prices, they should be debarred the privilege of disposing of large quantities of it at reasonable rates. I hope that some arrangement will be reached in the near future whereby the large surplus, which is an accumulating one in Ontario, will be made available to these fruit hungry people in the Northwest.

Mr. McNEILL : I am sure a few remarks will be in order just here without waiting for an invitation. I have been waiting for this opportunity for some time. I am really pleased to have a chance now to express myself plainly and clearly. I am sure that we must all have been pleased as fruit-growers with the earnest efforts of Dr. Saunders in this direction of making markets for us. It is that end of the fruit-growing business that must be attended to, and we are extremely obliged not only on this occasion, but on every other occasion, when he has had the chance to do something for us. At the same time he has given an opportunity to-night of saying a few plain things which I hope will reach the people of Manitoba. Here we are, fruit-growers of Ontario, with any amount of fruit, anxious to sell it and willing to give them the very best, and here are the people of the Northwest anxious to get it. But we cannot get our money out of it when we send it up to them. There are the plain facts of the case. Surely there is intelligence enough in this Association to get at the reason, and find out why it is that there should be such a discrepancy between the fruit-grower and the fruit-eater. These remarks come a little personal from the fruit men in Winnipeg to myself. I have shipped these last two years something like ten car loads of fruit to the Winnipeg market, and I know this, that many of the people in our section who have shipped very largely up there positively refuse to let one pound of fruit go to Winnipeg unless they got their money before the fruit left the station. Now, those are the hard facts of the case. I do not believe that every fruit merchant and every commission merchant is a rogue, but I do say we have been rascally swindled by some of the people of Winnipeg. They have spread reports about the manner of packing our fruit, and about the condition in which it got there, and I have every reason to believe—and I say this with the feeling that I shall be reported in Winnipeg—that the reason the reports were sent out were simply that they might have an excuse for sending us a less return than they otherwise would. Now our dealings with Winnipeg this year were much more satisfactory than usual, because most of us said, "Show us the color of your money before we send the fruit," and in most cases they did so. The fruit that went up from our section to Winnipeg—and we appear to be a little better situated than you are here in Niagara District for shipping of small lines of fruit, I don't know why—went up, the most of it having been paid for before it left our section; and strange to say, there were no bad reports, or very few bad reports, of any carloads that were paid for before they got there; but as to any carload that went up there that was not paid for before it got there, there was the most terrible muss with that car—it was mildewed, rotten, poorly packed, and everything that was bad about it. (Laughter). I do not mean to say but what that there was some foundation for these reports of badly packed fruit, but I say it is not all the fault of the packing. I personally packed a very large number of cars of fruit that have gone to Winnipeg, and we have packed those in freight cars, it is very true. I might say in that respect that we like nothing better, having tried refrigerator cars, and they were not at all satisfactory. We have tried it over the Northern Pacific, the Canadian Pacific, and we have tried the ordinary grain car, and we found that the best results came from the ordinary C.P.R. car with open windows in each end. We packed the grapes, for instance, in 10-lb. baskets, packed them in two layers, that is in two baskets five high, then put a heavy platform that separated the next tier of five high. Those were all packed in so securely that they could not move in any direction, and yet not so close but that the air could circulate freely through it. You can easily see that those baskets were packed so carefully that not even the ingenuity of the trainmen could stir them from their position; and yet they were not so tightly packed but that when the car was in motion there was a current of cool air—especially when they got up north—constantly passing through these baskets, and they got up there in good condition, where we had an independent report of it. Now, I have seen those cars packed. With any information I have from years of shipping up there I cannot suggest any better mode of packing the baskets than the method which is adopted; nor can the merchants themselves suggest to us any improvement. We have asked them personally to suggest some way by which we could pack our fruit more satisfactorily, and there has been no suggestion that came down from them that has not been adopted that proved good, and I think it is time that these reports of the bad packing of the Ontario people should cease. (Hear, hear). With regard to tomatoes there is no difficulty whatever in shipping our ordinary tomatoes up there, and in those years when they have no crop up there —which is about three years out of five—it is a very profitable trade indeed; but it is a trade that is rather delicate to handle, because it requires considerable experience to select the tomatoes that are fit for shipping. In regard to peaches, they are a little more difficult to ship; but with regard to pears there is no difficulty whatever, and the people of Winnipeg this year I know personally were supplied with pears, ton after ton of them, from our own section, and the returns we made were about thirty cents per bushel. Now, if the people of Winnipeg are not satisfied with pears that return to us only about thirty cents per bushel, they cannot be very fruit hungry— and the very best of pears at that. However, let it be understood that we are extremely obliged to Dr. Saunders, who has always been one of the best friends of this Association, and we hope he will do more of this missionary work for us.

Dr. SAUNDERS : I suppose human nature is pretty much the same all over the world. We heard these reports this afternoon from even such good people as the British people, that under certain conditions the apples were all slacks, and I suppose there are such people in this country perhaps, and under conditions where they are tempted financially to do so they make things appear worse than they really are. However, I may say that in coming through Winnipeg about the end of August I spent a day there, and spent a good part of it among the fruit shops, and I was shown three cars of fruit that came from Washington that had just been opened up, and some from California. I was also shown quantities of fruit from British Columbia, and some from Ontario. I suppose Mr. McNeill in his remarks refers principally to apples.

Mr. McNEILL: I have been engaged more largely myself in grapes and pears.

Dr. SAUNDERS: I did not see any Ontario grapes this time. The market seemed to be bare of them just at that particular period. I must say that I saw some very fine apples exhibited there for sale, and they were getting five dollars a barrel for them and they were going off very rapidly. Just at that time also there was a large quantity of Duchess apples that had been sent from Ontario, that had evidently been very ripe when they were sent, and they came in there on a Saturday afternoon, and in order to get rid of them they were obliged to sell them at about twenty to twenty-five cents a basket, which would not return anything to the shippers; but they were so far gone, if they had not been sold at that price they would have been dumped out on Monday morning, showing there are two sides to this question. While I saw some very good fruit, I saw also some that should not have been sent in such quantity and so far gone in ripeness. The fruit from British Columbia also was very variable. I found in many packages of plums perhaps three or four large plums on the top, and then mixed through some that would not be more than half the size, and here and there a partly decayed one. Such fruit as that does not impress a buyer favorably. If you have got a lot of small apples, grade them and put the small ones all in one box. If a man buying a box of plums sees one or two large plums, he naturally thinks they all ought to be that size, and then he says, "These others are inferior." Many of those California and Oregon plums that I saw were rather small in size, but they were all the same size in the same box, and hence did not give rise to any question or thought in the purchaser's mind about being inferior. I have no doubt a large part of the discredit that has attached itself to the shipment of Ontario grapes in the Winnipeg market arises from the fact of their being sent forward by freight instead of by express. Freight cars will take six or seven days at least.

Dr. SAUNDERS: I have travelled up very often with an express car, and it is only two and a half days from Ottawa. Toronto would be about the same. Well, three or four days makes a wonderful difference to fruits of that texture when they are really ripe, and makes all the difference sometimes between getting them there in first-class order and very poor condition; and if you have ever ridden in a freight car,—I have had some of that experience, too much of it—and been subject to the jarring and jolting that nearly knocks you off your feet when the cars collide, you would not wonder at the fruit being mashed in four days of that kind of jarring.

Mr. McNEILL: But the fruit by express was put into exactly the same car, only it was attached to a passenger car.

Dr. SAUNDERS: Exactly, but the passenger train is not jolted about the way fruit cars are. When you have an opportunity take a ride 50 miles in a freight car, and you will be perfectly satisfied my remarks are not fiction. (Laughter.) I believe the plan that would lead the fruit-growers of Ontario to the greatest good would be to make some arrangement with the express people, and I fancy they would be just as approachable to the Ontario people as they are to the people of British Columbia, and it is far better to pay 2½c. a pound to get your fruit through in good order than to pay a cent a pound and get it through in poor condition.

Mr. GREGORY: I do not believe it is altogether the fault of the growers or the fault of the commission men in Winnipeg why we do not receive better prices for our fruit. I believe one of the principal causes of that may be remedied if an effort is made by this Association. I think one of the crying evils of the fruit-growers of this country is the kind of cars in which we have to ship our fruit to the Northwest Territories and other points. The railway people have promised various times to build us ventilated cars such as are required to successfully ship grapes and fruits of that kind to the Northwest and other distant points, and they have neglected or refused to do so to the present time. I believe it is practically impossible for us to ship fruit with the cars that are now being provided, as box cars are totally unfit for the service. I do not see why the railway people should not build cars the same as the Northern Pacific people have built for California. The industry has grown here to such enormous proportions that it certainly would pay them to provide cars of a suitable kind to carry the fruit. I believe there is something in the package. but with the package such as suggested by Dr. Saunders, placed in suitable cars, we can send grapes by freight to get them through for one and a half cents. Their being on the road four or five days will not deteriorate them. They go through in good condition if it takes them five days to go through. This Association could take steps to induce the railway company to build cars suitable for the through traffic.

The PRESIDENT : This discussion is getting very interesting, but I am sorry to be obliged to shut it off at this time, but it would not be courteous to Dr. Mills, of Guelph, who is to follow, if we kept it open any later at present. The hour is already advanced, and while I recognize the importance of this discussion I do not think we had better continue it to-night any longer, but to-morrow morning if any member wishes I will arrange it so that the discussion can be resumed. Meantime think it over, and if there is any way you can suggest by appointing a committee to attend to it, embody it in a resolution and then we will put it in practical shape. The Fruit Growers' Association are only too glad to do anything of that kind ; that is their work.

HORTICULTURE AT THE ONTARIO AGRICULTURAL COLLEGE.

BY DR. JAMES MILLS, PRESIDENT O. A. C., GUELPH.

President Mills, of Guelph, conveyed greetings from the Agricultural College and congratulated the people of Ontario on having so great a variety and such an abundance of delicious fruit. Few people, he said, were better off in that respect ; and for one he could not forget the record made by Ontario in the fruit competition at the World's fair in Chicago—more points than Michigan, Ohio or New York, more even than California or any other state in the Union. Surely this was something worth recalling from time to time, and the facts of the case indicated how we should proceed in order to be successful in the future. Our natural advantages were not so great as in some states across the line ; but the intelligence of Canadian farmers and fruit growers was of a high order, and that was the most potent factor in production. So our hope for the future must rest on the wise and thorough training of the rising generation. We could not change our soil or climate, but we could do much to increase the industrial skill and aptitude of our people. By general and technical education, we could make them more skillful, progressive and successful workers—better mechanics, stock raisers and fruit growers ; keener, shrewder and more prosperous merchants and manufacturers. Much depended on the general education and special training of our young people. In general education, Ontario has done and was doing well ; but in the matter of industrial training, she was far behind. He would like to speak on the need and importance of having a good industrial High School in each county ; but time and place forbade.

A fruit grower needed to be an intelligent, wide awake man,—a man of good education who had learned how to use his head, his eyes and his hands,—a chemist, geologist, botanist and entomologist, a very keen observer and a man of sound judgment. The time had certainly come when fruit growers should understand the use of the microscope and be well versed in botany and entomology. The loss of crop from fungous diseases in the United States was from $150,000,000 to $200,000,000 a year. The proportion of loss from this cause in Canada was quite as great—from rust, smut, apple scab, black knot, pear blight, peach yellows, leaf curl, ripe rot, mildew, anthracnose, and many other diseases—all caused by minute vegetable organisms. How important, then, that farmers generally and especially fruit growers should be familiar with that branch of botany which deals with these low but very troublesome forms of plant life? The annual loss from insects, including San Jose scale, was perhaps greater, and it went without saying that fruit growers should be practical entomologists, men who know the character and habits of troublesome insects and could avail themselves of the best known methods of preventing their ravages.

At the College, they were giving horticulture more prominence than formerly. This was true as regards both teaching and practical work. Students of all the years had lectures, with a fair amount of practical instruction in ¦fruit growing, vegetable gardening and greenhouse work. A new orchard had been set out, their vineyard has been enlarged and a great number of variety tests had been made. The tests during 1898 had been with 15 varieties of red raspberries, 15 of black raspberries, 9 of blackberries, 13 of currants, 13 of gooseberries, 219 of strawberries, 11 of tomatoes, 270 of geraniums, and 30 of coleus. The results of these tests would be found in the next annual report of the College. The department had a complete set of greenhouses with an extensive collection of plants for use in lecture room and laboratory practice. The work done was abreast of the times; and it had reached a stage when they thought that they might say that it was of considerable practical value to the students at the College and to farmers and to farmers and fruit growers throughout the Province.

The College and the Fruit Growers' Association conjointly had charge of the Fruit Experimental Stations of the Province. Two representatives of the former and four of the latter constituted the Board of Control. At present there were thirteen stations, and two more would be established after the next meeting of the legislature. The new stations would be in the northern part of the Province, one on St. Joseph's Island and the other on the Government Farm at Dryden, about eighty miles east of Rat Portage. These stations were doing excellent work for the Province in testing varieties of fruit on different soils and under different climatic conditions, and in preparing a description o the Fruits of Ontario, a most valuable work containing good cuts, and a clear, reliable, description, with the strong and weak points of every variety of fruit grown in the Province. The next annual report of the Board would contain this description as far as it had gone.

The Fruit Growers' Association had done good work for Ontario in testing varieties, giving information about planting and cultivation, and keeping the subject of fruit growing before the people; but he was inclined to think that it had not done all that it was capable of doing and ought to do in the way of finding satisfactory markets for the fruit of the Province. It was important to grow good fruit, but no less important to find good markets for it; and this latter part of the problem demanded the most searching investigation and vigorous action by the Association at the present time; for was it not a fact whenever there was a really good crop of any variety of fruit in the Province, it was impossible to sell it so as to make anything like fair returns for the labor and capital invested. The grower very often had to choose between being robbed by commission men and letting his fruit rot on the trees. Was it not so in the case of both small and large fruits? If one had a special or permanent market, it was his interest to look carefully after it; and he could give it direct personal attention; but most growers had to place their fruit on the open market or markets of the country and rely upon the machinery of trade to dispose of it. All such needed the help of some organization or association to look after their interests—to direct their attention to the best markets, negotiate for cheap, rapid and suitable transportion, and work for the enactment of such rules and regulations as would be likely to secure something like a fair and honest disposal of the fruit sent to commission men. What about the northern parts of Ontario, the Province

4 F.G.

of Manitoba, and the Province of Quebec? Could any of our fruit be disposed of in these places, without allowing express companies and commission men to absorb the whole product? Could information be given to fruit growers through the press or by private circulars as to markets during the selling season? Here was a field for some committee or individual to be appointed by the Fruit Growers' Association—here was room for the exercise of the best business talent in the Association; and he took the liberty of commending the matter to their prompt, earnest and most careful consideration.

The PRESIDENT : I am sure we have listened to Dr. Mills' address with the greatest of pleasure, and I quite recognize that the points he brought out are points that should be taken into consideration and acted upon in a vigorous manner by the Fruit Growers' Association. I may say that while we may not have done as much as should have been done in the past in that regard, it is only within the last few years that the subject has been impressed upon our minds that we had over-production in fruit. There are a great many difficulties to be overcome in carrying out the suggestions which Dr. Mills has made, and time will hardly permit of my answering it altogether at the present time, although before the meetings close I hope we will find time to have a little further discussion of that subject, because it is one of vital importance, and there are points to be brought out to show that the officers of the Fruit Growers' Association have not been negligent in this respect. One point I will call attention to, and that is the fact that we have not had in the past years at our command any money with which to go about or undertake the fight which Dr. Mills has suggested. It takes money to do that sort of thing, and also it necessitates the co operation of every member of the Association. (Hear hear.) It cannot all be laid upon the Directors. You must understand, too, that the Association is only allowed a certain amount, and that it has devolved upon us to exercise the greatest of care as to every dollar we expend, and until we are in such a position—which we are rapidly obtaining, I am glad to say—we have not felt that we were able to undertake the contest that has been urged upon us ; but I believe that before this meeting closes means will be taken to enter into this matter, and that good will be brought about. I am very glad that the Doctor has so emphatically brought the matter before the members of the Fruit Growers' Association ; but I want to say to you, do not leave it all on the officers. It is in your power ; it is to you that the hints were thrown out by the Doctor to bring before the Association every point that you can think of, and also bring results before the Association, and your officers will act upon them. (Hear, hear.)

The SECRETARY read minutes of last meeting held in Waterloo in December, 1897 ; also letter from Rev. E. Burke, Prince Edward Island ; also letter from Winnipeg re Western Horticultural Society ; also letter from M. M. Black, regretting that he could not supply the paper asked for ; also from Mr. A. McD Allan, of Goderich, regretting inability to be present, he having been invited to speak on preparation for the Paris Exposition, 1900 ; also letters of regret from J. A. Morton, of Wingham, and Mr. Nicol, of Kingston.

The PRESIDENT : I am sure we are very much pleased to receive such correspondence, showing that the influence of the Society is extending to sister provinces.

The SECRETARY : I thought best this year, in order to give as much information as possible to all the members of our Association, to have a detailed account of the expenditures printed for distribution at the meeting. The premiums last year were larger and better than before, and a part of the money paid to Mr. Beall was due him for work done last year.

Mr. SCARFF (Woodstock) moved the adoption of the Report as read.

The motion was seconded by Mr. Murray Pettit, and carried.

Mr. A. H. PETTIT, as one of the auditors, read the Auditors' Report, finding a balance of $784.96, to which the bank's voucher is attached. He moved the adoption of the Report, which was seconded by Mr. Orr, and carried. The Report is as follows :

TREASURER'S REPORT, 1897-98

Receipts.		Expenditures	
Balance on hand Dec. 1, 1897	$ 266 02	Canadian Horticulturist	$1,941 87
Government grant....................	1,800 00	Salary secretary, editor and assistant..	1,200 00
Membership fees	4,147 13	Commissions	670 00
Advertisements	337 92	Premiums	455 78
Bound Vols. and binding..............	16 05	Illustrations	305 98
Back Nos. and samples...	7 37	Affiliated societies, organization and lec-	
Miscellaneous	11 45	ture course...........	385 07
		Directors' expenses....................	203 75
		Printing and stationery...............	139 13
		Postage and telegrams	135 86
		Committees	115 92
		Reporting.............	112 95
		Express and duty...............	45 50
		Auditing	31 00
		Collection and discount...	27 24
		Book binding	26 45
		Care of rooms	3 00
		Balance on hand...........	784 94
	$6,585 94		$6,585 94

DETAILS OF EXENDITURERS, 1897-8.

CANADIAN HORTICULTURIST—

Dudley & Burns, Toronto, November '97, $163.78 ; December, $134.07 ; index '97, $30.00 ; January '98, $154.15 ; February, $181.17 ; March, $176.00 ; April, $184.86 ; May, $177.10 ; June, $146.73 ; July, $147.15 ; August, $147.06 ; September, $153.40 ; October, $146.40. $1,941 87

SALARY—

Secretary-Editor, Assistant and Treasurer.......... .... 1,200 00

COMMISSIONS—

December '97, $20.83 ; January '98, $49.80 ; February, $20.95 ; March, $24.00 ; April, $24.60 ; May, $22.60 ; June, $8.50 ; July, $1.80 ; August, $4.95 ; September, $184.35 ; October, $247.10 ; November, $61.00................................ .... 670 00

PREMIUMS—

Morris, Stone & Wellington, $385.91 ; R. A. Nelles (postage for premiums) $28.36 ; L. Woolverton, (cost of packing premium plants and trees) $47.51...................... 455 78

AFFILIATED SOCIETIES—

Organization, Thos. Beall, $170.90 ; Lecture Course, Wm. Bacon, $51.37 ; M. Burrell, $29.80 ; Wm. Gammage, $22.50 ; G. C. Caston, $6.95 ; A. McNeill, $103.55 .... 385 07

ILLUSTRATIONS—

Grip Engraving Co., $278.06 ; Gardening Co., $5.80 ; Times Printing Co., $5.05 ; Globe Printing Co., $10.82 ; Stecher Lith. Co., $5.25..... .... 305 98

DIRECTORS' EXPENSES—

H. Jones, $23.50 ; G. Nicol, $20.35 ; W. Coulter, $20.35 ; Thos. Beall, $15.30 ; W. E. Wellington, $6.00 ; T. H. Race, $9.00 ; R. B. Whyte, $23.85 ; A. M. Smith, $6.50 ; L. Woolverton, $8.00 ; W. M. Orr, (Kingston Meeting) '96, $2.00 ; Zimmerman Hotel, Waterloo, (L. R. Taft) $1.50 ; A. McNeill, $15.70 ; J. S. Scarff, $10.80 ; M. Pettit, $11.90 ; R. L. Huggard, $11.00 .... 203 75

PRINTING AND STATIONERY—

A. M. Millward, (Printing) $109.75 ; R. A. Nelles, (Stat.) $8.30 ; J. A. Livingston, Printing) $17.00 ; Wm. Forbes, (Stat.) $1.20 ; Buntin, Gillies & Co., (Stat.) $1.20 ; A. F. Hawke, (Stat) 43c. ; Martin Bros., (Stat.) $1.25...... .... 139 13

POSTAGE AND TELEGRAMS.

R. A. Nelles, (postage) $99.70 ; Bell Telephone Co., $13.25 ; G. T. R. Agent, (telegrams) 71c. ; C. P. R. Agent, (telegrams) $1.97 ; stamps transferred from cash, $20.23........ 135 86

Committees—

W. M. Orr, (Tariff Guelph) $7.05 ; W. E. Wellington, (San Jose Scale, Ottawa) $21.10 ; A. H. Pettit, (Ottawa) $23.05 ; M. Burrell, (Ottawa) $29.55 ; E. D. Smith, Ottawa) $27.92 ; W. M. Orr, (Finance) $2.15 ; M. Pettit, (Finance) $2.10 ; A. M. Smith, (Finance) $2.00 . . . .　　115 92

Reporting—

Thos. Bengough . . . .　　112 95

Express and Duty—

R. A. Nelles, (Express and Duty) $41.19 ; J. S. Randall, (Freight) $2.90 ; J. Blair, (Freight) $1.91 ; L. Woolverton, (Cartage) 50c. . . . .　　46 50

Auditors—

G. E. Fisher, $11.00 ; A. H. Pettit, (two years) $20.00 . . . .　　31 00

Collection and Discount—

Bank of Hamilton, (Collections) $8.79 ; Bank of Hamilton, (Discount) $18.45 . . . .　　27 24

Binding "Canadian Horticulturist"—

o　　　　ros. . . . .　　26 45

Care of Rooms at Annual Meeting—

I. Hoffman, (Waterloo) . . . .　　3 00

　　$5,800 38

We, the members of your Finance Cemmittee, have carefully examined the accounts for expenditure made by the Secretary-Treasurer for the current year. And we beg to report that they were made in the best interests of the Association.

We have pleasure in stating that we found the accounts in perfect order for inspection.

Committee { W. M. Orr, M. Pettit, A. M. Smith.

REVISION OF THE CONSTITUTION.

Considerable discussion arose over the proposed changes in the constitution and by-laws. Amendments were made to articles 2, 4, 6 and 7 of the constitution, and clause 1 of the by-laws was amended and made article 9 of the constitution. A new clause was adopted as article 10. Clauses 3 and 4 were adopted as articles 11 and 12 respectively. A new clause was adopted as article 13.

Mr. Race moved that the following clauses and the closing recommendation of the committee be adopted as amended, and that the clauses of the amended and revised constitution and by-laws be numbered consecutively from the beginning, removing all "constitution and by-laws" distinction. (Carried.)

The constitution and by-laws as amended are as follows :

CONSTITUTION OF THE FRUIT GROWERS' ASSOCIATION OF ONTARIO.

1. The Association shall be called "The Fruit Growers' Association of Ontario.'

2. Its object shall be the advancement of the science and art of horticulture in all its branches and the encouragement of tree growing by holding meetings for the discussion of all questions relative to horticulture and forestry, by collecting, arranging and disseminating useful information, and by such other means as may from time to time seem desirable.

3. The annual meeting of the Association shall be held at such time and place as shall be designated by the Association.

4. The officers of the Association shall be a president, vice-president, a secretary and a treasurer, or a secretary-treasurer, and thirteen directors and two auditors, to be elected at each annual meeting.

5. Any person may become a member by an annual payment of one dollar, and a payment of ten dollars shall constitute a member for life.

6. This constitution may be amended as provided for by section 32, subsection 1, of The Ontario Agriculture and Arts Act

7. The said Officers and Directors shall prepare and present at the annual meeting of the Association a report of their proceedings during the year, in which shall be stated the names of all the members of the Association, the places of of meeting during the year, and such information as the Association shall have been able to obtain on the subjects of horticulture and forestry in the Province during the year. There shall also be presented at the said annual meeting a detailed statement of the receipts and disbursements of the Association during the year, which report and statement shall be entered in the journal and signed by the president as being a correct copy ; and a true copy thereof, certified by the secretary for the time being, shall be sent to the Minister of Agriculture within forty ,days after the holding of such annual meeting.

8. The Association shall have power to make, alter and amend By-laws for prescribing the mode of admission of new members, the election of officers, and otherwise regulating the administration of its affairs and property.

9. The Board of Directors at its first meeting shall appoint from among its own members or otherwise a Secretary and a Treasurer, or a Secretary-treasurer.

10. The President, the Vice-President and Secretary or Secretary-treasurer shall be *ex officio* members of the Board of Directors ; and the President, or in his absence, the Vice-President an *ex officio* member of all committees.

11. The President, Vice-President and Secretary shall constitute the Executive Committee of this Association, whose functions it shall be to manage the affairs of the Association, to control the finances and make the necessary disbursements throughout the year, and to bring a report of the same before the Board of Directors at each annual meeting for approval.

12. The Directors may offer premiums to any person originating or introducing any new fruit adapted to the climate of the Province, which shall possess such distinctive excellence as shall, in their opinion, render the same of special value ; also for essays upon such subjects connected with horticulture and forestry as they may designate, under such rules and regulations as they may prescribe.

13. The Secretary shall prepare an annual report containing the minutes of the proceedings of meetings during the year ; a detailed statement of receipts and expenditure, the reports upon fruits received from different localities, and all essays to which prizes have been awarded, and such other information in regard to horticulture and forestry as may have been received during the year, and submit the same to the Directors or any Committee of Directors appointed for this purpose and, with their sanction, after presenting the same at the annual meeting, cause the same to be printed by and through the Publication Committee, and send a copy thereof to each member of the Association and to the Minister of Agriculture.

14. Seven Directors shall constitute a quorum, and if at any meeting of Directors there shall not be a quorum, the members present may adjourn the meeting from time to time until a quorum shall be obtained.

15. The annual subscription shall be due in advance at the annual meeting.

16. The President (or in case of his disability, the Vice-President) may convene special meetings at such times and places as he may deem advisable ; and he shall convene such special meeting as shall be requested in writing by ten members.

17. The President may deliver an address on some subject relating to the objects of the Association.

18. The Treasurer shall receive all moneys belonging to the Association, keep a correct account thereof and submit the same to the Directors at any legal meeting of such Directors, five days' notice having been previously given for that purpose.

19. The Secretary shall keep a correct record of the proceedings of the Association, conduct the correspondence, give not less than ten days' notice of all meetings to the members, and specify the business of all meetings to the members, and specify the business of special meetings.

20. The Directors, touching the conduct of the Association, shall at all times have absolute power and control of the funds and property of the Association, subject, however, to the meaning and construction of the Constitution.

21. At a special meeting, no business shall be transacted except that stated in the Secretary's circular.

22. The order of business shall be : (1) Reading of minutes ; (2) Reading of Directors' report ; (3) Reading of Treasurers' report ; (4) Reading the Auditors' report ; (5) Reading reports of Standing Committees ; (6) President's Address ; (7) Miscellaneous business

23. The by-laws may be amended at any general meeting as provided for by section 32, sub-section 1, of the Agriculture and Arts Act.

24. The election of officers shall take place at the morning session of the last day of the annual meeting in each year, the newly-elected officers to assume their respective duties and responsibilities at the close of the said meeting.

25. The reasonable and necessary expenses of directors and officers in attending meetings of the Board of Directors and Committees, shall be provided from the funds of the Association.

26. It shall be the duty of the officers and directors of the Fruit Growers' Association of Ontario to encourage the formation of local fruit growers' horticultural societies in affiliation with the Ontario Association.

27. On the receipt of such members, with the required fees, the secretary of such local affiliated society may transmit their names and post office addresses, together with the sum of eighty cents for each to the Secretary of the Fruit Growers' Association of Ontario, who will enter their names as members of tha society, entitled to all its privileges, providing the initial number of such names be not less than twenty-five. -

28. Each local society so affiliating with a membership ot not less than twenty-nve shall be entitled to a visit from some member of the Board of Directors or other prominent horticulturist once a year ; it being understood that the railway expenses of such speaker shall be paid by the Ontario Society, and the entertainment provided by the local society.

29. The proceedings of such horticultural societies shall, on or before the 1st day of December of each year, be forwarded to the secretary of the Ontario Society, who may cull out such portions for the Annual Report of the Minister of Agriculture for the Province, as may seem to him of general interest and value.

30. Each local affiliated society is further expected to send at lea one delegate to the annual meeting of the Fruit Growers' Association.

The Director of the Fruit Growers' Association of Ontario, for the Agricultural District in which such society is formed, shall be *ex officio* a member of the Directorate of such local society and receive notices of all its meetings.

By-Laws for Affiliated Horticultural Societies.

(Prepared by Mr. Thomas Beall and Mr. L. Woolverton, as ordered by the Board of Directors of the Fruit Growers' Association of Ontario.)

This Society, known as the Horticultural Society of the   of   , organized under the provisions of the Agriculture and Arts Act of the Province of Ontario. Chap. 43, R.S.O. 1897, agrees to conduct its affairs in accordance with the several provisions of the said Acts, and with the following by-laws and regulations.—Sec. 13.

1. The members of this Society for any year shall be residents and ratepayers of this municipality to the number of at least fifty, and also others, who shall have paid one dollar into the funds of the society as membership fee for that year.—Sec. 7, s.-s. 1 (b).

2. The objects of this society shall be to encourage improvement in horticulture, and to secure to each member equal encouragement therein.—Sec. 9, s.-s. 2.

3. There shall be at least   public meetings in each year for discussing local horticultural matters, and for hearing lectures on improved horticulture.—Sec. 9, s.-s. 2, (a).

4. At any public meeting there may be an exhibition of such plants, vegetables, fruits and flowers as may be in season ; and wherever such an exhibition is held, there shall be present at least one expert gardener who shall give such information and instruction appertaining thereto as may be required ; but no prizes of value shall be offered for competition by the society at such meetings.—Sec 9, s.-s. 2, (e).

5. The annual meeting, and all other public meetings shall be open to the public free of charge. But members only shall have the right to vote at any meeting.

(a) When exhibitions are held at such public meetings, the public shall be invited to exhibit such horticultural products as may be thought suitable for the occasion by a committee appointed by the Board to superintend such exhibitions.

(b) This committee shall take such means as they think proper to secure exhibits for the occasion, and also procure proper conveyance for collecting and returning the same free of expense to exhibitors.

(c) These exhibitions shall be open to members and other exhibitors free of charge.

(6) A sum of money not to exceed   dollars may be offered in prizes in any one year for essays on any question of scientific enquiry relating to horticulture.—Sec. 9, s.-s. 2, (d).

7. Each member shall be given by this society a free membership in the Fruit Growers' Association.—Sec. 9, s.-s. 2, (b).

8. There shall be procured for each member, trees, shrubs, plants, bulbs or seeds of new and valuable kinds in each year, sufficient in quantity to exhaust the funds of this society after allowing for necessary working expenses.—Sec. 9, s -s. 2, (a).

9. The annual meeeing shall be held at half past seven in the evening of the second Wednesday in January, when there shall be elected a president, a first vice-president, and not more than nine directors, who together shall form the board of directors. At this meeting, the society shall also elect two auditors for the ensuing year.—Sec. 7. s.-s. 1 (e).

(a) At this meeting, only those members who have paid their subscription for the ensuing year shall be entitled to vote.—Sec. 10, s.-s. 1.

(b) At this and all subsequent public meetings, ten members shall constitute a quorum.—Sec. 10 s.-s. 1 (e).

10. The board of directors at its first meeting shall appoint a secretary and a treasurer, or a secretary-treasurer.—Sec. 7 s.-s. 1 (f).

(a) Five directors shall constitute a quorum for the transaction of business.—Sec. 14.

(b) Subject to these by-laws, the directors shall have full power to act for and on behalf of the society and all grants and other funds shall be expended under their direction.

At each annual meeting the directors shall present a detailed statement of the receipts and expenditures for the preceding year, and also a statement of the assets and liabilities of the society at the end of the year, certified to by the auditors.—Sec. 11, s.s. (c).

11. The said statements shall, when approved by the meeting, be placed on permanent record in the books of the society, and such portions thereof, together with what is further required by sub. sec. (a) of Sec. 11, shall be sent within one month to the Department of Agriculture.—Sec. 12.

12. The Director of the Fruit Growers' Association of Ontario for the Agricultural District in which this society is situate shall be considered an honorary member and receive notice of the meetings.

13. These by-laws and regulations cannot be altered or repealed except at an annudl meeting, or at a special meeting of the members of the society, of which two weeks' previous notice has been given by advertisement.

AGRICULTURAL DIVISIONS.

1. Stormont, Dundas, Glengarry, Prescott, and Cornwall.

2. Lanark North, Lanark South, Renfrew North, Renfrew South, Carleton, Russell, and the City of Ottawa.

3. Frontenac, City of Kingston, Leeds and Grenville North, Leeds South, Grenville South, and Brockville.

4. Hastings East, Hastings North, Hastings West, Addington, Lennox, and Prince Edward.

5. Durham East, Durham West, Northumberland East, Northumberland West, Peterborough East, Peterborough West, Victoria North (including Haliburton), and Victoria South.

6. York East, York North, York West, Ontario North, Ontario South, Peel, Cardwell, and City of Toronto.

7. Wellington Centre, Wellington South, Wellington West, Waterloo North, Waterloo South, Wentworth North, Wentworth South, Dufferin, Halton, and City of Hamilton.

8. Lincoln, Niagara, Welland, Haldimand, and Monck.

9. Elgin East, Elgin West, Brant North, Brant South, Oxford North, Oxford South, Norfolk North, and Norfolk South.

10. Huron East, Huron South, Huron West, Bruce North, Bruce South, Grey East, Grey North, and Grey South.

11. Perth North, Perth South, Middlesex East, Middlesex North, Middlesex West, and City of London.

12. Essex North, Essex South, Kent East, Kent West, Lambton East, and Lambton West.

13. Algoma East, Algoma West, Simcoe East, Simcoe South, Simcoe West, Muskoka, Parry Sound East, Parry Sound West, Nipissing East, Nipissing West, and Manitoulin.

R.S.O., 1897, c. 43, Schd. A.

ELECTION OF OFFICERS.

The report of the Nominating Committee was read by Mr. Race, and, on motion was unanimously adopted. The list of officers will be found on page 2.

COLD STORAGE OFFICIALS AND INSPECTION.

Mr. M. PETTIT moved "That the Secretary be authorized to communicate with the Montreal and Nova Scotia societies, requesting them to appoint one or more delegates to join a delegation appointed by this Association to interview the Government, and urge upon them the importance of appointing officers whose duties shall be to see that proper ventilation and greater care be given to the storage of apples and other fruit exported to Great Britain on ocean steamers, and that the Secretary shall make all arrangements and dates for meetings of such deputation." Mr. Pettit said: I regard this as very important work for this Association, and I believe if it is fully pushed, it will mean thousands of dollars to the fruit growers of this Dominion. This devil of Mr. Pattison's, that we heard about yesterday has one of his hiding places in the holds of these ocean steamers, and he can get up as much smoke, and steam, and heat there as any place else where it is found, and I think it is the duty of this Association to try and chase him out.

Mr. BOULTER seconded the resolution.

The SECRETARY.—It seems to me that the object of that Committee might be a little bit enlarged. This Association has often asked the Government to do a little in the way of inspection of fruit for export. It appears to me that it is practicable to do a little in that line now, because we are beginning a new business in exporting fruit in cold storage, and it is quite practical that everything that goes in this cold storage compartment should be inspected by a Government official. As a matter of fact, it has been done already in a small way. The special shipments that have been already made have all been inspected by Government officials, and marked "Inspected Canadian Fruit," and I think, if that work could be made permanent, it would mark a new era in our export trade. It is very important that the Government should be asked to act in this particular. Of course, we do not expect that every package will be inspected—they do not do that at the present time with our experimental shipments, but about one in ten is opened, perhaps one in one hundred, if you like, at random, but a sufficient number is opened to satisfy the inspector that the goods are up to the mark that is on the exterior of the package. We have certain grades which should be observed, and I think that every package should be guaranteed to be up to that grade, and it is very important that this Committee should be charged with asking from the Minister of Agriculture some provision in this particular. I do not suppose it is possible that all the outside general business of exporting apples in barrels should be thus controlled, as it would be too great an undertaking; but I think, in the special export trade in cold storage such as the Government has now adopted in cases, these could all be inspected, and it would be a great advantage to fruit growers to have all their fruit placed on the British market as inspected fruit. I would move that the words, " and to make provision for inspection " be also added to the objects of this Committee.

Mr. A. H. PETTIT.—You do not mean to make that compulsory?

Mr. BURRELL.—Do you think that an inspection of them by opening them up when carefully packed in tissue paper and so on would be advisable?

The SECRETARY.—Yes, I think just as soon as this special trade is thrown open to the public, a great many will put up fruit in improper shape. I do not know what provision could be made to prevent it, but I think we should ask the Department to make some provision.

Mr. HUGGARD.—In the resolution Mr. Pettit has just now presented, I think he hardly goes far enough in the way of invitation to these other societies to co-operate with the Committee appointed by this Association in the transportation of goods. Fruit growers know perfectly well that the rate of transportation, at the present time, is neither fair nor satisfactory.

Mr. BURRELL.—Excuse me, but I believe that question of transportation is coming up in a separate resolution.

Mr. A. H. PETTIT.—If the Secretary's clause in regard to fruit being inspected when sent forward means that the work will be entrusted to a man whom the Government might appoint to look after the shipment, and the matter made voluntary with those who request it, it could be accomplished, but to make it a compulsory matter would be a different thing.

THE SECRETARY.—I only ask that some provision be made for the inspection of fruit. I would far rather that all my packages of fruit should bear the inspection mark than have them shipped without that. I consider it a great advantage to me to have my packages marked " Inspected Canadian Fruit ; " but I would like to know how it would be possible for me to do that unless there is a Government official to do it. It would be of no gain to the British purchaser to know that a fruit grower inspected his own pack-age. If it is an advantage to me it is to every shipper to have some provision made by which, at some expense even—for I would not object to paying a small fee for the inspection of 100 packages—some provision should be made by which those who wish their goods placed on the British market as inspected fruit might do so.

Mr. BURRELL.—Does Mr. Woolverton think, for instance, that inspection will attain the ends that he imagines? My view of a Government inspection is that it is no good unless it is thorough—unless everything is inspected and inspected thorough. That is an impossibility, and if it is not thorough is it not almost valueless? Would it not be sufficient protection if every man was compelled plainly to brand his name on every package as it went on, instead of having a partial and therefore inadequate inspection? would it not defeat it own object?

Mr. M. PETTIT.—I have amended the resolution so as possibly to meet the views of the Secretary and others. (Resolution read as amended.)

The PRESIDENT.—I would suggest that you add " and branding." I believe every package of fruit sent out to any market, even the local market, should bear the fruit growers' name.

Mr. BUNTING seconded the motion as amended.

The Secretary read the motion as finally proposed by Mr. Pettit, seconded by Mr. Bunting, which was put to the meeting and carried.

The resolution was as follows :—" Resolved, that the Secretary be authorized to communicate with Nova Scotia, Quebec, and other Provincial societies, requesting them to appoint one or more delegates to join the delegation appointed by this Association to interview the Government and urge upon them the importance of appointing officers, whose duty it shall be to see that proper ventilation and greater care be given to the storage of apples and other fruits exported to Great Britain in ocean steamers, and that the Secretary shall make all arrangements and dates for meetings of said deputations ; and, further, this Committee shall discuss with the Minister the advisability of adopting some system of inspection and grading."

TRANSPORTATION OF FRUIT.

Moved by G. C. CASTON, seconded by M. PETTIT, that we the Fruit Growers Association of Ontario here assembled, believing that the transportation and marketing of raw fruits is the most important question affecting our Association at the present time, and that decisive measures to that end should be taken by our Association, hereby resolve that a Committee be appointed to be styled the Committee on Transportation and Markets, to be composed of the following gentlemen, viz. . W. E. Wellington (alternate W. M. Orr), Alexander McNeill (alternate E. D. Smith), M. Pettit (alternate T. H. P. Carpenter), W. H. Bunting (alternate R. W. Gregory), and that an appropriation be made from the funds of the Association, the limit of which shall be fixed by the executive to cover the necessary expenses of the committee.

Mr. CASTON, in speaking to the resolution, said that the reason for appointing alternates was that something might occur to prevent a person nominated from attending and it would be necessary that the locality particularly interested in this matter should be represented, and therefore it was wise to provide alternates. There are a great many details with which this committee will have to grapple. It is an old saying that corporations have no souls, and large corporations will have to be attended to; also the question of fast freights. It will be necessary for this committee to get together before they interview the railway and transportation companies so that there will be unanimity amongst them. Then with regard to securing more favorable rates, the distinction between the short and long haul is something enormous in this country. The competition is all over now ; the two railway companies have embraced each other. Then there is the question of re icing cars. I am told by a gentleman here that the cars are re iced at North Bay. That is not the place. I have known instances where the ice was all melted before they got to Winnipeg and the fruit was spoiled. They should be re-iced at Sudbury. Then the charges for icing are too high. In places where they have no cold storage the railway company should give a person a little chance. Where a man is willing to provide his own ice it is necessary for the fruit to be cooled down immediately it is picked before it is sent away. The railway company should give a person reasonable time to load, and for the fruit to be cooled down before shipping. One of the anomalies existing in the railway situation is that the competition between trunk lines is so keen that the business is cut down to small profits, and they calculate to make up for it on the short haul. I do not know whether this Committee can do anything in regard to that, but that is really the state of affairs, and the difference between the long and short hauls is simply outrageous in this Province.

The resolution was then put and carried.

REPORT OF COMMITTEE ON NEW AND SEEDLING FRUITS

Prof. Hutt gave the report of the Committee on New Fruits as follows: Nearly all our cultivated fruits are variations or improvements upon some wild type. The many choice varieties of pears now grown in our orchards or gardens have been brought about by gradual development and improvement one after another upon a wild form, which Downing speaks of as the "most austere of all fruits, the choke-pear of our fields, which seizes our throat with such an unmerciful gripe, really being a great improvement upon this wild species." These variations, or new varieties, as we call them, may arise in two different ways:

1. By bud-variation ; that is, when a single branch develops some striking difference from the tree or bush upon which it is growing, an example of which we have in the Golden Queen raspberry, which is supposed to be a bud variation from the Cuthbert.

2. By seedlings. This is by far the most productive source of all our new varieties.

Whenever a seedling or bud-variation appears which is possessed of any particular merit, it can be propagated or increased almost indefinitely by such asexual means of multiplication as taking cuttings, layering, budding and grafting. But on the other hand when a variety so propagated is allowed to propagate sexually, that is from seeds, it gives all sorts of varieties, or as we say, does not "come true from seed." It is this constant tendency to variation, with the possibility of something of superior value appearing, that gives to the work of growing and fruiting seedlings such interest. To many persons it is a work as fascinating and as exciting as a game of chance, and as usually carried on it is but little more than such.

That there is so much uncertainty about it is because so few of the players understand the game or put any skill into it. The great variety of the new varieties introduced from time to time are "chance seedlings," or "fence-corner varieties," of unknown parentage, brought up without care, and if they come into prominence it is because their inherent qualities have attracted kindly notice. Some few are the product of seed which has been selected and planted, and the young seedlings cultivated and cared for till they come into bearing. In the production of such a variety some degree of skill has been bestowed, and knowing the variety from which the seed was obtained we have a partial knowledge of its parentage. But those varieties upon which the greatest skill has been bestowed are the offspring of crosses, where both parents have been wisely selected, with a view to combining or improving in the resulting cross some of their particularly good qualities. Of such breeding are the Roger grapes, the Ontario apple and the Dempsey pear.

We do not wish to discourage the growing and introducing of chance seedlings, for many of our choicest fruits can boast of no other pedigrees, but we believe that much more would be accomplished, in a much shorter time, if greater attention were given to plant breeding. Let him who has the time and taste for such work make a study of the laws underlying plant breeding; let him not go at it hap-hazard, and wait to see what may turn out, but let him get before his mind some reasonable ideal, and then go to work systematically and make his ideal a reality.

It is during years of the greatest fruit production that the greatest number of seedling fruits are brought to notice. The year 1896 will long be remembered as producing the greatest apple crop on record ; and at our annual meeting that year nearly forty seedling apples were reported upon. The past season has, in some respects, been a fair one for fruit, yet it has not produced the abundance of other years, and the number of new fruits sent to your committee for inspection has been comparatively few.

In the following table we give, with brief notes, a list of what has come before us during the past year:

Sender.	Remarks.
SEEDLING APPLES.	
*Chas. Swinnerton, Barrie, Ont	Seedling of Duchess, but later.
*Dr. Saunders, C.E.F., Ottawa	"D'Arcy Spice"; as Eng. russet.
Rev. Prof. Campbell, Yoho Island, Muskoka	A Muskoka seedling, like a medium-sized well-colored Greening.
Dr. J. S. McCallum, Smith's Falls, Ontario	A good sized winter apple, much like Canada Red.
J. A. Mooney, Inverness, Que......	Of Alexander type, but smaller and of inferior quality.
John Joliffe, Rockwood, Ont........	Seedling of Duchess, but later. Quality not equal to Duchess.
*Joseph Knight, Renfrew, Ont.....	1. Resembling somewhat Scarlet Pippin; of high quality for dessert; season, October.
" " " "	2. Med. size; red; good quality; season, winter.
*James Rusk, Bracebridge, Ont	Large and handsome, resembling Duchess; fair quality; season of Wealthy.
SEEDLING PEARS.	
*F. W. Glen, Brooklyn, N.Y	"P. Barry"; like Clairgeau, but keeps till April.
Samuel Nelles, Grimsby ..... ·....	Med. size; color of Bartlett; a little coarse, but good flavor.
John McLaren, St. Catharines	Size and shape of Boussock, of bright yellow color and good quality.
M. A. Reid, Pt. Dalhousie	Like a small Clairgeau, but brighter colored.
SEEDLING PLUMS.	
*A. W. Peart, Burlington...........	"Ireland's Seedling"; med. size; dark blue; early, but too small.
A. W. Walker, Clarksburg..........	Med. size; dark maroon; early; good quality; freestone.
John Mitchell, Clarksburg	"Drake's Seedling"; size and color of McLaughlin; freestone; good quality.
*David Matheson, Ottawa	"Cooch"; large; dark red; fair quality; September.
J. K. Gordon, Whitby..............	Size and color of Lombard; good quality; freestone; August.
Harry Marshall, Hamilton.........	Med. size; round; red; fair quality; clingstone; August.
SEEDLING PEACHES.	
*Dr. Stewart, 152 Dowling Avenue, Toronto	Large; yellow flesh; good quality; later than Late Crawford.
*Mrs. Fairbrother, 119 D'Arcy St., Toronto.	Large; yellow flesh; handsome color; freestone; season of Early Crawford.
*R. T. Smith, Hamilton	1. Large; white flesh; red cheek; good quality; freestone; season after Hale's Early.
*R. T. Smith, Hamilton	2. Very large; 3 by 3 inches; handsome; good quality; yellow flesh; freestone; season of Rareripe.
Alex. Glass, St. Catharines.........	Peach much like Foster.
*M. Fitch, Grimsby, Ont........ ...	Large; yellow flesh; freestone; fair quality; season September 10th to 15th.
A. McLocklan, Guelph, Ont........	Med. Size; yellow flesh; freestone; fair quality; September 15th.
*Mrs. J. T. Ross, King Street East, Hamilton......................	Med. size; 2¼ by 2½ inches; yellow flesh; freestone; fair quality; October 20th.
SEEDLING GRAPES.	
*W. Bachus, St. Catharines, Ont....	White; size and flavor of Concord; early as Moore's Early.
*O. F. Wilkins, Bridgeburg, Ont	White; about size of Concord; good quality season of Moore's Early.
SEEDLING CHERRY.	
*John Gormley, Pickering, Ont.	Size and shape like Eng. Morello; bright red; flesh like a Bigarreau; firm, and a long keeper.

In the following paragraphs are given further descriptions of a few of the most promising seedlings above noted. Unless a seedling has about it some particular quality,

superior to named varieties of the same season, we do not think it is well to recommend that it be propagated and added to the already long list of named varieties.
Hence there are but few of the seedlings which can be so recommended.

APPLES.

SEEDLING APPLE. From Charles Swinnerton, Barrie, Ont., January 26th, 1898.
A large, handsome apple. A seedling of Duchess of Oldenburg; much like its parent
in appearance and quality, but a longer keeper. The tree, like the Duchess, is an early
and heavy bearer.

D'ARCY'S SPICE OR BADDOW PIPPIN. Received. from Dr. Wm. Saunders, January
24th, 1898, who received it from Ipswich, Suffolk, England. Mrs. Prof. Heaton, of the
British Association, says it is an apple held in very high esteem in Great Britain. The
apple is of medium size, with prominent ribs; color yellow, nearly covered with greyish
russet; stem, short in a small round cavity; calyx, nearly closed in a shallow uneven
basin, with five prominent crowns; flesh, white, crisp, juicy; flavor, rich, aromatic;
condition, excellent. Scions of this apple were sent to Mr. A. W. Peart, Mr. Freeman,
and Mr. W. H. Dempsey, and several were grafted at Gravenhurst. Mr. W. E.
Wellington says, under date of January 28th, that the apple is so much like Sharp's
Russet that he does not think it would be worth adding to our already numerous collection of varieties.

SEEDLING APPLE, from Joseph Knight, Renfrew. Sample came to hand October
22nd, 1898. Has the quality of a first-class table apple. Fruit of medium size, beautifully shaded with bright crimson on the sunny side, and light straw colour in shade
splashed and striped with light and dark red. Calyx closed in a small deep basin; stem,
short and thick, in a small, deep cavity with five deep grooves, somewhat resembling the
Scarlet Pippin; flesh, white crisp, tender; rich, peculiarly delicious, half-sweet aromatic
flavour; season, October-December; quality, first-class for dessert.

SEEDLING APPLE, from James Rusk, Bracebridge, Ont. Received, November 1st,
1898. A large, handsome apple, most likely a seedling of the Duchess, as it somewhat
resembles that variety in size, shape, and appearance. Quality, fair; season of maturity
about that of Wealthy.

PEARS.

THE P. BARRY. This is one of the promising new varieties which has been before
the public for the past few years, and is particularly valuable on account of its lateness.
Mr. Woolverton received samples of it this year on August 3rd from Mr. F. W. Glen, of
Brooklyn, N.Y., and makes the following remarks concerning it in the September number
of the HORTICULTURIST:—" At first we thought it like Beurre Clairgeau kept over in
cold storage, for it resembles that variety much in form and size. It is a winter pear,
ripening in April, very large; orange yellow when ripe; juicy, fine grained, and of
high flavour. Perhaps this will prove the very pear we want for export to Great Britain
in cold storage." It is now on trial at two or three of our Experimental Stations, and
will be reported on later.

PLUMS.

SEEDLING PLUM, from A. W. Peart, Burlington, Ont.. Known in the Burlington
district as "Ireland's Seedling." We have noticed this plum in Mr. Peart's orchard for
two or three years past, and he has given us the following notes concerning it:—"Fruit,
medium sized, nearly round, distinct suture, reddish purple, thick bloom, juicy and rich;
stone very small, flesh adhering slightly to it; season, last of August (this year
exceptionally early on account of drought); midway between Ogon and Bradshaw; has
tendency to rot as it ripens, and, therefore, has to be picked when firm." Tree, spreading;
moderate grower; close jointed; blossoms tender, variable in productiveness. In this
district, a crop perhaps once in three years; not as satisfactory and as sure a cropper as
some of our standard sorts. Its extreme earliness insures fair prices.

SEEDLING PLUM, from David Matheson, Ottawa, Ont., who suggests that, if it is entitled to a name, it should be called "Cooch," after the man who grew it. Mr. Woolverton gives a photograph, and the following description of it in the October number of the HORTICULTURIST :—" A plum of good size, measuring two inches long, 1¾ inches in width ; somewhat one-sided, with a very distinct suture on one side. In form it is somewhat broadened towards the apex. The stem is short, about half an inch in length, inserted in a shallow cavity. Colour, a very dark red, with greyish bloom. Flesh, greenish yellow, moderately juicy, soft of texture, moderately sweet. Quality, very good for cooking and market purposes. Season, late. Sample photographed came to hand September 10th."

PEACHES.

SEEDLING PEACH.—Raised by Dr. Stewart, 152 Dowling Ave., Toronto, and on exhibition at the Industrial, Toronto, September 9th, 1898. As shown in the accompanying photograph, this is a large round peach, measuring about three inches in diameter. The skin is light yellow with red cheek ; flesh, yellow, firm, of good quality ; freestone of the Crawford type. Originating in Toronto it may be that the tree will be hardier than Crawford ; at all events it is well worthy of trial. Buds were secured by Mr. A. M. Smith, St. Catharines, who is propagating it. This seedling will be tested as soon as possible at a number of our Fruit Experimental Stations.

SEEDLING PEACH.—Grown by Mrs. Fairbrother, 119 D'Arcy St., Toronto, and was exhibited at the Industrial, September 8th, 1898. A large, handsome, yellow peach, with bright red cheek ; flesh, yellow, juicy and of good quality ; freestone ; season of early Crawford. Worthy of trial.

SEEDLING PEACH, No 1, from R. T. Smith, Hamilton, Ont. Upon this Mr. Woolverton makes the following note in the September number of the HORTICULTURIST :—" A sample of this seedling was shown us on the 25th of August, at a season when good peaches are very scarce. 'Hale's Early' was just over, and 'Honest John' not yet ready. It is large, with beautiful bright red cheek ; has a distinct suture, a deep cavity and quite a depressed apex. The skin is easily removed without a knife. The flesh is white, very tender, sweet, rich and very juicy. A freestone and capital dessert peach."

SEEDLING PEACH No. 2, from R. T. Smith, Hamilton, Ont. The following account of this is given in the October HORTICULTURIST :—" On September 27th Mr. R. T. Smith, Hamilton, showed us another fine seedling peach of about the same season as Steven's Rareripe, and just in advance of Smock. It is very large in size, 3 x 3 inches ; almost round in form, with distinct suture; skin, yellowish green, with dull red blush on the sunny side ; flesh, tender, juicy, fairly sweet; freestone. A first-class dessert peach, and one which on account of its large size should be valuable for market."

SEEDLING PEACH, grown by Mr. M. Fitch, Grimsby. Sample shown September 13th, 1898. The following account of this appears in the October HORTICULTURIST :—" A beautiful peach, quite equal to Early Crawford in appearance, rounder in form ; size, 2½ x 2½ inches ; yellow, with deep red blush on sunny side, and partially suffused with red in the shade; down very perceptible to the touch ; skin, thick and easy to separate from the flesh; flesh, yellow, fine grained, juicy, but not quite so much so as Early Crawford, melting ; flavor, lucious ; quality, first-class for dessert or canning ; value, first-class for market, and probably a better shipper than Crawford ; season, September 10th-15th, immediately succeeding Early Crawford. A seedling worth testing."

SEEDLING PEACH, from Mrs. J. T. Ross, King St. East, Hamilton. Received October 20th. Medium in size (2¼x2½), greenish yellow skin, with faint coloring of red ; moderate down; deep and narrow cavity ; distinct suture ; flesh, dark yellow, juicy and of good quality ; freestone ; season, late in October. Promising as a late variety.

GRAPES.

SEEDLING GRAPE.. Grown by W. Bachus, St. Catharines. On exhibition at Industrial, Toronto, September 6th—10th, 1898. In size of bunch and berry, this seeding is about the same as Concord; in color it is like Niagara; quality, excellent; very early, about the season of Moore's Early. Worthy of trial.

SEEDLING GRAPE, from O. F. Wilkins, Bridgeburg, Ont. Received September 12th, 1898. Bunch of good size and form; berries, white, round, of medium size; flavor agreeable, somewhat foxy, but much sweeter and pleasanter than Concord; skin thin and tender; pulp, tender and separates readily from seeds. Is said to ripen with Early Ohio. Worthy of trial.

CHERRY.

SEEDLING CHERRY, from John Gormley, Pickering, Ont. Received July 22th, 1898. The following note on this seedling appeared in the August Horticulturalist. "On page 317, Vol. 20, we referred to this cherry as being of great promise. To day, July 12th, we have received another sample lot, and consider them even superior to those received a year ago. Being of Canadian origin, no doubt the tree is very hardy, and would succeed over a wide extent of country."

" The color is bright red like the Montmorency; the form about that of the English Morello, and the flesh like that of a Bigarreau, not very juicy; it parts easily from the pit, without dropping its juice; flesh, yellowish; a wonderful keeper, and therefore a good variety for distant shipment, Mr. Gormley writes, ' This is a seedling cherry-tree about 25 years old. I remember the tree coming up in a fence corner. It has never had any care, but has grown well under neglect. I would like to know if it is very valuable, as the quality cannot be excelled, and it bears every year '."

Mr. MORRIS. I would like to make a suggestion. That Report deals only with the seedlings of this country, and I suppose there is not one in a hundred that is worth propagating. Now, I think that it would add to the usefulness of the Committee's work, if they would extend their operations, and get every new fruit that nurserymen are offering for sale and report on them. I think that would be information that would be worth ten times more to this country than information on seedlings that are never grown afterwards or anything done with them. I think if they were to report on new fruits that nurserymen put in their catalogue it would give people information and a guide in the way of planting that would be valuable.

Mr. HUTT. That is a work of great value, which we are trying to do at our fruit stations. These are being tested. It would be difficult to get fruit of all these varieties. We might see a variety advertised in a nurserymen's catalogue, but the difficulty for this Committee would be to get a specimen of that so that they could pass on the fruit itself. We simply took note of any new Canadian seedling that came to our notice during the year.

Mr. MORRIS. Of course the work is very good that is being done at these experiment stations, but perhaps it will be six or eight years before we can have those fruits put on our lists. I do not think it would be difficult to get samples of any new fruit that is offered for sale by nurserymen. Perhaps the greatest hybridizer and the most successful that has ever been on the continent is Burbank, of California. He sends samples of his new plums to parties east whenever they are requested, particularly of this Japan class, and there is quite a number of new varieties coming up, although not even in the nurserymen's catalogue.

The SECRETARY. I am sure that the members of this committee are always pleased and glad to receive samples of new fruits that are grown by nurserymen that are sent to them. We shall always be pleased to receive them, and quite ready to report on them as well as on any other fruits that are sent in by any private individuals who grow them. I would move the adoption of this report for publication.

Mr. HUTT seconded the motion which was carried.

GRADING FRUIT AS TO SIZE.

By E. H. WARTMAN, KINGSTON, ONT.

The grading of fruit as to size has been one of the chief difficulties of packers. Having no standard to go by, but eye measurement, it is not to be wondered that we have so much irregularity in fruit grading; and that we find stunted, medium and superior size, all in the one package. But as the trade has recognized brands, designated XXX, No. 1 and No. 2 and have so often been disappointed, finding some packers of No. 2 equalled by other brands marked No. 1, and many a No 1 not equal to another packer's No. 2; the question is asked, how can we remedy this state of affairs. The remedy as to sizing all kinds of fruits properly, is simple, if the means are provided. At present there are fruit graders on the market, that will do the grading as to the size required in a most perfect manner, at perhaps a cost of 1c. per bbl. Each barrel is designated by a standard grade brand 2, $2\frac{1}{2}$, 3 or $3\frac{1}{2}$ inch diameter grade, or any other size that may be required. These fruit graders are durable, and cheap, and when fruit sized by them is put on the market it will bear being poured out and a striking uniformity is at once noticed. By the use of these machines, we do not propose to say to to the growers that we will not take their small fruit. We will be glad to get it and mark it as to size, and it will demand its relative price. But we must remember that in a year of an enormous crop we must set our standard higher than in a year of scarcity. Let a $2\frac{1}{2}$ inch diameter apple be the smallest size put on the market in a plentiful season, so that thousands of barrels being screened out, there will be a tendency to keep our markets steady. There are other ways of using our small apples more profitably than stuffing the centre of packages with this inferior grade. This imposition and fraud should be a thing of the past. Facing with large beautiful fruit, and putting inferior sizes in centre of packages, has been in vogue long enough. Buyers no longer credit barrels or boxes as to top facing, or being true to size throughout, but always pay a price for a second class size to be on the safe side. If these beautiful facers, top and bottom, were put in cases by themselves and marked as to grade, they would bring the top price in the market, whereas, used as they are, they only bring a second class price.

Some may say, "Sizing is very well, but what about color and fungus spots?" If apples are generally affected by spots, growers cannot afford to throw this class away; but grading this class to uniformity of size makes it very much more valuable to the trade. As to off color, if fruit is graded according to the scale, this class is not objectionable and will find a ready sale. In my experience of packing and shipping fruit for the last 25 years, the sizing has more often brought my stock into good repute than any other cause.

In trying to make sale of fruit, where you have no sample, the first question usually asked is, "How is your fruit for size?" If graded by a proper grader, and marked accordingly, how easily and truthfully is this question answered! I have a 100 bbls. Golden Russets $2\frac{1}{2}$ inch diameter grade. What does this mean? That there is not one apple in the 100 packages under this diameter. Is this not more satisfactory than saying they are a fair size, or average sample? For what one man may think extra, another may only call ordinary. The question of rebating on fruit not up in size and quality would be disposed of and all parties would be more satisfied with this way of grading as a more profitable, scientific, etc., up-to-date method.

For packers to say they can divide their fruit into two sizes by eyesight and draw the line as to size correctly is a mistake. You are always running too far towards small sizes and dropping culls in with your best grade. Large size mixed with culls was a very common occurrence in the old guess work style of grading. Graders relieve the eye of the task of measuring, so that the eye service can be devoted to picking out or detecting defective fruit, wich no machine can dispose of. Our old country market demands our best graded fruits. Our Canadian shipments have often been spoken of as inferior as to size, or as not strictly high class. Now, as we are living in the best province in the world for high class fruit, why not have our best apples put up in the best manner of grading, as well as put up in the best package for our English or foreign markets? And by so doing we will hold our own in all competition with other countries, and bring to ourselves much credit as well as large profits. While eighteen days in Glasgow, Scotland, watching auction sales of our Canadian Apples, I never saw our red varieties that were well graded sold at a low figure; always at from 15 shillings and upwards. But our yellow and green are not so much in favor. In competition for a prize for the best 12 apples or any other class of fruit, one strong point is in favor of the lot that has been graded as to uniformity of size and color. If size is uniform throughout the package, the same price can be obtained per peck or dozen, throughout package, relieving the merchant the trouble of grading after his purchase arrives in stock. It is hard to determine what a package or barrel of ungraded apples, as to size will realize a merchant, when put up by careless packers. As a proof that grading as to size combined with quality demands attention as well as secures top prices in Glasgow, I may say that a lot graded in this manner brought me a profit of over 100 per cent. The brokers who sold them, in sending my returns said, "Your grading as to size is a phenomenal success, and if you had sent them to our house in London your profits would have been larger." Some would say putting all even sized large apples together it would be impossible to keep them tight. But my experience in shipping Cabashea apples to London is to the contrary. Very large, even sized apples were opened in that city by myself and found perfectly tight and brought the top price in the market. I admit that this class are harder to keep tight than mediums, but long years of experience can overcome this difficulty. I have shipped to Glasgow in quantities with returns of only 4 per cent slack.

In conclusion I would say, that for export, never ship apples of any sort under $2\frac{1}{2}$ inches in diameter; and apples that generally grow larger, such as Kings, Spys, Greenings, etc., grade 3 inches in diameter, and you are most certain of success, as these sizes denote superior growth and will not cost more to export than inferior sizes. We, as fruit growers, packers and shippers, must remember we are living in an age of progress. We understand how to grow fruit and the kinds to grow for profit; but I am inclined to think as to packages and grading, we will, in the near future make long strides in the right direction, which will be a boon to growers as well as shippers and packers at large. At all times let our motto be:—

> We'll pack our best fruit,
> In uniform size,
> Never let top or bottom
> Beguile or tell lies.

The SECRETARY: I have been sizing my pears this year. I sent 400 or 500 cases of Bartletts to Great Britain this year, and graded them all for size. What we call No. 1 grade was the lowest grade of pears, and they were uniform from $2\frac{1}{4}$ to $2\frac{1}{2}$ inches in diameter. That meant just 100 pears in a case; you can put no more and no less than 100 in a case, so any one buying that package would know exactly how many pears he was getting. The next grade, A No. 1, measured in diameter $2\frac{1}{2}$ to $2\frac{3}{4}$ inches. That took just eighty pears to a case. Extra A No. 1 was three inches in diameter and took just sixty pears. On our apples a similar rule was observed. No. 1, $2\frac{1}{2}$ inches, average about eighty apples; A No. 1, 3 inches, about sixty apples; and Extra A, $3\frac{1}{2}$ inches, 48. I believe it is going to be more and more an important thing to size our apples. Whether we do it with a grader or not, we must have some way of making the grade uniform.

JUDGES OF FRUITS AT FAIRS.

Mr. RACE read the Report of the Committee of Fruit Exhibit, giving a list of competent Judges at Fairs, copies of this list to be sent to the Boards of the various Fairs.

Your Committee would recommend as competent judges on fruits at the agricultural fall fairs throughout the Province of Ontario the following :—

On Apples.—T. H. Race, Mitchell ; A. Mc. D. Allan, Goderich ; G. C. Caston, Craighurst ; A. H. Pettit, Grimsby ; E. Morris, Fonthill ; Dr. J. Harkness, Irena ; Henry Robertson, Morrisburg ; Harold Jones, Maitland ; H. A. Brouse, Ottawa ; Walter Dempsey, Trenton ; W. A. Whitney, Iroquois.

Pears and Plums.—A. Mc. D. Allan, Goderich ; A. M. Smith, St. Catharines ; A. H. Pettit, Grimsby ; Dr. Beadle, Toronto ; Chas. Van Duzer, Grimsby ; R. L. Huggard, Whitby ; E. O. Beman, Newcastle.

Grapes and Peaches.—M. Pettit, Winona ; W. M. Orr, Fruitland ; Alex. McNeill, Walkerville ; E. J. Woolverton, Grimsby ; W. W. Hilborn, Leamington ; A. M. Smith, St. Catharines ; Walter Forward, Iroquois ; W. A. Whitney, Iroquois.

Mr. CASTON : I suggest that this report be accepted as read.

THE LITTLE PEACH.

Mr. CARPENTER asked if any of the gentlemen knew anything of the new disease affecting the peaches seriously through the United States, particularly in Michigan. It is called " The Little Peach." I cannot find out any cause or any remedy. I have had a tree that had it last year similar to what is described in some of my papers in some very large orchards in Michigan. I noticed a few peaches on one tree. They ripen before they should naturally ripen, and they are very small, perfect in appearance in every respect with the exception of the kernel. I do not know whether they destroy the tree or what is wrong with it. I see by the papers they are cutting down large orchards of trees in Michigan just from this source ; and it was stated through the papers that some people supposed it to be this rosette in the peach, but it was denied. I have seen the rosette myself, and it is nothing like it.

Mr. PETTIT : I would suggest that our Secretary give us any information that he may gain through the " Horticulturist." I fancy we will not be able to gain any more information here to day.

CO-OPERATION IN FRUIT SELLING.

By Mr. ALEX. McNEILL, WALKERVILLE, ONT.

I do not propose to take all the time that in justice might be allowed to this subject, because there are other papers that must be heard, and I hope to reach you through the columns of the " Horticulturist," but I can assure you that this matter of co-operative selling is one that has been forced upon us, and one that must receive attention, and I hope that I at least will have the co-operation of my fellow fruit growers in this mode of selling. Co-operation is absolutely necessary in many things, but it is a good thing in almost all our fruit growing associations. It is unnecessary for me to point out the many advantages of it. In other lines of business co-operation has been found successful, and certain branches of farming have been almost created through this spirit of co-operation. Dairying, as we call it now in Ontario, would be almost an impossibility were it not for co-operation ; and that same spirit that has been so successful in connection with the production of cheese I believe can be introduced among the fruit growers and be equally successful there. Now it is an appeal for the development of this spirit of co-operation that I make here this afternoon. It is very true that to devise any system, any mechanism by which this co-operation can take place with regard to the selling of fruit, is somewhat more difficult than in other branches of agriculture ; but I am perfectly certain that with the intelligence we have represented in this profession it is not altogether

5 F.G.

impossible. I am sure that among us we can devise some scheme that will be practicable for us under our conditions. Of course it would be an easy matter for me to cite cases where co-operation has been successful among other people in the matter of selling their fruit. The peach growers in the nation to the south of us have long adopted this method in various sections of the country as a means of disposing of their productions, and it has been the universal testimony that where these co-operative associations have been worked with any degree of intelligence they have been successful. The peach growers of New Jersey and Delaware would think it almost impossible to conduct their operations now were it not for co-operation ; and I am sure we are all familiar with the great co-operative selling concerns of the fruit growers in New York State and Northern Ohio. The co-operative societies of Michigan have not been quite as successful as those of their eastern brethren, but even the Michigan men claim that co operation in selling has been an immense advantage to them. The fruit growers of California, particularly the grape grower, found that grape growing could be begun a few years ago only at a loss. Grapes are cheaper there even than they are with us, and though we are suffering now from the effects of growing grapes at half a cent a pound, they were even worse than that at California ; but due almost solely to the efforts of these societies the grape growers have forced grapes during this last year and 1897 to a very fair price—$21 a ton, I believe, was the average price in 1897, and 1 believe they realized quite good prices this year, almost solely through the efforts of co-operative societies. I cite these cases simply to shew that co-operation is possible with other people, and though the exact mechanism they have adopted might not suit our needs, I believe we have that within us that will enable us to devise the means that will suit us. The suggestion that I would make here this afternoon is that the different localities should be organized into associations, without any great amount of red tape or formality, but simply that the growers of a neighborhood should unite and appoint from among themselves a seller or a manager of the association, and should as largely as possible sell through this certain manager. Now that is just the plan in its bald outlines. There can be any mechanism introduced that you wish. You can incorporate if you think it necessary. It is not necessary at all, and associations of that kind are conducted in different parts of the continent without any formality except simply a meeting of the neighboring growers who ship from a certain railroad station, and who sometimes appoint a manager who is given power to sell their fruits. At other times the business is put in the hands of a committee of three or five whose business it is to meet the buyers and to arrange sales and other business of that sort ; and I believe that that can be done here, and we have concluded in our section to try this process next year, and we are willing to put our fruit in the hands of a manager. We are limiting it for next year to a special class of fruit, which are grapes, because the grape growers are not perhaps as numerous as the growers of other kinds of fruit, and they are grown in larger quantities by each individual grower. While there is an immense quantity of grapes grown in the aggregate in our section, the number of growers is comparatively few, so that the circumstances under which we co-operate are somewhat favorable. We propose to place the selling of our fruit in the hands of a certain individual under the direction, so to speak, of a committe of three of us, and all sales will be made through this manager and committee. We have drafted out a simple schedule on which we propose to have patrons—that is, those who unite with us—agree to give us the selling of this particular kind of fruit. It reads simply this way: " I hereby agree to place (naming a certain quantity of fruit) in the hands of this association for sale." The object of that is to know exactly how much we have to dispose of. We are acquainted with each other very largely, that is one of the essentials of this co-operative business. Our local associations are supposed to know the needs of each individual member, and as far as possible we unite in this matter for the sake of securing several objects : largely for securing better prices, but incidentally there will be other advantages—less competition among buyers, for one. Now in every neighborhood there are certain advantages that induce buyers to come. Buyers come to our neighborhood to buy grapes, perhaps not because we have better grapes there than anywhere else, though we claim to have, but buyers have the advantage of a number of growers of grapes in one neighborhood, and they come here to play off one grower against another. As a matter of fact I have evidence, which I submitted to my fellow growers after a transaction was over, that one of these large men from Winnipeg simply played off four or five of us in that way. He came to me and had an offer for grapes, asked me at what price I would put in my entire crop of grapes, which I estimated to amount to sixty tons ; and I made him an offer of $25 a ton in 10 lb. baskets. I am rather ashamed of the price ; certainly we should not have to take such a price for our fruit ; but it was the best we could get, and in my judgment, considering the competition all around me, I think $25 was the highest price I dared ask. He asked me if I would not take something less than that, and when I demurred a little he said, " Well, I will see you again before I leave," and I knew exactly what the process was going to be. He was going to my neighbor, Mr. Murgatroyd, and making the same offer and telling him that Mr. McNeil was going to take $25, would not he go $24 ? And Mr. Murgatroyd did what I would do under the circumstances—he took $24. Then he said to Mr. Murgatroyd that he would see him before he would leave. Then he went to Mr. Bennett, another neighbor, and Bennett agreed to put them in at $23. Then he came to me and said, " I would rather have these if you can put them in at a trifle under $23 ; " and I said, " I will go it at $22— (laughter)—and $22 I got. Now, that is the history of an actual transaction, not a freak of my imagination. I did not see him with the physical eye travelling around to these people, but I could trace him just as distinctly as though I had been following him around, and he came to me and saw me before he left, and he got satisfaction. If I could have paid my creditors dollar for dollar he would have squeezed me down a few cents less, but I thought I could not pay dollar for dollar at anything less that I took. There were certain advantages by buying from us that he could not get from any other people. For instance, he thought he could get a carload upon short notice. The agreement was that we should ship him a carload within twenty-four hours of his telegram, so that if he telegraphed this morning for a carload, ten tons, we expected to have it start to-night for Winnipeg. If we had been together I would have said, " The selling of this is in the hands of Mr. Murgatroyd." Mr. Bennett would have done the same, and Mr. Ferry would have also sent him to Mr. Murgatroyd. If he had that kind of a deal to go through then there would not be the competition of one against the other ; he could not play one off against the other in that way, so that there will be that advantage in this co-operation. Another advantage would be the lessening of the cost of sales. There are a certain number of expenses that must be undergone by each individual man. If I am selling a certain quantity of stuff I have to have telegrams to know the state of the market each day, These telegrams do not differ essentially. One would have done for the whole or half a dozen ; and there is a certain amount of correspondence, and , when you sell a large quantity of fruit correspondence becomes a serious matter. Most of us have not only to conduct the correspondence, but get out into the field and hustle during the shipping time, and we cannot delegate this matter of packing fruit to anybody else, and the correspondence in selling the ordinary crop of fruit is a serious matter, which might be lessened considerably by co-operation. Then this co-operation, even in this small way, would give us much better accommodation with the railway companies in the matter of cars and so on. That is a larger subject that I need not dwell upon. We all know that even where a dozen people are gathered together and are unanimous in demanding one thing they can secure what no individual or all the individuals acting individually could secure from the railway companies and truck companies and others with whom they deal. Each locality, too, has a certain market. Now, that market can be enlarged to a certain extent, but it is just possible it may cost considerable money to enlarge the market. Those of us who have tried to extend the market for our fruits have found that it did cost money to increase the market, and this increased cost could be materially lessened even by this small co-operation of each neighborhood that I speak of. It is a little too much to expect one man to open up a new field. Take, for instance, the northern part of Ontario. Some years ago I spent considerable money and time in opening up what I thought was a new market there, and I no sooner got a profitable trade—and I think I was the first person, certainly the first in our particular neighborhood, to take advantage of a certain freight rate that gave me access to three splendid towns, and I got a freight rate really where they had always been in the habit of paying express rate—but no sooner did I get that thing and spent considerable time and money in getting arrangements completed that all my neighbors had the advantage of the whole thing without any effort on their part I think I am a generous individual in most cases, but I thought it was a little hardship in that case, and I think co-operation would have been the grand thing if nothing more than to share the expense is such matters as these. Those who have had experience of this character are deterred sometimes from making these ventures on account of the expense ; but when we know that the expenses were shared by the community it would pay the community handsomely to undertake to open these new markets. These are only a few advantages of co-operation. There is another very important one—it would secure greater uniformity in the packing and grading of fruit. When these co operative methods are adopted it is positively essential that there should be some understand in regard to the quality of the fruit ; and the fact is, as some would say perhaps that now we grade the lower and grade down, but then the poorer fruit would be thrown out and nothing but the better class shipped ; the tendency of the grading is always upwards in these co operative associations and not downwards. That I consider a very important thing. The reputation of the association as such cannot be shirked so readily as that of the individual sometimes, because the whole mechanism is right at the criticism of the public. I would like to dilate further on the advantages of co-operation, but my object this afternoon is rather to open up the discussion and bring the thing before the members of this Association and see whether we cannot stir up a sentiment in favor of further co-operation. Of course you see that my object here is to endeavor to control the fruit at the shippers' end. Now it is a pleasure for me to say that the Niagara District Stock Co., a co operative concern, has done a great deal for the fruit growers in one way or another ; but they have commenced at the wrong end a little. They deal only with the sellers' end. Now, if these co-opera- tive societies and associations could work in conjunction with that, there we have a mechanism by which we can control the fruit at the shippers' end, and it is the only possible way of preventing gluts in the market. Unless we know and have some means of finding out what to be shipped and where to be shipped to, we have no means of pre- venting gluts in the market ; but if this Convention should take up seriously this matter of co-operation just as it has been taken up in the Dairymen's Association in connection with their cheese factories and creameries, we could make this matter so general that in a very few years we could develop a system of selling fruit by which we could control almost completely the shipping of fruit, so that no market would be over-supplied with fruit and no market would be under supplied. Now, I am sure there is not a fruit grower but feels that is a consummation devoutedly to be wished ; and I feel certain, if we can only induce the various members to think about this matter, to read what is said about co operative methods, and to so school themselves morally that they can work with their neighbors, much can be done by this Association in that direction. Old Dr. Johnston said, " There are some people that are so unclubable that it is almost impos- sible to work with them." Let us introduce the missionary and the Sunday-school and educate our neighbors to work co-operatively, and we have done a good thing. We can work co-operatively with success when we give it attention. I do not believe it is going to come suddenly—no good thing ever did—and I should depreciate a boom in co-opera- tive societies of this sort, because then mistakes would be made ; but let us proceed slowly, let us see how one works this year and then proceed along several years improv- ing year by year to work steadily for this particular object. I am sure any of you who have read broadly along these lines must believe along with me that co operation must come into our farm operations before we can get the benefit of our labors. We are sure that the ground principles are right. The only thing is the mechanism by which we can secure them. If we believe the general principle is right, it is our business as members of a community, as an association, to work for them carefully but energetically ;. to avoid the errors that we may see each year and improve for the year to come ; not to go ahead with the possible chances, with the certainty almost, of making very serious mistakes on a large scale, but to proceed cautiously and work towards the end, not dis- couraged by minor failures, but to proceed along the line knowing that we are right and going ahead just as fast as we possibly can without danger. I thank you for the attention you have given me, and hope that this may well receive your careful consideration. (Applause).

Mr. GREGORY.—l think that has been tried pretty well in this section. Mr. Bunting is best qualified to speak on that, and I would suggest his name.

Mr. BUNTING.—I can only say, that during the past few years in this vicinity we have endeavored to carry out some of the ideas that Mr. McNeill has expressed, and that we have met with considerable success, more particularly in connection with the railway people. We have succeeded, I think, in placing our goods here, in the market, in better way than before, and the returns received from the various markets where we have shipped have almost been invariably good. (Hear, hear.) There are times when reports that have come back have not been so favorable as we would have liked, but in looking at the details of the matter, we have been able to find out where the difficulty arose; and I think with Mr. McNeill, that co-operation is the true idea as far as fruit-growers are concerned. In taking up the matter in the Committee appointed this morning, it will be my duty to work this idea as far as I can, and in approaching the transportation companies in that matter, we will bring as much influence to bear as we can.

Mr. McNEILL —It is gratifying to have the first bit of experience in favor of this particular plan. I hope, in the years to come, it will be so common that we will not have to ask for experience along these lines.

NOTES ON EXPERIMENTAL SPRAYING IN 1898.

BY W. M. ORR, SUPERINTENDENT OF EXPERIMENTAL SPRAYING, FRUITLAND, ONT.

One learns quickly by means of the eye, and an ocular demonstration is always the most convincing. Spraying bulletins are excellent educators, but I fear the greater portion of the bulletin is seldom read. However, let a farmer once see the work of preparing and applying the mixtures, and let him be shown the different species of injurious insects on the trees, and the best method of dealing with them—and he will remember more about it than he would if he read a bulletin a dozen times. Realizing this, the Department of Agriculture for Ontario has for the past four years conducted a series of object lessons in spraying.

This year we worked at 30 points, covering the Province from Amherstburg to Renfrew. An agent visited each point seven times, and his dates were announced by poster, postal card, and in the press. The bulletin of 1897 was revised, and given to those wishing them at the orchards, beside a great many requests were received for them by mail.

That the farmers appreciate this effort of the Department to benefit them and demonstrate to them the best methods for caring for their orchards, is shown by the fact that the attendance this year was 3,538, beside many who visited the orchards, when the agent was not there, to see the results. This is about 700 more than attended last year, and almost double the number that attended in 1896.

Although the work for 1898 has only just closed, 31 applications have been received for the work next year, including two points where the work has always been done. These latter say, that the farmers had not realized how important it was, and wished for another opportunity to see the work.

Only one solution was used, Bordeaux mixture, according to the following formula:— Copper sulphate, 4 lbs.; fresh lime, 4 lbs.; water, 40 gallons. To this in every case was added four ounces of Paris green.

On account of the law which forbids the spraying of fruit trees when in full bloom, and on account of rain, many applications were lost, as the work had to be done at the date and hour named, so that the agent might reach his next point on time. However, the results in most of the orchards were satisfactory.

Allow me to give you a few of the actual results from this year's report. In estimating the percentage of perfect apples a part of the tree was picked clean, and the fruit carefully examined, every specimen which had a worm spot no matter how small, being rejected as imperfect.

In the orchard of Mr. Hugh Black, Rockwood, we had the following results :—

Snow—Sprayed, 64 per cent. clean ; unsprayed, 1 per cent. clean.

Ben Davis.—Sprayed, 100 per cent. clean ; unsprayed, 28 per cent.

Wagner.—Sprayed, 26 per cent. clean ; unsprayed, 2 per cent. clean.

Spy.—Sprayed, 100 per cent. clean ; unsprayed, 36 per cent. clean.

Greening.—Sprayed, 88 per cent. clean ; unsprayed, 24 per cent. clean.

Ribston Pippin.—Sprayed, 90 per cent. clean ; unsprayed, 80 per cent. clean.

Canada Red.—Sprayed, 72 per cent. clean ; unsprayed, no clean fruit.

This orchard has never been sprayed before. Concerning the work in his orchard, Mr. Black writes as follows, under date of Nov. 16th, 1898 : " In reference to the effect of spraying this season, I feel in justice bound to give you my impression, which is at follows : ' The effect on the foliage was plainly noticeable all season. The leaves were fresh and had that glossy appearance which indicates growth. The bark was smooth and looked like the bark of young trees, the moss and roughness on the bark almost entirely disappearing, and the trees have made more new wood than for some years past. The fruit was, on the sprayed trees, as nearly perfect as is reasonable to look for. In my experience, I never saw, even years ago, before so many enemies came to stay, so entirely good a crop of apples. I am safe in saying that in our Spys, which were sprayed, there was not one barrel of culls to 100 barrels of good fruit. I am convinced that our chances of growing apples profitably will largely be in proportion to the thoroughness with which we spray. Good cultivation, plenty of barnyard manure, and careful spraying will ensure us equally as good and abundant fruit crops as of yore. I might just add that we had in one place in the orchard, two Greening trees, well loaded, and *not a single cull apple* was found, neither worm, nor scab, nor mis-shaped. We cannot now grow potatoes without using Paris green—we must also realize that we cannot grow good fruit without spraying. The first spraying will almost entirely destroy the tent caterpillar. I hope that our Ontario fruit growers will accept the situation and spray their apples and other fruits thoroughly. Excuse the length of this letter. I am so convinced and satisfied I don't know where to stop praising it.' "

In the orchard of Mr. James Gray, Bolton, we had the following results :—

Snow.—Sprayed, 80 per cent. clean, heavy crop ; unsprayed, 23 per cent. clean, about half a crop.

Fall Pippin.—Sprayed 76 per cent. clean ; unsprayed, 4 per cent clean, one-half crop fallen.

Golden Russet.—Sprayed, 64 per cent. clean, this is the first clean fruit from these trees in four years.

Talman's Sweet.—Sprayed, 64 per cent. clean : unsprayed, 24 per cent. clean.

Colvert.—Sprayed, 84 per cent. clean ; unsprayed, 20 per cent clean, most of the fruit is fallen.

Spy.—Sprayed, 54 per cent. clean ; unsprayed, 20 per cent. clean.

Flemish Beauty Pear.—Sprayed, 90 per cent. clean ; unsprayed, 10 per cent. clean.

This orchard has never been sprayed before.

On June 30th, the agent writes : " Here are four Snow trees, two sprayed and two unsprayed, equally good last Spring and at blooming, standing side by side. Now, on the sprayed trees, the foliage is beautiful and the trees are well loaded with good-sized fruit, about 75 per cent. of which is free from scab ; while of the unsprayed trees, although the tent caterpillar has been gathered three times, the foliage is almost ruined, the scab is prevalent and the crop almost a failure."

In a letter written Nov. 15th, 1898, Mr. Gray says: "We noticed a marked improvement this year on Flemish Beauty Pears and Snow Apples, especially. The foliage on the sprayed trees was more luxuriant and stayed on longer in the fall. On the unsprayed tree there was almost no fruit free from scab, and very few fit for market; while on sprayed trees there might be about 90 per cent. of good fruit. Indeed all the varieties of apples sprayed showed a marked improvement when picking time came. It is our opinion that if the spraying is continued, year after year, that the fruit will be much improved, and that if this is not done very soon there will be little fruit worth gathering.

Mr. R. Govanlock's orchard at Seaforth we have the following results:

Spy—Sprayed, 70 per cent. clean, heavy crop; unsprayed, 20 per cent. clean, very light crop.

St. Lawrence—Sprayed, 80 per cent. clean; unsprayed, 50 per cent. clean.

Snow—Sprayed, 90 per cent. clean, heavily loaded; unsprayed, heavily loaded but not a clean apple.

King—Sprayed, 75 per cent. clean; unprayed, 50 per cent. clean.

Gravenstien—Sprayed, 100 per cent. clean; no unsprayed trees.

Greening—Sprayed, 88 per cent. clean; unsprayed, 32 per cent. clean.

Flemish Beauty Pear—Sprayed, 50 per cent. clean; unsprayed, no clean fruit.

Under date of Nov. 17th, 1898, Mr. Govanlock writes as follows: "With regard to my orchard prior to spraying, I may say that the fruit was badly spotted, misshaped and full of worms, but this year after spraying there is scarcely a worm in the apples and they are far more perfect in shape. I picked five sprayed Snow trees, and they packed 25 barrels, and left scarcely anything but the bruised apples, while the unsprayed trees were worthless, good for nothing but cider. There was a marked difference on all the other varieties. I consider the sprying a direct gain to me of least $50 in my small orchard. Of course I sprayed the balance of my orchard, but not so thoroughly. I am convinced that if every one would spray their orchard for a few years we could get rid of most of the pests."

Under date of Dec. 29th, Mr. Claude McLaughlin writes: "In reply to yours with reference to the spraying of my apple trees, I would say that in the fall of 1897 I was completely discouraged with the result of my apple crop, so I made up my mind to cut out all my trees (I have about 300). In fact I had cut some of them down, when I was advised by a friend to give them one more trial and to try spraying. The following spring I was making enquires about a spraying machine, when I received a notice from Mr. Orr calling a meeting of those interested in fruit raising in this section, and stating that it was the intention of the Government to conduct spraying experiments in different parts of the Ottawa Valley. I attended the meeting, and was so much pleased with Mr. Orr's explanations that I immediately offered my orchard for the experiments. Part of the trees were sprayed and part left unsprayed. With the result of the spraying I am more than delighted. The apples of the sprayed trees were sound and large, the foliage a good rich color, and the trees made more growth than ever before in one season. In the fall of 1897 I had no apples fit for use, all were small and scabby. In the fall of 1898, on all trees sprayed, I had perfect, large and sound fruit, and although the past season was an off year I had some of my trees propped they were so loaded. On the unsprayed trees the fruit was poorer even than in 1897, and perfectly useless. I have bought the machine with which the spraying experiment was conducted, and I intend using it next season, when I expect even better results as my trees were in very bad shape from the many insects that affected them. This fall they looked clean and healthy. I am fully convinced that with good systematic spraying and ordinary care of the trees, we can raise as good apples in this section of Canada, and better than in most sections. The spraying experiment by the Government was of very great value to this section and was much appreciated by the people."

In the orchard of Messrs. Freels Bros., Niagara-on-the-Lake, we had the following results :

Baldwin—Sprayed, very heavy crop, 48 per cent. clean, 90 per cent. fit for barrelling ; unsprayed, 4 per cent. clean, very light crop.

Snow—Sprayed, 16 per cent. clean, heavy crop, about 6 barrels fit to pack ; unsprayed, no clean fruit, about half barrel to the tree.

Astrachan—Sprayed, 90 per cent. clean ; unsprayed, 30 per cent. clean, dropped very badly.

Duchess—Sprayed, 90 per cent. clean, heavy crop ; unsprayed, 30 per cent. clean, dropped badly.

Fall Pippin—Sprayed, 80 per cent. clean, good crop ; unsprayed, no clean fruit and crop very light.

Harvest—Sprayed, 80 per cent. clean ; unsprayed, no fruit fit for market.

Spy—Sprayed, 40 per cent. clean, good size and about 6 barrels on the tree fit for packing ; unsprayed, no clean fruit, and only about one barrel per tree.

Mr. Freels says : " The sprayed trees were selected in different parts of the orchard, and that he had no right to expect a larger crop from the sprayed than from the unsprayed trees, and that if all his orchard had been sprayed this year with the same results as were obtained in the experimental trees it would have been worth over $1,000 to him.

Under date of Nov. 22nd, Messrs. Freels Bros. writes : " Your letter of the 12th inst , received requesting information as to the benefit derived from the spraying of the fruit trees. In reply thereto we have to say that the spraying of the trees did great benefit to them, and the yield of fruit was much increased thereby. However, we think that the spraying this year was not a fair test, owing to the wet and rainy weather, and we are satisfied that with favorable weather, the spraying of the trees would be of incalculable benefit. Our crop this year under the most unfavorable circumstances, exhibited increased yield, and, in comparison with orchards not sprayed, our showed the benefits of spraying."

In Mr. Hugh Gourlay's orchard, at Carp, the following results were obtained :

McIntosh Red—Sprayed, 100 per cent. clean ; no fruit unsprayed. This apple spotted very badly other years.

Snow—Sprayed, 105 per cent. clean ; unsprayed, 10 per cent. clean.

Baldwin—Sprayed, 100 per cent. clean ; no unsprayed fruit.

Under date of Nov. 17th, Mr. Gourlay writes : " Your letter received asking for information about my orchard, prior to the spraying and the result of this year's spraying. Last year and other years the foliage was often spotted and not healthy looking, and the tops of the limbs were often blighted. This year the sprayed trees presented a very healthy appearance the foliage being very green and most luxuriant, the trees making just about twice the growth they did other years. The fruit other years was more or less spotted ; much of it being badly shaped from the bites of insects, more than half the Snow Apples being unfit for sale. This year the sprayed fruit was much larger and better shaped than ever before, nearly free from spots, nine-tenths of it being sold as first class fruit. I sold all my first-class fruit at $3.00 per barrel. I attribute this all to the effects of spraying. The benefits derived from spraying are almost incredible. Some of my neighbors had their orchards striped bare by the tent caterpillar and were much pleased to see the good effects of spraying on my trees. I had not the faintest idea that spraying could produce such a marked improvement on an orchard in one season."

With a view to demonstrating that better results can be obtained where the work is properly and systematically carried on, year after year, we have for the last three years worked in Mr. Albert Pay's orchard, St. Catharines, spraying the same trees each year.

In 1896 the results were good. In 1897 Mr. Pay said that if all his orchard was as heavily loaded with as good fruit as were the trees which we had sprayed for two years, it would be worth $2,000 to him with apples at $2 per barrel. As to the results in 1898, writing under date of Nov. 25th, Mr. Pay says :

"In reply to yours of the 12th regarding spraying, I would say the row of trees sprayed by you showed a very a decided improvement over the row next it which has never been sprayed, both in foliage and fruit. This is the third season you have sprayed the same row in my orchard, and the Greenings and Northern Spys in that row have had a good crop every year and the Baldwins two good crops in three seasons. The Baldwins had a very heavy crop, in fact too many to get a good size. I picked eleven barrels off two Baldwins in the sprayed row, and not two barrels in the next row which were unsprayed. There was hardly a marketable apple on the unsprayed trees, while fully 90 per cent. of the sprayed fruit would class No. L. The Greenings and Northern Spys would be about the same. There has been a number of buyers through my orchard this fall before the apples were picked, and some saw the fruit before packing and they all spoke very highly of the stock and told me it was the cleanest and brightest fruit they had seen this year. There can be no question in my opinion as to the benefit of spraying, after the showing it made during the three years. I think, however, it should be done successfully with less than six applications. However, even with that many times, I fully believe it will pay to spray every year."

It is only fair that I should tell you of some of our failures as well as our successes. I will give you in addition to the results, extracts from the agent's note book made at the orchard on the days of spraying, so that you may be able to judge of some of the difficulties we encounter and the causes of our failure.

In Mr. R. S. Lang's orchard, Exeter :—

1st application, April 22nd.—Rained all day, so that it was impossible to work.

2nd application, May 4th.—Cloudy, followed by an all night rain.

3rd application, May 16th.—Fine. Many of the trees in bloom. Sprayed only some of the latter varieties. Bud moth and tent caterpillar bad on unsprayed trees ; found only one tent on sprayed trees.

4th application, June 1st.—Fine, fall apples well set, winter apples are light. Oyster-shell bark-louse, aphis, bud-moth and tent caterpillar at work in his orchard.

5th application, June 13th.—Rained all day. Scab showing badly on Snows. Agent writes on June 13th. "I am afraid that this orchard will be a failure. I have only had one good spraying here."

6th application, June 25th.—Rain in forenoon, but cleared and afternoon was fine. Found a few green fruit worms and Tussock moths. Foliage on sprayed trees decidedly better than on unsprayed.

7th application, July 9th.—Fine. Considerable scab but not many worms among sprayed fruit.

I inspected Mr. Lang's orchard and found :—

Greening—Sprayed, 50 per cent. clean ; no unsprayed trees.

Ben Davis—Sprayed, 10 per cent. clean ; unsprayed 10 per cent. clean.

American Golden Russet—Sprayed, 73 per cent. clean ; no unsprayed trees.

Snow—Sprayed and unsprayed about equal.

In a neighboring orchard I found American Golden Russet unsprayed 20 per cent clean and Greening unsprayed 20 per cent. clean. Mr. Lang says that he has never had any first-class fruit off this orchard. All the fruit has been scabby or wormy and not fit for packing. On Nov. 15th Mr. Lang writes, "Replying to your letter of Nov. 12th, would say :—The spraying of my orchard was a success this year in the way of destroying insects and worms. There was scarcely an apple but was free from worms, something very unusual for my orchard, but as for destroying the scab the spraying was not a success this year. There was so many wet days when your operator called to spray, that that may be the cause of the scab not being checked."

We had the common insect enemies to contend with this year. They were more numerous than usual, the dry hot weather being favorable to their propagation. The tent caterpillar was reported very bad on the 23rd of April. In many sections orchards were entirely defoliated by them. At one station where no spraying was done except on the experimental plot, they stripped the trees of their foliage, although the owner of the orchards said he had gone over the trees three times and destroyed their tents. The agent reported that the sprayed trees looked like monuments of mercy in the midst of sur. rounding desolation. However they were controlled without difficulty on the experi. mental trees.

The aphis was reported bad at some points as early as April 23rd, although it was not nearly so bad as last year. I am thoroughly convinced that to secure the best results we must begin treating the aphis and tent caterpillar much earlier than we have been accustomed to do. At Fruitland we have discovered aphis on the buds as early as April 8th and tent caterpillar on April 15th.

The green fruit worm a comparatively new-comer, and but little known here, is likely to become a serious pest. Some growers report from 20 to 30 per cent. of their apples and pears ruined by it. The agent reported on June 16th that it had destroyed much fruit.

The rose-beetle was reported as doing a great deal of damage at Niagara-on-the-lake, on June 11th. The agent says they were very destructive. especially on King trees. He says there was hardly an apple without one or more, and that he had found as many as six or eight on a single small apple. They had been in this orchard three years. Prof. Saunders says that they are destructive to the leaf of the apple, plum, cherry and apricot, but here they were working on the fruit and were especially destructive on the King.

The codling moth, the oldest and most formidable enemy which the apple and pear grower has to contend with, was very numerous this year, except in a few orchards in North-eastern part of the Province, in one of which, at Carp, twenty miles above Ottawa, owned by Mr. Hugh Gourley, and comprising twenty acres, varying from ten to twenty years old, not an apple injured by the codling moth could be found. Mr. Gourley says he has never seen an apple in his orchard injured by the codling moth.

The owners of every orchard in which we worked this year, with one exception, Mr. Curwen of Goderich, report that the moth was largely controlled by spraying.

In the southern portion of the Province the moth was very numerous and continued to propagate until the first of October. Early in this month, the young worm, scarcely visible to the naked eye, could be detected just burrowing through the skin of apples that up to that time were clean. As the last spraying was done about the middle of July, these latter broods were not destroyed by it. Had the whole orchard been sprayed the latter broods would not have been so numerous, as there was nothing to prevent the moths, which had bred on the unsprayed trees, propagating on the trees in the experimental plots, after the spraying had ceased early in July.

Mr. R. A. Dewar, of Fruitland, has a black Detroit apple tree eight inches in diameter, standing near his buildings, the fruit of which has for years been badly infested with codling moths. This year he sprayed it five times with Bordeaux mixture, adding four oz. of Paris green each time. The first spraying was done before the tree blossomed, and the other four at intervals of from twelve to fourteen days, ending about the 12th of July. Up to this date not more than five per cent of the fruit was injured by a worm, we examined the tree the 1st of August and found about 75 per cent of the fruit wormy. On the 25th of August we made another examination and could not find a clean apple. Many of the apples had three or four, and in one case five, worms in an apple. No two of them had entered at the same place, neither had they burrowed into each others unnels. There appeared to be no choice as to the place of entering the fruit. On the 5th of May a large coarse sack was bound to the trunk of the tree to trap the larvæ as hey were going up or down the tree. This was examined on the first of June but no arvæ were found. It was again examined on the 11th of August, and about 200 larvæ ere found, most of them in cocoons and about 50 in the chrysalis. A large number of npty cocoons from which the moth had emerged were also found. We put a number of 1ese chrysalis into a glass vessel and in a few days the moths began to appear. In eight : ten days we had over twenty beautiful specimens of the moth. A number of eggs, hich appeared like creamy spots about the size of a small pin head, were deposited on he glass. The bandage was replaced and left until the 27th of August, when it was ex- mined and 261 larvæ, mostly in unfinished cocoons and one chrysalis were found. It was again put on and left until the 15th of November, when 191 larvæ were found, all cocoons. After a careful examination no larvæ were found on the tree at this date, ex- cept in the folds of the sack, and in the crevices of the bark under the sack. In all 703 larvæ and chrysalis of the codling moth were taken from the bandage around this tree in addition to which quite a number escaped as could be seen from the empty cocoons. On October 11th we put socks on those trees where they were examined on the 29th of Nov- ember, sixteen larvæ were found on them.

It appears from the result of experimental work carried on throughout the Province that in the greater part of Ontario the codling moth can be controlled by spraying. However, in the southerly sections, particularly under the mountain between Hamilton and Niagara, they continue to do much damage after the regular spraying season is over. They are much worse directly under the mountain than they are on the lake shore two miles away or on the mountain. This is probably due to the large amount of fruit grown and the shelter afforded in that district. We propose next year, after the regular spraying has ceased, to continue the work in one or two orchards until picking time, using Paris green mixture, that we may ascertain whether the latter broods can be des- droyed this way.

No doubt it would be advantageous to supplement spraying with bandages. It costs but little, either for material or labor. Full instructions for doing the work may be found in Prof. Saunders' excellent work "Insects Injurious to Fruit." From our own experience we would consider it necessary to continue the work until the middle of October. The first wormy apples reported were June 28th.

The black or dead spot on the limbs of apple trees is quite bad in some orchards and appearing more or less all over the province. Mr. McGurn's orchard at Marysville is very badly affected, several trees being killed by it. He expects that the orchard will be ruined in a few years.

It appears from results obtained in experimental work, that from 65 to 80 per cent. of perfect fruit can be secured, when spraying is regularly and properly done, and when the conditions are favorable, such as an orchard standing high and dry or on well-drained land, away from buildings or hedgerows, and the trees planted far enough apart so that the limbs do not come within ten or twelve feet of touching, that they have an abundance of sunshine and free circulation of air. It is also important that the trees be properly trimmed, all rubbish removed and the land be properly fertilized, for it is a fact that two-thirds of the orchards in Ontario are starving. With good apples at the price they have commanded this year and last year, the orchard, if properly attended to, would be the most profitable part of the farm.

We have a fertile soil, the climatic conditions are favorable and the apple attains a degree of perfection in Ontario, not exceeded in any part of the world. We have an unlimited market in Europe for first class apples. All that is necessary is that we treat our orchards intelligently and give them the care and attention they require, thus secur- ing annual crops and avoiding over-production alternate years, which gives inferior fruit and taxes the trees. Then there will be no more difficulty of the market being glutted by an over-production alternate years, and with careful and honest packing our success is assured.

Mr. MILLS : Were all the results that you read from trees sprayed the same number of times ?

Mr. ORR : Yes, these men reported from the points where we did the work.

Dr. MILLS : You did this work that is reported on ?

Mr. ORR : Yes ; this is their own report of it apart from ours.

Dr. MILLS : How do you account for the great differences in the immediate neighborhood, in the same locality almost ?

Mr. ORR : We can account for the difference in the results from the location of the orchards and the conditions they were in.

Mr. MILLS : Are you sure the tops of the highest trees are always reached by the rod ?

Mr. ORR : We are sure sometimes that they are not. In some cases we have to do the spraying off a stoneboat. The trees were 40 feet high, and it is impossible to do the spraying in such a case.

Dr. MILLS : What is the length of the rod you used ?

Mr. ORR : From 12 to 14 feet. We had trees standing close together and interlacing and needing trimming very much, and in such an orchard as that you cannot expect to do perfect work.

A Delegate : Do you spray from one side of the tree, or both ?

Mr. ORR : We spray on both sides of the tree, and under it as well ; you get on a waggon and drive it up and down i   ray.

Mr. BRODIE : Do you not think if you used more Paris green you would have had less codling moth ?

Mr. ORR : You will notice we have been very successful with the codling moth up to the date that we ceased spraying. The principal damage done by the codling moth was after the spraying had ceased.

A Delegate : That is the second brood.

Mr. ORR : I think it was one continuous brood from the 15th May to the 13th October.

Mr. CASTON : The entomologists told us some years ago that there was only one brood of them. We are finding out there are a good many, especially in the Niagara Peninsula. I can corroborate what Mr. Orr has said about the sacking of the moths. I had a little experience just there. I had a piece of sacking, and I put it in the branches of the trees, and it remained there. Sometime about the beginning of November there was a young tree of twigs that was just beginning to bear, not near a peck of apples, and there would not be as many moths in the tree as in the larger tree, but I picked it up and examined it, and it had over a dozen nice fat codling moths ; and I thought, would not that be a good experiment to carry out, to take a few rags and put them in the trees and then examine them from time to time ?   I believe that would be one of the most successful ways of dealing with the codling moth. I do not think there is much of the Paris green gets into the calyx. I think there is apt to be chilly weather at the time the egg is deposited there, and the instinct of the insect leads it to deposit its egg in a protected place, but I do not believe our spraying will kill many in the calyx of the apple. If you find two apples lying close together on a limb you will find holes bored in from opposite directions, and where there is a leaf covering the apple you will find one or two holes under that, and this second brood is the most destructive of the whole. Another very valuable thing would be the introduction of hogs. When an apple drops, in ninety-nine cases out of a hundred there is a moth in it, and when the hog devours the apple that is the end of the moth, too. I think the hogs and the spraying would work admirably together ; two or three men have told me they do. I think we may congratulate ourselves on the fact that our manufacturers in this country have produced excellent spraying machines, and that in so short a time they have been so well perfected ; but I think there is room for a slight improvement, that is providing for a vertical spray to get at the insect that is on the under side, for example the aphis, because that is so destructive to the tree, and then to spray in the ordinary way, and as those insects insert their bill and suck the juice out of the leaf, Paris green is not of any use, and we have to apply something that will kill them by contact; we want something to get at them from the underside of the leaf.

Mr. BRODIE: My experience agrees exactly with Mr. Caston's in regard to hogs being turned into the orchard. I turn in my cattle to eat up the refuse, and we have hardly any codling moth. The only place where we have codling moth is where we cultivate our trees. In these orchards that are old in sod, we have no codling moth whatever.

SPRAYING FOR ORCHARD PESTS.

BY DR. JAMES FLETCHER, CENTRAL EXPERIMENTAL FARM, OTTAWA.

I heard Mr. Orr's report with a great deal of pleasure, and I believe it is a very valuable one. It is valuable because he gives us facts, and does not try to make conclusions from them; he gives us facts, which being true are scientific. I think it is a pity he was not allowed to read all the facts, giving the percentages, which would have showed fruit growers that it paid them to spray and to save crops in the best condition they could; but, of course, they know their own business best. Mr. Orr has given us this year, as he gave us last year, a report of very great value indeed, and if there were nothing else here to be discussed this afternoon, I think it would be one of the discussions that would mean more money in the pockets of the fruit growers than many other discussions which take up a great deal of time. One of the points which Mr. Orr asked about was the number of broods of codling moth in the course of a year. This is an important question, because it has been supposed that the experience of the first writers on the codling moth was going to be the experience of every experimenter or fruit grower in other parts of the country. Mr. Caston speaks of what the entomologists had told us. The entomologist, he told us, said there was one brood of codling moth in a year, and they told us perfectly correctly. The writer who made the first statement, which has been copied by thousands of writers since, was a New York man who wrote with perfect accuracy about New York. A few years later, Mr. Saunders wrote about London, and he wrote perfectly correctly fifteen years ago, when he said there were two broods, practically continuous after the middle of June, of codling moth. Later still, Prof. Cook. of California, says there was three broods; and they are all perfectly correct. According to the climate this insect changes its habits The appearance of the moth brood all during the season is only apparent and not actual. There are but two broods, and if Mr. Orr would look through his notes, or if some one else would make notes carefully next year, you will find that the first brood of the codling moth that lays the eggs appears just about the time when the young apples are formed. Mr. Caston's criticism about the egg being laid in the calyx, unfortunately is not founded on fact. The eggs are not laid in the calyx, and there is no reason why they should be. The eggs are laid any place, and unfortunately on the leaves, but the insects crawl on the apples, and the nearest channel by which they can obtain access to the interior of the fruit is through the calyx and into the pips. which they generally try to get at first, and where they do a great deal of their harm. The second brood, which appears in August and lays its eggs, which give all the after trouble, is there prolonged in the appearance of the moth. It is very much like the peach borer. The moths begin to appear after mid-summer, and keep on appearing right up till cool weather. It is all one brood; it is not a succession of broods. Some people say, "Why, how should eggs laid one time produce insects at another?" We cannot tell why, but we have proved it over and over again that that is the case. I know only one, namely, the caterpillar, where the eggs were laid on the 1st or 2nd July. They pass through three or four moults before they reach maturity. Some of them pass one moult and then lay in lethargy, and more remain in lethargy until next spring. Some of these caterpillars pass two moults, and some pass three moults, and next year the insects will appear very much sooner than those that only passed one. That will give several appearances, extending a month over the time that the codling moth will appear. There are two broods of the codling moth, but as they are brought out and appear during a long period, it makes the appearance of the young caterpillars very much prolonged in time, and it is practically the fact that young caterpillars may be found any time after the 1st of August until late in the year ; but it does not matter to horticulturists and fruit growers particularly what time these caterpillars appear ; they know that there is a certain danger-time in the year that they have to protect themselves against, and if they find that fact out that is all they want. It does not matter to the horticulturist where the codling moth lays the egg—in the calyx or on the apple. They know that the caterpillar is going to get inside the fruit and do harm. It is a matter for the entomologist to find out how it gets there, and for the horticulturist to prevent it. Mr. Orr, and Mr. Pettit before him, has shown in his report that a great deal of money can be saved by spraying. Spraying pumps have been improved so that we have nothing to complain of in our times. There are two sprayers here to day—the Spramotor and the Aylmer pump—excellent pumps, as good as any man wants to use. I do not say they are better than any others, but I say that they are all that a man wants. You need not stop spraying because you have not got a good pump. You should get a good pump, and use it. You know if you spray your trees regularly, and Mr. Orr's figures will show you the fact, that you are going to save a large percentage of your fruit. I maintain it pays every man to spray his trees, it does not matter whether he has two trees or two thousand it will pay him to spray those trees so that they will give good fruit, which will give him a good return. There are orchards in some parts of the country to-day which are not sprayed where hardly a good barrel of apples can be got, and adjoining those orchards, separated only by a fence, are orchards where fruit of A1 quality can be picked and give the owners big returns You are perfectly competent to know that by the very fact that you did not want your time taken up by all the figures Mr. Orr was prepared to read to you, because you knew that you could save from 60 to 80 per cent. of your fruit, and have it of the first quality by spraying. I say that report which Mr. Orr has given us is a very valuable one.

There is only one omission that I saw in it, and that was that he said nothing about the San Jose scale. We might infer from it that that San Jose scale was nothing to you growers up here. There is nothing more important than to prevent the introduction of the insect into the country. Your Government has put forth grand efforts to stamp it out, and as you know this Association is doing a good work in stamping it out. Mr. Orr last year drew attention to that pest and the enormity of it. It was of such importance that the Ontario Government and Federal Government undertook to pass measures, which were at first criticised, and which are now endorsed by the whole country, to stamp out this pest. I am surprised there is nothing said about it ; nor do I see anything on the programme about that insect which is doing so much damage, but which by the efforts of the Government has been brought down very materially. and to a greater degree than any one hoped for last year. The efforts that have been put forth are enormous, and the results, though they do not show now, will show, if they are kept up a little longer, that an enormous good has been done to the whole country. From the fact that people have not been ruined in the country some are arguing that too much fuss was made about it. I say, gentlemen, not one word was said where a hundred ought to be said, for such a pest as that is, can only be understood by going down to the southern orchards and seeing it. Last March I saw down in the State of Maryland acres and acres of magnificent fruit trees that had been killed as dead as possible in three years simply by that one insect having been introduced—one large orchard of 28,000 trees wiped out in three years —and yet people will say that too much fuss is being made about the San Jose scale. I am thankful to say that our Government did put into execution these Acts, which were discussed so fully in both Houses, and the good effects have been enormous.

Mr. ORR : I think there was no time of the year but what we could find a young odling worm just boring into the apple.

Prof. FLETCHER : That is after the middle of June ?

Mr. ORR : Yes.

Mr. A. H. PETTIT : There are a number of people here who have trunks and ranches of peach trees affected with the borer, with the gum oozing out quite freely. If ou will give them a little life history and remedy it would be helpful.

Dr. FLETCHER : The specimen on the wood that has been brought, and which when n attack is present is indicated by a large mass of gum that is produced and oozes, is a ery small beetle, one of the bark borers, which only bores into the bark and not into the ood. The best remedy is the Saunders wash with a little soda ash put into it—soft oap made thin enough to use with a large brush, and washing soda and water, then add o that carbolic acid sufficient to get a strong odor. It has been used by Mr. Karl Fisher, f Queenston, with great success. Put the first wash on in March, after that two appli- ations will be sufficient. One in March and the other about the end of May.

Dr. SAUNDERS : I wish to offer my word to what has been said of appreciation of his good work which Mr. Orr has been doing. I do not think there is any line of work which the Ontario Government has taken up which is likely to produce more permanent and lasting result than this work of spraying our fruit trees. The value of the apple crop in Ontario depends very much on the cleanness of the fruit and its quality, and we cannot have clean fruit now-a-days of good quality unless we adopt some regular system of spraying. Fungous enemies and insect enemies are multiplying to that extent that it is no use to look for good results as a rule unless the farmer and fruit grower will take the pains to meet these enemies by which he is surrounded. I know you occasionally meet with fruit growers who say, "I do not believe in spraying ; I have got just as good apples as my neighbor, and I have not sprayed, and he has." There may be exceptional cases of that kind. There are, no doubt ; because these people speak the truth. But there is no rule that has not exceptions, and these exceptions can be explained in every case without reflecting on the value of spraying. I was very much struck this autumn when visiting the Industrial Exhibition with the excellent demonstration which Mr. Orr made there on the value of spraying. I think there is nothing appeals to the mind of the ordinary and intelligent observer so strongly as a practical demonstration by object lessons, and I think Mr. Orr hit on a capital method of bringing together a large number of samples from different orchards where these experiments had been conducted, and showing fair representative fruit from sprayed and unsprayed trees. Sometimes when we get up to talk about these things at meetings, or talk about them to farmers individu- ally, they think we are allowing our imagination to run away with our judgment, and putting things in too strong colors ; but when they have the fruit put actually before them they can judge themselves of the results and the methods used ; and I think it was an admirable method of demonstrating the value of this most successful work. I think it cannot be commended too highly, and it has evidently fallen into good hands and been carried out very thoroughly. (Applause.)

Prof. MACOUN (Experimental Farm, Ottawa) : I listened with very great pleasure to Mr. Orr's reports, and I would like to add what results we have had this year at the Ottawa farm. In the Ottawa District we have not been very much troubled with scab ; in fact it is very rare that I have seen a case of it this year. Our spraying for scab did not improve the position to any great extent, but on spraying for codling moth, I observed that our early apples up to the Duchess were almost free from codling moth. From that time to the fall and winter apples were badly affected with codling moth. We sprayed our orchard five times this year ; but I have come to the conclusion that if we are to rid the orchard of codling moth, if we are to have clean fruit, that we must spray the winter apples later on in the season. It is impossible of course to spray some apples that ripen earlier, to spray them late on account of their color, but for winter apples I believe it would pay us to spray late in the season. I had an excellent opportunity this season of observing the good effects of spraying in Montreal. While there I had the pleasure of visiting my friend Mr. Brodie's orchard, and saw there the immense advantage which he had over his neighbors. Mr. Brodie has carefully sprayed his orchard for several years. His trees are in a far healthier condition than his neighbor's, and this year he tells me he produced 1,500 barrels of apples. Now, I saw the trees of his neighbor, and I saw there was scarcely any fruit on them, and Mr. Brodie tells me that they were none of them worth picking; in fact the man had nothing in his orchard. I think this example alone will show fruit growers how important it is to spray their trees thoroughly.

Mr. PATTISON : Some years ago, having some leisure about the 13th August, and noticing that the codling moth, the second brood, was working badly, I took the trouble to thoroughly spray the orchard with Paris green at that date. I am sorry to say that I found as far as I could see that it did no good whatever. I could not ascertain that I had benefitted in the slightest degree from it, and I am afraid that spraying at that time of year we do not seem to get at the insect sufficiently to do it any serious damage.

Mr. HUGGARD : I have a small orchard, about 80 apple trees, that I have sprayed some six or seven years. These last two seasons our first spraying was before the buds came out, and I consider is as important a spraying as there is the whole year for the black spots. Out of 130 barrels that we just shipped recently we did not have one bushel of wormy apples. I attribute the whole thing to careful and intelligent spraying at the right time.

Mr. TWEDDLE : I had some experience this year as well as years before in spraying, not only in my own orchard but in that of other parties, and I must agree with Mr. Orr that it was of a great deal of value. I was so unfortunate that I had to take to the road in selling spraying pumps. In my work I had a great deal of opposition from people whom I tried to sell to, and it occurred to me that I would try to take some means of convincing them from a financial standpoint that these things could be accomplished ; so I arranged with a neighbor to spray his orchard and pick the crop for one-half. He thought it was a good idea ; as he said " If you do not make anything I will not have to pay you, and it won't cost me much ; if you make anything I will make something." So he told me if I would spray his summer apples, Astrachan and Duchess, for nothing, give them a couple of applications, he would give me one-half of the balance. The orchard consisted of two parts of 10 acres each, both the same aged trees, about the same cultivation and the same kind of soil and everything alike as near as I could tell. The trees were not pruned sufficiently, or as thoroughly as I would have done. The arrangement was made about the 7th May, and I sent a rig down to work right away ; we put on what we could. Some of the trees bloomed before we got over it. In all we gave it four applications ; the last one was about the last of July. I think we finished on the 30th July, and when we picked the apples some of them had the Bordeaux mixture on them. We used more Paris green and lime ; we used six ounces of Paris green, forty gallons of water, and six lbs. of lime. When I finished on the 30th July the apples on both orchards, as far as size was concerned, seemed about alike, and in one orchard there seemed to be about as much crop as the other. I never went back to the orchard till about the middle of September, and I went into the nearest one first, and I was surprised to see the amount of fruit and the size and condition of them. I said to myself, " Why, here is a bonanza for me as well as for the owner," and I felt very well pleased. When I went over to the other orchard, where I expected to see three times as much fruit, I was very much disappointed in the quality and condition both in the variety and fruit. I could not understand ; I sprayed both orchards alike, and they looked to me just alike as near as I could tell, and cultivated alike ; but I found that the first orchard had been quite well manured with ashes and some barnyard manure, while the other had been pretty badly neglected in that way. From that orchard—and it was the off year—I took about 225 or 250 barrels, and the other orchard, instead of having three times as many, there were only 150 barrels of first-class fruit—hardly first-class ; we called it XX No. 1 and the other XXX. In the orchard which was not manured we took off about two carloads of peaches and one carload of Duchess, and one carload of the other, in all about forty-six tons. In the other orchard we took off about 480 barrels. That does not seem a large number of No. 1 fruit, but the unmanured orchard rendered a very small proportion of saleable apples ; there is where we had the loss. I may safely say that had that orchard been manured it would have yielded a thousand dollars more this year than it did. We shook down about fifteen tons of crop that were too small for sale, and my share of that orchard was $680, and it cost me about $275 or $280 for the spraying and packing and picking up of this fruit, cullage, etc., which left me just about $480 clear for the operation. I think this is a practical illustration that might do as much as any other illustration. There is nothing political about it. I got money out of it, and am very well satisfied. (Applause and laughter).

R. W. SHEPHERD (Montreal): The fruit growers in the Province of Quebec who have tested spraying thoroughly are I think all quite unanimous that spraying must be kept up and that it pays well to spray. In connection with my export business of apples in cases, I have to purchase at outside places ; I grow apples in different sections of the Province. I may say first of all that Fameuse is our leading apple in the Province of Quebec. You call it the Snow. It attains to great perfection in the Province of Quebec, and is our leading apple. It is by a long way the first and most profitable apple. It is also perhaps the most affected by the spot of any apple ; therefore in our Province it is an absolute necessity for us orchard men to continue spraying, and to spray well, and we must not neglect it. In connection with my export business of Fameuse apples in cases, I have to visit the different sections of the country in order to buy the fruit to fill my cases in the different orchards, and in one section of the Province I visited one orchard where a man of great experience had about 500 barrels of Fameuse. After going through his orchard I said to him, "I don't think you will be able to fill one of my cases out of your whole orchard." He says, "No, I don't think I will ; not good enough, not clean enough." I went to his neighbor on the next farm and he had sprayed his orchard the last three or four years and sprayed pretty thoroughly. I went through his Fameuse orchard and found very good fruit. He filled fifty cases. Further on a man who sprayed carefully filled 100 cases ; and it was only in the orchards that had been sprayed that I could get good enough Fameuse for my business. My own experience is that unless the spraying is kept up and thoroughly done every year the orchard men in the Province of Quebec may as well give up growing Fameuse ; and I think Mr. Brodie will bear me out in that, that in his section his orchard is in fine condition. His neighbors mostly French Canadians, have not bothered themselves about spraying, and they are cutting down their orchards. They found that Fameuse has become unprofitable, and the result is they don't want to learn I suppose, and they are going to some other kind of cultivation. That is the experience I had this year ; in the orchards that were not sprayed I could not get good enough fruit for my business, in fact I had to give up buying fruit because I could not get good enough in the sections where the spraying was not done.

Mr. CARPENTER : I would like to know, if Mr. Orr has experimented in some other directions of spraying than apples ? Many of us are interested in growing pears and plums and peaches and no apples. Is there the same good done in spraying of peach orchards ?

Dr. SAUNDERS : I may say in that exhibit in Toronto to which I referred, Mr. Orr exhibited some samples of the Flemish Beauty pears which had been sprayed, and some which had been gathered without spraying, and the one lot that had not been sprayed were badly cracked and diseased while the others were healthy. I have no doubt Mr. Orr has carried on experiments of other varieties of pears besides Flemish Beauty.

Mr. CARPENTER : Does the Government confine it to apples alone, Mr. Orr

Mr. ORR : Apples alone is our regular business. Of course I have been spraying all my fruits for the last 13 years at home ; that is experience apart from what I am doing in my regular work.

Mr. CARPENTER : Would it not be a good idea for the Government to give us a little benefit of the operation of spraying other fruit trees ?

Mr. ORR : Your crops are so regular and you make so much money out of them that your case is not demanding much sympathy from the Government. (Laughter.) If time

6 F.G.

would permit I could tell you something of my experience at home, but I hardly feel like taking up time when there are other papers on the programmes. I purpose giving my experience in spraying peaches in an article in the *Horticulturist.*

Mr. COLE (St. Catharines): There has been nothing said here to-day about the spraying of grapes. We all agree with Mr. Orr that it is very essential for fruit growers to spray their orchards. About six or seven years ago my vineyard—about 50 or 60 ton vineyard—was badly injured with black rot, something new to us in this section of the country; but we were advised to spray, and we did so next year with a great deal of benefit. My vineyard was hurt so badly that it took a great deal of time to repair it for the market, and then my crops were not in a very good condition; but I sprayed thoroughly that season, and out of 54 tons I am satisfied I did not have 500 pounds of culls, and I attribute the whole thing to the spraying. Since that we spray our vineyards thoroughly, which we feel it is a necessity to do in this vicinity in order that we may get first-class crops. It is as essential to spray our vineyards as it is apples.

Mr. ORR: The instructions for spraying apple trees apply to all other fruits. The necessity of spraying apples particularly is because we go over the whole Province, in sections where they have never seen the work done. You spray pear, peach, vineyards exactly in the same way and with the same material as apples. I will tell you what I did with my peach trees. I had heard that experimenters were spraying with a preparation of lime in the fall and winter to keep the buds back in the spring. They calculated by having the trees white that it would not attract the sun, and delay the blooming period a week or ten days. Last December I sprayed my peach trees thoroughly with preparation of lime alone, and in February and March they looked as white as snow. In the latter part of April and May, we sprayed the same trees with Bordeaux mixture. We just sprayed 100 trees with lime, and in the spring we sprayed all the orchard. The Bordeaux mixture I think was too strong for the narrow leaves or willow leaf peaches; after the spring came in they dropped the foliage and the crop, but all the rest of my peaches bore a good crop. I think when the trees were dormant that the Bordeaux mixture the regular strength did not injure them, but after the growth commenced I think it injured the wood so that they dropped their foliage. However, they got a new foliage and had a good crop of foliage later on, but they dropped their fruit. That was simply a few narrow leaf varieties. Where the broad leaf varieties took the material there was no harm done. I do not know of any peaches grown apart from what I had, and I attribute it all to spraying, preventing curling of the leaf which in my own case took the last leaf off the trees that were not sprayed.

A DELEGATE: What about the effects of the lime?

Mr. ORR: I was away from home, and I cannot tell you accurately as to that. Where they have been testing it for two years they claim they can hold buds back for a week or ten days.

Mr. PATTISON: Do you use any Paris green on peaches?

Mr. ORR: No.

Mr. PATTISON: What strength do you use if for plums?

Mr. ORR: I use the regular Bordeaux mixture, adding 4 ounces of Paris green to each 40 gallons of water for plums.

Mr. CASTON: There is one difficulty I have known in spraying with Paris green; if you stop with half a barrel of mixture and go to dinner, that Paris green goes to the bottom and I do not think there is an agitator made that would bring it up again if you do not use something else besides the agitator; and then when you come near the bottom you will have a very strong mixture. I would like to know Mr. Orr's experience as to that. When the Paris green mixes with the lime in the pump it forms a mass that you cannot get at with any ordinary agitator.

Mr. ORR: We never allow our appetites to drive us away with half a barrel of spraying (laughter); but if such a thing should happen I would not take the slightest hesitation in going right on with the agitators.

Dr. FLETCHER : There is this trouble, as Mr. Caston says, and even in spraying with all care it is well to wash your barrel out or stir it up with a broom after about three fillings. You can do it with a corn broom very well. In reply to the question as to spraying Paris green in the mixture, that is a very important one. I have never found it necessary to use any greater strength than one pound in 200 gallons, and have found excellent results with that. Mr. Brodie asked if it would not be better to have a stronger mixture than Mr. Orr uses. I would say it would be very dangerous to have it ever stronger than that. I think it was a lack of patience. Paris green is a slow killing poison, and it takes about two days to get the results.

Mr. BRODIE : In the meantime they eat up the whole of the potatoes. Laughter. I have heard from one of our Montreal fruit exporters that one of his farmers consigneed apples to him sprayed with raw petroleum and water and Paris green. Have you heard of such a mixture for preventing the apple scab, the fungi on the apple ?

Dr. FLETCHER : Yes, there has been a recommendation made during the last two years in the United States to use pure coal oil. At the present date, both in the States of Maryland and in New Jersey where it has been tried very carefully there are a great many injured trees from the application of that remedy. There is a special pump made by which the water and the coal oil are vaporized, broken up into very fine particles by the same machine. If anything gets out of order you are apt to do a great deal of injury, and hence they have not become very popular. The other remedy for the San Jose scale was to spray with pure coal oil on a bright day with a very fine nozzle. Anyone that has seen any spraying at all knows that if you have not fine weather the nozzle gets out of order very easily. It is better to use a weak solution and repeat it than to use a strong one and take the risk of losing all.

A DELEGATE : Tell us the solution for the San Jose Scale ?

Prof. FLETCHER : Two experiments in the United States have shown that the only remedy that has given what we may call even good results is this pure coal oil, which is too dangerous for anyone to adopt, and the other is caustic potash or whale oil soap as strong as two pints to one gallon of water, which is a very expensive application.

SHOULD ONTARIO BE REPRESENTED AT THE PARIS EXPOSITION ?

Mr. McNEILL : I am convinced that this Province should be represented at the Paris Exposition of 1900. It is on the back of the programme, and should be attended to at this session, as to-night is not a favorable opportunity, and I take the opportunity of making a motion in regard to it and offering a few remarks. I am sure it needs no words of mine to convince the people here that it would be to the advantage of everybody concerned that there should be a representative at the Paris Exposition ; not that we care particularly for our trade with the French people, but that we care with our reputation with the world, and the world will be there. Therefore I take for granted that every person in this hall to night would be glad if the Government would have a representative at this exposition. I therefore move :—"That the Provincial Government be requested to make an exhibit at the Paris Exposition of 1900." It is put very briefly, and I presume that the Secretary will transmit this to the proper channels, and that the proper means will be taken to make the opinion of this Association effective. I am perfectly certain too, that we are very anxious that our fruit exhibit should be creditable to us. We have a wonderful country here which has been misrepresented, and of late years much has been done, and successfully done, to combat the old ideas in reference to Canada, and the man who is put there to represent us will have a great deal to do with how this country appears before the world. I would therefore add to this motion, "that this Association recommend that William Orr be in charge as a representative of the fruit men in Ontario." I do this because of his long experience in fruit growing, because of his success in connection with the Chicago Exposition as far as he had charge of any part of it, and because of the experience that he has got throughout the province in connection with these spraying experiments. He has, perhaps more than any other man that I could name at the present time a knowledge of the exact resources of the Province in this line. I am sure you will all agree with me that no man is more worthy to represent us creditably there than the gentleman I have mentioned.

Mr. A. H. PETTIT: Allow me to second that resolution.

THE PRESIDENT: I do not think we have time for any general discussion unless there is any objection to this resolution, so I will just put it without discussion.

The resolution put and carried unanimously.

THE FRUIT GROWER OF THE FUTURE.

BY E. MORDEN, NIAGARA FALLS, ONT.

The fruit grower of the present is very often a failure. Very often he lacks scholastic training ; very often,he knows little of the sciences that underlie his particular industry· He lacks practical knowledge ; he lacks mechanical dexterity ; his soil is often unsuitable ; his location as respects markets is often wrong.

Often he is a city man, a business or professional man, a mechanic or a " transmogrified," slip shod farmer. Fruit growers must compete with men who are favorably situated.

The coming Fruit grower to succeed must be fully equipped. He will not be an ignorant man ; he will have a fair understanding of the laws of nature that are operating all around him. He will therefore study the sciences which underlie his business ; he will know of the elements and their combinations as found in the soil, the atmophere and the plants. He will be familiar with effects of heat, light and electricty. He will have a knowledge of insects of fungoid growths ; he will understand the insecticides and fungicides ; the whys and wherefores in their use will not be mysteries to him.

He will actively aid legislative measures for stamping out insects and diseases ; he will not stupidly refuse to destroy trees affected with peach yellows or other diseases because he has inherited some past theory from his grandmother. His wife will doubtless know why milk sours and thickens and cream rises ; why the bread or cake rises. through fermentation or the carbolic acid gas liberated from the carbonate of an alkali. She will know all about fermentation ; the sweetest of women should know how to make vinegar.

The coming fruit grower will have an accurate knowledge of fruits, their varieties culture and management. The coming fruitgrower will know how to handle his trees and do his work ; he will possess mechanical dexterity in his own particular line—very few, even of farmers, can handle a hoe properly ; he will see that the right thing is done in the right way and at the right season. He will not be a grower of weeds.

The coming fruit grower will not dabble much into other kinds of business, for although the general farmer has many advantages over other men, he cannot well be a general farmer and a general fruit grower. He may, however, successfully grow one or two kinds of fruit, A poor farmer does not make a good fruitgrower.

The coming fruit grower will operate with a suitable soil. He can buy good land far cheaper than he can make it. A hard clay, a poor sand, or a swamp, will be dear at any price.

The coming fruit grower will locate near to markets or shipping points. The farmer from away back, who expects to team berries for many miles and compete with a fully equipped fruit grower located near the city or town, courts disaster.

The coming fruit grower will plant varieties that will yield large crops suitable to the demands of consumers. Let us hope that the coming consumer will be educated to consider quality in making his purchases. To get the required varieties the grower will deal directly with responsible nursery men. He will when the fruit is produced hold that responsible nursery man to strict account for wrong fruit trees or plants furnished to him. The discouragements of present growers along this line should suffice for several generations.

The fruit itself will be reformed. The poorer samples will not cluster in the lower portions of the packages while their fairer friends are pushed up to the top. By some method of inspection or rejection the coming fruit will be what it seems.

The fruit commission-man will be reformed or extirpated. Growers cannot much longer produce fruit to increase the joys of express companies and commission men. The beautiful fruit which it has taken a lot of pickers' hours to prepare in good shape for transport is now shamefully and hopelessly bruised by express men in a few moments. Cheaper, better and more varied means of transportation we must have. When the future trolleys permeate our country in all directions reaching many villages and country places, fruit will be better distributed. How many farmers in the clay portions of Lincoln and Welland are supplied with peaches and many other fruits that are almost or altogether going to waste in the fruit growing sections.

We do not now reach the large home market in our own counties. In many of our counties there is no large production of the fruits generally. Their townspeople pay a pretty good price for the well bruised result of the express man's energy, while we pay him a high price for bruising it.

In the rural sections of much of Ontario where at least during the summer months fruit should constantly appear on the tables it is rarely seen. When the future farmer lives up to his best interests in this connection there will be a marvellous expansion of the home market. The commission man ought to become a direct buyer. In time his agents will meet the fruit growers at the stations and buy directly. Near the large American cities this system is in vogue. Growers there have had their fill of the commission business. We have had our fill. Emptiness is perhaps the proper word. The other fellows have been filled at our expense.

The coming fruit grower will recognize four principal points of the compass. The present one knows only three—east, west and north. He has not learned that there is a south which shelters millions of trained fruit eaters who, after their own season has passed, must get fruit from the north. The idea that southern fruit may find a northern demand is already well understood. The idea that later northern fruit may find a southern demand has not penetrated the cranium of the Canadian fruit grower. It will do so in time. From July 1st, 1893, until late in 1897, Canadian small fruit entered the United States free of duty. In the year 1896 nearly $36,000 worth of small fruit entered Buffalo. I have not the figures for Detroit and Niagara Falls, but I know that immense quantities were entered at those points. Buffalo and Detroit by what we should call a lucky chance are placed contiguous to the two principal fruit growing centres of Ontario. This southward current of Ontario fruit was increasing in volume at a rapid rate. With a free entry it would soon have counted many thousands and would have penetrated further and further south. Who would have been hurt by this state of affairs? Not the American fruit consumer ; not even the American fruit grower, because his season of fruit production would be past. The Canadian fruit grower was liable to suffer ; he would have been called upon to carry around a load of money which just now would be a queer experience. He would have perspired freely in producing fruit for those who wanted it ; now he perspires in his efforts to sell fruit to those who don't want it.

The effect of throwing back upon fully supplied local markets the $36,000 worth of small fruit that found an outlet at Buffalo is of course disastrous to us. What were our Canadian fruit growers doing during the fourteen years of free entry into the United States ? Clamoring for the exclusion of American fruits, and succeeding in their efforts,

Competing with the Americans in their own markets and asserting that we could not compete with them here.   At last our long-suffering neighbors gave us a dose of our medicine and it was not good to take.   When we come to the larger fruits we find that many of the western states will never produce them largely.   We can produce them.   Our winter apples are of good quality.   They keep well.   Our nearest and surest market is to the west and south.   Why should we refuse to occupy the markets that call for our fruit?   Why refuse to accept ordinary fruits from the south which mostly arrive when we have none.   We have all along given a free entry to the fruits of the extreme south.   These, arriving at all seasons, have done us much more harm than has resulted or would result from the influx of the more northern fruits.   Housekeepers who can secure a cheap supply of oranges and bananas do not, in most cases, *can* our summer fruits.

The coming fruit grower will not only enjoy free markets abroad, but will have a free market at home.   He will not be fined ten cents for feeding his fellow-countrymen who happen to live in towns or cities.   Just now in Ontario we find that hay, grain, dressed hogs, lumber, laths, shingles, wool, and under certain circumstances, butter, eggs and poultry, are exempted from the operation of the market fee tax.   Thus it will be seen that the general farmer is exempted while the fruit and vegetable grower is still taxed.   This unjustifiable discrimination against fruit growing should be remedied speedily.   The future fruit grower will pay his own municipal taxes, but will not be taxed by the town which he visits in order to sell his fruit.   The future fruit eater will not erect barriers to prevent himself from getting fruit to the very best advantage.

The fruit grower, in pursuit of his customers, meets with too many barriers without contending with Legislative barriers.

The PRESIDENT : Before closing the meeting there is a paper I would like to have read by Mr. William Armstrong of Queenston.

Mr. BURRELL : That is an important subject particularly to this district, because in spite of the talk of over production last year the peach industry is about the most important in this district, and 75 per cent. of the whole of the peaches that we produce were simply second grade peaches ; so we do not overproduce the good fruit, and this question of training and pruning properly to get good fruit is a very important subject to this section, and I feel that we should get that at once and properly explained by Mr. Armstrong in ten minutes.

The PRESIDENT : I have hurried through the programme with the view of giving Mr. Armstrong a place.

Mr. ARMSTRONG then proceeded to show his method of pruning peach, using samples of trees which he had brought in for the purpose.   In the absence of illustrations it is impossible to report his method.

HOUSE PLANTS.

BY WM. GAMMAGE, LONDON.

Fashions come and fashions go, but the fashion of cultivating plants and flowers is pre-historic.   It is ever on the increase, for as man's grosser wants are supplied, new necessities arise which must be satisfied, and what we considered luxuries a few years ago are the necessities of to-day.   The production of flowering plants is a recognized industry of the country.   A vast amount of capital is invested in it, and large numbers are employed in the production of nature's beauties.   Plants and flowers are now as much of a necessity to the complete furnishing of the modern home as are some of the more useful articles.   Nothing lends elegance to its surroundings or to the complete furnishing of a room like a perfect specimen of the palm family ; and the ease with which they are grown and cared for has not been generally known. Now that the public are becoming more acquainted with the case of their culture, the demand has increased until it requires thousands annually to supply the demand, where a few years ago dozens were ample. Nor is the demand confined to the Palm alone for house decorating, but Ferns, Ficus, Dracaena, Pandanus, Aspidistra, etc., each have their admirers. Failure or success in growing house plants depends almost wholly upon the person in attendance; situation, soil, water and pots are secondary considerations, but to be successful the peculiar requirements of each species must be studied, and even varieties of one species. In the ordinary living room the hot, dry atmosphere is certain death to most plants; therefore the cooler rooms should be selected. Do not attempt to grow flowering plants in a room where much gas is burned, that is if you want them to bloom; the amount of sulphur in the gas will cause the bloom to either drop before developing or develop an off color or a deformed flower. Gas has no effect worth mentioning on such plants as Palms, Ficus (rubber tree), Aspidistra, etc. Their only requirement is a sufficient and constant amount of care in giving light, air and water.

In the care of decorative plants, such as the above mentioned, avoid the use of commercial fertilizers, and that erroneous but widely practiced fad of dipping the plants with castor oil. The injudicious use of fertilizers has killed more valuable plants than it has ever been the means of benefiting. The use of castor oil, too, although not so quick in its action, is sure death to the subject. In my experience as a commercial florist I have found that when plants require feeding there is nothing like animal manures, and even with this mild form of stimulant too much care cannot be exercised in its use. When mineral or commercial fertilizers are used the time of application depends on the ingredients; if they contain nitrogen as the main manurial substance, they must be applied during the growing season, as plants assimilate this substance immediately; if phosphoric acid or potash is the main ingredient, then it should be applied before needed, or in other words should be incorporated with the soil in the compost heap. As plants take this form up slowly it is likely to remain in the soil until the roots take action upon them and make them soluble. It is a well known fact that all plants take their food in the form of solution, and almost exclusively direct from the soil by their roots. Nitrogenous manures are needed only to induce free growth of wood and foliage, the phosphates and potash give substance to the wood and color to the flower. In the preparation of the soil for decorative plants I would recommend the following as a compost : 50 per cent. clay loam sod, 20 per cent. jadoo fibre, 20 per cent. leaf mould, 10 per cent. well rotted cow manure. This mixture will answer for almost all varieties of palms, ferns, soft and hard wood decorative plants. For flowering plants, such as begonias, cyclamen, primuli, etc., a light rich, fibrous soil is required. As a rule, hard wooded plants require a heavier soil ; also geraniums, fuchsias, cinerarias, and all varieties of lilium, do better in a rich, heavy soil. Care should always be exercised to see that the soil is taken from some high and dry land ; a rich pasture or unbroken ground always being preferable. The more fibre your soil contains the less liable it is to sour, and the sooner your plants take hold of it.

Light, air, and water are indispensable to plants, as to man. Avoid the too frequent habit of crowding or huddling a lot of plants together, and thus producing the poor, puny, drawn, long-leggy plants that we see. Better to have a few, and have them sturdy, robust, and well matured. Give all the fresh air possible. Once a week is not too often to give them a total immersion, or to wash all the foliage. Perhaps the most important of all in the cultivation of plants is the knowledge of how and when to water; it is a knowledge that can be gained only by experience. It is one of the greatest difficulties we have to contend with in greenhouse work, to get men who thoroughly understand the art of watering. It is always safe to be on the dry side, for once the soil is soured by overwatering the growth is immediately checked, and will not again start, until chemical action has again taken place in the soil. Care must also be taken to see that the pots are not too large for the plants ; this is a common error, one that we meet with every day. A customer will come to the conclusion that a plant needs repotting, and immediately acts on the impulse of the moment, going out into the garden and taking the first convenient soil ; next a pot is selected two, or three, or perhaps four, sizes larger than the one from which the plant is to be removed ; no drainage is provided, but the already sickly plant is put into the large pot with the poor and too often sour soil, and then watered and watered ; then because it does not grow it is given stimulant in the way of liquid manure, whereas most likely the only thing that the plant required was to remove some of the soil, put it back into the same pot with fresh soil, and water sparingly until such times as it had made a new growth.

Bulbs for house culture give excellent satisfaction, commencing with Roman Hyacinths and paper white Narcissi, a succession of showy bloom can be had from early November until the spring. No special preparation of soil is required ; they do equally well in any kind of soil, or any situation. After being brought from the cellar they require an abundance of water and a moderate temperature to produce the best results.

Mr. WHYTE : What proportion of jadoo do you use ?

Mr. GAMMAGE : Twenty per cent.

Mr. WOOLVERTON : Is it easily got ?

Mr. GAMMAGE : Yes, from almost any seed house. It is sold at about three cents a pound, or $27 or $28 a ton. It has the appearance of peat. It undergoes some chemical process. It is imported from England. Speaking of watering plants Mr. Gammage said : Most people imagine that when a plant is potted in a large pot it needs plenty of water. That is not the case. After re-potting give it a thorough watering and allow it to dry sufficiently so that the roots will begin to work in it. If it is watered till the soil is soured the organic acid that is in the roots does not have power to make sufficient nutriment to take it up. People after watering plants think the soil is not rich enough and they go and give it liquid manure. This will almost always kill the plant.

Mr. BRODIE : Do you also attempt to use the bone meal as a fertilizer ?

Mr. GAMMAGE : It depends on what you are going to use it for. We use tons of it every year, but we mix it with our soil for months before we begin to use it.

Mr. WHITNEY : In potting lilies do you place sand around the bulb ?

Mr. GAMMAGE : Not necessarily. We use a proportion of sand in the soil, enough to cut it so that you can feel the sand.

Prof. HUTT : Mention the best dozen plants you consider most suitable for house collection.

Mr. GAMMAGE : In the way of decorative plants, the Palms, Ficus (rubber tree), Pandanus, Grevillea, etc. Here is one that will stand rough treatment in any situation whatever—the Aspidistra. The Begonia gives a good deal of satisfaction. Coming on at this time of the year we have the Cyclamen, and the Calla lilies. Nearly all the varieties of ferns are hardy ; Pteris tremula is probably the best.

Mr. WHYTE : You shook the flowers of the begonia to show the injury done by gas light ; was all that damage done since the flower came into this room ?

Mr. GAMMAGE : Yes.

Mr. WHYTE : Was it not on account of the uneven temperature of the greenhouse ?

Mr. GAMMAGE : No : take one of these begonias and put it into a room where there is a wood stove, and it will last for weeks and weeks without dropping either a leaf or a flower, but place it in a room where a gas or coal stove is burning, and oftentimes two hours will do it.

HARDY PERENNIALS SUITABLE FOR CULTIVATION IN ONTARIO.

By W. T. Macoun, Central Experimental Farm, Ottawa.

Flowers and fruit are so nearly akin that I think it is only right there should be one or more papers in connection with the Fruit Growers' Association on flowers. They are the most important, because if you had no flowers you could not have fruit. In travelling through Eastern Ontario and the Province of Quebec I noticed that our farmers have very few trees, shrubs or flowers growing on their farms. In olden times they began to clear away their woods, not thinking that the time would come when they would be glad of a few trees that they were so pleased to get rid of at that time. The result is that to-day in a great number of cases you will find that the farmhouse stands alone in a field without a tree for shade during the summer months, and with perhaps scarcely a flower to gladden the hearts of the wife and children and perhaps the householder himself. Now, I think this should not be, and it will be my aim always, whenever I have the opportunity, to impress upon farmers and fruit growers of the country how important it is to have some flowers in their place, and those of the best sort ; so that I am going to bring before you this evening what I consider are the best hardy plants for this Province.

The plant which grows from the seed, flowers, produces fruit and dies the same year ; or, in other words, an annual, does not possess, I think, the same charm as that which we have watched and cared for, perhaps for five years, and which, as time goes by, increases in size and beauty. Think of the old garden in which your younger days were spent, and there will come up in your mind's eye some favorite flowers and plants which had their places in some particular spot and which year by year appeared to gladden your heart and make your garden gay.

Many of the flowers which held a prominent place in the gardens of our forefathers are not to be surpassed to-day, but there are many more available since foreign countries have been opened up for exploration by our botanists and florists, and enthusiastic workers have produced others by selection and hybridization, until now we have a large and varied store of beautiful and many colored flowers. From this large number we can select those which please our fancy best and which are the most satisfactory.

It has been the aim at the Central Experimental Farm, Ottawa, to test as many species and varieties of perennials as possible, in order that the hardiest and best kinds would become known and be recommended to the farmers and horticulturists throughout Canada. The perennial border there is now more than half a mile long. It is on the east side of an Arbor Vitae hedge, and is twelve feet wide. There are three rows of plants—the latter being three feet apart each way. In this border there were living this autumn almost 1,200 different species and varieties of perennials. Notes are taken during the summer on the time of flowering, growth, color and other characteristics of the flowers, and the most promising sorts marked. In my report for 1897 a list was published of 100 of the best species and varieties that had up to that time been tested. A select twenty-five of these were marked with an asterisk for the convenience of those who had small gardens. There is reason to believe that this list has already proved of considerable value to intending planters.

The snow has barely left our fields and gardens when the Spreading Pasque flower (*Anemone patens*) throws up its flower stocks, at the ends of which are those large, deep, purple blossoms, which in the month of April help to relieve the otherwise dull appearance of the perennial border. Following this, in about two weeks, is the little Ox-eye (*Adonis vernalis*) which, with its large lemon-coloured flowers and finely cut foliage, is very attractive at this early season of the year. The Polemoniums or species of Jacob's Ladder, closely follow and are all profuse bloomers with flowers of various and delicate shades of blue. They flower in the following order :

Polemonium humile pulchellum, *P. Richardsoni* and *P. reptans*. *Polemonium coeru-leum*, or true Jacob's Ladder, does not bloom until the second week of June. All of these should be in every collection of 100 perennials.

The earliest white flower of note is the White Alyssum (*Arabis alpina*), which blooms in the first week of May. Were this to bloom later, it would be overlooked by lovelier flowers, but in the early spring its pure white blossoms are very attractive.

The most charming and graceful, perhaps, of all the early spring flowers, are the Barrenworts or Epimediums. Of these, the best are *Epimedium rubrum*, *E. pinnatum* (*sulfureum*) and *E. macranthum*. The brilliant coloring of *E. rubrum* and the bright yellow of *E. pinnatum* make a fine contrast. The leaves of these pretty plants are also very ornamental.

Most of our best composite flowers bloom in the summer and autumn, but the Leopard's bane is an exception. During the second week of May the Caucasian Leopard's bane (*Doronicum caucasicum*) begins to bloom. Its yellow flowers are very attractive at that early season of the year. Following this is *Doronicum plantagineum excelsum*, which is taller than the last and has still larger flowers and is the better of the two.

The Iceland Poppy (*Papaver nudicaule*) is now becoming more generally grown. Its yellow, white, or orange flowers are very pretty. Other chief points of merit are earliness and continuity of bloom, as the flowers appear early in the spring, continue through early summer, and, after a short rest, open again in the autumn. The Oriental Poppy, which is not in bloom until about three weeks later, is, I presume, well known to you all. Its immense scarlet flowers of great brilliancy make it a very effective plant.

Among the most showy of the spring flowers and the most attractive of those that bloom in the summer and early autumn are the Phloxes. The Moss pink (*Phlox Subulata* Syn. *P. setacea*) is one of the old-fashioned perennials which is still used for bedding or borders. Its deep pink flowers are very effective during the month of May. Other good early flowering sorts are : *Phlox amoena* and *Phlox reptans*. *Phlox ovata*, which begins to bloom in the first week of June, is very desirable. The flowers are of a lovely shade of pink and keep open for a long period. Those perhaps which are most grown are the varieties of *Phlox decussata*, usually known as the Hybrid Perennial Phlox. There are now so many named varieties of this Phlox that it is not difficult to find some which are satisfactory.

The old-fashioned but still popular flower, the Bleeding Heart (*Dicentra spectabilis*), is very showy during the latter half of May. It begins to bloom about the middle of the month and remains in flower for more than four weeks.

All the Columbines are lovely flowers, but there are a select few which are deserving of special note. The first to bloom of these is the Russian Columbine (*Aquilegia oxysepala*), distributed some years ago by the Ontario Fruit Growers' Association under the name of *Aquilegia Buergeriana*, which it was supposed to be at that time. The flowers are large, deep purplish blue with yellow and blue centres. Following this are *A. glandulosa*, deep blue with white centre ; *A. Stuarti*, deep blue with white centre, which is often a biennial, and *A. Canadensis*, our native wild Columbine. Toward the end of May, *A. coerulea*, one of the most delicately shaded and graceful species, is in bloom. The season of the Columbines is extended considerably by *Aquilegia chrysantha*, which does not bloom until about the fourth week of June. This is a magnificent species, attaining a height of four feet. The flowers are bright lemon yellow and very showy. There is a white-flowered variety of this which is also very fine.

With the opening of the pretty little dwarf Iris, (*Iris pumila*) during the third week of May, there begins a succession of lovely and many coloured species and varieties which go a long way to make our gardens attractive during the summer. Closely following *Iris pumila* is another dwarf species, *Iris Chamaeiris*, which is bright yellow with brown marking. The Siberian Iris with its numerous varieties now follows, and although these are not so graceful or pretty as some of the other sorts, they have their place in the rear of the border, for they attain a height of from three to four feet. During the first week of June, *Iris flavescens*, a beautiful yellow species with brown markings, begins to bloom, and following this are those wonderful and varied forms of *Iris germanica*, *I. neglecta*, *I. pallida*, *I. squalens*, and *I. variegata*, which rival the finest orchids in delicacy of colouring and grace of form. The Oris root (*Iris florentina*), which blooms about the same time, is a very handsome species. The flowers are large. pale blue or lavender, and sometimes white, and have a delicate perfume. This is one of of the most desirable species. Following these and beginning to bloom when they are almost gone, is the Golden Iris (*Iris aurea*). This is undoubtedly one of the most handsome species grown. The flowers are large and of a deep rich yellow color. These with a height of from 3 to 4 feet, give it a stateliness and beauty unsurpassed by any other yet tested at Ottawa.

The Japanese Irises, which are giving good satisfaction in a diversity of soils at the Experimental Farm, have an entirely different form from any of those previously mentioned. They have not the grace of many of the other species and varieties, but their colouring is exquisite, and they bloom during the month of July, when other Irises have disappeared.

The Globe flowers, or Trollius, which remind one of a buttercup, but which are larger and richer in colouring, begin to bloom during the third week of May and are the among the best of spring flowers. *Trollius Europœus, T. giganteus*, and *T. Ledebourii* are three of the best.

Time will not permit me to speak of other spring flowers, such as the Evergreen Candytuft, *Iberis sempervirens*, the Prophet Flower (*Arnebia echioides*). the Lily of the Valley (*Convallaria majalis*), and others.

During the first week of June the Spiraeas begin to bloom and keep up a succession of white, cream and pink flowers until well on in the summer. The best of these bloom in the following order : *Spiræa Filipendula* fl. pl., *S. astilboides, S. palmata elegans, S. Ulmaris*, and *S. Venusta*. Of these, *S. Filipendula* flore pleno and *S. Venusta* are deserving of special mention. The former has pure white double flowers and is about 2 feet tall ; the latter, has deep pink flowers and is 4 feet or more in height.

During the first week of June the bright scarlet flowers of *Heuchera sanguinea* begin to appear, and this charming and graceful plant continues to bloom until late in the autumn.

Most of the hardy perennial pinks have comparatively small flowers, but in some of the named varieties of *Dianthus Plumarius* flore pleno there are flowers which are almost equal to the best carnations. Mrs. Sinkins is one of these. The flowers of this variety are large, double white and highly perfumed. It is quite hardy and should be in every collection.

The Hemerocallis, or Day Lillies, contribute largely to the appearance of the perennial border during the summer months ; the best of these are : *Hemerocallis Dumortierii, H. minor* and *H flava*, which bloom in the order given. A new variety from Japan, *H. aurantiaca major*, promises to be a good introduction.

It is in June and July that most of the lilies are at their best, and there are so many varieties of these beautiful flowers that it is necessary to limit oneself to the very best. *Lilium canadense, L. tenuifolium, L. elegans, L. tigrinum, L. superbum, L. auratum* and *L. speciosum* make a succession of bloom from June until September.

There are several species of Coreopsis which enliven the flower border from the latter part of June until autumn. Of these the most satisfactory tested at the Experimental farm is *C. lanceolata*, the flowers of which are large and deep yellow. *C. grandiflora* is very fine. but has not proved perfectly hardy at the Experimental Farm. There is a variety of this Golden Glory which has been lately introduced, which we have not yet tested. *C. delphinifolia* is quite different from the two preceding species, the flowers having dark centres.

The Gaillardias are among the most satisfactory flowers as they continue to bloom for such a long time. Beginning about the third week of June, there is a continuity of bloom until late autumn. The flowers of *G. aristata grandiflora* are very large and of fine colouring, the petals being of a deep yellow more or less tinged with orange, and orange at the base. Some of the named varieties of this are still better, such as Superba and Perfection.

Other fine flowers which begin to bloom in June are : *Achillea Ptarmica flore pleno, Anthemis tinctoria kelwayi, Clematis recta. Dictamnus albus, Linum perenne, Oenothera Missouriensis,* and the hybrid Potentillas.

Most of the Campanulas begin to bloom in July. Of these, some of the best are : *Campanula carpatica, C. Persicifolia,* and *C. latifolia macrantha.* The Platycodons, which are closely related to the Campanulas, are very desirable plants with large, deep blue, striped or white bell-shaped flowers. They are all varieties of *P. grandiflora.* The beautiful Cashmerian Larkspur (*Delphinium cashmirianum*) is deserving of special mention. It begins to bloom about the first week of July, and its bright blue flowers continue to be seen until autumn. There is a pale blue form of this which is also fine. These Larkspurs only attain a height of from one and a half to two feet.

No garden is complete without a few pæonies. There have been such great improvements in these flowers of late years that the intending planter should make enquiries before buying, so as to get the very best varieties.

Perhaps no plant of recent introduction has become so popular, and deservedly so, as *Rudbeckia laciniata,* Golden Glow. Introduced only four years ago, this plant has now become almost as common as many of the old varieties. Unlike most plants of great merit, it multiplies rapidly, and it has thus been possible to supply all demands for it. It begins to bloom about the latter half of July and continues until late in the autumn. The flowers are large, very double and of a bright lemon-yellow colour, almost equalling a chrysanthemum of the same size and colour. It is a profuse bloomer and attains a height of from six to eight feet.

Some other fine flowers which begin to bloom in July, and which there is not time to take up individually, are : *Aconitum Napellus. Erigeron speciosus, Gypsophila paniculata, Helenium autumnale, Lychnii chalcedonica fl. pl., Rudbeckia maxima, Heliopsis pitcheriana, Scabiosa caucasica* and *Statice latifolia.*

During the months of August, September and especially October, the Michaelmas Daisies, or wild asters, help to extend the season of perennials. These flowers are now so common in our woods and waysides that they are not valued as they should be, but when brought into the garden they become most attractive during the autumn months. The best of our Canadian asters is probably *Aster Novae-Angliae roseus.* The flowers of which are bright pink. Several species and varieties which were obtained outside of Canada, and which are of the most exquisite shades of purple, pink, white and lilac, are : *Aster Amellus bessarabius, A. alpinus, A. Newry seedling, A. laeviagatus. A. undulatus, A. turbinellus,* the latter blooming until late in October.

There are a few other late blooming plants worthy of note, namely : *Aconitum Fishcheri* (*autumnale*), *Funkia subcordata* (*grandiflora*), *Helianthus doronicoides, Helianthus laetiflorus,* and *Hibiscus moscheutos.*

Though perennials thrive best when given good soil and good cultivation, a large number of them will also succeed with very little attention, and it is this fact which makes them valuable to the busy man, the lazy man, and the man who only grows them because he thinks it is the proper thing to have some flowers about his place. Once established, many perennials will hold their ground, though often shamefully neglected.

Mr. GAMMAGE : I suppose the varieties you have mentioned are all perfectly hardy at Ottawa ?

Mr. MACOUN : Yes. The great secret of preserving some perennials is to give them a good mulch of straw in the autumn when winter sets in. They can be got in the United States, or be got still cheaper by sending to Holland for them, and anyone wishing to get any of those can secure from me the names of firms in Europe or the United States who will supply them. First of all I would recommend you to apply to our Canadian nurserymen. Dr. Saunders reminds me that the seed can be had of a great many of them in the United States and in Europe.

REPORT ON HORTICULTURAL SOCIETIES FOR 1898.

The number of affiliated societies in operation as reported at the annual meeting of the Fruit Growers' Association of Ontario in December last was twenty-seven, with a total membership of 2,076. I now find from the list as published in the last Annual Report that the number of societies for the year 1898 is given as thirty-six, with a total membership of 2,610. Omitting from this list Burlington society where the membership is not given, and the Paris society, for sufficient cause, the true number of societies for 1898 is thirty-four and the membership 2,551. My work this year, which is now about concluded, will I venture to hope add several new societies to the list for 1899, which, if a corresponding aggregate is maintained, will make the membership from these societies something over 3,000 for the year 1899.

As the yearly aggregate and the yearly average of membership of each of the affiliated societies will be an increasingly interesting item for comparison with future years, I add the following comprehensive table commencing with the year 1895, which should be continued, or added to, for many a year to come :

Year.	No. of societies in affiliation.	Aggregate of membership.	Average per annum for each society.
1895.....................	11	798	72.5
1896......	17	1,197	70.4
1897......... ../........	27	2,076	77.0
1898.....................	34	2,551	75.0

I wish also to call the attention of the Board to the desirability of having a skeleton draft of by laws suitable for the guidance of the horticultural societies prepared as quickly as possible, and that a copy with the necessary instructions for their adoption be sent to each society.

Most of these societies are doing excellent service for our country and are deserving of every encouragement and assistance that can be given by the Fruit Growers' Association of Ontario.

THOS. BEALL.

In accordance with this suggestion, the directors afterward appointed Mr. Beall and the secretary a committee to draft the by-laws. (See page 54.)

REPORT OF COMMITTEE ON FRUITS ON EXHIBITION.

We, your committee, find on exhibition the following fruits :

Shown by T. R. Merritt, St. Catharines : Two varieties of Rogers, Niagara and Vergennes grapes in a good state of preservation and of fine quality ; fine samples of Columbia, Clairgeau and Lawrence pears ; Rhode Island Greening, Rox. Russett, Ben Davis, Baldwin and Fall Pippin apples , also a fine display of hot-house plants, including two specimens of Australian ferns.

A. M. Smith, St Catharines, has fine samples of Duchess d' Angouleme, Anjou, Lawrence, Josephine de Malines pears ; Champion quinces and Sutton Beauty apples, the latter a new claimant for public favor.

E H. Wartman, Kingston, shows thirteen varieties of apples grown by Jas. Russell, of Wolfe Island, namely, Cayuga Red Streak, Colvert, Blenheim Orange, Cabashea, R. 1. Greening, Tolman Sweet, Baldwin, Gilliflower, Snow, Seek-no-Further, Grimes Golden, all of excellent quality.

Robert Thompson, Grantham : Extra fine samples of Pomme grise and Baldwin apples.

Mr. Thomas Beall, Lindsay, shows fine Hulbert, Snow, Lawver, Ontario, Swazie Pomme grise, Ben Davis, Baldwin, Red Cathead, Nodhead and a Snow apple that appeared to be a relative ef the Duchess, but late and larger, of good quality, and evidently worth propagating.

Martin Burrell, St. Catharines, shows fine Vandevere apples, Lawrence and Duchess de Bordeaux pears, also a specimen of native of Japan chestnuts, showing a marked difference in size.

W. M. Orr, Fruitland, shows an excellent sample of Vergennes grapes, also Kieffer, Duchess and Clairgeau pears of the finest quality.

Jas Scarff, Woodstock, has Talman Sweet, Bellflower, Baldwin, Wagner, Spitzen-berg, King, Spy, Blenheim Orange, Russett, Snow, Cabashea, R I. Greening apples ; also fine samples of Duchess and Clairgeau pears.

The Experimental Farm, Ottawa, shows twenty-two varieties of hardy apples, most of them of Russian origin and particularly adapted to northern sections.

R. L. Huggard, Whitby, has eight varieties of apples and twenty-two of pears, most of them of fair quality.

Hugh Gourley, Carp, Ont., shows a fine collection of apples for that northern lati-tude, consisting of Winter St. Lawrence, McIntosh Red, Colvert, Canada Baldwin, Snow, Wolf River, and four varieties, names unknown, but of fine appearance, and several seedlings of Snow very similar to their parents.

There are also fine plants from the green-houses of Mr. L. D. Dunn, St. Catharines, and an orange tree in fruit from James Dunlop & Son, St. Catharines, also three plants from Mr. Groom, grocer, St. Catharines.

There was also shown a sample of Hawthorn jelly, exhibited by Mr. F. G. H. Patterson, Grimsby.

A. M Smith.
A. H. Pettit.

IN MEMORIAM.

Moved by Thos. Beall, seconded by M. Burrell,—" That we, the members of the Fruit Growers' Association, desire to place on record our sense of the loss the Association has sustained by the death of Mr. James Lockie, of Waterloo, and of Mr. Richard Trotter, of Owen Sound. Mr. Lockie, as President of the Waterloo Horticultural Society, did much to develop the growth and usefulness of that organization, and by his knowledge and enthusiasm contributed largely to the promotion of a healthy interest in horticulture generally.

" The late Mr. Trotter accomplished much useful work in the direction of organizing and testing varieties of fruit. He was also the leading spirit in organizing the Owen Sound Horticultural Society.

" We desire not only to testify to the sense of our own loss, but to express a very sincere sympathy with the relatives of these two highly-esteemed members of our Association."

LIST OF AFFILIATED HORTICULTURAL SOCIETIES.

Name.	President.	Secretary.	No. of members, 1898.
Arnprior	Claude McLachlin	G. E. Neilson	55
Belleville	W. C. Reid	W. J. Diamond	66
Brampton	A. Barber	Henry Roberts	115
Brockville	Samuel Reynolds	Geo. A. McMullen	85
Burlington	A. W. Peart	W. F. W. Fisher	....
Campbellford	J. B. Ferris	E. A. Bog	56
Carleton Place	A. H. Edwards	J. A. Goth	57
Cardinal	Wm. Beddie	E. E. Gilbert	58
Chatham	W. D. A. Ross	G. E. Massey	80
Cobourg	J. D. Hayden	H. J. Snelgrove	91
Durham	Chris. Frith	Wm. Gorsline	97
Grimsby	Mrs. E. J. Palmer	E. H. Read	51
Hagersville	Wm. Harrison	S. W. Howard	57
Hamilton	A. Alexander	J. M. Dickson	115
Iroquois	W. A. Whitney	A. E. Overell	65
Kemptville	Angus Buchanan	T. K. Allen	55
Kincardine	T. W. Perry	Joseph Barker	99
Leamington	J. D. Fraser	E. E. Adams	51
Lindsay	Alex. Cathro	F. J. Frampton	113
Meaford	O. Boden	A. McK. Cameron	71
Midland	Frank Cook	Miss M. Tully	56
Millbrook	George Sootheran	W. S. Given	56
Napanee	Mrs. W. H. Wilkison	James E. Herring	59
Niagara Falls South	W. P. Lyon	†T. J. Robertson	75
Oakville	T. C. Hageman	W. W. Paterson	128
Orangeville	John McLaren	Wm. Judge	75
Owen Sound	Ven. Arch. Mulholland	D. R. Dobie	57
Paris	A. G. H. McCormick	Gordon J. Smith	55
Picton	J. R Brown	W. T. Ross	75
Port Colborne	W. W. Kinsley	A. E. Augustine	52
Port Dover	James Symington	W. J. Carpenter	74
Port Hope	H. H. Burnham	A. W. Pringle	131
Sarnia	Hon. Alex. Vidal	T. J. Gordon	67
Seaforth	Wm. Ballantyne	F. G. Neelin	79
Simcoe	H. H. Groff	Henry Johnson	77
Smith's Falls	J. S. McCallum	W. M. Keith	110
St. Catharines	Judge E. J. Senkler	W. C. McCalla	59
Stirling	Mrs. Jas. Boldrick	David Sager	53
Thornbury	*J, G. Mitchell	*Miss H. Henman	53
Trenton	W. S. Jacques	S. J. Young	52
Waterloo	A. Weidenhammer	J. W. Winkler	167
Woodstock	D. W. Karn	J. S. Scarff	98
Windsor	Stephen Lusted	J. R. Martin	68

* Clarksburg P. O.   † Niagara Falls P. O.

INDEX.

FIFTH ANNUAL REPORT

OF THE

FRUIT EXPERIMENT STATIONS

OF

ONTARIO,

UNDER THE JOINT CONTROL OF THE

ONTARIO AGRICULTURAL COLLEGE, GUELPH

AND THE

FRUIT GROWERS' ASSOCIATION OF ONTARIO

1898.

(PUBLISHED BY THE ONTARIO DEPARTMENT OF AGRICULTURE, TORONTO:)

PRINTED BY ORDER OF THE
LEGISLATIVE ASSEMBLY OF ONTARIO

TORONTO:
WARWICK BRO'S & RUTTER, PRINTERS AND BOOKBINDERS, 68 AND 70 FRONT ST. WEST
1899

FIFTH ANNUAL REPORT

OF THE

ONTARIO FRUIT EXPERIMENT STATIONS

1898.

To the Honorable John Dryden, Minister of Agriculture for Ontario:

SIR,—We beg to submit to you the Fifth Annual Report of the Ontario Fruit Experiment Stations. You will notice the gradually increasing value of the reports of our experimenters as the various fruits come into bearing. We also submit to you the first compilation of work to date on " Fruits of Ontario," a volume which in the course of years is intended to contain reliable information and exact description of all fruits that are of interest to Ontario fruit growers.

We have the honor to be, Sir,

Your obedient servants,

JAS. MILLS,
Chairman.

L. WOOLVERTON,
Secretary.

BOARD OF CONTROL, 1899.

REPRESENTING THE COLLEGE.

James Mills, M.A., LL.D., Guelph..............................President.
H. L. Hutt, B.S.A., Guelph....................................Professor of Horticulture

REPRESENTING THE FRUIT GROWERS' ASSOCIATION FOR 1899.

A. M. Smith ....St. Catharines.
Alexander McNeill ....Walkerville.
W. E. Wellington ....Toronto.
L. Woolverton, M.A., Secretary .. ..Grimsby.

EXECUTIVE COMMITTEE.

Chairman—James Mills, M.A , LL.D.
Secretary—L. Woolverton, M.A.
Official Visitor—Prof. H. L. Hutt, B.S.A.

THE ONTARIO FRUIT EXPERIMENT STATIONS.

Name.	*Specialty.*	*Experimenter.*
1. Southwestern	Peaches	W. H. Hilborn, Leamington, Ont.
2. Niagara	Tender Fruits	Martin Burrell, St. Catharines, Ont.
3. Wentworth	Grapes	Murray Pettit, Winona, Ont.
Burlington	Blackberries and Currants	A. W. Peart, Freeman, Ont.
5. Lake Huron	Raspberries and Commercial Apples	A. E Sherrington, Walkerton, Ont.
6. Georgian Bay	Plums	John G. Mitchell, Clarksburg, Ont.
7. Simcoe	Hardy Apples and Hardy Cherries	G. C. Caston, Craighurst, Ont.
8. East Central	Pears and Commercial Apples	R. L. Huggard Whitby, Ont.
9. Bay of Quinte	Apples	W. H. Dempsey, Trenton, Ont.
10. St. Lawrence	Hardy Pears. Hardy Plums.	Harold Jones, Maitland, Ont.
11. Strawberry sub-station		E. B. Stevenson, Guelph.
12. Gooseberry sub-station		Stanley Spillett, Nantyr.
13. Cherry station and general collection of fruits or descriptive work	Cherries	L. Woolverton, Grimsby.

FRUITS OF ONTARIO,

DESCRIBED AND ILLUSTRATED BY

L. WOOLVERTON, M.A.,

SECRETARY OF THE ONTARIO FRUIT EXPERIMENT STATIONS.

1898.

1 F S.

FRUITS OF ONTARIO.

DESCRIBED AND ILLUSTRATED BY MR. L. WOOLVERTON, SECRETARY OF THE ONTARIO
FRUIT EXPERIMENT STATIONS.
1898.

Fruit growing has become so important an industry in the Province of Ontario, that it deserves every encouragement at the hands of the Department of Agriculture. The Canadian farmer who contemplates growing fruit asks for information on two points in particular, viz., (1) What fruits shall I plant, and (2) how shall I cultivate them ? The latter of these questions it is the province of the Ontario Fruit Growers' Association to answer through the Canadian Horticulturist and the Annual Report, while the former question is one that can be solved only by years of patient experimental work by our fruit experiment stations.

Of equal importance is some means of identifying all varieties now grown in our Province, and of knowing with some degree of exactness the size, color, general appearance and real value of these varieties aside from the catalogues of the nurserymen. To meet this latter need, the Secretary, with the advice and approval of the Board of Control, has begun the work of illustrating and describing the fruits of Ontario , and in this work he desires to acknowledge the valuable aid of the various fruit experimenters, and in particular the work of Mr. E. B. Stevenson, Freeman, Ontario, in describing strawberries. The illustrations are all new and original, having been engraved from photographs made the exact size of the fruit samples, except where otherwise specified, and in this way there will in time be made accessible to the Ontario fruit growers a complete guide to all the fruit grown in the Province. Such a work necessarily must be slow and tedious, but it is all important that it should be characterized by scientific accuracy, and the writer invites notes or criticism from pomologists generally.

NOTE.—In the following pages an attempt has been made to use the words instead of figures to describe quality and value according to the following scales :—

Quality.—1, very poor ; 2-3, poor ; 4-5, fair ; 6-7, good ; 8-9, very good ; 10, first class.

Market Value.—1-3, 4th rate ; 4-6, 3rd rate ; 7-8, 2nd rate ; 9-10, 1st rate.

APPLES.

ALEXANDER. *(Emperor Alexander.)*

ALEXANDER.

ORIGIN, introduced into England from Russia in 1817.

TREE, hardy, spreading, vigorous, fairly productive; bears early.

FRUIT, very large size; form, round, ovate, conical; skin, greenish yellow, russet dots, streaked or splashed with red; stem, $\frac{3}{4}$ inch long, set in a deep cavity; calyx, large, nearly closed, set in a deep, even basin.

FLESH, yellowish white, crisp, not very fine, moderately juicy; flavor, subacid, pleasant.

SEASON, September to November.

QUALITY, dessert, third class; cooking, first class.

VALUE, home market, first class; too tender for foreign shipments except in cold storage.

ADAPTATION. Quite general, the tree being hardy.

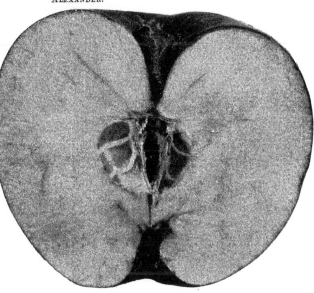

SECTION OF ALEXANDER.

[5]

BALDWIN. *(Steele's Red Winter.)*

The Baldwin originated in the State of Massachusetts and was for many years the most popular winter apple for either home or foreign markets. The average yield each alternate year

was about eight barrels per tree, and in some instances much larger. Large orchards of this variety were in consequence planted in the apple growing counties of middle and southern Ontario, but unfortunately for many years now these orchards have been almost barren, and many of them are being dug out as worthless. The cause may be poverty of soil, the lack of pollen of other varieties to fertilize the blossoms, or the prevalence of apple scab. If it is the latter, it may be overcome with the Bordeaux mixture ; if lack of potent pollen, by grafting in other varieties here and there through the orchard.

BALDWIN.

TREE, upright, spreading, vigorous grower, formerly very productive.

FRUIT, large, roundish, ovate ; skin yellow, shaded and splashed with crimson and red, dotted with some russet dots ; stem heavy, three-quarters of an inch long, in a broad cavity ; calyx, closed, in a deep plaited basin.

FLESH, yellowish white, tender, sub-acid ; quality, second class.

SEASON of use, January to March.

ADAPTATION. Not very hardy at Simcoe station or in North Ontario county ; further south and along the borders of the lakes this apple may be grown to perfection, if the scab can be kept off the trees.

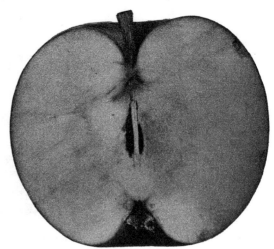

SECTION OF BALDWIN.

BEN DAVIS.

One of the most popular market apples in the southwestern and western states because of its great productiveness, hardiness, good color and its keeping and shipping qualities. Highly valued in some commercial orchards in Canada, but condemned by some growers on account of its inferior quality.

BEN DAVIS.

At the World's Fair in 1893, some of the finest apples shown by Iowa, British Columbia and Oregon were the Ben Davis. It is a profitable market apple.

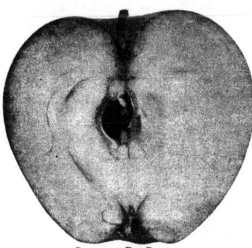

SECTION OF BEN DAVIS.

ORIGIN, brought from North Carolina to Kentucky with a lot of other seedling apples by Mr. Ben Davis. Scions taken from Kentucky to Southern Illinois about 1820.

TREE, spreading, fairly vigorous and very productive.

FRUIT, medium to large, roundish, truncated conical, unequal ; color, yellow, striped and splashed with red, having scattered areole dots ; stem, slender, one to one and a half inches long in a deep cavity ; calyx, erect, partly closed in a deep, wide basin.

FLESH, white, tender, mild, sub-acid.

QUALITY, dessert, poor; cooking, fairly good ; home market, good; foreign market, very good.

SEASON, January to May. (Bay of Quinte station.)

ADAPTATION. Succeeds remarkably well at the Georgian Bay and Bay of Quinte stations.

CABASHEA. *(Twenty Ounce Pippin).*

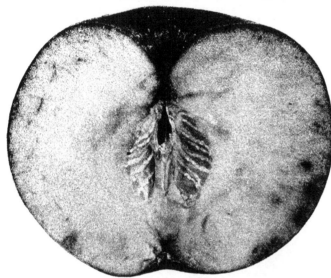

SECTION OF CABASHEA.

Not worth planting in Ontario. Through confusing its name with that of the Cayuga Red Streak, often called Twenty Ounce, this apple has been widely planted in our Province. The tree is unproductive and the fruit, though large and fine in appearance, drops early and is poor in quality. Twenty trees, at Maplehurst, twenty years planted, yielded about ten barrels of apples in 1895, the best so far.

ORIGIN, unknown.

TREE, vigorous, spreading, unproductive.

FRUIT, large, 3x4 inch, roundish, oblate, slightly conical; skin, yellowish green, shaded with dull red on the sunny side; stem, ⅝ of an inch long, stout, in a wide cavity of moderate depth; calyx open in a wide shallow basin; core medium.

FLESH, white, firm, coarse, sub-acid, only fair for cooking, useless for dessert.

SEASON, October to December. At Bay of Quinte station, season given from December to February.

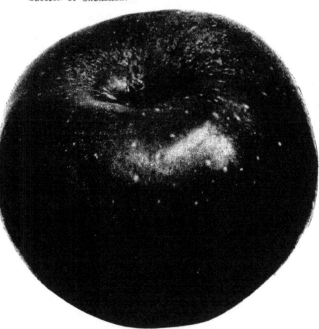

CABASHEA.

Tested twenty years, at Maplehurst, Grimsby.

CANADA RED.

(*Baltimore of Downing.*)

This apple is grown quite widely in Ontario under the name of Canada Red, and is valued as a profitable commercial variety, especially where Baldwin, Spy and Ontario do not succeed ;

for although only medium in size, it yields abundantly and the fruit is deeply colored, regular, clean and firm. There is an old variety of this name, which is now little grown, if at all, in Canada and which, though somewhat similar, is inferior to this variety, and consequently is undeserving of description.

ORIGIN. Unknown.

TREE. Vigorous, hardy and very productive.

FRUIT. Medium, roundish, slightly conical, regular ; color, greenish yellow, almost covered with red, sometimes splashed or slightly striped with darker red, having numerous large prominent

CANADA RED.

greenish areole dots which are smaller towards the apex ; stem, half an inch long in a small, deep, and often russeted cavity ; calyx small, closed in a shallow slightly corrugated basin.

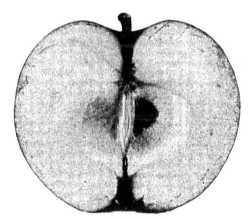

SECTION OF CANADA RED.

FLESH, greenish white, fine grained, firm, moderately juicy ; flavor, fair, mild, sub-acid.

SEASON, December to May.

QUALITY, dessert, medium ; cooking, medium ; home market good ; foreign market very good.

ADAPTATION. Reported hardy as far north as our St. Lawrence station near Prescott ; succeeds at Peterboro' and throughout all middle and southern Ontario.

CRANBERRY PIPPIN.

An apple that is worthy of being planted in southern Ontario as a fancy variety for export. Though the quality is ordinary and not suitable for dessert, its extreme beauty when opened in mid-winter, its large and even size, usual freedom from blemishes and the productiveness of the tree every alternate year, make it a desirable variety.

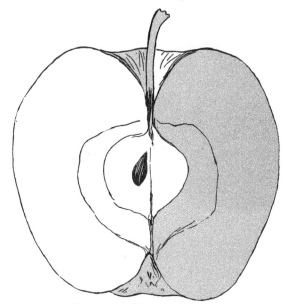

SECTION OF CRANBERRY PIPPIN.

At Maplehurst, Grimsby, in 1895, fifty trees of this variety, about twenty years planted, yielded 200 barrels of high grade apples, and in 1893, when other varieties were almost worthless, nearly the same quantity. Sometimes, however, this variety is subject to warts and knot which mar its beauty.

ORIGIN, accidental on a farm, near Hudson River, N. Y.

TREE, very vigorous, healthy, spreading, productive.

FRUIT, medium to large, roundish, oblate; skin, smooth, yellow shaded and striped with two shades of red; stem, slender, one one-eighth inches long in a deep cavity; calyx closed in a wide, wrinkled basin.

FLESH, white, firm, crisp, moderately juicy, sub-acid.

QUALITY, fair.

SEASON, November to February.

CRANBERRY PIPPIN. (Reduced.)

ADAPTATION. Southern portions of the Province, especially along the shores of the lakes

EARLY HARVEST.

The best apple of its season both for dessert and cooking, but of late years rendered worthless in Ontario by scab, which not only spoils its appearance but lessens its size and injures its flavor. The Early Harvest and Fall Pippin are the two apples which seem to be least able to resist this terrible fungus, and which most favor its spread. Unless therefore this fungus is checked by spraying with the Bordeaux mixture, this apple must soon be left out of the list of desirable varieties.

EARLY HARVEST. (Reduced.)

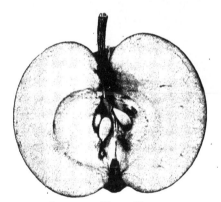

SECTION OF EARLY HARVEST.

ORIGIN, United States.

TREE, only medium in vigor, never attaining a large size, old trees averaging from one-half to two-thirds the size of Greening trees of the same age ; upright and spreading ; productive, considering the size of the tree and the fruit ; yield of full grown trees averages about four barrels every alternate year.

FRUIT, medium round, oblate ; skin, smooth, bright straw color when ripe, with a few faint dots ; stem, short, one-half to three-quarters of an inch, in a medium cavity, often russeted ; calyx closed in a shallow, sometimes slightly plaited basin.

FLESH, white, fine grained, juicy, crisp, tender ; flavor, rich, sprightly, pleasant sub-acid.

SEASON, first week in August ; in 1896, the last half of July.

Quality, dessert, best ; cooking medium ; home market, very good ; foreign market, useless.

ADAPTATION Thrives well on sandy loam in the Niagara district.

FAMEUSE.

(Snow, Pomme de Neige).

The most highly valued of all table apples, and but for one fault the Fameuse would be the most profitable of all to grow for profit, especially in the latitude of Montreal, where it attains its highest perfection. The fault is that it is quite subject to the apple scab, so that in some places the fruit is entirely worthless.

FAMEUSE.

ORIGIN, Province of Quebec, probably from seeds brought from France; it is often called Snow, from the color of its flesh, and its proper name signifies a famous apple.

TREE, moderately vigorous, moderately productive; hardy.

FRUIT, medium size, roundish; skin, light green, striped and shaded with two shades of red, often nearly covered with deep red; stalk, slender, half an inch long, in a small deep cavity; calyx, small, segmen's often recurved, set in a shallow, slightly plaited basin.

FLESH, snow white; texture, tender, very fine grained, breaking, juicy, aromatic.

QUALITY, dessert, first-class; cooking, poor.

VALUE, first-class for all markets, when perfect in form and free from spots.

SEASON, October to December

ADAPTATION. General in Ontario.

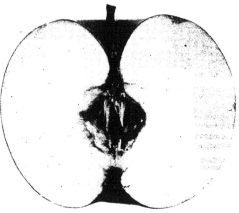

SECTION OF FAMEUSE.

GIDEON.

A very pretty apple, of about same season as Duchess, and less desirable, because it is inclined to rot at the core; it is also less highly colored. These faults will prevent its being popular as an export apple.

ORIGIN, by Peter M. Gideon, Excelsior, Minn., U.S.; of same parentage as Wealthy.

TREE, vigorous, hardy, holds fruit well, productive.

FRUIT, large, 3 inches by $3\frac{1}{2}$ wide, round or slightly conical; skin, white, with bright red cheek shaded with deeper red splashes; dots, white, obscure; cavity, broad, deep, regular or slightly corrugated; stalk, 1 inch, slender; calyx half closed, in a small, corrugated basin.

FLESH, white, flaky, tender, almost melting, yet crisp, fine, juicy, and of good flavor.

SEASON, September to November.

QUALITY, dessert poor, cooking fair.

VALUE, for home market, first; foreign, fourth rate.

ADAPTATION. Succeeds well on north shore of Lake Huron, in Algoma, and in Northeastern Ontario; trees loaded with fruit were found near Thessalon in 1898.

GREENING.

One of the staple varieties for profit in Ontario orchards. No one variety, except the Baldwin, was more widely planted in our Province previous to 1875, but since that time it has been

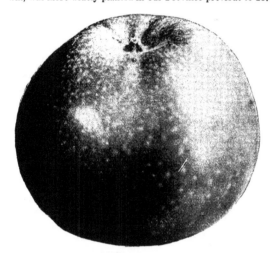

liable to scab some seasons, especially in cases where proper spraying is neglected. Its color is against it in foreign markets, and yet, as it becomes known, the demand for it increases. It has a tendency to drop early, especially south of Lake Ontario, and, therefore, needs to be gathered in good season, about the first of October, as a rule. Remarkable instances of productiveness have been reported. One large tree at Maplehurst, Grimsby, nearly one hundred years planted, yielded twenty barrels one season, and fifteen barrels another.

ORIGIN, Rhode Island.

TREE, very vigorous, spreading, a crooked grower, fairly

GREENING.

hardy, very productive, succeeds well on a great variety of soils.

FRUIT, large, roundish, sometimes a little flattened, regular, unless overgrown; color, green, becoming lighter as it ripens, often showing a blush when well exposed to the sun; dots light gray, areole, numerous toward the apex; stem, seven-eighths of an inch long in a smooth, narrow cavity; calyx partly closed in a nearly smooth shallow basin.

FLESH, white, with a greenish tint, yellowing as it matures; texture, fine grained, crisp, juicy; flavor, rich, slightly aromatic, pleasant, sub-acid.

SEASON, December to February.

QUALITY, dessert, medium; cooking, best; home and foreign markets, good.

ADAPTATION. Succeeds everywhere, except in northern sections.

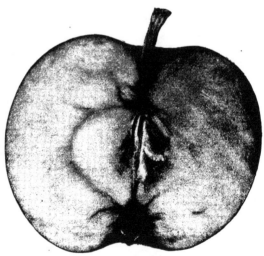

SECTION OF GREENING

KENTISH FILLBASKET.

An old English variety of great beauty of appearance and enormous size, often exceeding four inches in diameter. It is not, however, much grown in the commercial orchards of Ontario, being a fall apple, ill adapted to export, unless by cold storage, and of very ordinary quality.

ORIGIN, England; tree, vigorous, fairly productive, semi-hardy.

FRUIT, very large, three by four inches, globular, slightly ribbed; color, smooth, shiny, light green or pale yellow, sometimes almost white, and on sunny side splashed and striped with bright red; stem, stout, short, ¼ inch, set in a large cavity; calyx closed, set in a large plaited basin.

FLESH, fine, grained, tender and juicy; flavor, mild, subacid.

SEASON, October to December.

QUALITY, poor for dessert, good for cooking, good for home market, and poor for foreign market.

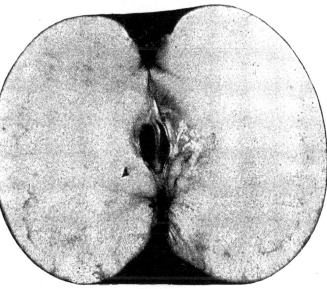

KENTISH FILLBASKET.

ADAPTATION. North shore Lake Ontario and Erie, east shore Lake Huron. The sample photographed was grown at our Bay of Quinte station in 1896.

KING. *(King of Tompkin's County.)*

Said to have originated in New Jersey. On account of its excellent quality for cooking, its peculiarly rich aromatic flavor, its beautiful appearance and large size, this apple is taking the highest place in the great apple markets of the world. Unfortunately the tree is a poor bearer, and consequently unprofitable as an orchard variety, unless under exceptional circumstances. Top-grafted on Talman Sweet, it is said to be more productive. For home use it is excelled by no apple.

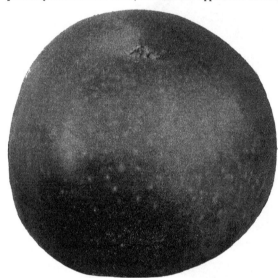

TREE, a vigorous grower, of spreading habit, but not long-lived.

FRUIT, large, roundish, uneven ; skin, yellowish, shading off from red to dark crimson ; stem, short and stout, inserted in a wide, d e e p, somewhat irregular cavity ; calyx closed in a broad, shallow, slightly corrugated basin.

FLESH, yellowish, white, crisp and juicy, moderately firm ; flavor rich, agreeable, aromatic ; quality first-class

SEASON, October to February in Southern Ontario ;

KING.

reported at the Simcoe station October to March for Northern Ontario.

ADAPTATION. Not hardy at Simcoe station unless top grafted on Talman Sweet, or some

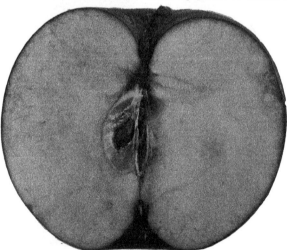

SECTION OF KING.

other hardy stock, and, therefore, it is not recommended for general planting in northern sections.

LADY.

(*In France, Api.*)

A beautiful little apple for the amateur's collection, and very highly valued where known for a dessert apple, having a pleasant flavor and great beauty. In Europe the apple is known as Api, but in America it has became known as the Lady apple. Some say it was so called because from its small size and beautiful color, it seemed just suited to a lady's mouth.

ORIGIN, France.

LADY.

TREE, upright habit and bears fruit in clusters, vigorous, only fairly hardy and productive.

FRUIT, very small, flat oblate. Color, green turning to yellow, half covered with a rich red cheek, and many tiny dots which are more numerous toward the apex. Stem, slender, half an inch long, set in a deep regular cavity. Calyx closed in a small wrinkled basin.

SECTION OF LADY.

FLESH, greenish white, fine grained, crisp and juicy ; flavor, pleasant.

SEASON, December to May.

QUALITY, dessert, best ; cooking, too small to be of any value ; market, high value in special markets.

ADAPTATION. Successfully grown as far north as the Bay of Quinte station.

2 F.S.

MANN.

The Mann apple is not very highly recommended for extended orchard planting in Ontario,

because of its rather unattractive green color in shipping season in Octo ber. The tree has the merit of being a productive variety and an early bearer, but the fruit is inclined to drop early, and to be small, when not thinned.

ORIGIN, New York State, a chance seedling.

TREE, hardy, vigorous, spreading, with slender branches; an early and regular bearer, inclined to overload.

FRUIT, of large size when thinned and well cultivated, $2\frac{3}{4}$ x $3\frac{3}{4}$ inches; form, roundish, oblate, regular; skin, dull green,

MANN

yellowing at maturity, nearly covered with light green dots; stalk half an inch long in a large slightly russeted cavity; calyx closed in a large plaited basin.

FLESH, yellowish, moderately firm, juicy, agreeable, sub-acid.

SEASON, January to April.

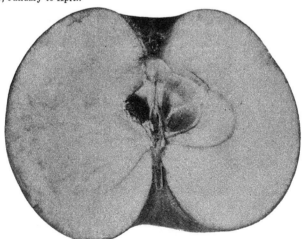

SECTION OF MANN.

QUALITY, dessert poor; cooking good.

VALUE. Good for home or foreign market, but its color is not favorable for best prices

ONTARIO.

This is a native of Ontario, as its name indicates, having been raised by crossing Wagener and Spy by the late Charles Arnold of Paris, Ontario. Its early and abundant bearing, the good quality and even size of the fruit, are the reasons why it is rapidly gaining in favor as an export variety. It has been tested in a commercial way for some years at our Bay of Quinte station, where it is counted one of the best for profit.

ONTARIO.

ORIGIN, Province of Ontario.

TREE, fairly hardy, moderately vigorous, somewhat spreading, very productive, an early bearer.

FRUIT, large, 2½ x 3½ inches, oblate, slightly ribbed, sides unequal; skin yellowish, nearly covered with bright red, with a few scattered small white dots with blush bloom ; stem, seven-eighths of an inch long, in a deep, russeted uneven cavity ; calyx closed in a moderately deep, corrugated basin.

FLESH, white with green tint, yellowing slightly as it ripens ; texture, fine grained, tender, juicy ; flavor, mild, sub-acid, sprightly, aromatic.

SEASON, January to April.

QUALITY, very good for all purposes.

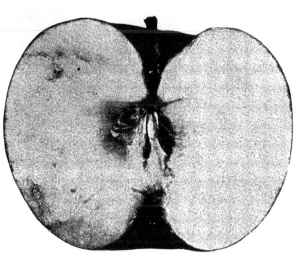

SECTION OF ONTARIO

ADAPTATION. Southern Ontario to north shore of Lake Ontario. Succeeds remarkably well at Bay of Quinte station.

RED ASTRACHAN.

Imported from Sweden to England in 1816, and widely planted in Southern Ontario for a summer market apple. Scarce another apple of its season equals it in beauty of appearance, for, in addition to its rich crimson color, it is often covered with a pale white bloom. Selected fancy grades of this apple are usually in good demand in our home markets, but sometimes there is a surplus, and prices even for Astrachans are very low. Promising for export in cold storage.

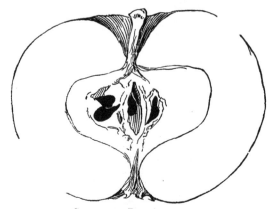

SECTION OF RED ASTRACHAN.

RED ASTRACHAN (Reduced).

TREE, upright ; very vigorous ; begins bearing early ; very productive.

FRUIT, medium to large, round, narrowing towards apex ; skin, deep crimson when exposed to sun, yellowish-green in shade, often covered with a thin, whitish bloom ; stem, stout, three-quarter inch long, in a deep narrow cavity ; calyx closed in a shallow, somewhat irregular basin.

FLESH, white, crisp, juicy, tender, becoming mealy when over-ripe ; acid, almost too tart to be counted first-class for either dessert or cooking ; quality, second class.

SEASON, 1st to 20th August.

ADAPTATION. In Niagara district perfectly hardy and productive. Two trees in 1895 at Maplehurst averaged ten barrels each. Not considered profitable at Simcoe station. Not very hardy in northern parts of Ontario county.

ROXBURY RUSSET.

(*Boston Russet.*)

One of the staple export varieties in many parts of southern Ontario, because of its long keeping qualities. It resists scab well, but is subject to the codling moth, unless well sprayed,

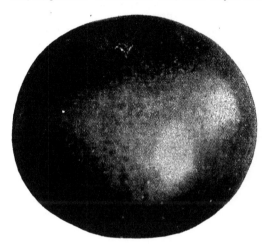

and is inclined to drop early from the trees, resembling the Greening in this respect.

ORIGIN, Massachusetts.

TREE, fairly vigorous, spreading like Greening, but flatter in form of top.

FRUIT, medium, roundish, oblate, sides not equal ; skin tough, green, nearly covered with russet, and having a brownish red cheek when fully exposed to the sun ; stem, half to three-quarters of an inch long in a medium sized, regular cavity ; calyx closed in round medium sized basin.

FLESH, yellowish white, almost coarse grained, moderately juicy ; flavor, mild, sub-acid, pleasant.

ROXBURY RUSSET.

SEASON, January to June.

QUALITY, dessert, fair ; cooking, good ; home and foreign markets, good.

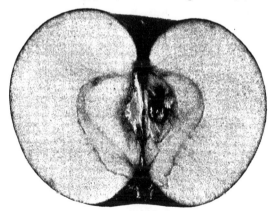

SECTION OF ROXBURY RUSSET.

ADAPTATION. Long tested in the Niagara district and found to be well adapted to it. As hardy as the Greening.

SPITZENBURGH.

(*Esopus Spitzenburgh.*)

One of the finest dessert apples for late winter use, and widely planted by early settlers throughout southern Ontario. It has proved to be unprofitable as a commercial apple, because the tree is liable to disease, and yields small crops in consequence.

ORIGIN, Esopus, on the Hudson river.

TREE, lacking in vigor, often showing dead or feeble wood ; upright, spreading, with drooping limbs when in bearing ; fairly hardy.

FRUIT, size, medium to large, oblong, slightly conical : skin, straw color in shade. but usually nearly covered with bright red, and dark red in sun, with a few stripes, and many obscure gray dots ; stalk, seven-eighths of an inch long in a narrow deep cavity; calyx, nearly closed, set in a narrow basin of medium depth, slightly corrugated.

FLESH, yellowish white ; texture, crisp, juicy, breaking ; flavor, brisk, rich, delicious.

SPITZENBURGH.

SEASON, December to March.

QUALITY, first class for all purposes.

SECTION OF SPITZENBURGH.

ADAPTATION. Succeeds well on sandy loam in southern Ontario.

SPY. *(Northern Spy.)*

The Spy stands in the very first rank of Canadian apples, whether for home or foreign markets. Originating in New York State on the line with the southern portion of the Province of Ontario, it succeeds here to perfection. Its beauty of coloring, half shaded by its delicate bloom, and its great excellence of quality for all purposes, justly claim for it its wide popularity. In Chicago, Canadian Spys are more sought for than any other variety, but, owing to tenderness of skin, which shows the slightest bruise, it is less popular for export to Great Britain than some other varieties. The tree is late in coming into bearing. often being fifteen years planted before yielding a crop, and this renders the variety somewhat unpopular with planters. Probably for fancy packages, selected Spys would be among the best.

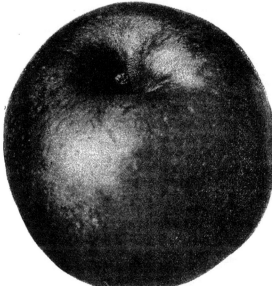

SPY.

ORIGIN, near Rochester, N.Y.

TREE, upright and spreading in habit; fruit spurs on interior boughs very vigorous, late in coming into bearing, but afterwards fairly productive in alternate years; blossoms late in spring and ho'ds its fruit late in the autumn; requires high cultivation and good fertility.

FRUIT, large to very large; form, roundish, slightly conical; skin, thin, light green, or pale yellow, sprinkled with light pink, striped and shaded with pinkish red, and thinly covered with thin whitish bloom; stalk slender, three-quarters of an inch long, in a wide. deep, sometimes russeted cavity; calyx, small, closed, in a narrow, moderately deep, abrupt, irregular basin.

FLESH, white, fine-grained, crisp, tender, juicy; flavor, rich, sprightly, subacid, fragrant.

SEASON, January to May.

QUALITY, dessert and cooking, first class; home market, first-class; a little tender for distant shipments.

SECTION OF SPY.

ADAPTATION. Sandy or clay loams in southern and middle Ontario; found tender at Simcoe Experiment Station and at the St. Lawrence Experiment Station.

SWAZIE POMME GRISE.

(Pomme grise d'or.)

There is no choicer winter dessert apple for the months of December and January than the Swazie Pomme Grise, especially when kept in a cool, dark cellar, as that its crisp texture and excellent flavor may be preserved. Unfortunately, It is not very productive, and, consequently,

SWAZIE POMME GRISE.

not profitable. One large tree at Maplehurst, seventy-five years planted, yielded only an aver age of four barrels each alternate year. It is well worthy of a place in the amateur collection.

ORIGIN, probably with Col. Swazie, near Niagara.

TREE, upright, fairly vigorous and not very productive.

FRUIT, small, round, oblate conical ; color, deep yellow, well colored with cinnamon russet and many whitish dots ; stem, three-quarters of an inch long, set in a deep cavity ; calyx, closed n a moderately deep, slightly corrugated basin.

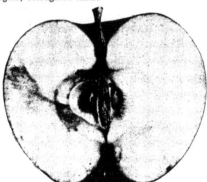

SECTION OF SWAZIE.

FLESH, white, fine grained, tender, crisp, juicy ; flavor, aromatic mild sub-acid, pleasant.

SEASON, December to March.

QUALITY, dessert, first class ; cooking, third class ; value for home market, poor ; value for foreign market, poor.

ADAPTATION. Succeeds in southern Ontario, especially in the Niagara district.

SWEET BOUGH.

(Large Yellow Bough of Downing.)

An excellent dessert apple, ripening about the same season as the Early Harvest ; not subject to scab, and a favorite with those who prefer a sweet to a sour apple.   Not profitable to grow for market, but it deserves a place in every collection for home use.   Baked whole it is delicious eaten with cream.

SWEET BOUGH.   (Reduced.)

ORIGIN, United States.

TREE, of medium vigor, never attaining a large size, and, therefore, even with a full crop, not very productive.   Bears full every alternate year ; head, compact.

FRUIT, large, ovate, conical ; skin smooth, greenish yellow ; stem one inch long, in a narrow, deep, regular cavity ; calyx open, in a shallow, irregular basin.

FLESH, white, fine grained, tender and juicy ; flavor moderately sweet, rich and agreeable.

SEASON, July 25 to August 10.

QUALITY, dessert very good ; cooking poor, except for roasting.
VALUE, home market, poor to good, foreign market, useless.
ADAPTATION, succeeds well in Niagara district.

WEALTHY.

This beautiful apple was distributed among the members of the Ontario Fruit Growers' Association in 1882 for trial, and has won for itself a good reputation in every part of the Province as a dessert apple of excellent quality, while in the northern portions it is especially

desirable on account of its hardiness. Mr. A. A. Wright, of Renfrew, says the tree endures 40° below zero without injury, and he advises planting this variety freely at the north. Mr. R. W. Shepherd, of Montreal, has grown it in that vicinity for years with success for export.

ORIGIN, St. Paul, Minnesota. By Peter Gideon.

TREE, vigorous, very hardy, over productive.

FRUIT, medium, roundish, oblate, regular ; skin, smooth, greenish ground, changing to pale yellow, rich red cheek, with stripes and splashes of red in the sun, sometimes nearly covered with crimson ; stem, one-half to three-quarters of an inch long in a deep regular cavity ; calyx, nearly closed in a deep, abrupt basin.

WEALTHY.

FLESH, white, fine grained, tender, juicy, sprightly, pleasant subacid.

SEASON, early winter.

QUALITY, dessert, very good ; cooking, good.

VALUE, for home market, very good ; for foreign market, very good.

ADAPTATION. Succeeds at Simcoe, Bay of Quinte, St. Lawrence and Niagara stations, also at Ottawa and Montreal

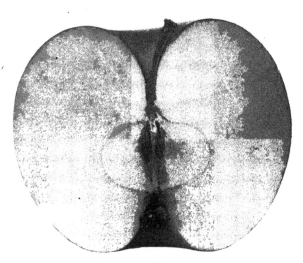

SECTION OF WEALTHY.

YELLOW TRANSPARENT.

An apple which may prove a substitute for the well-known Early Harvest, which is so subject to apple scab. This variety seems to be proof against fusicladium, both in leaf and fruit.

ORIGIN, St. Petersburg, Russia. Imported by the U. S. Department of Agriculture in 1870.

TREE, hardy, vigorous, upright, annual bearer, productive, began bearing at four years at Craighurst station.

YELLOW TRANSPARENT.

FRUIT, above medium, roundish, oblate, inclined to be conical ; skin, clear white, yellowish white when very mature ; dots, light green, obscure ; stalk, medium, in large cavity ; calyx closed in medium, slightly corrugated basin ; fruit hangs well on the tree.

FLESH, white ; firm till very ripe, then tender ; quality, second class.

SEASON, August 1st to 15th.

ADAPTATION. Tested at Maplehurst, Grimsby ; at Simcoe station, distributed widely by Ontario Fruit Growers' Association in 1886, and succeeds everywhere.

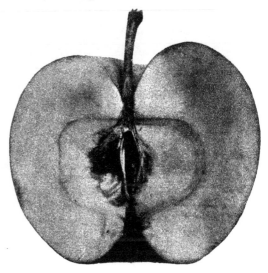

YELLOW TRANSPARENT. (Section.)

CHERRIES.

CHERRIES.

Classification.

In describing the cherries the following general classification is followed, though for convenience the varieties are arranged in alphabetical order. In some cases it is impossible to place a variety because of the crossing of one variety with another, which renders the classification almost useless.

I. Prunus Cerasus (Sour Cherry Class).

(a) *Kentish*—Pale red with uncolored juice.

(b) *Morellos*—Dark red fruits, with dark colored juice.

II. Prunus Avium (Sweet Cherry Class).

(a) *Mazzards*—European seedling cherries, of vigorous habit.

(b) *Hearts*—With soft-fleshed, heart-shaped fruit.

(c) *Bigarreaus*—Hard-fleshed, mostly light colored skin, and heart-shaped.

(d) *Dukes*—Tree of upright, vigorous growth, leaves fastigiate, fruit mostly acid or sub-acid.

BLACK EAGLE.

A very excellent dessert cherry, well deserving a place in [the home garden, but not sufficiently productive to be recommended for the commercial orchard. The average annual yield of large trees at Maplehurst is from twenty-five to thirty quarts. The fruit is usually in scattered clusters, and often borne singly, making the gathering expensive. In England this variety is more productive than in Canada.

ORIGIN, England, 1810, by Miss E. Knight, of Downton Castle, from Bigarreau and May Duke.

TREE, second rate in vigor, of a round spreading habit, third rate in productiveness; group Bigarreau.

FRUIT, medium to large, averaging about $1\frac{3}{8}$ long by $1\frac{5}{8}$ of an inch wide; form, obtuse heart-shaped, almost roundish oblate; skin, dark red, becoming almost black; stalk, slender, $1\frac{1}{2}$ to $1\frac{3}{4}$ inches long in a medium cavity: suture obsolete; stone, small.

FLESH, dark purple; texture, tender and juicy; flavor very sweet, rich and delicious.

BLACK EAGLE. (Reduced).

SEASON, July 8th to 15th (1897).

QUALITY, first-class for dessert.

VALUE, first-rate for near markets; second rate for distant markets because it soon decays.

[29]

BLACK TARTARIAN.

Of all our black cherries, this is one of the choicest, whether for market or for dessert on the home table. Of large size and delicious flavor, it is relished by all cherry lovers, and, being somewhat soft fleshed, it is very subject to the ravages of birds. On this account it is often necessary to harvest and ship it a little on the green side. It is not so productive as some others, but it makes up for this by bringing a higher price.

ORIGIN, Russia and Western Asia, introduced into England in 1796, and thence to America.

BLACK TARTARIAN.

TREE, erect, vigorous, attaining large size, fairly productive.

FRUIT, very large, $\frac{7}{8}$x1 inch, heart-shaped, of somewhat irregular outline ; stem, $1\frac{3}{4}$ inches long ; skin, bright purplish black.

FLESH, dark purple, tender and juicy ; flavor, rich and delicious.

SEASON, June 22nd to 30th.

QUALITY, dessert, first class.

VALUE, market, first-late.

ADAPTATION, South of Lake Ontario, and in sheltered places a little further north.

BELLE DE CHOISY.

(Ambree grosse " LeRoy.")

The most delicious of all dessert cherries, and one that should be planted in every amateur's garden, but of no value in the commercial cherry orchard, because not productive, and the tree is often short lived.

ORIGIN, Choisy, near Paris, 1760.

TREE, Duke, upright, foliage dark, hardy, not very productive.

FRUIT, medium to large, $\frac{3}{4}$ x $\frac{3}{4}$, obtuse heart-shaped ; skin, transparent, showing the structure of the flesh and the cells of juice within ; color, bright cornelian red in sun, pale red to amber in shade ; stem, slender, two inches long ; suture marked by a delicate line.

FLESH, very pale red, texture, soft, juicy ; flavor, sweet, very delicious.

SEASON, June 24th to July 1st.

QUALITY, dessert, first-class.

VALUE, market, fair.

BELLE DE CHOISY.

ADAPTATION, Southern Ontario.

CLEVELAND.

One of the finest Bigarreau cherries for dessert purposes, being of high quality and not too firm in texture. A good variety for commercial orchards, because of its high color and earliness of season, but not yet fully tested in this Province.

ORIGIN, by Prof. Kirtland, Cleveland, Ohio.

TREE, vigorous, of stout spreading habit, productive, fruited after three years planting at Maplehurst.

FRUIT, large, $\frac{7}{8}$ x $1\frac{5}{16}$ of an inch ; form, heart-shaped, sides unequal ; color, bright red moroon, on yellowish ground, dark rich red in the sun ; stem, stout, $1\frac{1}{2}$ inches long in a broad, uneven cavity ; suture, broad, half way round.

FLESH, light cream in color ; texture, almost tender, juicy, sweet, rich and delicious.

QUALITY, first-class for table.

VALUE, home market, first-rate ; distant market, first-rate.

SEASON, June 15th to 25th.

ADAPATATION. Southern Ontario.

CLEVELAND.

COE.

(Coe's Transparent).

A good variety for the home garden, but altogether too tender to be popular for the Commercial orchard.

ORIGIN, in Connecticut, with Curtis Coe, of Middleton.

TREE, healthy, fairly vigorous, with round spreading head, third rate in productiveness; group, Heart.

FRUIT, medium to large, about one inch long by one inch broad, round and regular in form; skin, thin, bright shiny amber, nearly covered with rich cornelian, marked with peculiar mottled blotches; stalk one and a half to two inches long set in a medium wide cavity; suture obscure.

FLESH, very pale yellowish tint; texture very soft and tender, juicy; flavor sweet and very good if not left hanging too long.

SEASON, July 7th to 14th (1897).

QUALITY, good for dessert.

VALUE, second rate for home market, fourth rate for distant market.

ADAPTATION, south of Lake Ontario.

COE'S TRANSPARENT.

KOSLOV-MORELLO.

Fifty trees, small seedling trees, of this cherry were sent to the Secretary of the Ontario Fruit Growers' Association by Jaroslav Niemetz, of Winnitza, Podolie, Russia, in 1889, and by him distributed among the directors.

Some of these trees were planted at Maplehurst, and, although still only bushes, they bore quite freely in 1897. Mr. Niemetz claims that it will endure almost any degree of cold, and that it begins bearing at the age of four or five years from the pit, which he claims is the best method of propagating it (see C. Hort., 1869, p. 218). They might well be grown in rows, 5 or 6 feet apart, just as we grow raspberries and currants. The fruit closely resembles that of the Morello (English).

TREE, bush form, very slow grower, slender; hardy; very productive; Morello.

FRUIT, fairly large, round, pointed at apex, dark red, turning black at maturity; stalk 1½ inches long in a slight depression; suture, barely traceable.

FLESH, red, turning dark red at maturity; texture, tender, juicy, acid, becoming milder as it hangs.

QUALITY, good for cooking.

SEASON, July 20th to August 20th.

KOSLOV-MORELLO.

ADAPTATION, the northern limit of cherry culture.

EARLY PURPLE.

(*Early Purple Guigne.*)

The earliest cherry is the Early Purple, a foreign variety known in France as the Early Purple Guigne. The tree is a vigorous, upright grower, and becomes quite productive as the tree acquires age. A tree at Grimsby, about thirty years planted, yielded in 1896, 144 quarts. They were harvested on the 11th of June, and sold in the wholesale market at an average of twelve cents per quart. This is the tree's best record, for usually the birds destroy the fruit before it matures, and if gathered as soon as colored red, it is little more than "skin and bones." The last few days of growth it fills out wonderfully, and becomes almost a so-called "black cherry." The branch which we photographed was taken from the tree above referred to and shows the habit of fruiting.

EARLY PURPLE.

TREE, upright, vigorous, healthy, productive when full grown.

FRUIT, medium size, roundish heart-shaped; skin dark red to purple; stem two inches long in a shallow cavity; suture obscure.

FLESH, red to purple; texture tender, juicy; flavor sweet and pleasant.

SEASON, June 13th to 25th, south of Lake Ontario.

QUALITY, dessert, good.

VALUE, market, 2nd rate.

ADAPTATION. Grown at Grimsby for thirty years and quite hardy; fairly hardy in Maine and Michigan; recommended for trial north of Lake Ontario.

3 F.S.

GOVERNOR WOOD.

This variety has proved itself a most satisfactory cherry for both dessert and market purposes. It is a very productive variety, and, though somewhat tender in flesh, is not nearly so subject to ravages by birds as Early Purple or Black Tartarian. Originated by Prof. Kirtland of Cleveland, Ohio, U.S.A.

GOVERNOR WOOD.

TREE, upright, spreading, healthy, vigorous and hardy wherever the peach succeeds.

FRUIT, medium to large, roundish-heartshaped ; skin, light, yellow, shaded with light to deep red ; stem 1½ inches long in a broad deep cavity ; suture, distinct on one side.

FLESH, yellowish, tender, juicy, sweet, aromatic and delicious.

SEASON, June 16th to June 25th.

QUALITY, dessert, 1st rate ; home market, very good ; distant market, good.

VALUE, market, 1st to 2nd rate.

ADAPTATION. Wherever the peach succeeds.

HORTENSE.

(*Reine Hortense.*)

One of the finest flavored of cooking cherries, and one which deserves the first place in the home garden. It is not as productive as the May Duke, but from its habit of fruiting singly is less subject to rot than that excellent variety.

ORIGIN, in 1832, by M. Larose, Neuilly ; first fruited in 1838.

TREE, of Duke habit, a vigorous and handsome grower and fairly productive ; Duke.

FRUIT, large to very large, roundish, elongated, sides slightly compressed ; skin, thin, light, shining red mottled with darker red, becoming richer in color the longer it hangs ; stock, slender, about two inches long.

FLESH, creamy yellow, nettled, very tender, juicy, ; flavor, slightly sub-acid, excellent.

SEASON, July 10th to 15th in 1897.

QUALITY, first-class for cooking.

VALUE, 1st to 2nd rate for market.

ADAPTATION, succeeds perfectly south of Lake Ontario.

HORTENSE.

KNIGHT.

(*Knight's Early Black*).

A delicious early, black cherry, ripening about a week in advance of Black Tartarian. It is a regular and even bearer, the average yield being from seventyfive to 100 quarts per annum. The fruit is borne singly or, occasionally, in pairs, and therefore is not gathered as rapidly as those varieties which grow in clusters. It is one of the most valuable dessert cherries, but not as productive as the Tartarian.

ORIGIN, England, by T. A. Knight, in 1810, from Bigarreau crossed with May Duke.|

TREE, healthy, fairly vigorous, with spreading head, second rate in productiveness ; Heart.!

FRUIT, medium to large, obtuse, heart-shaped, uneven ; skin, dark red or purple, becoming almost black if allowed to hang ; stalk two inches long in a rather large cavity.

FLESH, dark red to purple ; texture, tender and juicy, but firmer than Tartarian ; flavor, sweet, rich and delicious ; stone, small.

SEASON, July 1st to 6th (1897).

QUALITY, first-class for all purposes.

VALUE, for market, first-rate.

KNIGHT'S EARLY BLACK.

MAZZARD.

Black Mazzard (Downing), Merisier (Leroy), Corone (Hogg).

The common English black cherry, which is indigenous to the continent of Europe, and has now become naturalized in North America, is the original species from which the excellent heart cherries have originated. Seedlings of this class of cherries are grown extensively by nurserymen as stock upon which to propagate the finer varieties, as standards.

Mazzard.

The fruit of these seedlings varies considerably, often being small and rather bitter in flavor, and consequently of no value for market ; but occasionally we find one large enough to be worth cultivating, and of fairly good quality.

Origin, Europe.

Tree, very vigorous and healthy, often reaching thirty feet in height and spreading over an area as many feet in diameter ; Heart.

Fruit, small, heart-shaped, or round, a little flattened ; suture evident on one side ; skin, shiny black, thin ; stalk, inch and a half to two inches long.

Flesh. soft, melting, juicy, often somewhat bitter.

Season, July 10th to 25th.

Quality, very poor for dessert, poor for cooking.

Value, fourth rate for all purposes.

Adaptation, southern part of the Province.

MEZEL. (*Monstreuse de Mezel*, Bigarreau of Mezel.)

One of the finest of the late black cherries, of large size and great productiveness. Though a Bigarreau it has not the fault of its class of being especially subject to rot ; it is not so black in color as the Elkhorn, but dark enough a red to be classed with the black cherries.

ORIGIN, Mezel, France ; first introduced in 1846.

TREE, upright, spreading, a very vigorous grower ; one tree at Maplehurst forty years planted was thirty feet in height in 1897, and covered an area about the same number of feet in diameter ; first rate in hardiness and in productiveness ; group, Bigarreau.

FRUIT, very large, fifteen-sixteenths of an inch long by one inch in width ; obtuse heart shaped, slightly flattened, with a clearly-defined suture on one side, ending in a slight nipple ; skin, dark red at first, changing to dark purple at maturity ; stalk, two inches long, slender, set in good sized cavity.

FLESH, firm, juicy, breaking ; flavor, sweet, good.

SEASON, July 12th to 20th (1897).

QUALITY, for dessert, first class.

VALUE, for market, first rate.

MEZEL.

MORELLO. (*English Morello.*)

An old reliable variety for cooking purposes, known in England for nearly three hundred years, and deserving of wider cultivation in Ontario. Downing thinks the name Morello is from *Morus*, the Mulberry, from the dark purple color of its juice, which resembles that of the mulberry ; a profitable market variety.

TREE, habit, spreading, slender ; hardy and very productive ; vigor, medium ; Morello.

FRUIT, fairly large, roundish, nearly heart shaped, somewhat flattened on one side, with a slightly traceable suture.

SKIN, red, turning dark red or purple towards maturity ; stalk about $1\frac{3}{4}$ inches long, inserted in a shallow cavity ; stone small, slightly cling.

FLESH, very dark red, texture, tender, juicy, acid, becoming more subacid and agreeable the more it matures.

SEASON, July 20 to August 10, in 1897.

QUALITY, dessert, very poor ; cooking, first class.

VALUE, home market, second rate.

MORELLO.

NAPOLEON.

Napoleon Bigarreau, Royal Anne of California.

A valuable variety of foreign origin. Perhaps the most productive variety known, yielding fruit of the very largest size which is in good demand and, therefore, one of the most desirable varieties for the commercial orchard. It has one serious fault, namely, it is very subject to the rot, especially in wet seasons, and sometimes the whole crop of this variety is ruined by it.

NAPOLEON.

TREE, upright, spreading, vigorous, hardy on the south shore of Lake Ontario. Very productive.

FRUIT, very large, oblong heart shaped ; skin, yellow ground, light in shade, rich red cheek in the sun, sometimes mottled ; stem, $1\frac{1}{8}$ inches long ; suture plainly traceable.

FLESH, yellowish white, very firm, meaty, fairly juicy, good flavor, much esteemed for canning because it looks well in the jars and bears cooking well.

SEASON, July 8th to 16th.

QUALITY, dessert medium ; market, very good to best.

ADAPTATION, the southern part of the Province of Ontario.

MAY DUKE.

(*Early Duke, Royal Hative.*)

The staple variety of cooking cherry in its season, both for home use and market. The great productiveness, health and vigor of the tree, the mild acid of the fruit ripening over a considerable season, all tend to make this a favorite variety in all cherry-growing districts. The fruit is rather tender for distant shipments.

MAY DUKE

ORIGIN, Médoc, a Province in France, from whence the name is said to be a corruption.

TREE, upright, of fastigiate head, a habit especially noticeable in young trees ; vigorous, hardy, and productive ; Duke.

FRUIT, roundish, obtuse, heart-shaped, with traceable suture, and distinct indentation to apex ; grows in clusters ; skin, bright red turning darker at full maturity ; stalk 1½ to 2 inches long; stone small.

FLESH, red, tender, very juicy ; flavor, sub-acid, and very good.

SEASON, June 12th to 20th (1897).

QUALITY, good for dessert; first class for cooking.

OLIVET.

From tests in the experimental orchard, we judge the Olivet to be a valuable variety for the home garden. The tree is a fine grower, and the fruit large and attractive, with a mild acid flavor, while in season it immediately succeeds the Reine Hortense.

TREE, of French origin, usually classed with the Dukes, fairly vigorous ; hardy ; productiveness, second rate.

FRUIT, large, ¾ by ⅞, obtuse heart-shaped, almost round ; color, dark rich carmine ; stem, 1 to 1¼ inches, in a broad cavity, often in pairs.

FLESH, reddish ; texture, soft, melting, very juicy ; juice stains red ; flavor, very mild, pleasant acid.

OLIVET.

QUALITY, dessert, fair ; cooking very good to first-class.

VALUE, not yet determined in Ontario.

SEASON, June 24th to July 10th.

OSTHEIM.

(*Griotte d'Ostheim.*)

This and the Vladimir were distributed throughout the Province of Ontario a few years ago by the Fruit Growers' Association. The Vladimir is of little or no use, but the Ostheim is a fair size, productive enough to be profitable, and good for all purposes. Its hardiness should make it a special favorite in the colder sections, to succeed the Montmorency.

OSTHEIM.

ORIGIN, South of Spain, brought to Germany early in the 18th century, and cultivated near Ostheim, in Saxe-Weimar, whence its name.

TREE, third rate in vigor, almost a dwarf, first in hardiness, and second rate in productiveness ; Morello.

FRUIT, medium, about $\frac{9}{10}$ x $1\frac{3}{8}$ of an inch in length and breadth. The variety must vary, since Dr. Hogg describes it as large, and LeRoy describes the stalk two inches long set in a pronounced cavity. Round, slightly depressed at the side ; color, very dark purple, almost black when ripe ; stalk, one and three-eighths inches, in ones and twos ; suture not traceable ; pit, small, cling.

FLESH, very dark purple, tender, juicy, almost sweet when ripe, agreeable.

SEASON, July 18th to 30th, or even longer, improving in flavor the longer it hangs.

QUALITY, poor for dessert ; fair for cooking.

VALUE, for market, third rate.

ADAPTATION, quite general ; found fruiting freely in St. Joseph's Island, Algoma, in 1898.

VLADIMIR.

A Russian variety from Vladimir district, distributed by the Ontario Fruit Growers Association in 1887. It has been growing for these ten years at Maplehurst, and reckoned  unprofitable. The fruit is very scattered, smaller than the ordinary seedling Mazzard, and very subject to curculio. It is not to be compared in value with the Ostheim which is of the same season or a trifle later.

TREE, slow, weak grower ; rather a bush than a tree ; unproductive ; Morello.

FRUIT, small, round ; skin dark purple, almost black at maturity ; stalk 1⅜ inch long, in very shallow cavity ; stone very small.

FLESH, tender, purple, colored juice ; texture, melting, juicy ; flavor slightly sub-acid, fair.

SEASON, July 15th to 25th (1897).

VLADIMIR.   QUALITY, very poor.

VALUE, fourth rate for either home use or market.

ADAPTATION, general.

WINDSOR.

A valuable late cherry for either home use or market, its firm flesh making it a better shipper than most dark colored cherries. Indeed, from the middle to the end of July, when this cherry is at its best, there is no other to compete with it, the Elkhorn being just over. The tree is not an early bearer, and the fruit is subject to the curculio, but otherwise the Windsor stands among the very best.

ORIGIN, by James Dougall, Windsor, Ontario.

TREE, a vigorous, upright, symmetrical grower, healthy, very hardy and productive.

FRUIT, large, 1⅙ inch long by 1 inch wide ; form, round, obtuse, heart shaped : color, dark red turning darker as it hangs ; stem, 1½ inches long, set in a moderately deep cavity ; in twos and threes ; suture, obscure.

Flesh, yellowish, with reddish tint ; texture firm, moderately juicy ; flavor, rich and sweet.

WINDSOR.

SEASON, July 10th to 20th.

QUALITY, dessert, good ; cooking, good.

VALUE, first-rate for all markets.

ADAPTATION, farther north than most Bigarreau cherries.

YELLOW SPANISH.

Of all the Bigarreau cherries this is one of the finest, both on account of its great size and its delicious flavor. The tree grows to a very large size, surpasssing in this respect any other cultivated variety with which we are acquainted. It does not average very productive, because the fruit often blasts and drops, or is destroyed by Monilia. When, however, it does mature a good crop, the yield is enormous.

The variety is of European origin, and was introduced into the United States in 1800.

TREE, very vigorous, of large growth, spreading, productive.

FRUIT, very large and of a beautiful waxy lustre; form, round, obtuse, heart-shaped; skin, clear amber, nearly covered with red when exposed to the sun; stem, stout, $1\frac{1}{2}$ inches long in a wide cavity; suture, traceable.

FLESH, pale yellow; texture firm, juicy, breaking; flavor, sweet, delicious when well ripened.

YELLOW SPANISH.

SEASON, June 25th to 30th in 1896.

QUALITY, dessert very good.

MARKET VALUE. First-class.

ADAPTATION. Succeeds in peach sections, on well drained sandy soil.

CURRANTS.

CHERRY.

(Red Imperial, Fertile d'Angers—" LeRoy."

CHERRY.

The principal red currant grown in Southern Ontario for commercial purposes. Its large size, fine color and earliness, combine to make it the most satisfactory of all varieties for market, and many acres have been set out for this purpose. When well cultivated and well pruned back, a plantation of Cherry currants will continue very productive for at least twelve or fifteen years.

ORIGIN, Europe.

PLANT, vigorous, a stout stocky grower; productive; begins bearing the second year after planting; foliage thick, dark green.

BUNCH, usually short, but sometimes long and tapering; average length, two inches.

BERRY, very large, globuler, $\frac{1}{2}$ inch in diameter; bright red in color; acid.

SEASON, June 25th to July 25th.

QUALITY, fair.

VALUE, first-class for market and for jellies.

ADAPTATION, general, but succeeds better on clay loam than upon light sand.

FAY.

A variety that has been much advertised as superior to the Cherry, but, as a matter of fact, is very similar in fruit and in productiveness.

ORIGIN, New York State.

BUSH, vigorous, but sprawling, and somewhat subject to the borer where the shoots are not frequently renewed.

BUNCH, moderately close, loose toward the base ; length 2 to $3\frac{1}{2}$ inches.

BERRY, very large, globular, $\frac{1}{2}$ inch in diameter ; bright red ; juice, sub-acid.

SEASON, June 25th to July 25th.

QUALITY, good.

VALUE, first-class for market.

ADAPTATION, General

FAY.

HOLLAND.

HOLLAND.

(*White Holland, Long Bunched Holland.*)

The best bunched and the most showy of the white currants.

BUSH, vigorous, healthy and quite productive.

BUNCH, four to five inches in length ; loose at base of racemes, close toward apex.

BERRY, $\frac{3}{8}$ inch long by $\frac{1}{2}$ inch broad ; globular ; skin, thick, white ; flavor mild acid.

SEASON, July 10th to 30th.

MIDDLESEX.

(Saunders' No. 12.)

Among a collection of seedling black currants sent to Maplehurst by Dr. Saunders of Ottawa in 1896, we notice one which gives promise of greater productiveness than the others. Not only are the berries a good size, but, what is of greater importance with a black currant, the branches are full and hang pretty closely along the branch. If this variety continues its good qualities, we shall propagate it as being of sufficient importance to be distributed among our experimenters for farther test.

ORIGIN, Dr. Saunders, Ottawa, Canada.

BUSH, very vigorous, healthy, very productive for three successive years, viz., 1896, 1897, 1898.

BUNCHES, about 1¼ inches in length, compact.

BERRY, round, about half an inch in either diameter ; skin, jet black, thick ; flavor, good.

SEASON, July 8th to 16th, or later in Southern Ontario.

VALUE, first-class for cooking and market.

ADAPTATION, general.

MIDDLESEX. (Slightly reduced).

GOOSEBERRIES.

DOWNING.

This has been the most popular gooseberry of American origin for some years (1897) unless we except the Pearl, a variety of Canadian origin, very similar in size and appearance. It is very widely known and planted all over the continent of North America. It is not subject to mildew, and succeeds splendidly everywhere.

ORIGIN, with Chas. Downing, Newburgh, N.Y., a seedling of Houghton.

PLANT, healthy, first-rate in health and vigor [and] productiveness ; an upright grower.

FRUIT, size, medium, $\frac{3}{4}$ inch by $\frac{3}{4}$ broad, sometimes reaching $\frac{7}{8}$x$\frac{13}{16}$, when allowed to hang, not too heavily loaded ; form, round, often somewhat narrowed toward apex ; skin, smooth, transparent green with distinct light green ribs, and a thin whitish bloom.

FLESH, light green, tender, sweet and good.

SEASON of maturity, July 18th to 25th (1897.)

VALUE, for market, third-rate.

DOWNING. (Slightly reduced.)

PEARL.

The Pearl gooseberry has been widely planted in the commercial gardens of Canada and the United States. It is certainly a magnificent cropper, but it is very difficult indeed to distinguish the berry from the Downing, except that it averages a trifle larger.

—— PEARL.

ORIGIN, London, Ontario, with Mr. Saunders, a cross between Houghton and Red Warrington.

PLANT, healthy, not subject to mildew ; upright, spreading ; first-rate in vigor and in productiveness.

FRUIT, medium, measuring 1 inch long by 1 inch in breadth; round, often narrowed toward the apex ; skin, smooth, transparent green, with thin whitish bloom and light green ribs.

FLESH, light green, tender, sweet and good.

SEASON of maturity, July 18th to 26th, (1897).

VALUE, market very much the same as Downing.

ADAPTATION, nearly every part of Ontario.

NOTE.—The sample branch of Pearl from which our engraving was taken was grown by Mr. Thos. Beall of Lindsay, in July, 1898. The same engraving may stand for both Pearl and Downing, with the exception that the latter variety is a trifle smaller in size. Mr. Beall writes under date of September 22, 1898 : "The Pearl averages larger size; I have them growing side by side here at Lindsay. It is much more productive. I can find no difference in flavor until near or at maturity, at which time the Downing loses its flavor and becomes quite insipid, while the Pearl retains its good qualities to the end. The two varieties are so nearly alike that I think it almost impossible to distinguish individual berries; yet, when in quantities—say basket-fulls—the varieties are easily distinguished. The Pearl is larger, brighter in color, and, if well grown, a larger proportion of the Pearl berries will be somewhat elongated and decidedly pointed at the calyx end.

ENGLISH GOOSEBERRIES.

There are very few English varieties of gooseberries which are successful in Canada, chiefly on account of the mildew, which the American seedlings are much better able to resist.

Mr. A. Morton of Brampton has been testing these English gooseberries for many years, and has sent us samples, with notes, and from these we condense the following descriptions, with photographs.

CATHARINA.

An excellent table berry, highly recommended for family use by Mr. A. Morton of Brampton.

BUSH, medium size, vigorous, spreading, makes slender wood, fairly productive.

BERRY, large, long, yellow ; skin, a little hairy ; flavor, first-rate.

CATHARINA.

ADAPTATION, grown successfully for some years at Brampton.

CROWN BOB.

A profitable gooseberry.

BUSH, inclined to overbear, and thus exhaust its vitality ; drooping in habit.

BERRY, oblong, very large, especially if thinned before it is full grown ; skin, thin, hairy ; color, red ; of very good flavor.

CROWN BOB.

DUKE OF SUTHERLAND.

A first-class gooseberry.

BUSH, vigorous, large, spreading ; wood, long and slender ; foliage, dark green ; very productive ; grown free of mildew by Mr. A. Morton, Brampton.

BERRY, very large, oblong ; skin, dark green, smooth ; flavor, fair.

SEASON, late.

DUKE OF SUTHERLAND.

WHITESMITH.

One of the best of the English varieties for cultivation in Ontario; succeeds best on clay land, with northern aspect. On the sandy soil of the Niagara district it is much affected by mildew.

WHITESMITH.

ORIGIN, England.

PLANT, upright, fairly productive, fairly vigorous.

FRUIT, large, often $1\frac{1}{4}$ to $1\frac{1}{16}$ inches; oval, downy, with distinct regular veins; green, and when ripe sweet and agreeable.

SEASON, July 20th to August 10th.

QUALITY, first-rate for home uses.

VALUE, first rate for market.

LARGE SCOTCH RED.

BUSH, a free grower, healthy, large, productive.

FRUIT, large, sub-acid; a favorite table berry.

LARGE SCOTCH RED.

ONE OF THEM.

ONE OF THEM.

BUSH, very vigorous, with healthy foliage, moderately productive.

BERRY, very large, dark red when fully ripe.

QUALITY, first-class.

TWO TO ONE.

A desirable variety for family use. It is among gooseberries what the cherry is among currants in mode of growth.

BUSH, fairly productive; growth straggling.

BERRY, of the very largest size; fresh, tender; flavor good.

TWO TO ONE.

4 F.S.

GRAPES.

CONCORD.

The principal out-door grape grown for market in the Province of Ontario. Probably more than half the vines in the large commercial vineyards of the Niagara district, as well as in Essex and other parts of southern Ontario are of this variety.

The reason of this is (1) its comparative freedom from mildew, (2) its vigor of vine, (3) its productiveness. Four tons to the acre is not an uncommon yield, so that, even when it sells as low as 1½ cents per pound, there is yet a fair return for the investment. Still it is an open question whether in the near future it will not pay the grower better to plant varieties of higher quality that will bring a higher price, though they may be less productive.

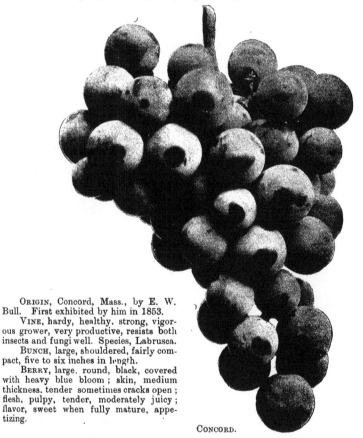

ORIGIN, Concord, Mass., by E. W. Bull. First exhibited by him in 1853.

VINE, hardy, healthy, strong, vigorous grower, very productive, resists both insects and fungi well. Species, Labrusca.

BUNCH, large, shouldered, fairly compact, five to six inches in length.

BERRY, large. round, black, covered with heavy blue bloom ; skin, medium thickness. tender sometimes cracks open ; flesh, pulpy, tender, moderately juicy ; flavor, sweet when fully mature, appetizing.

CONCORD.

SEASON, middle of September and October ; not a good keeper.

QUALITY, dessert, fair.

VALUE, near market, 2nd rate ; distant market, 3rd rate ; of no value for export.

ADAPTATION. Tested at Wentworth, Niagara, Southwestern and Bay of Quinte stations, in all of which it ripens well in the open air.

[50]

DELAWARE.

Universally acknowledged to stand at the head of all American grapes in point of quality. For the home garden a few vines of this variety are indispensable, for it is the most excellent of dessert varieties. It is also one of the highest priced grapes in our markets, often bringing more than double the price of the Concord. It is, however, not very much grown in our commercial vineyards, because the foliage is badly subject to thrip and the yield is only moderate. On rich deep soils, well drained, however, with high cultivation, thinning and close pruning, it is productive and profitable. It should be planted much closer than the Concord. Vines of the latter variety are usually planted ten feet apart, while the Delaware may be set five or six feet apart.

DELAWARE.

ORIGIN, unknown. Name from Delaware, Ohio, where in 1855 it was first brought into notice, though not disseminated until ten years later. It was first found in a garden in Frenchtown, N.J. The Bushberg Catalogue thinks it a natural cross between Labrusca and Vinifera, a native American and a European variety.

VINE, moderate grower, foliage delicate, subject to thrip; wood slender, hardy, regular, sometimes an abundant bearer.

BUNCH, small, compact, usually shouldered.

BERRY, small, round; skin, thin, beautiful light red, with whitish bloom, translucent; pulp, sweet, sprightly, aromatic; juice abundant, sweet, vinous.

SEASON, September.

QUALITY, dessert, 1st class.

VALUE, dessert, 1st rate; market, 1st rate.

ADAPTATION. Succeeds at the Niagara, Wentworth, and Bay of Quinte stations, and throughout the southern and middle portions of the province generally.

PEARS.

ANJOU.

(Beurre d'Anjou, Ne Plus Meuris of Le Roy.)

A fine market pear, succeeding admirably on the quince, but on the pear the tree is not so productive, nor the fruit so large. Its fine size, and melting, buttery texture, make it a favorite market pear for the month of December, and the experience of 1897 proves it a desirable variety to export to Great Britain.

ORIGIN, Louvain, Belgium, about 1823 ; named Ne Plus Meuris, after Father Meuris.

TREE, a vigorous, strong grower ; productiveness scarcely first rate even on the quince, third rate on the pear.

FRUIT, large, some samples in 1897 measuring $4\frac{1}{4}$ inches long by $3\frac{1}{4}$ wide ; form, obovate, blunt pyriform, sides often uneven, and samples not very uniform ; skin, thick, yellow at maturity, with greenish patches and brown dots, brownish red on sunny side ; stem, scarcely half an inch long, stout and fleshy ; calyx, open, set in a shallow basin ; core small, seeds few, if any.

FLESH, white, fine grained, buttery, melting ; flavor, pleasant, perfumed, not very sweet.

SEASON, November and December

QUALITY, table or cooking, good.

VALUE, home market, 1st class ; foreign market, very good.

ADAPTATION, succeeds admirably south of Toronto.

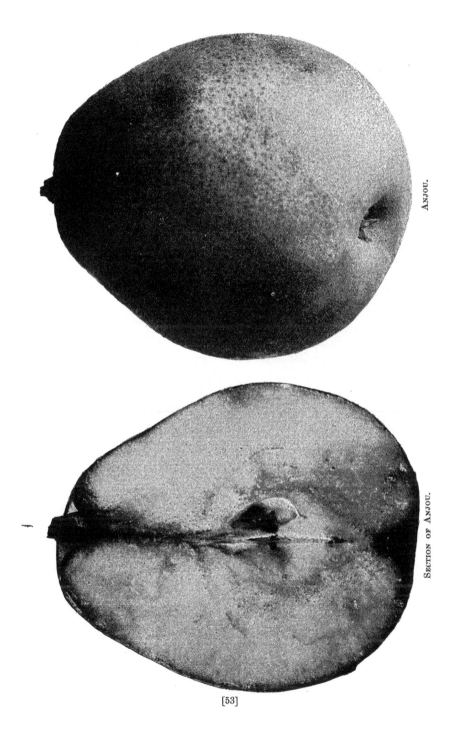

ANJOU.

SECTION OF ANJOU.

BARTLETT.

(In England, Williams' Boncretien.)

No pear of the same season equals in popularity the Bartlett, for either dessert or canning. Indeed, while it is in the market, no other pear compares with it in price or brings as much profit to the grower. Of late large orchards of this one variety have been planted in Canada and the northern States, and immense quantities of this pear are also shipped in car lots from California to our eastern cities, often causing the price to rule very low. In 1896 first-class Bartletts were sold in Toronto during a great part of September at from 30 to 40 cents a basket,

BARTLETT.

and ordinary stock for $2 and $3 a barrel.

ORIGIN, Berkshire, England, 1770, propagated by Mr. Williams, near London. Introduced into America and disseminated by Enoch Bartlett of Boston.

TREE, healthy, vigorous, half-hardy, overcomes blight better than most varieties, very productive.

FRUIT, large, oblong, obtuse, pyriform. Color, yellow, with very numerous minute brown dots, often russetted at the apex. Stem, $1\frac{1}{4}$ inches long, in a small irregular cavity. Calyx, open in an irregular basin.

FLESH, creamy white, fine grained, very buttery and juicy; flavor, sweet, perfumed, vinous.

SEASON, September 1st to 15th.

QUALITY, dessert, very good, market, best.

ADAPTATION, succeeds admirably in southern Ontario, and as far north as our Bay of Quinte station.

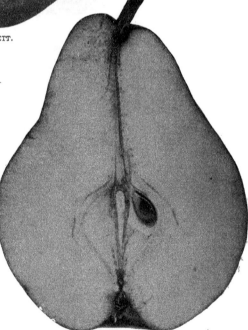

SECTION OF BARTLETT.

BOSC.

(Beurre Bosc, *Downing*.)

The Bosc pear is not as widely known among cultivators in Canada as its merits deserve. Though a russet, it yellows as it ripens ; the pear is large in size, and uniform on the tree as if thinned purposely ; and the texture is such that it can be exported in fine condition. In quality, a well grown Bosc is first-class. On the whole, we would place this pear among the valuable kinds for planting for export to the foreign markets.

ORIGIN. A chance seedling found in France, and dedicated to M. Bosc, the eminent director of the Jardin des Plantes at Paris, about the year 1835.

TREE. A vigorous grower, and a regular bearer, carrying its fruit singly

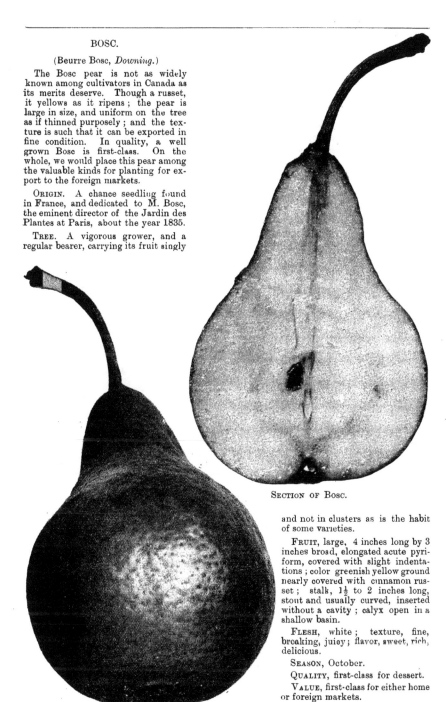

SECTION OF BOSC.

and not in clusters as is the habit of some varieties.

FRUIT, large, 4 inches long by 3 inches broad, elongated acute pyriform, covered with slight indentations ; color greenish yellow ground nearly covered with cinnamon russet ; stalk, 1½ to 2 inches long, stout and usually curved, inserted without a cavity ; calyx open in a shallow basin.

FLESH, white ; texture, fine, breaking, juicy ; flavor, sweet, rich, delicious.

SEASON, October.

QUALITY, first-class for dessert.

VALUE, first-class for either home or foreign markets.

ADAPTATION, southern Ontario.

BUFFUM.

Formerly this pear was much in favor as a profitable orchard variety, because of its productiveness and the wonderful hardiness and vitality of the tree, but of late years it is much less in favor with pear growers on acc unt of its small size and ordinary quality. Some trees of this variety at Maplehurst, forty years planted, have never shown the slightest tendency to blight, and have attained a great height, more resembling Lombardy poplars than pear trees.

ORIGIN, Rhode Island.

TREE, remarkable for its vigorous, symmetrical, erect habit of growth ; it is regularly and fairly productive, but unless gathered early the fruit drops badly ; not subject to blight.

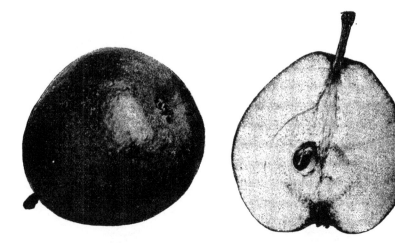

BUFFUM. (Reduced.)   BUFFUM. (Section reduced.)

FRUIT, medium size, obovate, slightly oblong, sometimes $2\frac{3}{4}$ inches long by $2\frac{1}{2}$ inches wide ; skin, rough, yellow at maturity, with bright or dull red or russet on sunny side ; dots, small, brown ; stalk, $\frac{3}{4}$ inch long in small cavity ; segments of calyx small, in a small basin

FLESH, yellowish white, crisp, not fine, not juicy, sweet with pleasant flavor.

SEASON, September.

QUALITY, dessert, fair ; cooking, fair.

VALUE, home market, poor , foreign market, very poor.

ADAPTATION, counted hardy in Bruce and Huron Counties ; slightly tender in North Ontario County.

CHAMBERS.

The Chambers pear has been grown at Maplehurst for about ten years on dwarf stock and commends itself as a fine market variety the beginning of August, for it is a good quality, large, and the tree is productive. Commended in Kentucky.

ORIGIN, brought from Maryland to Kentucky by Judge Wm. Chambers.

TREE, moderately vigorous, very hardy, productive.

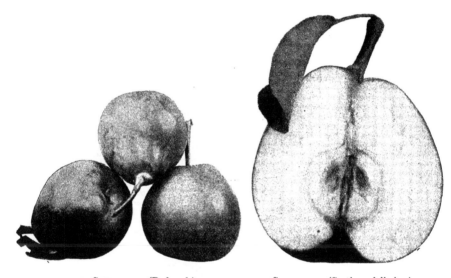

CHAMBERS. (Reduced.)   .   CHAMBERS. (Section, full size.)

FRUIT of medium size, $2\frac{1}{4}$ inches long by $2\frac{1}{2}$ inches in diameter; form obtuse, obovate, pyriform; color, pea green, turning yellow when fully mature, with numerous brown and green dots, and reddish brown cheek on sunny side; stalk, stout, 1 inch long, set on an angle in a flat cavity, often one shoulder prominent; calyx, small, half-open; seeds, few.

FLESH, white, half fine, tender, fairly juicy; flavor, aromatic, sweet and pleasant.

SEASON, August 1st to 10th.

QUALITY, good.

VALUE, for a near market, first rate.

CLAIRGEAU.

As a commercial pear, especially for a distant market, we know of no variety of the same season that is superior to this variety. Its large size, and the beautiful cheek which it takes on during the month of October, its excellent shipping and keeping qualities, all these combine to make it a profitable variety, and one that is easily grown, either as dwarf or standard, though usually large and fine sized as the former. The quality is variable according to the conditions of growth ; in France it is counted first quality ; in England, third quality ; with us, when well ripened, it is second rate.

ORIGIN, Nantes, in France, with a gardener named Clairgeau, about 1834.

TREE, first-class in vigor, hardiness and productiveness ; wood, stout, and upright in habit of growth ; branches, numerous, grown as a dwarf can be trained to make a fine pyramid ; an early bearer.

FRUIT, large, $4\frac{1}{2}$ inches long by $3\frac{1}{2}$ inches in width, one-sided, pyriform ; skin, green, turning pale yellow at maturity, almost overspread

with splashings and dots of russet, which completely covers it about the stalk and about the calyx ; orange red on sunny side ; stalk, $\frac{3}{4}$ inch long, stout, fleshy at the base, usually set at an angle with the axis ; calyx, small, open, in a shallow furrowed basin.

FLESH, white, coarse grained. juicy, with sweet, aromatic and vinous flavor.

SEASON, Oct. to January.

VALUE, home or foreign market, first rate.

QUALITY, cooking, good ; desert good.

ADAPTATION, succeeds admirably as far north as Thornbury ; and east as far as Prescott.

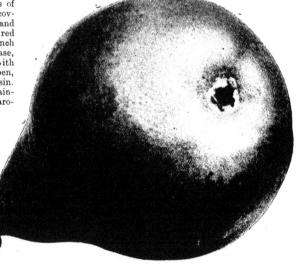

CLAPP'S FAVORITE.

Clapp's Favorite is a beautiful pear where well grown and well colored. It is also of good quality, so that it is well fitted to be a profitable market pear ; with one fault, that it soon passes out of prime condition, and, if allowed to ripen on the trees, it will rot at the core. On this account the fruit must be gathered as soon as full grown and well colored, and shipped while firm.

ORIGIN. Raised by Thaddens Clapp, of Dorchester, Mass., U.S.

TREE, upright, vigorous grower, somewhat spreading, forming a symmetrical top ; bears fruit of uniformly large size, pretty evenly

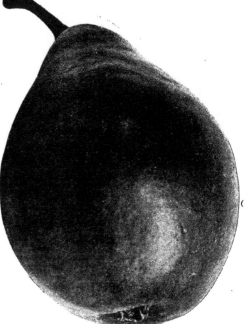

CLAPP'S FAVORITE.

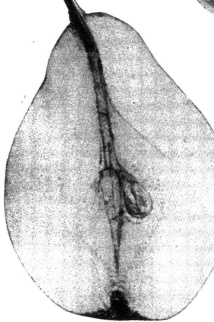

SECTION OF CLAPP'S FAVORITE.

distributed ; productive ; succeeds well as a dwarf on rich soil.

FRUIT, very large, pyriform, obovate, usually symmetrical, sometimes with unequal sides ; skin pale green changing to yellowish green, with dull red on sunny side, which becomes bright crimson at maturity, somewhat resembling the coloring of the well-known Louise ; stalk, stout and fleshy, obliquely inserted without cavity ; calyx, large, half open, in shallow basin.

FLESH, creamy white, fine, tender, juicy, with very agreeable flavor ; good to very good.

SEASON, August 20 to September 1.

QUALITY, good for dessert and cooking.

VALUE, good for home market.

ADAPTATION, hardy.

DEMPSEY.

A PLATE OF DEMPSEY PEARS (reduced).

The Dempsey was originated near Trenton in Prince Edward County, by Mr. P. C. Dempsey, the late well-known Director of our Association for that district. It was produced from a seed of a Bartlett, fertilized with Duchess d'Angouleme. The tree is a good grower and quite productive. The fruit is firm and consequently would ship well.

DESCRIPTION : Fruit large, oblong, obovate, pyriform ; skin smooth, yellowish-green, with brownish-red cheek in sun ; stem about one inch long, set in a fleshy base, and with almost no cavity ; calyx nearly closed in a moderately deep uneven basin, core small. Flesh white, fine grained, tender, almost melting, with sweet delicious flower. Season, last of October, November.

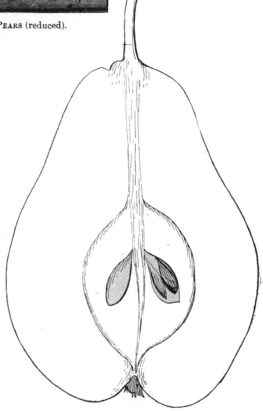

SECTION OF DEMPSEY PEAR.

DIEL.

A pear of ordinary appearance as grown in Southern Ontario, but of such size and excellent quality that it deserves a place in every collection, whether for home use or market.

ORIGIN, a chance seedling near Brussels, Belgium, named in honor of Dr. Diel, a German pomologist

TREE, very vigorous, hardy and productive.

FRUIT, large to very large ; obovate ; stem pale green, turning yellow at maturity, with numerous large brown dots and patches of russet ; stem, curved, stout, from 1 inch to 1¼ inches long, set. in an open uneven cavity ; calyx, open, in a basin of moderate depth and not very regular.

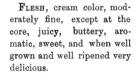

BEURRE DIEL.

FLESH, cream color, moderately fine, except at the core, juicy, buttery, aromatic, sweet, and when well grown and well ripened very delicious.

SEASON OF USE, November and December, just preceding the Lawrence.

QUALITY, dessert, very good.

VALUE, home market, second rate, because lacking in color ; foreign market, possibly first rate, because it carries well and has fine flavor, but not yet tested in this respect.

ADAPTATION, not yet proved (1897).

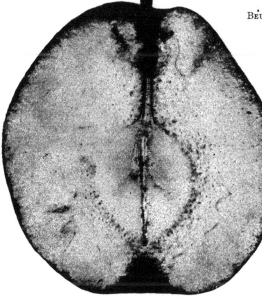

BEURRE DIEL (Section).

DUCHESS.

(Duchess d'Angoulême, LeRoy and Downing ; Angoulême, American Pomological Society ; Duchesse, common name in France.)

For many years this pear was counted among the best and most profitable varieties in Ontario, especially when grown on quince stock, and, in consequence has been largely planted ; but, since 1890, the Canadian markets for fruit have been overstocked, and prices for this pear have ruled low, even if held until December ; and the fruit itself has been inferior in size, and much knotted with curculio stings. Prime samples are excellent stock for export, carried in cold storage.

ORIGIN, Angers, France, in 1812, a chance seedling. In 1820 Andusson, the propagator, sent a basket of the fruit to the Duchess d'Angoulême, who authorized him to bestow her title upon the pear as its name.

TREE, a strong grower, succeeds best on the quince : variable in productiveness.

FRUIT, exceedingly variable in size, from three to five inches in either diameter, sometimes weighing a pound and a quarter ; form, obovate, large at the base ; surface, uneven, sometimes knobby ; skin, light green, patched with russet, and numerous grey dots ; stalk, stout, curved, one inch long, often swollen at point of attachment, deep set in an irregular cavity ; calyx, small, closed. in an uneven, often russeted basin.

FLESH, white ; texture, fine when well grown, but often coarse grained, melting, juicy, and, when properly matured, of a sweet and excellent flavor.

SEASON, October and November.

QUALITY, dessert, very good ; cooking, good.

VALUE, very good for either home or foreign market.

ADAPTATION. Hardy in southern Ontario, but only half hardy in Grey and Bruce, York, etc.

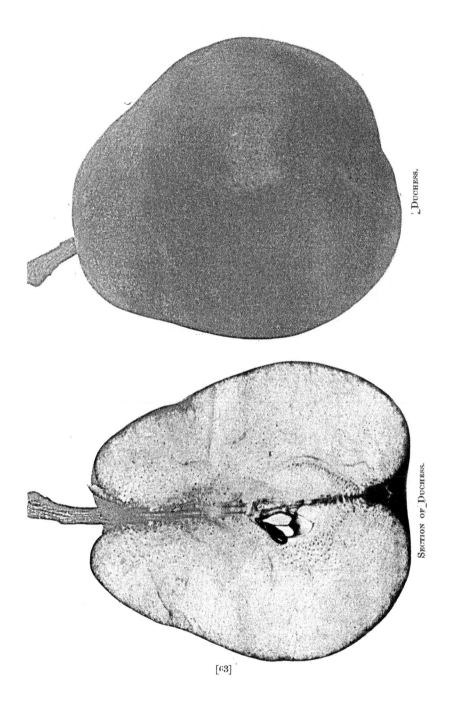

DUCHESS.

SECTION OF DUCHESS.

FLEMISH BEAUTY.
(Fondante des Bois of "LeRoy.)

F<small>LEMISH</small> B<small>EAUTY</small>.

A variety that has been a great favorite in Europe ever since the beginning of the eighteenth century, as is evidenced by the thirty-five synonyms which have been given it as shown in ".Dictionaire de Pomologie par Andre LeRoy." This and the Bartlett were among the first imported varieties of pears planted in Ontario, and it has been widely tested. In the northern sections, where it succeeds, it is a most popular variety, but in southern Ontario it has been of late so subject to scab and cracking of the fruit, that it has lost favor with growers, notwithstanding its excellent quality.

O<small>RIGIN</small>, discovered by Van-Mons about the year 1810 in Eastern Flanders, and distributed among his friends.

T<small>REE</small>, first class in hardiness ; almost first in productiveness ; an early bearer.

F<small>RUIT</small>, large, often measuring 3¾ long by 3¼ inches broad, averaging about 3 inches either diameter ; form, obovate, obtuse pyriform ; skin, light yellow when ripe, with frequent patches of brownish red on sunny side, with scattered minute dots ; stalk 1 inch to 1½ inches long, set in a narrow, deep cavity ; calyx open, segments short, in a small round basin.

F<small>LESH</small>, creamy white, melting, buttery, juicy ; flavor, rich, sugary, delicious.

S<small>EASON</small>. September 15 to 30. Should be gathered before quite ripe or it will drop and waste.

Q<small>UALITY</small>, first class.

V<small>ALUE</small>, first class where well grown, but counted second class on account of its being subject to fungus.

A<small>DAPTATION</small>. Quite general ; fine samples are grown at our Georgian Bay station and at our St. Lawrence station.

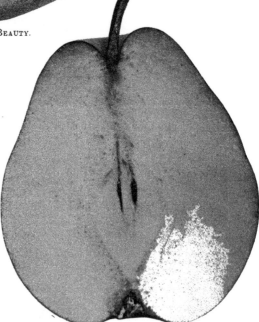

S<small>ECTION OF</small> F<small>LEMISH</small> B<small>EAUTY</small>.

HOWELL.

One of the best market pears of its season for southern Ontario, especially where grown on a standard. Its vigor of tree, regularity of bearing, clear skin, and good size and quality make it a desirable variety for the commercial orchard.

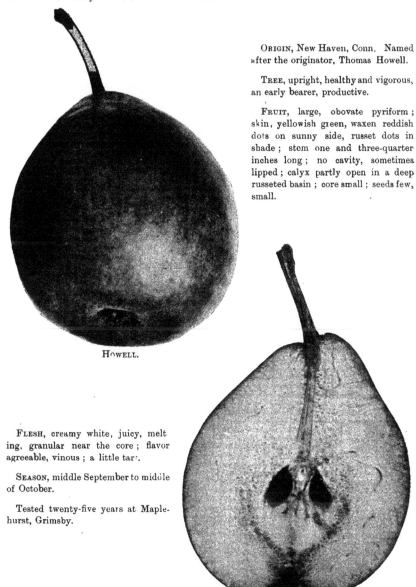

ORIGIN, New Haven, Conn. Named after the originator, Thomas Howell.

TREE, upright, healthy and vigorous, an early bearer, productive.

FRUIT, large, obovate pyriform; skin, yellowish green, waxen reddish dots on sunny side, russet dots in shade; stem one and three-quarter inches long; no cavity, sometimes lipped; calyx partly open in a deep russeted basin; core small; seeds few, small.

HOWELL.

FLESH, creamy white, juicy, melting, granular near the core; flavor agreeable, vinous; a little tart.

SEASON, middle September to middle of October.

Tested twenty-five years at Maplehurst, Grimsby.

SECTION OF HOWELL.

5 F.S.

KIEFFER.

There is perhaps no pear about which a greater diversity of opinion exists; some fruit men condemning it because of its lack of quality, and others insisting that its beauty of

appearance, its enormous productiveness, and its wonderful health and vigor of tree make it a profitable market variety, and that when properly grown and ripened it is quite a desirable kind, especially for cooking. Certainly the tree surpasses every variety in our collection for productiveness and vigor of growth; while the fruit is always uniformly perfect in form, free from blemishes, and, when the tree is cultivated and manured, large in size.

KIEFFER PEAR—EXTERIOR.

ORIGIN, by Peter Kieffer, Roxbury, Pa., a seedling of Chinese Sand pear.

TREE, wonderfully vigorous and healthy; an early and extraordinary bearer, often being laden with fruit after two years planting.

FRUIT, medium to large, averaging about 3 x 2½ inches; form, ovate, tapering at both ends, widest at middle, and narrowest toward stem: skin, light golden yellow, with bright cheek, and very numerous brown russet dots; stalk, one inch long, fairly stout, in a one-sided cavity; calyx, half open, in a medium sized irregular basin.

FLESH, yellowish white, half tender, half melting, not very fine, juicy: flavor, moderately sweet, poor.

SEASON, October, November and December to January.

QUALITY, dessert, very poor; for cooking good; valuable for canning.

VALUE, second rate for all markets.

ADAPTATION, very hardy.

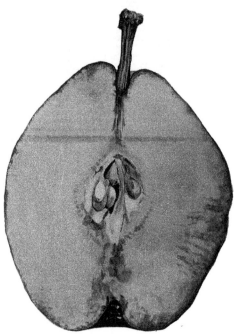

KIEFFER PEAR—SECTION.

PETITE MARGUERITE.

Among the desirable varieties of dessert pears for the home garden we would certainly include the Petite Marguerite, a pear of the highest quality for table use. At Maplehurst the tree has proved itself an abundant bearer and a good grower. The fruit is not large, but as size is not an object in a dessert pear, this is not a fault. Its season is immediately after the Giffard and just before the Clapp and the Tyson. As a market pear it is hardly to be commended, because of its small size and color ; and it will be a long time before we can convince the average dealer that size and color are not the chief considerations in a fruit.

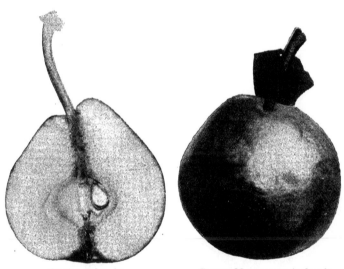

(Section reduced.)   PETITE MARGUERITE (reduced).

ORIGIN, Angers, France, in nurseries of Andre LeRoy.

TREE, second rate in vigor, and first rate in productiveness : succeeds as either standard or dwarf, but more vigorous as a standard.

FRUIT, medium size, about $2\frac{3}{8}$ in either diameter ; form, oblate, obtuse pyriform ; skin, light green, often tinged and mottled with bright red on sunny side, yellowing somewhat at maturity ; stalk, $1\frac{1}{4}$ inches to $1\frac{1}{2}$ inches in length, set in a narrow cavity, of which one side is often much higher than the other ; calyx, partly open, in a shallow corrugated basin.

FLESH, white, yellowish at core ; texture, fine, melting, juicy ; flavor, sweet, vinous, agreeable.

SEASON, August 20 to 30.

QUALITY, first rate for dessert, good for cooking.

VALUE, home market, second rate.

ROSTIEZER.

A small unattractive looking pear, of very high quality. It is the best of its season in quality for dessert purposes, and should have a place in the home garden. What the Seckel is in October, this pear is in August. Packed in small packages and labelled " extra quality dessert pears," the writer was able to sell them at a fancy price, but usually the pear sells far below its value on account of its ordinary appearance.

ROSTIEZER.   SECTION OF ROSTIEZER.

ORIGIN, foreign

TREE, healthy, vigorous, sprawling habits, shoots few, and need shortening in.

FRUIT, small to medium, obovate, oblong pyriform ; skin, green, sometimes turning yellowish, with reddish-brown cheek ; stem slender and nearly two inches in length ; calyx open ; basin small.

FLESH, juicy, melting, sweet, very delicious, of very finest quality.

SEASON, middle to end of August.

TESTED twenty years at Maplehurst.

SAPIEGANKA.

A Russian pear of fine appearance, scions of which were sent out to the Secretary of the Ontario Fruit Growers' Association in 1892, by Mr. Jaroslav Niemetz, of Winnitza, Podolie, Russia. It fruited at Grimsby in 1895 and 1896, ripening August 12th to 20th. Its fine appearance is in its favour, but its quality is inferior to other varieties of its seasrn, and, unless it should prove desirable on account of its hardiness, would not be worthy of general cultivation. Mr. Niemetz says, "In its home in Lithuania, old and large trees are met with which have endured many and severe winters in the Tamboff Government, it is the most hardy of all pears there grown, and, therefore, is certainly a hardy variety. The flavor of the flesh depends upon local conditions, for, though it is tasteful enough in the warmer districts, it is sometimes harsh; when grown in the north is juicy and buttery." Unfortunately the tree. is subject to blight.

SAPIEGANKA.

TREE, hardy, productive but subject to blight.

FRUIT, medium size, oblate, often somewhat flattened; color, brownish yellow, with brownish red in sun, with numerous small dots; stem, long in small cavity; calyx, sergments large, partly open in a broad, wrinkled base.

FLESH, white texture coarse, somewhat firm and juicy; flavor, sweet and agreeable.

SEASON, August 12th to 20th (1896.)

QUALITY, dessert, poor: cooking, poor.
VALUE, home market, fairly good; distant market, poor.

ADAPTATION, succeeds well at Grimsby. Tested by the Dominion Experimental Farm system and found tender in Manitoba and the Northwest, but perfectly hardy at Ottawa and in Muskoka.

SECTION OF SAPIEGANKA.

SHELDON.

One of the most delicious of dessert pears, if eaten just at the proper time.   Worthy of a place in every home garden, but not productive enough to be planted for market.

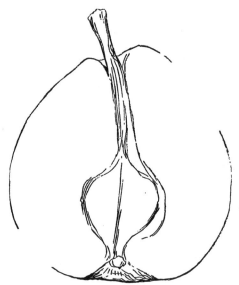

SECTION OF SHELDON.

ORIGIN, accidental on farm of Norman Sheldon of Huron, Wayne Co., N.Y.

TREE, vigorous, erect, not very productive, late coming into bearing.

FRUIT, above medium in size, roundish, obtuse obovate ; skin, yellowish-green, covered with thin light russett, brownish crimson in sun, russet dots ; stalk, short, stout, in a narrow cavity ; calyx nearly open, in a broad basin.

FLESH, creamy, buttery, juicy, sweet, aromatic.

SEASON, October.

Tested twenty years at Maplehurst.

SUMMER DOYENNE.

Doyenne d'Ete—*Hogg ;* Doyenne de Juillet—*Le Roy.*

For the home garden this pear is most desirable, not only for its good quality for dessert purposes, but because it has no competitor in the last half of July. It should be gathered before it is mellow to preserve its juiciness, for, if ripened on the tree, it becomes mealy and insipid. Its very small size makes it undesirable in the commercial orchard, especially now that we must compete with larger varieties from California which ripen earlier in that climate than they do with us

ORIGIN, Dr. Van Mons, Professor at Louvain, Belgium, about 1823, at which time he had on his grounds about 2,000 seedlings of merit.

TREE, vigorous young shoots, light yellowish brown, of upright slender habit, an early and abundant bearer ; dwarf trees two years planted beginning to fruit ; succeeds as dwarf or standard.

FRUIT, small, about 1¾x2 inches ; form, roundish, obovate ; color, green to lemon yellow with brownish red cheek on the sunny side, and numerous grey dots ; stalk about an inch long, stout, attached in a very slight depression ; calyx, small, half open, in a shallow plaited basin.

FLESH, white ; texture, fine, tender, juicy ; flavor, sweet and pleasant with slight aroma.

QUALITY, dessert, very good ; too small for cooking.

VALUE, too small for a market pear, except in limited quantities.

SEASON, 15th to 30th of July.

ADAPTATION, hardy in Southern Ontario ; fairly hardy in Bruce and Huron.

PEACHES.

ALEXANDER.

The earliest peach grown in the Niagara district and in Essex county. It is a clingstone, of poor quality for dessert purposes, and poor also for cooking. so that, in competition with yellow-fleshed Elbertas and Crawfords from southern peach orchards, it sells at a low price in our markets.

ALEXANDER (reduced).

ORIGIN, chance seedling, Mount Pulaski, Ill., on farm of A. O. Alexander.
TREE, vigorous, hardy, productive.
FRUIT, medium, globular, sides unequal ; color, greenish, suffused with dark and light red suture, broad ; apex, slightly sunken.

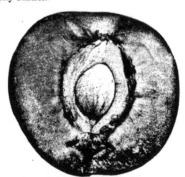

SECTION OF ALEXANDER.

FLESH, greenish white, firm. juicy, half melting, clings to stone ; flavor. sweet and fairly good
SEASON, July 20 to 30 (1896).
QUALITY, dessert, poor ; cooking. poor ; home market, poor ; distant market, very poor.
ADAPTATION. Succeeds at Niagara and Southwestern stations.

EARLY PURPLE.

For home use, as a dessert peach, this is one of the best of its season. Between 1860 and 1870 this variety was grown as the earliest market peach in Southern Ontario, but its extreme tenderness of flesh and rapid softening after maturity led to its giving place to other varieties.

TREE, thrifty, vigorous, hardy, fairly productive.

FRUIT, size 2½x2 inches ; form, irregular, ovate, one-sided ; skin, bright red, downy ; basin, deep ; stone, almost free.

FLESH, greenish white in color ; texture, very

EARLY PURPLE (Reduced).

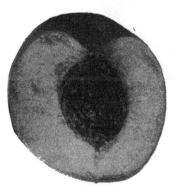

EARLY PURPLE (Section reduced).

tender. very juicy, melting ; flavor, sweet, rich, very agreeable.

SEASON, August 25th to September 1st (in 1897).

QUALITY, dessert, very good, cooking, poor.

VALUE, near market, third rate ; distant market, of no use.

ADAPTATION, Southern Ontario.

CRAWFORD'S EARLY.

Crawford's Early has long held its place at the head of the list of peaches both for home use and for market. Its beautiful golden color, its large size, its free stone and rich flavor all unite in giving it a just claim to this position. Its buds are a little more tender than those of some other varieties, and, consequently, many growers hesitate to plant it, but where high cultivation and plenty of fertilizer is given, fine crops of luscious fruit have resulted.

SECTION CRAWFORD'S EARLY.

ORIGIN, Middleton, N.J., by Wm. Crawford.

TREE, vigorous, productive under favorable conditions.

FRUIT, large to very large, oblong ; suture, shallow ; apex, prominent, swollen ; color, golden yellow, with rich red cheek.

FLESH, yellow, sweet, rich, free from stone which often parts in middle when nearly ripe.

SEASON, September 1st to 12th (1897).

QUALITY, dessert and cooking, very good ; market value, best.

ADAPTATION, Niagara district and parts of Essex county.

STRAWBERRIES.

ANNIE LAURIE.

(Perfect blossom.)

This is a very late variety, also one of the best quality. It may be taken as a standard for quality and flavor. A fine one for amateurs to pet.

ANNIE LAURIE.

ORIGIN, a seedling grown by John F. Beaver, of Ohio, in 1889.

PLANT, is very healthy and good grower, making plenty of runners for a fruiting row. No rust ; moderately productive.

FRUIT, berries are large and round, like the Jersey Queen, with gold seeds prominent. A very bright glossy scarlet, making fine appearance.

FLESH, pinkish white, of the very finest quality ; a fine table variety.

SEASON, late.

ADAPTATION, does better in some soils than others.

S.

AROMA.

(Perfect blossom.)

The Aroma is a good late one, taking the place that the old Gandy occupied. The Aroma is more productive, a good pollenizer for large late pistillates. Wherever grown it is a favorite.

ORIGIN. It was produced from seed of Cumberland by E. W. Cruse, of Kansas.

PLANT. It is a good vigorous grower, very healthy, no rust, making a good stand of large plants, quite productive.

FRUIT, is very large, bright dark red in color, fine looking berry, keeps its size well to the last picking, quite firm.

AROMA.

FLESH, pink, solid, and good quality.

SEASON, medium to late.

ADAPTATION, does well in all soils and climates.

[75]

BISMARCK.

(Perfect blossom.)

This is a seedling from Bubach, and in some respects an improvement, in others not as good ; its color is not as fine as Bubach. It is a good grower and productive.

ORIGIN. It was grown from seed of Bubach crossed with Van Deman, by J. C. Bauer, Arkansas.

PLANT, very healthy, strong, vigorous, resembles Bubach in color of leaf and style of plant ; it makes plenty of runners ; its foliage is fine ; fruit stalk is strong and medium to short ; plant quite productive.

BISMARCK.

FRUIT, large to very large, round, resembling Jersey Queen, but more conical ; gold seeds very prominent, light scarlet and bright looking ; sometimes hollow.

FLESH, pink in color, medium in firmness, good flavor.

SEASON, medium to late.

ADAPTATION, good accounts come from all places where it has been tried.   S.

BOYNTON.

(Imperfect blossom.)

This variety so closely resembles the old Crescent in its best days that it has been affirmed by some that it is the Crescent under a new name.

ORIGIN, said to be a cross between the Crescent and Sharpless. Comes from Albany, N.Y.

PLANT, is a strong, vigorous, and healthy grower, making a wild, matted row ; very productive.

FRUIT, is medium in size, light scarlet in color, medium in firmness.

FLESH, pink, acid, but fair quality.

SEASON, early, medium.

ADAPTATION, does well anywhere.

BOYNTON.

BRANDYWINE.

BRANDYWINE.

(Perfect blossom.)

ORIGIN, originated in Pennsylvania, from seed of Glendale, crossed with Cumberland, grown by E. Ingram. It was introduced to the public by Mathew Crawford, of Cuyahoga Falls, Ohio, in 1894. It is a fine variety, it's only fault is, it is not as productive as we would like.

PLANT, one of the most vigorous growers, making a wide matted row if allowed to do so, in fact it makes too many plants for its own good.

FRUIT, is large, heart-shaped, fine dark scarlet in color, golden seeds quite firm.

FLESH, red, tartish, but very good quality.

SEASON, medium to late.

ADAPTATION. It does well in most soils.   S.

BUBACH.

(Imperfect blossom.)

This is a grand stand-by and is very widely grown, is one of the largest and finest of them all   Plant is all that could be desired for fruit. Strong, deep rooted and healthy, one of the best for near-by market.

ORIGIN, it was grown by Mr. Bubach, of Illinois.

PLANT, the plant is a strong and deep-rooted one, dark red foliage ; no sign of disease of any kind ; makes plants enough for a good fruiting row ; fruit stem is short, strong and firm, productive and profitable.

FRUIT, is wonderful for its size and color ; the berry is bright and showy.

FLESH, pink ; medium in firmness and good quality.

SEASON, medium.

ADAPTATION. It does well in all soils.   S.

BUBACH.

CARRIE.

(Imperfect blossom.)

The Carrie would appear to have a bright future before it. It is one of the late sorts bidding for public favor. It is a good one.

CARRIE.

ORIGINATED from seed of Haverland, by Mr. Thompson, of Virginia.

PLANT, is large, vigorous and healthy, making long and strong runners and plenty of them ; it somewhat resembles Haverland ; not as productive.

FRUIT, the fruit is not so long as Haverland, very firm, almost as firm as an apple ; the color, bright scarlet, with gold seeds.

FLESH, white and solid, good flavor.

SEASON, medium.

ADAPTATION. Has done well wherever tried.   S.

CLYDE.

(Perfect blossom.)

Originated in Kansas, from seed of the Cyclone, about 1890, by Dr. Stayner, the Cyclone being produced from Crescent crossed with Cumberland. Thus we find out where the Clyde gets its great hardiness and productiveness, viz , from the Crescent. The first berries are as large as the Bubach and very productive. It grows very much like its parent Cyclone, also like the Haverland, but more vigorous than either. It has secured for itself very quickly a place among the standards, if it does not stand first, which place many are claiming for it.

PLANT, a strong and vigorous grower Perfect in every respect. No rust or trace of disease. Its fruit stalk is just the right length and strong enough to hold up the great load of fruit. In color, light, like Haverland. Strong, and has many runners that take root easily.

FRUIT, very large, as large as Bubach, roundly conical, bright dark scarlet in color, and very firm.

FLESH, pinkish white, fine eating, very pleasant to the taste, quality first-class.

SEASON, second early.

ADAPTATION. Does well everywhere and in all soils. S.

CLYDE.

ELEANOR.

(Perfect blossom.)

The Eleanor is one of the extra early ones ; a good healthy vigorous grower ; fruit, good size, fine shape ; in wet seasons it has a kind of mildew like on the Michel's.

ORIGINATED in New Jersey, a chance seedling found by Mr Coombe ; a good market berry.

PLANT, very healthy, vigorous grower, small and slender, dark in color, making many runners, quite productive.

FRUIT, color, dark scarlet or crimson ; medium in firmness.

FLESH, red, white centre ; acid, but good flavor.

SEASON, one of the earliest.

ADAPTATION, does well in most soils.

ELEANOR.   S.

GEISLER.

(Perfect blossom.)

This is a very fine variety ; it is new as yet, only having been introduced in 1897.

ORIGIN, a chance seedling found in Michigan, somewhat resembling the Seaford in shape and size.

PLANT, it is a very strong plant, making plenty of runners. The plant is very healthy, no sign of rust and quite productive. The plant is a very early bloomer, one of the first.

FRUIT, is large, bright dark scarlet, round to oblong in shape, berry is solid.

FLESH, light pink in color, medium in firmness and of good quality.

SEASON, early to medium.

ADAPTATION, seems well adapted for most localities.   S.

GEISLER.

GLEN MARY.

(Perfect blossom.)

This is a variety of great promise, it is one of th᷎ newer sorts. No doubt it will take a place among the standards on account of its size and productiveness.

ORIGIN, a chance seedling found by J. A. Ingram of Pennsylvania.

PLANT, a very large, strong, vigorous grower, making plants freely. No sign of any disease on it. Dark, rich foliage. An ideal plant. Fruit stem, medium in length, strong enough to hold up the very large berries. Very productive.

FRUIT, very large—the largest, dark crimson in color, ribbed like the Marshall, a hard, green seedy end that does not ripen well.

FLESH, pink to white, fair quality, inclined to acid.

SEASON, medium to late.

ADAPTATION, it has done well wherever tried.   S.

GLEN MARY.

GRENVILLE.

(Imperfect blossom.)

The Grenville is one of the best of the Pistillate or imperfect blooming kinds ; in some respects it is an improvement on the Bubach. It is a healthy, vigorous grower and quite productive, making it a good market sort.

ORIGIN, it is a chance seedling found in Ohio by Mr. Beuchly.

PLANT, very heavy and vigorous grower, making plants freely, very productive.

FRUIT, dark scarlet in color, large in size, heart shaped, medium in firmness and fine looking.

FLESH, pink to white, somewhat hollow, good quality.

SEASON, medium.

ADAPTATION, does well in all soils.   S.

GRENVILLE.

HALL'S FAVORITE.

(Perfect blossom.)

HALL'S FAVORITE.

When this variety was introduced it was claimed that it was as large as Bubach. It has not proved to be so. It is a fine, large berry.

ORIGIN, a chance seedling found by J. W. Hall, of Marion Station, Md.

PLANT, the plant is a good grower, healthy, vigorous, no rust, and makes plenty of plants ; medium in productiveness.

FRUIT, is large, not so large as Bubach, is firm, scarlet in color, the berry is solid.

FLESH, is a light scarlet, good quality.

SEASON, it is a medium season.

ADAPTATION. Does well wherever tried.

HAVERLAND.

(Imperfect blossom.)

Originated in Ohio by Mr. Haverland. Parentage unknown. Widely planted, and is one of the most productive. Its only fault is that in a wet season the fruit is somewhat soft. On the whole it is somewhat soft.

PLANT, very healthy. Vigorous grower, sending out strong runners. Its foliage is magnificent. Fruit stalk is very long and often not able to bear up the immense load of fruit the plant matures. Light in color of leaf.

FRUIT, large to very large, long, bright scarlet, medium in firmness.

FLESH, pinkish, sweet and good quality. -

SEASON, it is one of the first to ripen and continues all through the season.

ADAPTATION. It succeeds well everywhere and all soils suit it. S.

HAVERLAND.

JERSEY QUEEN.

(Imperfect blossom.)

ORIGIN, unknown. This is one of the best late varieties, frequently being the highest price. The berries are large and fine looking.

PLANT is a good one, very healthy one, no sign of rust ever appearing on it ; grows close to the ground, the foliage always fresh and green ; when well fertilized quite productive.

FRUIT is large, round and very bright scarlet in color with gold seeds, medium in firmness, very attractive in appearance.

FLESH, white to pink, solid and fair quality.

SEASON, late to very late.

ADAPTATION, does well in most soils.   S.

JERSEY QUEEN.

LOVETT.

(Perfect blossom.)

This is a great favorite in many places ; is a standard as a shipper and is thus favored by market growers.

ORIGIN, a seedling of Crescent and Wilson by J. H. Norris, of Kentucky.

PLANT is a good grower ; strong runners ; the plant sometimes rusts ; is quite productive.

FRUIT is large dark crimson, somewhat irregular ; somewhat resembling the Williams, but a better berry than the Williams ; a good market berry because it is firm.

FLESH is red, solid, good quality though a little acid.

SEASON, medium.

ADAPTATION, it seems to do well in most places.   S.

LOVETT.

MARGARET.

(Perfect blossom.)

MARGARET.

ORIGIN, the Margaret is a good one, will be a standard. It originated in Ohio, was sown from the seed of the Crawford by Mr. Beaver.

PLANT, the plant is large and strong, sending out the largest runners of any sort, plant is very healthy and quite productive.

FRUIT is large, very regular, crimson in color, seeds golden, solid and firm.

FLESH, red, inclined to tartness but good quality.

SEASON, medium.

ADAPTATION, will suit most soils.   S.

MARSHALL.

(Perfect blossom.)

This variety has perhaps received more favorable notice than most others of recent introduction. It is vigorous in growth, leaves very large and produces a quantity of very large, beautiful, dark crimson berries of fine quality.

ORIGIN, it is a chance seedling found growing on a stone heap by Mr. Ewell, of Massachusetts.

PLANT, a vigorous grower, large leaves, somewhat tender both in foliage and blossom and subject to rust, medium in color, first growth being yellow, fruit stem strong and able to bear up the immense berries, medium in production.

FRUIT, is of the largest size, dark crimson, firm and fine looking, quite regular in shape, *i.e.*, each berry is of same shape, but ribbed and tough seeds imbedded.

FLESH, red, with dash of white in centre, solid, fine quality, one of the best for dessert.

SEASON, early to medium.

ADAPTATION, only does its best in some soils and under highest cultivation ; a fine one for amateurs.   S.

MARSHALL.

MICHEL'S EARLY.

(Perfect blossom.)

This has been grown over a very wide extent of territory, but in many places it has been a failure.

ORIGIN, chance seedling, thought to be from Crescent, by J. G. Michel, of Judsonia, Ark.

PLANT, a very vigorous grower, making too many plants; a rampant grower; sometimes in some soils very little fruit is set, in some soils it is fairly productive.

FRUIT, is medium in size to small; dull reddish color; has a
MICHEL'S EARLY.   withered appearance; quality is good, the berry is tough and
leathery and so carries well.

FLESH, is pink, the quality is good, medium in firmness.

SEASON, extra early.

ADAPTATION, does well only in some places and on some soils.   S.

MASTODON.

(Imperfect blossom.)

This is very like Bubach both in plant and fruit, it is a good one, quite as good as Bubach. The plant is large and stony.

ORIGIN, it is also called Salzer's Late Mastodon, intro-duced by James Lippincott, Jr., Mount Holly, N.J.

PLANT, the plant is strong, large dark foliage; very healthy; makes plants freely enough for a good fruiting row; fruit stalk is short and thick and strong.

FRUIT, the cherry is very large and bright crimson and very showy.

FLESH, is pink, medium as to firmness and good quality.

SEASON, medium.

ADAPTATION, suited for all soils.   S.   MASTODON.

NICK OHMER.

(Perfect blossom.)

This is one of the best of all varieties lately introduced ; it promises to be a standard.

ORIGIN, a seedling of Widdifield by John F. Beaver, of Ohio.

PLANT, is a strong and stocky grower, sending out plenty of strong runners that root easily ; very healthy ; dark foliage.

FRUIT, is large ; bright crimson in color with gold seeds ; fine in appearance ; smooth and regular in shape.

FLESH, is pink at outside and white in centre ; solid and very firm and of best quality.

NICK OHMER.

SEASON, medium to late.

ADAPTATION, it seems to do well in most localities. S.

RUBY.

(Perfect blossom.)

This gives promise of taking a first place in many places, it has been an improvement on the Bubach.

ORIGIN, this sort is thought to be a seedling of Crescent and Sharpless by Mr. Riehl, of Illinois.

PLANT, is a strong vigorous grower ; under some conditions it rusts some but it makes plenty of plants and productive.

FRUIT, is large and plenty of it ; crimson in color ; quite regular in shape.

FLESH, is red in color, firm and best quality.

SEASON, mid-season.

RUBY.

ADAPTATION, good reports come of it from many places. S.

RIDGEWAY.

(Blossom perfect and large.)

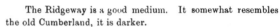

The Ridgeway is a good medium. It somewhat resembles the old Cumberland, it is darker.

ORIGIN, a seedling of Jersey Queen and Parker Earl, by Mr. Ridgeway, of Indiana.

PLANT, strong and healthy, stools out, would be a good one for hills or narrow rows, foliage free from rust, is quite productive.

FRUIT, the fruit is medium to large, highest scarlet color, prominent golden seeds, fine looking berry, medium in firmness.

FLESH, the flesh is red, solid and very good quality, fine flavored.

RIDGEWAY.   SEASON, mid-season.

ADAPTATION.   Good reports of it come from wherever it has been tried.   S.

SAUNDERS.

(Perfect blossom.)

This is one of the best market sorts, producing a good crop of large fine looking berries. The better it is known the more it is grown, taking the place of the old Wilson.

ORIGIN, it was originated by John Little of Ontario.

PLANT, is a vigorous grower, making many plants and healthy. Sometimes a little rust appears when grown under unfavorable conditions. Quite productive, blooms late, thus often escapes spring frosts.

FRUIT, is large to very large and firm ; color, bright crimson.

FLESH, red, firm, and very good quality, fine for table.

SEASON, medium to late.

ADAPTATION.   Has done well wherever it has been tried.   S.

SAUNDERS.

SEAFORD.

(Perfect blossom.)

SEAFORD.

The Seaford is a very good, medium season berry, one of the best. It is very productive, of large, bright, fine looking and better tasting berries.

ORIGIN, a chance seedling, and introduced by Slaymaker & Son, of Dover, Del.

PLANT, the plant is strong, vigorous grower and healthy, producing large clusters of fine fruit. It is also a good runner, making many plants, very productive.

FRUIT, is large and fine looking, bright crimson, with gold seeds imbedded. The berry is very solid and firm.

FLESH, is scarlet in color, very firm and of very good quality.

SEASON, early to medium.

ADAPTATION. It seems to do very well on all soils, it has been tried over a wide extent of territory. S.

SHARPLESS.

(Perfect blossom.)

The Sharpless has been before the public for a long time. In some parts it is still told to be one of the best, but in other places it is not productive enough to make it profitable for market.

ORIGIN, it was grown by Mr. Sharpless.

PLANT, a strong, vigorous grower, plant large and healthy, no rust, quite productive on some soils.

FRUIT, is very large, light scarlet in color, glossy, gold seeds prominent, does not color well.

FLESH, white to pink, firm and very best quality, fine for the table.

SEASON, medium.

ADAPTATION. Does very well in some places. S.

SHARPLESS.

SUNRISE.

(Perfect blossom.)

There are other kinds that are more profitable than this to grow. It does very well in some places.

ORIGIN, a seedling of Crescent and Sharpless from Massachusetts.

PLANT, is quite a vigorous grower, making a good row, quite healthy, medium in productiveness.

FRUIT, is scarlet, roundly conical, gold seeds, berry solid and of good size.

FLESH, is white, medium to soft, acid and fair quality.

SEASON, medium to late.

ADAPTATION. Does well in some places, not in all.   S.

SUNRISE.

STAPLES.

(Perfect blossom.)

This is one of the extra early kinds that will make it profitable for market, having a perfect blossom. It is a good color and quite firm and good quality.

Originated from seed of the Warfield by the late Mr. Staples of Ohio.

PLANT, quite healthy, making plenty of runners for a wide row, if needed, quite vigorous in growth, a good early staminate to fertilize early Pistillates with.

FRUIT, dark crimson in color, firm and good flavor. Color very like Warfield. Size, medium to large ; large for so early a berry.

FLESH, pink and solid, good flavor, somewhat acid yet spicy.

SEASON, extra early.

ADAPTATION. It seems to do well in most places.   S.

STAPLES

TENNESSEE PROLIFIC.

(Perfect blossom.)

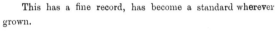

This has a fine record, has become a standard wherever grown.

ORIGIN, a seedling of Crescent and Sharpless ; grown by Capt. J. C. Hodges, of East Tennessee.

PLANT, is a vigorous, healthy grower, making many strong runners, very productive, an early bloomer.

FRUIT, is a bright crimson, medium to large in size ; the berry is sometimes double at the point, but quite firm.

FLESH, is red, very good quality and quite firm.

SEASON, early medium.

TENNESSEE PROLIFIC.   ADAPTATION. It does well wherever grown.   S.

VAN DEMAN.

(Perfect blossom.)

This is one of the earliest ; seems to do better in some places than others, some growers having discarded it while others look upon it as the best early.

ORIGIN, it comes from Arkansas, having been originated by J. C. Bauer, of Judsonia, Ark., from seed of Crescent crossed with Capt. Jack.

PLANT, is a vigorous grower, rusting somewhat in some soils ; fruit stalk is medium strong, able to hold up fruit ; dark in foliage ; quite productive, not a heavy picking at any one time but continuing through the season.

FRUIT, bright crimson in color, gold seeds ; very attractive, conical ; ripens and colors all over at the same time, best extra early for this.

FLESH, pink, very firm and very best quality.

SEASON, ripen with the first and continues to mid season.

ADAPTATION. Does better in some soils than others.   S.

VAN DEMAN.

WARFIELD.

(Imperfect Blossom.)

This variety has been a great favorite in many places. Nothing else was thought by some to be as good for a market crop. Where there is plenty of moisture it does well.

ORIGIN. Supposed to be a cross of Crescent and Wilson found growing wild by B. C. Warfield of S. Ill.

PLANT, is a vigorous grower; in some seasons it rusts somewhat; the plant cannot stand hot, dry weather; does not mature its crop; it is very productive, one of the most productive of all the varieties.

FRUIT, is dark crimson, very firm, medium to large in size, regular in shape, a good shipper.

WARFIELD.

FLESH, is red, firm and good quality though somewhat acid.

SEASON, early medium.

ADAPTATION. Does well in all soils. S.

WM. BELT.

(Perfect Blossom.)

ORIGIN, this berry comes from Ohio, having been originated by Wm. Belt, of that State. It is being grown largely as a fancy berry; large conical berry, the first berry being sometimes very large and very irregular.

PLANT, the plant is large and strong one, but rusts sometimes very badly; is quite productive.

WM. BELT.

FRUIT, large to very large, conical; bright scarlet in color, medium in firmness.

FLESH, pink slashed with white, nice mild flavor, fair quality.

SEASON medium to late.

ADAPTATION. Seems to do well in many different soils thus well suited for all sections. S.

WM. BELT.

WILLIAMS.

(Perfect Blossom.)

WILLIAMS.

This is a great favorite, in some localities prefer it to all others; it has some serious faults.

ORIGIN, a seedling from Sharpless, of Canadian origin, by Mr. Williams of Burford, Ont.

PLANT, is a vigorous grower, runners abundant, short, thus placing plants close together, rusts badly in some places; is quite productive.

FRUIT, is large, crimson, seeds imbedded, does not color well at the point, having white tip, berry firm.

FLESH, red, fair quality; the berry sometimes hollow.

SEASON, Medium to late.

ADAPTATION, seems to do well in moist soils, especially when it does not rust.   S.

WOOLVERTON.

(Perfect Blossom.)

Originated in Ontario by John Little, of Granton, about 1889, and sent out by him, it is now widely known as one of the best, not perhaps as productive as some, but the fruit is of the largest size and quite firm.

PLANT, a strong healthy grower; plant is large and deep rooted; dark in color; makes runners freely and root easily.

FRUIT, very large, as large as Bubach; crimson red seeds; flesh, red and solid.

FLESH, red, milk flavor, no acid.

SEASON, late.

ADAPTATION. It seems to do well everywhere; good accounts of it coming from all quarters.

S.

WOOLVERTON.

QUINCES.

ORANGE (OR APPLE.)

The leading market variety of Quince in Canada. Previous to 1870, this and the Angers were the only varieties of quinces known in Ontario, the former as a stock for budding dwarf pears, and the latter as a standard market variety. The Orange quince succeeds admirably in the Niagara peninsula, ripening well, taking on a beautiful rich golden color, and reaching a

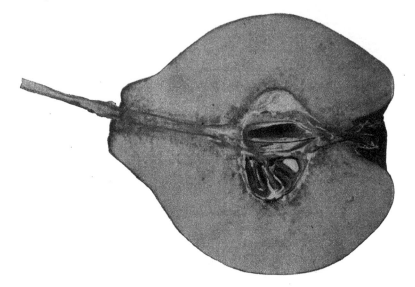

fine large size, either on clay or sandy loam. In old days this variety brought $6 or $7 per barrel in Toronto market, but in 1897 twenty-five and thirty cents per twelve quart basket was a common price.

ORIGIN, Southern Europe.

TREE, a slow grower, bushy, seldom attaining a height of more than twelve or fifteen feet ; hardy, will endure neglect but responds well to good cultivation and manure ; delights in moist land, without standing water ; fairly productive.

FRUIT, large and weighing from eight ounces to a pound ; form, somewhat like an apple, but with protuberance about the stem instead of a depression ; skin, golden yellow at maturity, with often a little greenish or russett color about the stem, which is set in a narrow cavity; calyx, large segment, which are leaf like, in a large deep, corrugated basin.

FLESH, tender : flavor good.

SEASON, October 1st to 15th, sometimes end of September.

VALUE, limited demand in Canadian markets.

CHAMPION.

A variety introduced betwen 1880 and 1890, probably raised from the Orange quince.
It grows to a larger size than the Orange, and ripens later. Season about the 20th of October.

This variety usually ripens well in Southern Ontario, but would be too late farther north.
Where it succeeds it is of more value for market than the Orange, on account of its large size, and freedom from blemishes. Not yet tested sufficiently for a full description.

FRUIT EXPERIMENT STATIONS OF ONTARIO.

MEETINGS OF THE BOARD OF CONTROL

At the annual meeting of the Board, held at Zimmerman House, Waterloo, December 14th, 1897, it was decided to send zinc labels to each experimenter for out-door use, because lead pencil marks on zinc are almost indelible ; to make a full exhibit at the Industrial ; and to send Prof. Hutt and Mr. L. Woolverton as a delegation to Algoma to consider the advisability of locating a fruit experiment station there.

Other business details were also considered.

On Monday, the 21st of February, the Board met at Toronto for the consideration of the estimates for 1898, the whole amounting to about $2,600. New forms were agreed upon for the experimenters.

It was also agreed that in view of the great number of varieties of trees and plants already distributed to the stations, the planting in the spring of 1898 should be confined to novelties such as are being offered in Canada, and to such stock as may be needed to fill vacancies.

On Friday, the 18th of November, 1898, the Board of Control met at the Walker House, Toronto. After reading of the minutes and correspondence, and other routine business, the report of the Visitation Committee to Algoma was read by Prof. Hutt, who explained that the report was a joint one, the part referring to St. Joseph Island having been written by Mr. L. Woolverton and that about the mainland by himself.

ALGOMA AS A FRUIT COUNTRY.

Your Visitation Committee left Toronto for Algoma on Saturday morning, July 23rd, having first called on the Minister of Agriculture for detailed instructions.

Reaching Richard's Landing, on St. Joseph Island, on Monday, the 25th, we were met by three representative men of the section, viz., G. Hamilton, Crown Lands Agent ; Chas. Young, President of the Farmers' Institute, and Mr. Richards, after whom the village was named.

About three days were spent on St. Joseph Island, in order to study its capabilities for fruit growing. Almost every orchard we could hear of was visited, and inquiries made regarding the varieties that are grown, and the success attending them. We found the soil on the island quite varied, from heavy clay to clay loam on the north side, to sand and sandy loam on the southwestern side. There is a good deal of limestone in the soil, and it responds well to good cultivation and manure. Although the ther. mometer often drops to 40 below zero in the winter, there are very few summer frosts, and the heavy snows of winter are a wonderful protection to the roots of trees, all of which showed a vigorous healthy growth, especially on the clay loam where well cultivated.

The forest growth on the island is vigorous, consisting largely of poplar, maple, larch, arbor vitæ, beech, basswood, yellow birch, oak, white spruce, hazel, etc., the latter being heavily laden with nuts; but the reckless destruction of forests prevails here as everywhere else in Algoma.

The Pin cherry grows wild everywhere and produces its small red fruit in great abundance. The High Bush cranberry is common, also two or three varieties of goose. berries, wild currants, red and black, and red raspberries. Summer frosts do not prevail,

7 F.S.

that of July 10th, which did so much mischief even in southern Ontario, was not felt except on low ground in St. Joseph Island. Of course the summer season is shorter, and only the earlier varieties of grapes could be expected to ripen, but the heavy snows, which cover the ground the whole winter, have much to do with the present capabilities of the island for fruit growing. This condition of things may be largely changed unless the people are instructed in the importance of forest protection which prevents the snow from being drifted off the land. As it is now, the ground seldom freezes, owing to the great depth of snow protection.

The following is a report of some of the orchards visited, and the varieties which have proven hardy in the island :

CHAS. YOUNG, Richard's Landing. The soil is clay loam, on high land, overlooking the lake. Mr. Young showed us fine trees of Transparent, Duchess, Alexander, Whitney No. 20, Charlemoff, Walbridge, and Longfield, all heavily laden with fruit. The trees were about five years planted, and so far were uninjured by winter, though often much affected with borer.

Mr. Young also had Late Kentish, Early Richmond and Ostheim cherry trees doing well and bearing abundantly. He has even planted a Yellow Spanish, and the tree has endured one winter, but it remains to be seen whether its fruit buds will endure the winter. Of grapes he has ripened the Janesville and found it quite productive.

Mr. Young has one hundred acres in his farm, and has a fine piece of ground sloping down toward the water, which he intends to devote to fruit culture.

A. RAINES, Sailors' Encampment. On the west side we visited the orchard of Mr. A. Raines, on the slope toward the west passage between the Sault and Mackinac. At his door we found dahlias in bloom, July 26th, and a tree loaded with common blue plums. Mr. Raines has clay land, well manured, and he has about one hundred apple trees, five years planted, growing vigorously, many of them laden with fruit, especially the Transparent, Duchess, Wealthy, Wolf River and Haas He said the Hyslop does particularly well, and one season he sold $8 worth of fruit off a single tree, twenty-five years old. He showed us a Kieffer pear tree making vigorous growth. He had planted trees of Baldwin, Greening, Spy and King but had found them a complete failure, not being sufficiently hardy.

WM. DUNN. On the south side we visited Mr. Wm. Dunn, whose farm is situated on a highland overlooking Mud Lake. Mr. Dunn's father settled in this section about eighteen years ago, and had united with our Fruit Growers' Association of Ontario, whose literature has been received every year since. Bringing a taste for horticulture from Scotland, he had at once begun gardening, and had made the mountain side attractive with fruits and flowers, now more or less neglected. Mr. Dunn says, however, that, if he could be relieved of his farm work, he could make some money growing fruit for the Sault, if only there were a nearer landing for the steamers. As it is, he loses the best part of a week whenever he takes a yacht load of fruit to that market. He has tested a good many varieties and finds the following to endure the winter and produce fruit :

Apples. Transparent, Duchess, Wealthy, Alexander, Golden, Russet, Walbridge, Scott's Winter, Pewaukee, Charlemov, Borsdorf, Gipsy Girl.

Plums Duane's Purple, Moore's Arctic and Lombard.

Cherries. Early Richmond and Ostheim.

Grapes. Janesville, Lindley and Delaware, all of which had ripened.

Pears. Flemish Beauty.

Mr. Dunn's apple trees were badly affected with the bark louse, which seems to increase very rapidly on them.

A. EDDY, Hilton. On the east side of the Island we visited the orchard of Mr. A. Eddy, of Hilton, whose son attended the O. A. C., Guelph, session of 1897-8, and who has six hundred acres of land on the Island. He planted an orchard of two hundred trees in 1897, all of which are growing well. The varieties are Duchess, Wealthy, Golden Russet, Snow, Longfield, Stark, Ben Davis and Scott's Winter.

ALGOMA AS A FRUIT COUNTRY.

Residence of Mr. Chas. Young, Richard's Landing, St. Joseph Island, Algoma.

Plot of ground at Richard's Landing proposed for Experiment Station—belonging to Chas. Young.

Throughout the Island we found a good many more small orchards, from fifty to one hundred young trees—for example, that of

Mr. A. CLIFFORD, on the A Line, who has two hundred and fifty acres, four and a half miles from Richard's landing. Here, in addition to the varieties above mentioned, we found the Montreal Peach apple in bearing, the Lombard plum heavily laden, though only two years planted, the Weaver plum, and, to our surprise, also the Shipper's Pride and the Abundance. The latter has withstood the climate for two years. The other plums were five years planted.

Mr. REESOR has a tiny orchard under good cultivation. In addition to the apples, he has the Lombard plum, Early Richmond, Vladimir and Ostheim cherries, and the Delaware, Niagara, Concord and Moore's Early grapes.

Near by we saw the finest black currants we ever saw, grown by Mr. Fish on clay soil. Never elsewhere have we seen this currant so productive, and we would judge that this fruit would be very profitable.

Messrs. AMOS and JOHN CHEER have heavy clay farms two miles north of Richard's landing, and have each about one hundred apple trees two years planted, some of which are already showing fruit. The varieties are Transparent, Duchess, Wealthy, Gideon, Stark, Walbridge, Ben Davis and Mann.

One of the peculiarities of the apple in this northern region is its earliness of bearing, probably resulting from a slower habit of growth than with us.

The great drawback to the fruit interests of the Island is the ignorance concerning suitable varieties. During the last fifteen years, thousands of dollars have been squandered on the Baldwin, Greening, King, Spy, etc., varieties altogether too tender, and which succumbed to the cold within a year or two after planting. Unscrupulous men have also done much harm, palming off novelties upon a too confiding public. The Deacon Jones apple, for example, was largely sold for 75 cents per tree throughout St. Joseph Island as a most desirable variety, and just now another kind is being pushed called the Arctic ; both untested varieties.

All agree in hoping that a fruit experiment station may be established to save them from such waste of money, and direct them in their future purchases.

On the mainland, or north shore as the islanders call it, we went over a central stretch of country about fifty miles long, from Bruce Mines east through Thessalon, Sowerby and Iron Bridge to Dean Lake Station—wheeling through country lying some distance back from the lake. Generally speaking the mainland is not so well settled or improved as St. Joseph Island, although a large portion of the land is evidently well adapted to farming. The principal crops grown are hay, oats, peas, spring wheat and barley. Nearly all of these were looking well. At the time of our visit farmers were in the midst of haying, which goes to show that their season is two or three weeks later than that in the southern parts of the Province.

The people, as a rule, seemed contented with their lot and prospects, and were hopeful for improvements. In the matter of barns many of them are ahead of their friends in the older settlements. Most of the barns now being put up are large and built on modern plans.

The soil on the mainland is not much unlike that on St. Joseph Island, but is generally inclined to be somewhat heavier. Just here it may be well to mention that the tourist passing through on the steamers and seeing the rock-bound shores, is apt to get a very wrong idea of the value of the land in this country for farming. There is, of course, plenty of rocky and hilly land to be seen inland, but there are also great stretches of fertile level land and rich valleys.

Some idea of the nature of the soil may be had from the character of the timber growing upon it. In the lowlands may be seen miles of tamarac, white spruce and white cedar. The original pine, for a number of miles back, has been cut off, and may be seen in immense lumber piles on almost every northern wharf. On the best loamy high lands the hard maple grows plentifully along with white birch and oak, but the tree seen most abundantly is the white poplar. This has sprung up wherever the original timber has been burned off.

Forest fires have been one of the greatest depredators in this northern section. The waste of valuable timber through fire has been deplorable, and even yet there is more or less waste from this cause every year. At one place we rode alongside of a fire about half a mile long, which had just started that morning.

The hazel, which is abundant everywhere on St. Joseph Island, is not so abundant on the mainland, but in its place may be seen acres upon acres of blueberries, the principal fruit crop of the Indian.

The climate on the mainland bordering the shore is not unlike that of St. Joseph Island, but as we go inland it becomes more severe. We were told that the thermometer often registered ten degrees colder on the mainland than on that island. Forty degrees below zero, however, is not an unusual temperature for either the mainland or islands.

One point claimed for the winters in this section is that they are steady, and that there is no January thaw and attendant loss of snow, which is often so injurious to vegetation in the more southern parts of the Province. The snow comes early, and is usually so deep that the ground beneath is seldom frozen. This naturally makes the country well adapted to the growing of strawberries and the low-growing bush fruits. The late spring and early fall frosts, which so frequently do great damage in other parts of the Province, are said to be not at all common in this district. We were surprised that none of the effects of the frost of July 10th, which did so much damage in inland parts of the Province this year, were to be seen in this northern section. In many gardens were to be seen good growths of potatoes, tomatoes, squash, cucumbers, etc., which would naturally be the first to show the effects of a frost.

In growing the fruit trees—apple, pear, plum and cherry—the settlers on the mainland have not as a rule attempted so much as their neighbors on the island. Many of them have not yet planted anything, but we found orchards enough to convince us that they can easily grow plenty of the more hardy varieties for their own use and home market, and probably in time also for the north-west market.

Most of the trees planted have been put out within the past four or five years, the extent of each orchard usually being from two to four dozen apple trees, and two or three odd trees of pears, plums and cherries.

Two of the finest orchards found in our travels were adjoining each other at Sowerby, several miles inland and about twelve miles east of Thessalon. In each of these were about 200 trees, which had been planted about six years ago. Among the varieties of apples in these orchards were Duchess, Transparent, Astrachan, Alexander, Wealthy, Snow, Wolf River, Gipsy Girl, Talman Sweet, Scott's Winter, Gideon and Longfield, and Martha and Whitney crabs. The Duchess, Transparent, Wealthy, Gideon and Longfield appear to do extra well in this section, and wherever seen were usually heavily loaded with fruit. Even little trees two or three years planted were to be seen bending under their load. In some cases the fruit had been thinned to save the trees, but more often the trees were propped to save the fruit. In one of these orchards we were surprised to find a Gueii plum tree, five years planted, quite as large and as heavily loaded as one would expect to find in a southern orchard. Mr. B A. Hagan and Henry McMillan, owners of these orchards, have promised to send a small collection of samples for exhibition at the winter meeting of the Fruit Growers' Association, to show what apples can be grown in Algoma

Near Iron Bridge, about twenty miles east of Thessalon, we found a young man, David Tait, who has started a nursery for the propagation of the hardier varieties of fruits for this section. He has two or three acres in nursery, and is budding and grafting his own trees on imported stocks He has a good collection of the hardy varieties of apples, pears, plums and cherries. The trees were well cared for and looked thrifty and healthy. We were pleased to find this, because many in this northern section who have bought trees from the agents of southern nurseries have been greatly disappointed with the results owing to the difficulty of getting trees in good condition. A nursery in their own district, supplying good trees of the hardy varieties, will be a great help towards successful fruit growing in Algoma.

All spoken to on the subject, were agreed that an experiment station, which would give them some idea of the most suitable varieties for this northern section, would be a great boon to all settlers. The general impression was that St. Joseph Island would be as suitable and as central a spot as could be selected, and that the results obtained there would be of value to all of the Algoma district.

L. WOOLVERTON,
H. L. HUTT.

The report was received and adopted, and it was agreed to recommend to the Department of Agriculture the advisability of locating a fruit experiment station at Richard's Landing.

A letter from the Hon. John Dryden was read suggesting the advisability of testing hardy fruits on the Pioneer Farm at Wabigoon. It was agreed to adopt this suggestion, and utilize the Pioneer Farm for this purpose.

INSPECTION OF THE ONTARIO FRUIT EXPERIMENT STATIONS.

BY PROF. H. L. HUTT, OFFICIAL VISITOR, O.A.C., GUELPH.

Since the establishment of the first stations five years ago, it has devolved upon me, as the representative from the College, to make an annual tour of inspection to each station, and to report upon the same to the Board of Control.

In previous reports I have made mention of the kinds of fruit which are being most extensively grown at each station, of the nature of the soil, of the capabilities of the men for carrying on the work, of the additional planting which has been done, and the care and attention which have been given to the work. Many of these points need not again be touched on. In this report, therefore, I have dealt more particularly with the progress of the work at each station, with the care taken of the stock sent for test, and with the condition of the crop upon which the experimenter has to base his report.

Previous to the enactment excluding American nursery stock the stations had been pretty well supplied with all the leading and promising varieties to be had from American as well as Canadian nurserymen. Consequently there was but little additional planting done this year at any of the stations, the little stock that was planted coming altogether from Canadian nurseries.

As far as possible each station was visited at the most opportune time for seeing at maturity the fruits specially under test. On account of the close attention which had to be given to our own experiments during the strawberry season I had not an opportunity of getting away to see Mr. Stevenson's plantation. Mr. Woolverton, however, spent a day with him and took photographs of a number of his leading varieties.

All particulars as to the value of different varieties I have left to be dealt with in the reports of the experimenters, where they can be more fully and properly given. I shall mention each station in the order in which they were visited during the season, beginning with the raspberries early in July, and ending with the grapes during the latter part of September.

THE LAKE HURON STATION.

Visited July 12th, 1898. At this station we have now under test a large collection of varieties of raspberries, and in addition quite a number of varieties of apples and plums, most likely to be of value in the section. Mr. Sherrington has been propagating from his stock of raspberries and setting out a new plantation, having a 20-foot row of each variety To prevent the suckering varieties from mixing, he is alternating these in the row with those which are propagated from tips.

Some varieties, like Shaffer, Gregg, Smith's Giant and Superlative, were more or less winter-killed last winter. Such points will be more fully noted in Mr. Sherrington's report, along with a record of the yields from the different varieties under test.

All of the plum trees, among which are several of the Japanese varieties, have so far come through the winters uninjured. These, and the young apple trees sent for trial, are making a good growth.

In the bearing apple orchard, the crop this year was light. The Northern Spys, however, were carrying a fair load.

All trees and plants sent to this station are being well cared for.

THE SIMCOE SUB-STATION.

Visited July 22nd, 1898. The collection of gooseberries under test at this station is not large, but it includes most of the American varieties and a number of the most promising English varieties. For the past two seasons Mr. Spillett has been having a very severe fight with the mildew, and in spite of repeated sprayings with the Bordeaux mixture it is still very bad on many of the English varieties. So far Pearl and Downing are the most satisfactory varieties in the collection.

THE GEORGIAN BAY STATION.

Visited August 3rd, 1898.—At this station we now have a fine collection of plums, made up of about 140 varieties. Eighteen of these have been bearing since the station was established. Thirty-five varieties put out three years ago are now beginning bearing. Among those most heavily loaded this year were Burbank, Abundance, Arch Duke, Saunders and Golden Prolific.

In another year or two the greater part of this large collection of varieties will be in bearing, when some valuable reports may be looked for.

So far all varieties of plums, as well as a number of varieties of pears and peaches, have come through the winter uninjured.

Mr. Mitchell is a first-class cultivator, and all of his trees have been well cared for.

On account of the severe drouth up till the time of my visit, it had been useless to sow crimson clover for the fertilizer experiment in the orchard, but after the rain at that time it would be sown at once.

THE SIMCOE STATION.

Visited August 4th, 1898. This being the most northern of all the stations it was thought wise to send here for trial a number of other fruits besides the specialties. Accordingly we have here a number of varieties of pears, plums, apricots, and a general collection of the small fruits, such as currants, gooseberries, raspberries, blackberries and strawberries.

The apple crop through this section this year is light, the winter varieties bearing little or nothing, but as usual there is a beautiful crop of Duchess and Wealthy, every tree of these varieties being heavily loaded.

The cherry crop was all off before the time of my visit, but Mr. Caston is much pleased with a number of the new varieties which begin bearing this year, and which will be dealt with in his report.

All the young trees set out four years ago, when this station was first established, have made a good growth, and a number of varieties, particularly among the plum trees, are beginning to bear.

The small fruits are now in full bearing, and will be reported on in Mr. Caston's report. The cultivation and attention given is all that could be desired.

THE BURLINGTON STATION.

Visited August 6th, 1898. With reference to this station we might say that it is as well stocked and as well managed as any fruit farm to be found in the country. Besides the raspberries, blackberries and currants, upon which Mr. Peart has been reporting, he has a good collection of varieties of grapes, plums, pears, peaches and apples.

As this station is situated in a section where fruits of all kinds are extensively grown, and where the conditions are quite different to those on the southern side of the lake, and from many of the other experiment stations, we think it would be well to enlarge Mr. Peart's specialty and ask him to report also on grapes, pears and plums.

His annual allowance should, of course, be proportionately increased, as he is at present barely paid for the full and excellent reports which he has been sending in.

Careful records have been made during the year of raspberries, blackberries and currants, a full account of which will appear in Mr. Peart's report.

THE SOUTHWESTERN STATION.

Visited August 26th, 1898. Mr. Hilborn's peach orchard is now probably one of the largest and finest in the Dominion, being over 100 acres in extent, and containing trees of over 150 varieties.

The peach crop in that section this year was said to be only about half an average crop, but, with the excellent cultivation given, Mr. Hilborn's orchard was doing much better than that. Very few of the young trees in the experimental plots are yet in bearing, although a great number of them should begin to bear next year.

The report from this station this year will, therefore, be based more particularly upon the yields from trees which were planted before the station was established.

THE EAST CENTRAL STATION.

Visited August 28th, 1898. The crop of apples and pears in this section this year was good, and Mr. Huggard's trees were generally well loaded.

The cultivation in the bearing orchard has not in the past been uniform. Part of the orchard has been given bare cultivation ; another part has been cropped with roots ; and a portion of it has been in sod for several years. Mr. Huggard is now convinced that early, clean cultivation is the best, and intends to give this in the future, using crimson clover as a cover crop, the seed of which will be sown about the beginning of August.

The young trees set out in the experimental orchard have been well cared for and have made a good growth. Some of them are already bearing a few specimens of fruit.

THE BAY OF QUINTE STATION.

Visited August 29th, 1898. At this station we have the largest collection of varieties to be found in the Province, and the reports from here should be of value to apple growers over a wide section of the country.

The young trees in the experimental orchard have been well cared for and have made a good growth. The older orchard has also been given first class cultivation all summer, but the scab came on very early in the season and the foliage on many varieties were so injured that they bore but little fruit. On account of the extremely severe drouth in this section for about two months all of the trees had suffered severely, and in many cases the fruit was not half its usual size. The varieties making the best show were Duchess, Alexander and Ontario. All the trees of these varieties were heavily loaded with very fair fruit.

Some of the grafts of new varieties put in three and four years ago are now beginning to bear.

THE ST. LAWRENCE STATION.

Visited August 31st, 1898. The young trees sent here during the past two years were planted in good rich soil, have been well taken care of, and have made a remarkable growth. So far most of the varieties have come through the winter uninjured.

In his bearing apple orchard Mr. Jones had a nice crop of Snows and Scarlet Pippins. There was some scab, but it had been pretty well held in check by spraying. The Scarlet Pippin was making a fine showing, and seemed less liable to scab than the Snow.

There had been more rain in this section, and the country looked much better than further west.

THE NIAGARA STATION.

Visited September 20th, 1898. At this station we now have a large collection of the more tender fruits, including peaches, plums, cherries, apricots, nectarines, grapes, etc., and a number of the most promising new varieties of nut trees, such as Japanese chestnuts, English walnuts, filberts, etc.

Everything at this station receives the very best attention. The trees have all been well cared for, and most of them have made a good growth. The nut trees have, so far, been the most unsatisfactory to transplant and grow. Mr. Burrell has been budding a number of the Japanese chestnuts upon seedlings of our native variety.

Very few of the experimental trees are yet old enough to bear fruit, but in the bearing orchards and vineyard there was a fine crop of fruit.

Crimson clover, as a cover crop in the orchards, has always given excellent results in this section, and Mr. Burrell usually succeeds in getting a good catch of it.

THE CHERRY STATION.

Visited September 21st, 1898. The experimental cherry orchard set out three years ago now presents a fine appearance. The trees have made a fine growth, and promise well for fruiting another year. Some varieties of the Morello type began bearing this year. Full notes on the growth and fruiting will be found in Mr. Woolverton's report.

THE WENTWORTH STATION.

Visited September 22nd, 1898. The young experimental vineyard set out here during the past three or four years is now pretty well established. The vines have all been trellised, and are beginning to bear. So far there are but few of the newer varieties that show signs of being equal to the old standard varieties.

In the old vineyards there was as usual an excellent crop. The cultivation and care given are all that could be desired. Some valuable reports on grapes may now be looked for from this station.

REPORT OF SOUTHWESTERN STATION, LEAMINGTON.

The peach orchards in Essex county gave but a partial crop of fruit this season. The trees ripened up both wood and fruit buds to perfection last autumn. They came through the past mild winter in perfect condition, and gave promise of a very large yield of fruit at the blooming period. Every variety was full of blossoms, none of which appeared to have been injured by the winter. The weather during spring was unusually cold for a length of time, thus retarding vegetation to a considerable extent. This condition of the weather was conducive to the growth of the curl leaf, and much injury resulted from this cause. Some varieties were injured much more than others. The same kinds suffered much more in some portions of the orchard than in other parts. As an instance, Barnard's Early in the south-western part of the orchard was injured to such an extent that they produced only about a dozen baskets to 100 trees. In the north-eastern portion of the same orchard, sixty roads away, 300 trees of that variety planted at the same time (six years) and receiving the same treatment throughout, produced a full crop of the finest fruit. The former lot of trees were on a somewhat higher elevation, and more exposed to the cold south west wind. This was the only cause I could detect to make the difference between the two lots of trees.

Among the varieties most injured are Champion, Elberta, Tyhurst, Lewis, Early Michigan and several others nearly as much affected. Young trees, three to four years planted, of nearly all kinds, were sufficiently injured to cause them to drop their fruit. Very little fruit was grown on trees less than five to six years planted. Among the kinds least injured may be named, Alexander Early, Rivers, Fitzgerald, Golden Drop, Hales' Early, Lemon, Smock, Longhurst, Hill's Chili and Salway.

During the time Early Rivers and Hales' Early were ripening the weather was warm, wet and showery, hence much injury resulted from the peach rot (Monilia).

As stated above, trees not more than four years planted produced no fruit, therefore those planted for experimental purposes were not old enough to produce fruit this season. All varieties have ripened up well this autumn and go into winter quarters in good shape.

Alexander is the first to ripen. It is very productive and has been planted in such large numbers in all peach-growing districts that the supply is greater than the demand. It being a cling stone and put on the market in such large quantities it injures the sale of later and better sorts. Those early cling-stone varieties are not good until they have been thoroughly ripened on the tree, and then they are not firm enough to carry to a distant market. For this reason most of them are sent to market in a half ripe condition, and are fit only for cooking, and for this purpose they are then of but poor quality. It would appear to be a mistake to plant many of those white fleshed early cling stone kinds. No doubt it would pay to take out a large portion of those already planted and substitute later and better varieties. The demand now is for large yellow flesh, highly colored sorts. Of this type the following may be named as among the most satisfactory market varieties, named in order of ripening : Crane's Yellow, St. John, Brigden, Crawford Early, Fitzgerald, Yellow Rareripe, Hinman, New Prolific, Engol's Mammoth, Longhurst, Late Crawford, Smock, Banner and Salway. The last named is too late, except for highly favored localities.

The Elberta is a very fine market peach, but has been so badly injured with curl leaf the past two seasons that it has had hard work to live.

Golden Drop has been one of the most profitable kind this season. It is only of medium size and not highly colored. It, however, produces such large crops of medium, even sized round clean fruit, that for canning or evaporating it has few equals.

Wager is a good peach when grown on healthy young trees. As the trees grow older they are liable to overbear, when the fruit spots and cracks to such an extent that it is of little value.

Lemon Free has in the past been one of the most satisfactory kinds grown. This season the fruit dropped bodily just before it was ripe enough to gather. This may be the result of the injury done by the curl leaf. While there was not sufficient injury to cause the fruit to drop while it was small, the indications are that the premature dropping at time of ripening was caused from that fungus.

Crosby gave a good yield of medium to large size fruit, of fine appearance and good quality on trees five and six years planted. On older trees it has a tendency to overbear, then the fruit is not so large or well colored.

Hinman is a very promising yellow flesh variety, ripening just after the Early Craw-ford. This is equally well colored, of as good quality, more hardy and will average larger than that old standard sort named above. This sort is well worth an extended trial.

Brigden is another of the Crawford type, ripens a little earlier, larger and equal to and surpassing that sort in all respects. Worthy of an extended trial.

Banner is a new variety originating in this (Essex) county. The fruit is large and round, skin bright yellow with red cheek, flesh fine grain and of the best quality of any variety of its season, which is with or just after Smock. The tree is hardy and very productive, one of the most promising late market varieties grown in this its native home. Well worthy of an extended trial.

W. W. HILBORN,
Experimenter.

REPORT OF NIAGARA STATION, ST. CATHARINES.

I beg to submit the following report of the work carried on at this station during the past season. As none of the trees planted on the experimental plots fruited this year, I am unable to present anything in the way of description of varieties. With the exception of the chestnuts, the trees generally have made a good growth, and under favorable conditions a large number of varieties should bear fruit next year.

I had intended to carry on again some experimental work in the thinning of peaches, but the failure of the crop rendered such work impossible. Last year the results of some experimental work against the peach ' borer ' were included in the report, and below will be found some additional notes on the same subject.

As the question of crimson clover is an important one for the horticulturist of the Niagara peninsula, I have embodied in this report the result of the work done here with this clover.

There were added to the experimental blocks this year three Japanese Walnuts, all of which have made a thrifty growth, also three seedling peaches from Georgia, and three of the variety ' Connecticut '; also, one each of the following varieties of plums : Large Golden, Lombard Improved, Stark's Gage, Normands, Coe's Violet, Bleeker's Gage, Moyer Seedling, and Glass Seedling No. 2.

LEAF CURL.—Owing partly to unfavorable climatic conditions and partly to the disease known as " curl leaf " the peach crop of this section has been largely a failure this year. Smocks and Late Crawfords yielded a fair crop in some orchards, but most varieties were very light indeed. Careful notes were taken here at the time "curl leaf" was at its worst, with the view of ascertaining what varieties were chiefly affected. The notes are the results of an examination of three trees of each variety, the trees being in their third year.

Very Badly Attacked. Crosby, Champion, Elberta, Early Barnard, Honest John, Jacques Rareripe, Golden Drop, Lord Palmerston, Late Crawford, Morris White, Old Mixon, Red Cheek Melocoton, Steven's Rareripe, Stump, Troth's Early, Tyehurst, Yellow St. John, Yellow Rareripe, Wager.

Moderately Attacked. Conkling, Early Crawford, Early Canada, Early Richmond, Fitzgerald, Hortense Rivers, Ostrander Late, Susquehanna.

Slightly Attacked. Early Rivers, Foster, Hale's Early, Hynes' Surprise, Garfield, Longhurst, Smock, Salway, Shumacher, Waterloo, Wheatland, Wonderful. Although a number of peach trees were sprayed with the Bordeaux mixture, partly to determine the effect on the curl leaf fungus, practically no difference was observed between sprayed and unsprayed trees. As a good deal of light has been thrown on this matter by recent investigations at Cornell, and at the Ohio Experiment Station, fresh experiments will be undertaken here next year. Professor Selby, of Ohio, and the assistant botanist at Cornell, have both obtained good results from the use of Bordeaux mixture, applied before the blossoms opened. Professor Craig also informs me that in Pennsylvania, Ohio, and California satisfactory work against leaf curl has been accomplished by the use of lime, and I hope to test this agency also in 1899.

The cherry crop of this district was lighter than usual. Common sour cherries bore a very small crop, and the sweet varieties suffered badly from rot, and were injured to a considerable extent by the black aphis. The better kinds of sour cherries, such as Early Richmond and Montmorency yielded a full crop.

PLUMS.—Plums, with the exception of Lombards, Imperial Gage, Prince's Yellow Gage, and English Damsons, were a failure here.

PEARS.—Pears, with the exception of Sheldon, bore well. Bartlett, Clapp's Favorite, Seckel, Beurre Clairgeau, Beurre Bosc, Duchess d'Angouleme and Lawrence may be especially mentioned.

GRAPES —Grapes were a good crop, and generally a clean sample. The varieties I found most profitable this year were Worden, Roger 44, Roger 9, Delaware and Niagara.

A seedling grape of unusual promise was recently brought to my notice. It is a white seedling of the Brighton, and probably fertilized by Moore's Early, a vine of which was near the parent Brighton Mr. Backus, the originator, lives about a mile from this station. He reports the grape to be ripe at least a week earlier than Moore's Early. The bunch is compact, not shouldered, berries as big as Lady, skin thickish, quality good. Vine not a rank grower, with slender, dark red wood, not unlike Pocklington. A few grapes had been left on the vine till October 10th, and I found no sign of shrivelling or cracking.

SPRAYING EXPERIMENTS.

Grapes—Mildew. Six vines were selected in a row of Brightons, which have always been more or less been subject to mildew. Two were left as check vines, two were sprayed with the 4, 4, 40 formula of Bordeaux mixture, and the remaining two received a light sprinkling of sulphur. There were three applications of both sulphur and Bordeaux mixture, the first on June 6th just before the blossoms opened, the second on June 24th, the third on July 9th.

The fruit was picked with following results :—

	Total grapes.	Badly mildewed.	Slightly mildewed.
Sprayed vines :—	24 lbs , 8 oz.	6 oz.	9 oz.
Sulphured vines :—	25 lbs.	....	5 oz.
Unsprayed :—	35 lbs., 8 oz.	3 lbs , 14 oz.	5 lbs., 4 oz.

The "slightly mildewed" were marketable, but not first-class. There was no brown rot on these vines, only the powdery mildew, against which sulphur would of course be far more effective than against the "downy" mildew. Lumping both "badly" and "slightly" mildewed, and reducing it to a percentage basis, the result would be—without going into decimals —

Sprayed :—96 per cent. clean ; Sulphured :—99 per cent.; Unsprayed :—74 per cent.

Cherries—for Rot. The May Duke variety was selected for experiment. Formula used "4, 4, 40," with the addition of 4 oz. of Paris green. Three sprayings were given on April 28th, May 31st and June 9th.

	Total weight.	Sound cherries.	Unsound.	Weight of good fruit.
Sprayed tree—	54 lbs.	4,058	2,020	39 lbs.
Unsprayed tree—	47 lbs.	2,974	2,385	27 lbs., 8 oz

Sprayed trees :—72 per cent. sound ; Unsprayed trees :—58 per cent. sound.

If four sprayings instead of three had been given better results would probably have been secured. Climatic conditions were extremely favorable for the spread of the monilia fungus this year on cherries and plums.

Plums. These were sprayed four times, but on Imperial Gage and Lombards the rot was exceptionally bad. A marked difference, however, will be noticed in the treated trees.

Imperial Gage :—

	No. unsound.	No. good.	Weight of sound fruit.
Sprayed—	330	465	28 lbs.
Unsprayed—	596	246	17 lbs.

Sprayed tree :—Sound, 71 per cent.; Unsprayed tree :—Sound, 41 per cent.

The spraying has also had a marked effect on the foliage of the trees. · At the present date (Oct. 18th) the sprayed trees retain nearly all the foliage, while those untreated have been practically bare of leaves for two weeks.

INSECTS.

Pear Slug (Selandria cerasi). Either from climatic causes, or an abundance of parasites, there was practically no sound brood of this injurious insect last year. This is probably the reason for the scarcity of the pest this year. I have not observed any serious injury from its work in this section.

Aphidæ. The currant aphis and black aphis of the cherry were both destructive during the past season, though the attacks of the latter were not so severe as in 1897. Good results were obtained here from a whale oil soap solution, 1 pound to 7 gallons. The solution is most satisfactorily made when the water is very hot. I would strongly urge those who have valuable sweet cherries to make an application even stronger than the one I mention before the blossoms open. It is an impossibility to thoroughly control this insect when it once gets established inside the leaf.

Peach Borer (Sannina exitiosa).—In the report of 1897 will be found the details of a number of experiments carried out against this enemy to peach trees. It was shown that the moths do not emerge in this latitude till about July 15th, and that eggs are laid from that time till well on in October. It was also demonstrated that no washes, except those of cement, will remain on the trees long enough to prevent the moth ovipositing. For this reason only the cement and skim milk wash was used this year. The use of paper wrapping was successful last season, but the slight additional expense and labour in putting them on, as compared with the washes, led me to discard them this year. There is also danger of " girdling " the trees by the wire or string with which they are tied on.

The cement and skim milk was applied to 45 trees this year on July 11th, all borers having been first removed. The trees were of various ages from three years to twelve years. On October 7th an examination was made and the wash found to be in fairly good shape. There were found—

On treated trees (45) :—Two very small borers evidently not very long hatched, one in a small cavity where the cement had failed to penetrate and the other where the wash had recently cracked.

On untreated trees (45) :—Nine borers were found, most of them half grown, and a considerable amount of damage had been effected.

The peach-borer has not been plentiful this season in the orchards here, otherwise I feel confident that results would have been still more marked. On the whole, I believe the cement wash to be the most satisfactory application that we yet know of to repel this destructive insect. Professor J. B Smith of New Jersey writes, under date October 14th : "The cement has been used quite considerably in our State this year, and, in general, with very good results." In making the wash it might be well to add enough crude carbolic acid to give a decided odor, the scent of carbolic being repugnant to a large number of insects.

CRIMSON CLOVER.

After an experience of four years with this clover, during which time it has been sown on plots of various sizes, from a third of an acre to two acres in extent, embracing different kinds of soil, I feel like strongly urging its claims on the fruit growers of this section.   It provides the cheapest possible way of obtaining a large and valuable supply of humus and nitrogen which our fruit lands too often lack, and, in spite of occasional failure, I am convinced that it would pay to sow as much ground as possible every year.   Last year a series of plots were experimented with, some of which were treated with manure, others with fertiliser, some with no manure of any kind, and some with crimson clover in full bloom plowed under.   Corn and potatoes were planted, and, though the details (published in the Montreal Weekly *Star* for July 5, 1898,) are too lengthy to insert here, I may say that the results were highly satisfactory, as showing the fertilising value of this plant.   With the exception of sowings in 1895 I have had no total failure during the last four years, and the fall of 1895 was exceptionally dry, and therefore unfavorable.   This year I have three plots on which dense mats of clover stand, from four to eight inches in height now (Oct. 18).   One is on a two acre block from which oats were cut for hay, and clover sown on July 28th ; the second on a strawberry patch turned under directly the fruit was picked, and the third on ground from which old peach trees were removed last winter.   A few conclusions from the four years experience may be helpful to those who wish to sow another year.

1. The best time to sow, if a really good stand is required, is from July 25th to Aug-5th—this is after a trial of dates ranging from the middle of July to the middle of September.

2. This clover is unlikely to succeed on clay soil, chiefly from the lack of moisture at the necessary time.   A sand, or light loam provides the best conditions.

3. Twenty to twenty-five pounds of seed to the acre is none too much—preferably the larger amount.   The seed is nearly twice as big as the ordinary clover, so this quantity is not as much as it seems.

4. It will thrive much better where the soil contains lots of potash and lime, because the micro-organisms, which secrete the nitrogen on the roots, flourish only when there is an abundance of those constituents in the soil.   For this reason we have never failed to get an excellent crop of clover on an old strawberry bed to which we always give a liberal supply of hardwood ashes.

5. In sowing in orchards it is advisable to leave a clear space of at least two feet next the tree rows, otherwise, in plowing under rank crop the following spring, more or less injury will undoubtedly be done to the roots.

6. It will pay to have the seed-bed in fine order, and put a light smoothing harrow or roller over the ground directly after sowing.

I might add, with reference to the chestnuts, that the " Spanish " chestnuts have made a much more vigorous growth this season than heretofore   From other peoples' experience and from that gained here during the last two years, it is evident that chestnuts thrive very slowly after transplanting. I have about eighty seedling chestnuts growing, many of which were budded this fall with Paragon, E. Reliance, and Spanish.   Budding is usually unsuccessful, and I fear not many have taken: those on which the buds fail will be crown grafted next spring, and it is hoped that a careful transplanting of the trees later on may be followed with good results.

MARTIN BURRELL,
Experimenter.

REPORT OF WENTWORTH STATION, WINONA.

The past season has been a favorable one for grape growing, the crop has been a good average, and the vines comparatively free from disease.

GRAPES.—Many of the newer varieties which have fruited are very disappointing, and not worthy of a longer trial than next year, being far inferior in vigour, productiveness, appearance and quality to many of the old reliable kinds.

Eight varieties have not proved true to name. Those marked Berckmans, Concord Chasselas, Concord Muscat and Grein's Golden, are Taylor, a small white wine grape of the Clinton type. Rochester is Catawba, Croton is Pocklington, Triumph is Lindley, and Janesville is Noah. Some of the newer varieties worthy of notice are :

Brilliant, a dark red, medium size, of most excellent flavor ; productive.

Dr. Collier, a black grape of Concord type. Although quite productive, do not think it could be grown as profitably as Concord.

Black Delaware, below medium size, fine quality with heavy blue bloom. The vine lacks vigour.

Eumedal, large clusters ; good flavor ; productive.

Watt, a dark red or maroon color, a little below medium size and of the very finest quality.

Mills, large black, goood quality, productive, and a very long keeper.

Moore's Diamond and *Winchell* are both early, productive white grapes of good quality, and could be profitably grown for market.

Woodruff Red is very handsome, bright red, productive, medium quality.

The annual record, giving yield and selling price, will show that many of the new varieties have produced a light crop for the age of the vine. This may be accounted for by some of them being small, one year old vines when planted. A test of the keeping qualities of about fifty varieties in open baskets in the cellar was made of last season's crop. The Mills far surpassed them all. On April 1st they were in fair marketable condition, firm, crisp and sprightly. Vergennes and Agawam stood next, but had shrivelled and lost considerable flavor. I would recommend planting the Mills for distant markets or for winter use at home.

PEACHES.—The experimental trees made a good growth last season and appeared in fine condition this spring, and bloomed very freely ; but as soon as the leaves appeared they were so badly affected with curl leaf that the crop was very light. Of those very badly affected were Carlisle, Crosby, Willett, Elberta, Jersey Queen and Michigan No. 1.

Those least affected were Stewart, Hilborn, Pratt, Michigan No. 8, Mt. Rose, Foster, Centennial and Early St John. After the weakening effect of the curl leaf the extreme dry weather during the growing season caused the trees to make a short growth. Bowslow's Late, Hilborn and Pratt were the most productive.

PLUMS.—The experimental plum trees have made a good healthy growth. Burbank, Carduc, Ogan and Willard were the only varieties that fruited—Ogan, the earliest, ripening the last of July.

SPRAYING.—Beurre Giffard pears, sprayed before budding, and three times after at intervals of about ten days, with Bordeaux mixture, yielded 20 per cent. more fruit, and 80 per cent. of that free from fungus, while the unsprayed had 30 per cent. clean. The same experiment with Flemish Beauty pears gave a higher percentage of clean fruit, but very little increase in quantity. With the same experiment on Lombard, Washington, Bradshaw and Yellow Egg plums, there was considerable rot on all after the spraying was discontinued, but much worse on the unsprayed trees ; while the leaves remained green and fresh for nearly three weeks longer on the sprayed trees.

M. PETTIT,
Experimenter.

REPORT OF BURLINGTON STATION, FREEMAN.

There are now under cultivation at this station over two hundred and twenty five varieties of fruits. Trees and bushes are, almost without exception, in a healthy, growthy condition. Upon the whole the season was not favorable to the production of much fruit. There were strawberries in abundance; grapes also were a good crop, but with these exceptions the output was very light. An almost unprecedented drouth set in early in June, which practically was unbroken for three months. In consequence fruit suffered severely, both in quality and quantity.

Raspberries and blackberries. The season was very unfavorable for these fruits, many varieties literally drying upon the bushes, and amounting to nothing. Among the former the red varieties stood the ordeal the best, and the black and purple the worst; while, of the latter the Kittatinny, Gainor, Early King and Early Harvest seemed to have the most strength. Wilson Junior is peculiar in its habit of growth. Like the black raspberry, its canes are long and slender, trailing more or less upon the ground; but unlike most raspberries and blackberries it appears to propagate by both tips and suckers. Child's Tree also slightly shows the same tendency. Reliance and London both promise well. The Japan Wineberry canes were frozen to the ground. Young suckers rapidly pushed up from the parent root, and bore some small, very acid scarlet colored fruit, the sole merit of the variety appearing to lie in its novel, oriental appearance. Among the medium and late blackberries the Gainor and Kittatinny took a first place. The Marlboro and Loudon probably fruited the heaviest and withstood the drought the best of all the raspberries.

Currants. The crop was very light, although the quality was good. Cherry still leads among the older varieties, while Raby Castle and Red Victoria promise well. The Belle de St. Giles gave a few remarkably fine large berries. Among the black varieties Champion takes first place, with Naples and Lee's Prolific but little behind. Collin's Prolific thus far has given a rank growth of wood with but little fruit.

Pears were also a light crop of rough uneven quality. The Kieffer only bore heavily. There was very little blight and scab, the Flemish Beauty alone suffering from the latter, The young trees, however, made a fair growth of wood.

Apples, too, were very light and poor in quality. The codling moth was very busy, Baldwins, Greenings and Roxbury Russetts suffering the most. Upon the whole the fruit was distinctly undersized. The Wealthy (a new variety here) is a fine early fall apple, but, unfortunately, like the Anjou Pear, it is not tenacious enough, dropping too easily.

Plums were a light crop of excellent quality. Very rarely indeed have they colored up and been so showy as they were this year. Among the Japan varieties the Satsuma is rather a curiosity, having a dark red flesh and a dull reddish skin. It is an oblong-conical plum, medium to large in size, flesh firm, but of inferior quality. It matures nearly two weeks later than the Burbank, ripening this year about the 7th of September. The Reine Claude is one of the best and most satisfactory plums grown here. There was considerable rot, many varieties having to be picked on the firm side in order to save them.

Peaches were very scarce.

Grapes were a good crop of fine quality. The Concord, Worden, Moore's Early, Moyer, Catawba, Delaware, Vergennes, Niagara and Wyoming Red especially, gave a fine yield of excellent fruit. Insects did but little damage, but the Brighton and Lindley were considerably damaged by mildew.

Fertilizing experiment. The crimson clover sown on one-half acre of apple orchard in 1897, passed through the winter without injury by frost. When vegetation was renewed it grew rapidly and on the first of June was a thick, splendid mass of showy crimson blossoms, beautiful to behold. It stood from fifteen to twenty-four inches high; and was, for about a fortnight, the Eden of bees and all nectar-loving insects. On the

6th of June the plot was sown with 50 lbs. of muriate of potash and 100 lbs. of bone-meal. The clover and fertilizers were then plowed under. The ground was next rolled so as to compact the soil, check the escape of moisture, and accelerate the decomposition of the clover. It was then harrowed lightly, in order to fill up spaces and level generally, then occasional surface cultivation to prevent weed growth and retain moisture. Fourteen lbs. of crimson clover were again sown upon the same plot on the 9th of July, 1898. The seed was harrowed in and the ground rolled, thus completing the circle. The season was too dry and hot for a good catch of seeds, and at this date (Oct. 27th) there is a thin setting of young plants about four inches high.

By next year I hope to be able to give some relative results as between this method and my usual treatment of an orchard.

. A. W. PEART,
Experimenter.

REPORT OF LAKE HURON STATION, WALKERTON.

The season of 1898 has been on the whole a very favorable one for the fruit grower. The apple crop was comparatively light, and very much scattered; but the crop was much better than was expected in the fore part of the season. While some orchards carried a full crop, others had less than a half and some none at all. The failure in the crop was, I think, owing to the heavy rains and cold weather during the blooming period. But the crop has been much better than last year, and the quality far superior. The winter of 1897-1898 was much colder than the winter of 1896-1897, the coldest being 13° below zero in the case of the former, while last winter it dropped to 20° below zero. My report as to hardiness of plants is based on that of 20° below zero, without protection.

There have been added to this experiment station this year eleven varieties of apples nine of pears, one plum, one apricot, one grape, five currants, one gooseberry, making a total of 61 varieties of apples, 28 of plums, 9 of pears, 12 of cherries, 1 apricot, 3 of grapes, 9 of currants, 6 of gooseberries, and 67 of raspberries and blackberries. All trees and plants are growing and doing well with the exception of one or two cherry trees.

INSECTS were very numerous this season, especially the tent and forest caterpillar—so much so that some of the orchards were entirely stripped of their foliage. A great many remedies were resorted to, coal oil being one of them, but to little effect; spraying with Bordeaux and Paris green was perfectly satisfactory. The codling moth has been bad; also one-third of the apples in some orchards are wormy.

FUNGI.—These diseases in their various forms have not been so destructive as last season, the apple spot being the most prevalent There was some anthracnose on raspberries and a little of the red rust. These diseases I never saw here until I received plants for the experimental work. The raspberries were all sprayed twice, once before growth started and again just before blooming, Bordeaux being used at each spraying with satisfactory results.

APPLES —The crop, as stated in report, was very scattered, some varieties, as the King, Blenheim Pippin, Twenty-ounce Pippin, were better than usual and the quality good. The Ontario is still giving great promise of becoming a first-class shipping apple. Fruit, large, of good form and free of spot. A few samples kept in an ordinary cellar until August.

PEARS —Were a fair crop, quality better than last year. The varieties chiefly grown here are Clapp's Favorite, Flemish Beauty, with quite a few other varieties in smaller quantities. Some very good samples of Kieffer and Duchess were shown at some of the fall fairs.

PLUMS.—Were a light crop. A few of the young trees are commencing to bear, but not worth reporting as to yield. All of the Japan varieties stood the winter without

8 F.S.

injury at 20° below zero. The Abundance and Burbank ripened a few plums of large size. The Abundance measured 2 inches long, $1\frac{7}{8}$ wide and $5\frac{1}{2}$ in circumference. It is a very thin skinned plum, and of fine flavor. Burbank is nearly as large as Abundance, but not of as good quality. They are all very vigorous growers, Burbank making over four feet of growth this season.

CHERRIES —Were light but the quality was good. Some of the young trees were full of bloom but failed to set any fruit ; but if the black knot is not looked after and the law made a little more strict there will not be a tree left in this district. It should be made imperative for township councils to appoint inspectors

RASPBERRIES.—The raspberry crop was very good considering the season, which was very dry, there being no rain from the 25th of June until the middle of August. After the crop was harvested quite a number of varieties were damaged by the winter frost, making the yield much less than otherwise would have been.

The Red Raspberries under experiment are grown on the hedge row system. Each variety occupying 18 feet long of row and 2 feet wide, and the yield from the Blackcaps is given in pounds and ounces. Estimating a pound to a box it will be readily under-stoods as to the yield per variety.

All-Summer has not fruited any as yet at this station ; it is of dwarfish growth, foliage large and healthy ; will give it another year's trial.

Brandywine is a red berry. So far it has proved to be hardy ; not very vigorous, but early and stands record in yield ; berry small and rather soft, but owing to its earliness it is a desirable variety for home market.

Brinckle's Orange. A yellow berry, medium size, soft, rather poor quality, not profit-able.

Cuthbert. Is without a doubt the best red raspberry under cultivation ; it is vigorous and hardy, good crops of large size berries, quality best.

Caroline. Plant vigorous ; hardy and a heavy yielder ; berry, medium size ; color, orange ; very soft and poor quality ; although this variety gave the largest yield it is not worth cultivation owing to the fruit being so soft.

Conrath. This is a blackcap of great promise ; plant very vigorous ; appears to be hardy and healthy ; fruit large and quality first-class.

Columbia. Is not holding its reputation as a vigorous grower ; the plant is not as vigorous as some of the blackcap varieties, it is a little tender, but yields well when not injured by the winter frost ; berry, large ; quality very good ; hangs well on the bush.

Golden Queen Plant healthy ; fairly vigorous and hardy ; color, orange ; medium size ; quality very good ; the best light colored variety.

Gregg. A blackcap ; strong grower ; a little tender ; fruit, large and of good quality ; covered with a heavy bloom.

Gault. Is not doing as well as expected at first. Plant fairly vigorous ; canes very large, but do not grow laterals enough ; fruit, large and firm ; quality very good ; color, black.

Hilborn The plants that I have under test of this variety I think are not correct. They are the poorest growers and weakest of those that are under test, while a row of Hilborns that was planted a year or two before are vigorous growers and good yielders. The berry is of medium size ; quality good ; color, black.

Hansell. A very early red variety. Plant about the same as Brandywine, a little earlier but as good a cropper ; berry, small and soft ; only good for near market.

Johnston's Sweet. Plant of the poorest growth and subject to disease. Berry, very small ; is not worth growing.

Kansas. Is a very promising variety ; plant, healthy and hardy, vigorous grower of strong canes ; it gave the largest yield among the blackcap varieties ; fruit, large, firm and of good quality.

Lovett. Plant, healthy ; poor grower ; fruit, black ; medium size ; quality fair ; season, medium.

Lottie. Plant, hardy ; fairly vigorous, but not as productive as it might be ; quality, very good ; color black.

Louden. Plant, healthy and hardy ; not so vigorous as some of the other varieties ; berry, large, of good quality ; color, red ; needs further trial.

Marlboro'. An early red variety ; plant, healthy and hardy ; dwarfish habit ; fruit, firm ; quality, medium ; yielded a little less than Cuthbert.

Miller. A red variety of vigorous growth, hardy and healthy ; season, medium ; berry, firm ; quality, only fair but does not yield well ; needs further trial.

Mammoth Cluster. The name is the best part of this variety ; it is simply worthless.

Ohio A blackcap ; vigorous ; a little tender ; fairly productive ; season, medium ; berry, medium size ; quality, fair.

Pioneer. Plant, fairly vigorous ; hardy and productive ; berry, medium size ; quality, very good ; color, black ; profitable.

Phœnix. Plant, moderately vigcrous ; healthy and hardy ; foliage, good ; berry; large ; quality, good but not productive enough to make it profitable.

Reliance. Plant, not so vigorous as some others, but hardy and healthy ; berry, rather small and soft ; color, red ; early ; quality, medium.

Rancocas. An early red variety ; medium grower ; healthy and hardy ; berry, rather small and soft ; quality, not quite as good as Reliance.

Red Field. Plant, vigorous ; hardy and healthy ; fruit, small, soft and of rather poor quality. This seems to be a cross between red and black, being purple in color.

Shaffer. Plant, very vigorous ; tender ; subject to disease ; fruit, large, firm ; quality, very good ; color, purple ; a good canning berry but not profitable.

Smith's Giant. A vigorous grower ; a little tender, but healthy ; berrry, large, firm ; quality, best ; color, black. This is a very promising variety if it will only stand the winter. It was damaged a little here last winter.

Superlative. Plant, rather weak and tender, but it has a beautiful foliage when healthy ; berry, very large and firm ; quality, very good ; color, red ; needs further trial.

Strawberry Raspberry. This is supposed to be a native of Japan. Plant, hardy and healthy ; the plant dies down to the ground every fall, growing up again in the spring in increased numbers to the height of twelve to eighteen inches ; the bloom comes out on the end of the canes ; the flowers are large and white, similar to the blackberry ; berry is red in color, large and of a handsome appearance ; the quality is of the poorest ; no use only as an ornament.

Turner. A very hardy variety, but not as vigorous as it might be ; healthy and of fine appearance ; color, red and quality good, but does not yield enough to make it a profitable variety.

Taylor. A blackcap ; plant, hardy ; fairly vigorous and healthy ; fruit, small ; quality, good ; but not profitable.

Thompson. A very early red variety ; plant, healthy and hardy, but not as vigorous as it should be ; berry, soft and small ; medium quality ; good for home use or near market

White Champlain. This is the lightest colored berry of its type ; poor grower ; fairly hardy, but not productive ; quality, fair

Zetler. This is a local berry of great promise ; vigorous and hardy. The season is about the same as Cuthbert, or a little earlier ; berry, large, firm ; quality, second rate ; color, red.

Fertilizing Experiment.—This experiment was commenced in 1897 by selecting half an acre of the bearing orchard containing a number of varieties. In the month of

August 25 bushels of ashes were applied, and 11 pounds of red clover seed sown. Later on 100 pounds of bone meal was also applied. The fall being very dry the clover did not make much growth, but stood the winter well, and was plowed under after attaining growth of ten to twelve inches. On the first of August of this season instead of the ashes I applied 50 pounds of muriate of potash, and 100 pounds of bone meal and 15 pounds of crimson clover seed. At date of writing this report, November 4th, the clover has attained a growth of six to eight inches. This I shall plow down this fall, as I fear the clover will not stand the winter. No perceptable difference can be seen as to the effect on the growth of trees as yet.

A. E. SHERRINGTON,
Experimenter.

REPORT OF GEORGIAN BAY STATION, CLARKSBURG.

There are now in test at this station 141 varieties of plums, including most of the leading Japans. All are doing well with the exception of a very few whose nature may possibly be to grow slowly.

This season's experience fully confirms that of the past two, that to make plum raising profitable, we must grow only the large and showy varieties. Even quality will not compete against size and appearance, as the actual sales have fully proved.

PLUMS.—The best selling plums this season were Bradshaw and Washington for early ; Glass, Quackenbos, Gueii and large Lombards for mid-season ; and Pond Seedling, Coe's Golden Drop, Yellow Egg, Reine Claude, and German Prune for late varieties.

Arch Duke. A rather slow grower; habit upright; a great bearer of uniformly large, dark, handsome fruit, with a heavy blue bloom ; a good shipper and keeper. Will make a valuable acquisition to our late varieties.

Abundance has done well with me this year for the first time. Three year old trees bore a full crop of most beautiful fruit. Size, medium to large. Shape, nearly spherical to distinctly sharp pointed. Color, yellow or amber, overlaid on the sunny side with dots and splashes of red, and in some cases, where most exposed, nearly covered with a deep blush red. Flesh, yellow, extremely juicy, with a peculiar sweet delicious flavor. Tree strong, upright grower. Fruit ripe this year ten days before Lombard.

Burbank. The most vigorous, spreading and sprawling grower in the orchard. A great bearer of strikingly handsome fruit. Seven eleven quart baskets were taken from three three-year old trees. It is only a few days later than Abundance here, and strongly resembles that variety in shape, but will average larger and rather better quality.

Diamond. A fine, large, late, dark plum ; good shipper ; tree moderately vigorous ; upright grower ; bears young ; very promising.

Grand Duke. Tree a moderately upright grower ; bears young. Fruit, large, dark purple, as large as Coe's Golden Drop, but a few days later. Will be a good shipper. Very promising.

Moore's Early. Valuable for its extreme hardiness. A regular bearer. Tree spreading with rather a scrubby top. Fruit medium size ; grows in clusters ; dark purple, with heavy blue bloom. Thin skin ; fine flavor. Stone very small, and almost free. Good for jellies, jams and preserves.

Golden Prolific. Tree very vigorous, upright grower. Fruit medium size. Skin, yellow with a light bloom. Stone, cling. Very productive, but a poor shipper. Quality, best.

Prune d'Agen. A foreign variety of excellent quality. Tree of moderate growth ; branches smooth. Apparently very productive. Fruit, medium sized, oval, slightly necked ; suture small ; skin violet purple, covered with a thick bloom. Flesh, greenish yellow, juicy, rich and delicious, slightly adherent to the stone. Best quality. Late September.

JAPAN PLUMS.—Contrary to my expectations, the Japan plums are proving themselves very promising. They all wintered well and several fruited a few plums, notably Abundance, Wickson, Red June, Chabot and Burbank, the latter setting fruit so thickly, that one could scarcely see the branches.

APPLES —The most profitable are the best varieties of commercial winter apples· What is wanted is high colored stock of good quality. The following do exceedingly well here, viz., Baldwin, Ben Davis, Northern Spy and King. The latter should be top-grafted. They will then bear regularly and abundantly.

PEARS.—Until recently pear growing here has been confined to but one or two varieties, viz., Flemish Beauty, Bartlett and Duchess. We have fruited successfully this season, Flemish Beauty, Bartlett, Clapp's Favorite, Belle Lucrative, Beurre Clairgeau, Duchess, Beurre d'Anjou, Howell, Kieffer and Wilder, and we have a number of others quite promising.

CHERRIES.—This was a good season for cherries. Everything we had did well, except Windsor, which made a wonderful show at first, but the fruit gradually shrank up and dropped off, so that very few matured. Only once in three or four years do we get a good crop of Windsor. Ostheim, a Russian variety, which for the past two years bore rather lightly, this year produced a very full crop. Montmorency, English Morello, May Duke, Wragg, and Yellow Spanish are varieties of much promise.

PEACHES —About seventeen varieties in test at this station. The wood wintered well to the last bud, and several bore a few stray fruits, notably, Bowslaugh's Late, Tyhurst Wonderful, and Smock. The peach "leaf curl" made its appearance here this spring on young Crawfords and Champions. We sprayed rather heavily with Bordeaux, which seemed to check it, for in about three weeks the trees appeared as healthy as ever.

INSECTS —We were exceptionally free from insects the past season. Curculio and codling moth were all we had to contend with. The usual remedy, Bordeaux and Paris green, was applied.

FERTILIZER EXPERIMENT.—This experiment was tried on one-half acre of bearing plums. Soil, deep sandy loam, in perfect condition. About July 1st, 1897, I spread about twenty-five bushels of unleached ashes and one hundred pounds ground bone. On 12th July I sowed ten pounds red clover. It was nicely up by July 20th. It made thick growth from eight to twelve inches high with a very heavy growth of roots. Plowed under Nov. 23rd. Result : trees this summer had a heavier and darker foliage ; fruit rather larger ; better color and more bloom than on those not similarly treated.

This experiment has been continued this year on the same half-acre, crimson clover being used in place of red. Further observations will be given in next report.

J. G. MITCHELL,
Experimenter.

REPORT OF SIMCOE STATION, ORAIGHURST.

I received this year for planting six standard apple trees, three standard pears, seven half standard cherries, one plum, one apricot, three currants, one grape vine and one gooseberry, twenty-three varieties in all, comprising the following varieties :

Apples : American Pippin, Aitken's Red, Peter, Winesap, Scarlet Cranberry, Yates' Red. Three of these are duplicates of varieties already growing in experimental grounds.

Pears : Bartlett Seckel, Dempsey, Eastern Belle.

Cherries : Kirsch, Orel 23, Russian 207, Red May, King Amarelle, Straus Weischel, Schattan Amarelle.

Plum : Gold.

Apricot : Harris.

Currants : Pomona, Victoria, Prince Albert.

Gooseberry : Red Jacket, Grape, Campbell's Early.

These have all lived, and although the season was very dry, have made a satisfactory growth. None of the experimental varieties of fruit have failed this year, but all are thrifty and doing well so far.

Strawberries : Many of the new and much lauded varieties are failures under ordinary field culture. While they may produce large specimens under special care and treatment, when they come into competition with some of the old well tried sorts they are not in it. The best all round berry I have tried, since the days of the Wilson, is the Williams. It is firm, withstands drouth well, is healthy in foliage, and maintains its size well to the close of the season. It is also a fairly good bearer, and barring its white tip, it comes well up to the mark as an all round up to date berry. Crescent is still the best bearer, with Haverland a good second. One of the best of the large varieties I have tested here is Little's 44. It has the healthiest foliage; it beats Bubach in this respect. It has a large, strong, vigorous plant, and a good bearer of very large berries; is a trifle soft, but of fine quality. Afton and Warfield are of poor quality, and total failures in a dry season. Hunn, a new variety from New York State, is a very late berry of fair quality and large size, but it is a pistillate, and there is no staminate variety late enough to fertilize it with. Under these circumstances it is handicapped, and only bears a few specimens. It only gets a little pollen from a few late blossoms of some staminate variety. But with a staminate variety beside it, late enough to fertilize it properly, I believe it would be quite an acquisition, as it would extend the season. It was beginning to ripen this year when other varieties were done.

Raspberries : The Cuthbert is still queen of the market, though I believe Louden and Miller will come pretty well up to it. They have not been sufficiently tested here yet, however. This was an off year for raspberries They may be said to have been almost a total failure, owing to the extreme heat and severe drouth. The Columbian was badly winter killed. It is a rampant grower, and does not ripen its wood sufficiently to stand our cold winters. It is not as hardy as Shaffer. I would advise planters in northern sections to go slowly on the Columbian. Turner is a worthless scrub berry. There are better ones growing wild. I am plowing mine under. Of the blacks, Smith's Giant is still to the fore as one of the best black caps tested here. Though the berry does not come up to the Older or Hilborn in quality, yet it is larger and firm. The canes are healthy, hardy and vigorous and a good bearer.

Blackberries : Agawam and Eldorado are the best tested here so far. Several new varieties have not fruited yet.

These, like the raspberries, suffered from the heat and drouth. I hope that next year we shall have enough in bearing for comparative purposes.

Currants : Fays, Cherry, Varsailles and White Grape give the best results. As to the black varieties, I am not sure as yet that the new varieties are any improvement on the older sorts.

CHERRIES.—Of all the varieties of fruits planted here, none seems better adapted to the soil and climate of this section than the Russian cherries. Some of those will no doubt turn out worthless as to quality, but experience so far has proved that there are many excellent varieties among them. The fruit is large and fine looking, and although very few of them will ever rank as dessert quality, they can hardly be excelled for canning and other culinary purposes. They are, both in tree and fruit, remarkably free from disease. Nine varieties planted in 1894 have not as yet shown any signs of black-knot, though there is plenty of it in the neighborhood. I believe in this connection that cherry and plum trees that are kept well sprayed over both limbs and trunk with Bordeaux mixture so as to cover the bark of the limbs well, will be little affected by the knot. One of the enemies of the cherry is a kind of slug that eats the leaves. It is easily destroyed with Paris Green. The green and black aphis is a more troublesome pest, as it sucks the juices from the leaves They are on the under side of the leaf and it is difficult to get at them. I would suggest an improved nozzle made to throw an upright or vertical spray so as to strike on the under side of the leaf. These insects can only be destroyed by spraying with something strong enough to kill by contact, such as kerosene emulsion, whale oil soap, tobacco water, etc. But the trouble is that these pests are at their worst at the time when the fruit is nearly ripe. This is especially true of the cherries, and I have found that spraying with kerosene emulsion at this time, in a dry season when there is no rain to wash it off again, leaves a very disagreeable taste on the fruit. The upper surface of a leaf may be covered with Bordeaux, yet the aphis will still thrive on the under side.

PLUMS.—In 1894, quite late in the spring, a bundle of sixteen plum trees were sent to me for planting, each a different variety. Though late and growth well advanced, they all lived, made satisfactory progress, and this year most of them came into bearing. We found little trouble with curculio. The chief enemies to contend with were slugs, aphis, shothole fungus, and, worst of all, plum rot. The variety most affected with rot was the Gueii. Fully a third of this variety was lost through this cause. The others were affected only slightly. Descriptive lists of those which fruited this year are given below.

Of the Japan plums tested here, *Burbank* is far the best so far. The trees of these, two years planted, have nearly a basket of very fine plums, and the growth of new wood on the leading branches measured thirty-two inches.

Abundance has not done very well, seems tender. Shensi also seems too tender for this section. Willard, Satsuma and Ogon promise well. Early Botan (mentioned in my report last year) bore a heavy crop this year, but the fruit was very small, and its main fault is in prematurely dropping from the tree. None of the plums planted here have failed, except three trees of Abundance and one of Shensi. There are several other that have not been planted long enough to describe.

The following plums fruited this year:

Burbank. Bloom on May 20, ripe Aug 30. Fruit conical, large. $1\frac{1}{2}$ by $1\frac{3}{4}$ in. diameter. Skin purple, covered with a delicate bloom turning dark red when ripe. Suture, obscure: basin broad, shallow; stalk short. Flesh, yellow, tender sweet, juicy, rich agreeable flavor; stone, small, cling. A very promising variety. Tree healthy, vigorous, spreading habit of growth; soil, warm loam cultivated with hoe crops, roots and small fruits between the trees. Fertilizer, stable manure and ashes. Planted in 1894.

Arch Duke. Tree spreading, healthy, moderately vigorous. Fruit large, $1\frac{1}{4}$ x $1\frac{1}{2}$ inches diameter, oblong, irregular skin dark blue covered with a thick bloom; cavity narrow; stem $\frac{1}{2}$ inch; suture deep distinct. Flesh slightly coarse, medium quality. Stone medium, cling. In bloom May 24th. Ripe Sept. 7th.

Middleburg. Tree upright, healthy, vigorous. Fruit large $1\frac{1}{4}$ x $1\frac{1}{2}$ inches diameter, oblong, slightly rounded at apex; skin purple, covered with a delicate bloom; cavity, small; stem stout, $\frac{3}{4}$ inch long; suture obscure. Flesh whitish, juicy, pleasant. Stem, medium. In bloom May 24. Ripe Sept. 10th.

Staunton. Tree spreading, healthy, vigorous. Fruit medium to large. $1\frac{1}{2}$ inches diameter, nearly round. Skin dark blue; cavity medium; suture none; stem stout, $\frac{1}{2}$ inch; flesh whitish. juicy, agreeable flavor, very good; stone medium. In bloom May 26th. Ripe Sept. 7th.

Black Diamond. Tree spreading, healthy, vigorous. Fruit, oblong, irregular, inclined to be lob sided, medium to large, $1\frac{1}{4}$ x $1\frac{1}{2}$ inches diameter. Skin dark blue, covered with thick bloom; cavity narrow; basin small; suture obscure; stem $\frac{3}{4}$ inch.

Flesh, whitish, juicy, agreeable flavor, very good.

In bloom May 20th. Ripe Sept. 10th.

In the above descriptions of plums, nothing is said of productiveness, as these were planted in 1894, and fruited for the first time this year, many of them only bearing a few specimens. They will require to be several years in bearing in order to determine their respective or comparative merits in regard to yield. Also, it must not be understood that these, or any of them, are recommended for planting in this district. That can only be determined by several year's trial. A very severe winter may kill most of them. I only describe them as they are this year, four years from planting. But they must have further trial before recommending them.

Gueii. Tree, healthy, vigorous. Fruit medium to large, slightly oblong. Skin dark blue covered with thick blue bloom. Suture obscure, $1\frac{1}{2}$ inches diameter. Basin shallow. Stalk $\frac{3}{4}$ inch, slender. Flesh sweet, tender, dry, agreeable flavor. Stone; medium, free. In bloom May 20th. Ripe Aug. 30th. Very badly affected with plum rot, fully a third of the fruit rotted, though sprayed with Bordeaux several times. Tree very productive.

Union Purple. Tree upright, vigorous, healthy. Fruit large, $1\frac{3}{4}$ inches diameter oblong ; suture, wide, shallow, obscure : stem $\frac{1}{2}$ inch, stout, set in a deep narrow cavity, basin shallow ; skin, dark purple covered with a purple bloom. Flesh, greenish yellow, juicy, rich melting aromatic ; stone, large, cling. In bloom May 20th. Ripe Sept. 1st. The best in point of quality yet tested.

Peter's Yellow Gage. Tree upright, vigorous, healthy. Fruit large, $1\frac{1}{2}$ inches diameter, oblong, roundish ; skin, greenish, deep yellow when fully ripe ; stem 1 inch ; cavity shallow : Suture, deep, distinct. Flesh greenish, yellow, juicy, sweet, rich ; stone large, cling. Very good to best. In bloom May 24th. Ripe Sept. 4th.

Prince of Wales. Tree upright, healthy, vigorous. Fruit large, $1\frac{1}{4}$ inches diameter, rounded, slightly conical. Skin, white, overspread with pink, and covered a delicate bloom. Cavity, broad, shallow ; suture obscure ; stem $\frac{1}{2}$ inch Flesh, greenish-yellow, sweet, juicy, agreeable ; flavor very good. Stone medium, cling. In bloom May 24th. Ripe, Sept. 4th.

PEARS.—For a number of years little attention has been given to pears in this district, owing to the belief that they, or most of them, were too tender to succeed here. While this is true to a certain extent yet I believe pears can be grown here quite successfully. Flemish Beauty is quite hardy here, and I am trying the experiment of top grafting more tender varieties on them.

The Russian varieties growing here, viz., Baba, Bessemianka, and Bergamot, seem as hardy as a Duchess apple. The fruit of these varieties I judge will not be up to the mark in quality. One, the Bessemianka, bore a few specimens this year. They were small and of poor quality. The others may be better, but I do not expect much in the way of quality from Russian pears. Their value will be in their hardiness, and suitability as stocks for top grafting. I am working on these, and a number of Flemish Beautys planted for the purpose. Such varieties as Bartlett, Anjou, Sheldon, Lawson, Lawrence, Clapps, Duchess, etc., and so far the experiment is proving successful.

Duchess, grown here as a dwarf on quince roots is not satisfactory. Nurserymen should never use quince roots for pears intended for Northern districts.

APPLES.—Several varieties of apples fruited for the first time this season, descriptions of which are given. One new variety, the Duchavoe, a Russian, is not described, for the reason that it so closely resembles the Hare Pipka, described in a former report, that I fail to see any difference in the two varieties. These two, with the Wolf River, are all akin to the Alexander. They have the same size and color, same texture of flesh and of about the same quality. Wolf River is if anything a little later. But all are apparently of the same origin. They are all fine, large, clean, attractive looking fruit of good cooking quality, and will be valuable as fall market apples.

There seems to be no new winter varieties that are likely to supersede such old tried varieties as N. Spy, Baldwin, Greening, King, etc., in public favor, and I would strongly advise those who are now planting out apple orchards in this section to plant such varieties as Tolman Sweet, Gideon and Haas, and top graft them with the above varieties, as they will in this way get the best and most valuable results in the line of winter apples. The Spy is the most popular winter apple to-day in Canada and the States, and we can never grow too many of them. They will never go begging for a market, and we are not likely to get a winter apple that will ever supersede it. At the same time there is more money in the Duchess than any winter apple, provided a market can be found for them, even if sold for a low price ; I have had more profit from the Duchess than any apple I have grown. And as long as I can find a market for them I will continue to grow them. But we must have winter varieties as well, and the advice given above with respect to varieties and the best and most profitable way to grow them is given from practical experience.

McIntosh Red, Fruit, rounded oblate, 2½ by 3 inches in diameter, color dark red when fully ripe slightly mottled with small light dots, stem short, set in a wide shallow cavity, calyx closed, basin small. Flesh white tender juicy mild sub-acid. Core small. Resembles the Fameuse somewhat but much larger. The specimen here described is probably above the average size being grown on a young tree.

Wolf River, Fruit large to very large, 3¼ by 4¼ inches in diameter ; roundish oblate, slightly ribbed, skin greenish-yellow overspread with crimson when fully ripe, with a few very small white dots. Stalk short, set in a deep russet cavity. Calyx nearly closed. Basin large deep often uneven. Flesh, white rather coarse, tender, mild, subacid, good for cooking. Season a little later than Alexander of which it is said to be a seedling, and which it resembles so closely that it is difficult to distinguish between them. A very fine handsome apple valuable for market

Magog Red Streak, Fruit, medium to large, 3 by 3½ inches, conical, slightly oblong. Skin, greenish yellow, marked with minute black dots and partly shaded and streaked with red. Stem short, stout, set in a medium cavity. Calyx closed. Basin deep, corrugated. Flesh yellowish, coarse, moderately juicy, sub-acid. Core medium.

The above fruits were grown on scions top grafted on seedlings and other trees and would likely be larger than the same fruit grown under ordinary conditions. But the shape, texture, flavor, etc., would be the same.

It must be remembered that the measurements given in these descriptions of fruit are of specimens grown on young trees and are no doubt larger than the same variety would be when the tree gets older and begins to grow heavy crops. Therefore the measurements here given, must not be taken as a true index of the average size of the fruit.

Also in giving the measurements of the season's growth of the varieties, the average growth is given as near as possible of the present year. While this will give a fair idea of the health and vigor of a tree, yet it is not always a sure index of the character of the tree, as a tree of open spreading habit, will have longer growths on the leading limbs than a closely brushy tree with fine willowy limbs, though perhaps not more vigorous.

G. C. Caston,
Experimenter.

REPORT OF BAY OF QUINTE STATION, TRENTON.

There are several of the new and old varieties of pears and apples, the scions of which were top grafted on bearing trees, that are fruiting, on which I give a few notes.

APPLES.

Boiken. Top grafted on Royals Jennett in 1895, first fruit last year, large, 3¼ B. 2¾ H. Yellow, some ripe Nov. 20, and some did not mature until April. First fruit very uneven in shape ; some fairly true, others ribbed. This year the shape is more true, color light straw with a little flush cheek in sun ; numerous russet dots. None ripe up to this date. Think they will keep better and mature more evenly. Abundant bearer.

White Pippin, grafted on Royals Jennett in 1895 ; fruited this year. Fruit whitish yellow ; numerous grey dots, very firm yet ; subject to apple spot ; has not made very strong growths.

Scott's Winter, top grafted in 1894 ; first fruit in 1896 ; fruit not good. 1897 fruit. medium, true in form. Stored in fruit house, kept until April 15th, 1898. Fruit roun. dish conical, striped, splashed with red, numerous russet dots ; pleasant sub-acid ; rather small to be of much value.

Cooper's Market, top grafted in 1895. Two imperfect samples this year.

Peck's Pleasant, top grafted in 1895. One specimen.

Jefferis, top grafted in 1895.

Washington Strawberry, top grafted in 1895, and only one apple.

Akin, top grafted in 1895.

Bismarck, tree planted in 1896. One apple.

Utter's Red, top grafted in 1895. First fruit in 1897, round ovate, whitish yellow, with but very little streaks of red on side next sun, but not enough to attract attention. Quality poor ; may improve, but the fruit is the same this season. Ripe now, Nov. 7th.

Longfield, planted in 1894. First fruit last year. This year 15 apples, ripened in. September ; very good ; whitish yellow with red on side next the sun.

Winter Banana, top grafted in 1896. A few one-sided specimens this year.

Wolf River,-top grafted in 1894. About one peck of imperfect apples this year.

Switzer, top grafted in 1894. One apple ripened in September.

PEARS.

Dr. Jules Guyot, two trees planted in 1895. One pear in 1896 ; one half peck in 1897. Similar in form to Bartlett, and nearly the same in color. Flavor clear sub-acid, good. Did not fruit this year.

Manning's Elizabeth, three trees planted in 1895. Two specimens in 1897 ; six this year. Fruit small, ripened in August.

Duchess Precoce, top grafted in 1895. Fruited in 1897, and this year a heavy crop. of fine, large pears ripened by September 20th. Very promising.

Dorset, top grafted in 1895. Fruit this year, large, fine; not ripe yet (November 7th.)

P. Barry, top grafted 1895, fruited this year, medium size, a winter pear.

Idaho, top grafted 1895, first fruit 1897, large, a fair crop this year of large pears. Some blight on limbs.

PLUMS.

Burbank is the only one fruiting, planted in 1895. Exceedingly rapid grower, and formed fruit buds on the main body of the tree within one foot of the ground, and from there all the way to the top of the branches. Came into bloom 2nd May ; fruit large, fine, very attractive. Ripe 1st September.

FERTILIZER EXPERIMENT.—In regard to the fertilizer experiment, the half acre|of orchard selected in 1896 for fertilizer experiment is a mixed block, containing Greenings, Baldwins, Seek no-further, Gravenstein, and one White Doyenne pear tree, all planted seventeen years, and fruiting. The whole of that part of the orchard received in 1895 a fair coating of bone meal, in 1896 the ½ acre received 100 lbs. of bone meal. July, crimson clover seed ; it came up good, but made very little top.

In the spring of 1897 all the clover was dead, plowed in May, sowed 100 lbs. bone meal. In July sowed red clover seed ; it came up fine, made a good cover. On May the 20th plowed it under, clover two feet high, sowed 100 lbs. bone meal. July 20th sowed 50 lbs. muriate of potash together with crimson clover, but the weather was so dry that. the clover did not come up till the last of August, the ground is well covered at present, November 4th.

The surrounding block had in 1897 a thin coating of stable manure, in 1898 a light dressing of ashes, about 40 bushels to the acre. Both blocks received the same thorough cultivation up to time of sowing clover seed. The surrounding block was cultivated twice after.

Results : The foliage was a little better color on the plot, no difference in growth, fruit yield the same, the only difference I could see was an added brightness in the fruit.

W. H. DEMPSEY, Experimenter.

REPORT OF ST. LAWRENCE STATION, MAITLAND.

For 1898 I beg to acknowledge the receipt of the following trees and plants, viz .—

Apples. American Pippin, Parlin's Beauty, Rome Beauty, Starr, Scarlet Cranberry, Winesap.

Pears. Bartlet Seckle, Eastern Belle, Petite Marguerite, Wilder.

Plums. Blood, Berckmans, Coe's Violet, Lombard Improved, Yellow Prolific, Normands, Stark's Green Gage, Seedling, Gold.

Apricot. Harris.

Grapes. Campbell's Early.

Currants. Pomona, Victoria Rd., Prince Albert.

All of which lived and made fair growth.

All the apples now on test, numbering about sixty varieties, have lived well and made satisfactory growth with the exception of one tree of Downing's Winter Maiden's Blush that was killed through accident. Yellow Transparent, planted 1896, and Magog Red, planted 1897, blossomed and set a little fruit, but it did not reach maturity.

In my commercial orchard Fameuse, Scarlet Pippin, Golden Russet and Tolman Sweet set well and gave a fair crop of well grown fruit.

Canada Red and Yellow Belleflower were white with bloom, but did not set two per cent. of fruit. Other varieties did not bloom with me this year.

The annual record attached to this report shows very promising for plums and pears. They are making a wonderful growth and have withstood the effects of two winters without injury, with the exception of one or two cases of blight as shown in report.

The insects were the worst on record this spring. Tent caterpillars destroyed so much foliage in unsprayed orchards that they looked as though they had been swept by fire. Bud moths were so thick that they destroyed the opening buds on young trees, killing them outright in some cases. Oyster shell bark louse are so thick that they overlap completely, covering the limbs on many trees and even the fruit was covered in the worst cases. Cigar case bearer and codling moth not bad. The black spot fungi about as bad as in 1897.

SPRAYING RECORD FOR 1898.

April 18, 19. Sprayed Bordeaux and Paris green ; buds opening.

May 11, 12. Sprayed Bordeaux and Paris green ; blossoms opening.

May 27, 28. Sprayed Bordeaux and Paris green ; blossoms fallen, bud-moth doing serious damage.

June 9, 10. Sprayed Bordeaux mixture and Paris green ; apples set fairly well, spot showing badly on fruit, particularly on east side of tree.

June 16. Bordeaux ; spot checked and apples growing rapidly.

July 11.   Bordeaux ; spot made no further development since June 10th.

July 11.   Unsprayed apples all badly spotted around blossom end.

Results of being sprayed six times :

Fameuse.   Sixty to 75°/₀ clean, well grown and colored; unsprayed, none clean, small and misshapen.

Scarlet Pippen.   One hundred per cent. clean, large and colored ; unsprayed, 50% clean.

Golden Russet.   One hundred per cent. clean ; unsprayed 60°/₀ clean.

Canada Red.   Ninety per cent. clean ; unsprayed 30₀/° clean.

Fameuse.   Sprayed three times ; last spraying, made May 27, 10₀/° clean.

Tent caterpillars were all destroyed with first and second sprayings and bud moth checked, but the Bordeaux had no effect upon the oyster shell bark louse, the sprayed trees are as badly infested as the unsprayed.   The trees on the half acre of bearing apple orchard that has been treated with twenty-five bushels wood ashes, 100 pounds of bone meal and sown with ten to fifteen pounds of clover annually for two years are in a very healthy condition and are making fair wood growth and setting fruit buds annually.

I can see no difference in the results between the above treatment and the plot under annual cultivation with the application of five tons per acre barnyard manure in the late fall.   But both the above mentioned plots are in far better condition than the plot in sod ; the bark is cleaner, wood growth more vigorous and foliage is of a dark green color, and nearly double the size of the leaves on the trees in sod and a dry summer or fall does not affect the foliage on the cultivated ground whereas the foliage on the trees in sod turn yellow and drop off in many cases before frost.   There is the same difference to be noticed in the fruit, with the exception that the fruit in sod is higher colored than on cultivated ground.

HAROLD JONES,
Experimenter.

REPORT OF STRAWBERRY SUB-STATION, FREEMAN.

The season of 1898 was very favorable for a good crop.   The crop was an immense one, and on account of this, no doubt, and strawberries having for two or three years paid the best of all small fruits, an enlarged acreage was planted.   Prices were low, but the fancy berries brought a good figure.   The fall of 1897 was favorable to the growth of plants, so that very wide rows were made.   These rows, if not thinned out and harrowed, would produce a very large crop of medium to small sized berries.   The standard varieties have held their place, while one or two new varieties have made a very favorable showing.

The Clyde did very well and easily stands at the head, the very best reports coming from all places where it is grown and no unfavorable ones.   In the list of those that did the best with me I would place : Bubach, Haverland, Saunder's, Woolverton, Margaret, Seaford, Nick Ohmer, Tennessee Prolific, Brandywine, Bisel, VanDeman, Beder Wood, Glen Mary, Splendid, Bismarck.

Among the new ones fruited for the first time are the following :

Bird.   Imperfect blossom.   A seedling of Manchester and Mount Vernon by W. F. Bird, of Ann Arbor, Michigan.   The plant is quite healthy and a good grower, making runners freely ; berry medium to large in size ; roundly conical ; scarlet in color ; flesh pink, medium in firmness ; fine quality and quite productive.   Worthy of a trial.

Cobden Queen.   Imperfect blossom.   A seedling of the old Wilson by John McCaffery, of Cobden, Illinois.   Is a good strong grower, a good runner, but has some rust at times.   The berry is round, crimson in color, seeds red, flesh pink and medium in firmness, fair quality, quite productive.   No better than many others.

Benoy. Perfect. Seedling of Bubach and Jessie by Mr. R. Benoy, of Indiana Plant a strong robust grower, somewhat like Sharpless ; makes runners freely and free from rust ; berry large as Sharpless, crimson ; seeds red and imbedded, flesh red, solid, firm and good quality. Worth trying.

Earliest. Perfect blossom. Very much resembles the Michel's Early in every respect, both in plant and fruit and season. If it is not the Michel's Early under a new name it is a seedling so closely resembling the Michel's Early that I cannot distinguish between them.

Geisler. Perfect blossom. Fine healthy plant and a good runner ; blooms very early. The berry is large, bright dark scarlet ; flesh light in color, medium in firmness, and good quality ; oblong in shape. Worth a trial.

Hall's Favorite. Perfect blossom. A chance seedling grown by J. W. Hall, of Maryland. Plant healthy, a good grower, plenty of runners. Berry medium to large in size ; scarlet ; flesh light scarlet, solid and medium in firmness ; obtuse at end something like Crescent : quality good ; medium in productiveness.

Jerry Rusk. Perfect bloom. Seedling from Bubach and Jessie, by Mr. Ran. Benoy, of Indiana. Plant a good strong grower, healthy and free from rust, makes many plants. The berry is rounding conical ; bright crimson ; golden seeds ; flesh red, medium in firmness ; good quality and quite large and productive. Worth trying.

Jersey Market. Imperfect bloom. Introduced by J. T. Lovett, of New Jersey. This variety was not in a good place, had not a fair chance, would not like to judge it by what it did with me under unfavorable conditions.

King's Worthy. A seedling of E. W. Cone. The plant resembles the Bubach ; healthy ; some fine large berries, but not productive enough.

Kyle No. 1. Perfect bloom. A chance seedling ; plant small and does not stand dry weather. The berry small and irregular, with neck. Not valuable.

Leheigh. Imperfect bloom. A good grower, coming from Pennsylvania, by W. B. K. Johnson. Only medium in size ; quite productive. Not valuable here with me.

Mayflower. A second Michel's Early ; about as good, no better.

Manwell. Perfect bloomer. Supposed to be a cross of Sharpless and Crescent by Allen D. Manwell, of Vinton, Iowa. The plant is a strong, healthy grower ; no trace of rust ; the berry is large, scarlet ; seeds pink, imbedded ; the first berries sometimes double and hollow ; medium in firmness, quite productive and worthy a trial.

Mastodon. Imperfect bloomer. Sent out by Mr. Saltzer. Plant a strong, robust, healthy plant, resembling the Bubach very much. A second Bubach in fact in all points. Berry is very large, beautiful bright scarlet, medium in firmness. In looking at a box of them you would say they are Bubach. I cannot distinguish between the two. It must be a seedling very closely resembling its parent Bubach.

Sixteen Nick Ohmer. Perfect bloomer. A seedling of Middlefield. The grower is Mr. G. Beamer of Ohio. The plant is a strong, vigorous, healthy grower, making runners freely, thus making a good row. The berry is large, roundly conical, bright crimson, gold seeds prominent, a beautiful looking berry ; flesh pink and firm ; very good quality and quite productive. A good one and worth trying.

Perfection. A seedling sent out by Mr. Saltzer. The plant is healthy and a good grower ; the berry is fair sized, with a neck ; very good quality ; somewhat rough ; medium in productiveness ; not very desirable.

Ponderosa. This is another seedling, I believe, of the Bubach. Plant healthy and a good runner, making many plants. The berry is quite large, but rough, resembling the Glen Mary a good deal ; dark crimson ; seeds golden and imbedded ; flesh red ; berry solid and firm and of good quality ; quite productive. The berry is like the Glen Mary.

Seaford. Perfect bloomer. A chance seedling. The plant is a strong, vigorous, healthy grower, a good runner, making plants freely. The berry is large, crimson in color, with golden seeds ; solid and firm ; flesh scarlet, very firm and very good quality. A good one and should be tried by all strawberry growers.

Shire. Imperfect bloomer. The plant is healthy and is a good strong grower. The leaves curl back like the Grenville The berry is medium to large ; dark scarlet ; round in shape ; flesh red, firm and good quality. Quite productive.

Seek-no-Further. Perfect bloom ; by Mr. J. M. Wickizer. Another of the Bubach type, but not so good by a long way. I desire to give a further trial before finally pronouncing upon it.

Two Teft Seedling. A good plant maker. A strong, healthy grower. The berry is medium in size, round and somewhat irregular ; scarlet is color with gold seeds prominent ; flesh pink, of fair quality and medium in productiveness. There are many others better.

Stahelin, Fred. Imperfect bloomer. A chance seedling found by F. C. Stahelin, of Bridgeman, Mich. The plant is very vigorous and healthy, making plants very freely. The berry is large, roundly conical ; bright light crimson in color with gold seeds ; flesh pink ; medium in firmness, good quality and quite productive. Worth a trial.

Planters cannot go astray in planting any of the above varieties as recommended worth a trial. The plants have not made as vigorous a growth this season as last year on account of the long, dry and very hot season. The rows are much narrower than usual, but I expect the fruit will be finer and larger on that account.

E. B. STEVENSON,
Experimenter.

REPORT OF GOOSEBERRY SUB-STATION, NANTYR.

The severe scourging the bushes received in 1897 when the foliage rotted early in the season affected the fruitfulness this year and most varieties bloomed very sparingly. Red Jacket, Downing, Pearl and Oregon Jumbo were less affected than any others and bore a nice crop this year, Autocrat also escaped fairly well and bore a large crop of fine berries. For eating, when ripe, this berry is hard to excel.

Spraying was commenced this year on March the 25th, by using four pounds of blue stone to forty gallons of water. Spraying with Bordeaux and liver of sulphur was kept up till fruit was fully grown, five sprayings being given.

No difference could be detected between those sprayed with Bordeaux and those sprayed with liver of sulphur, all being affected upon foliage and some spots upon fruit.

Being convinced that spraying for mildew must be largely preventive, I shall spray this fall with pure blue stone water, four pounds to forty gallons, and again in spring before leaves come out.

In spraying with Paris green in Bordeaux for gooseberry worm, I find four ounces of green to forty gallons not strong enough, so increased to six and to eight ounces to forty gallons, or a coal oil barrel full before it had the desired affect. Foliage was not injured.

Of the newer varieties under test, Red Jacket and Oregon Jumbo, which seem to be identical, are certainly the most vigorous, but so far are not equal to Pearl in productiveness. Success and White Crystal and a variety called Red Champion are too small. Crosby's Seedling is certainly a monster and a red one at that. It has vigor, too, which is shown by its bearing a nice crop this year after the experience of 1898. Dominick made a nice growth of wood but did not give a berry. Queen, Chautauqua and White-smith bore a few berries, each very much alike.

All my bushes made a fine growth of wood this season.

In spraying nursery stock of gooseberries for mildew upon foliage, I find it is no use spraying if mildew is permitted to get hold, as it turns the leaves affected black and they soon rot and fall off. Prevention is not better than cure in this case, but is the only *cure*.

The Champion, when not affected by mildew, is the most productive variety yet tested, and is fit to use green (for those who choose to use this fruit in this condition), at least two weeks earlier than any other. It was badly affected with mildew in 1897, and killed badly last winter as did Triumph.

S. SPILLETT,
Experimenter.

SIR,—I beg to report size and weight of some of the leading varieties:

Variety.	Size in inches.	Weight of 12 berries.
	inches.	ozs.
Autocrat	15/16 by 11/16	2 2/5
Chautauqua	1 " 15/16	3
Crosby's Seedling	1 1/4 " 1	4 1/2
Champion	14/16 " 12/16	1 5/12
Cook's Eagle	1 1/8 " 15/16	3
Downing	11/16 " 9/16	1 1/2
Green Chisel	11/16 " 11/16	1 1/2
Ingram's Ocean	1 1/16 " 14/16	3
London	1 " 14/16	1 1/4
Lancdolet	1 1/4 " 1 1/8	2 1/4
Red Jacket	13/16 " 11/16	2
Ontario	13/16 " 13/16	..
Pearl	12/16 " 12/16	1 5/12
Oregon Jumbo	13/16 " 14/16	2
Winham's Industry	1 " 14/16	2 3/4
Chance Seedling	1 " 14/16	3

APPLES.—*W. H. Dempsey, Experimenter, Bay of Quinte Station, Trenton, Ont*

Varieties.	Origin.	Habit of tree.	Fruit.								Flesh.		
			Size in inches of length and breadth.	Form.	Skin.	Stem.	Cavity.	Calyx.	Basin.	Co'or.	Texture.	Flavor.
Adam's Pearmain.	England, Herefordshire	U.S	$2\frac{1}{2}$, $2\frac{1}{2}$.	r. ov	y., partly rus. st., str. with r.	$\frac{1}{2}$ in.....	sh ..	open ...	pl.......	yh ..	crisp, juicy, rich.	sub-acid, aromatic.
Antonovka	Russia	S ..	$2\frac{1}{4}$, $2\frac{1}{2}$.	ov. c ...	wh., dark red in sun, sprinkled thinly with rus. d, covered with a rich ph. bloom.	$\frac{1}{4}$, often a mere nob.	b. s.	open ...	pl., even.	w ...	crisp, juicy .	sub-acid.
Cayuga Red Streak (20-ounce).	Connecticut, U.S	S. D	3, $3\frac{1}{4}$.	rh	gh. yel. str. and sp. with r.	$\frac{1}{4}$ to $\frac{1}{2}$ heavy.	d. w.	small, closed.	ang	w ...	coarse	brisk, sub-acid
Cellini	England (T. Phillips, Vaux Hall)	U.S	3, 3..	rh. ob ...	y, nearly covered with br. r. in shade with str. mot., da.c. in sun.	$\frac{1}{4}$........	d ...	open ...	pl.......	w ...	tender, juicy	brisk, pleasant sub-acid.
Colvert	America	S ..	$2\frac{1}{3}$, 2..	ob. con..	gh. y. str., sp. with dull r. in sun.	$\frac{1}{2}$	d ...	p. closed	w	gh. w	tender......	sub-acid.
Cox's Orange Pippin.	Mr. Cox, Colnbrook Lawn, Eng., supposed to be from seed of Ribston Pippin in 1830.	U.S	2, $2\frac{1}{4}$.	rh. ov....	y. str. and nearly covered with da. r. in the sun, rus. in cav.	$\frac{1}{2}$, fleshy.	n. d.	open ...	pl., sh...	yh ..	tender, crisp	juicy, rich, sub-acid, aromatic.
Cranberry Pippin.	Hudson, N.Y., U. S ..	S ..	3, $3\frac{1}{2}$.	rh. ob ...	y., br. r. with str. and sp. of da. r.	$\frac{1}{2}$ to $\frac{3}{4}$ ...	b ...	closed .	wr	w ...	coarse	sub-acid.
Early Harvest..	America	S ..	2, $2\frac{1}{4}$.	rh	y. or br. straw color, a few dots.	$\frac{1}{2}$ to $\frac{3}{4}$, slender	sh ..	closed .	even, sh.	w ...	tender	crisp, sprightly. sub-acid.
Early Joe	[illegible]ca	U.S	$2\frac{1}{2}$, $2\frac{1}{4}$.	rh. ob...	yh, str., st. with r.	$\frac{1}{2}$ to $\frac{3}{4}$ ...	n ...	closed .	even ...	wh..	tender	sub-acid.
English Codling.	England	S ..	3, $3\frac{1}{4}$.	ov	lemon y., some times flush cheek in sun.	$\frac{1}{2}$........	d ...	losed .	ang., fur	w ...	tender	pleasant, sub-acid.
Fall Jenneting .	America	S ..	3, $3\frac{1}{4}$.	ob. slightl[illegible]d	gh. y., with a dull blush on side next the sun.	$\frac{3}{4}$	d ...	closed .	even	wh .	tender	sub-acid.
Haas (Fall Queen).	America	U.S	$2\frac{1}{2}$, 3..	ob slightly con.	y., nearly covered with light r., with sp. and st. of darker r., nu w. dots, g. around cavity.	$\frac{1}{4}$........	d ...	closed .	even ...	wh., sta. with r. next skn.	tender	sub-acid.

Habit.
D.—Drooping. Ac.—Acute.
S.—Spreading. An.—Angular.
U.—Upright. Con.—Conical.
Cor.—Corrugated.
Ob.—Oblate.
Ov.—Ovate.
Tur.—Turbinate.

Form.
Obo.—Obovate.
Obl.—Oblong.
Obt.—Obtuse.
Pyr.—Pyriform.
R.—Round.
Rh.—Roundish.

Cavity.
B.—Broad.
D.—Deep.
N.—Narrow.
Sh.—Shallow.

Basin.
Ab.—Abrupt.
Ang.—Angular.
D.—Distinct.
Ev.—Even.
Fur.—Frrrowed.
Pl.—Plaited.
Rib.—Ribbed.
Wr.—Wrinkled.
W.—Waved.

Color.
D.—Dots.
Da.—Dark.
F.—Fawn.
G.—Green.
Gh.—Greenish.
Bl.—Blush.
Blo.—Bloom.
Biot.—Blot.
Br.—Bright.
C.—Crimson.
Clc
A.—Amber.
B.—Brown.
Bh.—Brownish.
Mar.—Marbled.
Mot.—Mottled.
Nn.—Numerous.
O.—Orange.
P.—Purple.
Ph.—Purplish.
Pa.—Pale.
R.—Red.
Rus.—Russet.
Sp.—Splashed or Splashes.
St.—Striped.
St.—Streaked.
Sta.—Stained.
Sun.—Sunny Side.
Spo.—Spotted.
V.—Violet.
W.—White.
Wh.—Whitish.
Y.—Yellow.
Yh.—Yellowish.

9 F.E.S.

APPLES.—Annual yield and selling price of varieties of apples at Bay of Quinte Station, 1898.

Varieties.	Age. (years)	Thinning—per cent, by hand or accident. (%)	Time of blooming.	Date of maturity.	Date of gathering.	Yield. (bush.)	Class 1.	Class 2.	Class 3.	Storage Place.	Temperature.	Date of decay.	Average price. (bbl.)	Remarks. On conditions of cultivation, spraying, manuring, etc.
Adam's Pearmain.	18	1	May 8	Jan	Oct. 18	2	1½	¼	¼	Fruit house	30 to 45	March 28	$2 00	Dwarf tree growing in sod.
Antonovka	18	5	" 7	Feb	" 18	2	1	¼	¾	"	"	May 15	1 50	"
Cayuga Red Streak (20-ounce)	25	5	" 8	Nov	" 7	7	5	1	1	Ship. to Montreal			1 25	Well cultivated.
Cellini	20	2	" 9	Nov	Sep	7	6	1	1	"			2 00	Dwarf tree growing in sod.
Bat.	25	5	" 8	Oct	Sep. 28	15	12	2		"			1 50	Well cultivated.
Cox's Orange Pippin	8 yrs topgraft	2	" 7	Jan	Oct. 6	5	4	¾	1½				3 00	Well cultivated and manured with stable, bones & ashes.
Cranberry Pin	22	5	" 8	Feb	Oct	7	6	1		Fruit house	30 to 45	March 28	3 50	Well cultivated, stable manure.
Early Harvest	35	5	" 6	Ju'y, Aug	July, Aug	8	6	1	1	"			75	
Early Joe	30	10	" 6	"	"	15	9	4	2				75	
English Codling	25	5	" 7	Aug., Sep	Aug. 20, Sep	8	7	1½	1½				75	
Fall Jenneting	15	5	" 7	Sep., Oct	Sep., Oct	6	4	1	1				75	Well cultivated; manured with stable and ashes.
Haas	15	2	" 8	Sep, Oct	20 Sep	6	4	1	1				75	" "

APPLES.

Yield and selling price of varieties of Apples at East Central Station, 1898

Varieties tested by R. L. Huggard, Wnitby.	Age.	Time of blooming.	Date of maturity.	Date of gathering.	Yield.	Class 1.	Class 2.	Class 3.	Place.	Temperature.	Average price.	Remarks on conditions of cultivation, spraying, manuring, etc.
American Golden Russet	22 years		Jan., May	Oct. 19	4½ bush	85	10	5			2 00	Hardy and profitable.
Astrachan	22 "		Aug. and Sept	Aug. 16	6½	65	20	15			1 25	No good demand for the stock.
Baldwin	22 "		Dec., March	Nov. 1	15	65	15	15			2 00	A splendid kind.
Bell Flower	22 "		Dec., Feb	Nov. 1	15	70	20	10			2 00	Good cooker and keeper.
Blue Pearmain	14 "		Nov., April	Nov. 3	11½	75	15	10			2 00	
Boston Star	22 "		Sept.	Sept. 20	16	75	15	10			2 00	Best yielder in orchard.
?a Red	18 "		Dec., April	Nov. 5	3	60	25	15			2 00	Poor cropper this season.
Chenango Strawberry	14 "		Sept	Aug. 27	6	60	20	20			2 00	Not much sale for this kind of stock
Duchess of ?rg	18 "		Aug. and Sept	Aug. 24	6	60	20	20			1 25	A profitable apple.
Early Harvest	18 "		Sept	Aug. 4	4½	90	10				1 00	Slow growing and poor bearing trees.
Fall Pippin	22 "		Oct., Dec	Sept. 29	7	70	15	15			2 00	Subject to fungus.
?'s Golden	22 "		O.t, Dec	Sept. 3	3	70	15	15			2 00	No use to plant largely.
Holland Pippin	22 "		Dec., March	Oct. 14	3	50	10	40				
Kentish Fillbasket	19 "		Oct., Dec	Oct. 29	4½	70	20	10			2 00	Very subject to fungus.
King of Tompkins Co.	22 "		Sept. and Oct	Sept. 12	5	60	5	35			2 00	A very fancy sort, not ?fable.
Haas	22 "		Oct. and Nov.	Oct. 15	5	80	15	5			1 50	A1 variety. ? bearer.
Minkler	19 "		Sept. and Dec	Sept. 29	15	75	15	10			2	A very ? ?ly, profitable variety.
McMahon's White	18 "		Jan., April	Nov. 4	12	85	10	5				Top grafted in 1895, makes good growth.
Maiden's Blush	18 "		Oct., Dec	Oct. 24	3 bush.	75	10	15			2 00	A nice fancy apple.
Northern Spy	22 "		Jan., March	Nov. 3	16	80	15	5			3 00	A ?lid apple, but slow ?lr.
Ontario	13 "		"	Nov.	6	80					2 50	A splendid ?le and ?le.
Pewaukee	18 "	May 22	"	Oct. 15	4	70	25	5			2 00	Dropped prematurely.
Princess Louise	10 "	" 20	Dec., Feb	" 10	4	60	35	5			2 00	Fruit ?le.
Rhode Island Greening	18 "	" 20	Jan., March	" 8	3½	95	3				2 00	Good for general planting.
Ribston Pippin	18 "	" 20	Nov., March	" 28	6	80	15	5			2 00	Dropped prematurely.
Salome	9 "	" 24	Jan., May	" 20	2½	80	10	10	Easru cellar	40° F.	2 00	A good profitable.
Seek No Further	19 "	" 20	Oct., March	" 29	5½	75	10	15			2 00	A medium ? ? ?.
? the Pomme Gris	10 "	" 20	Nov., Jan	" 29	3	80	12	8			2 00	A first-rate grower.
Swaar	22 "	" 24	Dec., March	" 10	5	70	20	10			2 00	Too small for market, but A1 for dessert.
?ly ? ?	22 "	" 24		" 15	3	60	20	20			2 00	Not a ?ry vigorous grower but bears well.
?an Sweet	22 "	" 26	Oct., March	" 12	6	60	30	10			2 00	Not a profitable apple to plant.
Wagener	22 "				6	70	20	10			2 00	To slow a grower.
Wealthy	12 "	" 20	Sept. and Dec	" 8	7½	70	20	10			2 00	Too abundant; fruit small.

APPLES.

Results of experiments in cultivation, pruning, spraying, at Bay of Quinte Station, 1898.

Varieties.	When planted.	Soil and cultivation.	Fertilizers used.	Pruning. Date, method & percentage of wood growth removed.	Growth in inches.	Vigor, scale 1-10.
Downing's Winter Maiden's Blush..	May, 1896..	Sandy loam with clay sub-soil; cultivated till July 12th then sowed to buck-wheat.	One quart bone meal to each tree.	Apl., pd.	24	8
Shackleford	" "	" "	" "	"	20	8
Barry	" "	" "	" "	"	25	8
Western Beauty....	" "	" "	" "	"	23	8
Walbridge	" "	" "	" "	"	26	9
Sultan's Beauty ...	" "	" "	" "	"	16	7
Star	" "	" "	" "	"	13	6
Walter Pease	" "	" "	" "	"	30	9
Beauty of Bath....	" "	" "	" "	"	30	9
Dudley's Winter....	" "	" "	" "	"	32	9
Talman Sweet	" "	" "	" "	"	20	8
Bismarck	" "	" "	" "	"	12	6
Boiken	May, 1897..	" "	" "	"	20	8
Peter	" "	" "	" "	"	17	7
Newtown Pippin ...	" "	" "	" "	"	14	6
Lankford	" "	" "	" "	"	18	7
Aiken's Red	" "	" "	" "	"	17	7
Milding	" "	" "	" "	"	16	7
Yates' Red	" "	" "	" "	"	26	9
Scarlet Cranberry ..	May, 1898..	" "	" "	" "	5	
Gano	" "	" "	" "	" "	8	

APPLES (CRABS). Tested at Simcoe Experiment Station.

Varieties.	When planted.	Soil and cultivation.	Fertilizers used.	Pruning. Date, method and percentage of wood growth removed.	Insects. Name.	Insects. Treatment.	Growth in inches.	Vigor, scale 1-10.
CRAB APPLES.								
Telfer Sweet	95	Loam clean.	Stable and ashes.	June ; about one-fifth removed.	Tent cater-pillar, web worm.	Bordeaux & Paris green	13	6
Martha	95	"	"				14	7
Whitney	95	"	"				18	9
Paul's Imperial....	95	"	"				14	7
Minnesota Winter..	95	"	"				15	7
Van Wycke	95	"	"				11	5
Picta Stricta	95	"	"				13	6
Quaker Beauty.....	95	"	"				18	9
Orion	95	"	"				15	7
APRICOTS.								
Apricots	96	Loam clean.	Stable and ashes.					
Purple	96	"	"				15	7
Alexander	96	"	"				16	8
Alexis	96	"	"				22	10
Gibb	96	"	"				21	10
Nicholas	96	"	"				22	10

Apricots not troubled with either insects or fungi.

APPLES.

Tested at Simcoe Station.

Habit. –D., drooping ; S., spreading ; U., upright.   Suture.—D., distinct ; L., large : Ob., Obscure ;
Obs., obsolete. Form.—Ac., acute ; An., angular ; Con., conical ; Cor., corrugated ; Ob., oblate ;.
Ov., Ovate ; Obo., obovate ; Obl., oblong ; Obt., obtuse ; Pyr., pyriform ; R., round ; Rh., roundish ;.
Tur., turbinate. Cavity.—Ac , acute ; Acu., acuminate ; B., broad ; D., deep ; N., narrow ; Sh.,
shallow.   Basin.—Ab., abrupt ; Ang., angular ; D , distinct ; Ev., Even ; Fur., furrowed ; Pl.,
plaited ; Rib., Ribbed ; Wr., wrinkled ; W., Waved. Color.—A., amber ; B., brown ; Bh., brown-
ish ; Bl., blush ; Blo., bloom ; Blot., blotched ; Br., bright ; C., crimson ; Clo., Clouded ; D., dots ;.
Da., dark ; F., fawn ; G., green ; Gh., green sh ; Mar., marbled ; Mot., mottled ; Nu., numerous ;
O., orange ; P., purple ; Ph., purplish ; Pa , pale ; R., red ; Rus., russett ; Sp., splashed or splashes ;
St., striped ; Str., streaked ; Sta., stained : Sun , sunny side ; Spo , spotted ; V., violet ; W., white ;.
Wh., Whitish ; Y., yellow ; Yh., yellowish.

Varieties.	Origin.	Habit of tree.	Size in inches of length and breadth.	Fruit.		
				Form.	Skin	Stem.
Duchavoe	Russia	S	3 x 3½	Con	Yellow, overspread with red.	Short, stout..
McIntosh Red..........	Canada	S	2½ x 3	Rh., Oh.	Da. R.	Short ......
Okabina...............	Russia	S	2¼ x 2½	R......	Light yellow, splashed with red	Long, slen-- der.
Magog Red Streak	Vermont, U.S..	U	3 x 3½	Con.Obl	Gh. Y., shaded and streak- ed with red.	Sh ....
Wolf River	Wisconsin, U.S.	S	3¼ x 4½	Rh. Ob.	Gh. Y., overspread with crimson.	Sh ....

Tested at Simcoe Station.—*Continued.*

Varieties.	Fruit.				Flesh.		
	Cavity.	Calyx.	Basin.	Core, stone, seeds.	Color.	Texture.	Flavor.
Duchavoe	D., N..	P. C	Pl	Med ..	White	Coarse	Sub-acid.
McIntosh Red.........	Sh	C	Small	Small .	W ...	Tender, juicy...	Mild, sub-acid..
Okabina	Sh	C	Sh	M	White	Tender, pleasant	Sub-ac'd.
Magog Red Streak......	Sh , N.	C	Deep.....	M	Yh.W	Coarse, moder- ately juicy.	Sub-acid.
Wolf River	D	Partly closed	Large deep rib	M	W ...	Coarse	Mild, sub-acid.

APPLES.

Results of experiments in cultivation, pruning, spraying, at Simcoe Station, 1898.

Variety.	When planted.	Soil and cultivation.	Fertilizers used.	Pruning. Date, method and percentage of wood growth removed.	Insects. Name.	Insects. Treatment.	Fungi. Name.	Fungi. Treatment.	Results.	Growth in inches.	Vigor, scale 1-10.
Anisim	95	Warm, rich loam, with a retentive sub-soil, or ginally very stoney; small fruits and other hoe crops are grown between rows of trees.	Stable and ashes.	June; pyramid forms; about ⅓ afterwards a few twigs annually.	Tent caterpiller. Aphis.	Bordeaux with Paris green.	Fusciladium slight.	Bordeaux.	Healthy foliage; no damage from Tent Caterpillar or other leaf-eating insects; slight damage from aphis. Bore a few samples of very fine, clean fruit. A very strong grower.	17	9
Bogandoff	94									18	9
Barry	94									18	8
Boiken	97									18	8
Belle De Boskoop	94									17	8
O's Met	96									18	8
Duchavoe	94									22	10
Enormous	94									23	10
Fallawater	96									20	10
Gideon	95									20	10
Gno	95									20	8
Haas	94									15	10
Hastings	95									20	8
Lubsk Queen	95									16	9
McIntosh Red	94									20	8
Longfield	94									15	9
Orel Not (Russian)	95									20	9
Ontario	95									20	9
Primate	95									20	7
Peerless	94									14	8
Romanskoe	95									18	10
Sweet Bough	95									19	8
Salome	95									16	8
Sherwood's Favorite	95									16	9
Shackleford	94									18	8
Stark	94									18	9
Shiawassee Beauty	24									15	9
Sutton's Beauty	94									12	8
St. Lawrence Winter	94									13	6
Titovka (Russian)	94									20	6
Vandevere	95									13	10
Wolf River	94									20	6
Yellow Transparent										20	10

An experiment showing comparative results with three leading varieties of apples

Four trees of each variety were selected, the Duchess as the leading early apple, the Though I could not get them all of the same age, for the obvious reason that the Spy them. Still it serves to show something of the comparative merits of the varieties.

APPLES.—Yield and selling price of three

Variety.	Age.	Thinning—per cent. by hand or accident.	Time of blooming.	Date of maturity.	Date of gathering.	Yield.	Grade per cent.		
							Class 1.	Class 2.	Class 3.
Four trees, Duchess	11 yrs., planted in '87·	....	May 18...	Aug. 20.	Aug. 20.	4 bbls.	95%	5%	....
" " Wealthy ...	10 " " '88.	....	May 25...	Sept. 25.	Sept. 25.	4 bbls.	50%	25%	25%
" " Northern Spy	17 " " '81.	....	May 30...	Oct. 15.	Oct. 15	8 bbls.	90%	10%	....

All received same treatment as to

CHERRIES.

HABIT.—D , Drooping ; S., Spreading ; U., Upright. SUTURE.—D., Distinct ; L , Large ; Ob., Ob-Oblate ;· Ov , Ovate ; Obo., Obovate ; Obl., Oblong ; Obt , Obtuse ; Pyr., Pyriform ; R., Round ; Rh., row ; Sh , Shallow. BASIN.—Ab., Abrupt ; Ang., Angular ; D., Distinct ; Ev., Even ; Fur., Furrowed ; Brownish ; Bl , Blush ; Blo., Bloom ; Blot , Flotched ; Br., Bright ; C , Crimson ; Clo., Clouded ; D., ous ; O., Orange ; P., Purple ; Ph., Purplish ; Pa., Pale ; R., Red ; Rus., Russet ; Sp., Splashed or W., White ; Wh., Whitish ; Y., Yellow ; Yh , Yellowish.

Varieties tested at Simcoe Station.	Origin.	Fruit.				
		Habit.	Size in inches of length and breadth.	Form.	Suture.	Skin.
Grenner Glass....	Russia	S	$\frac{5}{8}$	R	Ob.	Da. R.......................
Shattan Amarelle...........	"	S	$1\frac{1}{16}$	R	"	R...........................
Litham	"	S	$\frac{3}{4}$x$\frac{7}{8}$	Ob	"	Da. R., nearly black .....
Vladimir...	"	S	$\frac{1}{2}$x$\frac{5}{8}$	R	"	" " ......
English Morello	.. ..	D	$\frac{7}{8}$	Slightly con.	"	Br. Red ....
Ostheim	Germany ..	D	$\frac{5}{8}$x$\frac{7}{8}$	R	"	Da. R. ....
Bessarabian	Russia	S	$\frac{7}{8}$x$1\frac{1}{8}$	R	"	Red........................
Orel 24....	"	D	$\frac{7}{8}$x$1\frac{1}{8}$	R	"	Red........................
Dye-House	....	S	$1\frac{1}{16}$	Slightly con..	"	Red........................

was made this year.

Wealthy as the leading fall apple and the Northern Spy as the leading winter variety.
would not be in bearing at the same age as the others, and I had to take them as I had·
The results will be found in the tabulated statement.   *G. C. Caston, Craighurst.*

varieties of Apples at Simcoe Station, 1898.

Place.	Temperature.	Date of delivery.	Average price.	Remarks on condition of cultivation, spray-ing, manuring, etc.
shipped in refrigerator car...	....	....	$1.25, net $1 per bbl.	sprayed with Bourdeaux, cultivated, manur-ed with clover and ashes.
shipped	....	....	net, $1.25 per bbl...	trees overloaded, and half the fruit too small to be salable.
shipped in October..........	....	....	net, $2.00 per bbl ...	very fine samples of fruit, very clean and large.

cultivation, fertilizing, etc., etc.

CHERRIES.

scure ; Obs , Obsolete. FORM.—Ac., Acute ; An.; Angular ; Con , Conical ; Cor., Corrugated ; Ob.,
Roundish ; Tur., Turbinate. CAVITY —Ac., Acute ; Acu., Acuminate ; B., Broad ; D., Deep ; N., Nar-·
Pl., Plaited ; Rib., Ribbed ; Wr., Wrinkled ; W., Waved. COLOR.—A., Amber ; B., Brown ; Bh.,
Dots ; Da., Dark ; F., Fawn ; G., Green ; Gh., Greenish ; Mar., Marbled ; Mot., Mottled ; Nu., Numer-
Splashes ; St , Striped ; Str., Streaked ; Sta., Stained ; Sun., Sunny Side ; Spo., Spotted ; V., Violet ;

					Fruit.		
						Flesh.	
Stem.	Cavity.	Calyx.	Basin.	Stone.	Color.	Texture.	Flavor.
1½	Sh ...	. ....	......	M ...	Da. R..	Juicy	Sour.
1½	" ...	......	......	M ...	Da. R..	Red, juice............ ..	"
1½	" ...	......	......	Sm ..	Da. R.	" "	Pleasant.
1½	" ...	......	... ..	Sm ..	Da. R..	" "	Fair to small.
1½	" ...	......	......	M ...	R	Firm	Juicy, sour.
1½	" ...	......	......	M ...	R......	"	Pleasant when fully ripe.
1½	" ...	......	......	M ...	Wh	"	Mild sub-acid.
1½	" ...	......	......	Sm ..	R......	"	Firm, mildly acid.
1½	" ...	......	......	M ...	Wh. R .	"	Sub-acid.

APPLES.

Results of experiments in cultivation, pruning, spraying, at East Central Station, 1898.

Varieties under test by R. L. Huggard, Whitby.	When planted.	Soil cultivation.	Vigor, scale 1—10.	Pruning. Date, method and percentage of wood growth removed.	Treatment.	Results.
American Golden Russet	1876	clay loam ; clean cultivation	8	Pruned in March. Cut out suckers and interfering branches.	Sprayed May 2, copperas and lime. 12, Bordeaux mixture. 23, " June 10, "	4½ bushels per tree.
Astrachan	1876	"	7			6½ "
Baldwin	1876	"	10			15 "
Bell Flower	1884	"	6			15 "
Blue Pearmain	1876	"	10			11 "
Boston Star	1880	"	7			16 "
Canada Red	1884	"	5			3 "
Chenango Strawberry	1880	"	6			6 "
Duchess of Oldenburg	1876	"	8			6 "
Early Harvest	1876	"	6			4½ "
Fameuse	1876	"	8			7 "
Fall Pippin	1876	"	7			3 "
's Golden	1876	"	9			3¼ "
Hand Pippin	1876	"	9			4½ "
Kentish Fillbasket	1879	"	9			5 "
King of Tomkins Co.	1876	"	10			12 "
Haas	1879	"	*			3 "
Minkler	1880	"	9			16 "
McMahon's White	1880	"	7			6 "
Maiden's Blush	1876	"	9			5 "
Northern Spy	1880	"	6			4 "
Ontario	1880	"	8			6 "
Pewaukee	1888	"	6			3½ "
Princess Louise	1876	"	8			6 "
Rhode Island Greening	1880	"	8			6 "
Ribston Pippin	1889	"	8			31 "
Salome	1889	"	7			6 "
Seek No Further	1898	"	6			2¼ "
Swazie Pomme Gris	1879	"	8			5½ "
Swaar	1876	"	7			3 "
Twenty Ounce	1876	"	8			5 "
Talman Sweet	1876	"	8			3 "
Wagner	1876	"	7			6 "
Wealthy	1886	"	9			7½ "

* Top grafted in 1895.

BLACKBERRIES.

Descriptive table of blackberries, Burlington Station, 1898.

Size.—S, small; M, medium; L, large. Form.—R., round; C., conical; O, ovate. Color.—D, dark; R., red; P., purple; O., orange; B., bright; Bl., black. Flesh—F., firm; S., soft. Season.—E, early; M., medium; L, late.

Varieties	Origin	Plant — Canes — Habit of growth	Plant — Canes — Color	Plant — Canes — Freedom from disease, 1-10	Plant — Propagation by tips or suckers	Plant — Foliage	Plant — Vigor, scale 1-10	Plant — Hardiness, scale 1-10	Plant — Productiveness, scale 1-10	Berry — Size	Berry — Form	Berry — Color	Berry — Flesh h.	Berry — Flavor	Berry — Season	Berry — Size, inches	Remarks
Agawam		up. spr.	r. br.	9	S	Healthy	9	10	8	M	O. R.	Black	Firm	Poor	M.		
Ancient Briton		up. spr.	br	9	S	"	7	9	7	M	O. C.	"	"	Good	M.		Good.
Child's Tree		spr. up.	br	9	S	"	7	9	7	L	O. C.	"	"	Sweet, spr	M.		Offers
Dorchester		up. spr.	r. br.	9	S	"	9	10	7	L	O. R.	"	"	Sweet, spr	M.		
Early ..er		up.	br	9	S	Fair	9	7	9	M.	O. C.	"	"	Good	E.		
Early Harvest		up.	r. br.	9	S	Healthy	7	9	8	L	O. C.	"	"	Poor	E/M		Good.
Early King		up. spr.	br	9	S	"	7	8	7	S	O. R.	"	"	Good	M.		
Eldorado	Eldorado, Ohio.	up. spr.	r. br.	9	S	"	8	10	7	M	R. C.	"	"	Good, spr	M.		Good.
Erie		up. spr.	br	9	S	"	9	9	7	M.	O. R.	"	"		M.		Very promising.
Gainor		up.	br	9	S	Strong, healthy	9	10	9	L	O. R.	"	"	Fine, spr	M.		Hardy so far.
Kittatinny	Lovett, N.J.	up.	r. br.	9	S	Healthy	10	8	10	M	O. R.	"	M.f'm	The best.	L.		
..'s Best		up.	r. br.	9	S	"	8	10	8	S	O. R.	"	"	Fair	L.		
Maxwell		weak, spr.	r. br.	9	S	"	8	7	5	L	O. R.	"	"	Poor	M.		Too ..k.
Minnewaski		up. spr.	br	9	S	"	9	10	6	M	O. C.	"	"	Good	M.		Very large.
Snyder	..o	up.	r. br.	10	S	"	7	10	7	M	O. C.	"	"	Gd, spr	M.		One of the best.
Stone's Hardy	Wisconsin	up. spr.	r. br.	9	S	"	7	10	8	M	O. C.	"	Firm	Gd, sw't	M.		
Taylor	Indiana	up.	r. br.	10	S	"	7	10	8	S	O. C.	"	"	Gd	M.		
Wachusetts	Indiana	up.	r. br.	9	S	"	9	10	7	M.	O. R.	"	M. F.	Fine	M.		
..rn Triumph		up.	r. br.	10	S	"	9	10	6	S	O. R.	"	Firm.	Fine, sw't	M.		Very few thorns.
Wilson's Early		up.	br	9	S	"	10	9	8	L.	O. R.	"	M	Pleasant	E/M		Very ..thy.
Wilson Junior		spr., trailing	r. br	9	T. & S	(See note)	(See note)	8	6	M.	O. C.	"	Firm.	Sweet	M.		Some canes 11 feet long.

BLACKBERRIES.

Results of experiments in cultivation, pruning, spraying, at Burlington Station, 1898.

A. W. Peart, Experimenter.

Varieties.	When planted.	Soil and cultivation.	Fertilizers used.	Growth in feet	Vigor, scale 1-10.	Pruning, date, method and percentage of wood growth removed.	Results.
Agawam	1895	Gravelly loam plowed in spring, then frequent cultivation and hoeing until fruit is ripe. Banked up for the winter.	Stable manure.	7	9	Summer pruning of new canes late in July to 3½ to 6 feet long, according to vigor of variety; annual pruning, removing old canes and shortening laterals in March or early April.	A very short crop on account of the drought.
Ancient Briton	1897			5	7		
Child's Tree	1897			5	7		
Dorchester	1896			7	9		
Early Cluster	1895			7	9		
Early Harvest	1895			5	7		
Early King	1896			5	7		
Eldorado	1896			6	8		
Erie	1895			7	9		
Gainor	1895			7½	9		
Kittatinny	1895			8	10		
Lovett's Best	1895			6	8		
Maxwell	1895			3½	5		
Minnewaski	1897			6	8		
Ohmer	1895			7	9		
Snyder	1895			5	7		
Stone's Hardy	1895			5½	7		
Taylor	1895			7	9		
Wachusetts	1895			7	9		
Western Triumph	1895			7½	9		
Wilson's Early	1896			5	7		
Wilson Junior	1897			8	10		

Yield and selling price of varieties of blackberries at Burlington Station, 1898.

Varieties.	Planted.	Time of blooming.	Date of maturity.	Date of gathering berries (first and last).	Yield per hill.	Average price.	Remarks on conditions of cultivation, spraying, manuring, etc.
Agawam	1895	June 8	July 27	Ju'y 27—Aug. 10	⅔ lb.	6	There was practically no rain in this district from early in June until September—three months—so that the general blackberry crop was very short. The berries of many varieties dried up on the bushes. The Early Harvest, Early King, Kittatinny, Agawam, Eldorado, Gainor and Stone's Hardy seemed to have the most vitality and fruited the best; not more than 40 per cent. of a full crop.
Ancient Briton	1897	" 8	" 27	" 21— " 5	very few	....	
Child's Tree	1897	" 8	" 20	" 20— " 6	"	....	
Dorchester	1896	" 7	" 23	" 23— " 5	¼	....	
Early cluster	1895	" 11	" 25	" 25— " 10	1/20	....	
Early Harvest	1895	" 11	" 13	" 13— " 1	1	7	
Early King	1896	" 8	" 12	" 12— " 1	⅝	7	
Eldorado	1896	" 6	" 23	" 23— " 5	½	....	
Erie	1895	" 13	" 23	" 23— " 5	¼	....	
Gainor	1895	" 13	" 23	" 23— " 5	½	8	
Kittatinny	1895	" 10	" 23	" 23— " 15	⅓	8	
Lovett's Best	1895	" 11	" 30	" 30— " 10	1/20	....	
Maxwell	1895	" 11	" 20	" 20— " 1	very few	....	
Minnewaski	1897	" 10	" 25	" 25— " 5	"	....	
Ohmer	1897	" 11	" 23	" 23— " 5	⅓	....	
Snyder	1897	" 9	" 18	" 18— " 1	¼	6	
Stone's Hardy	1897	" 8	" 23	" 23— " 5	½	....	
Taylor	1897	" 8	" 23	" 23— " 5	⅓	....	
Wachusetts	1897	" 8	" 23	" 23— " 10	1/20	....	
Western Triumph	1897	" 6	" 23	" 23— " 5	⅓	7	
Wilson's Early	1896	" 13	" 20	" 20— " 5	1/20	....	
Wilson Junior	1897	" 4	" 20	" 20— " 5	very few	....	

CHERRIES.

Results of experiments in cultivation, pruning, spraying, at Simcoe Station, 1898.

Variety Dwarf Cherries.	When planted.	Soil and cultivation.	Fertilizers used.	Pruning, Date, method and percentage of wood growth removed.	Growth in inches.	Vigor, scale 1—0.
Bessarabian	1894	Clay loam....	Stable and ashes.	May ; dwarf ; thinned out about ⅛th	18	9
Brusseler Braum	1894	"	" "	....	18	9
Griotte Du Nord.........	1894	"	" "	....	20	0
Lustovka...................	1894	"	" "	....	19	9
Orel 24...................	1894	"	" "	....	18	9
HALF STANDARD CHERRIES.						
Dye House..............	1894	"	....	May ; dwarf ; thinned out about ⅛th	16	8
Ostheim...................	1894	" ..	....	....	15	7
Vladimir	1894	"	....	....	18	9
English Morello..........	1896	"	....	....	15	7
Litham	1896	"	....	....	16	8
Orel	1896	"	....	....	17	8

CHERRIES—

HABIT—D., Drooping ; S., Spreading ; U., Upright ; St., Stout ; Sl., Slender. SUTURE—D., Distinct ;
rugated ; H., Heartshaped ; Ob., Oblate ; Ov., Ovate ; Obo., Obovate ; Obl., Oblong ; Obt., Obtuse ;
B., Broad ; D., Deep ; N, Narrow ; Sh., Shallow. BASIN—Ab., Abrupt ; Ang., Angular ; D.,
COLOR—A., Amber ; B., Brown ; Bh., Brownish ; Bl., Blush ; Blo., Bloom ; Blot., Blotched ; Br.,
Moroon ; Mar , Marbled ; Mot., Mottled ; Nu., Numerous ; O., Orange ; P., Purple ; Ph., Purplish ;
Sun., Sunny Side ; Spo., Spotted ; V., Violet ; W., White ; Wh., Whitish ; Y., Yellow ; Yh., Yel-

Varieties tested at Maplehurst.	Origin and class.	Habit of tree.	Fruit.		
			Size in inches of length and breadth.	Form.	Suture.
Centennial					
Choisy	1 ; Duke	up., fas.		ob., h.	ob
Cleveland	Ohio ; Big	st., sp	$\frac{7}{8}$ x 15-16	h., sides unequal	d
Coe		r., sp		r , reg'r	obs
Dwarf Rocky Mt					
Dye House					
Eagle	England ; Big		13-16 x 15-16	obt., h.	
Early Purple	Europe ; B.	u., s	$\frac{7}{8}$ x $\frac{3}{4}$	acute, h.	obs
Elkhorn	Eur. ; Big	u., st.	$\frac{7}{8}$ x $\frac{5}{8}$	h., hollowed at apex.	obs
Elton					
Eugenie		u., fas.	$\frac{5}{8}$ x 3-16	h., irreg	d
Governor Wood	Cleveland, Ohio	r., reg	$\frac{3}{4}$ x $\frac{7}{8}$	obt., h.	d
Hortense					
Kentish (late)		s.	r. to m.	r., flattened	
Koslov Morello					
Late Duke					
Magnifique					
May Duke		u., fas.		r., obt., h	ob
Mazzard	England or France			r., h	
Mezel	Bigarreau (of Mezel), Europe.	u., s	15-16 x 1	obt , h., uneven	
Montmorency	Montmorency, France	s.	m. to l	r., flattened at base.	
Montmorency Ordinaire					
Napoleon		u., s	1 x 1	obt., h.	trac'able
Ohio					
Olivet		sl., sp	11-16 x $\frac{3}{4}$	r., slightly flattened.	obs
Ostheim	Russia	Morello bush	s. to m.	r., obt.	
Philippe					
Richmond	Europe	s.		r.	obs
Rockport					
Royal Duke					
Schmidt					
Spanish	Europe to America, 1800	sp	$\frac{7}{8}$ x 1 1-16	r., obt., h	ob.
Tartarian					
Windsor	Ontario, Canada		15-16 x 1	r., obt., h	
Wragg	Waukee, Iowa		m.	r.	obs

DESCRIPTIVE TABLES.

L., Large; Ob., Obscure; Obs., Obsolete. FORM—Ac., Acute; An., Angular; Con., Conical; Cor., Cor-
Pyr., Pyriform; R., Round; Rb., Roundish; Tur., Turbinate. CAVITY—Ac., Acute; Acu., Acuminate;
Distinct; Ev., Even; Fur., Furrowed; Pl., Plaited; Rib., Ribbed; Wr., Wrinkled; W., Waved.
Bright; C., Crimson; Clo., Clouded; D., Dots; Da., Dark; F., Fawn; G., Green; Gh., Greenish; M.,
Pa., Pale; R., Red; Rus, Russet; Sp, Splashed or Splashes; St., Striped; Str., Streaked; Sta., Stained;
lowish.

Fruit.

Skin.	Stem.	Cavity.	Flesh. Color.	Flesh. Texture.	Flesh. Flavor.
car		d.	l. r.	soft, juicy	sweet, very rich, with delicate aroma, most delicious.
br. r. m., dark rich red in sun.	st. $1\frac{1}{4}$ to $1\frac{1}{2}$	b. d. corr.	l. cream	tender, juicy	sweet, delicious.
b. shining a., nearly covered, b. r. blotched.	$1\frac{1}{2}$	m. b.	pale yh	soft, juicy	sweet, excellent.
d. r., becoming almost blk.	$1\frac{1}{2}$ to $1\frac{3}{4}$		d. p.	tender and juicy	very sweet, rich, and delicious.
d. r. to b	$2\frac{1}{8}$	s.	r. to purple	tender, juicy	sweet and pleasant.
dark moroon	$1\frac{1}{4}$	large, even	dark crimson	firm, juicy	sweet, rich, pleasant.
br. carmine	sl. $1\frac{1}{2}$	d	l. r.	soft, juicy	mild, acid, agr'able.
l. y. marbled and shaded with l. to d. r.	1 to $1\frac{1}{2}$	b	yh.	tender, juicy	sweet, aromatic, delicious.
b. r.		m		tender, juicy	very acid.
b. r. to d. r.	$1\frac{1}{2}$ to 2		r.	tender, very juicy	sub-acid, very good.
b	long and slender.	sh			
d. r. to b.	$1\frac{1}{2}$ to 2	m. d.	r.	firm, breaking juicy.	sweet and good.
b. to d. r.	$1\frac{1}{4}$ to $1\frac{1}{2}$, stout.	m. d.	yh.	soft, very juicy	sprightly, tart, mild when very ripe.
a., blotched or suffused with bright r.	$1\frac{1}{2}$		very pale yellow	firm, meaty, fairly juicy.	sweet, agreeable.
dark rich crimson	$1\frac{1}{8}$	b	l. r.	soft, juicy	mild, acid, agreeable.
red to dark r	$1\frac{1}{2}$ to $1\frac{3}{4}$		d. r. cling	tender, juicy, melting.	almost sweet when ripe, agreeable.
b. to d. r.	1		yh.	soft, very juicy	sprightly, tart.
clear waxen a., nearly covered with r. sun.	$1\frac{1}{2}$ to 2	b.	pa. y.	firm, breaking juicy.	sweet, pleasant, delicious.
d. r. to b.	$1\frac{1}{2}$	m. d.	yh. with rh. tint	very firm, moderately juicy.	rich, sweet, excellent.
b. r. growing almost b. at maturity.	$1\frac{3}{4}$ to 2		d. r.		

CHERRIES.—Results of cultivation, pruning, spraying, etc., at Maplehurst, 1898.

Varieties.	When planted.	Soil and cultivation.	Fertilizers used.	Insects.		Fungi.		Results.		
				Name.	Treatment.	Name.	Treat-ment.	Notes.	Height in feet.	Diameter of trunk in inches 1 foot from ground.
Cleveland	1896								10	2
Choisy	1896	Sand ; best	Ashes	Aphis	Kerosene			Cleared	10 1/6	2 1/8
Downer's Late	1896								9 2/3	2
Eagle	1896	Sand ; sod	Ashes	Aphis	Kerosene			Leaves burned with kerosene too strong ; ripened unevenly on account of aphis	8	2 1/4
Elkhorn	1896	Sand ; sod	Ashes	Curculio	Paris green	Rot	Bordeaux.	Badly stung	12	2 1/2
Elton	1896								11	2 1/4
Early Purple	1896	Sandy loam ; best cult.	Ashes	Aphis, curculio.	Kerosene	Rot	Bordeaux.	Cleared of aphis, but fruit ripened unevenly ; leaves burned with kerosene	10	2 1/4
Empress Eugenie	1896								11	2 1/2
Ida	1896								9 3/4	2
Koslov	1889	Sandy loam ; best cult.	Ashes	None.		None.		A bush ; quite productive		
Late Duke	1896								8 1/3	2
Magnifique	1896								7	2 1/8
May Duke	1896								11 1/4	2 3/4
Mezel	1868	Sandy loam ; best	Barn manure	Aphis, curculio.	Paris green, kerosene.			Ripened very unevenly on account of aphis		
Montmorency	1896	Same ; best	Barn manure and ashes	Curculio	Paris green			Healthy in foliage and in fruit.	7 2/3	2
M. Ordinaire	....									
Napoleon	1868			Curculio	Paris green.	Rot	Bordeaux.	Worthless from rot and curculio		
Ohio	1896								10	2 1/8
Olivet	1896								7 3/4	2
Reine Hortense	1896	Sandy loam ; best	Barn manure and ashes					Rotted badly as soon as ripe	9	2 1/5
Rockport	1896								13	3
Royal Duke	1896							No insects or fungi	9 1/4	2 1/2
Schmidt	1896								10 1/2	2 5/8
Spanish	1896	Sandy loam ; sod		Aphis, curculio.		Rot	Bordeaux.	Two-thirds rotten ; large number wormy ; almost worthless		
Tartarian	1896	Same		Aphis		Rot	Bordeaux.	Fruit blighted ; ripened unevenly ; very poor yield	9	2
Tartarian Improved	1896								9 1/3	2 1/4
Windsor	1896								10	2 1/2
Wood	1896	Sandy loam ; sod	Ashes							
Wragg	1896								7 1/6	2 1/4

MATURITY, SEASON AND YIELD OF CHERRIES AT MAPLEHURST, 1898.

Varieties.	Age since planting.	Maturity.	Season.	Yield.	Class 1.	Class 2.	Average price.	Remarks on conditions of cultivation, spraying, manuring, etc.
Cleveland	2 yrs		June 15 to 25				8	
Choisy	2 yrs		June 22 to July 2 or 4					
Dyehouse	3 yrs		June 20 to					
Eagle		July 8	July 4 to					
Elkhorn	40 yrs	" 15	July 11 to					
Early Purple	20¾ yrs		June 12 to 20	12 qts	8	4		With cultivation and spraying, one of the best late varieties for market
Knight's Early								⅓ taken by bugs, ⅓ by birds and rot.
Late Duke	3 yrs		June 26 to July 10 (no worms)					
May Duke	2 yrs		July 15 to July 6					
Mezel	30 yrs		July 2 to 15	108	100	8		A grand cherry if well cultivated and enriched.
Montmorency			July 2 or 3					
M. Ordinaire			July 2 or 3					
Ohio	3 yrs		June 16 to July 4					
Olivet	3 yrs		June 24 to July 5					
Richmond	3 yrs		June 24 to July 4					
Royal Duke			June 30					
Tartarian	3 yrs		June 28 to July 6				9	
Windsor	30 yrs		July 6					
Wood	30½ yrs		June 20 to 30					⅓ thinned by cherry rot while very small; controlled by Bordeaux.

VIGOR OF CHERRY TREES.

As shown after three season's growth at Maplehurst, 1898.

Varieties.	Height in feet.	Caliper measure in inches one foot from the ground.
Rockport Bigarreau	13	3
Elkhorn	12	2¼
Elton	11	2¼
Yellow Spanish	11	2¾
Empress Eugenie	11	2⅓
May Duke	11¼	2¾
Schmitz Bigarreau	10⅓	2⅝
Early Purple	10	2¼
Governor Wood	10½	2½
Windsor	10	2½
Cleveland	10	2
Ohio Beauty	10	2⅛
Belle de Choisy	10⅙	2⅛
Ida	9¾	2
Black Tartarian	9	2
Black Tartarian Improved	9⅓	2¼
Downer's Late	9⅔	2
Reine Hortense	9	2⅜
Royal Duke	9¼	2½
Late Duke	8⅓	2
Black Eagle	8	2⅛
Montmorency	7⅔	2
Olivet	7¾	2
English Morello	7⅙	1¾
Wragg	7⅙	2¼
Belle Magnifique	7	2⅛
Centennial	7½	1¼
Montmorency Ordinaire	6¼	1½

AGE OF BEARING FRUIT.

First fruitage of cherry trees in the experimental orchard at Maplehurst.

Two years planted.	Three years planted.
Cleveland.	Black Tartarian.
Dyehouse.	Black Eagle.
English Morello.	Belle Magnifique.
German Ostheim.	Belle de Choisy.
King's Amarelle.	Empress Eugenie.
Suda Hardy.	Elton.
Spate Amarelle.	Governor Wood.
Wragg.	Late Duke.
	Montmorency.
	May Duke.
	Ohio Beauty.
	Olivet.
	Purple.
	Reine Hortense.
	Royal Duke.

Descriptive table of currants, Burlington Station, 1898.

SIZE.—S., small ; M., medium ; L., large. FORM.—L., long ; S., short ; Sh., shouldered. COMPACTNESS.—C., close ; L., loose ; St., straggling. FORM OF BERRY.—R., round ; Ov., oval ; Ob., oblong. COLOR.—R., red ; B., black ; W., white ; G., green ; Y., yellow. SEASON.—E., early ; M. medium ; L., late.

Varieties.	Origin.	Foliage.	Vigor, scale 1-10.	Productiveness, scale 1-10.	Freedom from mildew, scale 1-10.	Diameter.	Form.	Size.	Color.	Flavor. (See Thomas.)	Season.	Dessert.	Market.	Remarks.
Belle de St. Giles		Healthy, thin.	7	5	8	inch.	R	L	R	Fine	M			
Black Victoria		Strong, healthy	9	6	8	"	"	L	B	Sweet	L			
Brayley's Seedling		Healthy	7	8	8	"	"	M	R	Dry acid.	E M			
Champion		Vigorous, healthy	10	9	8	"	"	V L	B	Acid	L			One of the best.
Cherry		Strong, healthy	8	9	8	"	"	L	R	Fine	M			Probably the best.
Collin's Prolific			10	5	8	"	"	V L	B	Very acid	L			
Fay's Prolific		Portland, N.Y., probably a cross, Cherry + Victoria										See catalogue of fruits.		
Gloire	England	Healthy, red	6	7	8	"	"	L	R	Acid	M L			Good.
Naples		Healthy,	8	8	9	"	"	V L	B	Acid	M L			Excellent.
New Victoria		Healthy,	9	9	8	"	"	L	R	Acid	M			Very largely grown [here.
North Star		Healthy, red	7	6	8	"	"	M	"	Good	E M			
Pomona	Canada	Healthy,	7	7	8	"	"	L	"	Spr. good.	M			
Raby Gale	N.Y., cross, Cherry + White Grape	Strong, vigorous.	8	5	8	"	"	L	"	Good	M			Promising well.
Red Cross		Healthy,	7	10	8	"	"	M	"	Acid, good				
Red Dutch		Healthy,	8	7	8	"	"	M	"	Good	M		,,	
Red Victoria		Good, healthy	8	7	9	"	"	M	"	Very good.	M		,,	Offers well.
Saunders		Healthy,	9	9	8	"	"	L	B	Fine	L		,,	
Versailles			7	6	8	"	"	M	R	Acid, good	M			
White Grape		Healthy, vigorous.	8	6	8	"	"	V L	W	Acid, good	E M			
White Imperial		Healthy.	8	8	8	"	"	L	W	Aid	E M			Very large berry.
Wilder	Irvington, Indiana, seedling of Versailles	Very, Medium.	8	8	9	½	"	L	R	Good	M			

10 F.S.

CURRANTS.

Results of experiments in cultivation, pruning, spraying, at Burlington Station, 1898.

A. W. PEART, EXPERIMENTER.

Variety.	When planted.	Soil and cultivation.	Fertilizers used.	Pruning, date, method and percentage of wood growth removed.	Insects. Name	Insects. Treatment.	Fungi. Name	Fungi. Treatment.	Results.	Growth in inches	Vigor, scale 1-10.
Belle de St. Giles	1896	Gravelly loam ; bushes plowed to in the fall and from in the spring, then frequent cultivation and hoeing until fruit is nearly ripe; no cultivation after middle of August.	Stable manure.	Late in March; the branches of red and white currants shortened so as to throw out laterals and fruit spears; the wood of black currants thinned out about 30 per cent.	Currant worm and borer in red and white currants ; borer in black.	For currant worm, paris green for first wood, hellebore for second; for borer, cutting out and burning injured stems.	Naples slightly injured by mildew.	Bordeaux.	Light crop save on two or three varieties (see table) but quality good.	12	7
Black Victoria	1896									16	9
Brayley's Seedling	1896									12	7
Champion	1895									18	10
Cherry	1896									14	8
Collin's Prolific	1896									18	10
Fay's Prolific	1896									10	6
Lee's Prolific	1896									14	8
Naples	1895									16	9
New Victoria	1897									12	7
North Star	1896									12	7
Pomona	1897									12	7
Raby Castle	1896									14	8
Red Cross	1896									12	7
Red Dutch	1897									14	8
Red Victoria	1896									14	8
Saunders	1897									16	9
Versailles	1896									12	7
White Grape	1896									14	8
White Imperial	1896									14	8
Wilder	1896									14	8

Yield and selling price of varieties of currants at Burlington Station, 1898

Variety.	Planted	Time of blooming.	Date of maturity.	Date of gathering berries (first and last).	Yield per hill.	Average price.
Belle de St. Giles	1896	May 10	July 8	July 8—13	½ lb.	Red currants, 4c per qt., black, 6c
Black Victoria	1896	" 16	" 8	" 8—20	½ "	
Brayley's Seedling	1896	" 10	" 8	" 8—13	1½ "	
Champion	1895	" 11	" 20	" 20—31	2 "	
Cherry	1896	" 9	" 6	" 6—12	1 "	
Collin's Prolific	1896	" 17	" 20	" 20—31	very few	
Fay's Prolific	1896	" 10	" 7	" 7—12	1 lb.	
Lee's Prolific	1896	" 12	" 12	" 12—20	⅜ "	
Naples	1895	" 12	" 12	" 12—20	2 "	
New Victoria	1897	" 12	" 4	" 4—8	very few	
North Star	1896	" 10	" 7	" 7—12	¼ lb.	
Pomona	1897	" 10	" 4	" 4—8	very few	
Raby Castle	1896	" 10	" 11	" 11—16	4 lb.	
Red Cross	1896	" 10	" 7	" 7.—12	very few	
Red Dutch	1897	" 10	" 4	" 4—8	3 lb.	
Red Victoria	1896	" 11	" 7	" 7—12	very few	
Saunders	1897	" 16	" 12	" 12—20	very few	
Versailles	1896	" 11	" 7	" 7—12	½ lb.	
White Grape	1896	" 10	" 7	" 7—12	¼ "	
White Imperial	1896	" 10	" 7	" 7—12	⅜ "	
Wilder	1896	" 10	" 7	" 7—12	¾ "	

GOOSEBERRIES. Tested at Gooseberry Station. S. Spillett, Nantyr, Experimenter.

Size.—S., small; M., medium; L., large. Form.—L., long; S., short; Sh., shouldered. Compactness.—C., close; L., loose; ISt., straggling. Form of Berry.—R., round; Ov., oval; Ob., oblong. Color.—R., red; B., black; W., white; G., green; Y., yellow. Season.—E., early; M., medium; L., late.

Varieties	Origin	Foliage	Vigor	Productiveness	Freedom from mildew	Size	Form	Color	Flavor	Season	Dessert	Market	Remarks
?at	Eng	Fair	7	8	8	L	O. B	G.	V. G	L	10	10	
?in	American	Good	9	10	7	M	O. V	G. W	Fair	M	6	7	
?'s ?in	Eng	Fair	3		8	L	O. O	G. W	G		9	10	
Crosby's Seedling	Foreign	Gdd	9	9	8	L	O. B	G. Y	G		9	10	
?n Bob	Foreign	Gd	8		8	V. L	O. V	R	G	M	10	10	
?hs	Eng	Good	8		8	L	O. B	B	G		9	10	
Cook's Eagle	Eng	?r	8		9	L		G.	G				
Downing	Eng	Fair	8	8	8	M	O. B	G. Y	G	M	9	10	
Dominion	Eng	V., Gd	8	9	9	R.	R.	G. Y	G	M	9	8	
?an Prolific	Foreign	?r	8		8	L	O. B	G. W	G	M	9	10	
Green ?el	Eng	Good	8	8	8	L	O. B	G. W	G	M	9	10	
Ingram's	Eng	Fair	7		1	L	O. B	R	V. G	E	10	10	
Keepsake	Eng	Good	8		9	L	O. B	G. Y	G	L	9	10	
Lancashire ?d	Eng	Fair	8	8	8	L	O. B	G. Y	G	M	9	10	
?ye Golden Prolific	Eng	Fair	8	9	8	M	R. V	R.	G	M	9	9	Oregon J. and Red Jacket are similar in every respect.
London	Eng	?r	8	9	9	M	O. R	R. W	G	M	8	9	
Lanceolet	Eng	?r	8		8	L	O. V	G. W	G	M	9	9	
Mrs. ?	Foreign	Gtod	9	8	9	M	O. V	G. R	G	M	10	10	
?on ? ?o	American	Gd	9	8	7	S	O. R	R.	G	M	9	6	Hairy, very.
Pearl	Foreign	?r	8	8	9	V. L	R. V	G. V	G	M	7	6	Not up in size, but in other respects a Downing.
Phoenix	American	Gtd	8	8	7	V. L	O. B	G. W	G	M	9	10	
Red Champagne	Eng	Fair	8	9	9	S	O. V	G. W	Fair	M	6	6	Too small.
Success	Eng	Good	8		8	L	O. V	G. Y	G	M	9	9	

GOOSEBERRIES.   Results of experiments in cultivation, pruning, spraying at Gooseberry Station, 1898.

STANLEY SPILLETT, NANTYR, EXPERIMENTER.

Varieties.	When planted.	Soil and cultivation.	Fertilizers used.	Growth in inches.	Vigor, scale 1-10.	Pruning. Date, method and percentage of wood growth removed.	Insects. Name.	Insects. Treatment.	Fungi. Name.	Fungi. Treatment.	Results.
	1890	Clay soil, which was stirred between rows every seven days with Horse Hoe and always as soon as practicable after a shower. Bushes are set 6x4, between bushes is stirred as rows with a long handle shovel.	Stable manure dug in the fall, ashes worked in during summer.	15	8	No cutting back any wood that is cut, is cut clean out.	Gooseberry worm.	Paris Green, 8 ozs, to 4 gals, of Bordeaux mixture, 8 ozs, to 40 gals, of Bordeaux mixture.	Mildew.	Bordeaux and liver of sulphur.	I can only report spraying for mildew a partial success. I can detect no difference in results between the two fungicides used. No fruit destroyed this year with mildew, but foliage effected in August.
	1893			20	9						
	1894			11	7						
	1895			10	6						
	1895			15	8						
	1895			12	7						
	1895			12	7						
	1896			23	4						
	1896			18	8						
Dominion	1896			10	6						
Green Prolific	1895			10	6						
Ingram's	1896			11	7						
Keepsake	1896			10	6						
Lancashire Lad	1896			11	6						
Large	1895			10	6		November 20th, 1897. Shrub system, about 6 stems allowed to grow, renewed every 3 years.					
London	1896			9	6						
Lanceolet	1896			11	7						
Ms.	1895			24	9						
Oregon Jumbo	1896			12	7						
	1896			21	8						
Pearl	1895			10	7						
Phoenix	1894			24	7						
Red	1895			6	9						
Red Champagne	1896			21	6						
Success	1896			14	8						
Triumph	1894			17	7						
	1892			18	8						
Was Industry	1894			3	8						
Yellow Scotch	1896			12	3						

GOOSEBERRIES. Annual Record, showing yield and selling price of varieties at Gooseberry Station, 1898.

Varieties.	Age. Years.	Time of blooming. May	Date of maturity. Aug.	Date of gathering. (Berries, 1st and last). Aug.	Yield.	Average price. cents.	Remarks. On conditions of cultivation, spraying, manuring, etc.
Autocrat	8	15	12	10 to 15	2 qts. per bush	7	Plants set 6x4 ft. between rows, ground was stirred every week with Planet Jr. Wheel Hoe; between bushes with shovel hoe, but always as soon as possible after a shower. First spraying March 82th with blue stone water, 6 lbs. to 40 gals, afterwards every 10 days and after heavy showers. Manure dug in in fall, hard wood ashes worked in during summer about each bush.
…in	5	10	10	10 to 15	few berries ; winter killed		
Ge's …in	4	15	12	10 to 15	few berries		
…n	4						
…y's Seedling	4	15	12	to 15	2 qts. to bush	8	
…n Bob	4	18	15		only few berries		
Gs.	2						
Gs Eagle	2	15	15	10 to 20	a few berries		
Downing	12	10	10	10 to 15	6 qts	5	
Dominion	3						
…J… Prolific	3	15	18	20	few berries		
…n … s.	2	18	15	15	"		
Ingram's …n	2						
Keepsake	2	18	18	20	few berries		
Large …n Prolific	3	15	18	20	few berries		
…n …n	2	18	15	20	"		
Ms.	2						
Oregon …o	3	10	12	15	few berries		
…l	3	15	18	20	only few berries		
Phoenix	6	10	12	10 to 15	6 qts. to bush	5	
…n …o	3						
Red …s…	4	10	15	20	few berries		
…d Champagne	4	12	12	10 to 15	2 qts		
Success	2	10	15	15	few berries		
…h …w	3				"		
…o Crysta	4	12	15	15	few berries		
…n's Ind	6	10	12	15	1 at	5	
…w Scotch	5	15	18	20	few berries		

GRAPES. Yield and selling price of varieties of Grapes at Wentworth Station, 1898.

TESTED BY M. PETIT, EXPERIMENTER, WINONA.

Varieties.	Age.	Thinned, per cent, by hand or accident.	Time of blooming.	Date of maturity.	Date of gathering, 1st and last.	Yield.	Grade, per cent. Class 1.	Class 2.	Average price.	Remarks. On conditions of cultivation, spraying, manuring, etc.
		Not thinned	The last three days of June			lb.	All sold as one grade	Those not carried out sold for wine at $15 per ton.	cents.	Ploughed in May and kept clean and mellow by frequent cultivation until August. Some stable manure and ashes used. Sulphur applied last week of June.
Agawam	11			October 5.	October 5–25	17½			2½	
Brill	3	"	"	September 15.	September 28	6	"		} Sold for wine.	
Black	3	"	"	" 15.	" 28	4½	"			
	3	"	"	" 10.	" 10	4	"		1½	
	16	"	"	" 15.	" 28	15½	"		} Sold for wine.	
Cambridge	3	"	"	" 10.	" 28	7	"			
	3	"	"	" 10.	" 28	8½	"			
	3	"	"	" 15.	" 20	6	"		1	
	24	"	"	October 20.	October 24	20½	"		2	
	15	"	"	September 15.	September 20	18½	"		2¾	
Dr.	3	"	"	" 15.	" 28	9	"			
Delaware	24	"	"	" 1.	" 20	17	"			
Early	3	"	"	" 10.	" 3	8	"		2	
	3	"	"	" 10.	" 23	10½	"			
	11	"	"	October 20.	September 12	16½	"		3	
Ms	12	"	"	September 5.	October 20	7¾	"		1	
Moyer	3	"	"	" 22.	September 5	6¾	"			
Niagara	15	"	"	October 10.	" 22	23½	"			
Opal	2	"	"	" 15.	October 20	8	"			
	3	"	"	September 1.	" 20	5	"			
	3	"	"	" 5.	September 28	6½	"			
	2	"	"	" 25.	" 28	4	"		2	
Salem	16	"	"	October 15.	" 29	3½	"			
Ulster Prolific	3	"	"	" 15.	October 24	19½	"			
W	16	"	"	September 8.	" 24	7	"		1¾	
Watb	16	"	"	October 20.	September 10	16½	"		1½	
	3	"	"		October 24	20	"			
						4½	"			

TABLE OF VIGOR. GRAPE VINES, TESTED BY M. PETTIT, WINONA, EXPERIMENTER.

SIZE.—T., thick; sl, slender. FORM OF JOINT.—S., short; M, medium.

Varieties.	Length, feet.	Size.	Form of joint.	Vigor.	Varieties.	Length, feet.	Size.	Form of joint.	Vigor.
Planted in 1894.									
…	8 to 12	T	S	8	…	10 " 15	T	S	10
Ar…	6 " 10	sl	M	7	…	6 " 8	Sl	S	7
…Giant	8 " 10	M	S	9	Man …	8 " 12	Sl	S	9
…	10 " 15	T	L	10	…	10 " 15	Sl	M	9
…alk	10 " 14	T	S	9	Man Seedling	4 " 6	M	S	5
Beacon	10 " 15	M	S	10	New Haven	5 " 8	Sl	S	6
Bell	4 " 6	Sl	S	4	…	6 " 8	M	S	5
…	7 " 10	M	sl	8	…	6 " 8	Sl	M	6
…	10 " 12	T	L	10	Requa	7 " 10	M	sl	6
… Muscat	4 " 6	M	S	10	Rockwood	7 " 10	M	L	7
Cottage	4 " 7	Sl	M	5	…	5 " 7	Sl	L	4
…	6 " 7	Sl	S	8	Watt	7 " 12	T	S	4
Cambridge	12 " 15	T	sl	8	Woodruff Red	7 " 10	Sl	S	5
Dr…	7 " 9	Sl	S	9	… Budded in 1895.				5
Elvira	6 " 8	Sl	S	6	Opal	10 to 12	Sl	sl	8
Early …tor	8 " 7	T	S	6	Presley	10 " 12	T	L	8
Early Ohio	8 " 8	M	M	5	… Budded in 1896.	6 " 8	T	S	6
…	5 " 6	Sl	M	8	…	6 " 8	M	L	6
Eumelan	8 " 12	M	M	6	Black July	4 to 5	T	S	8
…	4 " 6	M	S	5	Black Hawk	8 " 10	Sl	L	8
Eaton	4 " 5	M	sl	3	…	3 " 5	Sl	M	5
Esther	8 " 8	T	L	6	…	3 " 6	M	S	4
Etta	4 " 6	Sl	S	6	… Favourite	4 " 8	T	S	6
…	3 " 5	Sl	S	6	…	8 " 10	Sl	S	8
Grein's …	5 " 8	Sl	L	3	…	2 " 6	M	S	8
… Drop	8 " 9	Sl	L	5	Norton's Virginia	3 " 4	Sl	M	6
Geneva	7 " 10	T	S	8	…	2 " 3	M	S	5
…	9 " 5	Sl	S	9	Hayes	4 " 5	T	sl	7
Hermann	6 " 6	Sl	S	3	Kensington	3 " 6	Sl	S	6
Hayes	4 " 7	T	M	5	…	8 " 10	Sl	M	5
Ives	3 " 4	Sl	S	4	… Planted in 1897.				8
…	10 " 12	M	sl	2	Campbell's Early	4 to 6	T	S	8
Lo Rieseling	5 " 7	Sl	L	4	Canada	2 " 3	T	S	6
…	6 " 8	M	L	8	Delaware	3 " 4	T	S	5
…	6 " 8	M	M	5	Gazelle	4 " 5	T	sl	x
Moore's Diamond	4 " 6	T	S	5	Upland	3 " 5	M	M	5

PEACHES.

Varieties tested at South-western Station. W. W. Hilborn, experimenter.	Origin.	Tree.					
		Vigor Scale 1-10.	Hardiness Scale 1-10.	Productiveness, Scale 1-10.	Age of bearing.	Size by Scale 1-10.	Form.
Alexander	Ill	9	9	10	.....	5-6	R
Barnard	Ill	8	9	10	.....	5-6	R
Brigden	?	8	8	8	.....	8-10	O
Boyle's Yellow	Mich	8	9	10	.....	5-6	R
Banner	Ont	9	9	9	.....	8-9	R
Crane's Yellow	Mich	8	8	9	.....	7-8	R Ov.
Canada Early	Ont	9	9	10	.....	5-6	
Crawford Early	N. J	9	8	8	.....	8-9	R Ov.
Crawford Late	N. J	9	8	5	.....	9-10	R Ov.
Crosby	Mass	8	9	10	.....	5-8	R
Champion	Ill	8	7	6	.....	6-8	R
Dumont	?	8	8	9	.....	4-6	R
Engols Mammoth	Mich	9	9	10	.....	6-8	R
Elberta	Ga	7	5	6	.....	8-9	O
Frankford	?	8	8	8	.....	4-5	R
Fitzgerald	Ont	8	9	9	.....	8-9	R Ov.
Golden Drop	Mich	8	10	10	.....	5-6	R
Hinman	?	9	9	9	.....	8-9	R
Hale's Early	Ohio	8	9	10	.....	4-5	
Hill's Chili	N. Y	7	10	10	.....	5-8	O V C
Jersey Pride	N. J	8	6	7	.....	8-9	R Ov.
Jacques Rareripe	Mass	9	9	9	.....	7-8	
Longhurst	Ont	8	10	10	...	5-8	O V C
Lemon Free	Ohio	9	10	10	...	3-10	R O V
Lewis	Mich	8	9	9	.....	5-6	R
Moore's Favorite	Mass	8	8	7	.....	7-8	R
Marshall's Late	?	9	8	8	.....	7-8	B
Mt. Rose	N. J	8	8	7	.....	6-7	R
New Prolific	Mich	8	9	9	.....	8-9	R
Oldmixon Free	Am	8	6	4	.....	7-9	R
River's Early	Eng	8	9	10	.....	7-9	R
Smock Free	N. J	9	9	8	.....	8-10	O V
Smock Beer's	N. J	9	9	8	.....	8-9	O V
Salway	Eng	9	9	10	.....	7-8	R
Snow's Orange	Mich	7	8	8	.....	5-6	R
St. John	Am	8	8	9	.....	6-8	R
Stump	N. Y	8	8	7	.....	7-9	R
Tyhurst	Ont	8	10	10	...	5-6	R
Toledo Early	Ohio	8	9		.....	4-5	R
Yellow Rareripe	Am	8	7	6	.....	7-9	R
Wager	N. Y	8	9	10	.....	5-7	O V
Wheatland	N. Y	9	7	1	.....	8-9	O V

PEACHES.—*Con.*

| Fruit | | | | | Quality. Scale 1-10. | | Value. Scale 1.10. | |
Skin. Color.	Seeds or stone.	Flesh. Color.	Flavor.	Season.	Dessert.	Cooking.	Home market.	Foreign market.
				Begin to ripen.				
W R	Cling	W	Medium	July 23	3-6	3	3	2
Y R	Free	Y	Good..........	Aug. 29	7-8	9	7	7
Y R	Free	Y	Good	" 18	.9	9	10	10
Y R	Free	Y	Good..........	" 25	6-7	9	7	8
Y R	Free	Y	Very good....	Oct. 1.....	8-10	10	10	10
Y R	Free	Y	Good..........	Aug. 14	8-9	9	9	9
W R	Cling	W	Medium.......	July 23....	3-6	3	3	2
Y R	Free	Y	Good..........	Aug. 24	9	9	9	9
Y R	Free	Y	Good..........	Sept. 15...	9	9	10	10
Y R	Free	Y	Good..........	" 10....	8	9	9	9
W R	S Cling........	W	Good..........	" 5....	8-10	5	5	3
Y	Free ....:	Y	Good..........	" 8....	5 6	8	6	7
Y R	Free ....:	Y	Good..........	" 8....	8-9	10	10	10
Y R	Free	Y	Good..........	" 12..:	7-8	9	10	10
Y R	Free	Y	Good..........	" 4...	5-6	7	5	5
Y R	Free	Y	Very good....	Aug. 28	10	10	10	10
Y	Free	Y	Med to good..	Sept. 19....	6-7	9	7	7
Y Y	Free	Y	Good.... ...	" 4...	8-9	9	10	10
G W R	S Cling........	W	Medium.......	Aug. 14	5-6	5	4	4
Y R	Free	Y R	Med to good..	Sept. 12....	5-8	8	8	8
Y R	Free	Y	Good..........	" 6....	8-9	9	10	10
Y R	Free	Y	Medium.......	" 12....	5-6	7	8	8
Y R	Free	Y	Med to good...	" 12....	5-8	8	8	8
Y	Free	Y	Med to good...	" 28....	5-7	9	8	8
W R	S Cling........	W	Medium.......	Aug. 15 :...	3	3	3	4
W	Free	W	Good..........	Sept. 12....	7-8	8	6	6
Y R	Free	Y	Good..........	Oct. 5......	7-8	9	8	8
W R	Free	W	Good..........	Aug. 24	7-8	8	6	6
Y R	Free	Y	Very good....	Sept. 6	9-10	10	10.	10
W R	Free	W	Very good....	" 1.....	8-10	8	6-8	5-8
C W	S Cling........	W	Good..........	Aug. 5	6-8	6	6	5
Y R	Free	Y	Medium.......	Sept. 30....	5-7	8	9	9
Y R	Free	Y	Medium.......	Oct. 2......	6 8	8	9	9
Y R	Free	Y	Good..........	" 10.....	7-8	9	9	9
Y R	Free	Y	Good..........	Sept. 3	6-7	8	6	6
Y R	Free	Y	Very good....	Aug. 14	10	10	10	8
W R	Free	W	Medium.......	Sept. 28....	5-6	8	6	6
Y	Free	Y	Good	" 8	8	9	7	7
G W R	S Cling........	W	Medium.....	Aug. 15	5-6	5	4	4
Y R	Free	Y	Good..........	Sept. 6	8-9	10	10	9
Y	Free	Y	Good..........	" 8	5-7	8	6	6
Y R	Free	Y	Good..........	" 1	9-10	10	10	10

PEARS.

TESTED BY E. C. BEMAN,

Habit.	Form.	Cavity.	Basin.
D.—Drooping.	Ac.—Acute.	B.—Broad.	Ab.—Abrupt.
S.—Spreading.	An.—Angular.	D.—Deep.	Ang.—Angular.
U—Upright.	Con.—Conical.	N.—Narrow.	D.—Distinct.
	Cor.—Corrugated.	Sh.—Shallow.	Ev.—Even.
	Fla. —Flattened.		Fur.—Furrowed.
	Ob.—Oblate.		Pl.—Plaited
	Ov.—Ovate.		Rib.—Ribbed.
	Obo.—Obovate.		Sh.—Shallow.
	Obl.—Oblong.		Sm.—Smooth.
	Obt.—Obtuse.		Wr.—Wrinkled.
	Pyr —Pyriform.		W.—Waved.
	R —Round.		
	Rh.—Roundish.		
	Tur.—Turbinate.		

Varieties.	Origin.	Habit of tree.	Fruit.		
			Size.	Form.	Skin.
Ananas d'Ete.	Holland	S	Large	obt., pyr	y., bl.
Bartlett	England	U	L	obl., pyr	y
Bergamot, Gansel's	England	S	L	obl., fla.	y., b
Bergamot, Gansel's, late	England	S	Med	obl., r	y., rough
Belle Lucrative	Belgium	U	M	obv., obt., pyr	yh., g
Beurre Assomption	France	U	L	obl., pyr	y. and r.
Beurre Bose	Belgium	S	L	pyr., long neck	da, y. and rus.
Beurre Bachelier	France	S	M	obo., pyr	gh., y
Beurre Baltet Pere.	France	U	L	obo., obt., pyr	gh., y. with b. cheek.
Beurre Clairgeau	Nantes, France	U	L	pyr	yh., b. and r.
Beurre d'Amanlis	Belgium	S	M	obo	dull yh., g.
Beurre d'Anjou	France	S	L	obt., pyr	gh. rus., red'ish cheek
Beurre d'Aremberg	Belgium	S	M	short, pyr	gh., y
Beurre de Mortillet	France	U	L	obt., pyr	y., c. cheek.
Beurre Diel	Belgium	S	L	thick, pyr	y., some rus
Beurre Gris	France	S	M	obl , obo	yh., some rus
Beurre Golden of Bilboa.	Spain	S	M	obo., pyr	golden y
Beurre Goubalt	France	S	Sm	round, obo	gh., y
Beurre Hardy	France	S	M	obo., pyr	gh., b. and rus
Beurre Oswego	Oswego, N.Y.	S	M	obo., obo	gh., y. and rus
Beurre Robin.	Angers, France	S	M	r , obl.	gh., y. and rus.
Beurre Superfine	France	S	M	rh., pyr	gh., y
Blanc Perne	France	D	M	obo., pyr	gh., y
Black Worserter	England	L	obo., pyr	d , russety g.
Bloodgood	Long Island, N.Y.	U	Sm	tur., obo	y., some rus
Bonne d'Egee	France	S	M	obt., pyr	gh., y. and rus.
Bon Chretien, Summer	France	S	L	obl., pyr	y., o , bl
Brandywine	Pennsylvania	U	M	pyr	gh , y
British Queen	England	S	M	obo., pyr	y. and rus.
Buffum.	Rhode Island.	U	Sm	obl., obo.	deep y and r.
Catillac	France	S	L	broad, tur	y., b. cheek.
Calixte Magnot.	France	S	M	obo., pyr	gh., y
Church.	New York	S	M	r., obl.	gh., y
Clapp's Favorite	Dorchester, Mass.	S	L	obo., ov	pa., y. and r.
Comet	France	U	M	obo., pyr	rich y. and r.
Dana's Hovey	Roxbury, Mass	S	S	obo., pyr	gh., y. and rus
Dearborn's Seedling	Boston, Mass	S	S	r., pyr	light y
Dix	Boston, Mass	U	M	obl., pyr	y. and rus
Doyenne Boussock	Belgium	S	L	r., obo	deep y. and r.
Doyenne d'Ete	Belgium	S	S	r., obo	y. and r.
Doyenne Goubalt	France	U	M	obo , pyr	pa., y. and rus.
Doyenne Gris.	France	S	M	ov., obo	cinnamon rus
Doyenne White.	France	S	M	obt., obo	pa., y. and red.
Duchesse d'Angouleme	France	U	L	obl., obo.	gh., y. and rus.
Duchesse de Bordeaux	France	S	M	obt., pyr	y. and rus
Duchesse Precoce	France	U	L	pyr	lemon, y. and r.

PEARS.

NEWCASTLE, ONT.

Color.

A.—Amber.
B.—Brown.
Bh.—Brownish.
Bl.—Blush.
Blo.—Bloom.
Blot.—Blotched.
Br.—Bright.
C.—Crimson.
Clo.—Clouded.
D.—Dots.
Da.—Dark.
F.—Fawn.
G.—Green.
Gh.—Greenish.
Mar.—Marbled.
Mot.—Mottled.
Nu.—Numerous.
O.—Orange.
P.—Purple.
Ph.—Purplish.
Pa—Pale.
R.—Red.
Rus.—Russet.
Sh.—Shaded.
Sp.—Splashed or Splashes.
St.—Striped.
Str.—Streaked.
Sta.—Stained.
Sun.—Sunny Side.
Spo.—Spotted.
V.—Violet.
W.—White.
Wh.—Whitish.
Y.—Yellow.
Yh.—Yellowish.

Fruit.

Stem.	Cavity.	Calyx.	Basin.	Flesh.		
				Color.	Texture.	Flavor.
1¼	Sh	open	sh		buttery and melting	sweet, high flavor.
1¼ stout	Sh	open	sh., pl	w	fine grained, buttery	sweet, aromatic.
¾ stout	B	open, small.	br., sh	w	melting, juicy	sweet, rich.
1	D	large, open	sh.		juicy, granular	vinous, astringent.
1¼	N	short, open.	med. depth		very juicy, melting	sugary, rich.
¾	N	large, open	med	w	juicy, half melting	vinous, acid.
1½	no cavity	small.	sh	w	juicy, buttery.	rich, sweet, aromatic.
1	Sh	partly closed	sh		juicy, melting	vinous.
¾	N	large, open	med. depth		juicy, breaking	sweet.
1 stout	no cavity	open, short	sh	yh	juicy, granular	vinous, variable.
1¼	Sh	open, broad.	sh	yh	juicy, melting	sweet, variable.
½ stout	Sh	small, open.	sh., smooth	wh	juicy, melting	rich, vinous.
¾ stout	Sh	short, small.	d., n	w	buttery, melting	vinous, sub-acid.
1 stout	Sh	open	sh	w	juicy, melting	sweet, aromatic.
1¼ stout	B	closed	sh, br	yh., w	coarse grained, juicy	sweet, rich.
1¼ stout	no cavity	closed	sh	gh., w	melting, juicy	vinous, acid.
1½	Sh	small, closed	sh	w	fine grained, melting	vinous, acid.
1½	Sh	large.	sm		melting, juicy	sweet, not rich.
1 stout	Sh	large, open	sh		melting, juicy	sugary, vinous.
¾ stout	D	closed	sh		melting, juicy	sweetish, vinous.
1½	B	partly closed	b	wh	coarse, juicy	vinous, aromatic.
1¼ stout	no cavity	partly closed	sm		juicy, melting	vinous, sub-acid.
1¼	Sh	large	sh	yh., w	crisp, juicy	sweetish.
1½	no cavity	erect	sm		hard and coarse.	astringent.
1¼	no cavity	open	very sm	yh., w	buttery, melting	rich, aromatic.
1¼ stout	B	small, open.	sh	w	juicy, melting	sugary, rich.
1¾	Sh	large	sh	yh	coarse, juicy	sweet, musky
1	Sh	open	sh	w	juicy, melting	sugary, vinous.
1 stout	N.	small	sh	yh., w	fine grained	sugary.
1	Sh	small	sm	w	buttery, rather dry	sweet.
1	N	small	wide, deep	reddish	hard, coarse	very poor.
1¼	Sh	open	sh	w	juicy, melting	insipid.
1¼	N	small	b., sh	w	juicy, melting	sweet, rich.
¾	S	closed	sh., pl	w	juicy, melting	sweetish, vinous.
1	S				juicy, melting	very poor.
1	S	open	sm	yh	juicy, melting	sugary, aromatic.
1¼	S	open	sh	w	juicy, melting	sweet, sprightly.
1¼	S	small	sh		juicy, granular	rich, sweet.
1 stout	B	open	sh		buttery, juicy	sweet, aromatic.
1¼	S	small, open.	sh	w	juicy, melting	sweet, pleasant.
¾	S	small	sh		juicy, melting	sweet
¾	N	small, closed	sh	w	fine grained, melting	rich, perfumed.
1	S	small, closed	sh	w	fine grained, melting	rich, high flavor.
1½ stout	D	small	uneven	yh., w	buttery, juicy	usually poor.
1½	none	open	med	w	moderately juicy	sweet, pleasant.
1	S	small	sh	w	juicy, melting	sub-acid.

PEARS.—*Continued.*

Varieties.	Origin.	Habit of tree.	Fruit.		
			Size.	Form.	Skin.
Flemish Beauty	Belgium..............	S	L	obt., pyr	pa., y. and red b...
Forelle	Germany	U	M	obl., ov............	y. and r............
Fondante de Malines.....	Belgium	U	M	obo., pyr	pa., y. and vh. rus..
Garber	United States	S	L	ov	lemon y., sh. with r.
Glout Morceau...........	Belgium..............	S	L	obt., pyr	gh., y............
Goodale	Saco, Maine..........	U	L	obl., obo., pyr	pa., y. and bh. r....
Graslin	France	S	M	obo., ov., pyr	gh., y. and rus.....
Harvard	Cambridge, Mass.....	U	M	obl., pyr..........	olive, y. and rus ....
Howell	New Haven, Conn ...	U	L	rh., pyr	light y. and r.......
Idaho..................	Idaho, U. S..........	U	M	ob	gh., y............
Jaminette........	Metz, France	S	L	obo	gh., y. and rus .....
Jargonelle English........	France	S	L	long, pyr.	gb., y. and b ......
Jones	Pennsylvania	U	S	obo., pyr	y and rus..........
Josephine de Malines	Belgium..............	S	M	r., obl....... ...	gh., y. and rus.....
Kieffer	Pennsylvania	U	M	ov	deep y ....
Kirtland	Ohio	S	M	obt., obo..........	y and rus.. ......
King Sessing	Pennsylvania	U	L	obt., pyr..........	gh. and y..........
Lawrence	Long Island.....	S	M	obt., pyr.........	pa. y. ....
Louise Bonne de Jersey...	France	U	L	obl., pyr.........	yh., g. and b ......
Madeline.....	France	U	M	obo., pyr	yh , g............
Marshall	U. S	S	M	r., obo............	deep y. and rus.....
Madame Eliza........ ..	Belgium...	S	L	pyr	pa., yh., g.........
Mons. Herberlin..........	....	U	L	obt., pyr..........	y. and r ....
Mount Vernon	Roxbury, Mass.......	S	M	obt., pyr..........	y., ph., rus........
Nouveau Porteau........	Belgium.............	S	L	obo., pyr..........	g. and rus.........
Onondaga	Conn....	S	L	obt., oval, pyr	rich y.............
Osband's Summer........	New York...........	U	S	obo., pyr	y. and r...........
Ott	Pennsylvania	U	S	r., obo............	gh., y. and rus.....
Passe Colmar....	Belgium.............	S	M	obt., pyr..........	yh., s. and rus.....
Paradise d'Antomne	Belgium.............	S	L	pyr	rich, y. and rus.....
Pitmaston....	Pitmaston, England ..	S	L	obl., obo..........	y. and rus ......
Pound	....	S	L	pyr	yh., g. and b.......
Pratt	Rhode Island	U	M	obt., pyr..........	gh., y............
Rostiezer	....	S	S	obl., pyr..........	dull y. and b ....
Rutter	Pennsylvania	S	M	r., pyr...	gh., y. and rus.....
Seckel.	Philadelphia, Pa	U	S	obo	yh., b.............
Sheldon	Wayne Co., N.Y	S	M	obt., obo	gh., y. and b.......
Souvenier du Congress	France	U	L	obt., pyr..........	y. and r ....
Steven's Genesee	Livingston Co., N.Y..	S	M	obt., obo	y..............
St. Germain..............	France	S	L	long, pyr	yh., g. and b.......
St. Ghislain	Belgium.....	U	M	pyr	y.............
Triomphe de Vienne.....	....	S	L	pyr	yh., rus ....
Tyson..................	Pennsylvania	S	S	acute, pyr........	deep y. and r.......
Urbaniste	Belgium.............	S	M	obo., pyr..........	pa., y. and rus.....
Vicar of Winkfield	France ....:	S	L	long, pyr ....:...	pa., y. and b........
Washington	Delaware.............	S	M	obo	pa., y. and red dots.
Winter Nelis	Belgium.............	S	S	r. pyr	yh., g. and grey rus.
Wilmot	Newcastle, Ont.......	S	M	obo..............	y. and some rus....

PEARS —*Continued.*

Fruit.						
				Flesh.		
Stem.	Cavity.	Calyx.	Basin.	Color.	Texture.	Flavor.
1½	N	short, open.	small, round	yh., w.	juicy, melting	sweet, rich.
1 slender	S	small	n	w	buttery, melting	vinous, not rich.
1½	Sh	large, open	sm	w	juicy, melting	sweet, perfumed.
1¼	D	large, open	deep	w	juicy, granular	sub-acid.
1¼	Sh	large, open	irr	w	fine grained, melting	sweet, variable.
¾ stout	D	small, closed	deep	w	juicy, melting	sweet, vinous.
1½	Sh	open	sm	yh	juicy, buttery	sweet.
1 stout	none	small	n	w	juicy, melting	sweet, variable.
1¼ stout	Sh	open	uneven	w	juicy, melting	brisk, vinous.
1 stout	Sh	open	sh	wh	juicy, buttery	sweet, perfumed.
1 stout	none	open, small.	med.	w	juicy, granular	sweet, pleasant.
1¾	none	open	sm	yh., w.	juicy, granular	sub-acid, variable.
1¼	none	open	sh	yh	buttery, granular	sweet, brisk.
1¼	Sh	small, open.	b	pink'h w	juicy, buttery	sweet, aromatic.
¾	N	open	n., pla.	w	juicy, granular	sub-acid.
¾	Sh	open	sh		juicy, melting	sweet, aromatic.
1¼	B	closed	sh	wh	melting, granular	sweet, perfumed.
1¼	Sh	open	b	w	juicy, melting	sweet, aromatic.
1½	none	open	sh	yh., w	juicy, melting	rich, sub-acid.
1¾	N	small	sh	w	juicy, melting	sweet.
1¾	B	open	sh	wh	juicy, buttery	sweet, variable.
1¾	none	small	sh	w	buttery, melting	sweet.
1¼	N	open	sh	w	juicy, buttery	sweet, perfumed.
1	none	small, closed	sh	yh	juicy, granulated	vinous, aromatic.
¾	Sh	closed	n	w	buttery, juicy	sweet, vinous.
1¼ stout	Sh	small, closed	n	wh	juicy, granular	rich, vinous.
1	N	partly closed	b., sh	w	juicy, melting	sweet, pleasant.
1¼	Sh	open	sh	wh	juicy, melting	sweet, rich, aromatic.
1½	Sh	open	sh	yh., w.	juicy, buttery	sweet, aromatic.
1½	none	open	sm	w	juicy, buttery	vinous, aromatic.
1½	N	open	sh	w	juicy, buttery	sub-acid, pleasant.
2	none	crumpled	sh	wh	firm, solid	harsh, astringent.
1¼	N	open	sh	w	juicy, melting	sweet, vinous.
1¾	none	open	sm	wh	juicy, melting	rich, sweet, perfumed.
1¼	Sh	closed	sh	w	juicy, granular	sweet, vinous.
1¾	Sh	small.	sh	wh	juicy, buttery	sweet, spicy, rich.
¾	D	open	b	wh	juicy, melting	sweet, vinous, rich.
1¼	Sh	open	sh., pl	w	juicy, melting	sweet, musky.
1	Sh	open	sh	w	half melting	sweet, aromatic.
1	none	open	sh	w	juicy, granular	sub-acid, variable.
1½	none	open	sh	w	juicy, buttery	sprightly, variable.
1¼	none		sh	wh	juicy, buttery	sweet, aromatic.
1¾	none	open	sh	w	juicy, melting	rich, sweet, aromatic.
1	B	closed	n	w	juicy, melting	rich, sub-acid
1¼	none	large, open	sh	gh., w.	juicy, buttery	sub-acid, astringent.
1¼	Sh	small	sh	w	juicy, melting	sweet, perfumed.
1½	N	open	sh	yh., w.	juicy, melting	sweet, aromatic.
1¼	Sh	open	sh	w	juicy, breaking	sweet, brisk, vinous.

PEARS.

Results of experiments in Cultivation, Pruning,

Varieties under test by R. L. Huggard, Whitb'.	When p'anted.	Soil and cultivation.	Fertilizers used
Bartlett	1887	clay loam	none
Buffum	1889	"	"
Belle Lucrative	1889	"	stable manure
Beurre Clairgeau	1891	clover sod	
Beurre d'Anjou	1889	clean cultivation	
Beurre Supeifine	1887	"	stable manure
Beurre Antoine	1889	"	
Brockworth Park	1889	"	stable manure
Clapp's Favorite	1887	clover sod	
Doyenne d'Ete	1889	clean cultivation	stable manure
Duchess d'Angouleme	1887	"	ashes
Flemish Beauty	1887	"	stable manure
Glout Morceau	18-7	"	none
Grey Doyenne	1889	"	"
Graslin	1889	clover sod	"
Goodale	1889	"	"
Howell	1889	"	ashes
*Idaho	*	clean cultivation	stable manure
Josephine d'Malines	1890	"	"
Keiffer	1887	clover sod	none
King Sessing	1889	clean cultivation	stable manure
Louise Bonne d'Jersey	1887	"	"
Lawrence	1889	clover sod	none.
Mt. Vernon	1889	clean cultivation	ashes.
Laconte	1890	"	stable manure
Pres. Drouard	1889	"	"
Ritson	1892	clean cultivation	stable manure
Rostiezer	1887	"	"
Sheldon	1876	"	none
Souvenir de Congres	1887	"	stable manure
Seckel	1894	"	"
Winter Nelis	1889	clover sod	none

*Top grafted in 1894.

PEARS.

Results of experiments in cultivation, pruning, spraying, at East Central Station, 1898.

New varieties planted 1896 that fruited this season, having from three to a dozen samples each.

Varieties tested by R. L. Huggard, Whitby.	When planted.	Soil and cultivation.	Fertilizers used.	Pruning. Date, method & percentage of wood growth removed.	Treatment.	Remarks.
Rutter	1896	Clay loam; land was root cropped.	Stable manure.	March. Cutting out interfering branches.	Sprayed twice well, May 12 Bordeaux mix. May 23, Bordeaux mixt.	large deep green, excellent.
Krull	1896					resembles Keiffer's.
Comice	1896					large yellow and fine.
Winter Nelis	1896					small and dark color.
Idaho	1896					very fine and large. [ity.
Japan Gold Russet	1896					beautiful russet flavor, qual-
Easter Beurre	1896					only medium, not No. 1.
P. Barry	1896					disappointingly small.

PEARS.

Spraying, at East Central Station, 1898.

Pruning. Date, method and percentage of wood growth removed.	Treatment.	Results.
March		gcod, clean fruit.
"		light crop.
"		"
..		fair crop.
..		no crop.
		1½ bushels to tree.
"		1½ " "
young wood cut out		medium crop.
no pruning		3½ bushels to tree.
cutting back		2 bushels.
young sprouts cut out		2 "
no pruning needed		2½ "
" "		1½ ::
		2 "
none		½ bushel.
cutting back		½ "
no pruning required		4 bushels.
thinning sprouts	Sprayed May 2nd, 12th, 23rd, June 10th, copperas and lime, Bordeaux mixture.	1½ bushels per tree.
cutting back	" "	1¼ " "
no pruning done		5 " "
cutting back		no crop.
no pruning done	" "	4 bushels per tree.
"		½ bushel "
thinning	" "	no crop.
cutting back		½ bushel.
none required		2 bushels per tree.
"		no crop.
thinning		½ bushel.
none required		3 bushels.
cutting back		½ bushel.
no pruning		1¼ bushels.
thinning shoots		¾ bushel.
none		½ "

PEARS.

Yield and selling price of Pears at East Central Station, 1898.

Varieties under test by R. L. Huggard, Whitby.	Age.	Date of maturity.	Date of gathering.	Yield.	Grade. Per cent.			Storage.		Average price.
					Class 1.	Class 2.	Class 3.	Place.	Temperature.	
Bartlett	11 years	Sept.	Sept. 16	3 bush.	90	10				$1.50 per bushel.
Bo...	9 "	Gb	Oct. 4	½	100					$1.20 "
Be...ve	9 "	Gov.	Oct. 25	⅔ bush.	70	20	10			$1.25 "
Be...au	7 "	G.	" 25	1 bush.	80	20				
Beurre...	9 "	Nr. to 15	" 27	1½	80	20		Barn cellar	40° F.	$1.00 "
Beurre Superfine	11 "	lae	" 28	1¼-1½	75	25				$1.00 "
Be...o	9 "	Dec.	" 28	½½	100					5c "
Brockw...h Park	9 "	la, dn	" 28	3½	80	20				$1.50 "
Gs...	11 "	Aug. nd Sept.	Aug. 18 nd 19	2	80	10	10			$1.50 "
Doyenne d'Ete	9 "	July	Jy 10	2	70		30			$1.50 "
...	11 "	Nov.	Oct. 28	1½-1½	75	25				
Flemish	11 "	Dec	St. 20	1½	60	40	0			$1.15 "
Glt...	11 "	Jy nd Aug	Gt. 27	1¼	90	10				$1.50 "
Gay Gn...	9 "	Gt., Nov	Jy 2	¼ bush.	90	10	20			90 "
Gle...	9 "	Gt., Nov	Gt. 28	4	70	15				$1.25 "
Howell	9 "	Oct., Nov	Gt. 8	1¼	85	20				
Idaho	9 "	lae	G. 4	1¼	95			Barn cellar	40° F.	
Keiffer d'Malines	8 "	Dec., Jan	Dec. 7	5	60					1.60 "
King Sessing	11 "	Dec.	" 1	4 bush.	90	10	10	No crop.		1.85 "
L Bonne de Jersey	11 "	G., Nov	Sept. 20	½	50	50	10			
L Mt V...n	9 "	L, Feb	Oct. 2	2	75	15		No fruit.		
Le...e	9 "	G., Nov	Oct. 16	½ bush.	65	25		Barn cellar	40° F.	$1.50 "
Pres...d	8 "	Dec., Jan	" 27	2	100			No fruit.		$1.20 "
President	9 "	Nov	Oct. 7	½ bush.	80	20				$2.00 "
Ritson	6 "	Sept	Aug. 16	3	70	30	10			$1.50 "
Rostiezer	11 "	Oct	Sept. 30	1	95	5				
Mon...	22 "	Gt.	" 30	1¼-1¼	45	55				
Souvenir du Congres	11 "	Dec., Jan	Oct. 8	½	75	25				
Seckel	4 "	L, March	" 29	1¼-1½						

PEARS.

Results of experments in cultivation, pruning, spraying at Bay of Quinte Station, 1898.

Varieties tested by W. H. Dempsey, experimenter, Trenton.	When planted.	Soil and cultivation.	Fertilizers used.	Growth in inches.	Vigor, scale 1—10.	Pruning. Date, method and percentage of wood growth removed.
White Doyenne............ ..	1895			17	7	
Giffard....................	1895			23	7	
Duchess d'Angouleme	1895			14	6	
Louise	1895			12	6	
Dorset.....................	1895			10	6	
Ansault........	1895			14	6	
Lady Duke	1895	Sandy loam, with some clay and clay sub-soil; cultivated. Planted to potatoes.		36	10	
Pound.....	1895			14	9	
Fred Clapp	1895			18	7	
Souvenir d'Esperen............	1895			26	9	
Andre Desportes....	1895			18	6	
Summer Doyenne.............	1895			12	6	
Kieffer	1895			36	10	
Easter Beurre	1895			14	6	April.
Manning's Elizabeth..........	1895		Stable and ashes.	12	6	
Brandywine ....·.	1895	Sandy loam, with clay sub-soil, cultivated.		15	7	
Dr. Jules Guyot	1895			16	7	
Barry.......................	1895			14	6	
Fred Beaudy.................	1895			16	7	
Lady Clapp.	1895			16	7	
Winter Nelis................	1895			20	8	
Duchess Precoce.....	1895			16	7	
Lincoln ....·.	1895			30	9	
Wilder	1897	Sandy loam with clay sub-soil, cultivated.		21	8	
Koonce....	1897			20	8	
Seneca	1897			22	8	
Margaret.....,..........	1898			22	8	
Petite Margaret	1898			3	2	
Bartlett Seckel.	died	.. ..	....	......	... ..	

PEARS.

Result of experiments in Cultivation, Pruning, Spraying, at St. Lawrence Station, 1898.

By Harold Jones, Maitland, Ont.

Varieties.	When planted.	Soil and cultivation.	Fertilizers used.	Growth in inches.	Pruning. Date, method & percentage of wood growth removed.	Insects. Name.	Insects. Treatment.	Fungi. Name.	Fungi. Treatment.	Results.
Baba	'97			36	April, thinned out and cut back ¾ new wood			None		Healthy.
Beurre	'96			3	No trimming	None		"		Blight has affected all three trees.
	'96			18	"	"		"		Healthy.
Beurre Hardy	'96			6	Cut back ¼ new wood	"		"		Very little growth.
Favorite	'96			26	"	"		"		Healthy.
	'96			20	"	"		"		"
	'96			27	"	"		Fungi spots on leaf		
	'96			16	No trimming	"		None		
Gle	'96			15	"	"		"		Fruit Bs and twigs injured last winter.
Gn	'97			8	"	"		"		hy.
	'96			20	Cut back ½ new wood	"		"		Ge tree kl by blight.
	'96			6	No trimming	None		"		Healthy.
	'96			28	Cut ½ new wood	"		"		Inclined to blt.
	'96			24	"	"		"		ly.
Le	'97			30	No trimming	"		"		Ge tree did in July possibly blight.
				5	"	"		"		Healthy.
	'96			19	Cut back ½ new wood	Slug	Paris green	"		"
	'96			16	No trimming	None		"		
	'96			13	"	"		"		
Beauty	'96			24	Cut ¼ new wood	"		"		One tree killed with blight.
Wier	'97			32	"	"		"		Healthy.

Soil clay loam. Planted to strawberries and potatoes, and given clean cultivation.

Barnyard manure when planted to potatoes. Yard manure and ashes when in strawberries.

PEARS.

Result of experiments in Cultivation, Pruning and Spraying, at Burlington Station, 1898.

By A. W. PEART, EXPERIMENTER.

Varieties.	When planted.	Soil and cultivation.	Fertilizers used.	Growth in inches.	Vigor, Scale 1–10.	Pruning. Date, meth'd and percentage of wood growth removed.	Insects. Name.	Treatment.	Fungi. Name.	Treatment.	Results.
1. Anjou	1880	Gravelly loam. Ploughed in fall or spring, then clean cultivation until last of July. In young orchard, potatoes or root crop grown, with liberal manuring and clean cultivation.	Stable Manure.	10	5	March—Heading back young trees up to five or six years old, to make them stocky, and compact in the top, and cutting out cross branches. 20 per cent.	Slug, codling moth and curculio.	Paris green and lime, two pounds of lime to one of Paris green, to prevent injury to the leaves, these in 200 gallons of water.	Pear blight and scab, the former affected the Duchess, Bartlett and Clapp's Favorite ; the latter the Flemish Beauty.	Cutting out and burning for blight. For scab the Bordeaux mixture.	A light crop of pears of rather inferior quality.
2. Bartlett....	1880			10	5						
3. Beurre Bosc	1896			20	9						
4. Beurre Giffard	1896			20	9						
5. Buffum	1897			10	5						
6. Clairgeau	1896			15	7						
7. Clapp's Favorite ...	1889			15	7						
8. Doyenne Boussock ..	1896			20	9						
9. Duchess	1889			10	5						
0. Easter Beurre	1897			15	7						
1. Flemish Beauty.....	1880			11	6						
12. Howell	1896			18	8						
13. Idaho..............	1896			18	8						
14. Josephine d'Malines.	1896			20	9						
15. Kieffer	1896			24	10						
16. Lawrence	1896			24	10						
17. Lawson	1896			20	9						
18. Louise Bonne	1897			15	7						
19. Osband's Summer...	1897			14	7						
20 Petite Marguerite...	1896			24	10						
21. President Drouard...	1897			15	7						
22. Seckel	1897			20	9						
23. Sheldon	1889			18	8						
24. Souvenir de Congress.	1896			15	7						
25. Sudduth	1897			12	6						
26. Summer Doyenne...	1896			15	7						
27. Tyson	1897			20	9						
28. Vermont Beauty	1896			20	9						
29. Wilder.	1896			18	8						
30. Winter Nelis........	1896			18	8						

Yield and selling price of varieties of Pears at Burlington Station, 1898.

By A. W. PEART, EXPERIMENTER.

Varieties.	Age.	Time of blooming.	Date of maturity.	Date of gathering. (Berries, 1st and last).	Yield per tree.	Grade per cent Class 1.	Class 2.	Class 3.	Average price.
1. Anjou	18 years..	May 13 .	Nov., Dec.	Oct. 5..	½ bush .	50	30	20	$3.50 per bbl.
2. Bartlett	18 "	" 16 .	Sept.	Sept. 5..	½ "	45	30	25	3.00 "
3. Clairgeau	2 "	" 16 ..	Nov.	Oct. 6..	.....	..	..	..	
4. Clapp's Favorite	9 "	" 18 ..	Aug.	Aug. 25..	½ bush .	70	30	..	45c. per bkt.
5. Duchess	9 "	" 14 ..	Oct., Nov ..	Oct. 1..	½ "	50	35	15	$2.50 per bbl.
6. Flemish Beauty	18 "	" 16 ..	Sept.	Sept. 6..	½ "	10	40	50	25c. per bkt.
7. Howell.	2 "	" 13 ..	Oct	Oct. 7..	....	..	..	..	
8. Kieffer	2 "	" 13 ..	Oct., Nov ..	Oct. 7..	....	..	..	..	
9. Lawrence	2 "	" 17 ..	Dec.	Oct. 15..	....	..	..	..	
10. Petite Marguerite.	2 "	" 16 ..	Aug.	....	....	..	..	..	
11. Sheldon	9 "	" 13 ..	Oct., Nov	Oct. 5..	½ bush .	..	..	..	
12. Winter Nelis	2 "	" 17 ..	Dec	Oct. 15..	....	..	..	..	

PEARS.

Vigor of Pear Trees tested at St. Lawrence Station.

Varieties.	Year of planting.	Inches of new growth and habit.	Vigor, scale 1-10.	Diameters of leaf.	Color of foliage.	Young growth.	Condition.
Baba	1897	36—U	5	4 x 2¾	D.G.	Strong	Healthy.
Winter Pear	1897	32—U	4	3 x 1¾	D.G.	"	"
L. Lecteur	1897	5—U	3	3 x 1¾	D.G.	Poor	Blight.
Sudduth	1896	16—Up	5	2 x ¾	Pale green	Medium	Healthy.
Ritson	1896	19—U.S.	4¾	2 x 1½	L.G.	Strong	"
Lincoln Conless	1896	30—S	4½	2½ x 1½	D.G.	"	One tree healthy, 2 died in 1897 blight.
Victorina	1896	13—U	1½	1½ x 1	D.G.	Medium	Healthy, 3 years from the graft.
Lincoln	1896	24—U.S.	3¾	2¼ x 1¼	L.G.	"	Blight.
Bessemianka	1896	18—S	3¾	2 x 2	L.G.	"	Healthy.
Kieffer	1896	28—U.	4¼	3½ x 2	D.G.	Strong	"
Golden Russett	1897	8—U	2½	5 x 3½	L.G.	Poor	Blight and tender.
Bergamot	1896	6—S.D	4¾	2¼ x 1¼	Pale green	"	Blight.
Vermont Beauty	1896	24—U.	3¾	2½ x 1½	L.G.	Medium.	"
Howell	1896	20—U.S.	5	3 x 1½	D.G.	Strong	Healthy.
Dempsey	1896	27—U.	3¾	3 x 1½	L.G.	"	"
B. Hardy	1896	26—U.S.	5	2¼ x 1½	D.G.	"	"
Clapp's Favorite	1896	20—U.S.	4¼	3½ x 2	D.G.	"	"
F. Beauty	1896	16—U.S.	6¼	2½ x 1¼	L.G.	"	Healthy, fungi.
Goodale	1896	15—U.	4½	2¾ x 1½	D.G.	Medium	Healthy.
Idaho	1896	6—U.S.	3¾	2½ x 1½	D.G.	"	Blight.
B. Clairgeau	1896	1—	3	2½ x 1½	L.G.	Poor	Blight all 3 trees.

PEARS.

Results of experiments in cultivation, pruning, spraying at Simcoe Station, 1898.

Varieties tested by G. C. Gaston, Craighurst.	When planted.	Soil and cultivation.	Fertilizers used.	Growth in inches.	Vigor, scale 1—10.
Baba (Russian)	1895	Warm loam, originally very strong. Hoe crops grown between rows of trees.	Stable and ashes.	20	10
Bergamott (Russian)	1895			17	9
Kieffer	1895			22	10
Bessemianka	1895			18	10
Flemish Beauty	1895			18	10
Sudduth	1896			15	8
Bartlett on Flemish Beauty	Grafted spring of 1898.			32	10
Ogon do				20	10
Sheldon on Bessemianka Russian				35	10
Lawrence do do				25	10
Lawson do do				29	10
Winter Nelis do do				21	9

☞The trees were pruned in June on the pyramid style, about 1.7 per cent. of wood growth being removed.

☞Insects found: slugs ; treatment: Bordeaux Paris Green ; results: very healthy in both foliage and wood.

DESCRIPTIVE TABLE OF PLUMS.

Habit.	*Suture.*	*Form.*
S.—Spreading.	D.—Distinct.	Con.—Conical.
U.—Upright.	Ob.—Obscure	Ov.—Ovate.
		Obl.—Oblong.
		Pyr.—Pyriform.

arieties tested by J. G. Mitchell, Huron Station, near Clarksburg.	Origin.	Habit of tree.	Fruit.								
			Size in inches of length and breadth.	Form.	Suture.	Skin.	Stem.	Core, Stone, Seeds.	Flesh.		
									Color.	Texture.	Flavor.
Arch Duke	English	U	2 x 1¼ in.	Obl.	D	Black	¾ inch.	free	yellow	[illegible]	fair.
Abundance	Japanese	U	2 x 1½ in.	Con.	D	Amber		c ing	yellow	juicy	melon-like.
Burbank	Japanese	S	2 x 1⅓ in.	Ov.	D	Cherry red	¾ inch.	cling	yellow	juicy	sweet.
Diamond	Japanese	U	2 x 1¼ in.	Obl.	D	Black	1 inch.	cling	yellow	[illegible]	fair.
Grand Duke	English	U	2 x 1¼ in.	Obl.	D	Deep purple.	¾ inch.	cling	greenish yellow	juicy	fair.
Moore's Arctic	Aroostock Co, Maine	S	1½ x 1 in.	Ov.	D	Dark purple.	¾ inch.	nearly free	yellow	firm	fair.
Golden Prolific	European	U	1¾ x 1½ in.	Pyr.	D	Yellow	¾ inch.	cling	greenish yellow	juicy	sweet.
Prune d'Agen	French	U to S	1½ x 1 in.	Ov.	Ob	Violet purple	⅞ inch.	slightly cling.	greenish yellow	[illegible]	rich.

PLUMS.

Results of experiments in Cultivation, Pruning

Varieties tested by Harold Jones, Experimenter, Maitland. Ont.	When planted.	Soil and cultivation.	Fertilizers used.	Growth in inches.
Abundance	1897	Soil clay loam, planted to corn and potatoes. and given clean cultivation.		42 ..
Col. Wilder	"	"		56 ..
Chas. Downing	1896	"		20 ..
Communia	....			24 ..
Deaton	1897			29 ....
Field	"			40 ....
Forest Rose	"			60 ....
Forest Garden.	"			36 ....
Gneii	1896			39 ....
Green Gage	1897			45 ....
Grand Duke..............	"			36 ....
Glass Seedling...........	"			18 ....
Hugh's Seedling...	1896			36 ....
Lincoln	1897	"	Barn yard manure when planted to potatoes. Barn yard manure and ashes when planted in strawberries.	24 ....
Lombard	1896			31 ....
Milton	"			36 ....
Moore's Arctic....	"			29 ....
Montreal	"			24 ....
Pond's Seedling	"			28 ....
Prince of Wales	1897			30 ....
Rockford	"			36 ....
Shippers' Pride	"			34 ....
Saunders	1896	"		18 ....
Tatge	"			31 ....
Whitaker	"			38 ....
Weaver	"			40 ....
Wolf	1897			24 ....
Wyant	"			42 ....
Yellow Egg	"			46 ....
CHERRIES.				
....	... .			21 ....
....	.. ..			20 ....

PLUMS.

and Spraying at St. Lawrence Station.

Pruning.	Insects.		Fungi.	Results.
Date, method and percentage of wood growth removed.	Name.	Treatment.	Name.	
April, cut back ⅔ of new wood.	None....	....	None..........	healthy.
"	....	kerosene emulsion	....	"
Cut back ⅔ new wood...	Aphis ..	....	....	Growth checked by aphis in early spring; one spraying removed the trouble.
¼	....	....	shot hole fungi.	Very slight attack of fungi; no treatment given.
" ¼	....	....	"	"
" ¼	....	....	"	"
" ¾ "	....	....	....	"
" ⅔ "	....	....	shot hole fungi.	healthy.
April, cut back ⅔ new wood ..	....	....	none	"
Cut back ¼ new wood	....	....	"	"
No trimming....	....	....	"	"
Cut back ¼ new wood........	....	....	"	"
" ¼ "	....	....	"	The aphis attacks this variety in the bud early in the spring and destroyed one tree before it was noticed; kerosene emulsion saved the others.
" ¾ "	Aphis ...	kerosene emulsion	....	healthy.
No trimming................	....	....	"	
Cut back ½ new wood	....	....	shot hole fungi	"
" ¾ "	....	....	none	"
" ¼ "	....	....	"	"
No trimming................	....	....	shot hole fungi.	
Cut back ½ new wood	....	....	"	
" ¼ "	....	....	none	"
" ¾ "	....	....	"	..
" ¼ "	....	....	"	
No trimming......	Aphis...	kerosene emulsion	"	
Cut back ½ new wood	" ..	"	"	
" ¾ "	" ..	"	Blight.........	
" ¾ " ..	....	....	none	healthy.
" ¾ "	....	....	"	"
" ¼ "	....	....	....	"
" ½ "	....	....	"	
No trimming................	Slug	Paris green......	"	
"	"	"	"	

PLUMS.

Results of experiments in cultivation, pruning, spraying at Simcoe Station, 1898.

Varieties tested by G. C. Caston, Craighurst.	When planted.	Soil and cultivation.	Fertilizers used	Growth in inches.	Vigor, scale 1-10.	Pruning. Date, method and percentage of wood removed.	Insects. Name.	Insects. Treatment.	Results.
Burbank	96	loam, clean	stable and ashes.	32	10	June, slight	slugs ...	Bordeaux, Paris green.	foliage very healthy, and uninjured by fungus or insects.
Willard	96	"	"	22	10				
Ionui	96	"	"	20	9				
Gia	96	"	"	15	8				
Pride	96	"	"	18	9				
H' Pride	96	"	"	16	8				
Ogon	1896	"	"	20	9	Kills back to some extent in winter.			
Black Diamond	1894	"	"	24	10				
Union Purple	94	"	"	18	9				
Prince of W ds	94	"	"	20	9				
Prince's Gie	94	"	"	18	9				
Peter's Yellow Gage	94	"	"	20	9				
Grand Bie	94	"	"	17	8				
Quackenbos	94	"	"	19	9				
Staunton	1894	"	"	11	6				
dr on Prune	1894	"	"	24	10				
Yellow Egg	94	"	"	13	6				
Hudson dr Purple Egg	1894	"	"	11	6				
Middleburg	1894	"	"	22	10				
Gueii	94	"	"	10	5				

PLUMS.

Results of experiments in cultivation, pruning, spraying at Bay of Quinte Station, 1898.

Varieties tested by W. H. Dempsey, Trenton, Ont.	When planted.	Soil and cultivation.	Fertilizers used.	Growth in inches.	Vigor, scale 1-10.
Imperial Gage	1895		Stable	16	7
Jefferson	"			16	7
Italian Prune	"			12	6
Victoria	"			20	7
Orange Prune	"			12	6
Yellow Gage	"			24	8
Smith's Orleans	"	cultivated till August.		16	7
Burbank	"			40	10
McLaughlin	"			30	9
Willard	"			24	8
Reine Claude	"			18	7
Wild Goose	"	clay sub-soil,		36	10
DeSoto	"			36	10
Hulings Superb	"			24	8
Reine Claude Violette	"			18	7
Wickson	1897	Sandy loam,		36	10
Lincoln	"			7	4
Chabot	"			36	10
Spaulding	"			6	4
Grand Duke	"			15	7
Abundance	"			20	7
Gold	1898	Sandy loam cultivated	Stable	12	6
Harris (Apricot)	"		"	8	4
Yellow St. John (Peach)	"			20	7
Bessarabian (Cherry)	"			6	3

PLUMS.

Tables of Vigor, by H. Jones, St. Lawrence Station, Maitland.

Varieties.	When planted.	Average wood growth.	Habit.	Girth.	Leaf. Length, & width.	Leaf. Color.	Vigor.	Notes on condition.
		inches.		inches.	inches.			
Weaver	1896	40	S	4½	4 x 2	Light green	Fair, slender	subject to attacks of aphis and sometimes suffers from twig blight.
Lombard	1896	31	U S	4½	3 x 1½	D G	strong	on black knot in 1897, aphis and shot hole fungi.
Gueii	1896	39	U	6¼	4 x 2½	D G	very strong	healthy.
Montreal	1896	24	U	5	3 x 2½	L G	medium	healthy.
Ponds Seedling	1896	28	U	6¾	3½ x 2	L G	strong	shot hole fungi.
Saunders	1896	24	S D	5½	3 x 2	L G	medium	aphis.
Hughes Seedling	1896	36	U	5	3 x 1¾	D G	strong	healthy.
Moore's Arctic	1896	28	S	6½	3½ x 3	D G	strong	healthy.
Milton	1896	36	S	6	4½ x 1½	L G	strong	healthy.
Abundance	1897	44	U	5	4½ x 2¾	D G	strong	healthy.
Lincoln	1896	22	S	4	3 x 3	L G	poor	healthy.
Col. Wilder	1897	56	S D	3¾	5 x 2	L G	strong	healthy.
Whitaker	1896	38	S	7½	4 x 1½	D G	strong	healthy.
Tatge	1896	31	U S	7	2½ x 1¾	D G	strong	healthy.
Communia	1896	21	U S	4¼	3 x 1½	D G	medium	healthy.
Hammer	1896	36	U S	5	5 x 2	L G	strong	aphis, healthy.
Chas. Dowing	1896	20	S D	5¾	4 x 1½	D G	strong	aphis, healthy.
Rockford	1896	36	U S	2½	4 x 2	L G	strong	healthy.
Wyant	1897	42	U S	2½	4 x 2	L G	strong	healthy.
Forest Rose	1897	60	U S	3½	5 x 2½	L G	strong	healthy.
Forest Garden	1897	36	U S	2½	4½ x 2	D G	medium	shot hole fungi.
Prince of Wales	1897	30	U	3	4 x 3¾	D G	poor	shot hole fungi.
Glass Seedling	1897	18	S	4	2½ x 1¾	D G	medium	healthy.
Wolf	1897	24	S	2	3½ x 2	L G	medium	healthy.
Grand Duke	1897	36	U	3¼	3 x 2½	D G	medium	healthy.
Field	1897	40	U	4	3 x 2½	D G	medium	shot hole fungi.
Deaton	1897	29	U	2¾	2½ x 2	D G	poor	shot hole fungi.
Green Gage	1897	45	U	5	4 x 2½	D G	strong	healthy.
Yellow Egg	1897	46	U	4½	4 x 2½	D G	strong	healthy.
Shippers' Pride	1897	34	U	4	2½ x 1¾	D G	strong	shot hole fungi.

STRAWBERRIES.

Yield and selling price of varieties of strawberries at St. Lawrence No. 10 Station, 1898.

Varieties tested at Maitland, Ont., by Harold Jones, Experimenter.	Age.	Time of blooming.	Date of gathering berries (first and last).		Yield from 12 plants in ozs.	Average price.	Remarks. On condition of cultivation, spraying, manuring, etc.
						cts.	
Aroma	1 year	May 19.	June 17,	July 4..	200	5½	
Beulah	1 "	" 15..	" 13,	June 24 .	104	5½	
Brandywine	1 "	" 20..	" 17,	" 30..	179	5½	
Beauty	1 "	" 19..	" 20,	" 30..	110	5½	
Belle	1 "	" 19..	" 20,	" 30..	174	5½	
Beder Wood	1 "	" 18	" 13,	July 4..	205	5½	
Clyde	1 "	" 19..	" 15,	" 30..	87	5½	
Grenville	1 "	" 13..	" 15,	" 27..	85	5½	
Haverland	1 "	" 18..	" 15,	" 27..	76	5½	
Marshall	1 "	" 19..	" 15,	" 30..	64	5½	
Margaret	1 "	" 21..	" 17,	" 4..	40	5½	
Maple Bank	1 "	" 23..	" 20,	" 4..	....	5½	
aunders	1 "	" 22..	" 17,	June 27..	94	5½	
Ten Prolific	1 "	" 21..	" 20,	" 30..	89	5½	
Wm. Belt	1 "	" 19..	" 20,	" 30..	132	5½	
Warfield	1 "	" 19..	" 15,	" 27..	38	5½	
Woolverton	1 "	" 20..	" 17,	" 30..	194	5½	
Williams	1 "	" 22..	" 17,	July 4..	282	5½	
Van Deman	1 "	" 14..	" 13,	" 22..	13	5½	

Aroma	gave 200 ounces	from 12 plants,	200.		
Beulah	" 104	"	12	"	104.
Brandywine	" 179	"	12	"	9.
Beauty	" 110	"	12	"	110.
Belle	" 174	"	12	"	174.
Beder Wood	" 205	"	11	" or 223 ounces from 12 plants.	
Clyde	" 87	"	10	" 104	" 12 "
Grenville	" 85	"	12	" 85	" 12 "
Haverland	" 76	"	12	" 76	" 12 "
Marshall	" 64	"	12	" 64	" 12 "
Margaret	" 40	"	6	" 80	" 12 "
Maple Bank	" 16	"	3	" 64	" 12 "
Saunders	" 94	"	12	" 94	" 12 "
Ten Prolific	" 89	"	5	" 212	" 12 "
Wm. Belt	" 132	"	12	" 132	" 12 "
Warfield	" 38	"	7	" 65	" 12 "
Woolverton	" 194	"	12	" 194	" 12 "
Williams	" 282	"	12	" 282	" 12 "
Van Deman	" 13	"	5	" 30	" 12 "

RASPBERRIES.

Results of experiments in cultivation, pruning, spraying, at Burlington Station, 1898.

A. W. PEART, EXPERIMENTER.

Varieties.	When planted.	Soil and cultivation.	Fertilizers used.	Growth in feet.	Vigor, scale 10.	Pruning. Date, method and percentage of wood growth removed.	Insects.		Fungi.		Results.
							Name.	Treatment.	Name.	Treatment.	
1. All Summer	1895	Gravelly loam. Ploughed in the spring, then frequent cultivation until fruit is ripe. Banked up for the winter.	Stable manure.	3½	6	Annual pruning early in April, summer pruning early in August, of young canes to make them stocky and throw out laterals. Old canes removed at annual pruning.	The Marlboro' so newhat injured by the raspberry slug.	Hellebore.	Some anthracnose in Shaffer's Colossal, Columbian, Kansas and Hilborn.	Cutting out and burning after crop is gathered.	A light crop on account of the great drought.
2. Columbian	1895			6½	9						
3. Cuthbert	1894			8	10						
4. Golden Queen....	1896			5½	8						
5. Gregg	1896			6	9						
6. Hilborn	1895			5	8						
7. Japan Wine	1896			6	8						
8. Kansas	1895			6½	9						
9. Kenyon..........	1897			4	7						
10. Lottie	1897			5½	8						
11. London	1896			5	8						
12. Lovett	1895			4¼	7						
13. Marlboro	1894			4	7						
14. Miller	1897			3½	6						
15. Mills	1897			5½	8						
16. Ohio	1896			7	9						
17. Older	1895			5½	8						
18. Palmer	1895			6	8						
19. Phœnix	1897			3	5						
20. Progress	1895			5½	8						
21. Redfield	1896			5	8						
22. Reliance	1896			4¼	8						
23. Royal Church....	1897			8½	6						
24. Shaffer's Colossal.	1895			6	9						
25. Smith's Giant....	1896			7½	10						
26. Souhegan	1896			4¼	7						
27. Thompson	1895			3½	6						
28. Winant	1897			3	5						

Yield and selling price of Raspberries at Burlington Station, 1898.

Variety.	When planted.	Date of blooming.	Date of maturity.	Date of gathering. (Berries 1st and last.)	Yield per hill.	Average price.	Remarks On conditions of cultivation, spraying, manuring, etc.
1. All Summer	1895	June 6..	July 8..	July 8—Oct. 15	Very few		In comparing yields of varieties with those of 1897, the general crop this year was short by at least 50 per cent. Some varieties which cropped heavily last year, gave little or no fruit this season, as notably the Palmer; the drought was so severe that the fruit dried upon the bushes. The black and purple varieties suffered more than the red.
2. Columbian	1895	" 15..	" 13..	" 13— " 28	1½ lb.		
3. Cuthbert	1894	" 13..	" 13..	" 13— " 31	1 lb.		
4. Golden Queen	1896	" 10..	" 5..	" 5— " 20	½ lb.		
5. Gregg	1896	" 7..	" 13..	" 13— " 31	Very few		
6. Hilborn	1895	" 9..	" 5..	" 5— " 20	1¼ lb.		
7. Japan Wine	1896	" 23..	" 25..	" 25— " 31	Very few		
8. Kansas	1895	" 6..	" 5..	" 5— " 20	1⅜ lb.		
9. Kenyon	1897	" 13..	" 12..	" 12— " 25	Very few		
10. Lotta	1897	" 6..	" 10..	" 10— " 25	"	9 cents per quart.	
11. London	1896	" 13..	" 13..	" 13— " 31	½ lb.		
12. Lovett	1895	" 10..	" 10..	" 10— " 25	Very few		
13. Marlboro	1894	" 6..	" 5..	" 5— " 25	2 lb.		
14. Miller	1897	" 13..	" 12..	" 12— " 23	Very few		
15. Mills	1897	" 10..	" 9..	" 9— " 20	"		
16. Ohio	1896	" 6..	" 3..	" 3— " 31	¼ lb.		
17. Older	1895	" 6..	" 8..	" 8— " 25	Very few		
18. Palmer	1895	" 4..	" 1	" 1— " 20	Dried up		
19. Phœnix	1897	" 13..	" 12..	" 12— " 25	Very few		
20. Progress	1895	" 3..	" 3..	" 3 - " 20	Dried up		
21. Redfield	1896	" 13..	" 10..	" 10— " 20	Very few		
22. Reliance	1896	" 8..	" 8..	" 3— " 31	½ lb.		
23. Royal Church	1897	" 15..	" 13..	" 13— " 31	Very few		
24. Shaffer's Colossal	1895	" 15..	" 10..	" 10— " 25	1 lb.		
25. Smith's Giant	1896	" 6..	" 13..	" 13— " 31	½ lb.		
26. Souhegan	1896	" 4..	" 8..	" 8— " 26	Dried up		
27. Thompson	1895	" 9..	" 8	" 8— " 91	½ lb.		
28. Winant	1897	" 9..	" 10..	" 10— " 25	Very few		

RASP

SIZE.	FORM.	COLOR.
S—Small.	R - Round.	D—Dark. O—Orange.
M—Medium.	C—Conical.	R—Red. B—Bright.
L—Large.	O—Ovate.	P—Purple.

		Plant.				
			Canes.			
Varieties tested by A. E. Sherrington, Walkerton, Ont.	Origin.	Habit of growth.	Color.	Freedom from disease, 1-10.	Propagation by tips or suckers.	Foliage.
All Summer................ ..	....	up	l. green	10	S......	rank, healthy.
Brandywine	....	up	d. red..	10	S......	good ....
Brinckles Orange.............	....	up	purple.	10	S......	heavy ....
Cuthbert	Riverdale, N.Y....	strong, up..	d. red..	10	S......	good, healthy.
Caroline.......................	....	up	r......	10	S......	plenty ......
Conrath.............	....	strong, up.	brown.	10	tips ...	good, healthy.
Columbian	Oneida, N.Y	up	red ...	10	tips ...	fair.........
Golden Queen	New Jersey	up	red ...	10	S......	rank
Gregg	Indiana	strong, up.	d. red.	9	tips ...	good ... .
Gault	Ohio	up	p.....	8	tips ...	fair.
Hilborn	Leamington, Ont..	up	b	8	tips ...	fair.........
Hansell	....	up	red .	10	S......	good ....
Johnston Sweet	....	up	d. red	4	tips . .	poor ......
Kansas	Kansas	up	d. red..	10	tips ...	good, healthy.
Lovett	New Jersey	up	d. red..	10	tips ...	good ....
Lottie.......................	....	up	d. red..	10	tips . .	fine...... ..
Louden	Janesville, Wis....	up	d. red.	10	S......	healthy.....
Marlboro	Marlboro', N.Y....	up	red ...	10	S......	heavy, healthy
Mammoth Cluster............	....	up	d. red..	3	tips ...	poor ....
Miller.......................	....	up	red ...	10	S......	good, healthy.
Ohio	Ohio	up	brown.	9	tips ...	fair.........
Pioneer	....	up	d. red.	9	tips ...	good ....
Phœnix	...'..........	up	d. red.	10	S......	good, healthy.
Reliance	New Jersey	up	brown.	9	S......	fair.........
Rancocos]...................	....	up	red ...	9	S	good ......
Redfield	......,.........	up ,......	d. red..	10	S & tips	rank
Shaffer's Colossal	Monroe Co., N.Y..	strong, up.	brown.	7	tips ...	good ....
Smith's Giant	St. Catharines, Ont.	up, strong.	d. red.	10	tips ...	good, healthy.
Superlative	....	up	brown.	7	S	large ....
Strawberry Raspberry	. ...	dwarf ...	......	10	S......	good, healthy.
Turner	....	up	red ...	10	S......	large, healthy.
Tang'er	. ...	up	d. red..	9	tips ...	good ....
Thompson...................	Ohio	up	d. red.	10	S......	good ....
White Champlain	....	up	o /.....	9	S......	fair.........
Zettler	....	up	d. red..	10	S......	good, healthy.

BERRIES.

FLESH.	SEASON.
F.—Firm.	E.—Early.
S.—Soft.	M.—Medium.
	L.—Late.

Berry.							Value Scale 1-10.	
Size.	Form.	Color.	Tenacity (*i.e.* to calyx or receptacle).	Flesh.	Flavor.	Season.	Market.	Remarks.
								has never fruited.
M	R	R	free	S	4-5	E	7-8	
M	SC	Y	M	S	6-7	M to L	4-6	
L	C	R	M to good	F	10	L	9-10	best red berry.
M	R	Y	F	S	2-3	M to E	1-3	
L	R	D	good	F	8-9	M	9-10	very promising.
L	R	P	good	F	8-9	L	7-8	
L	C	Y	M	M	5-7	L	4-6	best yellow berry.]
L	R	D	F	F	10	L	9-10	
L	R	D	M	F	6-7	L	7-8	
M	R	D	M	F	6-7	M	9-10	
M	R	R	M	M	6-7	E	4-6	
S	R	D	F	F	1	M	1-3	useless.
L	R	D	M	F	8-9	M	9-10	best blackcap.
M	R	D	F	F	6-7	M	4-6	
M	R	D	M	F	8-9	M	4-6	
L	R	R	G	F	8-9	M	7-8	
L	R	B	free	F	8-9	E	7-8	
S	R	D	F	M	2-3	M	1-3	no good.
M L	R	R	M	M to F.	6-7	M	7-8	
M	R	D	F	F	4-5	M	7-8	
S	R	D	F	F	6-7	M	7-8	
M S	R	R	F	F	8-9	E L	9-10	
M	R	R	F	M	4-5	E	4-6	
S M	R	R	M	S	6-7	E	4-6	
S	R	P	F	S	1	L	1-3	
VL	SC	P	F	M F	6-7	M	4-6	
L	R	D	M	F	10	L	9-10	a good one.
L	C	R	M	M	8-9	M	9-10	
L	R	R	G	F	2-3	M L	1-3	
S	R	R	F	S	8-9	E	7-8	
S	R	D	F	S	4-5	E	4-6	
S	R	R	F	S	4-5	E	4-6	
M	R	O	M	S	6-7	M	4-6	
L	C	R	G	F	6-7	M L	7-8	very promising red

CATALOGUE

OF THE VALUES OF

THE FRUITS AND FRUIT TREES OF ONTARIO

ALSO SHOWING

THEIR ADAPTABILITY TO THE VARIOUS PARTS OF THE PROVINCE.

DESIGNED TO AID PLANTERS IN SELECTING SUITABLE VARIETIES.

SUBJECT TO ANNUAL REVISION.

COMPILED BY THE SECRETARY OF THE FRUIT EXPERIMENT STATIONS

AND

PUBLISHED BY THE ONTARIO DEPARTMENT OF AGRICULTURE, TORONTO

12 F.E.S.

CATALOGUE OF FRUITS FOR THE USE OF PLANTERS.

APPLES.

Key to Quality:
1 Very Poor
2–3 Poor.
4–5 Fair.
6–7 Good.
8–9 Very Good.
10— First Class.

Key to Market Value:
1–3 4th Rate.
4–6 3rd Rate.
7–8 2nd Rate.
9–10 1st Rate.

Key to Adaptation:
*—Desirable.
**—Especially Desirable.
†—Promising.
0—Undesirable.
00—Not Hardy.

Key to Stations:
1. Southwestern.
2. Niagara.
3. Wentworth.
4. Burlington.
5. Lake Huron.
6. Georgian Bay.
7. Simcoe.
8. East Central.
9. Bay of Quinte.
10. St. Lawrence.
13. The Secretary's Fruit Farm.
14. Algoma.

Varieties tested at Bay of Quinte Station. W. H. Dempsey, Trenton.	Season in use.	Tree				Fruit					Adaptation — Southern Stations					Middle Stations				Northern Stations		
		Vigor, scale 1.10.	Hardiness, scale 1-10.	Productiveness, scale 1-10.	Total value of Tree.	Quality, scale 1-10 — Dessert.	Cooking.	Value, scale 1-10 — Home market.	Foreign market.	Total value of fruit.	No. 1.	No. 2.	No. 3.	No. 4.	No. 13.	No. 5.	No. 6.	No. 8.	No. 9.	No. 7.	No. 10.	No. 14.
Albury	Jan.-Feb.	7	8	8	23	9	9	9	9	36						*			**	*		
	Aug.-Sept.	8	10	6	24	6	6	4		16				*			*	*		0	*	
	Sept.	10	10	8	28	4	9	9	9	31				0*		*	*	**	**	*	*	
	Mar.	8	10	6	24	8	8	7	9	32						*	*	*	*	*	*	
	Feb.-Mar.	8	8	8	24	7	7	4	4	22				*		*	**	*	0		*	
Bailey Sweet	Aug.-Sept.	9	10	8	27	8	8	7	1	24				**	*	0	**	*	0	0		
Baldwin	Nov.	6	8	8	22	4	8	4	4	20				*	**	*	*	*	0	00	*	
Beauty of Kent	Jan.-Mar.	6	7	8	21	4	6	8	8	26				*	*	*	**	**	*	**	*	
Ben Davis	Oct.-Nov	10	10	10	28	4	6	8	8	26						**	**	*	0*	**	*	
Benoni	Mar.-May	8	10	8	28	10	8	6	9	26				**	**	*	*	**	*	**	*	
Blenheim	July-Sept.	8	10	8	26	6	8	4	7	25					**	*	*	*	0*	*	*	
Blue ?main	Nov.	10	10	10	30	8	7	9	9	29					**	*						
Bogdanoff	Oct.-Feb.	8	10	6	24			8	9	31					0	*			0	*		
Boston Star	Oct.-April	10	10	8	28	8	8	7	9	32							*	*		*	*	
Bietigheimer	Dec.-Feb.	8	10	10	28	8	9	7	7	38				*	**	*				*		
Bismarck	Oct.-Dec.	9	10	10	29	6		7	8	30						*	*		0	0	*	
?he Beauty	Aug.-Sept.	7	8	10	25	9	9	7		25						*			0	0		0
Ga. ?ette	Oct.-Nov	10	10	5	25	2	6	6	6	20					0	*			0	0*	0	00

CATALOGUE OF FRUITS.—APPLES.—*Continued.*

Varieties tested at Bay of Quinte Station. W. H. Dempsey, Trenton.	Season in use.	Tree.				Fruit.						Adaptation.													
		Vigor, scale 1-10.	Hardiness, scale 1-10.	Productiveness, scale 1-10.	Total value of tree.	Quality, scale 1-10 Desert.	Cooking.	Home market.	Foreign market.	Value, scale 1-10	Total value of fruit.	Southern Stations. No. 1.	No. 2.	No. 3.	No. 4.	No. 13.	Middle Stations. No. 5.	No. 6.	No. 8.	No. 9.	Northern Stations. No. 7.	No. 10.	No. 14.	
APPLES.—*Con.*																								
	Aug.-Sept.	10	10	10	30	6	9	10	9		34				* * *	* *	* *	* *	* * * *	* * * *	* *	* * *	‡	
	Jan.-Mar.	8	9	10	27	9	9	9	9		36				* * *	*		*		* * *	*	*		
	Jan. Mr.	10	10	8	28	7	9	8	8		31							0		*	0 *		
	Feb.	6	7	9	22	8	6	8	9		31					0				0			
	Dec.	8	9	10	27	4	4	4			13									0			
	Jan.	8	10	10	29	5	5	5	5		15									0			
	Dec.	9	10	10	25	5	4	5	10		19						*	*		*			
	Mar.	6	7	6	20	10	8	9			37				*			*		*	*		+
Salome	May	7	7	8	22	6	7	8	8		29				*		*		*			*	
Sutton	May	8	9	7	24	9	6	8	10		33				*		0		*	*		*	
Stump.	Oct.	8	8	8	24	6	9	6	5		22						0		*				
Scarlet		9	10	8	29	10	7	10			29				*		0	0		0	*		
Seek No	Mr.	8	8	7	24	4	4	4	8		30				*		0		*	*			
Sops of		8	9	8	24	2	7	8			12						0	*	*	*			
Sour	Aug.-Sept.	10	9	10	27	8	9	9	6		17				*					0			
St.	Aug.-Sept.	10	10	10	30	7	6	6	6		32				*		*	0	*	0			+
Stuarts	Sept.-Oct.	8	9	10	27	4	6	6	8		25					0				0			‡
Stark	Feb.-May.	10	10	10	30		6	6			24				*	0		*	*		0	*	
Swaar.	Mar.	8	8	7	23	8	7	8	9		32				*	*	*			0		*	
Swazie.	Nov. Jan.	7	9	9	24	9	8	5	7		22				*	*	*	*	*	*		*	
Sweet Bough.	Aug.-Sept.	7	10	8	24	8	8	5	7		23				*	*	*		*	*		*	
Sweet	Aug.	10	10	9	29	6	6	4			20						*		*				
Us Red		9	9	5	24	7	9	6	4		22				*		*	*	*	*		*	0
Wealthy	Sept. Dec.	9	9	10	28	8	8	9	8		33				*	0	*	*	*	0	*	*	*
	Dec.	7	8	10	25	8	8	9	7		32				*	0	*	*	*	*	0		*
	Dec. May	6	8	9	23	7	5	7	7		26				*	*	*			*		*	‡
Yellow	August	10	10	8	28	6	8	6	4		20					*		*		*	0 *	*	+
Yellow	Dec.-Mar.	8	8	5	19	9	8	7			24				0	0		0		0	00 *	*	
Yellow																								

CATALOGUE OF FRUITS—BLACKBERRIES—RASPBERRIES.

Tested at Burlington Station.	Season in use.	Bush.				Fruit.					Adaptation.											
		Vigor, scale 1-10.	Hardiness, scale 1-10.	Productiveness, scale 1-10.	Total Value of Tree.	Quality, scale 1-10. Dessert.	Cooking.	Value, scale 1-10. Home market.	Foreign market.	Total Value of fruit.	Southern Stations. No.1. No.2. No.3. No.4.				No.13.	Middle Stations. No.5. No.6. No.8. No.9.				Northern Stations. No.7. No.10. No.14.		
BLACKBERRIES.																						
Agawam	July 27-Aug 10	9	10	8	27	6		6		12				*	*							
Ancient Briton	" 21- 5	7	9	7	23					14				o								
Childs' Tree	" 20- 6	7	9	7	25	7		7		14				o								
Dorchester	" 23- 6	9	9	7	26	7		7		16				o	*							
Early	" 25-10	9	10	7	26	6		8		17				o								
Early Harvest	" 13- 1	7	7	9	24	8		8		15				*	*							
Early King	" 12- 5	7	9	8	23	9		8		19				+								
Eldorado	" 23- 5	8	8	7	26	7		9		20				o	*							
Erie	" 23- 5	9	10	9	28	10		9		11				*								
Gainor	" 23-15	9	10	7	29	10		10		13				+	*							
Kittatinny	" 30-10	10	9	9	26	6		5						o								
..'s Best	" 20- 1	8	10	10		5		8						o	*							
Maxwell	" 25- 5	5	7	8	22					16				+								
Minnewaski	" 23- 5	8	10	6	26	8		8		16				*	*							
Snyder	" 18- 5	9	10	7	25	8		8		16				+								
Stone's Hardy	" 23- 5	7	10	8	26	8		7		16				-	*							
Taylor	" 23-10	9	10	8	25	9		7		17				*	*							
Wachusetts	" 23- 5	9	10	7	28	10		9		17				o	*							
Western Triumph	" 20- 5	7	9	6	23	8		9		17				*								
..'s Early	" 20- 5	10	8	6	24	8		8						o								
Wilson, Jun														o								
RASPBERRIES.																						
All Summer	July 8-Oct 15	6	9	7	22	8		8		16				*	*							
Columbia	" 13-28	9	10	9	28	7		8		15				*	*							
Cuthbert	" 13-31	10	10	8	28	10		10		20				*	*							
Golden Queen	" 5-20	8	10	7	25	9		6		14				*	*							
Gregg	" 13-31	9	10	7	26	7		7		13				*								
Hilborn	" 5-20	8	9	7	24	6		5		10				o								
Japan Wine	" 25-31	8	6	4	18	5		8	0													
Kansas	" 5-20	9	9	9	28	10								*								
Kenyon	" 12-25	7	8	7	22	10		8		18				*								

CATALOGUE OF FRUITS—RASPBERRIES—CHERRIES.

Tested at Burlington Station.	Season in use.	Tree or bush.				Fruit.					Adaptation.											
		Vigor, scale 1-10.	Hardiness, scale 1-10.	Productiveness, scale 1-10.	Total value of Tree.	Dessert.	Cooking.	Home market.	Foreign market.	Total value of fruit.	S. No.1	S. No.2	S. No.3	S. No.4	S. No.13	M. No.5	M. No.6	M. No.8	M. No.9	N. No.7	N. No.10	N. No.14
RASPBERRIES.—Con.																						
Lottie	July 10-Oct. 25	8	8	7	23	8		8		16				+								
Loudon	" 13- " 31	8	10	8	26	6		8		14					**							
Cuit	" 10- " 25	8	9	7	23	7		10		17				**								
Marlboro	" 12- " 25	7	10	10	27	9		8		17												
Mier	" 5- " 23	6	9	7	22	4		8		12				*								
Mills	" 9- " 31	8	9	7	24	9		8		17				*								
Ohio	" 8- " 25	9	10	8	27	8		8		16				*								
Cer	" 1- " 20	8	9	6	23	9		8		17												
Palmer	" 11- " 25	8	10	8	26	9		9		18				+	+							
Felix	" 3- " 20	5	9	7	21	5		8		13				+								
Progress	" 10- " 20	8	10	5	23	8		8		16				*								
Redfield	" 10- " 31	8	10	7	25	7		7		15				+	+							
Reliance	" 13- " 31	8	10	8	26	5				12					0							
Royal Church	" 10- " 31	6	9	7	22									*	*							
Shaffer's Colossal	" 13- " 20	9	8	9	27									+	0							
_'s Giant	" 8- " 31	10	10	7	24									0	0+							
Souhegan	" 10- " 25	7	10	7	22										***							
Thompson	" 8- "	6	10	6	22										*							
Wet	" 10- " 25	5	7	3	15										*							
CHERRIES.																						
Tested at Maplehurst.																						
Choisy	June 24 to July 4	6	9	4	19	10	4	5	4	23												
Cleveland	June 15 to 25	9	8	8	26	10	5	9	8	32												
Coe	June 25 to July 6	10	8	6	24	6	5	6	2	19												
Dyehouse																						
Eagle	July 1 to 10	7	8	4	19	10	4	8	7	29						**	*	*		**		
Early Purple	June 15 to 25	9	9	5	23	8	2	8	8	26												
Elkhorn	July 10 to 20	8	8	10	26	5	6	10	10	31								*				
Elton																						
English Morello	June 20 to	9	10	7	26	6	10	6	6	28					*	**	*	**		**		
Eugenie																						
Hortense	June 20 to	4	10	4	18	2	7	6	6	21					*	**	*			*	*	
Kentish (late)																						
Knight	June 20 to 30	7	8	6	21	10	5	9	9	33		**			*	*	*			*		

Variety	Dates												
Koslov Morello	July 10 to...												
Late Duke		8	9				7	24	7	9		8	34
Magnifique	June 15 to 30.	10	10	10		8		24	4	2		10	4
May Duke	July 1 to 12.	8	8	10	2		8	28	10	10		10	35
Mazzard	July 4 to 15.	10	10		7	10	3	24	8	7		7	26
Mel ...	July 1 to 10.	6			9								
Mercy													
M. ordinaire	July 4 to 12.	9	9			9	5	27	10	9		9	31
Napoleon		8	8	10	10	7	4	25	7	7		7	28
Olivet													
Orel 24	July 8 to 16.	4	10	8		7		21	7	7			26
Ostheim													
Philippe	June 20 to 30.	4	10	8	9		6	20	6	7			26
Richmond													
Rockport	July 4 to 12.	10	8	8	8	8	10	24	8	8		8	32
Spanish		8	8	10	7	10		23	8	10		10	37
Tartarian													
Vladimir		8	10		5	8		26	8	10		10	33
Windsor		7	8		5		10	23	8	8		7	30
Wood	June 20 to July 4												
Wragg													

CURRANTS.
Tested at Burlington.

All hardy thus far.

Variety	Dates							
Belle de St. Giles	July 8–13.	7	5	10	9	12		10
Black Victoria	" 8–20.	9	6	9	6	15		9
Brayley's Seedling	" 8–13.	7	8	8		15		8
Champion	" 20–31.	10	9		9	19		10
Cherry	" 6–12.	8	9			17		10
Collins' Prolific	" 20–31.	10	5		9	13		9
Fay's Prolific	" 7–12.	6	7		7	15		9
Lee's Prolific	" 12–20.	8	8			16		9
Naples	" 12–20.	9	9			18		9
New Victoria	" 4–8.	7	6			13		9
North Star	" 7–12.	7	7		7	14		9
Pomona	" 4–8.	7	5			12		9
Raby Castle	" 11–16.	8	10		7	18	14	9
Red Cross	" 7–12.	7	7		8	14	4	8
Red Dutch	" 4–8.	8	8		7	15	7	6
Red Victoria	" 7–12.	8	7		9	17	9	7
Saunders	" 12–20.	9	9			15	19	9
Versailles	" 7–12.	7	6		7	13		8
White Grape	" 7–12.	8	6		7	16	16	7
White Imperial	" 7–12.	7	8		10	15		8
Wilder	" 7–12.	8	7		7	16		10

(a) Those varieties left blank not as yet sufficiently tested.

CATALOGUE OF FRUITS—GRAPES.

Key to Quality:
1 Very Poor.
2–3 Poor.
4–5 Fair.
6–7 Good.
8–9 Very Good.
10 First Class.

Key to Market Value:
1— 3 4th Rate.
4— 6 3rd Rate.
7— 8 2nd Rate.
9—10 1st Rate.

Key to Adaptation:
*—Desirable.
**—Especially Desirable.
+—Promising.
0—Undesirable.
00—Not Hardy.

Tested at Wentworth Experimental Station by M Pettit, Winona.	Season in use.	Tree					Fruit			Adaptation — Southern Stations					Middle Stations				Northern Stations	
		Vigor, scale 1-10.	Hardiness, scale 1-10.	Productiveness, scale 1-10.	Freedom from disease, scale 1-10.	Total value of Vine, max. 40.	Quality, scale 1-10.	Value, Home market, scale 1-10.	Total value of fruit.	No. 1.	No. 2.	No. 3.	No. 4.	No. 13.	No. 5.	No. 6.	No. 8.	No. 9.	No. 7.	No. 10.
Adirondac	September	3	2	2	2	9	9	2	11		**		*	**			**			
Agawam (Rog. 15)	Oct.-Nov.	9	9	8	8	30	9	9	18								0			
Alvey (Hagar)	Oct.	7	8	6	8	29	2	9	4								*			
Amber	Oct.-Nov.	6	6	3	4	19	2	2	4					0						
Amber Queen	September	7	6	5	6	24	6	5	11					0						
Anna	October	6	8	7	7	28	6	5	10				*				*			
August Giant	September	8	9	6	7	30	2													
Bacchus	October	8	9	7	8	31	5	7	14								*			
Barry	September	9	9	8	8	34	2													
Berckman's	September	6	9	8	7	33	7													
Black Delaware	"	4	6	5	7	24	7									**				
Black Eagle	"	7	7	4	6	22	8				*		0	**		**	*			
Black Pearl	"	9	5	6	9	21	8	2	4								*			
Brighton	October	8	9	9	6	36	8	7	15		*		0	*	*	*	*			
Brilliant	Oct.-Nov.	8	9	7	7	31	8						**	**	**		*			
Cambridge	September	8	10	8	6	30	10													
Catawba	Sept.-Oct.	7	8	8	5	31	8	10	20		*		0	0	**	*	*		*	
Concord	September	10	7	10	8	39	6	10	16		*		**	**	**		*			
Cottage	September	6	10	3	9	25	4	4	8		*		0	0*		0	*			
Clinton		10	10	6	6	32	6													
Crevelling	September	6	7	6	6	25	8		10											
Cynthiana	October	7	8	5	6	26	2													

Delaware	September	5	8	8	8	6	27	10	10	20		*
Diana	October	9	9	7	6	6	31	6	6	12		
Dracut	September	6	8	7	6	6	28	2	4	6		
Dr.	October	7	9	8	4	7	30	4				*
Duchess	"	6	8	6	5	8	25	5	6	11		
Early Ohio	August	7	5	6	9	7	31	9	6	15		0
Eldorado	September	8	8	8	4	8	26	4	4	8		*
Empire State	"	7	8	6	7	7	26	5	5	12		0
Eumelan		6	7	4	7	7	34	7	7	11		
Goethe (Rog. 1)	October	9	9	6	8	8		4				
Herbert												
Jefferson	Oct.-Nov.	4	5	5	7	7	21	6	6	12		**
Janesville												
Lady	September	2	10	9	2	6	20	8	8	16		0
Lady Washington	October	9	9	7	7	5	30	4	4	8		*
Rey (Rog. 9)	September	9	10	8	8	8	35	9	9	18		**
Lutie		7	8	9	9	8	32	2				
Marion	October	8	8	7	4	6	31	7	4	11		0
Martha	September	4	6	4	2	6	31	8	7	15		
Massasoit (Rog. 3)	"	10	9	6	7	7	28	8				
Mills												
Merrimac												
Missouri Riesling	October	7	8	7	4	5	29	3	7	7		*
Moore's Diamond	September	6	8	6	7	7	27	7	7	14		**
Moore's Early	"	5	9	4	6	7	27	8		15		**
Moyer												
Niagara	October	9	9	10	5	2	33	3		5		*
		8	7	8	7	5	30	5	5	8		
Oneida	September	8	8	7	7	6	27	7	6	8		**
Perkins	October	5	6	6	8	5	24	7		13		0
Pocklington	"	7	7	5	8	6	25	8				
Poughkeepsie Red	September	6	6	6	5	6	13	6	10	10		**
Prentiss	"	3	9	3	6	3	33	3	4	13		
Rebecca	September	10	7	9	1	1	33	1		16		*
Requa (Rog. 28)		7	8	8	6	6	30	6				
Rockwood	October	10	9	9	9	6	32	8	9	17		0
Salem	September	9	9	8	8	7	28	9	2	4		+
	October	9	7	3	9	8	35	9				**
Triumph	"	7	8	9	9	6	27	8				*
Transparent	"	7	7	7	7	7	30	7	8	14		+
Ulster Prolific	"	7	6	8	8	7	27	7				**
Vergennes	Oct.-Nov.	7	9	6	6	7	26	6	8	15		*
Victoria	September	7	9	9	9	8	30	8	8			+
	"	7	9	9	7	9	34	9	6	17		+
Woodruff Red		9.7	9	7	8	8	32	8	9	10		*
Worden	September	8	8	7	7	4	31	4				+
Wyoming Red	"											

CATALOGUE OF FRUITS.—PEARS.

Tested by E. C. Beman, Newcastle, Ont.	Season in use.	Tree.				Fruit.				Remarks.
						Quality.				
		Vigor.	Hardiness.	Productiveness.	Total value of tree.	Dessert.	Cooking.	Home market value.	Total value of fruit.	
Ananas d'Éte	Sep., Oct.	7	6	7	20	8	6	8	22	Very subject to blight.
Bartlett	Sept	8	8	9	25	9	10	10	29	One of the best for market.
Bergamot Gansels	Sep., Oct.	6	9	5	20	8	5	5	18	
Bergamot Gansels, late	Jan., Mar.	6	8	8	22	2	5	4	11	Not worth growing.
Belle Lucrative	Sep., Oct.	7	6	7	20	8	6	6	20	Very good, subject to blight.
Beurre Assomption	Sep	7	5	6	18	6	7	8	21	Not sufficiently hardy
Beurre Bosc	Oct., Nov.	8	7	8	23	9	7	10	26	Very fine for market.
Beurre Bachelier	Oct., Nov.	7	8	8	23	5	5	6	16	Not valuable
Beurre Baltet Pere	Nov., Dec.	6	6	8	20	5	6	6	17	
Beurre Clairgeau	Nov., Dec.	6	5	8	19	5	6	8	19	Very showy.
Beurre d'Amanlis	Sep	8	9	9	26	5	5	4	14	
Beurre d'Anjou	Nov., Dec	9	10	4	23	9	6	10	25	Not productive
Beurre d'Aremburg	Dec., Jan.	8	8	7	23	6	6	5	17	Sometimes astringent.
Beurre de Martillet	Sep	7	6	7	20	7	5	7	19	Rots at core, handsome.
Beurre Diel	Nov., Dec.	7	8	6	21	8	7	7	22	Liable to rot.
Beurre Gris	Sep., Oct.	6	7	6	19	6	6	5	17	Very valuable. usually poor.
Beurre, Golden of Bilboa.	Sep	7	5	6	18	5	6	6	17	Very showy, but poor.
Beurre Goubalt	Sep	5	5	7	17	4	5	3	12	Not worth growing.
Beurre Hardy	Oct	8	8	6	22	7	6	7	20	
Beurre Oswego	Oct., Nov.	8	9	8	25	6	5	5	16	Spots and cracks.
Beurre Robin	Sep	9	8	8	25	5	5	6	16	
Beurre Superfin	Oct	8	10	6	24	8	6	6	20	
Blane Perne	Dec., Ap'l	6	7	8	21	2	6	4	12	Not worth growing.
Black Warserter	Dec., Mar.	9	8	10	27	1	4	2	7	Of no value.
Bloodgood	Aug	5	7	7	19	9	5	5	19	Fine for home use.
Bonne d'Eyee	Sep., Oct.	5	6	6	17	8	6	5	19	Identical with Buckworth.
Bon Chretien, Summer	Sep	7	9	7	23	5	8	5	18	Spots and cracks.
Brandywine	Sep	8	8	5	21	7	4	5	16	Rots at core.
British Queen	Nov	7	6	5	18	7	6	6	19	
Buffum	Sep., Oct.	8	7	8	23	6	5	5	16	
Catillac	Dec., April	6	5	7	18	1	6	3	10	
Calite Mignot	Nov., Dec.	7	6	10	23	2	4	3	9	
Church	Sep., Oct.	7	8	6	21	7	5	6	18	
Clapp's Favorite	Sep	9	7	9	25	9	8	9	26	Subject to blight.
Comet	Aug	8	7	8	23	2	4	5	11	Beautiful but very poor.
Dana's Hovey	Nov., Dec.	8	8	6	22	9	4	5	18	Very fine for home use
Dearborn's Seedling	Aug	7	8	7	22	8	6	5	19	
Dix	Oct., Nov.	8	8	6	22	7	6	6	19	Liable to spot and crack.
Doyenne Boussock	Sep., Oct.	9	8	7	24	7	6	9	22	
Doyenne d'Ete	July, Aug.	7	7	8	22	7	4	4	15	
Doyenne Goubalt	Dec., Mar.	5	5	4	14	6	5	6	17	
Doyenne Gris	Oct., Nov.	6	7	7	20	8	6	4	18	Spots and cracks.
Doyenne White	Oct	7	8	8	23	8	6	5	19	Spots and cracks.
Duchess d'Angouleme	Oct., Nov.	5	5	8	18	4	6	6	16	Season too short.
Duchesse de Bordeaux	Jan., Mar.	7	7	6	20	7	6	5	18	Good for home use.
Duchess Precoce	Sep	7	8	10	25	6	10	10	26	Fine for market.
Flemish Beauty	Oct	10	8	9	27	8	7	8	23	Spots and cracks.
Foselle	Nov., Dec.	6	5	6	17	4	4	5	13	Beautiful but poor.
Fondante de Malines	Sept., Oct.	5	6	8	19	3	6	7	21	
Garber	Nov	10	7	10	27	4	8	7	19	
Glout Morceau	Dec	5	4	6	15	5	6	4	15	Subject to blight.
Goodale	Oct	8	9	9	26	7	7	8	22	
Graslin	Oct., Nov.	8	6	8	22	6	6	7	19	
Harvard	Sep	8	9	7	24	5	5	6	16	Rots at core.
Howell	Oct	7	7	9	23	6	7	8	21	
Idaho	Oct	8	7	8	23	7	8	5	20	Very subject to blight
Jaminette	Dec., Mar.	9	7	8	24	7	6	7	20	Good for long keeper
Jargonelle, English	Aug	7	6	7	20	6	5	3	14	Subject to blight and
Jones	Oct., Nov.	8	8	10	26	8	5	7	20	rots at core.
Josephine de Malines	Dec., Feb.	7	7	8	22	9	6	7	22	

PEARS.—*Continued.*

Tested by E. E. Beman, Newcastle, Ont.	Season in use.	Tree.				Fruit.				Remarks.
		Vigor.	Hardiness.	Productiveness.	Total value of tree.	Quality.			Total value of fruit.	
						Dessert.	Cooking.	Home market use.		
Keiffer.	Nov., Dec.	7	7	10	23	5	10	6	21	Rots at core.
Kirtland	Sep	8	6	7	22	7	6	5	18	Unproductive.
King Sessing	Sep	7	8	5	20	7	7	6	20	
Lawrence.	Nov., Jan.	7	7	8	22	9	7	7	23	
Louise Bonne de Jersey	Sep., Oct.	7	7	9	23	7	9	7	23	Subject to blight.
Madeline	Aug	7	6	7	20	6	4	5	15	
Marshall	Sep	7	8	7	22	6	5	6	17	
Madame Eliza.	Nov	9	8	8	25	5	6	5	16	Subject to blight.
Mons. Haberlin	Sep	7	6	5	18	7	6	6	19	
Mount Vernon	Nov., Dec.	8	8	7	23	8	6	7	21	
Nonreau Poiteau	Nov	7	6	8	21	6	7	7	20	Sometimes astringent.
Onondaga	Oct., Nov.	8	6	7	21	6	6	7	19	
Osband's Summer	Aug	6	7	6	19	7	5	4	16	
Ott	Aug.	7	6	8	21	9	5	5	19	Variable in flavor.
Passe Colmar	Dec., Jan.	8	6	8	22	7	6	5	18	
Paradise d'Automne	Sep. Oct	8	7	9	24	8	6	7	21	Subject to blight.
Pitmaston	Oct., Nov.	7	6	8	21	6	8	8	22	
Pound	Dec., Mar.	7	7	6	20	1	6	4	11	
Pratt	Sep., Oct	8	7	9	24	6	6	7	19	Very fine for home use.
Rostiezer	Aug., Sep.	8	7	6	21	9	5	6	20	Best dessert pear grown.
Rutter	Oct., Nov.	7	7	8	22	6	5	7	18	
Seckel	Sep., Oct.	7	9	8	24	10	6	7	23	
Sheldon	Oct	9	8	7	24	9	7	9	25	Subject to blight.
Souvenir du Congres	Sep	7	6	7	20	7	8	8	23	Subject to blight.
Steven's Genessee	Sep	7	7	8	22	6	5	6	17	
St. Germain	Nov., Dec.	6	7	7	20	6	7	5	18	
St. Ghislain	Sep., Oct.	7	7	8	22	7	5	5	17	
Triomphe de Vienne	Sep	8	8	9	25	8	7	8	23	
Tyson	Sep	10	9	7	26	10	5	5	20	Variable in quality.
Urbaniste	Sep., Oct.	7	7	6	20	8	7	8	23	
Vicar of Wakefield	Nov., Feb.	8	6	8	22	2	8	6	16	
Washington	Sep	7	7	9	23	8	5	6	19	
Winter Nelis	Dec. Jan.	6	7	8	21	9	5	9	23	Variable in flavor, sometimes astringent.]
Wilmot	Sep., Oct.	10	10	10	30	8	6	8	22	

CATALOGUE OF FRUITS.—PEARS.

Key to Quality.
1—Very Poor.
2-3—Poor.
3-4—Poor to Good.
5-6—Good to Very Good.
7-8—Very Good.
8-9—Very Good to Best.
10—Best.

Key to Adaptation.
*—Desirable.
**—Especially Desirable.
†—Promising.
0—Undesirable.
00—Not Hardy.

Varieties tested at East Central Station. R. L. Huggard, Whitby.	Season in use.	Vigor, scale 1-10.	Hardiness, scale 1-10.	Productiveness, scale 1-10.	Total value of tree.	Quality, scale 1-10. Dessert.	Quality, scale 1-10. Cooking.	Value, scale 1-10. Home market.	Total value of fruit.	No. 1.	No. 2.	No. 3.	No. 4.	No. 13.	No. 5.	No. 6.	No. 8.	No. 9.	No. 7.	No. 10.	No. 14.
Ananas d'Ete	September,	8	6	4	48	4	4	5	13		**		**	**	**	**		0		00	00
Bartlett	September,	7	7	9	23	9	5	10	24		*		*	*	*	*	**	**	+	00	
Belle Lucrative	September, October.	6	7	8	21	8	4	7	26					**	*		**	0			
Beurre Antoine	Or, December.	7	7	7	21	8	4	6	25					*	*		*	**	+		
Beurre Bosc	September, October.	8	9	6	23	7	6	8	31		**		**	**	**		†	**	*		
Beurre d'Anjou	Or,	8	9	6	23	8	6	8					**	*			*	*			
Beurre Diel	September, December.	9				8											*	*			
Beurre Easter													*								
Beurre Giffard	August	7	7	7	21	10	6	9	25		**		**	*	*		*	**	*		
Beurre Hardy	September,	10	10	9	30	8	8	9	25		*		*	*		*	*	0	*		
Beurre Clairgeau	Or, July.	9	8	9	26	8	7	8	32					*			*	*			
Beurre fine	Or.	7	8	8	23	8	4	6	26		*		*	*		*	*	**			
Brandywine	August, September.	8	8	7	23	7	6	6	19					**	*			*			
Brockworth Park	December,	9	9	6	24	7	5	7	19					*			*	*			
Buffum	Last of September	10	7	9	26	10	7	9	26		*		**	*	**		**	*	*		
...'s Favorite	August, September	9	7	8	24	8		8						**	*		**	**	*		
Doyenne d'Ete	July																				
Dempsey	Or,										*		*	**	*		*	**	*		
Doyenne Boussock	September,	10	10	10	30	9	9	9	26				**	**			*	*			
Duchess ...	Or.	8	8	7	23	8	8	8	24		*		**	**	*		**	**	**	+	
Duchess de Bordeaux	December, February.																	0	+	+	
I ... Precoce																					
Dorset																					

		Month						
D'Jules Guyot		....						
Eastern Belle		....						
*Flemish Beauty		September	9	9	8	8	26	7
Goodale		October	8	8	7	8	23	8
Kut Morceau		December	8	7	6	6	22	8
Graslin		December	8	6	8	8	23	7
Grey Doyenne		July	7	6	6	9	19	8
Howell		Mar, November	8	6	7	7	21	8
Idaho		Mar, November	8	6	2	8	24	9
Josephine de Malines		December, January	7	9	7	8	22	7
**Kieffer		Mar	10	7	8	8	30	8
Lawrence		December	6	10	10	9	19	7
Louise Bonne		September, October	7	8	5	7	24	8
Lawson		October		8	9	10		
Le conte		....						
Manning's Elizabeth		November, December	9	7	8	8	24	7
Mount		....						
Margaret		....						
Osband's Summer		December						
P. Barry		August	7	9	7	7	23	5
Petite Marguerite		December, January	9	10	8	8	27	6
President Druard		October, November	10	9	8	10	26	
Ritson		August, September	9	7	8	10	23	8
Rostiezer		October	8	7	7	7	23	9
Sheldon		August, September	7	10	8	9	25	8
Souvenir du Congres		August, September						
Tyson		August, Mar	7					
Vicar of Wakefield		August, Mar						
Winter Doyenne		September	6	6	6	7	19	7
Winter Nelis		December, January	8	10	9	8	27	7

* Scabs badly at Southern Stations.   ** The Secretary does not agree with Mr. Huggard's value of Kieffer for dessert.   All these values will be revised next year.

CATALOGUE OF FRUITS FOR THE USE OF PLANTERS.

PLUMS.

Key to Quality:
1 Very poor.
2—3 Poor.
4—5 Fair.
6—7 Good.
9—9 Very Good.
10— First Class.

Key to Market Value:
1—3 4th Rate.
4—6 3rd Rate.
7—8 2nd Rate.
9—10 1st Rate.

Key to Adaptation:
*—Desirable.
**—Especially Desirable.
†—Promising.
0—Undesirable.
00—Not Hardy.

Varieties tested at Georgian Bay Station. J. G. Mitchell, Clarksburg.	Tree.					Fruit.					Adaptation.												
	Season in use.	Vigor, scale 1-10.	Hardiness, scale 1-10.	Productiveness, scale 1-10.	Total value of tree.	Dessert.	Cooking.	Home market.	Foreign market.	Total value of fruit.	No. 1.	No. 2.	No. 3.	No. 4.	No. 13.	No. 5.	No. 6.	No. 8.	No. 9.	No. 7.	No. 10.	No. —.
						Quality, scale 1-10.		Value, scale 1-10.			Southern Stations.					Middle Stations.				Northern Stations.		
Abundance	Last of Sept	8	10			6	8			27		**		*	*	+	*	**		+	†	†
Duke	Aug	9	8	8	25	8	9	10				**					*			+		
Bradshaw	Sept	10										*			*		*			++++		
Burbank																				+		
Bleeker's Gage	Sept.-Oct	4	8	8	20	7	10	10		24		*		*	*		*	*		+		
Bingham	Sept	10	8	10	28	8	9	10		27		**			**		**	*				
		9	10	10	29		7	4		11		*		*	*		*	*	*	+	*	
Coe's Golden Drop	Sept	9	8	5	22	7	7	7		21							*	*	*	*	
Damson	August																					
Duane's Purple	August																					
De Soto		10	9	6	25	7	8	10		25		*			*		**	*	*		
Fellemberg	Sept	10	10	9	29	4	8	7		19		0		0	0		**	*		*	
General Hand	Sept	8	7	8	23	6	9	8		20		**		*	*		**	*	*		
Bass	Aug	7	7	7	20		7			17		†				+	*	**		+	
Goliath	Sept.-Oct																					
German Prune		10	10	8	28	5	7	7		19		0		0	0		**	*	*	*	
Red Duke	Aug	8	10	8	26	6	9	6		24		*		*		+	*	*		*	*
Gueii	Sept.-Oct																					
Howard's Favorite		10	9	9	27	10	10	10		30		**		**	**	**	**	**		+	*	+
Huling's Superb	Aug	8	6	6	19	10	10	10		30		*		*	*		*	**		*		
Imperial Gage	Early Sept																					
Jefferson																						

Lawrence's Favorite	Aug									10	8	8	8	26	10	10	7	27	
Lincoln								*											
Lombard	Sept							**		10	10	10	10	30	8	9	8	25	
McLaughlin	Aug							**		8	7	6	7	21	10	10	9	29	
M's Arctic	Early Aug								**	7	10	10	6	27	6	5	8	14	
New ...	Sept									9	9	10	10	28	8	8		21	
Niagara ... Gage																			
Ouillin's	Aug							*		9	8	8	8	25	4	6	8	18	
Orange	Sept							**		6	7	6	6	19	8	9	10	27	
Prince of Wales	Aug							*		7	6	4	4	17	8	8	8	24	
Peach	Last of Sept									10	10	10	8	28	4	7	10	21	
Pond Seedling																			
Peter's Yellow Gage	Early August									9	10	8	8	27	6	7	7	19	
Prince's Yellow Gage																			
Purple Egg	Sept							**		10	10	9	9	29	4	8	7	19	
Quackenbos	Sept.-Oct							**		10	10	8	8	28	10	10	10	30	
Reine ...																			
Reine ... Vi...																			
Red ... Bonum	Aug.-Sept									10	10	9	9	29	6	9	9	24	
Saunders	September									8	8	8	10	24	10	8	9	29	
Smith's Orleans	Aug.-Sept									9	7	8	10	24	10	10	10	30	
Spaulding																			
St. Catharine	Sept									8	8	6	8	22	8	8	10	18	
Washington	Aug									6	7	8	7	21	10	7	7	24	
Willard																			
Wild ...																			
Yellow Egg																			
Yellow Gage																			

CATALOGUE OF FRUITS FOR THE USE OF PLANTERS.—RASPBERRIES.

Varieties tested at Lake Huron Station. B A. E. Sherrington.	Season in use.	Tree				Fruit			Adaptation (No. 5, Middle Stations)	Remarks.
		Vigor.	Hardiness.	Productiveness.	Total value of Tree.	Quality, Dessert.	Value, Home market.	Total value of fruit.	No. 5.	
All Summer	July 5–July 28	4	10	2	14	9	8	0	0*	
Brandywine	" 4	8	10	10	28	7	8	17	*	
Brinckle's Orange	" 11–Aug.	7	10	5	22	6	4	11	*	
Caroline	" 6	10	10	10	29	10	10	20	*	
Cuth	" 11–	10	10	10	30	4	4	8	+–	
Columbian	" 13–July 28	10	5	4	17	9	10	19	*	Badly winter killed.
Golden Queen	" 22–Aug.	8	10	9	26	8	8	16	+–+*	Best yellow berry.
Gregg	" 11–	7	7	5	21	8	8	16	+*	
Hilt	" 16–	9	8	6	21	10	10	20	*	
Hilborn	" 22–	8	10	3	17	7	5	15	0*	Don't think this is the true Hilborn.
Hansell	" 13–July 28	5	10	9	27	5	7	10	*	
Johnson's Sweet	" 2–	8	4	3	12	10	4	14	*	
Kansas	" 16–Aug.	8	10	9	29	1	10	5	*	
Lovett's	" 13–	8	7	8	23	9	9	20	–+*	
Lottie	" 16–	1	10	4	23	7	9	14	*	
Loudon	" 16–	1	10	1	21	3	9	15	0*	
Marlboro	" 9–	4	10	4	26	7	9	18	*	
Mammoth Cluster	" 11–	4	10	7	26	7	5	16	+–*	
Ohio	" 13–July 28	8	10	8	18	4	8	9	*	
Pioneer	" 16–Aug.	9	8	8	25	6	9	14	0*	
Phenix	July 11–Aug.	7	10	5	26	7	7	15	+–*	
Reliance	" 8–July	8	10	7	23	7	6	18	*	
Rancocas	" 2–	8	10	6	25	7	2	14	0+	
Redfield	" 20–Aug.	9	10	6	26	2	7	13	+–+–	
Shaffer	" 16–	10	4	5	19	6	10	13	0*	Badly winter killed.
Smith's Giant	" 1–	9	8	7	24	10	10	20	*	"
Superlative	" 13–	5	5	4	14	9	9	18	*	
Strawberry Raspberry	" 28–	8	10	6	21	9	0	0	*	
Turner	" 2–July 25	8	10	5	23	6	9	18	*	
Taylor	" 9–	8	10	8	26	6	6	12	*	
Thompson	" 2–	7	10	8	25	7	7	13	*	
White Champlain	" 26–	6	9	4	19	7	5	12	**	Row not full.
Zettler	" 11–Aug.	9	10	9	28	7	9	16	**	A local berry.

TWENTY-NINTH ANNUAL REPORT

OF THE

ENTOMOLOGICAL SOCIETY

OF

ONTARIO.

1898.

(PUBLISHED BY THE ONTARIO DEPARTMENT OF AGRICULTURE, TORONTO)

PRINTED BY ORDER OF

THE LEGISLATIVE ASSEMBLY OF ONTARIO.

TORONTO:
WARWICK BRO'S & RUTTER, Printers and Bookbinders, 68 and 70 Front St. West
1899.

CONTENTS.

WILLIAM HAGUE HARRINGTON, F.R.S.C.

President of the Entomological Society of Ontario, 1893-5

JOHN DEARNESS, I.P.S.

President of the Entomological Society of Ontario, 1895-7

TWENTY-NINTH ANNUAL REPORT

OF THE

ENTOMOLOGICAL SOCIETY OF ONTARIO,

1898.

To the Honorable John Dryden, Minister of Agriculture.

Sir,—I have the honor to present herewith the twenty-ninth annual report of the Entomological Society of Ontario. It contains an account of the proceedings at our annual meeting, which .was held in the City of Montreal, on the 8th and 9th of November last. The change from London, the usual place of meeting and the head-quarters of the society, was made in order that the members generally might join in the celebration of the twenty-fifth anniversary of the formation of the Montreal Branch. The report includes the financial statement of the Treasurer and the reports of the various sections, branches and officers of the society, as well as the papers and addresses delivered during the course of the meeting.

The *Canadian Entomologist*, the monthly magazine published by the society, has now completed its thirtieth volume and begun the issue of the thirty-first. The volume contains a large number of valuable original papers contributed by the most eminent writers in this department of science in Canada and elsewhere. Great attention, it may be observed, has been paid to scale insects and a great many new species from different parts of North America have been described.

I have the honor to be, Sir,

Your obedient servant,

CHARLES J. S. BETHUNE,

Editor.

Trinity College School,
Port Hope.
1 EN.

OFFICERS FOR 1898-9.

President.....................HENRY H. LYMAN, M.A....................Montreal.
Vice-President................REV. T. W. FYLES, D.C.L., F.L S. ....South Quebec.
Secretary ....W. E. SAUNDERS ....London.
Treasurer.....................J. A. BALKWILL..................... .....London.

Directors :

Division No. 1 ....W. H. HARRINGTON, F.R.S.O. ....Ottawa.
      "   2 ....J. D. EVANS ....Trenton.
     ..   3 ....ARTHUR GIBSON........................Toronto.
     ..   4 ....A. H. KILMAN ....Ridgeway.
     ..   5 ....R. W. RENNIE......................London.

Directors ex-Officio (ex-Presidents of the Society) ....
> PROF. WM. SAUNDERS, LL.D., F.R.S.O., F.L.S.,
>   Director of Experimental Farms ....Ottawa.
> REV. C. J. S. BETHUNE, M.A., D.C.L., F.R.S.C.,
>   Head Master Trinity College School ....Port Hope.
> JAMES FLETCHER, LL.D., F.R S O, F.L.S.,
>   Entomologist and Botanist, Experimental
>   Farms ....Ottawa.
> JOHN DEARNESS, I.P.S ....London.

Director Ex-officio (Ontario Agricultural College)....
> PROF. WM. LOCHHEAD......................Guelph.

Librarian and Curator........J. ALSTON MOFFAT.......................London.
Auditors...................J. H. BOWMAN and W. H. HAMILTON ....London.
Editor of the "Canadian Entomologist" ....
> REV. DR. BETHUNE ....Port Hope.

Editing Committee ....
> DR. J. FLETCHER ....Ottawa.
> H. H. LYMAN...........................Montreal.
> J. D. EVANS............................Trenton.
> W. H. HARRINGTON...... ....Ottawa.
> JAMES WHITE .... Snelgrove.

Delegate to the Royal Society ...REV. DR. FYLES ....South Quebec.
Delegates to the Western Fair ..J. DEARNESS and W. E. SAUNDERS............London.

Committee on Field Days....
> DR. WOOLVERTON, MESSRS. BALKWILL, BOWMAN,
>   ELLIOTT, LAW, PERCIVAL, RENNIE, SAUNDERS,
>   and SPENCER ....London.
> DR. HOTSON ....Parkhill.

Library and Rooms Committee
> MESSRS. BALKWILL, BETHUNE, DEARNESS, MOFFAT, and SAUNDERS.

[2]

ANNUAL MEETING OF THE ENTOMOLOGICAL SOCIETY
OF ONTARIO, 1898.

The thirty-fifth* annual meeting of the Entomological Society of Ontario was held at Montreal, in the Museum of the Natural History Society, on Tuesday and Wednesday, November 8th and 9th, in order that the members might join in the celebration of the twenty-fifth anniversary of the formation of the Montreal Branch. At the request of the President, Mr. Henry H. Lyman, the chair was occupied by the Rev. Dr. Bethune, of Port Hope.

The meeting was called to order at 2-30 p.m. on Tuesday, when the following members were present: Dr. Wm. Saunders, Director, and Dr. James Fletcher, Entomologist and Botanist, Experimental Farms, Ottawa; Messrs. John Dearness and W. E. Saunders (Secretary) London; Mr. Arthur Gibson, Toronto; Rev. C. J. S. Bethune, Port Hope; Mr. J. D. Evans, Trenton; Rev. Dr. Fyles, South Quebec; Messrs. H. H. Lyman, A. F. Winn, J. T. Hausen, Lachlan Gibb, M. Waring Davis, G. C. Dunlop, D. Brainerd, A. E. Norris, H. Brainerd, J. B. Williams, Chas. Stephenson, Rev. Dr. Campbell, and others, Montreal.

The President read letters expressing regret at their inability to attend the meeting, from the following prominent American entomologists: Dr. L. O. Howard, Director of the Division of Entomology, U.S. Department of Agriculture, Washington, D.C.; Rev. Dr. W. J. Holland, Chancellor of the Western University of Pennsylvania, Allegheny, Pa.; Professor F. M. Webster, Wooster, Ohio; Professor M. V. Slingerland, Cornell University, Ithaca, N.Y.

The report of the Librarian and Curator, Mr. J. Alston Moffat, was read by the Chairman, showing 47 additions to the Library, which make the total number of volumes 1,553, and satisfactory work in the increase of the collections.

The Chairman next read the report of the Treasurer, and explained that the large balance in hand on the 1st of September last, when the books were closed, would be greatly reduced by the payments that became due between that date and the end of the year. A discussion upon cork and pins then ensued. Dr. Fyles exhibited a sample of a substitute for cork that had been placed upon the market. Dr. Fletcher enquired why the quality of the cork recently supplied by the Society was so poor. The Secretary replied that he thought a better quality could be procured by paying a higher price for it. Dr. Fletcher considered that we should have the best obainable, as the present supply was unsatisfactory. Mr. Lyman exhibited some specimens of English-made steel pins, both gilt and black enamelled, and the Secretar was authorized to procure a moderate supply in order that the members might use t em if they wished.

The Report of the Botanical Section was then read by the Chairman. Dr. Fletcher made enquiries as to *Cuscuta epithymum*, a dodder which has been found upon clover in the County of Middlesex. Mr. Dearness assured him that it had been correctly identified. He then said that it was a true annual, growing from seed each year.

The Report of the Microscopical and Geological Sections were next read by the Chairman, who remarked that London had become a headquarters of scientific research for the western peninsula of Ontario, in consequence of the good work done by the Society and its sections. It was certainly an unique matter that so many branches devoted to different departments of science should be affiliated together in connection with the Entomological Society of Ontario.

The Reports of the local Branches of the Society were next read; that of the Montreal Branch by its Secretary, Mr. Lachlan Gibb; the report of the Toronto Branch

* By an error it is stated in the last annual Report that "the thirty-fifth annual meeting" was held n 1897. As the Society was founded in 1863, this is manifestly a mistake.

also by its Secretary, Mr. Arthur Gibson; and the report of the Quebec Branch by its President, the Rev. Dr. Fyles. These reports all gave evidence of much good work accomplished, and steady progress in interest and numbers.

The Report of the Delegate to the Royal Society of Canada was read by Mr. John D. Evans, of Trenton, who represented the Entomological Society at the last annual meeting in May. It contained a brief record of the work that had been done during the previous year.

The Report of the Council of the Society was read by the Secretary, Mr. W. E. Saunders, of London, as follows:

REPORT OF THE COUNCIL.

The Council of the Entomological Society of Ontario submits herewith its Annual Report for the year 1897–8.

The Council is pleased to be able to report that the three Branches of the Society in Montreal, Toronto, and Quebec, are in an active and vigorous condition, much good work having been done in all of them during the past season. The membership of the Branches, the meetings held, and the particulars of their work will be found in their respective reports.

The twenty-eighth annual Report on economic and general Entomology was presented to the Minister of Agriculture for Ontario, at the end of December last, and was printed and distributed at the close of the session of the Legislature. It contained one hundred and four pages, and was illustrated with fifty-six wood-cuts and two full-page plates, in addition to an account of the proceedings at the last annual meeting. The report contains the annual address of the President, Mr. John Dearness, and the following valuable and interesting papers : "The Locusts of the Bible," by Rev. T. W. Fyles ; "A Study of the Gryllidæ (Crickets)," by Mr. Wm. Lochhead ; "The Value of Systematic Entomological Observations" and "Protective Resemblances," by Mr. J. A. Moffat ; "On Butterfly Books, by Mr. H. H. Lyman ; "Some Household Pests," by Rev. C. J. S. Bethune ; "On the Entomological Results of the Exploration of the British West India Islands by the British Association for the Advancement of Science," by Dr. L. O. Howard ; "The Work Against the Gypsy Moth, 1897," by Mr. A. H. Kirkland ; "Notes on the Insects of the Year," by Messrs. Harrington, Bethune, Moffat, Fyles, Gibson and Grant ; "The San Jose Scale," by Dr. James Fletcher ; and a short account of the proceedings at the annual meeting of the Association of Economic Entomologists. The report on the whole contains a larger number than usual of distinctly practical and popular papers that cannot fail to be of great value to the community. These papers were specially prepared by members of the Society in order to afford useful information on a great variety of insects, free as far as possible from scientific and technical language, to farmers, gardeners, fruit-growers, and others affected by the ravages of destructive insects.

The *Canadian Entomologist*, the monthly magazine published by the Society, completed its twenty-ninth volume in December last. Eleven numbers of the thirteenth volume have been issued ; they contain 296 pages, and are illustrated with six full-page plates, one of which is colored, and a number of original wood-cuts. Among the many valuable papers may be mentioned a series of articles on "The Classification of the Horntails and Saw-flies of the World," by Mr. William H. Ashmead, and "The Descriptions of a Number of New Species of Scale Insects," by Mr. T. D. A. Cockerell, and others.

Friends of the Society will note with pleasure, that one of our officers, Mr. Wm. Lochhead, has been appointed to the important position of Professor of Biology, in the Ontario Agricultural College, at Guelph. The College is to be congratulated on having made so wise a choice in filling the vacant position.

Since our last meeting, great efforts have been made by the Legislature of Ontario and the Federal Government, to eradicate such colonies of the San Jose Scale as have been found in Canada, and to prevent further introductions of this injurious pest. In our last report will be found the Federal and Provincial Acts bearing upon this subject. These Acts have been vigorously enforced during the past season, and orchards, in districts where the Scale has been found, have been subjected to a rigid inspection. Exceptional efforts have been made by the Provincial Government, to wipe out all traces of this pest, the increase of which, as everyone who understands the matter knows, would be a national calamity.

The members of the Council are gratified to know that the excellent work of one of its oldest and most esteemed members has been recognized by the University of Bishop's College, Lennoxville, Que., the Rev. Thomas W. Fyles having received, at its hands, the degree of D.C.L. The excellent work of Dr. Fyles in encouraging the public taste for Entomology, by his popular papers on insects, and by the formation, in 1897, of the Quebec Branch of the Entomological Society is well known to all our members.

The Council profoundly regrets the loss by death of Prof. Panton, of the Ontario Agricultural College, at Guelph, who at the time of his decease was Vice-President of the Society. He was highly esteemed and respected by the members, both for the efficient assistance he has rendered the cause of Practical Entomology in Canada, and the agreeable and courteous manner which ever characterized his intercourse with all who came in contact with him.

The Council has much pleasure in stating that entomological books can now be imported into Canada free of all Customs duty, and that this concession was obtained through the representations of our Society. Early in the year, the President called the attention of the Council to the fact, that under item No. 464 of the tariff, books upon the application of science to industries of all kinds could be imported free of duty, and suggested that an effort should be made to secure the placing in the same category books upon entomology, on account of the close connection between that science and the successful prosecution of agriculture. This was unanimously approved by the Council and a Committee consisting of the President and Drs. Bethune and Fletcher, was appointed to prepare a memorial to the Government. The memorial having been approved, was signed by the President and Secretary, and was duly forwarded to the Finance Minister on the eve of the introduction of the budget, but owing to the pressure of other business was held over until the prorogation of Parliament. It was referred to the Minister of Customs, who requested the President to furnish more information, and to submit samples of books. On this being done, the Hon. Mr. Patterson, at once decided that such books should be admitted free under the item above referred to.

The Society was represented at the meetings in Boston, in August last, of the Association of Economic Entomologists of North America, and the American Association for the Advancement of Science, by its President, Mr. Lyman and the Rev. Dr. Bethune.

The Council desires to express its entire satisfaction with the efficient manner in which the Librarian and Curator, Mr. J. Alston Moffat continues to discharge the duties of his offices.

All of which is respectfully submitted,

HENRY H. LYMAN,
President.

The adoption of the report of the Council was moved by Mr. Dearness, who also said that it would be interesting to have inserted in the report of the Montreal Branch, some details regarding their Saturday afternoon lectures for young people ; upon being seconded by Mr. L. Gibb, the motion was put to the meeting and unanimously adopted.

REPORT OF THE LIBRARIAN AND CURATOR FOR THE YEAR ENDING 31st AUGUST, 1898

The bound volumes received in exchange from Government and public institutions during the year were 9: By gift—From Miss Ormerod, through Dr. Fletcher, Kollar's "Treatise on Insects Injurious to Gardeners and Farmers," and from Rev. Dr. Bethune, "The Life and Adventures of Audubon." By purchase—"A Systematic Arrangement of British Plants," and Grote's "Illustrated Essay of 1882." The number of volumes bound was 34. The number of volumes added to the library during the year was 47. The full number now on the register is 1,553. The number of volumes issued to local members was 19.

Several valuable additions have been made to the collection of native lepidoptera during the year by Mr. J. W. Bice, from his captures at electric light.

An important extension was made in the exotic collection by the receipt of a large number of attractive Japanese butterflies and moths in excellent condition from the Rev. H. Loomis, Yokohama, Japan.

Respectfully submitted,

J. ALSTON MOFFAT,
Librarian and Curator.

REPORT OF THE BOTANICAL SECTION.

The President and Council of the Entomological Society :

GENTLEMEN,—During the season just past, the meetings of the Botanical Section have been held with good regularity, beginning with April 20, and continuing every second week until midsummer was over. The members have been actively engaged in the study of the various departments and three plants new to the district of London have been found and exhibited to the meetings, namely, *Linaria minor, Galium cinereum, Fraxinus quadriangulatus ;* and others of particular rarity have been noted :—Asclepias similar to Purpurea but whose species was not satisfactorily determined, *Melissia officinalis* and *Ranunculus bulbosa,* Fleshy Fungi have been the recipients of considerable attention on the part of some of the members and a more general interest has been awakened in this branch.

Some points brought out at the meetings which are of sufficient interest to be mentioned in our report are as follows :—*Lactuca scaevola* is reported from various quarters and is said to be spreading throughout the County of Middlesex and others adjoining. It is said to be a pernicious weed and some farmers complain very much of its abundance and troublesomeness.

Cuscuta epithymum, a dodder which has been found flourishing only on clover, and of which there were several reports last year, was found again in the same localities this year.

The lateness of the present summer season is also worthy of note. At the time of writing (Oct. 22), wild specimens of *Liatris cylindracea* are in bloom, and in the garden *Anemone Japonica* is full of buds and flowers, while the Phloxes, annual and perennial, and also roses and carnations are still yielding flowers ; apple, pear and peach trees in the gardens, maples, elms, and even the ash trees are still in almost full leaf, many of them, particularly the three former, being quite green. Local records show that not for 17 years has there been so late and open a season.

Respectfully submitted for the Botanical Section,

I. BOND,
Chairman.

W. E. SAUNDERS,
Secretary.

REPORT OF THE MICROSCOPICAL SECTION.

The President and Council of the Entomological Society of Ontario:

GENTLEMEN,—I have the honor to present the report of the Microscopical Section of the Entomological Society of Ontario.

Meetings were begun in November, officers being elected as follows, Chairman, J. A. Balkwill; Sec'y, W. E. Saunders; Committee, Messrs. Rennie, Saunders and Balkwill.

Nine. meetings were held at which five sets of papers were given, a good attendance recorded and much interest manifested. A good many slides were mounted by the members and a great deal of interesting and instructive discussion on microscopical subjects was engaged in.

The papers read comprised,—

Shine moulds, by J. Dearness, London.

Bacteria, by Dr. H. A. Stevenson, London.

Radiolaria, by R. W. Rennie, London.

Diatoms, by J. Dearness, London.

Marine Algæ, by R. Lees, M.A., St. Thomas.

Submitted on behalf of the Section,

J. A. BALKWILL,
Chairman.

W. E. SAUNDERS,
Secretary.

REPORT OF THE GEOLOGICAL SECTION.

To the Entomological Society of Ontario :

The Geological Section of the Entomological Society of Ontario begs leave to present the following report :

The section continued to meet weekly throughout the year. A special study of the fauna of early geological time was made through the medium of fossils from the Silurian and Devonian formations as developed in south-western Ontario, assisted by charts of the characteristic organic life of these periods.

Special trips to interesting points in our western peninsula were made by various members of our section, and reports of their observations were subsequently made. Among other places visited were the following :—Kettle Point (Cape Ipperwash), by Dr. Woolverton, the chairman of the section ; the Crystal Cave at Put-in Bay, Ohio, by Mr. Percival ; the bituminous shales of Alvinston, Lambton Co., Ont., by Mr. Sangster ; the new oil fields in Sarnia township, Ont. ; the Guelph formation as developed at Galt, Ont., by Mr. Goodburn. The chairman of the section also visited the new oil fields at Dutton. Commendable interest was manifested in the general study of geological science.

Appended are abstracts of the reports made of field observations.

Dr. Woolverton's report on Kettle Point and its concretions :

" To the lover of natural history, and especially to the geologist, there is no place in our western peninsula that is of greater interest than this.

" Kettle Point is composed of bituminous shales which overlie the Hamilton formation and which are here the highest member of the Devonian series. The chief feature of this point is the large number of concretionary bodies strewn along the shore, washed there from the shales which extend as shoals far into Lake Huron. These concretions vary in size from a foot to five feet in diameter. Their composition is limestone, colored by bituminous matter. They are crystalline and radiate from a centre. They resemble fossilized wood. When exposed to the action of the air they usually divide through the centre forming hemispheres.

"As they are being wantonly destroyed by visitors there should be legislative protection provided for these curiosities as soon as possible.

"The shales here present a fine tesselated appearance. The vertical cleavage runs in parallel straight lines at different distances, and the general appearance is much the same as it would be had these shales been placed in position by skilled workmen. Quantities of pyrites are found in these shales. The iron oxidizing tinges with red the boulders along the shore.

"By decomposition of the shales, quantities of alum are produced. This the Indians, from time immemorable, have used as medicine and a commodity for barter. Many years ago fire raged among these shales and consumed a great part of the peninsula which previously had extended far into the lake."

Mr. Percival's report on the celestine grotto at Put-in-Bay :

"It having been reported to the section that a curious crystal cave had recently been discovered on an island at the western extremity of Lake Erie, I decided to visit it and report. The cave was discovered a year ago by workmen engaged in digging a well. At a depth of about twenty feet a fissure was discovered at one side of the well, and further excavation revealed a beautiful little cavern everywhere lined with crystalline strontium sulphate (celestine). The owner having lighted the well by electricity the effect is very fine. The crystals are rhombic, of a beautiful azure blue, and vary in size from one inch to twenty inches in transverse axis. As the cavern is everywhere lined by these crystals it may be considered a gigantic geode. The cave is semi-circular in form and about forty feet in perimeter. The arch of the roof however is low owing to the vast deposit of crystals, said to be more than twenty-two feet in thickness, on the floor of the grotto.

"Crevices at several points together with other indications lead to the opinion that this is only one of a series of similar caverns in that vicinity. The owner proposes to continue excavating during the ensuing winter, and probably next summer there will be several grottoes open to the inspection of visitors.

"Strontium is a somewhat rare mineral and occurs nowhere else in large quantity. The element was isolated about a century ago. It is whitish in color, oxidizes readily, decomposes water with explosive violence, and never occurs in organic bodies. It gives a remarkable band of light in the spectrum, by which it is readily detected. Strontium was named after Strontian, in Argyle, Scotland, where it is found as a carbonate. It is also found in Sicily in small quantity. Here however the quantity in sight is quite large. Sr. nitrate is used to give a crimson tint to a flame, and is the chief material used in making Bengal fire (red). Strontium salts are also used in sugar refining to hasten the crystallization of sugar."

Mr. Percival placed beautiful crystals in our geological cabinet in the Entomological Society's rooms, where they may be inspected at any time.

MR. SANGSTER'S REPORT ON ALVINSTON SHALES.

The outcrop measures 1,400 feet in length, and borings made at various points prove that the depth is sixty feet. The river has eroded the bed to a depth of about eight feet. The shales are similar to those exposed at Kettle Point, but contain no concretions. They are highly carbonaceous and contain much iron sulphide. The shales are capped by a stratum of clay forty feet in thickness.

Experiments made with this shale prove it to be a most valuable material for the manufacture of vitrified brick. A leading manufacturer of paving brick declared no better material for the purpose had hitherto been discovered on this continent. As a company is being formed to manufacture brick from these shales, it is hoped that soon they will rank among the developed economic products of this Province.

Mr. Sangster exhibited fine specimens of vitrified brick manufactured from these shales.

Mr. John Law, who spent some time among the Catskills, southern New York reported that veins of copper, also platinum, besides traces of gold and silver, had been discovered in these regions. He exhibited specimens of drift boulders from this location ; gneiss appeared to be the predominating material. He also exhibited a photograph of a famous drift rock called Eagle Rock. He thinks that prospectors would find it a favorable field for exploration.

Mr. Goodburn visited Galt and reported as follows :

The rocks at Galt are dolomite (in some cases pure) and belong to the Guelph group. They vary in colour, from a dirty yellow to a beautiful grey (the grey being the lowest in the series), and are of a peculiar crystalline texture. They furnish excellent building stones. The Guelph group varies here in thickness from 90ft. to 160ft. The underlying mass is the Niagara group. The upper portions of strata are much broken up, and contained many specimens of the Megalomus Canadensis. This bed was about 15ft. thick. The lower beds were quite compact, and also contained many fossils. One Meg. Can. which I secured is perfect, six inches in length, and larger than any figured in Nicholson's Palæontology. I also found a very good specimen of Megalomus compressus four inches long and a little over one inch in thickness, a portion of the outer spiral and, the whole of the inner cast of a Murchisonia Loganii. The quarry whence I obtained my specimens is near the Grand Trunk track, and about 200 yards from the Grand River.

The Chairman visited the oil fields at Dutton, Elgin Co., Ontario, and reported that the pioneer company operating there had seven producing wells.

Mr. Kirk reported on another new oil field situated in Sarnia Township, Lambton Co., Ontario. One company operating there had thirty producing wells scattered along a line about two miles in length. These produce from 15 barrels per day downwards. They propose to thoroughly develop this tract, and sink a well every 200 feet. The producing area is about one mile in width. Another company working in an adjoining neighbourhood have very recently obtained some good wells, one of which pumps 25 barrels a day. The producing wells are all situated along anti-clinal, which, however, does not appear at the surface, being deeply covered by clay. Oil is obtained here at a depth of about 475 feet. The borings pass through clay 100ft., hard rock 15ft., shale 150 ft., upper lime 15 ft., shale 150 ft., lower lime and sandstone about 45ft. In order to obtain oil each well must be torpedoed, the charge being from 20 to 50 quarts of nitro-glycerine. These new oil fields seem to be a northwesterly extension of the petroleum oil belt. The oil is found along a line trending northwest and southeast.

GEO. KIRK,
Secretary.

THE REPORT OF THE MONTREAL BRANCH.

The 215th regular and 25th annual meeting of the Montreal Branch of the Entomological Society of Ontario was held in the rooms of the Natural History Society of Montreal, on May 10th, 1898.

The following members were present : Messrs. H. H. Lyman (President), A. F. Winn (Vice-President), E. T. Chambers, J. B. Williams, Dwight Brainerd, L. Reford, O. Stevenson, G. A. Moore, and L. Gibb ; visitor, Mr. M. Waring Davis.

The chair was taken by the President, and the minutes of the previous meeting were read and confirmed, also the last annual report.

The President then submitted the following report of the Council for the past year :

In presenting their twenty-fifth annual report the Council have much pleasure in being able to congratulate the Branch upon having enjoyed a continuous and fairly prosperous existence for a quarter of a century. This, in view of the small number interested in the pursuit of this particular branch of science, coupled with the fact that in this country almost everyone has to work for a living, is, we think, a highly creditable showing.

During the season eight meetings have been held, at one of which we had the pleasure of the attendance of Dr. Fletcher, and at another of that of Rev. Mr. Fyles, and the following papers were read :

Annual address of the President.

Notes on the Collecting Season of 1897—Dwight Brainerd.

On the Food of the common Grass Snake—J. B. Williams.

A late Autumn Ramble on the Mountain—A. F. Winn.

On the Mounting of Lepidoptera—H. H. Lyman.

The San Jose Scale—Dr. James Fletcher.

Further notes on the Genus Chionobas—H. H. Lyman.

Our books and original papers—A. F. Winn.

Our native Pieridæ, a theory—Dwight Brainerd.

Introduction to the Classification of Insects—Rev. T. W. Fyles.

An Arctian : what is it ?—Rev. T. W. Fyles.

Life History of Tæniocampa alia, Gn—Rev. T. W. Fyles.

The Dytiscidæ—A. F. Winn.

During the season a number of our members again took part in the course of short lectures to young people on Saturday afternoons at the Natural History Museum. This work is now fairly established, and should be productive of good results in the future.

Our small library, which had suffered greatly in the past through the Branch having no permanent quarters, has received some valuable additions through the kindness of one of our absent members, Mr. Jack, and the Cabinet of the Natural History Society has been materially added to by two of our members, Messrs. Winn and D. Brainerd.

Our Branch has also presented a copy of Comstock's Manual for the study of Insects to the library of that Society as a slight return for privileges accorded to our Branch.

Steps have been taken to secure as far as possible the interchange of papers between the different branches of the Society, that all may get the benefit of such papers. Should this scheme be successfully carried out, it should add materially to the interest of the meetings, and cause the several branches to take more interest in each other's work.

At the last annual meeting of the parent Society our Branch was honored by having one of its members elected to the presidency.

The Treasurer's report shows that the finances of the Branch are in a satisfactory condition.

Respectfully submitted on behalf of the Council,

HENRY H. LYMAN,
President.

The Treasurer then submitted his report, which showed an accumulated balance in hand of $38.68.

Upon the motion of Mr. J. B. Williams, seconded by Mr. L. Reford, the reports of the Council and Treasurer were received and adopted.

The President then read his annual address, giving a resume of the past year's work, and suggesting the holding of a conversazione in the autumn to mark the completion of the 25th year of the Montreal Branch.

The following officers were then elected for the ensuing year :

President—Henry H. Lyman ; *Vice President*—A. F. Winn ; *Secretary-Treasurer*— Lachlan Gibb ; *Council*—G. C. Dunlop, J. B. Williams, Dwight Brainerd.

L. GIBB, Secretary-Treasurer.

REPORT OF THE TORONTO BRANCH.

The second Annual Meeting of the Toronto Branch was held in the Education Department (Normal School) on Friday evening, the 1st April, 1898.

The following members were present : Messrs E. V. Rippon, President : Arthur Gibson, Secy-Treas : H. D. Chipman, C. T. Hills, C. H. Tyers, A J. Cherry, H. C. Austen, S. R. Carter, E. M. Fenwick and Frank Welch.

The minutes of the previous regular meeting were read and approved.

REPORT OF THE COUNCIL : The Secretary read the following report of the Council for the year ending 31st March, 1898.

The Council of the Toronto Branch of the Entomological Society of Ontario take pleasure in presenting the second Annual Report of the proceedings of the Branch for the year ending 31st March, 1898.

Since our previous Annual Meeting one new member, Mr. E M. Fenwick, has been added to the roll of membership, and it is earnestly hoped that throughout the year now commencing, the members will endeavor to obtain as many new additions to the roll as possible.

During the year, eighteen regular meetings have been held, and the following papers, contributed by the members, tended considerably to add to the interest manifested in, and the success attending these meetings.

" Parasitic Forms of Insects " by Mr. E. V. Rippon.

"Collecting in and about Kingsville, Ont." by Mr. C. T. Hills.

"Some of the Insect Pests of the Niagara District " by Mr. H. O. Austin.

" Muscular Powers of Insects " by Mr. H. D. Chipman.

" The Mosquito " by Mr. A. J. Cherry.

" On the Noctuidæ Occurring at Toronto" by Mr. Arthur Gibson.

On the 23rd November last the Branch had the pleasure of contributing an illustrated lecture on " Our Friends and Foes of the Insect World ", through the kindness of one of our members, Mr. T. G. Priddey, to the eleventh Section of the Boys' Brigade. About 200 boys were present, most of whom took an interest in the discourse, and it is hoped that some stray seed may have fallen into good ground.

During the collecting season three field days were held, viz., on the 24th May to " Trout Creek", on the 19th June to "Trout Creek " and on the 1st July to Forks of Credit.

The Branch is indeed pleased to place on record the appreciation it feels towards the Minister of Education (Hon. G. W. Ross) and the Education Department for Ontario, for their kindness in granting the Branch the free use of a room, in which to hold meetings and store the collection and library.

The report of the Librarian-Curator shows that during the year quite a large number of valuable Government publications have been donated to the Branch, also that the collection of insects is steadily increasing.

The Treasurer's report shows the balance carried forward to be on the right side.

All of which is respectfully submitted.

E. V. RIPPON, President.

The report of the Treasurer was presented, as also that of the Librarian-Curator, submitted by Mr. H. D. Chipman. On motion of Mr. Hills, seconded by Mr. Austen, the reports of the Council, Treasurer, and Librarian-Curator, were adopted as read.

The election of officers for the ensuing year resulted as follows:

President—Mr. R. J. Crew; Vice-President—Mr. C. T. Hills; Secretary-Treasurer— Mr. Arthur Gibson. (accl.); Librarian-Curator—Mr. H. D. Chipman; Members of Council—Messrs H. C. Tyers and E. M. Fenwick.

The retiring President, Mr. E. V. Rippon, then addressed the meeting. He referred chiefly to the work done during the past year, and while pleased with the result, said he would like to see the members take a more active interest in the work. As regards the collection of insects he hoped the members would contribute as many specimens as they possibly could during the coming season, and pointed out the advantage to all the members in having a representative collection in the possession of the Branch. Of course, it would not be expected that the members would neglect their own private collections, but with a little extra work on the part of each member, he felt satisfied that much progress could be made in the collection during the approaching season. He also referred to the reading of papers at the meetings, and hoped that the members would make an effort to contribute more papers in future. During the past year only six papers were contributed by the members. He encouraged those present to make more notes during the coming season, feeling sure that if such were done more papers would be contributed at the meetings. He mentioned that the outlook for the Branch's future was much brighter than ever before, as the Education Department for Ontario had very kindly granted the Branch the free use of a room in which to hold meetings, and store the collection and Library. He also touched upon the membership and hoped that those connected with the Branch would endeavor to have some new names added to the roll during the ensuing year.

The meeting then adjourned.

ARTHUR GIBSON, Secretary.

REPORT OF THE QUEBEC BRANCH.

The annual meeting of the Quebec Branch of the Entomological Society of Ontario was held on the 26th of February, 1898. Eighteen members were present, the President, the Rev. T. W. Fyles, occupying the chair.

PRESIDENT'S REPORT. The Quebec Branch of the Entomological Society of Ontario is to be congratulated on the success which has attended it during the first year of its existence. Its numbers have increased, its meetings have been regularly held and well attended, and considerable interest in natural history has been awakened in the community through its proceedings. The pleasures of its monthly meetings have been enhanced by the hospitality of its members. This has been so far extended that its gatherings have taken as much of a social as of a scientific character: though the objects of the association have never been lost sight of—"Philosophy in sport" having been made "Science in earnest."

In the course of the summer a number of rare and interesting specimens were taken, and these were afterwards exhibited and identified. Among them were some the names of which were new to the Quebec lists.

The thanks of the members are due to the authorities of Morrin College for the countenance and encouragement they have given to the association.

The Branch was represented by its President at the annual meeting of the Entomological Society of Ontario held in London, Ont., on the 12th of October. On this occasion many hearty good wishes for the prosperity of the Branch were expressed.

The parent society has reached the 35th year of its existence. Its 28th annual report is now in the press. Its monthly organ, *The Canadian Entomologist*, which has now reached its 30th volume, ranks as one of the leading Entomological publications of the day, and has an extensive circulation, not only in Canada and the United States, but in Europe and other parts of the world. Flourishing branches of the Society exist in Toronto and Montreal. The Quebec branch will, we trust, be no less prosperous than these.

The Society has experienced a great loss by the death of its Vice-President, J. Hoyes Panton, M. A., F. G S., Professor of Natural History and Geology, in the Ontario Agricultural College, Guelph. He was the author of a useful handbook entitled "Our Insect Foes and How to Destroy Them." His valuable article on "Entomology for Rural Schools," which appeared in last year's report of the Society, is, no doubt, fresh in the minds of many of you. His useful career was cut short while he was yet in his prime. The American Entomological Society has also sustained a great loss by the death of its President, Dr. George H. Horn. The *Entomological News*, of Philadelphia, thus speaks of him :

"The entomological world has lost a shining light and American Coleopterology its greatest votary. As a systematic coleopterist he probably did not have a superior in the world. His large collection of beetles was considered the finest extant in the field he cultivated. It, with his library, and five thousand dollars for the care of the former, he willed to the American Entomological Society."

Entomology in the United States has made great strides. The Division of Entomology in the Department of Agriculture, Washington, D. C., has been of vast benefit to the agriculturists and horticulturists of this continent. Its present able director, Mr. L. O. Howard, and his efficient staff, are not merely supporting, but raising more and more the high character that its services have won for it. Among the valuable bulletins that it has lately issued are :

"The Gypsy Moth in America," by L. O. Howard.

"Revision of the Tachinidæ," by D. L. Coquillet.

"Some Little-Known Insects Affecting Stored Vegetable Products," by F. H. Chittenden.

"Insects Affecting Domestic Animals," by Herbert Osborn.

The insects that are causing the greatest alarm in America at the present time are the Gypsy Moth (*Porthetria dispar*) and the San Jose Scale (*Aspidiotus perniciosus*) Comstock. Specimens of the former species escaped in 1869 from the residence of Professor Trouvelot, at Medford, near Boston ; and for eight years the insects increased in numbers without exciting much attention. The species has now extended its ravages through a district of 220 square miles, and the State of Massachusetts has expended $775,000 in the effort to exterminate it.

The pernicious scale insect was first noticed in the San Jose Valley, California. It has now located itself in spots from Florida to Canada, and from Washington to New Jersey. Its wide and rapid spread is owing to the fact that it has been 'shipped' with fruit and with nursery stock in all directions. It infests deciduous fruit trees, and, unless prompt measures are taken, an orchard attacked by it will be completely destroyed in a very few years. Our Canadian Department of Agriculture has taken the alarm, and posters, drawn up by Dr. Fletcher have been widely distributed to draw the attention of fruit-growers to the danger.

But Entomology has not only to deal with insects, more or less obnoxious to man ; it brings to our notice the beneficial labors of hundreds of other kinds. It holds up to our admiration the marvellous beauty with which the Creator has gifted many of his lesser creatures, and it brings home to us the teaching that " His tender mercies are over all His works." As it is in grace, so it is in nature, " He that seeketh findeth." The works of the Lord are great, *sought out* by all them that have pleasure therein.

REPORT OF THE COUNCIL   In presenting this, the first annual report of the Quebec branch of the Entomological Society of Ontario, your Council finds that the branch, although not eleven months in existence, has succeded very well in the objects for which it was instituted, viz. : the inculcating and promoting a lively interest in entomology, the collection and classifying of specimens, and bringing the members together in social intercourse, through entomological excursions, lectures and gatherings at each other's houses.

Our membership is now twenty-six, viz. : eighteen adults and eight juniors.   We have grounds for hope that, during the present year, it will be largely increased.

Meetings have been held monthly, with exception of the midsummer months, in Convocation Hall of Morrin College, by kind permission of the College authorities, for which courtesy our sincere thanks are due.

Papers have been read and lectures illustrated by diagrams, delivered in the same Hall, which have been numerously attended.   Instruction has also been given as to the killing, mounting and preserving of specimens, which has been much availed of ; and we are glad to see it, especially amongst our Junior members.   Several nicely-mounted specimens, taken during the summer campaign by members of our branch, have been shewn at our meetings and evince keen interest in the study of entomology on the part of almost all.

Papers have been read and lectures given on land beetles, two winged flies, flesh flies, mycetophylidæ (mushroom flies), bombilidæ, parasites, especially those infesting cattle, horses and sheep, and the best means of their extermination (most useful information to the farmer and grazier), as well as the tiger moths—Arctiidæ—Colias interior, etc.   The caterpillars have not been forgotten and our "woolly-bear" friend, " Phragmatobia rubricosa," as he sturdily scampers over the snowdrift, lets us know that life is by no means lacking in even the smaller things of creation during a Canadian winter, for he early shows himself, a harbinger of spring.

The want of a proper cabinet for the conservation of insects arose, and through the kindness of a few of the members and friends of the Association, a very handsome one has been obtained, which is placed in Morrin College, and has already received its first instalment of insects.

Before closing what must necessarily be but a brief report, owing to the short time since the organization of the branch, we must call your attention to an item very interesting to our hive of workers, viz : the treasurer's report, which shows that, after remitting to the parent society the necessary honorarium and paying expenses, we have, out of our subscription list, a balance in hand of $6.70.

JOSEPH EVELEIGH TREFFRY,

Secretary.

The officers elected for 1898 were :

President—Rev. Thomas W. Fyles ; *Vice-President*—Miss Macdonald ; *Council*— Hon. Richard Turner, Mr. J. Eveleigh Treffry, Prof. H. Walters, Mrs. R. Turner, Miss Bickell, Miss B. Winfield ; *Secretary-Treasurer*—Lt.-Col. Crawford Lindsay ; *Curator*— Professor H. Walters.

Since the annual meeting in February the branch has held four regular meetings, and five field-days. On the latter occasions very happy excursions to the Gomin, the Island of Orleans (twice), and Beauport were made.

The branch now numbers twenty-eight adult members and fourteen junior.

CRAWFORD LINDSAY,

Secretary-Treasurer.

QUEBEC, Nov. 5th, 1898.

REPORT FROM THE ENTOMOLOGICAL SOCIETY OF ONTARIO TO THE ROYAL SOCIETY OF CANADA.

Having the honor to represent the Entomological Society of Ontario, I beg leave to submit the following report of its work and proceedings during the past year.

The Society still maintains its former position as to its increasing membership. Its Branches are doing good work, and have given a very considerable impetus to the study of insect life. The Toronto Branch having been inaugurated, commenced its life with the New Year, and later a Branch was formed in Quebec, under the most favorable auspices. The Library has been augmented by an unusually large number of additional volumes, numbering no less than eighty-eight; the total number on the register now being 1,506. Important additions were also made to the Society's collections of insects.

"The Canadian Entomologist," the official organ of the Society, maintains its prestige among its class of literature. The twenty ninth volume of 306 pages was issued during the past year (1897), its contributors numbering forty-four, of whom thirty reside in the United States of America, one in Mexico, one in Germany, and the remaining twelve in Canada. These contributed seventy-six articles, in which were described twenty new genera, one new subgenus, ninety-one new species, and six new varieties.

The following are a few of the more important papers above referred to, viz. :

On the Mexican Bees of the genus Augochlora.—By T. D. A. Cockerell.

The Coleoptera of Canada.—By Prof. H. F. Wickham. Continued through nine numbers, and being also a continuation of a series of articles on the same subject which have appeared during the past three years, making an extremely useful compilation for students in Canadian Coleoptera.

A Generic Revision of the Hypogymnidae (Liparidae)—By Harrison G. Dyar.

Catalogue of the Phytophagous and Parasitic Hymenoptera of Vancouver Island—By W. Hague Harrington, F.R.C.S.

Some new species and varieties of Lepidoptera from the Western U.S.—By Wm. Barnes, M.D.

Descriptions of some new Genera and species of Canadian Proctotrypidæ—By Wm. H. Ashmead.

Synonymical and descriptive notes on North American Orthoptera—By Samuel H. Scudder.

On rearing Dragon Flies—By James G. Needham.

Contribution to the knowledge of North American Syrphidae—By W. D. Hunter.

Preliminary Studies of North American Gomphinæ.—By Jas. G. Needham.

A Generic Revision of the Hypocritidae—By Harrison G. Dyar, Ph.D.

Notes on the Life History of Colias Interior (Scud)—By H. H. Lyman.

The Life History of Epirranthis Obfirmaria, Hbn.—By Rev. Thos. W. Fyles.

Notes on Grapta Interrogationis Fahr.—By H. H. Lyman and A. F. Winn.

Also there appears a number of book notices, correspondence, etc., etc.

The thirty-fifth annual meeting of the Society was held in its new room in the Young Men's Christian Association Building in London on Tuesday and Wednesday, October 12th and 13th, 1897.

The annual report published by the Society to the Department of Agriculture of the Province of Ontario consists of 104 pages, in which is contained a full report of the proceedings of the annual meeting above mentioned, together with the annual address of its President. (The reports and papers contained therein were here enumerated.)

JOHN D. EVANS,
Delegate.

REPORT OF THE TREASURER FOR THE YEAR ENDING 31st AUGUST 1898.

RECEIPTS.		EXPENDITURE.	
Balance on hand September 1st, 1897....$	575 52	Printing ....$	597 85
Members' fees	335 13	Report and meeting expenses	214 00
Sales of Entomologist	196 46	Library	35 92
Sales of pins, cork, etc	74 06	Expense account, postage, etc..........	133 49
Government grant	1,000 00	Rent	175 00
Advertisements........................	26 50	Salaries	300 00
Interest	23 87	Pins, cork, etc	36 03
		Balance on hand August 31st, 1898......	739 25
	$2,231 54		$2,231 54

We, the auditors of the Entomological Society of Ontario, hereby certify that we have examined the books and vouchers of the treasurer and find them well kept and correct and that the above statement is in accordance with the accounts.

W. H. HAMILTON, } Auditors.
JAS. H. BOWMAN,

STATEMENT OF RECEIPTS AND EXPENDITURE FROM SEPTEMBER 1st, 1898, TO 31st DECEMBER, 1898.

RECEIPTS.		EXPENDITURE.	
Balance on hand September 1st, 1898......$	739 25	Printing ....$	206 45
Members' fees	86 90	Report and meeting expenses	155 73
Sales of Entomologist	15 47	Library....	22 51
Sales of pins, cork, etc....................	11 58	Expense account, postage, etc.............	22 53
Advertisements ....··	7 00	Rent	100 00
Interest	13 80	Salaries	50 00
		Pins, cork, etc	9 44
		Balance on hand 31st December, 1898	307 34
	$874 00		$874 00

J. BALKWILL, Treasurer.

THE PRESIDENT'S ANNUAL ADDRESS.

By Henry H. Lyman, M.A., Montreal.

Gentlemen,—It is with much pleasure that I welcome you to the thirty-fifth annual meeting of our society, and especially is this pleasure enhanced by the fact that our meeting is held in this city in celebration of the twenty-fifth anniversary of the formation of the Montreal branch.

It is a subject for much congratulation that our society, which started from such small beginnings, has grown to such a large number of members, with associate members all over the world, and that its monthly journal takes so high a place in the field of entomological periodicals. But I think that we in Montreal have some reason to be proud of the fact that we are the third oldest entomological association on this continent, and, without any monetary grant or assistance from Government, have been able to keep our meetings up with great regularity through a quarter of a century.

Two hundred and seventeen meetings have been held, and over 200 original papers have been read by our members, and about 80 of these have been published.

But, to turn to matters of more general interest, when an amateur entomologist, with extremely little leisure to devote to this science, has the honor, or perhaps I should say the misfortune, to be elected to the distinguished position of president of so important a society, the question what he is to do for an annual presidential address becomes at once a serious bugbear.

We amateurs have to take our science in so scrappy a fashion, in such small mouthfuls, that it is generally impossible for us to follow out any continuous line of investigation or experiment, and our work is of too fragmentary a nature to afford material for an important address. True, by reading and study, we might familiarize ourselves sufficiently with the work which has been done in some particular line by other entomologists to enable us to give a fairly accurate review of such subjects, but that seems hardly desirable, unless one can add something of interest from one's own observations.

Many of my predecessors in this office have devoted much of their addresses to a review of the principal injurious insects of the year, but I feel that this subject can be so much better handled by those who are by profession economic entomologists that I prefer to leave that task to them.

It has occurred to me that there are many subjects, some of them small in themselves, perhaps, but which for all that are not without their interest, and I have therefore determined to invite your attention to a sort of entomological omnium gatherum or olla podrida.

But before taking up any of these subjects, it is my painful duty to refer to the sad event which so early in the season, and in the maturity of his powers, deprived our society of our highly respected vice-president. Prof. Panton was elected at the last annual meeting, though unable to attend on account of illness, but I do not think that any one at that time anticipated a fatal termination, and I, certainly, looked forward with pleasure to meeting him at this annual meeting.

But the greatest loss to entomology in America, using the latter term in a wider sense than our neighbors generally use it, which has occurred during the year was unquestionably that sustained in the death of Dr. George H. Horn, who since the death of Dr. J. L. Leconte has been facile princeps among American coleopterists.

By the death of Dr. J. A. Lintner, American economic entomology has suffered a great loss, and I am sure his memory will be cherished by all who had the privilege of his acquaintance. He was a very able entomologist and a kindly, unassuming gentleman.

Among other losses by death especial mention should be made of Prof. Kellicott, of the Ohio State University, but whom I had not the privilege of knowing.

But to turn to less mournful subjects : If I were asked to state what I consider the chief characteristic of entomologists, I think I should say their patience. Surely a man deficient in this virtue would not continue long in the pursuit of this science. Are we ever thoroughly discouraged ? Does not hope spring ever fresh in our hearts ? We may secure the eggs of a species whose life history we are anxious to enravel, and after carrying the larvæ nearly through, and just when success seems about to reward our patient care, a mysterious disease may sweep the whole brood away, and yet we only say, " I must try it again ; better luck next time."

When I think of the myriads of species whose life histories are waiting to be unravelled, of the comparatively few who are engaged in this work, of the few life histories which we can work out in a single season, and of the very few seasons we have in which to do this work, I am inclined to think that the way we go at this task is almost sublime.

But this reflection leads me to what is perhaps a delicate question, and that is— Would it not be better if some of our friends, when working out these life histories, would give less time to debating as to more generalized and more specialized forms?

Surely it will not be contended that a more specialized form is necessarily higher than a more generalized one ? There is evolution downwards as well as upwards, specialization towards degradation as well as towards advancement.

I confess that when I find able entomologists laying such great stress upon such minutiæ as one vein being slightly more appressed to another vein in one genus than in some other genus, or the presence or absence of some minute veinlet, when it is admitted that even individuals of the same species show variations in these matters, which fact has to be accounted for on the convenient doctrine of reversion, or when it is proposed to classify families as higher or lower chiefly upon the single characteristic of having or not having the fore pair of legs aborted, my share of the patience to which I have alluded tends to wear thin.

While not a champion of the New Woman, I certainly believe in the doctrine of the equality of the sexes in the case of the Lycænidæ, and protest strongly against any attempt on the part of the gentleman Lycænid to lord it over his spouse on account of his aborted fore legs. The bear has a plantigrade foot, and the domestic fowl is a biped, but it is hardly probable that these facts would lead any systematist to place these animals next to man in the order of classification. We shall never have a natural, and therefore scientific and satisfactory classification of these creatures until we know them in all their stages, when our classification will be based upon the sum of their characteristics.

There is one word which I would like to say to our professional friends, and that is, that I think they might show a little more consideration for the amateurs in the way of giving the reasons for any necessary changes of name. Amateurs have neither the time nor the opportunity to keep up in detail with the tremendous output of entomological literature, and when one takes up a number of a journal containing an instalment of a " revision " of some group, and finds that some well-known name has entirely disappeared, and after a protracted hunt finds, let me say, such an old acquaintance as *Euchœtes Collaris*, Fitch, disguised under the name of Cycnia Tenera, Hübner, and this without a word of explanation of this wonderful discovery, one can hardly be blamed for exclaiming " A plague on all your revisions."

In entomology, as no doubt in other branches of natural science, some men are lumpers and others are splitters. To the latter I would say that the describing of new species should certainly not be done on the chance of their proving distinct, and to the former that once a form has been described as a new species it should not be lumped except upon overwhelming proof. As an example of most unwarrantable lumping may be instanced the case of *Euchœtes Collaris*, Fitch, which on the authority of some wiseacre was known for many years as "the common white variety of *Euchœtes Egle*," because, forsooth, entomologists were too lazy or too stupid to secure the eggs and rear the species.

But I find a very curious tendency in many men to be both lumpers and splitters, lumpers in dealing with the work of others, but splitters in their own work.

A man takes up some group with the view of monographing it, gathers specimens from far and near, inspects all the types to which he can gain access, and finally announces that what have passed for half-a-dozen distinct species are merely slight local varieties of one world-pervading species.

Now this may be all right, though I think that such lumping might, perhaps, better be deferred till the forms in question had been bred through all their stages. But look what follows : among the material gathered together he finds one specimen slightly different from any of the named forms, and two other specimens which agreeing together differ slightly in some other direction, and upon these three specimens two new species are founded, although the divergence does not appear to be greater than in the case of the forms which he has just lumped ; and thus we have a patent lumper and splitter combined.

What I have already said of the difficulty, especially for amateurs, of keeping up with the literature of the subject leads me to suggest that it would be a great assistance if an annual list of all the new genera and species of North American insects, with the references as to where described, were published in the January number of the "Canadian Entomologist," and I feel sure that our journal would thereby become of greatly enhanced value to all working entomologists.

The insufficient indexing of some publications is a frequent source of vexation and loss of time, and adds materially to the difficulty of those who need to refer to articles some time after their publication. If the index of every journal were begun with the issue of the first number, each article being cross indexed as soon as issued, the work would not be heavy, and when the last number was in type a thoroughly satisfactory index could be completed in a very short time. The late Dr. Lintner placed a very high value upon a thoroughly complete index, and spared no pains to make the indexes of his Reports as perfect as it was possible to make them.

From 1868 to 1873 inclusive we had an Annual Record of American Entomology, edited by Dr. Packard, with a number of leading authorities in the different orders as associate editors. It was a very useful work, and it is, I think, much to be desired that we should have some sort of an annual index of American Entomology. The difficulties in its way are, I know, very great, but if it were possible for it to be undertaken by the Division of Entomology of the Department of Agriculture at Washington, it would be a great assistance to all the working entomologists of the continent.

Another point of great importance is the care of important collections, and especially the preservation and accessibility of types. It is not reasonable for any one to expect types to be lent for study as the risk of loss or damage is too great, but they should certainly be accessible to those who visit for this purpose the museums or private collections where these types are preserved. It is certainly disappointing when one has made an expensive journey for the purpose of examining a collection, or studying certain types, to find that one's journey is wholly or partly in vain, either through the caprice of a museum curator, or through the collection being in too crowded a condition to permit of an examination being made with safety.

To any one who augments his collection by either exchange or purchase, the different styles of pinning and spreading specimens of Lepidoptera are matters of serious concern, as one generally has to reset all specimens so obtained, unless one is willing to have one's specimens at all sorts of heights, and spread in all sorts of ways. The late Mr. Morrison, who collected so extensively for his patrons, used to insert his pins so that there was frequently very little more than a quarter of an inch above the thorax, and as he used very small sized pins, which bent easily, it was very difficult to handle the specimens without knocking off the antennae.

It was a great step in advance when all the principal makers of microscopes were induced to accept the Microscopical Society's screw, as any objective could be used on any stand. Is it too much to hope for, that entomologists on this continent should adopt a standard length of pin, and a standard height at which to place the specimen on the pin, a standard spreading board for Lepidoptera and a standard style of setting? And this brings me to the most important suggestion which I desire to make, and that is, that North American entomologists might with advantage follow the example of the ornithologists and form a "Union" with a limited number of full members, and an unlimited number of associate members, the full members to be chosen from the leading entomologists of the continent, but associate membership to be open to every entomologist.

The American Ornithologists' Union has been a marked success, and I see no reason why a similar union should not work equally well among entomologists. There are many subjects with which such a union might deal, and if its decisions were generally accepted, as I have no doubt they would be, I am sure it would do a great deal to harmonize the work in this branch of science.

To mention a very few of the things which might be dealt with in addition to those which I have already mentioned I may suggest the capitalization or otherwise of specific names, the nomenclature or numbering of the veins in the wings, the designation of the various segments of larvæ, as well as all the questions in regard to nomenclature. If it be objected that ornithology is practically one subject, while entomology is a whole collection of subjects, I answer, "True, but the same principles apply to all the branches." Take the case of the capitalizing or otherwise of specific names. Some capitalize all specific names, as Mr. W. H. Edwards, with whom on this point I entirely agree, others use capitals for names derived from persons and small letters in other cases; others, and I am afraid the large majority, use the lower case letter in all cases. Would it not, however, be better in such a matter as this to waive our personal predilections and for the sake of uniformity accept an authoritative ruling by such an organization as I have suggested.

With regard to venation the question of uniform designation is of much greater importance, as it is impossible for an amateur to familiarize himself with all the systems in vogue, and hence many generic descriptions or articles on structure are quite unintelligible to many readers. The old system of named veins and veinlets or nerves and nervures seems certainly preferable to me to the confused systems of numbering now in use by different authors, and surely this is a matter which could very profitably be settled by such a body, while in the realm of general nomenclature the field is so vast that the Union would have abundant material for business at its annual meetings for many years to come.

Another point in the same connection may be mentioned, and that is in regard to the official organ of such an association. There have been at different times so many different entomological journals started and carried on for a few years only to die out again. There are many entomologists who cannot afford to subscribe to more than one journal, and it might be better if instead of so many journals with small circulations competing for subscriptions there were fewer in the field, but those more generally subscribed to.

But lest I weary you with suggestions which may be regarded as savouring of presumption in an amateur, I would now invite your attention to a rapid glance at a portion of the work which is being carried on by some of the leading entomologists of the continent. While, as I said, I prefer to leave to others who are so infinitely better qualified the task of giving a review of the insect depredations of the year, I can hardly avoid referring somewhat briefly to some of those which have attracted the widest attention.

As Canadians we are naturally especially interested in the work which our own official entomologist is engaged in. Dr. Fletcher is certainly untiring in his work, travelling about the country from the Atlantic to the Pacific to attend meetings of farmers, fruit growers and dairymen, for the purpose of interesting and instructing them in the importance of economic entomology, and in regard to the economic value of particular grasses, and the people are thus being brought to see that the aim of the experimental farms is not the providing of handsome residences in a charming locality for a certain number of scientific gentlemen, but that there is a very real money value to the agricultural interests of the country in the work and investigations which are being carried on there. But naturally from the large sums annually devoted by the Central Government at Washington and the various States to the prosecution of economic entomology by a large and highly trained force of entomologists, the work in that country must necessarily overshadow what we are doing in Canada, though I think it is also undoubtedly a fact that from our more northern latitude we are much less subject to insect depredations of a devastating character.

The attack which in recent years has caused the most widespread alarm on account of the serious nature of the damage likely to result from it is unquestionably that of the San José Scale. This most injurious insect appeared in California late in the seventies, was brought east on nursery stock to New Jersey in 1887. or 1888 and had by 1893, when its presence in the Eastern States was discovered by Dr. Howard, spread through portions of almost every one of the Eastern and Middle States causing the death of thousands of trees before its presence became known. Naturally it soon became a subject of discussion at all meetings of agriculturists and entomologists and has been the subject of legislation by sixteen of the States.

From this very necessary publicity it was naturally to be expected that other countries would take alarm and endeavor to protect their agricultural interests from so great a danger. The first country to do so was Germany, the German Emperor issuing a decree on the 5th February last prohibiting the importation of fruits and plants from America, which prohibition was subsequently restricted to living plants and fresh fruits which might be found to be affected by living scale.

Following shortly after the action of Germany came the passing by our Canadian Parliament of the San José Scale Act on the 18th March last, by which Act it was provided that nursery stock should be excluded when imported from such infected countries as might be designated by the Governor-General in Council, and the United States, Australia, Japan and the Hawaiian Islands were immediately so designated, the plants not subject to the attack of the Scale being exempted from the operation of the Act.

A month later the Government of Austria-Hungary issued a decree barring out living plants, grafts and layers, as well as the packings and coverings, but not excluding fruit except such as might upon examination be found to be infected. Following this the Government of the Netherlands sent an expert to the United States to investigate and report, and Sweden also sent an expert partly for the purpose of making a similar investigation.

The Legislature of Ontario has passed a law for the destruction of badly infested trees and providing reasonable compensation for loss so incurred, while in the United States a bill governing inter-state commerce in nursery stock and providing for quarantine in the principal ports of the country was reported favourably upon by the Committee on Agriculture at the last session of Congress and will doubtless become law at an early date.

In this connection attention may be directed to the obvious limitations of the use of natural enemies of insect pests, the attempted introduction of Californian beetles into New Jersey in the hope of their multiplying and checking the San José scale having proved a failure, as has also the attempt to infect the scales with a parasitic fungus from Florida.

The present year has been an important periodical cicada year, the broods occurring this year being the brood XVII. of the Septendecim race and brood VII. of the Tredecim race. In this connection especial attention should be called to the very important pamphlet upon this subject prepared by Mr. C. L. Marlatt, First Assistant Entomologist at Washington, and issued as Bulletin No. 14 of the new series of the U. S. Department of Agriculture. This paper extending to 148 pages copiously illustrated, is certainly the most important contribution which has yet been made to our knowledge of this wonderful and interesting insect.

Last winter, the Legislature of Massachusetts appropriated $200,000.00, the full amount asked for, to continue the work of exterminating the Gypsy Moth, and as a consequence very remarkable progress has been made in this work during the past season, and it now seems probable that if similarly liberal appropriations are continued for several years longer this important, but tedious, work will be crowned with success. The work of destroying the Brown-tail Moth has also been intrusted to the same force and is being carried on in connection with the Gypsy Moth work.

Other work in Economic Entomology which may be referred to is the progress made by the Division of Entomology at Washington in the accumulation of data concerning the distribution of injurious insects in the United States.

Mr. Pergande, in furtherance of his investigations of the Lecanium scales affecting the fruit trees, spent the summer in Europe and collected large material.

In the early spring, Dr. Howard visited Mexico to investigate the possibilities of preventing the introduction of the Morelos Orange Fruit Worm into California.

Mr. R. A. Cooley, an assistant to Prof. Fernald, has been at work upon the genus Chionaspis and has accumulated an enormous amount of material, and it is anticipated that his paper, when published, will give more than twice the number of species formerly known.

Fig. A. Operation of the first category. A compound pupa and a compound moth of P. Cynthia.

But while the economic side of the science is that which is of chief interest and importance to the community, I confess that my own interests lie rather in the direction of the purely scientific side of the subject.

From this point of view the experiments of Mr. Henry E Crampton, Jr., of the Department of Zoology of Columbia University, are of surpassing interest.

Mr. Crampton, following up the experiments of Mr. G. Born upon frog and toad embryos, determined to try similar experiments in grafting upon Lepidoptera in the pupal period and has obtained some truly marvellous results Mr. Crampton selected the pupæ of the large Saturnians, Cynthia, Cecropia, Promethea and Polyphemus as being the most suitable, though he also experimented with success upon Vanessa Antiopa, but had no success in his operations upon Danais Archippus.

The butterflies are not so well suited to these experiments as these large moths, partly because of their status being higher than that of the moths, and in the case of those which winter either in the larval or imago state, the chrysalis period is too short.

Naturally, failure resulted in a good many cases, the average of successful operations amounting to about ten per cent.

Fig. B. Operation of the second category. Union in "Tandem" of P. Cynthia, anterior, and C. Promethea, posterior.

The operations were of great variety, the anterior end of one pupa being joined to the posterior end of another either of the same or of a different species, or they were joined in tandems or in pairs back to back, while in one case the tip of the abdomen of one moth was grafted to the upper side of the abdomen of another. One pupa had had its head cut off and was still alive and the abdomens of some were cut off about the middle to see if any regeneration would take place. No cases have been successful where the division has been made longitudinally through the centre of the pupæ, and the nearer this line is approached the fewer there are which are successful, and conversely the less that is taken off the more likely are the subjects to survive.

The modus operandi is to slice the pupæ with a razor and effect the junctions with melted paraffin. The paraffin ring cannot be removed, as the coalescence is only effected between the interior portions, the two portions of the pupa case never uniting. The paraffin ring naturally tends to prevent the imagos emerging and they have to be helped out when they seem, from the papery condition of the pupa case, to be ready for emergence, the case being picked off bit by bit.

In general, the wings fail to expand and as a consequence the abdomen remains distended by the hæmolymph. In some cases the wings, or a majority of them, expand very well, one, perhaps, being aborted. In the case of a tandem junction, the anterior one may expand and the posterior one not. In such a case the former had only lost the tip of its abdomen, while the lower one had lost its head. In one case where two portions of pupæ were joined laterally, one eye in one part had coalesced with the neighbouring one in the other part to form a common eye. As a rule, the operations greatly retarded the development of the specimens.

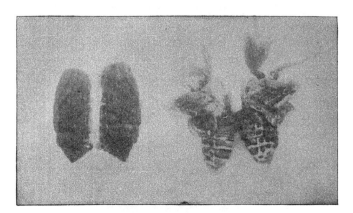

Fig. C.   Operation of the third category.   United pupæ and united imagines of S. Cecropia.

One of the objects of these experiments was to see what effect, if any, the unions would have on the colours of the resulting moths, but the results were rather negative, as nothing very definite was obtained.

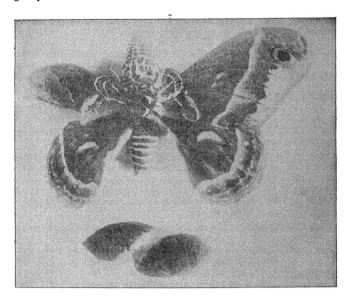

ig. D.   Operation of the third category.   United pupæ and united imagines of S. Cecropia

Another object was to ascertain if it would be possible to breed from such monstrosities, but though some individuals had shown symptoms of desiring sexual connection, no union had ever taken place, and so no eggs had been obtained, and as these operations must greatly lower the vitality, of the subjects, it seems very improbable that any attempts at breeding from these monstrosities could ever be successful*.

Another man who is doing good work, though in a much less startling field, is Dr. Otto Seifert of New York, in his experiments with heat and cold applied to the pupæ of butterflies and moths. Following up the work of Dorfmeister, Weismann, Edwards, Stange, Merrifield, Standfuss, and Eimer he has made extensive experiments upon a considerable number of species.

Pyrameis Atalanta, which seems very susceptible to these influences, Papilio Asterias, P. Turnus, Colias Philodice, Grapta Interrogationis, Melitæa Phaeton, Danais Archippus, Limenitis Disippus, Vanessa Antiopa, Junonia Coenia, Arctia Arge, A. Nais, Philosamia Cynthia, and Samia Cecropia have all been experimented upon with more or less success.

The operations were carried on by means of an incubator and an ice chest, the temperature in the former being maintained as nearly as possible at 38° C. equal to 100° F. while in the latter it varied between 4° C. and 6° C. equal to 39° F. and 43° F.

In summarizing his results Dr. Seifert informs me that the effect seemed to depend more upon the susceptibility of the individual than upon the length of the exposure to these artificial conditions, as in some cases chrysalides kept ten days on ice produced more aberrant forms than resulted from others kept for thirty days on ice.

Cold and heat did not always have opposite effects in some particulars, as for instance Limenitis Disippus exposed to heat was deepened in colour along the costa to the middle of the wing, the mesial band of secondaries narrowing or being omitted altogether. Subjected to cold the colour was turned darker also but in a different way, the darker tone being chiefly produced by many black scales along the veins, and the mesial band on secondaries being more marked.

While heat in general tends to produce a more marked or defined design, when accompanied by an excess of moisture Dr. Seifert found a tendency to almost destroy the colour but never to affect the design.

Heat and cold were also found to affect the shape of the wings, in some cases the apex of primaries becoming more pointed, while in P. Turnus and G. Interrogationis cold caused a remarkable development of the scallops and dentations of the wings.

Cold changed the rounded secondaries of Junonia Coenia to a form more elongated towards the anal angle, while heat shapes the wings of Limenitis Disippus nearly to those of Danais Archippus.

Pyrameis Atalanta was affected in the most interesting manner by cold, the red transverse band on primaries above being broken up into four spots while below the secondaries are much changed in appearance, the buff tone of the lower two-thirds of the outer margin being greatly strengthened and spread inwards, while a violet bloom tends to spread over the wing.

In Arctia Arge the prominent black spots on the abdomen vanish entirely or are much diminished by heat, and the black marks on primaries are also reduced.

By cold the black spots on the abdomen are enlarged, sometimes in the female becoming transverse bands, while on the secondaries blackish streaks originating from the base spread outwards towards the margin.

Dr. Seifert also experimented upon eggs but could only find that heat hastened development while cold retarded it. Eggs of Colias Philodice exposed to a temperature of

*The cuts illustrative of these experiments have been copied from those in "Biological Lectures," published by Messrs. Ginn & Co., of Boston, by the kind permission of Mr. Crampton, who delivered the 11th lecture at the Marine Biological Laboratory of Wood's Holl in the summer session of 1897.

100° F. hatched in 36 hours, while cold if not carried too far, 8-10 days, merely retarded the hatching, but eggs of A. Luna exposed to cold for 20 days were all killed.

The chief point which Dr. Seifert is seeking to elucidate is whether the variations obtained can be transmitted to the offspring and become hereditary. This field of investigation, while much less startling than that in which Mr. Crampton is working, certainly seems likely to prove more fruitful.

Among the most important publications on the Lepidoptera of North America which have appeared during the year must be mentioned Prof. Fernald's monograph of the Pterophoridæ, with its sixty-two pages of text and nine plates devoted altogether to structural details, which work has been accorded the highest praise by those best able to judge of its merits.

Mr. Beutenmüller has laid us under a further debt of gratitude by the issue of his "Descriptive Catalogue of the Bombycine Moths found within Fifty Miles of New York City," which appeared last month. This is on the same plan as his previous catalogues of Butterflies and Sphingidæ, and extends to ninety-six pages, with nine excellent plates. One hundred and eighty-one species are described, of which ninety-three are illustrated, but from lack of space the author had to omit all generic descriptions. At present this work is only available to those having access to the "Bulletin of the Amerian Museum of Natural History," or are so fortunate as to receive a copy of the author's edition, but I am glad to be able to announce that Mr. Beutenmüller, on completion of the series, contemplates re-issuing the whole in book form, which will then be generally available.

Mr. Beutenmüller, in addition to carrying on this important work, is also engaged upon studying various genera of the Lepidoptera with a view to revision, and has recently issued a review of the genus Euchloë or Anthocharis, to be followed later by a paper on Argynnis.

Dr. Dyar has been carrying on his important studies on structure, especially of larvæ, and is engaged in conjunction with Dr. J. B Smith upon a monograph of Acronycta, and is also at work upon a new catalogue or check list which, it is promised, will render the Lepidoptera scarcely recognizable by those who have accustomed themselves to Dr. Smith's Check List of 1891.

Dr Ottolengui of New York has taken up the Plusia group and has gathered specimens of nearly, if not quite, all the known North American forms, and has secured either specimens closely agreeing with all types which he has not been able to see or, where this was impossible, carefully executed colored figures of such types. He is thus in a position to monograph the group, and has discovered some extraordinary errors which have been current for many years. If I may be pardoned for saying so, his work has been carried on on precisely similar lines to my study of the Callimorphas some years ago, namely, by finding out first what each author meant by his description, fixing the types absolutely, and then working from that basis, instead of taking things for granted and going by guesswork, and this, I contend, is the only true method.

In Coleoptera, as I am informed, the illness and death of Dr. Horn has produced almost a standstill.

In Hymenoptera valuable contributions have been made chiefly by Mr. Ashmead, aided by Dr. Howard, Mr. Marlatt and Dr. Dyar, the latter in Tenthrenid larvæ, and the growth of knowledge in this order has been almost phenomenal, while Dr. Smith has been engaged in most interesting work on the underground forms, the Digging Bees, by means of the plaster cast method.

In Diptera the works of Messrs, Coquillett and Johnson, especially the very important "Revision of the Tachinidæ" by the former, have added much to our knowledge, and it is encouraging to note the increase in the number of students in this order.

In Orthoptera the event of chief interest has been the issue of Dr. Scudder's most important "Revision of the Melanopli," a work which must have involved an immense amount of labor and research, extending as it does to over 400 pages, and illustrated by twenty-six plates. In connection with this order attention may be called to the interesting discovery that the large Mantid, Tenodera Sinensis, Saussure, from China and Japan, has been introduced into the United States and has been breeding for at least three years in the vicinity of Philadelphia.

In regard to Hemiptera, I have already referred at some length to the San José Scale and the work in connection therewith, but mention should also be made of Prof. Cockerell's pamphlet on the other scale insects closely allied to the San José Scale and liable to be confounded with it.

The completion early last year of Mr. W. H. Edwards's magnificent work on the Butterflies of North America, which was undertaken in 1868, caused something like a pang to those who for so many years had been receiving as they appeared the successive parts of this splendid work, and the hope has been expressed on many sides that the talented author might be willing to undertake the issue of a supplementary volume of, say, twenty-five plates, for which he has ample materials, provided one hundred subscribers at $1.00 per plate could be secured.

But if the closing of Mr. Edwards's labors produced a temporary lull in the issue of beautiful illustrations of our North American butterflies, we are now about to see issued a work which is surely destined to popularize the study of the Lepidoptera on this continent if anything can.

Dr. Holland, the talented Chancellor of the Western University of Pennsylvania, who has amassed an enormous collection of Lepidoptera, including that of Mr. Edwards with all that author's types, has undertaken the publication of a large edition of a popular book on the North American butterflies, to be called "The Butterfly Book, A Popular Guide to a Knowledge of the Butterflies of North America," and has authorized me to make the following announcement in regard to it:

It will be brought out, probably about the end of November, by the Doubleday & McClure Co. of New York,* and will be illustrated by forty-eight coloured plates done by the same system of photographic reproduction and printing which has become so familiar through the publication on Birds issued monthly by the Nature Study Publishing Co. of Chicago and New York. These plates will represent 526 species of diurnal lepidoptera, in many cases giving both the upper and under sides of the insect. The figures are, in the main, taken from the type specimens contained in the Edwards collection, and many of the species are represented for the first time, having never previously been figured. In addition to the representations given of the imago, Dr. Scudder has most kindly granted permission to reproduce the plates contained in his Butterflies of New England in which the early stages of these insects are represented. There are, furthermore, to be about 200 cuts in the text, representing anatomical details of structure which are useful in the determination of genera. A cut representing the neuration of each genus is given, and in some cases additional cuts showing the subgeneric forms. Brief descriptions of the imago, egg, caterpillar and chrysalis, when the latter are known, are given in the text. Interlarded in the somewhat dry technical details are extracts from the writings of other authors, which are calculated to interest the general reader, and quotations amusing and pathetic, gathered from out of the mass of butterfly lore.

All this is to be put before the American and Canadian public in good binding for the sum of $3.00, but it will be necessary to sell 7,000 copies of the book, unless a monetary loss is to result, but surely among the 70,000,000 of the United States and the 5,000,000 of Canada there should be no difficulty in disposing of 7,000 copies of such a book at such a price.

A fair idea of the character of the plates can be obtained from the rough proofs which Dr. Holland has sent to be shown at this meeting.

---

* A Canadian edition has been published by Mr. William Briggs, 29-33 Richmond St. West, Toronto.

In regard to the publication "Birds," which title has recently been enlarged to " Birds and all Nature," and which has begun giving excellent illustrations of butterflies and mammals in addition to the plates of birds, it seems a great pity that with such beautiful plates it is not considered worth while attempting to make the text of some scientific value.

Another popular book under the name of " Every-Day Butterflies," from the facile pen of Dr. Scudder, is announced and will contain familiar and fully illustrated accounts of sixty or more of the commonest butterflies, taken in the order of the season.

In conclusion I have to express my indebtedness to Dr. Howard, Dr. Smith and Prof. Fernald for the kind manner in which they responded to my inquiries, and for the valuable information afforded and suggestions offered, which have materially contributed to any interest which my address may possess, and to you, gentlemen, my acknowledgments are due for the patience with which you have listened to me.

Dr. FYLES, in rising to move a vote of thanks to the President for his valuable and interesting paper, said that he approved of the address with one exception namely, that when so good a worker, so good a collector, read so good a paper as the address just given, he should not call himself an amateur. Dr. Wm. Saunders seconded the motion He had listened with great pleasure to the address, so full of admirable suggestions showing the keenest interest and deep insight into the needs of the active entomologist. He called attention to the many interesting statements of the investigation now progressing. *Carried.*

Mr. Lyman briefly acknowledged the vote, saying that as he was not a professional entomologist he must be an amateur.

Mr. W. E. SAUNDERS, referred to the President's suggestion of the formation of an American Entomologists' Union, and spoke of the good work done by the American Ornithologists' Union, in preventing needless changes of nomenclature and in other important matters. Mr. A. E. Norris spoke on the importance of uniformity of setting, strongly approving the President's suggestion of a Union to authoritatively settle all such matters. He would favor the giving of greater attention by the societies to the working out and making complete exhibitions of the life histories of insects, as such exhibits are at once the most interesting and instructive.

A paper entitled " Some International features of Economic Entomology " by Prof. F. M. Webster, Wooster, Ohio, was then read by Dr. Fletcher.

SOME ECONOMIC FEATUES OF INTERNATIONAL ENTOMOLOGY.

By F. M. WEBSTER.

When that massive ridge of Archæan rock, the backbone, so to speak, of the future American continent, was first laid down, stretching away from northwest to southeast, it is hardly to be supposed that it was cut in twain from east to west by some huge chasm, which, in future ages, was to separate from each other two distinct worlds of animal life, with no inter-communication between them.

Nor is it more likely that, after the ponderous ice sheets of the Glacial Period had plowed their way from the far north, crushing and grinding the solid rock and transporting huge boulders from the area that we are now pleased to term Canada, far to the southward, and depositing them along what is now the Ohio River, there should have been thrown athwart this pathway an invisible barrier across which animal life could not by any possibility make its way.

It was nature that hollowed out the beds of the great, turbulent lakes and furrowed out the course of gigantic Niagara, but it was uncivilized man who first chose to make these barriers between himself and his enemies ; and while civilized man has followed the example thus set for him, this is no part of nature's handiwork. Though the Cross of St. George may now proudly float from the one side, and the Stars and Stripes as proudly respond to the northern breezes from the other side; though there may be martialled, armed hosts on either side, the coats of one being red and the other blue, this is but following in the footsteps of the uncivilized aborigine, and not in the pathway of nature.

The feathered migrants of the air will, each recurring spring, make their way from the far south and rear their young in your woods and fields and along your inland lakes and streams, gathering their progeny together and making their way southward again in autumn, though a Queen might issue her edicts and a President promulgate his orders to the contrary. Again, the finny tribes of the sea and lakes seek their food and deposit their spawn wherever their inclinations and a favorable situation may tempt them, wholly unconscious of the tribulations that they bring upon the enthusiastic angler from the cities of the United States, who suddenly finds himself and his craft in the hands of British law in case he attempts to follow them. The moose, the wild deer, the wolf and the bear are no less free to go and come, roving northward or southward as their inclinations prompt them, totally ignorant of the terrors lurking in invisible, arbitrary lines and the questionings of custom house officers; for these are the belongings of men and not of nature.

In the light of what has been stated, then, it may be said that at present Canada and the United States are separated by an imaginary, arbitrary, political line, which we as subjects of two powerful nations are bound to respect in matters outside of natural science, but it seems to me that the naturalist must be permitted to demand that this condition is not allowed to extend farther. We are dealing with nature, and nature, as has been shown, knows no national lines. With us, as entomologists, the fact that we are all Americans must stand paramount to any other considerations. America is separated more or less widely from other portions of the world by depths of sea, which form a far more effective barrier to insect migrations than any that human minds can conceive or human hands erect. Unaided by man or his agents, but few insects could make their way from the eastern to the western hemisphere, or vice versa, though those neo-tropical might and probably have, unaided by man, spread from thence northward into the nearctic regions. Two illustrations of these last will suffice, one the Harlequin Cabbage Bug, *Murgantia histrionica* (Fig. 1), known to inhabit Central America and the West Indies, has lately pushed its way northward, in Ohio, to within twenty miles of Lake Erie, or to about Lat. 30° 15′ N , while the Chinch Bug, *Blissus leucopterus* (Fig. 2, highly magnified), in all probability originally a neo-tropical species, has,

Fig. 1.

Fig. 2.

as you know, spread northward over a portion of the Dominion of Canada, and while it has not as yet been known to depredate upon your crops to any noticeable degree, yet it may do so in the future, in which case it may be expected to first make its presence known in your timothy meadows rather than in your grain fields, and quite likely will work considerable injury before it is recognized by your agriculturists. Another phase of this problem of insect migration is illustrated by the Colorado Potato Beetle, *Doryphora decemlineata*, which at one time was restricted to the country about the base of the Rocky Mountains, and its food-plant consisted of vegetation having no economic value. But now came the eastern emigrant farmer with his indispensable potato, a plant closely allied to the natural food-plant of this insect, and thus the potato patches of the settlers became as so many stepping-stones to the beetles and enabled them to make their way eastward to the Atlantic coast and Canada, transcontinental railways probably hastening their arrival, as they are shown to have appeared along the lines of railways earlier than elsewhere. So much for this aspect of the problem, but let us now turn our attention toward some other phases of a more international character.

Many years ago, probably about 1856 or 1857, the Cabbage Butterfly, *Pieris rapæ* (Fig. 3), was introduced about Quebec, and possibly also again about 1891, since which time it has spread westward and southward until it now extends from the Atlantic to the Pacific and nearly to the Gulf of Mexico, even its numerous parasites not being able to entirely prevent its ravages. The Codling Moth, *Carpocapsa pomonella*, was in all probability first introduced into the United States, but Canada has as you all know sustained her full share of injury from its ravages. These two species have been brought to our shores from the mother country, and they are by no means the only ones that have been introduced from Europe or Palæarctic regions, and, I fear, those that we now have with us will not be the last to

Fig. 3.

come this way. The latest and most serious introduction of all, the San Jose scale, *Aspidiotus perniciosus*, is in all probability another contribution from the Palæarctic region, as I have been able to prove almost conclusively that it came to us from Japan, and we therefore received it from the west instead of the east. Recent experiences are amply sufficient to show that it will destroy the orchards of Canada as well as those of the United States, within whose domains it first made its unwelcome appearance.

The foregoing illustrations will certainly be sufficient to convince anyone that we cannot by simple Legislative or Parliamentary enactment erect a Chinese wall, so to speak, that shall keep Canadian insects, whether native or introduced from making their way into the United States, or similar species escaping from the latter into Canada. We in the United States are more likely to import more insect pests than you, and, owing to our geographical situation, will suffer most from their depredations, but, put the matter as we will, we are much in the position of a large family threatened with an attack of some contagious disease ; if one member contracts it all will be alike exposed, and to attempt prevention by individual isolation, will result in no end of trouble and aggravation without accomplishing the end desired, precisely as we have found our State laws to do. What we need, primarily, is an international quarantine measure that shall apply uniformly to all North America. A judicious, properly enforced measure that shall mean the same from the mouth of the St. Lawrence to the mouth of the Rio Grande, and from there to Vancouver or the mouth of the Yukon, and as far beyond as is found necessary. It is all very well for your Canadian law-makers to say that it is none of Canada's affair what is done in the United States, and our politicians will make the same plea, but we who are continually dealing with these problems of nature know better ! We know that there is a power higher than that of our combined nations, that rules these natural elements, which power we cannot control, but, may oft'times utilize to our advantage. International entomology and international insect legislation are matters that we are being confronted with for the first time—matters of the future rather than of the past—but the next century will see them brought to the front. There will arise important questions which must be settled calmly, judiciously and justly, and entomologists must be ready to advise and counsel in these matters. The Entomological Society of Ontario ought and will have its influence in solving these international problems, as these come up one after another for solution and in accordance with nature's unyielding laws. I look for the time to come, and in the comparatively near future, when these matters will become far more important factors in international law than they are at present, as, indeed it seems impossible that the situation can be otherwise.

If we look about over the world at the present time, we find Cape Colony prohibiting the importation of all American nursery stock, whether from the United States or Canada. Several European nations have gone even farther and attempted to prohibit American green fruits from being brought within their respective domains. Queensland quarantines against New Zealand, South Australia against New South Wales, and Tasmanian fruit is condemned and destroyed in Melbourne; British Columbia destroys infested fruit from the United States as well as from other parts of British America, while

Canada prohibits the importation of nursery stock from the United States; at the same time several of these States have enacted laws which enforced to the letter would become quite prohibitory in their effects. The most of this trouble has come from the appearance of that pernicious little pest the San Jose Scale, *Aspidiotus perniciosus*, which we, in all probability, first received from the west.

Now, this method of dealing with the problem of insect control cannot be said to be all wrong, as some of it is quite necessary and proper, but there is certainly a great deal of misdirected effort being put forth and commerce is suffering therefrom to a considerable extent. It is the beginning of insect legislation, and first attempts at anything are usually more or less crude and capable of improvement. It is all right for Cape Colony to protect her growing fruit interests by keeping certain fruit pests out of South Africa, by prohibiting the importation of nursery stock, liable to infection, and keeping these Acts in force until such time as the pests have either become exterminated or some method discovered whereby the nursery stock can be effectually disinfected and rendered safe. If the Australasian Colonies had, years ago, united on a uniform code that would apply to all ports alike and admitted nursery stock and green fruits after an examination and disinfection, as has been done at the port of San Francisco, California, during the last few years, they would not now be contending against each other. If we in America had taken similar steps in the matter of insect legislation fifty years ago, we would in all probability have escaped much of the insect depredations of the present, as the major part of our seriously injurious species in this country are of foreign origin.

It is of course, too late, now, to prevent what has already been done, but it is not too late to take measures to prevent further importations from both east and west. In our efforts to suppress the insect pests that we already have with us, we are overlooking the greater problem of prevention of future similar introductions. We are laying altogether too much stress upon individual effort, as put forth by States, Colonies or Provinces against each other, and entirely losing sight of the international aspects of the problem. We cannot seem to disabuse our minds of the idea that political lines have something to do with the management of these natural organisms, and cannot apparently grasp the idea that natural barriers may be utilized by one or more nations acting in unity, and for the direct benefit of all thus acting. Sometime in the future, though neither you nor I may live to see it come to pass, these arbitrary, imaginary lines will, in problems of this sort, be lost sight of, and there will appear in their stead lines of another sort, far less imaginary and more natural, and these will encompass not one nation alone, but one or many as the case may be. We shall then designate these areas by a term now unknown, except to scientific ears, viz., Zoogeographical Regions, and while these may vary somewhat from the outlines laid down by Wallace, in his "Geographical Distribution of Animals," yet they will probably cover much the same areas as there indicated. There will probably continue to occur cases like that of the Colorado Potato Beetle, where a species may spread from one section of a Zoogeographical Region over, and become destructive in, many portions of the remainder, yet these phenomena are likely to occur but rarely. We may learn that the Almighty can make a better barrier, over or around which insects cannot make their way, than the wisest of men or the mightiest of nations. There are phenomena connected with the geographical distribution of insects for which we cannot, with our present knowledge, account. There are boundaries beyond which certain species do not make their way, though to the human eye and mind there are no obstructions in the way of their doing so. The science of applied entomology is yet in its infancy, and we have very much to learn even of our most common species of insects, but we can even now see the unnatural and impractical methods that we are trying to apply toward their control, as between one portion of the world and another. We try to erect legal barriers where none exist in nature, and ignore those which nature has provided. All of this, of course, applies to protection from future importations, and not to such as have already gained a foothold, these last being beyond the scope of my paper, as I have restricted it, and the management of these will depend largely upon the energy and care of the people inhabiting the territory over which such species are now distributed. There is, however, a very important phase of the problem of controlling these pests, already imported from foreign countries, and which will be discussed later on in my paper. While it has not been deemed best to discuss, in detail, legislative control of such destructive species as have already been colonized here in this country, and many of them widely diffused, yet their possible control in many cases at least, by the application of nature's own forces seems to me to constitute a very important feature of International Entomology.

Forms of both plants and animals, unaided by the influences of man, make their way over the face of the earth but slowly if at all, and it is probable that a species often becomes so influenced by the change that it loses its specific identity and takes on new characters, so that the specialist rechristens it and gives it another name. The result of all of this is that wherever a species makes its way, naturally, its enemies usually follow, or else while undergoing the process of adaptation, new enemies come to exert their influence. In other words, the difference between an artificial and a natural introduction is much the same as suddenly dumping an iceberg into a pond, as against allowing the same amount of water to make its way into the pond, from the same source, but through a small spring or brook. In the former case both equilibrium and temperature are disarranged, while in the latter the effect is too gradual to cause any radical changes.

The legitimate introduction of plant life from one country into another has come to be a matter of vast commercial importance, and, adding as it does to our health, comfort and pleasure, such introductions are in every way commendable. Accidental introductions may, however, not always prove so satisfactory. Now, all of this brings me to the second phase of the subject of International Entomology, viz., the intentional, if not indeed necessary, introduction of exotic insects in order to re-establish the equilibrium that has been upset by the importation of plant life, or, as is sometimes the case, to enable the plant introduced to become permanently established.

Of species of insects purposely introduced from one country into another, there are those whose products constitute articles of commerce, of which the honey bee and silk worm are well known illustrations. The importation of large quantities of the ova and imagines of two species of American aquatic hemiptera, *Corixa mercenaria*, Say, and *Notonecta americana*, Fabr., from Mexico, where they are used for human food, into England, where they are to be used as food for birds, game, fish, etc., is another illustration of a different feature of this commerce in insect life.

The relations of insect to plant life are, however, so various and intimate; and, because of their reaching out over the face of the globe for the fruits, grains and ornamental vegetation of other climes, men are finding themselves more and more driven to import insects foreign to their respective countries. In some instances it has been found impossible to permanently establish an exotic plant without insect assistance. We all remember how impossible it was to get the red clover plant established in New Zealand until humble bees were also imported to fertilize the bloom, as the plant is not one that will perpetuate itself indefinitely from the roots ; and at present we in the United States are unable to grow the perfect Smyrna fig owing to a lack of the good offices of a little foreign insect, *Blastophaga pensens*, which actually represents the male element in its fertilization.

Lastly, we come to what appears to be the most important of all insect importations, viz., the introduction of foreign, carnivorous insects, whose office in their native country is to prey upon and destroy those that are destructive, which last we have unintentionally imported into this country on trees, plants and shrubs, or in the fruits and grains coming to us from these same countries. That is to say, when we find that we have introduced a destructive species of insect, we are to go to the native habitat of this and there secure its native insect enemies, and introduce these to hold the former in check, as they do at home.

Parasitism is nature's insecticide—one of the forces that is employed by nature to restore equilibrium, so to speak, among natural organisms in point of numerical strength. The observing entomologist may every year witness proof of this, for he will observe some species to increase very rapidly during a short time, and, knowing of their fecundity, will often be led to predict a serious outbreak. But at the opportune moment, Presto! a change! and the species that was but yesterday, as it were, literally swarming, is now reduced to a minimum, while the dead are everywhere thickly scattered about. Two instances of this sort have, the present year, come under my own observation. Early in May, the females of the grain aphis, *Siphonophora avenœ*, appeared on the growing wheat and were soon surrounded by their young. These insects were in a short time as plentiful as they usually are, at that season, in years of excessive abundance, and there seemed every indication of an outbreak of the pest. But now there appeared a little Braconid parasite, *Aphidius avenaphis*, and within ten days there were few living adults to be found, though the distended, brown bodies of those that had succumbed to their minute enemy were everywhere plentiful. It was as if a Mighty hand had been stretched forth accompanied by the command, Peace! be still. During August and early September

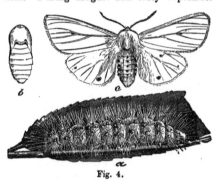

Fig. 4.

there were great numbers of caterpillars of *Spilosoma virginica* (Fig. 4, *a* caterpillar, *b* chrysalis, *c* moth) and to a less degree of *Arctia acrœa*, in Northern Ohio, and, if they had all developed moths, there would have been much injury caused by the caterpillars next year. But this was not to be, as by September 20th the dead and dying were hanging to weeds, grass and fences, in myriads, having been attacked and killed by a fungous enemy, probably *Empusa aulicœ*, Reich., and neither of these caterpillars will probably be at all abundant with us next year. The same phenomenon was noticed in Ohio six years ago.

Scattered through our entomological literature, are hundreds of such illustrations of the value of parasites in holding in check the hordes of destructive insects that occur in this country, and there is hardly a working entomologist who cannot add to these from his own unpublished notes.

Of our most destructive insect pests nearly all have been brought to this country from abroad. Lack of their natural enemies here, together with the fact that, in many cases, these introduced pests are not known as such in their native homes, leads us to

Fig. 5.

conclude that we, in our importations, have left these enemies behind. The case is much as though we were to import from some foreign country a huge piece of machinery, but on its arrival we find that the balance wheel has been omitted, and in such a case what are we to do? Cable back for the missing wheel, or attempt to run our machine without a balance wheel? There are, doubtless, instances where introduced species can not be subdued in this manner, by the importation of their ancient enemies, but, generally speaking, this appears to be the rational method of accomplishing this end. The history of the introduction of the Orange Scale, *Icerya Purchasi* (Fig. 5), from Australia into California, is probably familiar to most, if not all, of those present. The orange industry of the United States and, as was afterwards learned, of other countries also, was threatened with a most destructive enemy to citrus fruits. In California orange groves were being destroyed to such an extent that it looked as though the cultivation of this fruit would have to be abandoned. But a natural enemy of this pest was discovered in Australia and imported, artificially, into this country, and as a result the pest has been subdued, and with us, before it had spread beyond the Pacific coast. Not only this, but

3 EN.

this natural enemy, one of the Coccinellidæ, has been sent wherever the Orange Scale has been introduced and the effect has been the same as in this country.   All of this has been an object lesson in the application of Nature's forces in overcoming the evil results of man's influences in the artificial diffusion of destructive insects.   In North America, and also in Australasia, men are at present wrestling with another important pest, allied to the Orange Scale, and introduced into California many years ago, but in this case probably from Japan.   I refer again to the San José Scale, *Aspidiotus perniciosus*, which has, with us, spread over a vast range of country and already caused great losses.   From all that I have been able to learn by observation of this pest, both in the orchards of the United States and on nursery stock immediately on its arrival from Japan, and also from the writings of others, it would appear that the natural enemies of this pest have been left in their native homes.   Probably, as with the Orange Scale, these are Coccinellids whose habits are such that it would be impossible to get them in connection with their hosts at the time when the trees are packed for shipment to this country, as this is done at the season of the year when these insects have finished their development and abandoned the trees, if not wholly, remaining only in the adult state and would promptly desert the trees on being disturbed.   If there had been important internal or fungous enemies we should certainly have gotten these with the host insect long ago.   Now, it would certainly seem that in the introduction of Aspidiotus and its suppression we have a problem in applied international entomology, precisely like that presented by Icerya, and it would as certainly appear that, with our past experience, the very course of all others to pursue would be to learn what the natural enemies of this insect are in its native home and then introduce these as promptly and diffuse them as widely as possible, not only in one state or province, not in the United States or British America alone, but in North America *   It is Americans that are suffering from the ravages of this pest, where they are located, geographically or politically, does not matter in the least. . International boundary lines cut no figure in this problem whatever, and have no more influence on these natural objects than they have on the winds.   We should seek to introduce living organisms from the Palæarctic Life Region into the Nearctic Life Region, no matter what or how many nations may lay claim to the territory of either one or both of these regions.   What we are really trying to do is to help natural selection to keep pace with artificial selection, and, if we accomplish anything in this direction, it will be by aiding nature and not in any sense by attempting to circumscribe her by imaginary lines of separation which have no existence in fact.

Now, lest I be misunderstood, let me say that true naturalists can only exist among loyal men and women. We must, all of us, be true to the nation that protects us by its wise and judicious legislation.   Science stands for truth and right and honesty, and, for this very reason we must stop whenever and wherever these national lines cease to represent the truth, and be guided by others.   In matters political, we must respect political lines, but in dealing with natural phenomena, we must abandon these and be guided by such as have been laid down by the hand of the Creator, who outranks either Queen, President or any other human potentate,   Therefore, we must lose sight of national boundary lines and unite upon those laid down by nature.   Here, in North America, there should be the closest relations between the United States Department of Agriculture and similar Departments of the various Provinces of British America, and absolute unity of action wherever this is possible.   This quarantining of one State, Province or Nation against another may possibly do in cases of isolation, like New Zealand or Cuba, or as applied to some of the ills that we already have with us, but this sort of work will never protect in the sense that a combination certainly would, if we were to throw aside

*Note—Since the above was written I have received the following from the Rev. H. Loomis, of Yokohama, Japan, which will be of interest in connection with this paper. "I see in the *Canadian Entomologist*, for July, an article in which you recommend that some one be sent to Japan to make a study of the enemies of the San José Scale.   I think it a most excellent suggestion.   There are many varieties of Lady Beetles here, and I am quite sure that it is due to them that the Scale is not more injurious in Japan.   I am strengthened in this opinion because the Gypsy Moth is found all over Japan, and yet it is not especially harmful.   This is entirely due to a parasite that feeds upon the larvæ so universally as to prevent its rapid increase.   I have watched the results with great interest and would recommend that both insects be made a matter of careful study."

arbitrary lines and unite on others laid down by nature. This is a phase of international entomology that will sooner or later be thrust upon us by the necessities of international commerce in articles that harbor injurious insects. We must have broader measures of protection than we have had in the past. We must take necessary precautions against the introduction of injurious species, and, after the most thorough and searching investigations, introduce the beneficial species. In all of these matters, Canada and the United States are one, and, this being true, there must be no lines of separation between the entomologists of these two countries. We must work together, shoulder to shoulder, and God speed the day when we shall do this, to even a greater degree that we are now doing! The coming century will be fraught with work for the entomologist, and his loyalty to his country will be best shown by his careful, conscientious labors.

On concluding the reading of this paper Dr. Fletcher said that he thought it was one of unusual importance and particularly so just at the present time when such great efforts were being made to prevent the spread of the San Jose Scale, a danger the magnitude of which was by no means appreciated by the fruit growers and fruit consumers of the Dominion. It was, too, eminently proper that the subject should be introduced by the writer of the pages which he had had the honour of reading to the meeting, for few people had done so much to present the subject to the public of America as Prof. Webster. It was well pointed out that the political limits of the two great countries mentioned were not recognized by the natural denizens of the faunal and floral zones which we had as naturalists to study, although by accident owing to the great lakes this was somewhat the case. International economic entomology was only in its infancy, but it was being rapidly acknowledged at its right value of importance owing to the vast interests at stake. Dr. Howard, in his letter regretting that he could not be with us to-day, had been good enough to say that he considered the relations existing between the entomologists of the Dominion and of the United States to be of an ideal nature. The speaker felt sure that all present would agree with him that this was actually the case, and further, that this happy state of affairs was largely due to the constant and unfailing courtesy of Dr. Howard himself and his assistants at Washington, too numerous to mention now by name separately, but well known to every student who required help with regard to any special family of insects; to such men as the late Drs. Riley and Lintner, to Professors Webster, J. B. Smith, Comstock, Slingerland, Hopkins, Alwood, Johnson, Cockerell, Fernald, and many, many others who were not only always ready to help, but had in the past frequently helped with most valuable papers published in our reports and in the *Canadian Entomologist.* In his official position he was brought frequently into contact with these gentlemen and found invariably the utmost kindness and ready assistance. Last spring he had by invitation taken part in a conference of economic entomologists, fruit growers and nursery men held at Washington, for the purpose of laying before Congress the advisability of passing legislation for the suppression of the San Jose Scale. A committee waited upon the Congressional Agricultural Committee and explained the wishes of the conference and a favourable report was made by the Agricultural Committee to Congress. Legislation would undoubtedly have been enacted almost identical with our federal San Jose Scale Act but for the unfortunate outbreak of the Spanish-American War—Canada however had done her part and Dr. Fletcher believed that this law was a most useful provision. The Minister of Agriculture had considered the matter most carefully and the present popular measure was due to the minister's careful enquiries and legislative skill. The Hon. John Dryden had also put forth strenuous efforts for the protection of the fruit interests of the Province of Ontario. Too much could not be said of the excellent work of Mr. W. M. Orr the Superintendent of Spraying and of Mr. G. E. Fisher who had pushed most energetically and tactfully the inspection of orchards for the San Jose Scale.

Dr. Fletcher congratulated the members of the Montreal Branch on the splendid work they were doing; he paid a well merited tribute to the persistent work which Mr. Lyman the president had been doing during many years and characterized the many papers which had appeared from his pen as being prepared with the greatest care as to detail, complete.

ness as to research, and richness as to scientific facts they contained; his example had done much to stimulate the other members of the Branch to continue the good work they were doing for the Science of Entomology, particular attention being drawn to some of the collections exhibited at the present meeting, as those of Mr. Dwight Brainerd, who had prepared some beautiful cases illustrating the life-histories of several species of insects, of Mr. A. F. Winn, Mr. Dunlop, Mr. Williams and Mr. Norris, all of which contained many specimens of great interest. In conclusion the speaker begged to move a hearty vote of thanks to Professor Webster for his suggestive, timely and valuable paper.

This being seconded by Rev. Dr. Fyles, was carried unanimously.

NOTES ON PAPILIO BREVICAUDA, SAUNDERS.

By A. F. Winn, Montreal.

This species is either extending its habitat or has always had a wider range than credited to it, for I can now record its occurrence at Kamouraska, Que., a village on the south shore of the St. Lawrence about 85 miles below Quebec. (Lat. 47° 33" N.)

Its locality as given in Scudder's Butterflies is "Newfoundland and the shores and islands of the Gulf of St. Lawrence both north and west," but I think Percé (Gaspe Co.) is the only recorded place on the south coast.

In July, 1889, a specimen was sent to me from Bic (Rimouski Co.) and arrived in a battered condition, but during the many seasons that I have spent my fortnight's vacation at Metis, about 30 miles further down, I have never seen the butterfly on the wing.

Rev. Dr. Fyles stated that a specimen had been taken last summer on the Island of Orleans, P. Q., by Mrs. Turner, of the Quebec Branch.

In 1896 I had not made up my mind where to spend my holidays and wrote Mr. L. Reford at Metis, asking him whether he was finding any good specimens and whether there was any hotel accommodation. He replied that he had taken a number of good things, among others a Papilio larva, and that there were plenty more to be found on a beach plant resembling celery.

I left for Metis on August 16th and found on my arrival that most of the larvae were nearly full grown, but a few were in their third stage. Some that Mr. Reford had in his house were just entering the chrysalis stage. We boxed all the mature larvae we could find and left the younger ones to feed on the archangelica plants during our stay, and before starting home gathered all we could find along with a supply of growing plants in tomato tins. The plants stood the journey well and grew nicely in the garden and we had no difficulty in getting all the larvae into chrysalis, but neither of us was successful in breeding a butterfly. All of my chrysalids were attacked by the parasite, which destroys so many P. asterias chrysalids—*Trogus exesorius.*

Thinking the species might be different I sent a specimen to Mr. Harrington of Ottawa, who has kindly determined it as the dark form of T. exesorius.

From larvae obtained the following year (1897) Mr. Reford managed to get one fine imago, which hatched in midwinter.

During the past summer I spent my vacation at Kamouraska, arriving there on August 13th and remaining until the 28th, spending part of 13th with Dr. Fyles at Levis. On the morning of the 14th while walking along the beach I noticed some rocks of the same slate formation that we had found the food plant of *brevicauda* among at Metis and after a few moments was pleased to find two or three plants but could find no larvae. A few yards further on, however, there were a number of plants and on them several larvae in their second stage, some in the first and some eggs.

The eggs are pale yellow, smooth and spherical except that the base is considerably flattened, and are attached mostly to the upper surface of the leaves, but sometimes to the lower side and on the stem and a few were on surrounding objects including a stick which lay across the rocks and on the rock itself.

Before hatching the egg becomes slate color. The larva has already been described and is so like P. asterias in all its stages that I could observe no points by which the two species could be distinguished.

I sent some larvae to Dr. Fyles at Levis and some eggs to Mr. Brainerd of Montreal, keeping a few eggs myself, and of these the first hatched August 15th and the first chrysalis was formed August 31st, making a larval period of 16 days—a remarkably short one, as Scudder observes, for such a high latitude. A number of larvae and eggs were found during the whole of my stay and when I examined the plants for the last time on the 28th the full grown larvae were crawling over newly laid eggs, and larvae of all sizes were side by side.

The first butterfly I saw was on the afternoon of the 14th, a little way back from the shore, but I afterwards found that the foodplant grew in a ditch in the same field. I failed to capture this female, and saw no more until the following Sunday (21st) when a party of us went to Tache's Point, a rocky promentary covered with trees, about a quarter of a mile north of the church. Several broken males were caught, but not having my net I could not catch the few that were in good condition. After lunch I returned with my net and caught one male in fair condition, and a number that were otherwise. On the 22nd I took a run on my bicycle along the main road towards Riviere du Loup, and got off at the bridge crossing the St. Paschel river, and followed the dyke, which the farmers have built to keep the sea out of their fields, and along the dyke the Archangelica grows in profusion. Eggs and larvae were plentiful, but in no case more than four larvae on one plant. I put my net together and waited for butterflies, but a strong wind was blowing which almost made me give up for the day, when a female fluttered through the fields, stopping to lay an egg here and there. I saw that the specimen was a damaged one, and thought that it would be best to watch it for a while, so got into a ditch where the food plant was most abundant, and the butterfly soon settled close to me and laid an egg on the top of a leaf, then went underneath and laid another, and finally crawled down the stem, or rather backed down, laying a third egg at the juncture of the three footstalks of the leaves. As it was flying off I caught it and boxed the eggs. Two of these hatched August 31st, the third did not hatch, although the larva was fully formed within. The egg stage is thus about nine days, and from laying of eggs to chrysalis is less than a month under favorable circumstances.

Regarding the feeding habits of larvae, Scudder says (authority Mead) that "they are very susceptible to cold, prolonged darkness, or confinement of any kind, and when not feeding they either rest on the leaves in full sunlight or bask on the hot stones." My experience at Metis and Kamouraska does not corroborate these statements, for not having any proper breeding cages with me I kept my larvae in the absolutely light-proof boxes used for photographic plates, and though I had at times as many as sixty in a box, I never had a healthier lot of larvae. The young larvae when at rest certainly lie on the top of the leaves in the sunshine, though you will rarely find a full-grown one in this position, but search the stem and the old ones are easily seen, and smelt too. Several times I visited the plants before breakfast, about 6.30 a.m., and found that all were at work and none at all on the stems, and on August 26th some were seen feeding at 8.30 p.m., though moonlight is not good for observation of this kind.

In the chrysalis there are two distinct forms, the green and yellow, and the light and dark brown, and I find that all my larvae which suspended themselves on stems of the plant have produced green pupae, while those that crawled into boxes and shelters that I provided for them have assumed the brown form.

The species is regarded as single brooded, quoting Scudder again, "flying in June and the first half of July, and is most abundant the latter half of June. Eggs have been obtained from June 14th for a month, some chrysalids carried south gave out the butterfly the same year, one in eighteen days."

If in the northern part of its range the butterflies fly through June and begin to lay eggs before the middle of the month, it seems probable that it should occur in a warmer region, such as Kamouraska, even earlier, and there would be ample time for a second brood before the middle of August, but to settle this point it would be necessary to see the butterflies on the wing and eggs laid in June, and chrysalids in July, and some member of our newly formed Quebec branch could easily solve the matter. Finding the species in so many stages at the same time seems to me to favor the idea that there are two broods, as in my experience in species that are single brooded the imagos appear for a short period with great regularity, and in the early stages the moulting and pupating of all are within a comparatively short time of one another, but in two brooded species the first brood is regular and the second not, while in many brooded species, such as *Pieris rapae* and *Grapta interrogationis*, the last broods seem hopelessly mixed up.

The last female that I saw on the wing at Kamouraska seemed to be a perfect specimen and if single brooded must have spent at least eleven months in the chrysalis, which Gosse states (Can. Ent. XV, 45) is the period of this species in Newfoundland.

Dr. Fyles, in commenting on the paper, said that he had received some of the larvæ from Mr. Winn, with a supply of food-plant; when this was exhausted he endeavored to find a substitute, but the larvæ were very hard to please. Eventually he succeeded in getting them to eat the leaves of parsnip, though they would not touch carrot, on which the larva of *P. asterias* feeds. He found that the chrysalids formed on the stem of the plant were like it green in color, while those which transformed in the box were brown. (Specimens of both were exhibited). He had five chrysalids in good condition, from which he hoped to obtain the butterflies,

Dr. William Saunders, the original describer of the species, upon being called upon said his specimens were sent to him from Newfoundland by a collector there, and he had never met with it personally. He was very much interested in the careful work detailed by Mr. Winn; just such work should be done in every species, studying it in every stage until its life history was completely known. The society has shewn by its publication of so many original papers in the *Canadian Entomologist* that it fully appreciates this line of work, and he believed that in no other publication had so many and such valuable papers appeared as in our own magazine.

The meeting then adjourned, it being six o'clock p.m.

THE CONVERSAZIONE.

On the evening of the 8th November a very enjoyable Conversazione was held at the Natural History Society's Museum.

This was got up by the Montreal Branch in celebration of the 25th anniversary of its formation, and with the kind assistance of the Natural History Society and Microscopical Society of Montreal and the Parent Entomological Society, which all gave grants towards the expenses as well as other assistance.

Unfortunately there were other powerful attractions as Lord and Lady Aberdeen were making their farewell visit to Montreal and it was also the opening week of the much advertised new theatre, Her Majesty's, but in spite of these other attractions about two hundred guests accepted the invitation. The guests were received by Mr. Henry H. Lyman, President of the Entomological Society, and Mrs. Clarence Lyman, Dr. F. J. Adams, President of the Natural History Society, and Mrs. Adams, Mr. Albert Holden, President of the Microscopical Society, and Mrs. Holden. Among those present were noticed Mr. Samuel Finley, a Governor of McGill University, and Mrs. Finley, Dr.

and Mrs. Wm. Saunders of Ottawa, Mr. and Mrs. Fysshe, Mr. and Mrs. Beaudry, Dr. Girdwood, F.R.S.C., Prof. of Chemistry in McGill University, and Mrs. Girdwood, Rev. Dr. and Mrs. Campbell, Mr. J. H. Joseph, Prof. MacBride, Prof. of Zoology in McGill University, Mrs. Cox, Mr. Sumner, Mr. J. D Evans, C.E. of Trenton, Mr. and Mrs. G. O. Dunlop, Prof. and Mrs. Donald, Mr. F. S. Lyman, Q.C. and Miss Lyman and Miss Cassels, of Washington, Mr. and Miss Scott, the Messrs. and Miss Brainerd, the Misses Dunlop, Dr. Shirres, Dr. Deeks, Mr. Winn, Mr. Clarence Lyman, Mr. Walter Lyman, Mr. and Mrs. Plimsoll, the Misses Redpath, Mr. and Mrs. Lighthall, Mr. De Sola, Mr. and Miss Cramp, Mr. and Mrs. Gibb, Mr. C. T. Williams, Mr. Stevenson Brown, Mr. J. B. Williams, F.Z.S., Mr. Dearness and Mr. W. E. Saunders, of London, Mr. Gibson, of Toronto and many others.

Shortly after 9 o'clock the three presidents proceeded to the platform, which was decorated with palms and chrysanthemums, along with Rev. Dr. Bethune of Port Hope, Dr. Fletcher of Ottawa, and Rev. Dr. Fyles of Quebec. Mr. Lyman called the gathering to order, the guests seating themselves to listen to the addresses, and in a brief address welcomed the guests to this celebration and traced rapidly the history of the Branch from its formation on the 16th October, 1873, pointing out that so far as he could ascertain it was the third senior existing entomological society in North America, being only antedated by the American Entomological Society of Philadelphia and the parent society at London, Ont., and stating that 217 meetings of the branch had been held, at which over 200 original papers had been read, of which some 80 had been published.

Mr. Lyman briefly referred to the vast economic importance of the study and as an illustration mentioned that during the current year the State and Federal authorities of the United States were devoting no less a sum in the aggregate than about $350,000.00 to the prosecution of economic entomology.

Mr. Lyman expressed his regret that he had been unable to secure the attendance of any entomologists from the neighbouring Republic although pressing invitations had been sent to Dr. Howard, Dr. Holland, Prof. Webster, Mr. Slingerland and Mrs. Slosson.

After announcing that Dr. Bethune, Dr. Fletcher and Dr. Fyles would also deliver addresses, Mr. Lyman resigned the chair in favour of Dr. Adams.

The Rev. Dr. Bethune, Port Hope, one of the founders of the original society, and second President, spoke briefly of the work done by the parent society, and of the rise and progress of entomology in Canada.

Dr. Fletcher, the Dominion Official Entomologist, Ottawa, touched upon the economic aspect of the subject, and the value of a knowledge of entomology.

The Rev. Dr. Fyles, President of the recently formed Quebec branch, spoke briefly of the work done in that city. He also presented greetings from his branch to the Montreal branch.

On the conclusion of the addresses the majority of the guests repaired to the museum up stairs, though some lingered in the reception hall to examine the many beautiful objects, chiefly of an entomological character, which were exhibited under a large number of powerful microscopes by members of the Microscopical Society. The stairway and entrance to the museum had been tastefully decorated with flags, butterfly nets and other entomological paraphernalia, two long handled nets for working electric arc lights being especially noticeable.

The orchestra under the direction of Mr. Charles Reichling, which had been playing during the reception of the guests, took up a position in the gallery and discoursed sweet music during the remainder of the evening.

In the museum hall a fine exhibit of insects, chiefly Lepidoptera, was displayed the show cases being further embellished with potted plants.

The exhibits were chiefly furnished by the members of the Montreal branch, Mr. Lyman, the President and Mr. Winn, the Vice-President, each showing 30 cases exemplifying all the families of North American Lepidoptera except the micros. Mr.

Brainerd showed six cases beautifully illustrating the life histories of a number of interesting species, while Mr. Dunlop contributed an equal number of cases of striking exotic species. Mr. Norris showed about half a dozen drawers illustrating Montreal species as well as the method of preparing and spreading lepidoptera, while Mr. J. B. Williams exhibited an interesting case showing the life history of the Walking Stick (Diapheromera Femorata). In addition to these exhibits by members of the branch, the Museum Committee of McGill University contributed six large cases of strikingly beautiful tropical butterflies mounted on the Denton tablets, while the Natural History Society showed its collection of Canadian Coleoptera and a few drawers of exotic Lepidoptera.

Refreshments were served about half past ten o'clock and a very enjoyable evening was brought to a close shortly after 11 p.m.

ELECTION OF OFFICERS.

After a meeting of the Council had been held for the transaction of business, the general session of the Society was resumed at 11 o'clock a. m., Dr. Bethune occupying the chair at the request of the President. The first proceeding was the election of officers for the ensuing year, which resulted as follows : See page 2.

THE FARMERS' GARDEN AND ITS INSECT FOES.

Rev. Thomas W. Fyles, D.C.L., F.L.S., South Quebec.

Once upon a time some new tenants came to a farm-house in the neighborhood in which I was residing. A former owner of the place had enclosed a piece of ground on one side of the house and had formed a lawn and flower-beds, and planted fruit bushes and ornamental shrubs. The place was a quarter of a mile from my home; and one day I walked down to see the new-comers. I found them busily engaged in driving half-a dozen hogs into the enclosure I have mentioned. I ventured to suggest that the animals would play sad work with the flowers. This was the reply—"from a heart as rough as Esau's hand,"—"Flowers, flowers! The only flowers we care about are cauliflowers!" The answer expressed the prevailing contempt, in that comparatively new settlement, for everything like home adornment. I ought not to say *everything*, for an exception must be made in favor of bed-quilts. The females of that neighborhood spent much of their spare time in the manufacture of bed quilts. The choicest kinds were white, and had Turkey-red flowers and fruits, and intensely green leaves of impossible shapes trailing all over them. The possessor of a dozen varieties of such "spreads" was a proud woman. She would occasionally hang her art-treasures in the open space in front of her house, to excite the envy and admiration of her female neighbors, who would occasionally light their pipes and stroll round to examine the patterns.

The typical farm-house, at that time, and in that part of the country, was a story-and-a-half, oblong building, covered with rough, unpainted, hemlock boards. The main door was at one end and opened into the living-room. It and a trap-door into the cellar were, in some instances, sheltered by a rude veranda. In the door, near the bottom, was usually found a circular hole with a lengthened slit above it, in which a light shutter fitted to the opening, was suspended on a wire to allow egress and ingress to the cat. A story was told of a man who had two such openings made—a larger and a smaller—for the convenience of the cat and the kitten.

This primitive dwelling usually stood on a knoll in a yard open to the road. The yard, which was the receptacle for the refuse of the house thrown from windows and doors, was encumbered with logs drawn up for fuel, and was littered with chips. It was the common play-ground—if I may be allowed so to *generalize*—of the poultry, pigs and pickaninnies ; and in it, in the summertime, one or two "smudges" were kept burning to drive away the mosquitos and black-flies.

The vegetables used by the people of that locality at that time were chiefly of field growth,—potatoes, Swedish turnips and pumpkins. The fruits were apples, from seedling and ungrafted trees, and the wild berries of the country,—strawberries from the meadows, raspberries from the pastures and roadsides, and " high-bush " cranberries from the swamps. The raspberries were spread on sheets of hemlock-bark, and dried in the sun for winter use ; the strawberries and cranberries were preserved with maple-sugar. I remember my only experience of cranberry jam. It was at a party to which I was invited. I found myself incommoded by the large, flat, crustaceous seeds with which the preserve abounded. I stole a glance around to see how my neighbors disposed of these seeds and I found that the orthodox plan was to swallow them whole. I tried this for the occasion, but from that day forth I carefully avoided " cranberry sass "—as it was called in the vernacular.

Happily the race I have spoken of have passed away. Many of them were seized with the " Western fever," and moved to North Dakota and other distant places, to retard civilization in them. Their rude dwellings also are gone, or have been altered out of recognition. The succeeding generation is more enlightened and refined. The change has been largely brought about by the agricultural association and county fairs, which, through their prizes given for the best-cultivated farms, the best gardens, the finest vegetables, fruits, and flowers, and the choicest productions in the arts of life, have done a vast amount of good. Improved schools, superintended by well-trained teachers, have fitted the rising generation to appreciate the agricultural and horticultural literature that has been widely circulated—reports and bulletins from our Experimental Farms and Scientific Associations ; papers and magazines on rural affairs ; and last, and I venture to say not least, illustrated catalogues from our seedmen and florists. These last have done much to create and foster a taste for horticulture. Now moreover improved machinery and garden implements enable the farmer to carry on his gardening operations with ease and expedition ; so that good results around the homestead may be obtained without detriment to the operations on the farm at large.

My ideal of a farmer's homestead is this : a house facing the road, but a little back from it, having convenient verandahs—that to the front being furnished with wide-meshed wire netting extending from its base to its roof, for the support of such climbing plants as the English honeysuckle and Jackman's clematis. The Virginia creeper, which is a favorite on account of its free growth, is apt to hold moisture and rot the wood-work. If grown at all it should be often trimmed.

Behind the main building should be an extension connected with the dairy, wood-shed, etc., and facing this a yard, approached by a sideroad, and bounded by a shed for vehicles. Beyond this shed should be the cattle-yards with shelter for the animals, and then the barns.

In the lee of the buildings, though not in their shadow, I would have the ground for small fruits, and beyond it the orchard. The bushes should be planted in rows, and far enough apart to allow a steady horse with a cultivator to pass between them. Nothing is gained by crowding plants. The use of the cultivator and hoe should keep the ground around and under the bushes clean.

The kitchen-garden proper should be unincumbered with bushes and permanent paths, so that the manure carts may be driven anywhere over it, and the ground thoroughly ploughed in the fall, and again in the spring. I would have no partitions of beds except such as might be made with the hoe or shovel as occasion required.

The drive to the front of the house should come with a sweep round the central bed, and be flanked with flower-borders. Beyond these would be the lawn, with ornamental shrubs planted singly or in clumps : syringas, Tartarian honeysuckle, viburnum plicatum, the purple-leaved berberry, and lilacs white and purple.

In the front bed the house-plants moved from the windows when the green blinds were replaced would find suitable summer quarters, and a vase in the centre of it containing trailing and other plants would add to its beauty.

For the flanking beds, plants that require little attention and make a good show are desirable. To my mind the old favourites are the best—low shrubs like the Mahonia, moss-rose, and flowering currant; St. Joseph lilies; perennials such as iris, Chinese pœony, dicentra, perennial phlox and bee-larkspur; biennials as the Sweet William, Canterbury bell, foxglove and hollyhock—the last named, judiciously placed, produces a fine effect. Such plants require but little time for their cultivation. The forking in of a dressing of manure, an occasional shifting of place and dividing of them to prevent overgrowth, are the main operations required.

Around the whole should be a sheltering belt of evergreens—young pines, hemlocks, and Norway spruce. A few inexpensive rustic seats placed here and there under the trees would give an air of repose to the scene.

Supposing the buildings, yards, gardens and orchard to occupy five acres out of a hundred acre farm, the space will be well and profitably taken up.

Now what insect foes would the owner of such a property have to contend with The insect spoilers are numerous. For convenience we may group them into—

    (I.) Those that suck.
    (II.) Those that bite.

Each group may be sub-divided into—

    (1) Open workers.
    (2) Hidden workers.

And the methods to be taken against them may be spoken of as:

    (a) Preventive.
    (b) Destructive.

Of insects that suck the different kinds of plant-lice and scale-insects are most to be dreaded. They belong to the families APHIDÆ, COCCIDÆ and COCCINÆ in the order HEMIPTERA.

Some species of them are familiar to many persons. Their fondness for house plants has brought them into notice; and the difficulties experienced in exterminating them have created a desire for further information as to their nature and habits.

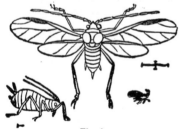

The perfect male and female aphides appear late in the year (Fig 6). The female deposits egg-like capsules upon the stems and branches of the food plant of her kind. Each capsule contains a perfect louse, which, in early Spring, bursts from its envelope and becomes a stem-mother capable of producing 90 or 100 creatures after her own likeness, and as prolific as herself. Seven or eight generations of such agamic producers succeed each other—their numbers increasing by geometrical progression till they count up to billions.

Fig. 6.

The stem-mother of the aphis has a flask-like body from which project two small spouts. Its head is furnished with a proboscis, which the inscet drives into the substance of the leaf or bark of its food-plant, for the purpose of imbibing the sap. In the process of digestion, the sap imbibed is converted into the "honey-dew" which the insect now and again ejects from the spouts above metioned.

The plant is injured, in the first place by the withdrawal of nourishment from it, and in the second, by the clogging of its stomata, or breathing-pores by the accumulation of the viscid honey-dew.

Now it is evident that the aphides cannot be assailed through their mouths by poisonous spraying, as the leaf-eating insects can. They cannot be poisoned, but they can be suffocated. Whatever effectually closes their spiracles brings death to them. Spraying with kerosine emulsion, applications of whale-oil, size, pyrethrum, tobacco smoke, are all effective.

To witness the deadly effects of oil upon an insect, apply with a feather or camel's-hair brush a drop of linseed oil to the body of a troublesome hornet or bumble-bee buzzing in the window. The end comes quickly ! The oil is not taken into the stomach of the insect, but is spread over its body, and clogs its breathing-pores, and the insect dies.

The aphides left to run their course, at length give rise to a generation of winged insects ; and these proceed to make the preliminary arrangements for the next year's round of aphidean gatherings and festivities.

The aphides are named according to the plants they frequent. Thus we have :—
The aphis of the apple, *A. mali*, Fabricius.
"   "   plum leaves, *A. prunifolii*, Fitch.
"   "   currant, *A. ribis*, Linnæus.
"   "   cherry, *Myzus cerasi*, Fabricius.
"   "   cabbage, *A. brassicæ*, Linnæus, etc, etc.

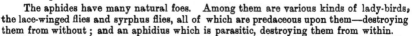

An easy way of smoking a house-plant is to turn an empty flour barrel over it, at the same time inserting a suitable vessel containing two or three pinches of tobacco and a small live coal. The smoke will soon do its work.

For the destruction of that troublesome insect the woolly aphis or "American Blight" (*Schizoneura lanigera*, Hausmann) (Fig. 7) which is found in white patches on the apple trees, the use of a scrubbing brush with diluted soft soap is recommended. By this means the insects are crushed and the tree cleansed at the same time. The house plants may be freed from that trouble-pest, the common mealy-bug (*Dactylopius adonidum*, Linnæus) by more gentle treatment of like nature.

Fig. 7.

The aphides have many natural foes. Among them are various kinds of lady-birds, the lace-winged flies and syrphus flies, all of which are predaceous upon them—destroying them from without ; and an aphidius which is parasitic, destroying them from within.

Insects even more difficult to deal with than the aphides are the scale insects. The scrubbing-brush and soft soap may be used for their discomfiture. All the insects that we have yet considered work in the open air. There are others that live by suction, but operate under ground. The most formidable of these is the Dog-day Harvest Bug, *Cicada canicularis*, Harris.

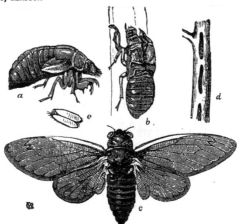

Fig. 8.

I made acquaintance with this insect many years ago, in Montreal. I was walking up Mountain Street, and, when near the top of it I saw a very seedy looking individual of the bug tribe creep from the soil at the foot of a large elm-tree (Fig. 8a) and begin to climb the trunk. I sat down and watched it. After ascending about two feet it dug its claws (It was very well provided with claws!) into the irregularities of the bark and took a firm hold. It then commenced to writhe and twist as if it were taken with a violent internal disorder. Surely something will come of all this commotion I said to myself; and something did result—its skin was suddenly rent from the head to the abdomen (Fig. 8b), and the creature began coolly to crawl out of its own skin, drawing out its legs as if it were taking off its boots. When quite free it shook out its wings, and in a few moments presented the appearance of a perfect cicada. (Fig. 8c.)

The female cicada is furnished with a remarkable organ, one part of which resembles a double key-hole saw. With this she cuts into the bark of the tree and forms a receptacle for her eggs. These eggs she carefully deposits. After a while they hatch, and the larvæ which come from them find their way to the roots of the tree, into which they thrust their beaks. Then commences the work of suction that lasts for a length of time—the juices of the tree being the only nourishment the creatures receive. One species of cicada (*C. septemdecim* Linneus) spends 17 years at this employment.

It is in orchards of some standing that the cicadas are most likely to establish themselves; and it may be that the operations of these hidden foes have more to do with the occasional shortage of fruit than people have an idea of. How to reach the spoilers is a problem. Probably one of the best suggestions that has been made is, to enclose the orchard with a sufficient fence, and then, to do as the people above-mentioned did with the garden—turn the hogs into it. The animals will grub (*grub* is a very appropriate word!) about the roots, and destroy a variety of larvæ and pupæ. They will loosen the sod and let in the air; and their droppings will help to fertilize the soil. The use of the bush-harrow and the rake, and the scattering of a little grass seed after the animals have been removed will repair the damage they may have done.

Against the biting insects the campaign should begin after the leaves have fallen. The fruit-trees should then be carefully examined for the eggs of some kinds and the cocoons of others. The beadlike eggs of the Brown Vapourer (*Orgyia antiqua*, Linnæus,) attached to the vacated cocoons of the mother insects, and the egg-patches of the Gray Vapourer (*O. leucostigma*, A. & S.), covered with a protective that resembles sugar frosting, will be found readily enough where the creatures are plentiful. The brown elongated masses of the eggs of the Lackey Moths (*Clisiocampa Americana*, Harris, and *C. disstria*, Hubner,) should be looked for on the twigs (Fig. 9), and when found cut away and destroyed, as should also the cocoons of the Saturnians.

As soon as the buds appear in the spring, Paris green and water well stirred should be applied to the fruit trees by means of a force pump and spraying nozzle. This spraying will destroy the injurious "bud-worms," "leaf crumplers," "canker worms," etc., and later applications will overcome those troublesome pests the "tent-caterpillars" and "fall web-worms," and other less conspicuous foes.

Fig. 9.

White hellebore, applied with a dredger, or mixed with water and sprinkled with a can over the fruit-bushes will kill the larvæ of the "currant saw-fly" (*Nematus ventricosus* Klug) Fig 10, and those of the span-worm (*Enfitchia ribearia* Fitch) Fig 11. A like application to the rose bushes will free those plants from "slug-worm" (*Selandria rosæ* Harris), and from the leaf-crumpling caterpillars of the pretty little brown and white Tortrix *Penthina nimbatana* Clemens).

With one notable exception our butterflies can hardly be said to be injurious. The larvæ of most of them feed on weeds or plants of little value. A few of them feed on cultivated plants.

Papilio turnus Linnæus, feeds on the apple, etc.

P. asterias Fabricius, feeds on the parsnip, carrot, etc.

Pieris oleracea Bd. feeds on the potherbs.

Grapta interrogationis Fab. feeds on the hops, etc.

G. progne Cramer, and *G. gracilis* G. and R. feed on the currant.

Thecla strigosa Harris, feeds on the plum.

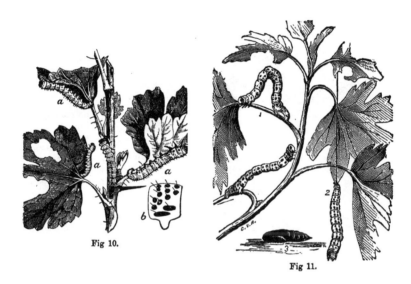

Fig 10.

Fig 11.

But these insects are few in number, and so widely scattered, that they do little, if any, harm.

Fig 12.

The one exception is *Pieris rapæ* Linnæus, the " cabbage-butterfly " (Fig 2). This is an exceedingly troublesome insect. The best method to check its ravages that I know is to set an intelligent child to work to pick off the caterpillars (Fig 12 a) from the plants, and to crush them under foot. The chrysalids (Fig 12 b) of this species, and of others, may often be found attached to fences and buildings.

I lately had the opportunity of witnessing the proceedings of a Papilio brevicauda larva when about to change to a chrysalis. It spun, on the side of a twig, a little pad, to which it attached itself, having climbed into a proper position for doing so. When it had settled itself, it turned its head to its back and ejected, through its mouth, a drop of mucous which it drew out in a silken thread, and attached to the twig. It then turned its head round on the other side, and deposited another drop on the same spot, drawing it out and fastening it as before, thus making a complete loop. The ends of this it strengthened with a branching web. Having completed its arrangements it curved its shoulders, drew in its head, and remained quiescent for two or three days—that is, till its loop and other fastenings were firm and dry. Then its skin was rent at the thorax, and, by a succession of heaving and swaying motions, was worked back, segment by segment, till it reached the extremity or cremaster, from which, in a little while, it fell away, leaving a delicate green chrysalis with a row of yellow knobs on either side, and with pretty salmon-coloured spiracles.

The farmer no longer dreads the Colorado potato-beetle, *Doryphora decem-lineata*

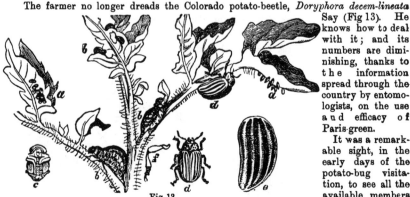

Say (Fig 13). He knows how to deal with it; and its numbers are diminishing, thanks to t h e information spread through the country by entomologists, on the use a n d efficacy o f Paris-green.

It was a remarkable sight, in the early days of the potato-bug visitation, to see all the available members of a farmer's house-

Fig 13.

hold busily engaged in beating off the "bugs" with small sticks, and catching them in milk cans; now and again emptying their prey into the fire over which soap was in the making, or pig's food in the cooking. "*All was fish that came to net*," and so beetles and their parasites—"friends and foes," were—

——— "in one red burial blent."

Men are sometimes surprised to find the potato-beetles feeding on the tomato and tobacco plants in their gardens. The insect in its native haunts fed on the wild potato, *Solanum rostratum*. Of the *Solanceæ*, or Nightshade Family, to which the potato belongs, there are in north America six genera—not counting the South American genus Petunia, now so largely cultivated in gardens. They are (1) *Solanum*, nightshade; (2) *Physalis*, ground cherry; (3) *Nicandra*, apple of Peru; (4) *Hyoscyamus*, henbane; (5) *Datura*, thorn apple; (6) *Nicotiana*, tobacco. The first of these includes the potato, the egg-plant, and the tomato, all of which are eaten with avidity by the beetle. Deprived of its favourite supplies, the insect turns to such other members of the family as may grow within its reach. I have found it upon Physalis and Datura, as well as upon Nicotiana.

Of enemies working covertly, the cut-worms are among the most troublesome. They are larvæ of certain kinds of Noctuid, or night-flying moths. Whenever a farmer sees a

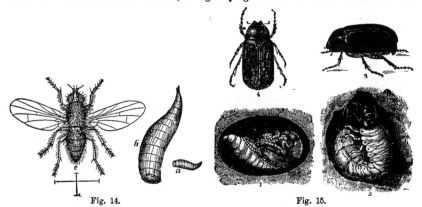

Fig. 14.   Fig. 15.

blade of corn falling over and turning yellow, or a cabbage-plant bitten off near the ground, he may be very sure that a cut-worm is working there, and should use a spud or pointed stick to unearth the spoiler. To foil these pests the young plants should be earthed up as soon and as far as possible, for the creatures crawl over the surface, at night, and cannot ascend a mound of crumbling earth.

Young onions are damaged both by the cut-worms and by the maggots of the onion-fly, *Phorbia ceparum* Meigen (Fig. 14). The former work singly ; the latter, in groups. Both should be carefully dug out and destroyed. Dry soot scattered over the onion-bed is believed to be serviceable in keeping away the fly.

The "white-grubs," or larvæ of the May-beetle, *Lachnosterna fusca*, Frohl. (Fig 15) are well-known pests. In the fields the plough unearths them ; and the poultry, follow-ing in its wake, hold high carnival, and become fat and well-liking. In a thoroughly-worked garden the grubs find but little harborage.

The hidden pests above mentioned can be dealt with moie easily than some others.

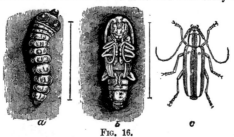

FIG. 16.

The apple-tree borer, *Saperda candida* Fab. (Fig. 16), works near the ground, in young trees, and so weakens the stems that sometimes, in a high wind, the trees are snapped off. The larvæ betray their presence by their *frass*. When this is the case a wire should be thrust into the tunnels, for the destruction of the occupants. A thick wash of soft shap applied to the stems in June will deter the beetles from laying their eggs upon t em.

There are other borers that injure other trees. It is in search of these that the woodpeckers work so systematically around the stems. The woodpeckers are among the fruit-grower's allies, and should not be molested.

Fig. 17.

The borer of the currant stems is the larva of a pretty little clear-wing moth, *Ægeria tipuliformis* Linnæus (Fig. 17). Late in the fall all un-healthy-looking stems in the red, white and black currant-bushes should be cut out and burned. The moths appear in June, and consort for safety with the small black wasps of the genera *Odynerus* and *Gorytes*, which they somewhat resemble. A child can soon learn to distinguish them from these, and can spend a few bright midday hours profitably in capturing the moths with a butterfly net. The capture of one female will save many currant stems from damage.

We have, then, glanced at some of the worst of the insect pests that frequent the farmer's garden. The study of them in their native haunts will be found full of interest and a knowledge of their proceedings and the various methods of counteracting them' will prove of great value, and ought not by any to be lightly esteemed.

ON THE NOCTUIDÆ OCCURRING AT TORONTO.

By Arthur Gibson, Toronto.

For some time past, in fact ever since the season of 1896, I have considered the Noctuids to be my special favourites amongst the Lepidoptera, and in view of this I thought a few remarks under the above heading might interest those present.

The Noctuidæ comprise that large family of Lepidoptera known as the "Owl-let" moths, or night-flyers. As a rule, the members of this family feed by night and rest during the daytime. Some of the larvæ of these moths, commonly known as cut-worms, are amongst the most destructive of our caterpillars. The ravages which they have been recorded as making, resulting in the losses of certain agricultural products, have been enormous. Around Toronto, as far as I know, their devastations have not amounted to very much, comparatively speaking. In the regions most infested with these pests, the loss to agriculture is tremendous, but the ravages thus caused have been reported so fully in Government publications that it is not necessary for me to say anything further about their destructive propensities. It might not be out of place, however, to mention that on account of these larvæ being night feeders, all of their devastations are perpetrated after dark, in the daytime the caterpillars hiding under crevices, stones or any other article under which they can escape notice.

To the collector of these moths there are various novel ways of procuring specimens. The two most indulged in, in Toronto, are taking advantage of the electric lights, especially in the outer districts, and by the still better way of "sugaring" the trees. In the early part of the season, say until towards the last week in June, the Noctuids that are then flying seemingly prefer the electric lights to the "sugar"—such is my experience. By the first of July they start to come to the "sugar," and from then until the end of August, and even beginning of September, lots of good work can be accomplished. Some Noctuids which are often taken at "light" are seldom captured at "sugar," while on the

Fig. 18.

other hand specimens like the catocala are generally taken at "sugar." Relicta (Fig. 18) is about the only catocala which I have noticed around the lights to any extent. During the end of August of last season quite a number of Relictas were to be seen at "light," while I have, as yet, only met with one specimen at "sugar." Collecting with the aid of "sugar" is much the better way, not only as regards the number of specimens taken, but also in view of the variety of Noctuids secured. The season of 1897 was an ideal one for "sugaring" purposes in Toronto. One evening as many as 26 specimens of catocalæ were taken by Mr McDunnough and myself while out together, besides a large number of smaller interesting Noctuids.

It is safe to say that among the Noctuids we find some of our most beautiful moths, but on the other hand some of them are most inconspicuous in color, being of a dull gray, brown, or black, or these colors combined.

In North America, according to Prof. J. B. Smith's List of Lepidoptera of Boreal America, there are recorded no less than 1841 distinct species of this great family of Noctuidae, and since the compilation of this list there have been several new species described. On my list I have marked off about 160 different species, which I have taken at Toronto, besides quite a number of unnamed species. Probably there occur several hundred more representatives.

Among the various genera there are to be found some very interesting species. The first thing I have marked of on my list is Raphia frater. This moth is of uncommon occurrence, the specimens I have being taken at light.

The genus Acronycta is an interesting one, some of the members being beautiful insects. Around Toronto, I have taken 10 different species, viz., occidentalis (Fig. 19),

Fig. 19.   Fig. 20.

morula, populi, Americana, dactylina, hastulifer, luteicoma, brumosa, superans (Fig. 20), and funeralis. Of these probably funeralis is the most rare, while morula, dactylina and luteicoma are very scarce.

Harrisimemna trisignata, the only one of the genus, is a rather pretty moth; the three specimens I have were taken at light.

It is not necessary for me to mention every species of Noctuidae which I have taken, so I will just confine myself to the names of those which to me are considered of rare and of uncommon occurrence in the neighborhood of Toronto. In cases where it is possible I have mentioned whether the specimens were taken at "light" or at "sugar."

Microcoelia diphtheroides, fairly rare, taken at light.

Rhynchagrotis cupida, at sugar, very few taken. First time I took it was in 1896; very scarce since then.

Semiophora tenebrifera, one specimen at light.

Feltia venerabilis, only one specimen, taken at light.

Dicopis Grotei, one specimen taken at sugar, 13 June, 1896.

Mamestra imbrifera. Took one specimen of this beautiful insect, resting on the trunk of a tree, on the afternoon of 18th July, 1896.

Mamestra purpurissata, 1 sp. at light.

Mamestra grandis, 2 sp. at light.

Mamestra adjuncta, 1 sp. at light.

Mamestra latex, 1 sp. at light, 30th May, 1895, and one 9th May, 1896.

Mamestra rosea, very rare, two sp. at light, last capture 26th May, 1897.

Hadena lignicolor, rather uncommon, taken at sugar in June and July, 1895.

Dipterygia scabriuscula, 2 sp. taken at sugar.

Prodenia flavimedia, one sp. at light.

Trigonophora periculosa, 1 sp. at sugar and 1 at light.

Helotropha reniformis, fairly common, at sugar in 1896, rather scarce since then.

Hydroecia velata, 1 sp. taken at light.

Hydroecia cataphracta, 1 sp. at light, 9th May, 1894.

Pyrrhia umbra, 2 sp. at light, 4th May, 1896, and 2 sp. of the variety angulata on 20th June, 1896.

Orthosia ferruginoides, 2 sp. taken 21st Sept., 1895.

Scopelosoma Moffatiana, one of the early appearing Noctuids, 2 sp. taken at light, 20th April, 1896; also observed last season.

Scopelosoma ceromatica, also an early Noctuid, 4 sp. taken at light, 20th April, 1896. I have never taken either of the last two named, in the fall of the year, although I understand they hibernate in the imago state.

4 EN.

Calocampa curvimacula, very nice thing, 2 sp. taken at light, 20th April, 1896, and 1 sp. 17th May, 1897.

Cucullia asteroides, 2 bred specimens.

Cucullia intermedia, 3 sp. at light, 2 on 20 April and 1 on 16th April, 1896.

Among the Plusias there are some fine things. I have taken 8 different species marked off on my list, viz, ærea, aereoides, balluca (Fig. 21), striatella, bimaculata,

Fig. 21.   Fig. 22.

precationis, ampla, and simplex (Fig. 22), together with one un-named. Of these striatella, balluca, and ampla are the rarest, with simplex and precationis the commonest. All my Plusias were taken at light.

Heliothis armiger, one sp. taken 22nd Sept., 1895.

Alaria florida, very pretty moth, 4 specimens taken at light in 1894, never very common.

As to the Catocalas, I have taken 14 different species at sugar, the principal captures

being, grynea, ultronia (Fig. 23), a beautiful variety of ilia, briseis, relicta, (Fig. 18), habilis, neogama (3rd Aug., '96) and retecta. The season of 1896 was by far the best I have yet experienced in collecting Catocalas, such species as ilia, cerogama, uniguga, and parta (Fig. 24) being very common. During the past season I did not notice a single specimen of ilia. I understand that O. cara was taken in Toronto last season.

Panopoda rufimargo, one specimen, taken at light.

Fig. 23.

Homoptera nigricans, one specimen at light.

Bomolocha baltimoralis, 2 sp. at light.

Brephos infans, one specimen taken on 11th April, and one observed on 16th April, 1898.

I have brought to the meeting some of the species mentioned in my paper, also a few "uniques" which, as yet, I have not got identified. Some of these will no doubt interest certain of the members present.

FIG. 24.

At a future date I may be able to relate, in a much better manner, something on the "Noctuidae occurring at Toronto," which may be of more interest than the article I have just read.

Mr. Gibson also exhibited specimens on the following very rare butterflies which he was so fortunate as to have captured at Toronto : Thecla Ontario, Pamphila Baracoa and Brettus ; also Pyrameis carye, which was taken by Mr. Tyers. T. Ontario has only been twice taken before in the Province from which it is named ; the other three are new to our Canadian list.

Mr. D. Brainerd disagreed with the writer of the paper regarding the superiority of light to sugar as an attraction for moths. Mr. Winn said that he had found sugar the best bait until June 15th, but after that flowers were the most attractive. He had taken 160 specimens between 7.15 and 8.15 one evening.

THE COLLECTOR
AND HIS RELATION TO PURE AND APPLIED ENTOMOLOGY.

By F. M. WEBSTER, WOOSTER, OHIO.

The insect collector may or may not be a professional entomologist. He may be a minister, doctor, lawyer, merchant, soldier or sailor. He may be confined within the walls of a counting-room, bank, office, study or other place of occupation, during eight or ten hours of the six days of the week, for eleven months of the year, or he may be camped for months in the wilderness, or spend months on the sea, with an occasional respite of a few weeks on shore. There are few professional collectors, the major portion of these being engaged in other pursuits, and spending the time generally devoted to rest or recreation by the majority of people, in the collection of insects, in itself a most pleasing and healthy sort of recreation, provided ones tastes trend in that direction. Thus it occurs that a collector may be confined to a limited area, or he may be able to carry on his work in widely distant localities. I know of a soldier, wounded and in a hospital, who managed to make a considerable collection of insects and especially such as are readily attracted to light, and another whose business, that of a commercial traveller, takes him from one end of the country to another. I have in my own collection, specimens taken at almost all hours of the day or night, under almost every condition imaginable, and in as great a diversity of localities.

Outside of professional entomologists, the collection of insects is largely a labor of love, with no hope or expectation of any compensation whatever. This, then, would appear to be the proper place to discuss the value of these self imposed labors to the science of entomology.

While much has been said and written, both pro and con, relating to the value of the services of those men and woman who collect but do not study insects, it has always appeared to me that in this, as in almost everything else, we should make a distinction between the careful collector and the one who, strictly speaking, could hardly be termed a collector at all. Of course industry and energy here as elsewhere, count for much, but care, neatness and accuracy are imperative. Then, again, there has existed a certain condition of affairs, happily now fast disappearing, under which a collector was obliged to humbly submit his hard earned material to a specialist for determination, which specialist, after condescending to go over it, retained the specimens for his trouble, and in the case of new forms, frequently forgot to give credit to the collector when naming and describing them. It was thought sufficient to state that specimens were from Canada, California or Texas. The description being sometimes drawn up from a single specimen, thought to be typical of course, because it was the only one in the hands of the describer, was often faulty, so that the danger to the pure science from discolored or deformed material getting into such hands was very considerable. It goes without saying if you place a lot of carelessly collected and prepared material in the hands of a specialist, who is simply a species maker, and whose judgment and accuracy is not above question, the result will be not only n. gen. et sp., *ad infinitum*, but time has shown that the sort of entomology that such work represents had best be spoken of in connection with an ?.

But this is one extreme and one that is fast being eliminated, all specialists of repute now giving full credit to the collector for material placed at their disposal, and frequently this is done at the request of the specialist himself. It seems to me that this is one of the most encouraging evidences of progress in entomological research, as the collector soon finds that with credit there, invariably, goes more or less responsibility, and we therefore get better and more careful collecting, while the specialist or systematist is placed in possession of better material and more elaborate data, and is thus better enabled to avoid mistakes and synonyms. But we must not lose sight of the fact that this material and data must be supplied by the collector, who may be so situated that he is not able to work up his material properly, while the systematist is often equally unable to secure these by his own efforts; and we thus have a division of labor, which, if faithfully carried out by both parties, can only result in much good, and material progress in our beloved science.

For my own part, I have come to look upon the labors of the careful collector, as having much the same relation to the science of entomology, as those of Livingstone and Stanley have to the advance of civilization in Southern Africa. These latter gentlemen did not fell trees and plow and sow, but they paved the way for these, and made civilization possible. The collector is the advance discoverer, who must be followed by the systematist before the biologist can commence his labors. We first must get our species, and then so define it as to prevent its being continually confused with other forms, else we cannot study either its own life or its relation to other species. In the history of the advance of civilization we have, first, the discoverer, next, the pioneer agriculturist with his log cabin, followed by cities and schools and churches and railways, all the accompaniments of civilized life, but all preceded by the one who first made his way through the trackless wastes and told of what he saw.

Now, about the collector and his work. He who cares nothing for habits, variations and geographical distribution, will accomplish the least for the advancement of the science, though, as has been stated, industry and push are neither one to be despised, and it is better to know that certain species are to be found in Canada, California or Texas, than not to know of their existence at all. It would be much more satisfactory to know just where in these areas the species were found, as all extend over a wide area and great variety of country. But just here let me call attention to a serious defect, and one that does not seem to be confined to the careless or inexperienced, viz., giving as localities of occurrence, isolated points, having local names which are unknown a few miles away, and are not to be found indicated on any of our maps. Such give no clue whatever to the one who is engaged in tracing out the geographical distribution of a species, as I have myself experienced after hours of fruitless search, finally giving up in despair. In all cases it is better to give exact localities with reference to their proximity to some point which is indicated on our maps; the approximate latitude and longitude will be the most stable and valuable of all, as the information can be used in any country and by the aid of very ordinary maps and charts. To those who object to taking the trouble to do this, let me suggest that other entomologists will there take up our work after we have followed Harris, Fitch, Riley, and more recently, Lintner and Maskell, on that long journey from which none return. We cannot, now, see what problems those who are to follow us may have to solve, nor can we determine the nature of the data that will be required for such solutions. Then, too, the foreign entomologist has frequently to turn to us for information regarding the distribution of both species and genera, and it is but justice to our fellows if we present our data in a manner that will be most intelligible to them. Some very good collectors, and not all of them American either, have overlooked this matter, and as a consequence we are sometimes left in the dark where we most needed light, and our colleagues really intended to supply it to us.

Altitude will not come amiss when you go over your notes, possibly twenty years hence, while food plants, food habits, relative abundance, and, indeed, almost any facts relative to the "sociology" of a species will be sure to be of use sometime, for someone. I am continually using data secured ten, fifteen, or twenty years ago, some of it at the time seeming to be hardly worth recording, but it is surprising how many good things in the way of specimens and facts we are continually turning up, by accident, as it were, oftentimes not realizing the full value of our "find" until years afterwards. A careful, faithful observation is never without value, as it either brings a new fact to light or else substantiates an old one. Insects do not necessarily act alike over the entire area of their distribution, and the man or woman who uses their own eyes is almost sure to see something that has not before been observed. Why ! I have gone to your fellow member, Mr. W. H. Harrington, again and again for facts regarding some of our insects that I have been observing for years, but he, with his close observation, has observed things that, if they were to be seen in my locality, were overlooked by me. We do not see everything going on about us, by any means, even we that are most in the field, and I have gone several hundred miles from home, and found certain insects there doing certain things that they were not observed to do at home, but as soon as I returned they were found to be engaged in precisely the same way that I had observed them elsewhere, and probably had been doing so all the time, but I did not happen to be a witness to the fact.

Of late we are hearing much relative to life zones, and, while it is hardly probable that we have at the present time sufficient definite information regarding the exact localities of occurrence among insects to enable us to say much in regard to these, as it is very easy to say too much, yet we all know that our species are not all of them generally distributed. Almost every collector will get species in his immediate neighborhood, sometimes in abundance, that are to be found rarely, if at all, elsewhere. There are certainly areas, over which a certain species will be found to occur in a greater or less abundance, while a few miles away it will appear to have given way to another. In almost every locality there is sure to be some particular spot that will be found especially rich in insect life. These favored spots may be a bit of woodland, a bank, a shaded ravine or a secluded valley, to which one can go with the assurance that he will secure something rare or new. The vegetation here may not differ materially from that of hundreds of other places, seemingly equally favored also by climate and elevation, yet a greater number of species seem to have gained a foothold, so to speak, here than elsewhere, and, somehow, are able to retain their hold. Just why this is true is not exclusively an entomological problem, but involves animal and vegetable life as a unit, and the insect collector can, if he will, pile up facts that will go a long way toward the settlement of problems not at present considered in connection with entomology at all. In other words, before we can do much with mapping out life zones, we must have a vast amount of information that can only be secured by the careful collector and observer. Not only must this data be secured, but it must be made available by being placed on record where it can be found by the great army of scientific men and women. I am well aware that there is in some quarters, an aversion to publishing detatched notes and observations and a tendency to hold fast to all such until a mass of material is thus secured sufficient for an extended and exhaustive discussion, but it has always appeared to me in a different light. Let us suppose that the science of entomology is an immense vase, as large as Ætna or Vesuvius, and this is shattered into fragments and scattered over the face of the earth, and entomologists, without definite knowledge of its original form or dimensions, are set to work to gather up these scattered fragments and reconstruct the vase. The fragments will of course be of every conceivable size and form and when brought together fit into each other perfectly, but many of them will be much alike in form so that the misplacing of a fragment will not infrequently occur, the mistake only being discovered by the proper one being found and fitted into place. A fragment may include a species, or any fact connected with its life history or habits. Now, let us suppose that a collector in Canada or elsewhere discovers a new species, while an entomologist in some distant part of the world discovers an allied form. Here are two fragments of science, separated, how widely we cannot know, until the intervening space has been filled in by collections, breedings and observations carried on by perhaps a dozen different individuals, possibly speaking half as many different languages, each contributing his fragment that is to fill in the space that divides the two forms and cements the two together, so to speak. Let me illustrate again, taking this time *Diaspis amygdali,* which has recently been discussed by Mr. Cockerell, Mr. Tryon, Mr. Lounsberry and myself, each presenting some new phase of its habits in various parts of the world. But one of my contributions related to a parasitic foe, described by Dr. Howard and reared by myself from the Coccid just mentioned, on trees recently imported from Japan, and also by Professor Marchal in Paris, Mr. E. E. Green in Ceylon, the late Mr. W. M. Maskell from Coccids received by him from Sydney, New South Wales, and at the United States Department of Agriculture, from an Aspidiotus from Georgia. Here we have fragments of our imaginary vase gathered from all quarters of the globe, not only fitting into the Diaspis fragment, but into others as widely separated as well. But suppose each one had kept his fragment to himself until such time as he could secure sufficient material for an exhaustive paper ; how long would each have stood in the way of the other in attempting to make use of his information ? " Rushing into print " is not to be commended, but a collector owes it to his fellows, and to entomology in general, to collect carefully and make all possible observations in connection with his material, placing the former on record for the benefit of his colleagues. The value of such work as is being done by Messrs. Harrington, Kilman, Bean, Fletcher, Lyman, Fyles and other Canadian entomologists, is not to be measured by our present knowledge, nor are the facts gained by these gentlemen to be taken separately, for, individually, they may be nearly or quite worthless and yet contain the very missing link that some other worker is hunting for, and through the lack of which he is unable to proceed in the solution of his own problem. Isolated from his fellows, working for the love of nature with little or no encouragement from those about him, it is not to be wondered at that a collector should think only of himself and his individual pleasure, becoming satisfied with dried corpses pinned in his cabinet and caring nought for the habits of these forms of life when active. But there is a world of riches at the door of every collector, isolation frequently becoming a blessing in disguise, for if he will but keep his eyes open and tell the world what he sees, he will ere long be surprised at the wealth of facts that he will accumulate.

The unknown in entomology may be likened to an ocean whose shores are lost in infinity, while the known is as a mill pond. There is so much to observe, so much to learn and life is so short. The collector, more than any one else, has opportunities for observation such as, if made with care and accurately recorded, may outweigh volumes of compilations that are too frequently permeated by the opinions of men, while original observations come direct from the hand of the Creator.

In conclusion, then, if there is any kind word of encouragement or of admonition that I can offer to the collector, whether he be located in city or country, let me do so here. Gather up these fragments of which I have been telling you, as you would grains of gold from among the sands, for sooner or later there will be a mint open for their reception and you will be surprised at their value. You will be more than once astonished to find that what you took for a worthless, fragmentary observation, will really turn out to be the keystone of an arch which has long been unfinished for lack of your fragment.

ENTOMOLOGY IN SCHOOLS.

By Wm. Lochhead, Ontario Agricultural College, Guelph.

The Annual Reports of this Society for 1896 and 1897 contain several very suggestive papers relating to the study of insects in our schools. Ex-President Dearness dealt somewhat fully with the subject in his two Presidential addresses, and the late Professor Panton outlined a method of presenting the subject from an economic standpoint. These three addresses, I remember, gave rise to a discussion among the members present on those occasions, and showed plainly that the time was ripe for introduction of nature-study into our schools. The members were unanimous in the opinion that insect life should form a portion of the children's study, at least, in our rural schools.

Mr. Dearness deserves much credit for his efforts towards the introduction of nature-study in his own County of Middlesex, and, in a general way, throughout the Province of Ontario. It is to be hoped that a little leaven will leaven the whole lump, and that every County Inspector will endeavor to the utmost to further this most desirable object. The compulsory study of Botany in the lower forms of our High Schools has already paved the way to a partial recognition of nature study as one worthy a place in our school curricula.

As a teacher of science for several years in some of our largest Collegiate Institutes, I may be permitted to use whatever influence I possess in urging on this good work, and towards this object this paper has been prepared.

This paper will consider the subject under the headings *Why?*, *How?*, and *When?*, *i.e.*, why should teachers introduce the study of insect life into their schools? Supposing its introduction is a wise procedure, how should it be taken up? and when should it be taken up?

WHY?

1. Because the study of insect life trains the eye to see, and the mind to draw proper conclusions from certain observed facts. The child learns clearly the relationship between causes and effects. It is remarkable the number of people who jump at conclusions without taking the time to relate cause and effect. Traditions and superstitions are still rampant, and many erroneous ideas of our forefathers are still too often accepted as truth in spite of the great advances that science has made during the last fifty years.

Pupils properly guided in their observations of nature will soon correct for themselves many of the errors that imperfect observers have made, and which have been handed down as truths. When the pupils have grown older, and have become engaged in the various pursuits of life, where alertness of mind, close observation, and accurate deductions count for much in the struggle for wealth, those who have been most carefully trained while young will, other things being equal, be most likely to succeed. It is a case of survival of the fittest in a struggle for existence. Comparisons, relations and judgment which are cultivated by a proper study of insect life are indispensable to the successful farmer, merchant and statesman. "If the farmer's boy learns how to accurately observe the process of nature with which farm produce deals, and the foes with which agriculture has to contend, are not the chances vastly increased that he will be successful in managing nature so as to get the greatest favors from this coy mistress of his life and fortune?"

2. Apart from the direct bearing on a successful life from a commercial standpoint, the study of nature reveals beauties and wonders all about us. Our eyes are opened to the wondrous transformation of insects, to the inter-relationships which exist between plants and insects, and among insects themselves. These are subjects of perennial interest, and the persons who have observed nature carefully will find in her not only " a resource and recreation, but an ever-faithful friend holding out comforting arms to those who are weary in soul and body." I think no one can be unhappy who has a true friend in nature, and can establish a living sympathy with everything about him, for Coleridge says :

> " He prayeth best who loveth best
> All things, both great and small ;
> For the dear God who loveth us,
> He made and loveth all."

A writer with wide experience says : " The element of education which is at present most lacking in our common schools is the training of the powers of observation. The children need above all things else to be taught to observe carefully and correctly and to state their observations in clear and terse language. The ordinary child, whether on the farm or in the town, actually sees comparatively little in the world about him. The wonders of the trees and plants in park or meadow, of birds and insects flying about the house, float like shadowy visions before his eyes. " Seeing, he sees not." He needs a teacher who can open his eyes and fix his mind on the realities among which his daily life is passed. This accurate observation of natural objects and facts is the only foundation on which scientific attainments can rest. The scientist is chiefly a man who sees better than his fellow men. But it is also a great help in practical life.

3. " No branch of science means more in actual dollars to the people of the country than Entomology. At least one-tenth of our crops is lost owing to the depredation of insects." It is surely a proper thing to instruct our children about the insects. They should learn to distinguish insects which are enemies from those which are friends. If our farmers and gardeners understood the method of dealing with the foes, and acted promptly and efficiently, the money value of this knowledge and action would equal the richest Klondike ever discovered. When Governments spend millions, and individuals risk their lives in opening up a mineral Klondike, it is not unreasonable to ask that more attention be paid to this insect Klondike at our doors. Let us educate the children to take an interest in insects, for in a few years they will have the control of the great money-producing areas, viz., the farms of our land. Dr. Fletcher has already treated of the value of Entomology from an economic aspect at a previous meeting of this society, and Mr. C. C. James, the Deputy Minister of Agriculture of Ontario, has also ably handled the subject in several addresses before Farmers' Institutes.

How.

Every good teacher will have his own method of presenting the subject, the one best suited to his own individuality, but there are general principles which he must follow :

1. As far as our rural schools are concerned, Entomology should be studied " without reference to systematic order or relationships." The whole study should be thoroughly informal in every respect ; it should be natural. No stated lesson should be assigned as a task beyond the general collecting of insects which the teacher may ask to be done occasionally. At first the teacher will simply guide the pupils by adroit questions such as these : Where did you find it ? What was it doing ? On what plant did you find it ? Did you see it fly ? How did it fly ? Did you hear it sing or chirp, etc. The difference in structure among insects brought before a class should also be studied by means of questions put by the teacher, the number of wings,

Fig. 25.

Fig. 26.

legs, and eyes, (Fig. 25) its mouth, and its breathing apparatus. The pupil will soon see that insects are unlike in many features, the observation of which will tend to increase his interest.

Occasionally injurious caterpillars will be caught in the act of eating leaves (Fig. 26); this occasion should be well used by the skilful teacher, and useful lessons learned. It is wonderful what a variety of insects will be forthcoming when the interest of the pupil is thoroughly aroused. Very often the best teacher will be incompetent to answer all the questions asked him by the curious naturalists, but that should not deter him in his work, for even experts will very often tell of their ignorance in matters relating to insect-life.

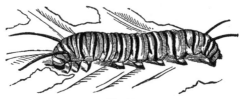

Fig. 27.

2. Encourage the pupils to make collections. Mr. Dearness has explained very clearly in his last year's Presidential address the simple method of collecting, so that every teacher who feels a living interest in this informal work, will find no difficulty in equipping both himself and his pupils with the necessary appliances.

Fig. 28.

3. Encourage the study of life-histories, for after all this part is the most important in every respect. The wonderful transformations should excite intense curiosity, and accuracy as to the observations forms one of the most valuable trainings to be obtained in any department of science. (See Figures 27-32).

Fig. 27, the caterpillar ; fig. 28, the caterpillar changing into a chrysalis ; fig. 29, the chrysalis ; fig. 30, the perfect butterfly.

Fig. 29.   Fig. 30.

4. Make this nature-study the basis of composition lessons, and informal talks, where good English form and style must be insisted upon. A child full of enthusiasm for a subject cannot help but talk, and write too, if required to do so. Let abstract and foreign topics alone till his reading has become wider and his mind more fully developed

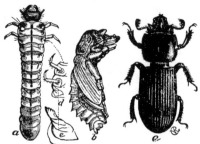

Fig. 31, grub, pupa and beetle (Passalus Cornutus).

The logical expression of the sequences in the development in insect life, if repeated frequently, will become one of habit, and will tell powerfully in many other ways. Not long ago the Principal of one of our largest Model Schools stated to me during a conversation, that almost invariably he could pick out the teachers-in-training under him who had received a science training in the High Schools. Science-trained pupils could develop a lesson along natural lines in proper logical order, so that they were thoroughly pedagogical in all their work.

5. Let the study of insects be one of relaxation from the more arduous duties of the school. The pupil must never have "Examinations" on the subject, else the knowledge of facts will soon be considered by pupils the chief aim of the study. Even the observations to be made must be incidental, just as the questions must be informal.

The child mind craves for informal instruction along such lines, and "the school becomes a delightful place, and the teacher an angel of light."

WHEN ?

The amount of time allotted to this study should not be much. Let it creep in whenever the teacher feels that there is a need of relax-

Fig. 32, transformations of a Dragon-Fly.

ation, or when he has material for a good lesson. Some have advocated devoting a period to the work on Friday afternoons, but I would not limit the period to any particular time. It should not appear at all in the programme of studies. The youngest child is not too young to make observations and to try to give explanations.

TEACHER'S EQUIPMENT.

The greatest difficulty at the present day is to secure properly equipped teachers. This difficulty will gradually disappear as nature-courses are placed on the curricula of Normal and Model Schools, but a few words, I think, will not be out of place here regarding books with which the nature teacher should be familiar.

1. Comstock's *Insect Life*, published by the Appletons, is the best hand-book of suggestions, directions and methods for teachers that we have in America. Outlines of studies are given on pond life, brook life, orchard life, forest life and roadside life, while methods of collecting and preservation of specimens are sketched very clearly. Price $2.50.

2. Comstock's *Manual for the Study of Insects* takes easily first place as an Identification Book, and should be in every Entomologist's library. It contains keys to the

orders, and families, and gives brief descriptions and engravings of nearly all the commonly occurring insects. Price, $3.75.

3. Prof. Panton's *Insect Foes* (30c.) is a very convenient book for the busy man who would like to know the most injurious insects and the methods used in destroying them.

4. *Insecta*, by Hyatt & Arms, is a very neat and interesting book for beginners, and pays much attention to the anatomy of types from each of the orders. Price, $1.25.

5. Scudder's *Guide to Butterflies* and *Life of a Butterfly* are very useful books. The former pays much attention to identification of larvæ. Price, $1.50. Also Dr. Holland's *Butterfly Book*, with 48 coloured plates. Price, only $3.00.

6. Other special works are : *Williston's Diptera*, $2.25 ; *Cresson's Hymenoptera*, $3.00 ; *Leconte & Horn's Coleoptera*, $2.50 ; and *Banks' Neuropteroid Insects*, 50 cents ; and *Packard's Works*.

7. In Economic Entomology there are Saunders's Classic Work, *Insects Injurious to Fruits*, price, $2.00 ; Harris' *Insects Injurious to Vegetation* ; Smith's *Economic Entomology*, price, $2.50 ; Weed's *Insects and Insecticides*, price, $1.50.

8. Last, but not least in importance, are the *Annual Reports* of our own Entomological Society, in which will be found splendid accounts of the injurious insects from year to year. Every teacher should subscribe for the Canadian Entomologist, $1·00 a year ; for in doing so he would get twelve monthly numbers of the Magazine and a copy of the Annual Report of the Society's Proceedings.

TWO AVIAN PARASITES: NOTES ON THEIR METAMORPHOSES.

By R. Elliott, Bryanston, Ont.

In the month of April, 1897, I noticed among the feathers of a Broad-winged Hawk which I was making up as an ornithological specimen several examples of a medium-sized fly that, judging from its peculiar structure, the faculty it possessed of passing rapidly through and hiding among the feathers, its reluctance to leave although provided with well-developed wings, must be a parasite, alive and well and quite at home.

Looking at a species of the highly organized order Diptera, in which the metamorphosis is complete, my first surprise at seeing the insect there soon merged into the second wonder : If the parasite remains for life on the host, and the metamorphosis is complete, in what manner is the routine of reproduction carried on ? One could easily imagine eggs deposited on the feathers, an excellent environment to ensure development. But then, what would become of the larva ? One could scarcely conceive of a maggot as living on the exterior of a living bird.

[In a Catalogue of Insects, under the family *Hippoboscidae*, I found *Olfersia Americana* Leach noted thus :—" Lives on *Bubo virginianus* and *Buteo borealis*."]

As the Broad-winged Hawk is a near relative of the last-named, is in fact *Buteo latissimus*, I assumed that I had found the name of the insect.

In September of this year, while manipulating a White-throated Sparrow for the same purpose as my hawk, I found another parasite fly, possibly of the same family, but of a different species from the first-named. It measured about five millimeters in length, with wings nearly, if not quite, as long as head and body, The thorax was flat and smooth ; the skin leathery and tough ; the legs (a light olive-green) long and strong and provided with curved hooks—an admirable contrivance to enable the parasite to travel through the maze of feathers while the troubled host travelled through the mazes of the northern forest.

Through the kindness of my friend, Mr. Dearness, I am enabled to present herewith a drawing made by him under the microscope, which shows the structure of the fly's foot. (Fig. 33.)

The most interesting feature of the particular specimen described above lay in the fact that when found its condition gave me hopes that I might receive some light on its method of reproduction. Its abdomen was much larger in proportion than that of its congener found on the hawk.

Having placed the fly, living and uninjured, in a small phial, I watched and awaited developments. Within twenty hours I found the fly dead at the bottom, and a single large pupa (Fig 34) sticking to the side of the bottle. As it appears incredible that the young could have subsisted by itself in such a place, it seems reasonable to conclude that the egg and larval stages were passed within the body of the parent, thus accounting for two important phases in the course of its life. The pupa measured $2\frac{1}{2}$ x 2 millimeters, blackish brown, smooth and shining, flattish, oval, suggesting in form and outward structure some minute trilobite.

Fig. 33.
Foot of Parasite of
White-throated Sparrow.

Fig. 34.
Form of the
shining black
pupa.

Mr. J. Dearness submitted the specimens of the two parasitic insects, and the curious larva, adding the following notes :

With the specimens submitted herewith, Mr. Elliott has afforded some of us our first opportunity of examining a pupiparous insect. He shrewdly suspected the curious fact in the life history of the insect under notice that the earlier metamorphoses take place in the abdomen of the parent, and that the young insect emerges therefrom in the pupal stage. The adhesiveness of the pupa, as shown by its sticking to the side of glass bottle, may be an important agent in keeping the pupa among the feathers during the brief time between its expulsion and its exit as an imago.

The only book I had at hand at the time of making these notes which relates anything of the Pupiparæ was Van der Hoeven's. Speaking of the Pferde-laus (*Hippobosca equina* L.) he says : "If we were told that a bird laid an egg that produced a young one at once as large as the mother we should think the account fabulous and ridiculous ; the fabulous part would not be diminished were the bird ever so small, or even a winged insect. Of this insect—the Pferde-laus—the story is actually true."

The smaller of the two parasites was the one that deposited the pupa in the bottle ; it is in the genus *Ornithomyia*, Latr., and is characterised by having distinct eyes, ocelli usually three, wings distinct, claws of tarsi tri-dentate. Hippobosca has no ocelli, and the tarsi are bi-dentate.

The author above quoted says of the family to which these insects belong that they lay no eggs, but are viviparous. That which seems to be an egg laid by these insects, and which is sometimes as big as the abdomen of the mother, ought to be regarded as a pupa. From it the perfect insect (imago) comes to view after an interval of time dependent upon the temperature to which the pupa is exposed.

A BIT OF HISTORY.

By J. Alston Moffat, London, Ont.

Early in 1898 the Rev. Dr. Bethune had received an enquiry from Mr. H. Bird, of Rye, N.Y., concerning certain specimens in the Society's collection. The Doctor naturally referred him to me. Shortly after I received from Mr. Bird a letter enquiring if *Hydrœcia appassionata* Harvey, was represented amongst the species of that genius in our collection. I replied that it was not, and that I suspected that there was but one specimen of it extant; and that one was in the the British Museum; and that a re-discovery of it would be a matter of very great interest; and this opinion I afterwards found was also entertained by Mr. Bird.

This *Hydrœcia appasionata*, Harvey, is a species that was taken at London, by Mr. E. Baynes Reed, and described by Dr. Leon F. Harvey in the August number of the *Canadian Entomologist* for the year 1876, page 155, under the generic title "Gortyna." The date of the description indicating that the capture had been made the previous year at the latest. There is no mention made of the number of specimens taken, or upon which the description was made; the presumption is, that it was a unique. At all events, a type specimen had gone into Mr. Grote's collection; Mr. Grote's collection went to the British Museum, and that specimen went with it, and there I presume it is now. It has generally been considered that some of the species of this genus are rather variable and run closely into each other. Reference is made by Mr. Bird in his paper (*Can. Ent.* Vol. 30, p. 130) to the difficulty that seems to have been experienced by the describers in deciding to which species certain forms belonged. Guenee is reported as considering *Marginidens* Guen and *Limpida* Guen as possible varities of *Rutila* Guen, whilst Walker regarded *Marginidens* as a doubtful variety of *leucostigma*. I have read somewhere a statement made by Dr. J. B. Smith, that as the genus then stood a specimen might be yellow or mouse-colored, with or without spots and yet be the same species. Dr. Smith had been convinced that the genus was in a most unsatisfactoy condition and wanted revision, and he undertook the task. The first thing to be done was to get as much material together for study as possible, so early in the year he requested the loan of the Society's specimens of that genus for comparison. I replied, that then they would have to be sent by express, and that he would remember that the unreasonable demands of the U. S. Custom officers had erected an effectual barrier to anything more being sent in that way. I sent to him a list of the genus as it was represented in the Society's drawers, and from these he choose those he wanted most to see, and they were sent to him by mail. Amongst them were three specimens which I had under the specific name "Rutila." One was from my former Hamilton collection. Another was taken by Mr. C. G. Anderson, of London, in 1895. And as it did not correspond to anything I could find, it was sent for determination and returned as "Rutila." The other was a specimen taken by Mr. Bice in 1896, of which he took several that season, and as I could not identify it, I sent it also for a name, which was also returned as "Rutila." This I considered was an illustrious example of the variability of the species, and quite confirmatory of Dr. Smith's statement already referred to.

In due time the specimens were returned with Dr. Smith's determination of the various forms attached to them. In his letter to me of August 15th, 1898, announcing his returning the specimens he remarks: "The specimen of *Appasionata* is the only decent example known to me in collections. *Circumlucens* is a new species of which there are only a few other examples known to me. So, though the lot was small it was not without interest." So there had been an example of the long lost *Appasionata* in the collection and I did not know it. This specimen of *H. Appasionata*, Harvey is Anderson's capture of 1895. *H. Circumlucens*, Smith, is the specimen from my old Hamilton collection, and "*Rutila*" is the 1896 capture of Mr. Bice. It would then appear as if "*Rutila*" had been a kind of general repository for anything that was known not to belong elsewhere. I believe there are two or three other specimens of *H. Appasionata*, Harvey in collections in London.

By my ordinary method of collecting fall moths, searching for them in the daytime, or beating bushes and weeds; all species of *Hydroecia* seemed to be rare and difficult to find, except *Nictitans*, which is more or less plentiful every season; whilst other species are obtainable only in single specimens at long intervals. In Mr. H. Bird's valuable paper on this genus (*Can. Ent.* Vol. 30, P. 126,) mention is made of *Nitela* as being a well known species; here it is seldom taken, and its variety *Nebris* has yet to be reported present. Referring to *Cataphracta*, Mr. Bird says: "At light the Imago would be considered a rarity." Here it is the most abundant form presenting itself at light. Dozens of it might have been taken in the season of 1897. It was less plentiful in 1898. *Inquaesita* would come next in point of numbers. This is an illustration of changed results in different localities.

THE GYPSY MOTH.

By E. H. FORBUSH.

Ever since the Gypsy moth exterminative work was placed under the management of the Massachusetts Board of Agriculture the plan of operations has been to work from the outermost limit of the known infested region toward the centre.

Obviously such a method, if properly executed, would best carry out the purpose of the State law, first, for the prevention of the spread, and second, for the extermination of the moth. In accordance with this plan it has been the policy of the Board to clear the outer towns from the moth and, at the same time, to reduce, so far as the money granted would permit, the number of the moths in the central towns. It was hoped that when the outer towns were cleared the force could largely be concentrated in the inner towns, clearing them also. If the Board had each year received the sums it has deemed necessary and annually requested this policy would by to-day, it is believed, have been carried on to complete success. But since the necessary legislative grant annually asked for by the Board has been cut down year after year from one-third to one-half, the moths have so increased in the central towns that they have been scattered into and have seriously threatened the towns cleared or nearly cleared in the outer belt.

Under these circumstances it has been found necessary during the seasons of 1897-98 to concentrate large bodies of men in the central towns to prevent a further wide dissemination of the larvæ into the outer towns; the outer towns, meanwhile, receiving less than their full share of attention.

The present year the full amount asked for ($200,000) was granted for this work by the legislature. Unfortunately the grant was so delayed that much of the necessary work of egg-destruction (by burning, before hatching time) could not be done. The heavy rains, too, which prevailed through May and June greatly hampered the spraying. Nevertheless, the burlap-work, which was done more extensively than ever before and over most of the territory known as infested, proved so successful that nowhere in the whole burlapped territory were any considerable number of trees stripped by gypsy moth larvæ.

We have also this summer done extensive burning, beginning in August; burning will be continued where needed.

On the whole, the granting this year of the full sum asked will make it possible for us to accomplish far more in 1898 than has been accomplished in any previous year.

While it is true that two colonies of the moth (one in Lincoln, discovered in 1897, the other in Manchester, discovered this year) are known, immediately outside of the limits of the territory hitherto defined as infested, these discoveries, under all the circumstances, do not in the least surprise me, since I have believed from the first that a few of such extra-limital colonies might confidently be looked for. Still these discoveries emphasize the necessity of far more inspection work outside the limits of known infestation. We have been absolutely unable in past years, with the money hitherto granted, to do nearly all that needed to be done in this line of work. This year as much as possible was done in this line, revealing, however, no infestation.

Efficient work has been done both in Manchester and Lincoln. The centre of the Manchester colony appears to be stamped out. Much work will be necessary in its immediate vicinity this fall and the country surrounding it must be carefully watched next year. The Lincoln colony has been brought to such a condition that there is little danger of dissemination from it.

Nevertheless the moth is scattered through hundreds of acres of woodland there and extermination in Lincoln and the adjoining town of Weston, into which a few larvæ have been dispersed, will be costly.

The work of spraying and burning the past season has been greatly facilitated by improved apparatus prepared under the direction of Mr. E. C. Ware, of the Department, and in part invented by him.

Information about the Gypsy moth has been widely scattered through the region adjacent to the infested territory. People have learned to dread the moth and are on the watch for it. The Lincoln and Manchester colonies were discovered and reported to us by citizens. To secure still further the intelligent co-operation of citizens in this work, it is planned to distribute from house to house, within the towns immediately bordering the infested region, an illustrated bulletin descriptive of the Gypsy moth, its habits and something of its history.

In no previous year have we been able to speak so confidently of progress so early in the season. The great wooded tracts, especially in the eastern, western and northern divisions of the infested territory are now in excellent condition. More than ever this year have I been impressed with our power to cope with and in due time to utterly extirpate the Gypsy moth, when we are sufficiently supported by Legislative grants.

If the Legislature promptly provides for several years to come an appropriation strictly limited to the Gypsy moth work and equal to the amount granted this year, there can be no doubt of the final extermination of the Gypsy moth from Massachusetts.

Dr. Bethune, in commenting on the paper, said he had visited in August last the scene of operations of the Gypsy Moth Commission, and had been shewn all their appliances and methods of operation in carrying out the work of controlling and ultimately exterminating the destructive insect. He described the spraying of the foliage of tall trees with poison in order to kill the caterpillars, the scraping off and destroying egg-clusters, the burning by means of a hose discharging blazing kerosene of weeds and rubbish in rough localities which were known to be infested, and also the banding of trunks of trees with burlap. The apparatus employed was of the most perfect description and was largely the invention and product of the members of the force. He was especially impressed by the magnitude and thoroughness of the work; in traversing many miles of the State in different directions he noticed that every tree, large or small, whether in private gardens, public streets and parks, or woods and swamps, had its trunk wrapped round with burlap and a code mark painted upon it indicating the dates when it had been inspected. He felt sure that if the Commission is maintained with its present staff of workers the extermination of the insect will before many years be accomplished.

It was then moved by Mr. Dearness, seconded by Mr. J. D. Evans, and resolved : That the thanks of the Society be conveyed to Prof. Forbush for his interesting paper, and that this Society desires to place on record its admiration of the work done by the State of Massachusetts, under the able direction of Professors Fernald and Forbush, to restrain the spread of this most destructive insect, and if possible to exterminate it eventually. Had not such energetic measures been taken the consequences to neighboring States and even to our own country might by this time be appalling.

THE COTTON BOLL-WORM IN CANADIAN CORN.

By J. Dearness, London, Ont.

On the 10th of October Mr. E. T. Shaw, residing near Dorchester Station on the G. T. R., east of London, drew my attention to a larva which he said was damaging his corn by burrowing from the top downward between the rows of grain on the ear. I went over into the field—one of about four acres—and with his assistance soon obtained a number of specimens of the larva. I estimated that in the part of the field we were collecting them that about one ear in five was affected.

On taking the larvæ home I was surprised to find that it agreed exactly with the descriptions of the Cotton Boll worm (*Heliothis armiger* Hubn) and that in a Canadian latitude it could be so numerous as to possess an economic interest.

On making further inquiries I learned that the "worm" was reported in the corn-fields of most of Mr. Shaw's neighbors and indeed was said to be much more prevalent and injurious in a large corn-field of Mr. McNiven's than in Mr. Shaw's.

Last week Mr. Paul Hunter informed me that he had been husking corn in a field near Gladstone, Ont., a village in another part of the same township, and that "nearly every ear had a worm in it." He described the insect so well without any suggestions from me that I felt sure it was the same that had attracted the attention of the Dorchester Station farmers.

I visited Mr. Shaw's farm again on the 3rd instant (November) in the hope of find-ing some more specimens, the numbers of my first collection having been reduced by cannibalism. In confinement the larvæ seem to prefer the tissues of each other's bodies to the corn I placed in the jars with them. Possibly, indeed probably, they could not bite the rather hard shelled corn placed in one of the jars. In another jar in which two or three ends of ears of corn had been placed, when I returned after a week's absence only one specimen was living. Therefore, as just stated, I went last week to Mr. Shaw's to collect some fresh specimens to bring to this meeting. He happened that day to be hauling in unhusked corn. In the load just brought in we found relatively few affected ears, not more than one in twenty or thirty, but in the next load they were quite common, one in every two or three ears.

The affected ears usually had but a single larva in them, the largest number I saw in one ear was three. The damage done to affected ears by the burrowing and milling of the grain is not very great, less than five per cent., but some of such ears showed a mould that had made an entrance and was following the channel burrowed between the rows of the injured grains.

Dr. Fletcher informed me last night that a farmer near Orilla had reported dam-age to 75 per cent. of the ears of his corn by an insect which the doctor found to be the same species as the one under consideration. He will doubtless refer to it in his Notes of the Season.

The life-history of this interesting insect has been so well studied and so fully reported in the Fourth Report of the U. S. Entomological Commission and in subse-quent bulletins of the Division of Entomology of the U. S. Department of Agricul-ture that but little remains to be done by Canadians. However its appearance here in the role above described may justify a brief synopsis of what has been recorded of its history and habits.

From the elaborate report of the Commission above cited we learn that in many parts of the Southern States the Boll-worm is regarded as more destructive to cotton than all other insects combined and that in some parts of the Southern and Western States it has been very injurious to corn. In the three years preceding the labors of the Commissioners they reported very marked damage to corn all through the South and West, it being a common experience to find fields in Virginia and southward in which almost every ear was pierced.

Glover, in 1866, wrote that a dissection of a female boll-worm moth showed that it contained about 500 eggs. Mr. F. W. Mally, who made an exhaustive study of this insect for the U. S. Division of Entomology obtained 687 eggs from one moth. The egg is oval in shape, whitish in color, and beautifully sculptured, fifty of them side by side would make a line an inch long. The eggs are laid singly on various plants, but preferably it would seem on the young silk of ears of corn. This preference is taken advantage of by the cotton growers who plant patches of corn here and there in the plantations to serve as a trap crop, the corn being harvested at a time when the planters think they will effect the maximum destruction of the larvæ. The egg hatches in 2 to 4 days. The larva which is variable in color undergoes well marked changes in its earlier moltings, some of these are noticeable in the specimens exhibited. The mature worm is an inch to an inch and a half in length and rather less than a fifth of an inch in diameter, the head is amber colored and the body is strikingly marked by a dark stripe along the back centred by a fine white line. On either side of the dark stripe on the back are paler ones and on the side a very distinct and whitish stripe in which the spiracles are found. On the sides are three or four rows of tubercles each bearing a rather stiff hair. The two legs (the six on the anterior segment of the body) are dark in color and the prolegs have each fifteen small hooks.

The first food of the young larva is its own egg shell, but it soon settles to work devouring the tissue of its host plant, whether that be cotton, corn, tomato or some other. In August it is said to pupate in about 21 days, and the pupal stage then to extend over two or three weeks The last brood hibernates in the pupal stage. These remarks on the life history are condensed from Mr. Mally's reports.

The perfect moth like the larva is variable in color. It is fully described and well illustrated in the 4th Report of the Entomological Commission.

The series of specimens in our collections at London were taken by Mr. Moffatt, at Hamilton, some years ago. I do not find any Ontario record of it since until this year.

Although this year it is present in sufficient numbers to warrant the attention of the economic entomologist, I do not suppose there need be much apprehension on the score of serious injury in the future. The unusually prolonged season in Ontario may have permitted the development of an additional brood as compared with other years. Were it to remain and extend its area it would be most unwelcome as the question of remedy is obviously difficult. Its presence in the green ear of corn can be detected by an observant eye. When observed the tedious remedy of pinching or hand-picking might be resorted to. Obvious difficulties stand in the way of spraying with poisonous solutions.

After the members present had examined the specimens brought by Mr. Dearness, Mr. Dwight Brainerd reported that he had met with the insect in Massachusetts this year for the first time. Mr. Winn said that a few specimens had been found in Montreal and referred to the mention of the insect in Mr. Gibson's list of moths taken at Toronto. Dr. Bethune had found it this year also at Port Hope, where the larva burrowed into the fruit of the tomato.

MUSKOKA AS A COLLECTING GROUND.

By ARTHUR GIBSON, TORONTO.

In the month of August last I had the pleasure of spending two weeks in the "Highlands of Ontario," Muskoka, my destination being Port Sydney.

Port Sydney, with a population of about 50 inhabitants, is about 138 miles due north of Toronto, being situated at the southern extremity of Mary Lake, which is about 5½ miles long and 2 or 3 wide.

To a person who has never visited Muskoka, the Lakes which abound everywhere in that district, and which as a rule, are filled with numerous small islands, beautifully arranged, so to speak, and the mainland with its wild picturesque scenery, the sight that meets the eye is truly wonderful, and worth going some distance to see.

5 EN.

In Mary Lake there are seven small islands of various sizes, one probably covering an acre or even two, while another would only contain about enough room upon which to build a fair sized house. These islands for the most part are composed of solid rock, with only probably a few feet of earth on the surface. In fact throughout the whole district there is nothing but rocks, rocks, rocks. On some of the islands there is a considerable growth of trees, shrubs etc., while others seemed to be quite bare. A curious sight often observed in the Muskoka country is large trees growing out of a crevice in what appears to be solid rock. To a casual observer there is considerable mystery in this, and as I have not looked into the matter, I am unable to throw any light thereon.

Certain rocks, on the islands, as well as on the mainland, sink, as it were, straight down into the water often to a depth of 30 feet and more. These rocks are not loose, in the ordinary sense of the word, but are a part of and joined to the mainland or island as the case may be, and often reach a height of probably one hundred feet or more. It will be readily seen, therefore that even the most delightful resorts, are not always the safest, but have their treacherous surroundings, and it is a wonder more drowning accidents do not occur throughout the many lakes that make Muskoka the attractive place it is.

From an entomological point of view, Muskoka ought to offer grand inducements to the collector, as vegetation in most places is simply in the wild state, and many good captures could no doubt be recorded. The month of August, the time of the writer's visit, is too late for general work, but for the collector of Noctuidae there should be a good harvest during that month, as there are numerous good places for " sugaring " purposes. About the 1st of July, I think, would be the most profitable time to visit Muskoka, as insects generally are most to be had about that time.

However, during my vacation at Port Sydney I noticed the following species of butterflies, viz Argynnis Cybele, Atlantis, Aphrodite and Myrina, all of which seemed fairly common, with Myrina the most plentiful. The first three named were mostly worn specimens, only a few of those taken being presentable   Pieris rapae, Colias Philodice and Chrysophanus Hypophlaeas were also common. The latter was the commonest of all those noticed. Everywhere this little butterfly was to be seen flitting about, and the majority of the specimens were in good condition. A few specimens of Danais archippus (Fig. 30), and Grapta progne (Fig. 35), were observed, and of the Limenitis, disippus (Fig. 36) seemed fairly plentiful,

Fig. 35.   Fig. 36.

whilst but a single specimen of Arthemis came to view, no doubt owing to the lateness of the season. Besides these I noticed quite a number of specimens of Feniseca tarquinius, but could not manage to secure a single one. These interesting butterflies have a peculiar habit of flying anywhere but in the direction the collector is looking. They were all flying in close proximity to the alder bushes, on which their larvae feed upon a species of aphis.

Among the moths I took Catocala relicta and concumbens, also a few other noctuids, some of which were new to me, and I noticed the wings of Euprepia caja lying upon the sand, the body of which some enemy had secured.

Besides the above, some beetles were secured with the aid of the sweep net, but as everything was burnt up with the heat, nothing much was to be done. I did not take any notice of any of the other orders, so cannot say anything about them ; grasshoppers seemed quite plentiful, however.

Dr. Wm. Brodie of Toronto, the well-known entomologist, has, I believe, visited Port Sydney on several occasions and I understand has explored the neighboring vicinity. He stopped at a farm house a few miles down the Muskoka River from Port Sydney, the owner of which is an enthusiastic naturalist, his principal hobby being ornithology. In a conversation with Mr. Crew the doctor stated that during his recent visit during the latter part of June and first week or so in July he had made some interesting captures. One specimen of Euprepia caja was secured by him as well as another moth very similar to caja and probably of the same genus. Dr. Brodie spoke of the plentifulness of Limenitis Arthemis, and reported having taken quite a number of a Chrysophanus, which I understand does not occur at Toronto, and which appeared to be very common ; most

of the specimens taken, however, were more or less in a damaged condition. Debis portlandia (Fig. 37) also appeared to be of common occurrence, the Dr. taking some 5 or 6 specimens. The habits of this butterfly are very similar to Neonympha Eurytris, which is our commonest representative of the "ringlets." On the whole the Doctor considered the past season to have been a poor one in the vicinity of Port Sydney, but I am satisfied that with a good season much interesting work could be accomplished there.

Fig. 37

The country to the north of Port Sydney and Huntsville which is about 12 miles from Port Sydney, contributes some fine specimens of insects. Mr. Tyers has received quite a large number of lepidoptera from the Muskoka region about 25 miles north of Huntsville, among which are some very nice things in the Noctuidae, which are not included in our local fauna, and the majority of which have not, as yet, been identified.

No doubt there are new species yet to be found in that country, which has not, as far as I know, been worked up to any great extent.

RANDOM RECOLLECTIONS IN NATURAL HISTORY.

By J. Alston Moffat, London, Ont.

The aphidivorous habit of the larvæ of *Feniseca Tarquinius* has been well observed and recorded. The striking portraiture of a monkey's face in the form and markings of the chrysalid has also been commented on, and even photographed, yet no one can form a correct conception of its wonderful naturalness until they have seen it. But there is a habit of the butterfly which it at all times indulges in that I have not seen noticed in print, which is quite in keeping with the peculiarities of its previous stages, and, as far as I know, is unique. A favourite situation for this butterfly to rest on, either singly, or in groups, is the open side of a wood, or the leafy branch of a tree projecting into an open space. I have seen a single individual take its position on the extreme point of such a branch, and from there it would dart a little distance to the one side of where it had been sitting, then back to about as far on the other side of it, then back and forth a number of times before it returns to rest on its perch again. The distance it traverses in this movement may be about ten foot, and at right angles to the branch on which it had been sitting. It brings up at each end with a perfect snap, and a perceptible rustle of the wings. It seems to throw itself with great violence, and stop as suddenly, as if it had struck a board ; then off to the other end of its course and back again, to and fro with such rapidity that the eye can scarcely follow it ; then after a short rest it will repeat its performance.

Whether it is the male or female that indulges in this sport, I cannot say, or if it may not be confined exclusively to either sex. I had the good fortune to see the performance enacted three different times, in two of which the exhibition was brought to a fatal termination, but no attention was paid to the sex of the performers. I should be inclined to surmise that it is the male and he only.

When reading some remarks upon the parasitic worms of the genus *Gordius*, more commonly called "Hair Snakes," from the belief entertained by many that they are horse hairs transformed in water into snakes; the writer animadverted upon the ignorance and superstition that still prevailed on this subject, which was considered not at all creditable to the superior education of the present day; which brought back to my recollection something of the tedious process by which my mind was relieved of its ignorance in this matter, and set me a-thinking that if the writer had been possessed of some further information it might have tended to moderate his estimate of himself and others; for there are few erroneous notions in natural history entertained by the multitude, that have such a reasonable excuse for their existence, in nature and in fact, as this one about "Hair Snakes." And seeing that a knowledge of facts is a more certain way of abolishing both ignorance and superstition than the denouncing of either; and as it seems to me that there are extenuating circumstances connected with this subject that are not as well known as they ought to be, I shall give an account of what I at one time saw.

When I was a small boy living in the country, which was at that time "Backwoods,' and having no playmates of my own kind, I naturally sought for companionship with other kinds; passing my time in the woods and fields in search of something new, curious or attractive to me, and especially in observing the works and ways of living creatures, in which I found my chief enjoyment. On one hot summer day after heavy and continued rain I was amusing myself in a pasture field that had never been cultivated : and in which were numerous little hillocks with hollows on one side of them, indicating that there, in the long-by-past, trees had grown, been uprooted and decayed. The hollows were filled with pure water from the recent and frequent showers. Their bottoms were smooth and bright green, whilst their clear and crystalline waters reflected every passing cloud that floated over them in the brilliant sunlight. Whilst dreamingly watching the rapid passing of small white clouds reflected in one of these pools, my attention was aroused by an agitation of the water at one side; and upon examination I found a tuft of yellowish white hairs, which had evidently come from some cow's tail, partially in and partially out of the water. The hairs may have been between eight and ten inches in length, and there may have been fifteen or twenty of them together. There was about two-thirds of their length in the water, and the rest on dry ground. The part of them that was on land was a compact mass, as if they had been plucked out together and dropped there; whilst that part of them that was in the water had each individual hair as widely separated from its fellow as it possibly could get, whilst each and all of them were animated by an undulating eel-like movement which they kept up incessantly, as if they were making an effort to get off and could not.

I had seen *Gordius* before that, and upon inquiry had been informed that they were " Hair Snakes," from which I inferred that they were hairs turned into snakes; and here sure enough I thought I had found a bunch of them in the process of transforming; but how one portion of a hair could become a living snake, whilst the other part still remained a dead hair, was to me a perplexing and mighty mystery, and remained so for many years afterwards. In some of my promiscuous reading I at length came upon a satisfactory solution of the enigma. It seems that there is an animalcule of some kind that breeds in water, and is in the habit of attaching itself to objects floating in the water, and if these creatures are sufficiently numerous, and the object sufficiently pliable, they can by united action produce an undulating movement, and give to the object an appearance of individual life; and this is what I had seen. Not quite an ocular delusion, but a mental deception of the most convincing kind. I had noticed when looking at the hairs, that the portion in the water appeared stouter than the other, but I satisfied myself with the thought that a living thing should grow; and in after years when I learned that an object in water appeared thicker than when out of it, I wondered if I had not been deceived in that way, but there was an apparent roughness of their surface which I could not account for, as I knew that hairs did not soften and swell in water; but what I had read explained most satisfactorily everything I had seen in connection with them.

If that tuft of hairs had been wholly in the water, and their full length endowed with motion as part of it was, each hair would have been moving independently of the others, and would likely have been scattered all over the pool; then in all probability my attention would not have been particularly attracted by them, further than to think that "Hair Snakes" were unusually numerous in that pool; and so I would have missed an instructive lesson, for what I read would not have impressed me as it did, but for what I had seen previously. This is an experiment that anyone favourably situated for obtaining the right conditions could easily carry out for themselves, and then they would have ocular proof of what a reasonable excuse there does exist for the belief that "hairs do turn into snakes."

Fig. 38.

When engaged at one time in an effort to bring some chrysalids of the Tomato Sphinx (Fig. 38) to maturity, and obtain the moths, I noticed that one of them was dead, so laid it aside for a time. Upon my next handling it I found the outer skin dry and shrivelled, and upon removing a portion of it, which was an exceedingly thin and brittle scale, I saw that the moth within had been fully matured up to the point of emerging before it died, so finding that I had an excellent subject upon which to operate for discovering the position and arrangement of the various parts of the insect, as they were disposed of in the chrysalid prior to its assuming an active life, I commenced investigating. Carefully removing the outer covering, which came away as freely and as clean as if it had never been in any way attached to the corpse within, but upon which had been distinctly impressed every external feature of the coming moth, the matured pupa was disclosed scaled and coloured complete. The winglets, which were about three-quarters of an inch in length, pressed firmly—in what seems to be an unnatural position—on its breast, instead of on the sides where they are to be afterwards; and the long legs compactly gathered together under the winglets, occupying the least space possible. The external loop on the chrysalid, in which the proboscis, or sucking tube, generally called "tongue," is partly contained, interested me the most, so I gave special attention to it.

Upon removing the outer scale of the loop—which has often been compared to the handle of a pitcher, and to which it bears a striking resemblance—I found that the proboscis within was double. It leaves the head and reaches about two-thirds the length of the chrysalid in the loop, where it touches and is united to the covering of the abdomen; here it is doubled back upon itself, not sharply, but with an open curve, which produces that knob at the lower end of the handle. It then presses closely to the under, or inner side of the descending portion till it reaches the head, where it passes inward to the body of the moth, whence it proceeds downward again, under the folded legs and winglets of the moth to its full length of four and a half or five inches, tapering gradually but perceptibly from base to apex.

If such a chrysalid was broken open when newly transformed from the caterpillar, it would be found to be an unorganized fluid mass, seemingly held together only by the outer integuments—which parted so freely from what was inside, when matured—and upon which, even at that time, is imprinted all the external outlines of the coming moth, and from which the internal organical structure of the future solid body seems to radiate, and take on form and consistency. What a wonderful transformation is herein brought about by time and favourable conditions! From an unorganized fluid, to a diversified and complicated organism, adapted to a vigorous, active life. And the sucking tube, so delicately and yet so powerfully constructed, that the creature can extend it to its full length of five inches, or roll it up into a coil at its pleasure, not the diameter of a five cent piece. And yet more wonderful if we go back to the egg from which it all came, and within which lay "the power and the potency" for producing all that was to follow. "Never deviating from its course, but always producing a being like the parent." The proboscis is constructed of two longitudinal pieces with a groove on the inner side of each, which forms the cavity through which the moth takes its nourishment. These two pieces are firmly held together side by side by means of interlacing fibres, which yet admit of elasticity to the tube and allow the cavity to expand when food is passing through it, and may be used by muscular pressure in assisting to force it into the gullet. What wonderful adaptations of means to an end are to be observed in nature for the production of organs suited to the requirements of the creatures using them. One can at times see something like the exercise of the inventive faculty in evading or overcoming obstacles in the way of reaching the end required, when these are somewhat out of the ordinary, and with admirable success; impressing the mind with the thought that there must be somewhere, intelligent direction and supervision for the accomplishing of it.

THE PREPARATION OF SPECIMENS FOR THE EXHIBITION OF LIFE-HISTORIES IN THE CABINET.

BY DWIGHT BRAINERD, MONTREAL.

My brother and I arrange our cases in a rather peculiar way, and were complimented by being asked to describe it for the "Report."

The point that bothered us, was to break the lines ordinarily found in a drawer. We have four sizes of cardboard oblongs, cut proportionately, and use them instead of the common name labels. They are placed above each species, should be about half as long again as the wing span, and contain the bleached wings, frass and eggs corresponding to the name across their left hand margin. (See Plate).

Life Histories shewn in a Cabinet (D. Brainerd).

By this method, the drawers are cut up into little squares, each large enough to hold a series together with the caterpillar, ichneumons, etc. One can put a good deal of taste into the arrangement and the effect is certainly good. Outside of looks, I do not know that the system has anything to recommend it. Of course with white cards, the drawer covering must be colored : we employ a rough buff wall paper.

I am asked for some remarks on inflating and wing bleaching. Many books give instructions, but for novices it may be said that caterpillars are inflated or blown by slightly cutting the anal orifice, ventrally, squeezing everything out by the hole so made while holding them between the fingers in a soft cloth ; binding a tube in this hole and drying them, inflated by a current of hot air. It is well to have a piece of blotting paper to absorb the drop or two of liquid ejected when the cut is first made, and care must be taken to clean the neck. Neglect of this makes an ugly black blotch.

Benzine is the best thing for killing, as some kinds of caterpillars seem to fatten on chloroform. The stripping and drying should be done immediately the caterpillar is dead. If not, it draws up into all sorts of knots, and if left until relaxed, is too tender. Partially dry the skin before giving it much air pressure or it will get out of shape, and stiffen up the tail end before paying much attention to the head.

I never could make much success of the straw recommended by experts, and always use a glass tube drawn to a point to furnish the air. Lap it with silk three or four times, run slightly into the caterpillar, make a turn or so in front of the last pair of legs and fasten the silk back on the tube. With very small things, this glass can afterwards be cut off by a file, and a headless pin, bent at right angles, stuck in with a drop of gum. Larger species should be slipped off by the thumb nail and pinned through the middle.

The less heat used, the better will be results. A lamp chimney fastened horizontally on a metal coat hook, makes a first class oven. And a candle is the best source of heat as by snuffing it the temperature can be regulated. The flame should be kept at least two inches below the oven, and the segments you are working held over the hottest place. Druggists sell a double bulb inflator now, which is much better than the breath for giving the empty skin its shape.

In bleaching wings, to show the veins, the only suggestion I can offer is the use of wood rather than common alcohol for washing. The oil in it increases the transparency. If bleaching has not been described in past Reports, the wings are torn or snapped off close to the body, soaked a minute in alcohol, and then, to remove the color, in Labaraque olution. When clear, wash again in alcohol, dip in water and mount on a card.

THE BROWN-TAIL MOTH (*Euproctis chrysorrhœa*, L.).

BY DR. JAMES FLETCHER, OTTAWA.

The specimens of the new pest of fruit and forest trees in Massachusetts which I am able to show to-day, have been kindly supplied for this purpose by Mr. A. H. Kirkland of the Gipsy Moth Committee. They consist of the male and female moths, the egg mass, the full-grown larva and the hibernaculum in which the larvæ pass the winter.

This insect is well known in Europe and has about the same range as the Gipsy Moth. Thirty years ago, when I was a boy, it was not an uncommon species for one season at Rochester, Kent, in the south of England, but I learn that it is now rare. The first notice of its occurrence in America was when Prof. Fernald announced that he had been working on it in Massachusetts in 1897, but it had been noticed by some for four or five years before that date. It is thought to have been imported with nursery stock perhaps as early as 1885. Early last spring it was sufficiently abundant for Mr. Kirkland to point out to me several of the winter nests of the larvæ as we travelled from Boston by railway to Malden, Mass. Most of these nests seemed to be in pear trees. Prof. Fernald has published a bulletin on the subject, and also an extensive article in the proceedings of the last meeting of the Association of Economic Entomologists which was held at Boston. Both Prof. Fernald and Mr. Kirkland consider this insect as a serious pest and urge that drastic measures should be adopted to exterminate it. The latter writes under date, Oct. 5, 1898 :—

"The Brown-tail Moth was not a severe pest here the past summer because of the thorough work done last winter in destroying the winter webs of the young larvæ. Where this was neglected the caterpillars proved quite a scourge and from these neglected spots no doubt the moths spread to no small degree in the flying season. The female, you will remember, flies freely. A hopeful feature is the parasite help. We found the pupae parasitised to quite an unexpected degree by *Diglochis omnivorus,* Walker, and by a few larger hymenopterous parasites. Of course, I have only two years' experience to go by, and from this as a basis no strong predictions can be made, but I should not be surprised to see this insect spread gradually over New England and become a pest of about equal rank with the Tent Caterpillar, perhaps worse. Since the female flies so well and is doubtless carried on gales of wind, I can see no prospect of exterminating the insect. While we know that the insect breeds well on many shade and forest trees, I doubt if it becomes a pest at any great distance from orchards."

Köllar, the Austrian entomologist, in his "Insects Injurious to Gardeners, Foresters, etc.," says of this insect which he treats of under the name of the Yellow-tailed Moth : "It may justly be reckoned among the most destructive insects of the orchard. The larvæ often infesting fruit trees to such a degree that not a leaf or fruit remains uninjured, as was the case in the year 1828."

The caterpillars have a very wide range of food plants including nearly all of the large and small fruits ; they will also attack a great many of the common perennial plants. The favourite food seems to be the pear. Compared with the Gipsy Moth, as both the male and female moths fly easily, the Brown-tail Moth has greater powers of spreading. The life history of the species is as follows. The winter is passed by the partially grown caterpillars, which hatch in August and feed for about six weeks upon the upper surface of the leaves, stripping them of the skin and cellular tissue in the same way as is done by the Pear Slug, leaving the skeletonized leaves brown and dead. The winter shelter consists of several leaves spun together with silk, and a colony of the young caterpillars retires into this shelter in the latter part of September and remains dormant until the following spring. They revive again just as the buds are bursting and do much harm at that time, devouring the young leaves, flowers and forming fruit. When full-grown in June they spin light cocoons among the leaves, and the moths emerge about three weeks or a month later. The moths appear in July and the curious and beautiful egg masses covered with golden fur-like down may be found on the leaves during this month. They are elongated, depressed, and rounded above, more regular in outline than the egg masses of the Gipsy Moth, but like them protected by a densely felted covering consisting of the golden brown hairs from the anal tuft of the female. Not only are the caterpillars of this insect voracious feeders upon the foliage of many kinds of trees and plants; but they are also the cause of much annoyance from the stinging hairs of the larvæ and pupæ. This stinging is of much the same nature but more intense than that caused by the hairs of the species of *Halisidota.* Prof. Fernald states that many persons in the infested region suffered so severely as to require the aid of a physician and the irritation was so annoying to some of the Gipsy Moth employees that the chemist was directed to investigate the matter to discover the cause and to find out if possible an antidote. Prof. Fernald concludes his article (Bull. 17, New Series, U. S. Dep of Agriculture, Div. of Ent.) as follows. "The nettling of the skin may be caused by contact with the caterpillars, both old and young, or the cocoons, but in the latter case contact is not necessary, as the hairs from the cocoons are blown about by the wind. An English journal mentions the fact that travellers are often affected when the wind blows strongly from infested hedges along the side of the road."

By examining the specimens which I have here, it will be seen that the egg mass is about half an inch long by a quarter of an inch wide. The eggs cannot be seen under their furry covering, but they are round, of a golden color, and there are between 200 and 300 in a heap. The caterpillars vary in appearance during the different moults. The young caterpillars are described as of a dirty yellow color, with a black head and a black ring around the neck. They are thickly covered with hair and have four rows of black dots along the back. They are social in their habits throughout their larval life. From the first they spin a web over themselves, and as a leaf is destroyed another is attached to it by silken strands and gradually becomes part of the nest. The leaves attacked are also fastened securely to the twigs. The nest is never entirely forsaken ; when the caterpillars get larger they sally out in search of food but return from time to time to their refuge. The mature larva (as exhibited) is rather a handsome creature, velvety black lined with brown and bearing on each segment tufts of golden brown bristles. Along each side is a conspicuous lateral interrupted white stripe with tufts of curious hair-like processes. On segments ten and eleven are spherical reddish yellow tubercles, one on each segment, similar to those found on the Gipsy Moth. These the caterpillars can elevate or depress at pleasure. The head is black mottled with brown, and the full-grown larva is nearly an inch and a half in length.

Köllar speaks of pupation taking place by preference upon damson trees, the caterpillars leaving apple and pear trees to pupate upon the damsons. He also speaks of the mode of pupation as follows : " After the last moult, which the caterpillars undergo either in the old nests under the new web or in the open air, they disperse over the different fruit trees in the garden. Pupation takes place in June ; several again unite, roll some leaves together into a ball, make for themselves jointly a brownish web and become dark brown pupæ. There are from four to twelve in a ball."

Among remedies, this author recommends highly the collecting of these balls, which are generally found either on damson trees or, when these are not present, upon the lower branches of the trees which have been attacked. The Brown-tail Moth is a night flying insect which is very active at night, but sits quietly without movement during the day time. The four wings and thorax are of a snowy whiteness; the antennæ are golden brown, white above, and in the male widely pectinate. The abdomen is dark brown in both sexes, that of the female bearing at its posterior extremity a round mass of golden yellow hair, which entirely disappears by the time egg laying is completed, the component hairs having been deposited by the female over the mass of eggs as a covering.

The work which has been done in connection with the Brown-tail Moth is another instance of the grand service which is being rendered to the State, the Union and the cause of economic entomology by the Gipsy Moth Committee. The laws which have been enacted in Europe, and already in Massachusetts, show the necessity of attending to this enemy at once before it gets beyond control. It is well for the country that chance has introduced it within the area so well watched by the expert entomologists and officers of the Gipsy Moth Committee. The careful experiments which have been carried on by these gentlemen show that the destruction of the webs in winter and the spraying of trees when 'the caterpillars are active, supplemented with lantern traps, are effective means of keeping down the numbers of this insect, and, further, that if the matter is neglected we have in this new pest an enemy with great capabilities for spreading and doing harm, which should stimulate effort on the part of everyone living in the infested areas to do what is advised by the Committee promptly, so that, if still possible, so destructive an enemy may be prevented from spreading over a large area of country. The experience of some districts which were systematically worked by destroying the conspicuous winter shelters with the caterpillars inside them in 1897-8, is very instructive, for there were practically no moths in these districts last summer; but in adjacent places where no effort was made, the moths have increased to such an extent that these cleared districts will probably be re-infested and all the work will have to be done over again.

INJURIOUS INSECTS IN 1898.

By Dr. James Fletcher, Ottawa.

The crops of the Province during 1898 have not suffered generally from any unusual or even locally severe outbreak of injurious insects. There have been, of course, losses in all crops from the ordinary annually-recurring pests; but the wide awake Ontario farmer now knows pretty well what to do or where to get the necessary information, when he notices an unusual abundance of an insect enemy. We may again be thankful for a season of good crops, and for the most part these were got in in good condition. The general results of the year are given concisely in the excellent Crop Reports for November, issued by the Deputy Minister of Agriculture, Prof. C. C. James. The only drawbacks of the season were exceptionally hot weather with drought in some sections in July and August and a rather wide-spread and almost unheard of frost in the month of July, which affected some tender crops. The autumn was long and fine, with no severe early frosts, thus allowing all root crops and fodder to pick up well.

Cereals.

The cereals throughout the Province have made an excellent showing. Owing to the increase in the price of wheat last autumn, a large area was sown to this staple crop. The hot, dry period referred to, although it ripened up some oats rather prematurely, produced wheat of exceptionally fine quality. Mr. W. Scott, of the McKay Milling Co'y of Ottawa, a large buyer of grain, tells me that he has not seen for many years wheat of such high quality as he has this year received from some parts of the Ottawa Valley, some samples running as high as 64½ lbs. to the bushel, without any sign of injury by the Wheat Midge or other insect enemies.

"Poor yields were exceptional, and large yields were common. The plumpness of the grain is frequently alluded to, in many cases the weight going over the standard, and as high sometimes as 63 or 64 lbs. to the bushel. Here and there only did correspondents complain of rust, midge, or other injury to the crop. The yield is 24 bushels per acre for Fall Wheat. . . . . The crop of spring wheat has been over an average in yield, and the quality is also good. The yield is 17.7 bushels per acre."—(November Crop Report, Ont. Bureau of Industries, p. 2.)

Barley yielded heavily, and the sample, for weight and color, has seldom been surpassed. I have not heard of any injury by insects.

Oats were in places light, and in some localities suffered from the attacks of the Grain Aphis, Wireworms, and Cutworms. The injury by the first of these was light. As is usually the case, the parasites which invariably accompany this plant-louse, increased in enormous numbers and the plague stopped. The parasite which did best service was *Aphidius granariaphis*, Cook.

Devastating Dart Moth. A rather bad attack of the Glassy Cutworm (*Hadena devastatrix*, Brace), Fig. 29, the caterpillar of the Devastating Dart Moth, occurred on the farm of Messrs. J. Yuill & Sons, at Carleton Place.

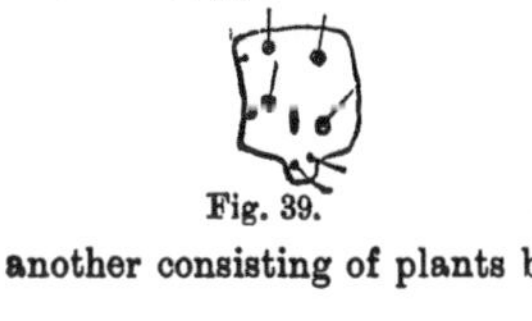

Fig. 39.

When insects attack a crop of grain it is always difficult to apply any remedy to the standing plants and the only resource is the practising of agricultural methods founded on the known life-history of the pest. Most insects feed upon closely allied plants; the wisdom, therefore, is apparent of following an infested crop belonging to the grass family with another consisting of plants belonging to a different botanical family.

Among the Cutworms, the two worst enemies of grain crops in Ontario are the species referred to above and the AMPUTATING BROCADE MOTH (*Hadena arctica,* Bois.), and although it is probablethat the latter of these may feed on other plants, the favorite food plants seem to be members of the Gramineæ or true grasses, upon the roots and lower stems of which they feed in a similar manner to the Glassy Cutworm.

This Cutworm is a more troublesome pest when it attacks grain crops, from the fact that the caterpillar does not become full-fed until some time later. In an attack of this kind it is, of course, necessary to examine the caterpillars to see how nearly they are full-grown. In the case referred to above the cutworms of the Devastating Dart Moth from Carleton Place were found to be full-grown by the end of the first week in June, and the owners of the field, who wished to sow their land again to oats, were advised that this could be safely done. The land was cultivated at once, and on the 8th of June was seeded down again to oats and grass. This crop was not attacked at all because the caterpillars were all in the chrysalis condition. This would not have been the case if the infesting Cutworms had been the caterpillars of the Amputating Brocade Moth.

Even less amenable to remedial treatment than the above are the various species of WIREWORMS (Fig. 40), which attack grain crops particularly on timothy sod. No satisfactory remedy for these has as yet been discovered. Sowing rye or barley on infested land has been found useful by some, and late ploughing is highly recommended; but no applications to the land or poisoning of the seed are of any avail.

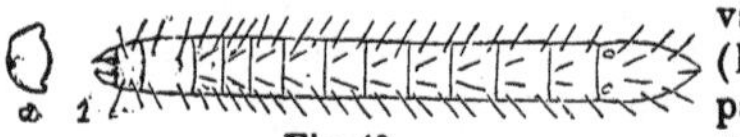

Fig. 40.

An interesting discovery has been made during the past summer at Toronto, by Mr. C. W. Nash, and at Norwood, Ont., by Mr. T. W. Wilkins, of a parasitic fungus belonging to the genus *Cordyceps,* which was in both places destroying the wireworms in considerable numbers. This fungus was much more slender than the one which is frequently figured as the parasite of the White Grubs (*Cordyceps melolonthæ,* Tulasne) (Fig. 41). So far, the identity of the wireworm destroying species has not been obtained. It is probable that it is an undescribed species.

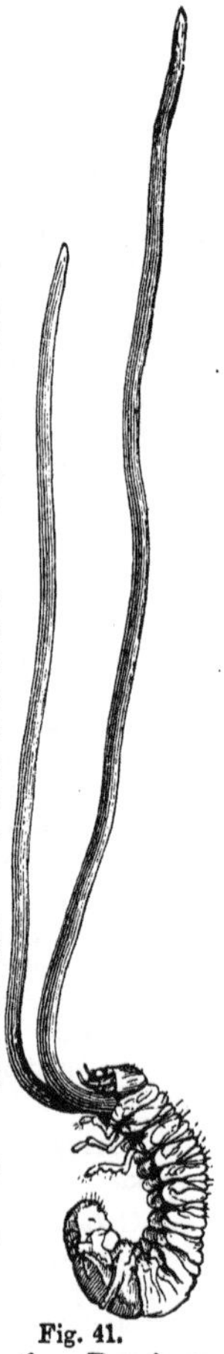

THE WHEAT MIDGE (*Diplosis tritici,* Kirby), which a few years ago worked such havoc in the wheat crop, seems almost to have disappeared from Canada; however, one district seems to have suffered severely from this pest last season. This was along the shore of Lake Ontario in the Niagara peninsula. Another pest, which did not appear at all in 1898, is the American Frit Fly (*Oscinis carbonaria,* Loew.),   Fig. 41. which in 1890 injured wheat very much in the eastern portions of the Province. For three years before that it had also been an enemy of meadow grasses.

THE WHEAT-STEM MAGGOT (*Meromyza Americana,* Fitch), although present in most localities where looked for, seems lately to have gone back to a large extent to its natural food plants, the wild native grasses.

The most important attacks upon wheat, and these were by no means extensive or severe, were by the old and well-known culprits, the Hessian Fly (*Cecidomyia destructor,* Say) and the Joint-worm (*Isosoma tritici,* Riley).

Fig. 42.

THE HESSIAN FLY (Fig. 42—greatly magnified) is probably more prevalent than it is generally thought; but as its depredations in most places are not serious they are not observed. The injuries to fall wheat in the autumn are greater than by the more conspicuous attack on the stem during the summer by the spring brood. Occasionally the spring brood attacks the wheat plants in the succulent root shoots just as is done by the autumn brood; this would be due I think to a late spring holding back the development of the wheat plants, The eggs would be laid on the leaves, and the young maggots might attack the shoots too severely to allow of them developing into stems. It has been frequently noticed that insects are not belated to the same extent as plants by cool spring weather,

THE WHEAT JOINT-WORM (*Isosoma tritici*, Fitch). (Fig. 43—the fly highly magnified). In 1895 specimens of injured wheat straws bearing many galls in the bases of the sheathing leaves of the stems were sent from Meaford, on the Georgian Bay, by Mr. Thomas Harris; these were considered to be *Isosoma hordei*, Harris. The injury to the infested crop amounted to 5 per cent.

There was no recurrence of the attack last year at that place; but a somewhat similar attack upon wheat appeared at Verdun, Bruce Co., on the opposite side of the peninsula. Many specimens were sent to me by Mr. William Welsh, both in the autumn of 1897 and last spring. The galls were different from the Meaford specimens in that there was little swelling, and the cells of the larvæ were almost entirely in the tissues of the stem proper, short sections of which were rendered hard, woody, and brittle by the operations of the insects. From some of these stems a large number of the

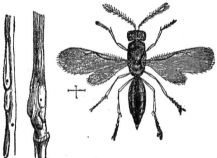

Fig. 43.

flies were reared. These have been identified by Dr. L. O. Howard and prove to be *Isosoma tritici* of Fitch. The injury was serious, attacked stems producing fewer and smaller grains than the others. From the Verdun material, in addition to the gall makers, two kinds of parasites were reared, *Homoporus chalcidiphagus*, Walsh, and *Eupelmus epicaste*, Walsh; but these were not present in sufficient numbers to affect the outbreak to any appreciable degree. During the past summer loss from this Joint-worm was not so great as in 1897, so it is to be hoped that its natural enemies may have increased. The eggs of the joint-worms are inserted into the young green straws in June by the female flies. Wheat, oats, rye and barley are damaged. There is only one brood in the year, a few of the flies issuing in the autumn, but most of them not till the following spring. Most of the galls are situated in the first or second joints of the stem above the root, and, as the normal time of emergence is in the spring, any treatment of the stubble such as burning over or ploughing down deeply, by which the insects are destroyed or smothered, must reduce their numbers considerably. Mr. Welsh noticed that many of the hardened portions of the stems were broken from the straw in threshing and were found among the rubbish or in the grain. These pieces from half an inch to one inch in length contain from five to ten larvæ. This shows that, besides treating the stubble, these pieces of stem as well as the straw must also be attended to. The broken-off hardened pieces should be collected at threshing and cleaning and burned. Likewise straw from fields where the joint-worms have been found should be destroyed by either feeding or some other means before the time at which the flies should appear.

THE PEA WEEVIL (*Bruchus pisorum*, L.). As in previous years many inquiries have come in for the best means to kill the "pea bug" in seed pease. The life-history is well-known; the eggs are laid on the young green pods; the grub on hatching eats its way in and penetrates one of the forming pease.   There it remains until full-grown, consuming the interior of the pea and passing through all its stages from a white fleshy grub to the chrysalis and then to the perfect beetle.   A small proportion of the beetles emerge the same autumn and pass the winter under rubbish or in barns and other building.   The larger number, however, remain in the pease and do not emerge until the next spring, so that they are frequently sown with the seed.   The perfect insects fly easily and resort to the pea fields about the time the blossoms appear.   They feed for some time on the flowers and leaves, and egg-laying takes place as soon as the pods are formed.

Remedies.—The best remedy for this insect is, undoubtedly, to treat the seed with bisulphide of carbon.   Nearly all the large seed houses have special buildings for this purpose, and few seed pease are sold which have not been treated.   Should it be found, however, when sowing pease, that they contain living weevils, it is an easy matter to treat them.   Perhaps the most convenient way for farmers is to take an ordinary 45-gallon coal oil barrel.   Into this 5 bushels of pease may be put at one time.   According to the quantity of seed to be treated, use 1 ounce of bisulphide to every 100 pounds of pease; therefore, if the barrel is filled, put 3 ozs. of the chemical in a flat, open saucer or basin on the top, or pour it right on the pease; cover up the top quickly with a damp sack or other cloth and put some boards over that.   Bisulphide of carbon is a colourless liquid which volatilizes readily at ordinary temperatures; the vapour which is quite invisible, but has a strong, unpleasant odour, is heavier than air, therefore sinks readily and permeates the contents of any closed receptacle.   This liquid is very inflammable; so great care must be taken with it.   The pease should be treated under a shed out of doors, and should be kept tightly closed up for 48 hours.   No light of any kind must be brought near, or an explosion may occur.

The late sowing of pease is sometimes practised to avoid the weevil; but this plan is not approved of, as the crop is small and is then frequently attacked by mildew.

Seed pease may be held over without injury for two years, and this is a sure remedy against the Pea Weevil; for the beetles must emerge the first spring, and if the pease are tied up in paper or cotton bags, as they cannot eat through these materials, they will all be dead before the second spring.   Weevilled pease should not be used as seed, as they produce, if they grow at all, weak, spindly plants.

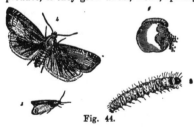
Fig. 44.

THE PEA MOTH (*Semasia nigricana*, Steph., Fig. 44).   For many years pease in all parts of Eastern Canada have been much injured and sometimes rendered quite unfit for the table by the caterpillars of a small moth.   The large, late garden pease have suffered most.   Although its injuries were so considerable, it was only last year that the moth was reared and its identity determined.   Maggoty pease are well known to the housekeeper; but it is only at intervals of some years that they are abundant enough to cause much complaint.   The caterpillars are whitish and fleshy, with dark heads and some dark tubercles on the segments, from each side of which a slender bristle springs.   When full-grown they are about ¼ inch in length; they then eat their way out by a small round hole through the pod and enter the ground a short distance, where they spin small oval cocoons in which they pass the winter, and the perfect moths do not appear again until nearly the middle of the following July.   Dr. J. Ritzema Bos, in his Agricultural Zoology, says of the same or a closely allied European species : " The moths fly about in large numbers around the pea blossoms, always a short time after sunset.   The females lay one, two, or at most three, eggs on a very young pod.   In fourteen days the caterpillar is hatched, bores into the pod, and attacks the pease.   The pease attacked are covered, while in the pod, with the coarse-grained excrement of the caterpillar and are often united, two or three together, by a web."   The perfect moth is a modest-coloured but pretty species, ¼ inch long when the wings are closed, mouse-coloured, bronzed towards the tips of the wings, silvery gray beneath. The only markings are along the front costa and at the apex of the fore-wings. The costal marks consist of 10 or 12 short, black streaks separated by similar clear white dashes; near the apex is a flask-shaped mark which bears 4 or 5 short, longitudinal, black dashes. Last year the attacks of the Pea Moth upon pease in Ontario were considerable, Mr. John McMillan, M.P for Huron, even putting the loss at one-third of the crop in his district.

Remedy.—As a remedy, deep ploughing has been recommended. It has also been found that early sowing and the cultivation of early varieties enable the pease to mature before the moths are on the wing. The perfect insects have been reared both in 1897 and last season. In the former year all the specimens emerged between July 12 and 15, and in 1898 between July 13 and 15. These specimens were kept under natural conditions, and these dates probably agree with the time the moths appear naturally in the field.

The Bean Weevil (*Bruchus obtectus*, Say, Fig. 45). From time to time notices appear in reports of entomologists and in the newspapers in the United States of injury to seed beans by a weevil similar to the Pea Weevil, but rather smaller. This is the Bean Weevil, a small, very active beetle, at one time thought to be a native of America but now considered to be a cosmopolitan species, which has been imported into this

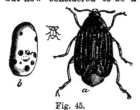

Fig. 45.

country through commerce. Authentic instances of this pest having occurred in Canada in injurious numbers have not, I believe, been recorded until this year, when it was found at Strathroy, Middlesex Co. As in the case of the Pea Weevil, the Bean Weevil occurs in the seed and is sown with it. The eggs are laid on young forming pods and the grubs eat their way inside and attack the seeds. There is, however, one important difference in the life history, namely, the bean weevils are able to propagate in the dry, stored seed, and two or three broods may come to maturity and entirely destroy the beans, whereas in the case of the Pea Weevil the young grub can only begin life in the soft, green pease; again, there is never more than one weevil in a pea, while in the case of the Bean Weevil, ten, twelve, or more, may occur in a single bean, according to its size.

Remedy.—The remedy for this new enemy of the bean is precisely the same as for the Pea Weevil, viz., to fumigate the infested seed with bisulphide of carbon. If, however, it is found that the beans have been badly bored before the injury is detected, it is far better to destroy the whole by burning and procure new seed without going to the trouble and expense of fumigating.

FODDER CROPS AND ROOTS.

Fodder crops of most kinds have been remarkably heavy in most parts of the Province during the past season. In the Ottawa Valley such crops of clover have never before been seen, and with the exception of a little injury by the Black Army-worm, *Noctua fennica*, Tausch. in the spring, both crops were exceptionally heavy and were saved in the best of condition. In the west one or two occurrences of the Clover weevil (*Phytonomus punctatus*, Fab.) were mentioned but no appreciable effect upon the crop was made.

The Clover-seed Midge (*Cecidomyia leguminicola*, (Lintner) did a good deal of harm in the seed growing districts and some farmers speak of turning their attention to the Mammoth Red Clover and Alsike, because these varieties are not injured by this troublesome insect. The remedy of feeding off or mowing the crop before the 20th June has been found satisfactory by those who have tried it, because the maggots (Fig. 46) of the first brood mature and leave the clover heads to enter the ground and complete their changes soon after the date given, and if the clover is fed or cured before that date the larvæ are destroyed If left later the maggots leave the clover heads and produce the second brood which matures just as the second crop, from which the seed is reaped, comes into flower. About the time

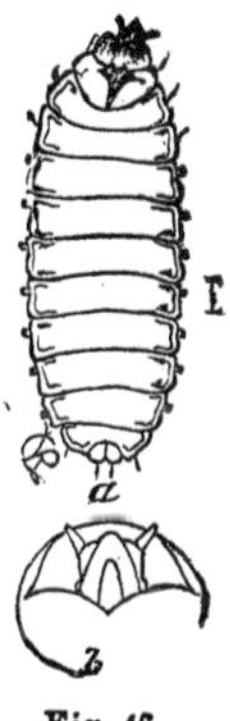

Fig. 46.

the seed is ripe these leave the clover and pass the winter in the ground, to emerge again the following spring just at the time the clover blossoms.

The hay crop has been little injured by grasshoppers or other pests. In old worn out meadows "Silver top," caused by leaf-hoppers and other sucking insects, has been noticed; but well worked land with a good rotation of crops suffers little from this injury.

Potatoes have been less attacked by the COLORADO POTATO-BEETLE than usual. Early in the season some correspondents thought that this pest was dying out, but the hot weather of midsummer soon brought it up to its usual abundance. The well tried remedy, Paris green, in either wet or dry applications, is now too well known to require more than a reference.

Injuries by White Grubs and Wireworms were more serious than is often the case, and unfortunately little can be done to counteract their operations.

THE CUCUMBER FLEA-BEETLE, Fig. 47, (*Crepidodera cucumeris*, Harr.) which fre quently does great damage to potatoes by perforating the leaves, has been successfully treated again this year by spraying the plants with Bordeaux mixture and Paris green made with the formula 6 lbs. of copper sulphate, 4 lbs. of fresh lime and 45 gallons of water, to which ½ lb. of Paris green is added. This remedy is now becoming well known, and on account of its usefulness widely used by our wide awake farmers to prevent the loss which is still enormous from the ravages of the Potato-rot. The first spraying should be done in Ontario not later than the 1st August, and this should be followed by two more applications on 15th August and 1st September. These sprayings also, of course, render unnecessary the treatment of the potatoes for the Colorado Potato-beetle, as those insects are killed at the same time.

Fig. 47.

A rather unusual injury to potatoes was this year reported from Carrville, York Co., by Mr. J. Lahmer. This was by the FOUR LINED LEAF-BUG (*Pœcilocapsus lineatus*, Fab.), and occurred at the end of May. The attack was, however, restricted in area and did not continue late into the season. The life-history of this pest has been worked out by Prof. Slingerland, of Cornell University. The eggs are laid in the terminal twigs of currant and other bushes in the autumn and do not hatch until the following spring. The bugs attack the leaves of the currant and some other shrubs to a certain extent, but are more injurious to various herbaceous perennials. The plants most often noticed as injured by this insect are Sage, Mint, Gooseberry, Currant, Dahlias, and the Japanese Honey-suckle (*Weigelia*), Potatoes and some other plants less frequently. It is hardly likely that this insect will ever prove a serious enemy of the potato crop. The mature insect is a bright greenish yellow bug three-tenths of an inch in length, with two black spots on the thorax and four stripes of the same color down the back. It is very quick in its movements.

Remedies.—As the eggs are laid in the twigs of bushes and are comparatively con spicuous, owing to the white tips protruding, wherever the bugs have been troublesome the eggs should be looked for and destroyed during the winter. The bugs and larvæ can be killed or driven away by dusting with pyrethrum insect powder, or by spraying with kerosene emulsion or whale-oil soap solution.

THE TURNIP APHIS or CABBAGE APHIS (*Aphis brassicæ*, L.). Turnips in many sections have been badly injured by this plant-louse, which has been one of the worst enemies of root crops during the past season. Although much loss is due to this pest every year, as a rule, nothing is done by farmers to remedy the evil, many volunteering the in formation that nothing can be done. This, however, is not the case, for successful experi ments have shown that, by spraying the plants bearing the first colonies which appear early in August, much may be done to protect a crop. At the time of thinning and hoeing turnips the colonies are small and may be easily treated by means of a knapsack sprayer with kerosene emulsion (one part to nine of water), or with whale-oil soap, one pound in eight gallons of water; or even by hoeing out the infested turnips and covering them with soil, an easy matter at that time with the hoe in hand.

VEGETABLES.

Vegetables in gardens suffered locally from the usual pests of the garden, Cutworms, Flea-beetles, Onion, Radish and Cabbage maggots. For cutworms, banding freshly set out plants with paper or tin collars was quite effective; and for plants grown in rows, bran poisoned with Paris green was most effectual, either slightly dampened so as to make the poison adhere and then distributed in small heaps along the rows, or with more bran added until it was almost dry and then drilled along the rows. Flea-beetles (*Phyllotreta vittata*, Fab.) on radishes, young cabbages and turnips were speedily disposed of by dusting the plants with Paris green, 1℔. in 25℔s. of perfectly dry land plaster. The ROOT MAGGOTS were unusually abundant and many experiments were tried to find a good remedy. Dusting Hellebore and Insect powder well down among the plants gave perhaps the best results with radishes and onions. For the cabbage maggot Hellebore 2 oz and Kainit 2 oz. were mixed in a pailful of water; about half a teacupful poured around the root of each cabbage after pulling away some of the earth, gave considerable protection but was not a perfect remedy. Kainit used alone, dissolved in water, or applied dry close to the roots of cabbages, onions and radishes and then covered with soil, or dusted on the surface close to the roots, had the effect of protecting the plants for a time, but did not give with me results sufficiently good to allow of its being recommended in the way some American growers have done. Last season, however, was an exceptionally bad one for all of the root maggots; radishes, onions and cabbages all being attacked severely from early in the spring until right up to the hard frosts of autumn. Kainit however is a quick acting fertilizer and a decided insecticide. Further experiments have been planned, and growers of vegetables can use it with advantage in ordinary years.

THE CARROT RUST-FLY (*Psila rosœ*, Fab). An attack upon carrots which has re-cently called for attention in Canada is by the European enemy of the carrot, called the Carrot Rust-fly. This has come under my notice occasionally during the last ten years in parts of Ontario, Quebec and New Brunswick, in all cases doing much harm in restricted localities, but as a rule disappearing after a year or two. The outbreaks, how-ever, are, I fear, becoming gradually more numerous. During the past autumn infested carrots were sent to me from Knowlton and Beauce in Quebec Province and from Ottawa in Ontario. The attack is easily recognized. Early in the season the leaves of young carrots turn reddish and the roots will be found to be blotched with rusty patches, par-

ticularly towards the tip These carrots when stored for winter use, although some-times not showing much injury on the outside, may be found to be perforated in every direction by dirty brown burrows, in which are many semi-transparent yellowish maggots about $\frac{1}{4}$ of an inch long. These maggots are blunt at the tail end, but taper toward the head, where is a black hooked tip, forked at the base, by which the maggot makes its way through the roots. The pupparium is reddish-brown, and the maggots, as a rule, leave the carrots before

Fig. 48.—The Carrot Rust-fly—natural size (1, 5, 7), and enlarged (2, 6, 8).

assuming this form. The fly and its work are shown very well in the figure (Fig. 48) by John Curtis, which I am able to present herewith through the courtesy of Miss Ormerod and Messrs. Blackie & Sons. The mature fly is two-winged, $\frac{1}{4}$ of an inch long, bright shiny black, with yellow legs and red eyes. The wings are beautifully iridescent. The winter is passed either as a maggot or in the puparium.

Remedies.—The methods which have given the best results in preventing injury by the Carrot Rust-fly are (I). Late sowing. Carrots which have been sown late have been found much freer from attack than those sown at the ordinary time. When grown as a field crop it is usual to sow carrots as soon as possible, but for table use carrots of excell-ent quality may be obtained from seeding as late even as the middle of June. If field carrots grown for stock are only moderately attacked they can be fed but, of course, are not as

6 EN.

good as sound roots. (II.) Preventive remedies consist of applications of strong smelling substances by which the characteristic odor of the carrots is masked. For this purpose, sand tainted with coal oil or carbolic acid, has been used to good effect. Kerosene emulsion diluted 1 to 10 and sprayed along the drills by means of a knapsack sprayer, also gave comparative immunity. In localities where the fly is known to have occurred, the ordinary precaution of sowing carrots as far as possible from the infested land will occur to all growers Where carrots have been stored away during the winter in sand or earth, this soil should be treated to destroy the pupæ, which leave the roots and enter it to pass their pupal stage. A convenient method is to put the soil into a wet manure pit, or, if this cannot be done, it might be buried in a deep hole, specially dug for the purpose, and, after covering up, the top soil should be firmly tramped down.

THE CORN-WORM (*Heliothis armiger*, Hbn.). Several correspondents have complained of the unusual abundance this autumn of the caterpillars of what Prof. Lugger calls the Sweet-Corn Moth or Tassel Worm. These are both good names, but the insect is far more generally known as the Corn-worm. It is also the same as the notorious Boll Worm of the cotton, to which crop it frequently does great damage. Unfortunately, no very good, practical remedy has been discovered for application in the cotton field. The injuries of the Corn-worm are in Canada almost confined to the fruit of tomatoes and to sweet corn, particularly the late varieties. Late in October, Mr. C. L. Stephens, the Secretary of the Orillia Horticultural Society, sent specimens of the caterpillars and injured ears of corn, with the information that the caterpillars had been very destructive, injuring as much as 95 per cent. of the ears of both sweet corn and yellow field corn. It was a new outbreak in the locality, and was the cause of considerable anxiety. Specimens were sent also from Sombra (Lambton Co., Ont.), and two rather bad occurrences came under my notice at Ottawa. The caterpillars do not appear until late in the season. In the month of October they were found of all sizes eating the young grains of corn, mostly near the tips of the ears. There were sometimes five or six caterpillars in a single ear, many of which were rendered quite unfit for the table. As the larvæ approached full growth, they would occasionally eat their way out of one ear by a neat round hole and travel to another ear. They were very variable in color, from $1\frac{1}{4}$ to $1\frac{1}{2}$ inches in length, of a pale-greenish or dark-brown color, marked with longitudinal dark stripes and with a conspicuous stigmatal band, white mottled with pink, the body bears the ordinary tubercles, which are distinct and black, each one supporting a slender bristle. The whole upper surface is marbled with white and the whole surface velvety, by reason of numberless and very short bristles, black and white in about equal numbers. When full grown, these caterpillars eat their way out of the ears and, entering the soil, spin cocoons, within which they change to chestnut-brown pupæ. This moth is by no means a common species in Canada, and all the specimens I have seen have been taken late in the year. Prof. Lugger states that the insect does not winter in Minnesota, but that all are killed late in the fall. This, he points out, would mean that the insect has to be re-introduced every summer from the South, where it can successfully hibernate. Whether this is also the case in Canada, I am not sure, but I think that some must with us pass the winter as pupæ. The moth, like the caterpillar, is very variable in color. It is usually of a pale, dull, ochreous yellow, with variable olive or ruddy markings on the forewings. The yellowish hind wings have a broad black band and are edged with pink. These moths expand a little more than an inch and a half. The caterpillars of the Corn Worm feed, besides, upon a great many other kinds of plants than those mentioned, such as pumpkins, tobacco, beans, peas and a large number of weeds and garden plants.

Remedies.—The only remedy which can be suggested is the hand-picking of the caterpillars. The destruction of the moths by lantern traps has been also recommended : these consisting of a lamp standing in an open pan containing water and a little coal oil. These traps are placed at night in fields where the caterpillars have been abundant. When an ear of corn is attacked, the silk shows the effect of the injury going on beneath the husks by being discolored prematurely. As soon as this is noticed, the leaves of the husk should be pulled back and the marauders destroyed. Fall ploughing will, doubtless, break up the cocoons and expose many of the pupæ to various enemies.

FRUIT CROPS.

Notwithstanding several adverse circumstances, the fruit crop of the Province was a good one, and satisfactory profits were realized. If the crop was short in one section it was abundantly made up somewhere else. "Notwithstanding all disadvantages, the returns from all over the Province, with the exception of a few northerly counties, show that the supply of fruit, more especially apples, was considerably more than sufficient for home consumption, very large shipments having been made to England and the United States from the western fruit growing section. Pears, peaches, plums and smaller fruits were also shipped from many localities." (*November Crop Report.*)

Insect enemies were the cause of much loss; but most convincing evidence was again given this year of the value of spraying, and undoubtedly one of the most instructive and interesting exhibits at the Toronto Industrial Fair was the display of fruit gathered from sprayed and unsprayed trees in the same orchard. These orchards were those in which Mr. W. M. Orr, the Provincial Superintendent of Spraying Experiments, had carried on his work during the summer of 1898, and were situated in twenty-four different localities. There were in all 250 plates of fruit. The owners of the orchards were in no way interested in trying to prove that spraying was or was not beneficial, but were practical men anxious only to know how to get the largest returns of money from their property. They would, therefore, be the very people to acknowledge poor results. The superintendent had nothing to do with the selection of the actual fruit shown, and did not see it until it arrived in Toronto, where he took charge of it and displayed it to good effect as a most convincing proof of the efficiency of spraying. At the last meeting of the Ontario Fruit Growers' Association at St. Catharines on December 2nd, 1898, Mr. Orr read his report on the results of the experimental spraying work carried on for the Ontario Government under his direction during the year. This is a most valuable document, and will be published in full in the Report of the Fruit Growers' Association. Mr. Orr explains his method of work and gives extracts from the letters of some of the owners of the orchards. In estimating the percentage of perfect apples, a part of the tree was picked clean and the fruit carefully examined ; every specimen that had a worm or a spot, no matter how small, being rejected as imperfect. Some of the facts given and the figures which substantiate them will certainly convince many that spraying does most decidedly pay. The spraying must, however, be done properly, without stint of labour or materials, with the best obtainable apparatus and at the proper time. I am more and more convinced that failure to protect crops by spraying is due to lack of skill or carelessness in applying the spray, disregard as to the exact date when the successive applications should be made and misdirected economy as to the pump and nozzle used. Occasionally, good, careful fruit growers find that spraying does not always give the results which they expect ; Mr. Orr, however, says, "The owners of every orchard in which we worked this year, with one exception,—Mr. Ourwen, of Goderich—report that the Codling Moth was largely controlled by spraying."

I give the following quotation from Prof. L. H. Bailey's recent pamphlet, "Impressions of Our Fruit-growing Industries," because it bears directly on this point, he says : " Does spraying pay ? The past season has given strange results in spraying ; in very many instances spraying seemed to do no good. Does spraying pay, then ? Certainly, the same as tillage and pruning do. We do not know why there were so many unsatisfactory experiences in 1898, but this does not lessen the fact that bugs and fungi should be killed. That spraying pays is as well demonstrated as it is that apple worms, tent caterpillars and potato blight are injurious. Markets often fail, but it does not follow that markets are a nuisance. The surest way is to make it a rule to spray everything every year." (*Cornell Bulletin 153*, 1898.)

In summing up the results of the spraying work of the season, Mr. Orr said at St. Catharines : " It appears from results obtained in experimental work that from 65 p.c. to 80 p.c. of perfect fruit can be secured when spraying is regularly and properly done, and when the conditions are favourable, such as an orchard standing high and dry on well-drained land, away from buildings or hedgerows, and the trees planted far enough apart so that the limbs do not come within 10 or 12 feet of touching, and have an abundance of sunshine and free circulation of air. It is also important that the trees be properly trimmed, all rubbish removed, and the land properly fertilized, for it is a fact that two-thirds of the orchards in Ontario are starving: With good apples at the price they have commanded this year and last, the orchard, if properly attended to, would be the most profitable part of the farm."

If the fruit-growers of Ontario, generally, can be made to appreciate the above statement of Mr. Orr, who is a practical fruit-grower, and will follow his advice, enormous advantage must accrue to the country from the good work which the Provincial Minister of Agriculture, the Hon. John Dryden, has done by having the spraying experiments and other work on injurious insects carried out. In fact, it is hard to find in the whole Provincial expenditure anything which has given such manifest and quick returns for the small amount of money expended. The great interest which was taken in this work of spraying is shown by the fact that over 3,500 fruit-growers attended the meetings when the spraying was being done, in order to see the work, to ask questions and to learn the the proper way to carry on operations for themselves. This was almost double the number that attended two years ago.

Spraying with arsenical poisons, such as Paris green, London purple, arsenate of lead, etc., was done, first of all, to lessen injury by the Codling Moth on the apple, and by the Plum Curculio on plums and cherries ; but it is now used against all foliage eating insects. It has lately also become the custom to spray many plants with a combined mixture which will destroy both insect and fungous pests. For this purpose, the best mixture known is Bordeaux mixture and Paris green. The formula most widely adopted is one which is very easy to remember, as all its parts contain the figure 4. It consists of copper sulphate, 4 lbs., quick lime, 4 lbs., Paris green, 4 ozs., water 44 gallons.

Owing to the large amount of capital necessarily invested in and required to operate a fruit farm, and the permanent nature of fruit plantations, more attention has been given to those causes upon which failure and success depend than has been the case with ordinary farm crops, which change from year to year ; consequently, more perhaps is known and more enquiries are received with regard to orchard pests than any other class of insects. The common enemies which occur year by year in orchards have been treated of over and over again in our annual reports, and there would be no advantage in speaking of them now at any length, but attention may be drawn to some of the more serious or unusual outbreaks.

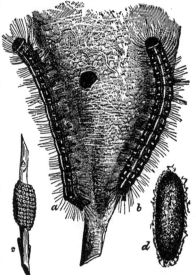

Fig. 49.

Tent Caterpillars have been even more abundant than last year in almost every province of the Dominion. In the Ottawa district groves of basswoods, maples, and aspers were stripped of every vestige of foliage, as well as the underbrush, consisting of numerous kinds of shrubs. Although the Forest Tent Caterpillar was slightly more numerous, the American Tent Caterpillar (Fig. 49), it was noticed, occurred with it in almost equal numbers, and, notwithstanding that close search was made for parasites, in this number of egg clusters were collected to see if the young caterpillars contained in the egg were in a healthy condition. These were kept in a warm office, and by the 1st of January hundreds of young caterpillars had hatched and were gathered together in a large mat-like cluster on the side of the jar.

There is no indication of the presence of either egg parasites or fungous disease, and as the trees throughout this district bear enormous numbers of the egg clusters, the outlook is ominous ; special effort must be put forth by fruit growers and gardeners during the present winter and next spring, or there will certainly be serious loss next season.   The remedies which give the best results against these insects are (I.) the collection and burning of the egg cluster during the winter, (II.) the cutting off and burning of the nests of young caterpillars early in spring, when they may be easily detected by the conspicuous white tents which they spin in the crotches of branches, and (III.) the spraying with Paris green of all trees liable to be invaded in an infested district. The sooner the application is made the more effective it will be, for many insects which can be controlled while young are much more difficult to poison after they have reached a certain size.

THE APPLE APHIS (*Aphis mali*, Fab.) appeared in large numbers early in spring, and many enquiries were received about it from the western part of the Province.   Little harm, however, was done either in the spring or late in the autumn, when most of the damage due to this insect generally occurs.

THE PLUM APHIS (*Aphis prunifolii*, Fitch) was less abundant by far than last year, although reported from a few places.   Specimens of another plum aphis, (*Hyalopterus pruni*, Fab.,) were received from one or two Ontario localities.

THE BLACK CHERRY-TREE APHIS (*Myzus cerasi*, Fab.) was certainly less wide-spread in the Niagara district last season than in 1897, and reports concerning it were very contradictory ; nevertheless considerable damage was done, particularly in orchards of sweet cherries.   It has been noticed that the dark-coloured plant-lice are more difficult to kill than the green ones.   Of several remedies which have been tried, the one which has given the best results is whale-oil soap solution, one pound of Good's Caustic Potash Soap No. 3 in six gallons of water, applied warm as a spray.   Kerosene emulsion, also an excellent remedy, must be used as strong as one part to six of water for these plant-lice. The eggs of the Black Cherry-tree Aphis are laid upon the twigs, particularly on the fruit spurs, by the last autumn brood.   There is no doubt, therefore, that good work could be done by spraying the trees during the winter, or better still, early in spring before the buds burst.

Another enemy of the cherry, as well as of the plum and pear, which when neglected did much harm was THE CHERRY AND PEAR SLUG (*Eriocampa cerasi*, Peck).   The remedy which gives the surest relief is the prompt spraying of the trees with Paris green, one pound in ·200 gallons of water, adding in all cases an equal amount of fresh lime with the arsenical poison, Paris green, to counteract its caustic effects on the foliage.

THE GREEN FRUIT-WORMS.—The caterpillars of three very similar moths belonging to the family *Xylina* did much injury to apples and pears, attacking specially the young fruit.   These caterpillars are not regular pests of the orchard, but appear in numbers at long intervals ; but, as they have a special taste for the green fruit, attacking it in preference to the foliage on fruit trees, ·the damage they do is much more important than that done by many other injurious insects.   In addition to fruit trees they attack maple trees.   At Niagara and at Aylmer, Que, near Ottawa, shade and forest trees, particularly the Silver Maple *Acer dasycarpum*, Ehrh.), were terribly disfigured and almost defoliated by these caterpillars over large areas.   It was pleasing to see at the end of June that thousands of them were being destroyed by various insect-eating birds, chiefly warblers, but especially by the English Sparrow.   In the streets of Niagara they were so vigorously assailed by the sparrows in the branches, and by chickens which waited for them below, that few could have escaped to complete their changes.   Mr. Orr writes of the occurrence of this pest in the Niagara peninsula :— "The Green Fruit-worm, a comparatively new comer, and but little known here, is likely to become a serious pest : some growers reporting from 20 to 30 per cent. of their apples and pears ruined by it.   By the middle of June it had destroyed much fruit."

Mr. N. H. Cowdry also writes of its depredations on the fruit of apples and pears at Waterford, Ont. The same complaint came from Mr. J. A. Link, of Sombra, Ontario.

Remedy.—The only remedy is early spraying, while the caterpillars are small and while they are feeding on the buds and young foliage. Luckily for the fruit grower these caterpillars are always accompanied when in large numbers by parasitic enemies.

THE ROSE BEETLE (*Macrodactylus subspinosus*, Fab.), Fig. 50.—This well-known enemy of the fruit grower, which every year does so much harm by eating the flowers of grapes, apples, pears, roses, plums, raspberries, blackberries, and in fact all plants belonging to the Rose family, as well as many other kinds of trees, did some harm this year in the hotter western sections of the Province. It occurred in large numbers near Niagara upon the young fruit of apples, in some cases actually covering the fruit. There is only one brood of this pest, the mature beetles last for about five weeks. There is perhaps no fruit insect known more difficult to combat than this is. The ordinary insecticides have little effect on it. Covering rose bushes with netting and beating the beetles from

Fig. 50.

the bushes into pans containing coal oil can be practised on a small scale. The only remedy which so far has been found at all effective on a large scale "is to spray grape vines and fruit trees with a wash made by adding three or four pecks of freshly slaked lime and a quart of crude carbolic acid to 50 gallons of water." Dr. C. M. Weed.)

THE RASPBERRY SAWFLY (*Monophadnus rubi*, Harris), was more than usually abundant in the western counties of the Province, but where promptly sprayed with Paris green and water, and later when the fruit was forming with white hellebore, was easily disposed of.

SCALE INSECTS.—The advent of the San José Scale in Ontario had a remarkable awakening effect on the fruit growers of the province, and, as a consequence, there has been during the past season far more enquiry with regard to injurious insects than has ever been the case in a single year before. The vigorous policy of the provincial Government and the excellent conscientious work done by the Inspector, Mr. George E. Fisher, and his assistants, backed up by a rigorous application by the Federal Government of the San Jose Scale Act has undoubtedly had a good effect not only among the thinking fruit growers of the Dominion, but upon statesmen in other countries who have made several enquiries as to what steps were being taken in Canada to stamp out this most injurious insect and prevent further importations from infested countries. Having had ample opportunity of examining the districts which were infested, I can bear testimony to the great success which has attended these efforts. The investigations in connection with the San Jose Scale have brought to light other scale insects where their presence was not suspected ; both the Forbes Scale and the Putnam Scale have been found to be widely distributed, but in very few instances have they occurred in injurious numbers. These two scales are of particular interest owing to their very close superficial resemblance to the San Jose Scale ; the microscopic difference of structure, however, can at once be discovered when the scale-insects are taken from their scales and after proper preparation examined under the microscope. In addition, both of these species lay eggs at certain times of the year, while the San Jose Scale, it is alleged, never does so. The Forbes Scale (*Aspidiotus Forbesi*, Jnsn.) and the Putnam Scale, (*A. ancylus*, Put.) can be successfully combated by spraying the trees with whale-oil soap, one pound in two gallons of water. The best time to make the application is early in spring before the trees are covered with foliage.

THE SCURFY BARK-LOUSE (*Chionaspis furfurus*, Fitch.), Fig. 51., wide-spread, but not very abundant nor injurious has been found in many localities in the western part of the province, and, like the the very injurious Oyster-shell Bark-louse, can be destroyed with the whale-oil soap solution mentioned above, followed by high culture and good horticultural treatment of the trees.

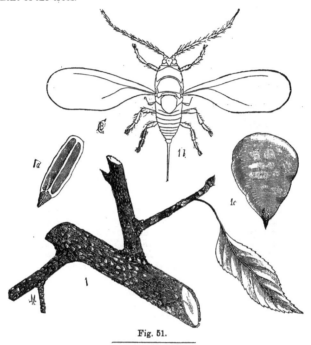

Fig. 51.

NOTES ON INSECTS OF THE YEAR   DIVISION NO. I., OTTAWA DISTRICT.

By W. Hague Harrington, Ottawa.

The first insect to attract attention in the spring was the larva of the little Arctian *Phragmatobia rubricosa*, Har., the fuscous little woolly bears of which may be found scurrying over the snow in day time or coiled up in some small depression where they had rested from their wanderings of the day before. On bright days in April, *Aphodius prodromus*, Brahm, filled the air. This species has only been noticed at Ottawa for the last four or five years, but is now as common as *Aphodius inquinatus*, Hbst.

Cutworms.—The Black Armyworm (*Noctua fennica*, Tausch.) was abundant in some localities as near Hull, Quebec, and on the Central Experimental Farm, attacking many plants, but especially clover and peas in fields, and also doing much harm in gardens as a cutworm. This is an early developing species which is full-fed about the end of May, and consequently plays great havoc in beds of young seedlings of early vegetables, sometimes cutting off as many as six or eight peas, or mowing down eight or ten inches along a row of onions or carrots in a night. Occurring with this caterpillar, as cutworms in gardens, were the larvæ of the White Cutworm (*Carneades scandens*, Riley), uncommon at Ottawa, and our commonest cutworm. The Red-backed Cutworm (*Carneades ochrogaster*, Gn.). These caused considerable loss in gardens among young vegetables and seedlings of flowers. This latter is also a large species when full-grown; but as the eggs laid the previous autumn do not hatch till the following spring the caterpillars do not become full-fed till much later in the season than the Black Armyworm and the White cutworm, both of which pass the winter half-grown. For some reason the White Cutworm did not revive from hibernation last year till much later than many ther cutworms. Poisoning with traps made of bundles of weeds, grass, or clover dipped

in a strong mixture of Paris green and water, or with poisoned bran, were very success‐
ful.   Cabbages, tomatoes, and other young plants were easily protected at the time of‐
setting out with rings of paper or tin.

THE CODLING MOTH (*Carpocapsa pomonella*, L.) was unusually prevalent and injur‐
ious in unsprayed orchards.   The standard spray for this insect is the poisoned Bordeaux
mixture, with which not only the fungous disease "Black Spot of the Apple" is treated,
but all foliage-eating insects, as well as the Codling Moth.   The formula is copper
sulphate 4 lbs., fresh lime 4 lbs., water 40 to 44 gallons, and Paris green 4 ozs.

TENT CATERPILLARS.—The most remarkable occurrence of the season was of the two

common species of Tent Caterpillars *Clisiocampa
americana*, Harr. (Fig 49) and *C. disstria*, Hbn.
(Fig. 52).   These two kinds of caterpillars which
were about equally abundant, stripped bare many
acres of Aspen Poplar, Basswood and Maple
groves along both banks of the Ottawa River and

Fig. 52.

along the Canadian Pacific and Canada Atlantic Railways in the counties of Carleton.

THE ASH-GRAY PINION.—Maples were also extensively injured at Aylmer, Que., and
at Hull, Que., by the green caterpillars of *Xylina Grotei*, Riley, and *X. antennata*,
Walker.   These caterpillars are known as Green Fruit Worms, on account of their de‐
structive habit of eating large holes in the sides of young apples and pears.   In the
Ottawa district they did little harm in orchards, but stripped almost bare large forest
trees at the two places mentioned.   This is an uncommon attack which has not occurred
in anything like the severity of last season since 1885.   The ashy-gray moths do not ap‐
pear until late in the season.   There are three species very similar in general appearance.
All of these may be taken at sugar in the Ottawa District in September and October.

The caterpillar of the Eye-spotted Bud-moth (*Tmetocera ocellana*, Schif), Fig. 53,
was rather common on apple trees in company with the Oblique-banded Leaf-roller
(*Cacœcia rosaceana*, Harr), Fig. 54. The Cherry Web worm (*Cacœcia cerasivorana*, Fitch),
Fig. 55, was extremely abundant on the wild bird cherries on the Laurentian mountains,

Fig. 53.    Fig. 54.    Fig. 55.

near Chelsea, Que., the unsightly webs attracting attention along the sides of the moun‐
tain road.   Although so abundant on the wild cherries, this insect did no harm to culti‐
vated varieties.

THE OYSTER SHELL BARK LOUSE.—(*Mytilaspis pomorum*, Bouche), Fig. 56, is
very common and destructive in this district, occurring not only on apple trees
but also on many other kinds of shrubs and trees in the garden and forest.   It
was noted as injuriously abundant on red and black currants, lilac, spiræas,
ash, dogwood (*Cornus*), mountain ash and hawthorne.   The Forbes scale was
found on the fragrant currant (*Ribes aureum*, Pursh), and the Putnam
scale on the elm.

The White Cedar Lecanium (*Lecanium Fletcheri*, ckl.) and "Red
Spiders did some harm to cedar hedges.

Canker worms were noticeably less abundant than usual, but the Bass‐
wood Looper (*Hybernia tiliaria*, Harr), Fig. 57, was very common, the deli‐
cate male moths drawing the notice of the least observant by their clumsy
flight and the late season at which they appear.

THE CURRANT SAW FLY (*Nematus ribesii*, Scop), was as usual abundant
and destructive where the bushes were not treated with the well-known
remedies, Paris green or White hellebore.

Fig. 56.

THE CURRANT APHIS (*Aphis ribis*, L.) was the most destructive insect on currants and gooseberries this season, many bushes being so much injured that they dropped their leaves and the fruit was ruined.

Fig. 57.

THE GRAPEVINE LEAF-HOPPERS (*Erythroneura* species) did much harm to Virginian creepers and grapevines, but particularly to the former. These insects, like the grapevine, flea-beetle (*Haltica chalybea*, Illiger), seem to prefer the Virginian creeper to the grape. This is sometimes very apparent where the creeper and wild grapevine are trained together over arbours.

Two more enemies of the Virginian creeper not often referred to as such, but which both occurred in some numbers this season at Ottawa in the same arbour, were *Saperda puncticollis*, Say, a beautiful longicorn, velvety black with golden yellow stripes down the edges of the wing cases and with spots on the thorax. These emerged from the larger living stems of Virginian creeper, while from younger stems many specimens of *Psenocerus supernotatus*, Say, were reared.

The Mourning Cloak Butterfly (*Vanessa antiopa*, L.) and the Interrogation Butterfly (*Grapta interrogationis*, Fab) were destructively abundant on elms planted as shade trees. The caterpillars of the former also stripped large branches on willow bushes.

ROOT MAGGOTS in cabbages, radishes, turnips and onions were remarkably destructive right through the season.

Two injurious insects which it was hoped had "run their course" and which for the last year or two had not been nearly so abundant as in previous years, this year again showed up in decidedly increased numbers. These were the imported Larch Saw fly (*Nematus erichsonii*, Hartig) and the Cattle Horn fly (*Hæmatobia serrata* Rob-Desv). For the Horn fly perhaps the most convenient remedy is 1 lb, of pine tar mixed with 10 lbs. lard. A small quantity of this ointment rubbed lightly along the back and sides of cattle once a week during the fly season will have the effect of keeping flies away and will also have a healing and soothing effect upon any sores due to rubbing or licking.

NOTES ON INSECTS OF THE YEAR, DIVISION NO. 2, BAY OF QUINTE DISTRICT.

BY J. D. EVANS, TRENTON, ONT.

Throughout this district the only crop which has suffered to any extent from insect foes during the past season (1898) is the seed pea crop.

For a number of years the cultivation of fancy or seed pease in this section for foreign markets has been very extensive, while a good demand and high prices ruled for such, extra precautions were taken by growers to have the weevil (*Bruchus pisorum*) killed by the seedsmen before they arrived at maturity or had destroyed the pease ; but during the past three or four years, when prices have become lower, ordinary grades of pease have been grown to a greater extent than formerly and the grower becoming careless in housing and dilatory in marketing his crop, the weevil has greatly increased in numbers. This occurs not so much along the Lake front of the County of Prince Edward as in inland sections. While many farms may be entirely free from the pest, others will lose fro n 15 to 30 per cent., while instances occur, although rarely, in which the loss is 40 per cent.

Another destructive agency to the pea crop is a blight said to be caused by a fungous growth which oftentimes will utterly destroy a whole field in a single night. This disease has been very prevalent during the past season and has caused a great loss to the farming community.

NOTES ON INSECTS OF THE YEAR, DIVISION NO. 4, NIAGARA DISTRICT.

BY A. H. KILMAN, RIDGEWAY, ONT.

The past season has not been marked by any great insect depredations, at least as far as my personal observation and inquiry have reached, in this locality—Niagara District—but variations in the occurrence of insect pests, pointing either to an increase or a decrease or in the more startling direction of the approach of new foes, is always of interest to students of Entomology and to farmers and fruit growers.

Contary to expectation, the Northern Army-worm, *Leucania unipuncta*, was less in evidence than during 1896-7. In late August, when the imagines of this insect are nearly always to be found, none were observed. The grass-hopper, (*Caloptenus femur-rubrum*) was also conspicuously absent.

Cabbage butter-flies *Pieris rapae*) during the drought in the earlier part of the season, were scarce but late cabbages were much injured by the larvæ of this insect. Similar observations were made in regard to the Colorado potato-beetle. Early potatoes were not materially injured and unwary gardeners, deceived by the non-appearance of the slugs, relaxed their efforts and paid the penalty by seeing the plants of the later crop "sailing under bare poles."

Raspberry canes have been seriously injured in some localities, by a cane borer, probably *Oberea bimaculata*.

An inconspicuous green worm, doubtless the Raspberry Saw Fly (*Selandria rubi*, Harris), operated in spots all over the fruit section, completely destroying some patches of red-raspberries near Niagara Falls.

Neglected vineyards on sandy soil suffered an entire loss of crop from the ravages of the Rose Beetle (*Macrodactylus subspinosus*, Fabr.)

In this locality plums failed to blossom. The Curculio (*Conotrachelus nenuphar*), attacked the later cherries with the result that the fruit was wormy and useless.

Apples, especially in neglected and unthrifty orchards, were scarred by insects and fungi and wormy by larvæ of Codling moth.

The Tussock Moth (*Orgyia leucostigma*) is on the increase here. In the neighboring city of Buffalo, it has become a scourge, defoliating the horse-chestnut trees, and attacking other trees as well. To gather and destroy the cocoons or egg masses in winter seems to be the most feasible method of checking the ravages of this insect.

The birch trees in the parks are attacked by a new pest, an Agrilus. The species will be determined next summer.

Crioceris asparagi, Linn., the Asparagus Beetle, (Fig. 58) which according to Dr. A. S. Packard, is not a native but an introduced species has advanced in its attack upon asparagus plants as far north as Niagara River. Mr. Reinecke informs me that he has found the beetles in abundance on asparagus at Buffalo.

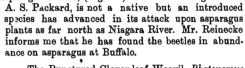

Fig. 58.

The Punctured Clover-leaf Weevil, *Phytonomus punctatus*, Fabr., in August last, appeared in great numbers on the side-walks and fences and on the shores of Lake Erie, but though I have repeatedly examined the clover fields for the purpose of determining the amount of injury done by this particular insect, thus far I have failed to find either the imago or the larvæ on a clover plant.

NOTES ON INSECTS OF THE YEAR.—DIVISION No. 5, LONDON DISTRICT

By R. W. Rennie, London, Ont.

In submitting my report as director for Division No. 5 for 1898, I am very glad to state that there have been no additions to the number of injurious insects in this district, with two exceptions ; in fact there has been a falling off in numbers of older pests that in previous years played great havoc with certain crops.

One exception is the Cottony Maple scale (*Pulvinaria innumerabilis*, Rathvon)—Fig. 59—which appeared in very large numbers this last spring; in fact, in such large numbers did they appear that on one of the finest streets in this city (London), the trees appeared to have been sprayed with white-wash.

Fig. 59.

In the fifth report of the U. S. Entomological Commission, there is an article copied from Prof. Riley's report as U. S. Entomologist for 1884, page 412, in which he states that the females, before the falling of the leaves, migrate to the branches and twigs, and there fix themselves, generally on the underside. Such has not been the case in this city. They were found occasionally on the branches and twigs, but the vast majority were noticed round the spot where a branch had been cut or broken off; indeed, so thickly that they almost overlapped each other. They have not confined their attacks to the maple, but have also been working on the grape vine.

It has apparently been quite a study to find out in what manner this spreads. Some think that it is due to planting infested trees, others by birds, insects, water, etc., but if you were to get a colony under the microscope you will soon find out how they spread.

I have a table three feet in diameter on which I use the microscope. One evening I placed a colony on a glass slip under the microscope, which was at one edge of the table, and probably examined them for ten or fifteen minutes, and there left them. Going back again in about twenty minutes, there were none on the slip, but they could be found at the extreme edge of the table. They do not seem to care what they walk over, anything and everything is the same to them. How many reached the floor I do not know, but from the number left on the table fully two-thirds had got away. Take any insect as small as this is that will walk over three feet in the course of twenty minutes, or less. Surely there can be no doubt as to how they spread, particularly when they do not care what they walk over.

As to the means proposed for destroying this pest, they are various, such as heading in of the branches. (What is the good of this if they do not confine themselves to the branches?) Also spraying with whale oil soap this may be effective, but it is also very expensive. In my own opinion there is nothing better than kerosene emulsion, which I think is one of the best destroyers of insect life that can be used without excessive expense. There are also parasitic enemies, as there are in every other branch of animal life.

About the 24th of May last I noticed a small larva feeding on the eggs, but was unable to identify it in this stage. Mr. Balkwill, the treasurer of our Society, succeeded in rearing a few, which were identified by Mr. J. Alston Moffat as Hyperapsis signata.

The other exception is *Graptodera chalybea* (Fig. 60), commonly known as the grape vine flea beetle. This insect appeared in great numbers this spring in this

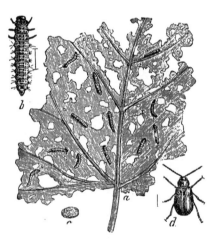

locality, although this is not a grape-growing district. This insect passes the winter in a mature state, attacks the buds of the vine as soon as they begin to grow, destroying both fruit and foliage at once. In about three or four weeks the mature insects disappear, but their place is taken by a small, insignificant looking larva, generally black in colour, which very soon makes its presence known by eating holes through the leaf, making the leaves look like sieves ; not eating like some larvæ do, starting at one part and continuing until the whole leaf is devoured. They move from place to place on the leaf, apparently selecting parts in the leaf that are most acceptable to the palate of an epicure (as such they undoubtedly are.)

These larvæ attain their full growth about the end of July, pupate in the earth, and emerge in from ten days to two weeks in the mature state. The greatest injury is done in the spring by the mature insect.

Fig. 60.

The most effective remedies for this insect are : To remove all fallen leaves in the fall, and whatever other decaying vegetable matter has accumulated around the vines, and burn it ; also in early spring to syringe the vines with a weak mixture of Paris green and water. Hellebore may be used in the summer against the larvæ.

In regard to other destructive insects, as I mentioned in the first part of my report, they have been less numerous than usual.

After remarks had been made by many of those present on the abundance or rarity during the past season of many familiar insects, the following resolution was moved and unanimously adopted :—

"That a most cordial vote of thanks be tendered to the members of the Montreal Branch for the exceedingly generous reception they have given to the Entomological Society of Ontario on the occasion of their annual meeting."

A FEW OF THE MOST TROUBLESOME INSECTS OF THE PAST SEASON
(1898).

READ BEFORE THE COLLEGE OFFICERS' LITERARY AND SCIENTIFIC SOCIETY, BY H. L. HUTT, B.S.A., ONT. AGRICULTURAL COLLEGE. GUELPH, ONT.

As far back as I can remember, I have always taken a great deal of pleasure in studying insect life. On more than one occasion can I remember being punished and disgraced in school, for investigating the jumping capabilities of a grasshopper, or squeezing an involuntary song from a captive cicada. But that was in days gone by. Now the policy of the Educational Department is to encourage the study of such subjects as were then discouraged by hard knocks.

At this institution Entomology has probably always been a part of the regular course. When I began to study it systematically about ten years ago, under the direction of Prof. Panton, it appealed to me at once as one of the most interesting and practical subjects on the curriculum. And the first summer I spent at home after leaving the College, all the available beehives, boxes and glass-topped section cases were converted into breeding cages, where all transformations could be watched in the specimens within. My collection that year was not confined to insects alone, but it contained a variety of creatures from batrachians and lepidopterous larvæ to milksnakes and their eggs. And I might add that one of the most interesting methods of studying this most interesting subject is to watch the transformation and habits of the insects themselves, either in confinement, or as they occur in nature.

As there is no class of society that is exempt from the losses and annoyance caused by insects, a knowledge of their life history and habits is important to all, but to none is it of greater importance than to the farmer and fruit-grower.

During the past summer I received a great many letters enquiring about insects affecting a wide range of crops. To deal fully with all mentioned would necessitate writing a book, but as the subject of this paper I have taken a few of the more common ones that have been the most troublesome, and these, it will be noted, represent fairly well most of the orders into which insects are usually divided.

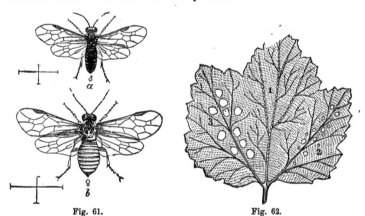

Fig. 61.   Fig. 62.

1. THE CURRANT SAW-FLY, (*Nemátus ribésii*). One of the earliest insects to make its appearance was the Currant Saw-Fly (Fig. 61, *a* the male, *b* the female). This belongs to the Hymenoptera, or membrane winged insects, and is closely related to that most industrious and beneficial of all insects—the honey-bee.

It passes the winter usually in the pupa state, in a slight papery cocoon spun beneath the surface of the ground or under rubbish or leaves. From its winter quarters it emerges early in the spring, about the time of the opening of the buds of the currant and gooseberry. Last spring they appeared in unusual numbers, and during the warm parts of the day might be seen in swarms about the bushes.

In appearance this saw-fly is a little smaller than the common house-fly, and has a yellow body. The male is considerably smaller than the female and is somewhat darker in color. During bright, warm days they are very active, but early in the morning or when the weather is cool and cloudy they are sluggish and may be easily captured.

Saw-flies are so called because of the saw-like ovipositors of the females. Speaking of these, Prof. Comstock says, "This is at least one instance of where the female wielding of a saw is done most skilfully, for the female saw-fly uses these nice tools in a very efficient manner, to make slits in the leaves and stems of plants in which she places her eggs." The eggs are deposited, from 20 to 40 in number, upon the back of the ribs and veins of the leaf, usually upon the lower leaves of the bushes (Fig. 62) They hatch in about ten days and the young larvæ begin to feed at once upon the tender leaves. They grow rapidly, and if unchecked will in a short time entirely strip the bushes of foliage. In the course of about three weeks, the larvæ become full grown (see Fig. 10), when they leave the bushes, spin small papery cocoons, and enter the pupa or resting state. From these the adult saw-flies emerge in a short time, and a second brood of larvæ follow, which strip the bushes again the latter part of summer.

This is probably one of the easiest insects to hold in check, as it feeds upon bushes that are easily got at, and it is readily destroyed by stomach poisons, such as Paris green or hellebore. The most important points in fighting it are to begin early, as the young larvæ are usually well at work by the time the leaves are full grown, and to force the spray up from the under side of the bushes so that it will reach the lower leaves where the caterpillars begin operations.

2. THE LARCH SAW-FLY (*Nemátus Erichsonii*). On the 24th of June last, my attention was directed to the scorched appearance of the foliage on the clump of European larches in the field in front of the College. Upon going to examine them closely, I found that they had been almost entirely stripped of their needles by some kind of insect. Upon further investigation I found one or two small trees on the west side of the clump upon which a few of the larvæ were still at work. It was a smooth, glaucous green worm which I had never seen before, but from certain characteristics, such as the seven pairs of prolegs and the curling under of the last segments of the body, I recognized it at once as the larva of some species of saw-fly. Upon consulting Packard's excellent report on "Forest Insects" I found it fully described as the Larch Saw-fly (*Nematus Erichsonii*), a new and much-dreaded enemy in the larch and tamarack forests.

Like the Currant Saw-fly, it is supposed to have been imported from Europe. The first notice of it on this continent was in 1881 by Dr. Hagen upon specimens found in Massachusetts. Two or three years later it was found in vast numbers in Maine, New Hampshire and other New England States, where it had stripped all the tamarack forests. In the report of the Ontario Entomological Society for 1885, Prof. Fletcher of Ottawa gives an excellent account of its life history, and of the devastation it had made in the tamarack swamps of Quebec and the Maritime Provinces.

It was then noted that the most western point that it had at that time reached was about Casselman, on the Canada Atlantic, about 30 miles east of Ottawa. Its appearance at Guelph last June would indicate that it had made considerable progress westward. In my travels over the Province last summer, I was particular to watch for indications of its presence, and I noticed from the scorched appearance of the tree tops, that it had stripped the tamaracks in many places between here and Walkerton, and that in the large tamarack swamp south of Bradford the trees in July were as bare as if a forest fire had swept through them.

The adult insect is a handsome saw-fly, somewhat resembling the Currant Saw-fly but is a little larger and darker colored, being mostly black with an orange band around the middle of the abdomen. The female deposits her eggs in incisions made in the young terminal shoots. The young larvæ feed voraciously upon the tender needles and develop with wonderful rapidity. Some idea of their voraciousness, vast numbers, and rapidity of growth may be gained from the fact that the active larval state lasts but a single week, and during this short time they often strip bare vast forests of tamarack.

When mature, they drop to the ground and pass the winter in a dark brown, oval cocoon spun in the moss or grass beneath the trees.

So far as we have learned, there is but a single brood of them during the season, and this is quite enough. As it is, the defoliated trees throw out a second set of needles, and are thus enabled to survive one or two attacks, but when they are stripped of their foliage repeatedly the results cannot be otherwise than fatal. One or two natural enemies have been found preying upon the larvæ, and it is hoped that they may be able to hold them in check, because it is usually impossible to fight them by any of the modern means of insect warfare on account of the inaccessible nature of the places in which they breed. On single trees they may easily be destroyed by spraying, or even by shaking them to the ground, as they cannot crawl back upon the trees again.

3. THE TENT CATERPILLARS (*Clisiocàmpa americàna and C. disstria*). Among the Lepidopterous, or scale-winged insects, none attracted more attention last year than the Tent-Caterpillars. There are two species of these common to this part of the continent, one known as the Apple-Tree Tent-Caterpillar, and the other as the Forest-Tent-Caterpillar. The latter appeared last year in several parts of the province in vast armies. At one place on the W.C. & B. they were reported in the papers as having been in such vast numbers that they stopped a train. And judging from the plague of them which I saw on St. Joseph's Island, I am quite prepared to believe the reports.

A comparative study of the life histories of the two species is of interest. The adult insect in each case is a reddish brown moth measuring when the wings are expanded from one and a half to one and three-quarters inches across. In this stage they have no power of taking food, and live only long enough to provide for the generation to follow. The eggs are laid about the middle of July in ring-like clusters encircling the small twigs, usually from 200 to 300 eggs in each cluster. The eggs of the *Clisiocampa Americana* may be distinguished from those of the *Clisiocampa disstria* by the oval form of the clusters, those of the latter being squarely cut off at each end. In both cases the egg masses are covered with a thick coat of tough varnish which renders them waterproof, a wise provision of nature, as it is nearly nine months before the young caterpillars emerge from them. During the first warm days of spring they make their appearance, and after taking their first meal from the gummy substance which has protected them for the winter they begin to feed upon the opening buds.

The most striking difference in the two species now becomes apparent in the habits of the young caterpillar. Those of *Clisiocampa Americana* spin a tent in the nearest large fork of the branch upon which they are hatched. Into this they retire at night, during stormy weather, or when they are not feeding, in warm weather they often repose in a black mass upon the outside of it, leaving it regularly once in the forenoon and again in the afternoon to feed. Each caterpillar spins a silken web along the branch wherever it travels. Thus they never lose their way home although they may forage all over the tree. The caterpillars of the other species do not dwell in tents and are more disposed to lead a wandering life. When young they often march from place to place in single file close procession. From the time they are half grown until they reach maturity they are wonderfully active and move about as if they were in a great hurry and had no time to lose.

Both species reach maturity in about six weeks, and are then handsome hairy caterpillars, about two inches in length. *Clisiocampa disstria* has a row of white spots down the centre of the back, which distinguishes it from the other species, in which the white line is unbroken.

The Forest Tent-Caterpillar is a general feeder, living on a great variety of forest trees and often doing considerable damage in orchards. The Apple-tree Tent-Caterpillar is not such a general feeder, and is more frequently found on the apple or wild cherry. For the latter it has a particular preference. In our forest plantation where there are 15 or 20 different species of trees, it was noticed last spring that every tree of the wild cherry had two or three nests of these caterpillars, while not another tree in the plantation was affected.

Another difference between these two insects appears in the construction of their cocoons. Those of *Clisiocampa Americana* are formed of a double web, the outer one loosely woven and filled with a powderly substance resembling sulphur. They are usually hid in some out of the way place, as under rails, boards or rubbish. Those of *Clisiocampa disstria* have none of this powdery substance and are more frequently formed inside of the leaves hanging on the trees. On St. Joseph's Island last summer, I saw hundreds of maples and other forest trees upon which every leaf contained one of these concoons, even the native spruces were so full of them that they appeared as if packed in wool.

4 CANKER-WORMS.—(*Paleacrita vernáta* and *Alsophila pometária.*)—Canker-worms have been very abundant in many parts of the country for a number of years past. There are also two species of these, but they resemble each other so closely that to the causal observer they differ only in name. One is known as the Spring Canker-Worm (*Paleacrita vernáta*) (Fig. 63), and the other as the Fall Canker-Worm (*Alsophila pometária*) (Fig. 64). One of the most noticeable differences in the two species appears in the egg stage. The eggs (Fig. 63 *a* and *b*) of the Spring Canker-Worm are oval in form and are laid in the spring in irregular patches hidden under loose bark or in expanding buds.

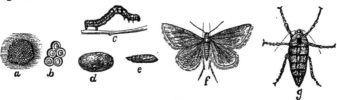

Fig. 63.

Those of the Fall species are shaped like miniature flower pots, are ranged in regular rows in masses (Fig. 65, *a, b, c*), and deposited in the late autumn in some prominent place on the tree. The larvæ of both species (Fig. 63 *c* and 65 *f*) make their appearance with the opening of the leaves in the spring. They reach their full size in about three weeks and are then about an inch in length. On account of their peculiar method of travelling, by alternately looping and extending their bodies, they are commouly spoken of as "measuring worms." They have another peculiar habit when disturbed of suddenly dropping from the tree and suspending themselves in mid air by a delicate silken web which is spun as they drop. Their appearance in this position is graphically described in the following letter which I received from a correspondent last June :—

Fig. 64.   Fig. 65.

BRIGHTON, June 6th, 1898.

DEAR SIR,—Last evening my husband said, "Come with me, I wish to show you a sight." We went into the orchard. "Now," says he, "see that tree over there, the leaves are all eaten up." "Worms," says I. "Yes," says he, "but not the kind you know." He took a stick and gave a limb a tap, and in an instant one hundred worms were hanging by tiny webs. He then went around hitting all the limbs he could reach, and I think there must have been a million worms suspended in the air beneath that tree. "Now, May," says he, "what am I to do? I have manured and thoroughly worked this orchard for two years, have had it trimmeed, and the worms' nests all taken out of it once this spring, now just look at it." "I'll tell you," says I, "I'll write to the Agricultural College and see what they advise." An answer would be gratefully received, as the orchard is no small item in our accounts.

Yours truly;

———— ————.

In an orchard that is regularly sprayed they can give little or no trouble, as they are easily destroyed by Paris green, but in large shade trees, which are some-times attacked, and where the spraying cannot easily be done, strategic measures have to be resorted to. From the fact that the female moth in both species is wing-less, and after emerging from the pupa in the ground has to climb the tree to deposit her eggs, the placing of a tar band or other barrier upon the trunks of the trees at once suggests itself as a remedy.

5. THE COLORADO POTATO BEETLE.—(*Doryphora decem-lineáta.*)—The potato bug, or more properly, the potato beetle (Fig. 13) is with us yet, and he seems to be here to stay. Out of about ten thousand species of Coleoptera common to this coun-try, the potato beetle stands out prominently as the one most generally troublesome. We have become so familiar with it that we seldom think of it but to kill it, yet a few facts as to its history in this country may be of interest. To the late Dr. C V. Riley, of Washington, we are indebted for the best account of it that has anywhere been published, and I have made free use of his little book on "Potato Pests," in the preparation of these notes.

The Colorado Potato Bug, as it has been commonly called, was first described under the scientific name Doryphora decem-lineata, by Thomas Say, in 1824. It was then to be found only in Colorado and the North-Western States, just this side of the Rocky Mountains. Its original food plant was the Sand Bur (Solanum rostratum) a species of wild potato peculiar to that region.

As civilization advanced westward and potatoes began to be grown in its native home, it gradually acquired the habit of feeding upon the cultivated potato, and began its eastward march from potato patch to potato patch. In 1859 it had reached to within 100 miles of Omaha City in Nebraska. In 1861 it invaded Iowa, and gradu-ally during the next three or four years it spread eastward over the whole State. In 1864 and 1865 it crossed the Mississippi into Illinois, at four or five different points coming on in a column about 200 miles broad from north to south. It was then travelling at the rate of fifty miles a year and it was predicted that it would reach the Atlantic Sea board in 1881. On this side of the Mississippi, however, the potato fields were more plentiful and it began to make better time, actually arriv-ing on the Atlantic coast in 1874, seven years ahead of time, its average rate of progress being 88 miles per year. This rate, however, was not uniform, the northern columns of the army made the most rapid progress; the southern columns travelling through a country where potatoes were not so much grown, and under a broiling hot sun, lagged far behind.

The invasion of Ontario began in July of 1870, at two points on the western frontier, namely, near Point Edward and near Windsor. During 1871 they came on in increasing numbers, and it was said that during that summer the Detroit river was literally swarming with them. They were crossing on ships, chips, staves, boards, or any other floating object that presented itself. By June of that year they were common around London, and, Mr. Squirrel informs me, that later that year they had reached as far as Galt. I can well remember the first one I ever saw ; it must have been in the summer of 1872.   I was then a little chap attending school on the historic battle field of Lundy's Lane, and I little knew then that I had met an enemy that would refuse to be driven from the country, for their invasion was one not only of conquest but colonization wherever they went.

A few beetles were sent to us last summer which were covered with a very interesting parasite known as *Uropoda Americana*.   These are little mites about the size of a small pin-head, and of a flax seed brown colour.   Each beetle was so thickly covered with them that hardly any part of its body was visible.   The infested beetles were placed upon a potato plant along with some of their healthy relatives in hopes that their enemies might increase and subdue them, but after a few days the infested beetles had disappeared and the parasites with them, while the healthy beetles fed on serenely.

6. GRASSHOPPERS.—The grasshoppers belong to the Orthoptera or straight-winged insects.   Of these we have a great many species, but they may all be grouped into two families—the Acridiæ or short-horned grasshoppers, and the Locustidæ or long-horned grasshoppers.

There has been much confusion of terms in the common names applied to these insects. The term locust properly applies to the first family, and not to the Locustidæ, or long-horned grasshoppers.   The term locust is also improperly applied to the Cicada, which belongs to another order altogether.   To all but entomologists, however, the members of both families are usually known as grasshoppers, and for convenience in this paper we shall use that general term.

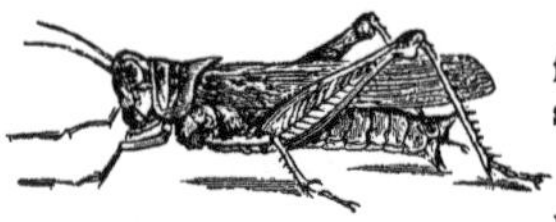

Fig. 66.

The most common species with us is the Melanoplus, femur-rubrum, the red-legged grasshopper, or, more properly speaking, locust.

The females of this species deposit their eggs in holes made in the ground by means of their ovipositors.   The eggs are laid in masses in the fall of the year, and hatch during the following spring or early summer.   The young do not undergo complete metamorphosis, or change of form, as do the insects of the other orders we have mentioned. There is no larval stage ; the young make their appearance as little grasshoppers without wings.   They pass through several moults, and the wings gradually develop.   With the last moult they become full fledged, and their destructiveness is then increased by their increased powers of locomotion.

Grasshoppers are more or less troublesome every year in all parts of the country, but they are usually particularly plentiful in localities where there is much waste land or poor farming.   Two years ago I wheeled through the country from Walkerton to Clarksburg, a distance of about fifty miles   There was then in many places through which I passed almost another plague of locusts or grasshoppers.   In conversation with a farmer whom I met I learned there were in some sections of that country quite a number of abandoned farms, where grasshoppers had been breeding year after year unmolested.   Upon these farms they ate everything bare and then spread to adjoining farms.   Good farming with clean cultivation and short rotation of crops is one of the best means of avoiding a grasshopper plague.   On the College farm here Mr. Rennie tells me that since the fences have been removed, the permanent pastures broken up, and a short rotation of crops adopted, hardly a grasshopper could be found, whereas the old fence bottoms and permanent pastures were formerly alive with them.

7. APHIDS, OR PLANT-LICE.—Probably the most widely distributed and generally injurious insects during the past two years have been the Aphids, or plant-lice.   They are members of the family Aphididæ, belonging to the section Homoptera, in the order Hemiptera.   This section or sub-order Homoptera includes not only the Aphids but all of the bark lice, scale insects, mealy bugs, and leaf hoppers, some of the most injurious insects, and at the same time some of the most difficult to fight.

They are characterized, in common with all the other insects of this order, by a suctorial mouth, with which they take all their food in a liquid form, sucking it as juice from the plants upon which they feed. They are further remarkable for their insignificant size and the wonderful rapidity with which they breed. There are a great many species of plant-lice, and they infest in one form or another a great variety of trees and plants. The tendency has been to name these according to the tree or plant upon which they feed. One of the most destructive species in this and many others sections last year was the *Aphis brassicae*, or cabbage aphis, which affects cabbage, turnips, rape, and other brassicaceous plants. Another was the Aphis mali, or apple aphis. On the cherry there was a very troublesome black species known as Mysus cerasi, or the cherry-tree aphis. These are only a few of them, but they are all alike very troublesome in sucking the sap and reducing the vigor of the plants upon which they feed.

Many species like those on the cherry, apple and plum, excrete a sticky liquid substance known as "honey dew," upon which ants, bees, and flies regale themselves. The presence of ants running up and down the trees is almost a sure indication that aphids are at work upon the leaves. Other species, like those infesting the cabbage and turnip, excrete a white powdery substance which covers their bodies. In the woolly aphis infesting the roots of apple trees, this excretion is so fluffy that the insects appear to be covered with wool.

The life history of plant lice is peculiar. The various species differ considerably in the details of the transformations, but the following may be given as applying to most of them. The eggs which are shiny black are very large for the size of the insect, are laid in the fall upon the food plant. From these hatch in the spring wingless females, which without the intervention of the males soon begin to bring forth living young. In five days or six days these young aphids begin to reproduce in the same way. This process of agamic reproduction and compound multiplication goes on so rapidly that in a short time the progeny of the original "stem mother" mounts up into the millions. If this production of wingless forms continued long, it would mean the starvation of all, by the destruction of the plants upon which they were feeding, but Nature provides for this by the development after a time of winged forms which "hie away to fresh fields and pastures new," and in this way they spread. Often in the fall the air is so full of these flying aphides that a person riding or driving quickly becomes covered them. As the cold weather approaches and vegetation ceases, sexual forms, male and female are developed, the females being wingless. Eggs are again produced to carry the species over to another year.

From the fact that Aphids and other insects of this order insert their beaks and suck their food from the interior of the leaves or stems, it is evident that the application of stomach poisons such as Paris green can be of no avail in destroying them. The material supplied must be something that will kill by coming in contact with their soft bodies. The kerosene emulsion, so generally recommended, has been found to be more or less satisfactory, because of the frequent injury it does to the foliage upon which it is applied. Another remedy much more satisfactory, is a strong decoction of tobacco, made by boiling a pound of tobacco waste in five gallons of water, and this is made doubly effective by dissolving in it a quarter of a pound of whale-oil soap. This should be applied as soon as the aphids appear, as after a time it becomes difficult to reach them because of the curling over them of the leaves upon which they are feeding.

Nature's most active agents in holding plant lice in check are the Lady Birds. Last summer these and their larvæ could be found actively at work devouring the lice upon almost every tree and plant infested.

7. HOUSE-FLIES.—(*Musca domestica, et al.*) Of all the insects that bother and annoy the house keeper none are more common than the house flies. And notwithstanding this fact the woman, or man either, who can give a full account of the life history of these flies is as rare as the one whose house is free from them during the summer season.

All true flies belong to the order Diptera or two-winged insects. There are several species commonly found in houses, although but one of these should properly be called the house-fly. This is the Musca domestica, a medium sized grayish fly too well known to need description.

The life history of this species, which is fairly typical of the majority of them, may be briefly outlined as follows : It passes the winter in the house or some other building, hiding in sheltered spots anywhere between the cellar and the garret. A few specimens in the warmed rooms occasionally hum about in the winter, reminding us that they have seen better days. In the early spring the few sole survivors of the swarms of the preceeding year make their appearance. These are mostly females ready at once to become mothers and by the end of the season their children and great great grand children extend to the tenth and twelfth generations. Each female lays on an average about 120 eggs at a time, which are deposited in irregular masses usually in horse manure. The eggs hatch in about twenty-four hours and the larvae coming from them are white footless maggots about half an inch in length. In this stage of its existence the fly is beneficial as a scavenger. In from five to seven days the larvæ attain their full size, and enter the pupa or resting state. In its outward appearance the pupa is a smooth brown oval shell about a quarter of an inch in length and less than half of that in diameter. In manure heaps these may often be gathered by the shovel-full. In some investigations conducted at Washington last summer, as many as 1,200 larvæ and puparia were counted in one pound of horse manure. The pupa stage also lasts only from five to seven days. So that to produce a full fledged fly from the laying of the egg requires only about ten days or two weeks.

To trace the development of the fly through all of these stages is very easy, but to ascertain the length of life of the adult fly is more difficult, and as yet I have seen no data on the subject. The Washington experimenters declared that this was a bit of information almost impossible to obtain correctly, because of the inability of the fly to live in close confinement. Here then is a point in the life history of one of our commonest insects about which we are yet more or less in the dark.

A few of the other species of flies commonly found in houses may be mentioned· The one most closely resembling the house fly in appearance is the *Stomoxys calcitrans*, or stable fly, so troublesome on horses and cattle. The most important difference in this species is that the mouth parts are formed for piercing the skin. A bite from one of these is just as painful as the sting from a bee, but it has not the same poisonous after-effects.

One of the largest species found in houses is the *Calliphora vomitoria*, or "blue-bottle fly," that big, blue, buzzing, bummy, beggar that goes tearing through the house from room to room as though he owned the premises. He is capable in a few minutes of arousing more fight in a woman than all the other flies combined. A favorite place for this species to lay its eggs, is in meat that has been exposed for a short time. As with most other flies, the time required for development is short, and the rate of increase is so rapid that it has given rise to the saying that a pair of these flies will devour an ox more rapidly than a lion,

One of the smallest species seen in houses, the *Homalomya canicularis*, is sometimes called the small house-fly. This species is largely responsible for the prevalent but erronous idea that little flies become big ones.

In closing this paper we should like to enter a plea for a more general study of this most interesting branch of natural history. In none do we find a greater range for observation and research, and in none can practical investigation be turned to more profitable account.

NOTES OF THE SEASON OF 1898.

By J. Alston Moffat, London, Ont.

One of the most noticeable pecularities of the Entomological year about London, was the scarcity of diurnals ; many of the more common forms being to all appearance entirely absent. There were some noticeable exceptions to the rule, *Pieris rapae* for instance. From the early part of May to the end of the month, it was in unusual abundance for the spring brood. More like what one is accustomed to see in the autumn about cabbage and turnip fields ; indeed it was more plentiful in the spring than at any other time of the year, something unusual in its history, and starting the inquiry, what had become of its faithful attendant parasite *Pteromalus puparum ?* The yellow swallow-tail *Papilio turnus,* appeared in moderate numbers, also *Limenitis ursula,* whilst that nearly ubiquitous butterfly *Colias philodice* that helps to give life and animation to every rural scene was rarely seen. I am not certain that I saw a Milkweed butterfly, *Danais Archippus* about London until the middle of September. The larger silver-spotted frittillary *Argynnis* were noticeably scarce ; and so on through the entire list of common forms ; which made the meditative contemplation of a landscape dull and uninteresting by reason of their absence.

Collecting at electric light commenced early and continued good up to the end of June, many interesting and attractive specimens being obtainable by that method. The early geometers and some species of the noctuids were in abundance, whilst hybernated specimens of Scopelosoma and Lithophane were plentiful, and many of them were in excellent condition. *L. antennata* must be a very hardy insect, and capable of enduring extremes of cold ; Mr. Bice having found specimens of it about the lights during the months of January, February and March ; the least indication of mildness in the weather was sure to bring it out. July and August were characterized by more their usual unprofitableness to the collector, giving him plenty of hunting but little collecting. There were no reports of any serious injury having been done in this locality to crops or fruits from insect pests. Many of the ornamental bushes and shade trees of the city were rendered unsightly by the presence in great numbers upon their branches of the Cottony Scale, *Pulvinaria innumerabilis,* but the attack passed off without any apparent injury resulting.

On the 2nd of June I received from J. D. B. Mackenzie, Esq , of Chatham, N. B., a letter, stating that he had sent to me for identification, some insects that had appeared upon his cherry trees and literally stripped them of their foliage in two or three days. The insect proved to be *Ademonia rufosanguinea,* Say, of the Chrysomelid family ; an innocent enough looking little beetle that would not be suspected of being capable of working such destruction. It must surely be a rather unusual occurrence ? Their numbers must have been great. He also wished for information as to where he could get a description of its life history ? That I could not give him.

On the 27th of July I received from Clinton, Ont., a box six inches long by four wide and one and a half deep, filled with the remains of Web-worm moths, *Clisiocampa Americana* and *disstria* mostly ; said to have been the result of one night's capture in one street lamp—kind of lamp not stated, electric probably. I had read in the newspapers earlier in the season, accounts of the running of railway trains being interfered with in some localities, by reason of the swarms of caterpillars on the track ; that may have been one of the localities. At all events, that boxful gave evidence of great negligence on the part of those interested, in their dealings with their tent caterpillars.

On July the 22nd, I took a trip to Lake Erie Shore. I had heard a good deal about ' Rondeau,' the Government reserve and the public park there, and that it was easily reached by rail from Chatham, Ont., so I thought it might be a profitable place to spend a day or two. In anticipation I was going to a place well wooded and wild; but instead, I was landed far out upon a sand-bar almost entirely destitute of vegetation. This sand-bar is what separates Rondeau (round water, admirably descriptive) from Lake Erie, whilst the Government reserve is on the opposite side of the bay, nine miles or so away in a straight line and no convenient means of reaching it ; and as my time was limited I made no effort to do so. The sand-bar is being utilized for summer residences with its excellent boating and bathing privileges, and is locally known as ' Erieau,' a euphonious combination but lacking in correct significance. In such conditions there was but little opportunity for me to indulge in my favorite pursuit ; yet even there I came upon two insects which I had never met with alive before. One was that highly ornamented little dragon fly, *Celithemes Eliza,* Hagen, which was quite plentiful amongst the straggling milkweeds and wild rice growing along the bay side of the shore, and was in fine condition as if recently emerged. The abdomen of one sex is ornamented with bright red, the other with yellow, but their brilliance disappears in drying. In company with it, but in greatly inferior numbers was *Celithemes Eponina*, Drury, which used to be plentiful in one locality at Hamilton. The other find was that attractive Hemipteron *Lygaeus fasciatus*, Fab. Although milk-weeds were to be found for hundreds of yards along the bay shore, there was but one spot where I saw it, and that was a small clump situated between two cottages, and from which by frequent visits I secured seven of them. There I observed on the wing as the first of the season, a few fine fresh specimens of the milk-weed butter-fly, *D. Archippus*, Fab.

In July, Dr. W. J. Stevenson brought to me a fresh maple tree borer, *Plagionotus Speciosus*, Say, (Fig. 67) the first living specimen of it I have seen taken at London. I could obtain it at Hamilton by the dozen where the shade trees are nearly all hard maple, whilst in London they are as nearly all soft maple ; and to that as a cause I have always attributed its absence here.

During the autumn there was the usual appearance in abundance of two or three species of the Cut-worm moths at light, whilst amongst them was to be obtained an occasional rare and desirable specimen of other kinds. About the end of September Mr. Bice secured a number

Fig. 67.   of that attractive Pyralid, *Eudioptis hyalinata*, Linn. It was on the 29th day of September, 1881, that I saw at Hamilton my first specimen of it on the wing, and so far as is known, very few have been taken in Ontario since, and not more than a single specimen in a season. This disclosure of such a marked increase in numbers is of considerable importance to the community, as indicating the possibility of its becoming here, such as it has proved itself to be in the Western and Southern States a first class pest to the cultivators of that delicious fruit, the musk melon. In the Eleventh Report of the New York State Entomologist for the year 1895, after giving an account of the total destruction of some melon patches in the south, which had been cultivated for the market, at page 138 it is stated : " It would appear from the limited literature accessible, that *Eudioptis hyalinata* is more especially a southern insect. I have examples in my collection from Texas. It has also been taken in Michigan, is not uncommon in New Jersey, and has been taken in Canada. I have no knowledge of its occurrence in the State of New York." That it had not been reported from New York State was to me rather a surprise, and I started the question whence came it to us ? It would seem as if it must have reached Ontario by way of the west, having found the conditions most favorable for its spreading in that direction. It is the habit in some quarters to speak disparagingly of " mere collectors." But an occurrence of this nature brings forcibly to view the great loss, that even now, our department of science is suffering from the want of more collectors ; for it is upon their labors and observations that we are largely depending for our knowledge of the introduction and spread of injurious species. A knowledge of the flora and fauna of any particular district is of great general interest and advantage to all students of nature, whether the individual disclosing it has any time, inclination or ability to devote to the technicalities of the subject or not, and is well deserving of the grateful acknowledgements of all.

Almost the same time as the preceding, Mr. Bice took several specimens of another Pyralid, *Pilocrosis ramentalis*, Led. This species was represented in the Society's collection by a single specimen taken by me at Hamilton, and named for me by Mr. Grote, then of Buffalo, who had much of interest to tell me of the peculiarities of this insect, one noticeable thing about it is the long scales covering the costal margin at base of the front wings of the females, which can be raised so as to disclose the membrane. Mr. J. Johnston of Hamilton informed me that these two species are represented in his collection by a single specimen of each, taken by him there many years ago. Recently I have seen a specimen of *E. hyalinata* amongst some material sent to me for determination by Mr. C. E. Grant, of Orillia. In September the Tomato Sphinx, *S. quinquemaculata*, Hub, was quite plentiful, which suggests some interesting queries concerning the life history of this species. It is considered to be single brooded in this latitude ; but it is known to mature occasionally in confinement the same season as produced. Were these

September specimens from eggs of an early brood, or were they from belated chrysalids of the previous summer's production? It has been observed that there is a great differance in the time of their appearance in nature, some showing themselves in early June, whilst fresh specimens may be obtained at the end of July; the location of the winter quarters of the pupæ influencing the time of maturing to some extent most likely. Again, if these late comers produced ova could they pass the winter safely? If not, then it would help materially to reduce the numbers for the following season. Of Sphingidae less frequently met with in this locality, Mr. Bice took specimens of *Ampelophaga versicolor* Harr. The Tobacco Sphinx, *S. Carolina*, Linn., and *S. Cingulata*, Fab., or *Convolvuli* of Linn. One thing secured by him, and determined by Dr. J. B. Smith, which is new to the Society's collection, is a single specimen of *Hydroecia limpida*, Guen., whilst several other Noctuids of the season's capture are not yet identified.

THE FREEZING OF INSECTS.

By Henry H. Lyman, Montreal.

In the 22nd Report of the Entomological Society of Ontario, being that for 1891, there appeared a paper from my pen under the title, " Can Insects Survive Freezing?"

I have recently come across further records of observations upon this subject, and deem them of sufficient interest to be republished.

In looking over an interesting book of travels, entitled " A journey from Prince of Wales's Fort in Hudson's Bay to the Northern Ocean, undertaken by order of the Hudson's Bay Company for the discovery of copper mines, a North West passage, etc., in the years 1769, 1770, 1771, and 1772, by Samuel Hearne," published in 1796, I came across the following interesting notes on page 397. :—

" Frogs, Grubs, and other Insects."

" Frogs of various colours are numerous in those parts as far north as the latitude 61°. They always frequent the margins of lakes, ponds, rivers, and swamps; and as the winter approaches they burrow under the moss at a considerable distance from the water, wher they remain in a frozen state till the spring. I have frequently seen them dug up with the moss (when pitching tents in winter) frozen as hard as ice; in which state the legs are as easily broken off as a pipe stem, without giving the least sensation to the animal; but by wrapping them up in warm skins, and exposing them to a slow fire, they soon recover life, and the mutilated animal gains its usual activity; but if they are permitted to freeze again they are past all recovery, and are never more known to come to life. The same may be said of the various species of Spiders, and all the Grub kind, which are very numerous in those parts. I have seen thousands of them dug up with the moss, when we were pitching our tents in the winter; all of which were invariably enclosed in a thick web, which Nature teaches them to spin on those occasions; yet they were apparently all frozen as hard as ice. The spiders, if let fall from any height on a hard substance, would rebound like a grey pea; and all the Grub kind are so hard frozen as to be as easily broken as a piece of ice of the same size; yet when exposed to a slow heat, even in the depth of winter, they will soon come to life, and in a short time recover their usual motions."

In Dr. H. Guard Knaggs' Lepidopterist's Guide, on page 44 of the 1871 edition, under the heading of " Ailments of Larvæ," I find the following :—

" Frost Bite.—It is well known that larvæ, which have been so stifly frozen that they might have been easily broken, have afterwards recovered. The chief thing to be remembered in the treatment of such cases, is that the thawing should be effected very gradually, rapid thawing being dangerous."

ODOUR OF THE SAN JOSE SCALE, *Aspidiotus perniciosus*

By F. M. WEBSTER, WOOSTER, OHIO.

In the many accounts of this insect I do not recall that attention has been called to the odour that is associated with this insect and which in cases of excessive abundance, can be detected at a considerably distance away. Where the air is quiet it is often possible to detect the presence of a badly infested tree a yard away, and I presume that with more acute olfactories, such as insects are supposed by many to possess, even the presence of a more limited number of the scale might be detected at a much greater distance. As ants do not appear to be at all partial to this Coccid, at least in this country, it is not easy to understand what influence this odour can have in the economy of the species. It is possible that, in its native home, this odour might attract other insects and thus afford a means of diffusion, not at present so available to the scale in this country.

THE ODOUR OF COCCIDÆ.—Prof. Webster's interesting note leads me to offer a few remarks. The species of the subgenus of *Toumeyella* of *Lecanium* have quite a strong musky odour ; but ordinarily I have been unable to detect any marked odour in species of Coccidæ. I suppose, however, that all possess some odour, and that its purpose is to attract the males to the females. This seems the more probable when we remember that in many species the male puparia are not on the same part of the plant as the females. Here at Mesilla Park, also, I have lately seen a male of *Margarodes hiemalis*, Ckll. ined , run over the ground until it detected a spot where a female was buried, and then dig down to the female. It must certainly have detected its mate by the sense of smell

T. D. A. COCKERELL.

LIFE HISTORY OF THE SHEEP SCAB-MITE, *Psoroptes communis*.

By C. P. GILLETTE, FORT COLLINS, COLORADO.

I am not aware that the full life-history of this insect has been published, though I shall not be surprised to learn that such is the case.

In order to know how long a time should intervene between the first and second dippings for the cure of scab, we must know the period of incubation and also the entire time elapsing from the deposition of the egg up to the time that the mite from that egg, if a female, may be itself depositing eggs. These points were determined in a series of experiments conducted by the writer one year ago and were reported in a local paper, the " Fort Collins Courier," last spring. I took seventy-five eggs from a lock of wool drawn from the back of a badly infested lamb and, after dividing them in two nearly equal lots, placed them at once on the skin of the backs of two lambs that were not infested with the mites at the time. In order to irritate the surface a little and better prepare it for the little mites that would begin at once to hatch, a lock of wool was drawn in each case from the particular spot where the eggs were placed.

Mr. Ball, assistant in my department, made a special examination of these "cultures " once a day until the mites from the eggs were fully grown and themselves laying eggs.

At the first examination a few young mites were found, which was to be expected as a few eggs among so many would be about ready to hatch. At the end of the fourth day all the eggs had hatched. At the end of the ninth day a few individuals were found in copula, and on the eleventh day eggs were found. As it required four days for the newly deposited eggs to hatch, the entire time elapsing from egg to egg would be fourteen or fifteen days.

As there would be eggs in all stages of incubation upon a sheep when the latter is dipped for the cure of scab, I have set the limit of time for the second dipping at not sooner than five days and not later than ten days after the first dipping. If the second dipping comes at a time outside this limit, there will probably be eggs upon the sheep again.

OBITUARY.

PROFESSOR J. HOYES PANTON, M.A., F.G.S.

It is our sad duty to record the death of Professor Panton, which took place at Guelph, on the 3rd of February, 1898, after a long and very painful illness, which he bore with the utmost patience and resignation. He was born at Cupar, in Fifeshire, Scotland, and was brought out to Canada when a child ; his father settled in Toronto at first, and removed, after some years, to Oshawa. He was educated at the Whitby High School and Toronto University, where he graduated with honors in Natural Science in 1877. The following year he was appointed Professor of Chemistry in the Ontario Agricultural College, but after a few years resigned the position and removed to Winnipeg, where he became principal of the Collegiate Institute. In 1885 he accepted the invitation of the Ontario Government and returned to Guelph, where he filled the position of Professor of Natural History and Geology in the Agricultural College till the time of his death. His work there had special relation to economic entomology and botany, on which subjects he issued many useful bulletins to farmers and fruit growers. He also published two small works on Economic Geology and "Insect Foes," which are valuable manuals of an elementary character. In 1896.Professor Panton attended for the first time the annual meeting of the Entomological Society of Ontario, though he had long been a member, and on that occasion read very interesting and useful papers on "Entomology for Rural Schools " and " Two Insect Pests of 1896—the Army Worm and the Tussock Moth." At the annual meeting in October, 1897, he was elected vice-president of the Society, but was unable to attend owing to the illness which had already seized upon him. The following resolution of condolence was adopted at a meeting of the Council held in March : " The members of the Council of the Entomological Society of Ontario have heard with profound regret of the death of their highly respected colleague and vice-president, J. Hoyes Panton, M.A., F.G.S., Professor of Biology and Geology in the Ontario Agricultural College, Guelph. They desire to place on record their admiration for his talents and attainments in natural science, and their deep sense of the loss which economic entomology in this Province sustained by his removal in the maturity of his powers and at an age when he was capable of performing much useful work. They beg to offer to Mrs. Panton and family their respectful sympathy in the great bereavement which has befallen them."

On the 18th of February, 1898, Mr. JOHNSON PETTIT died at Buffalo, N.Y., and was buried a few days later at Grimsby, Ont. For many years Mr. Pettit was a most diligent and successful collector of Coleoptera in the neighborhood of Grimsby, and was well known amongst entomologists both in this country and the United States. After forming a very complete collection of the beetles of Ontario so far as known at that time, he gave up the pursuit and turned his attention to geology. Subsequently he sold his cabinet of insects to the Entomological Society of Ontario at a nominal price, in order that it might be kept in a place of safety and preserved from destruction. His work was characterized by remarkable neatness and painstaking accuracy.

PROFESSOR DAVID SIMONS KELLICOTT was born at Hastings Centre, Oswego County, N.Y., January 28, 1842, and died at his home in Columbus, Ohio, April 13, 1898. In his boyhood his frail constitution and delicate health required him to spend much of his time out of doors, and it is to this, no doubt, that in part at least his love for nature may be traced. He graduated from Syracuse University with the degree of B. Sc., while the institution was yet known as Genesee College, teaching one year in Southern Ohio prior to his graduation. After graduating, he taught one year in Kingston Normal School, Pennsylvania, after which he was connected for seventeen years with the State University, at Buffalo, N.Y., being Dean of the College of Pharmacy, and also Professor of Botany and Microscopy. He came to the Ohio State University in 1888, where, for ten years, he has occupied the chair of zoology and entomology. At the time of his death he was General Secretary of the American Association for the Advancement of Science, President of the American Microscopical Society, and Treasurer of the Ohio Academy of Science. He had served as President of the Buffalo, N.Y., Academy of Science, and the Ohio Academy of Science.

Animal parasites of fishes, and the rotifera, from time to time claimed a considerable portion of Professor Kellicott's attention, but his entomological work won for him the admiration of the entomologists of America. Patient, conscientious and utterly devoid of selfishness, he was one of the most kind and loveable men the writer has ever met. Faithful and just with his colleagues and the idol of his pupils, seeking patiently and industriously after the truth, he won esteem while living, and in his death he has left numberless friends to mourn his loss. If there was ever a man who deserved the reward: "Well done, thou good and faithful servant," that man was David S. Kellicott; and the fruits of his labors will stand as an enduring monument to his faithfulness among his fellow men. He began to contribute to the Canadian Entomologist in 1878, his last article appearing in 1896.   F. M. WEBSTER.

DR. JOSEPH ALBERT LINTNER.

By the death of Dr. J. A. Lintner, which occurred at Florence, Italy, on May 6th economic entomology has lost one of its oldest, ablest, and most distinguished devotees. He was of German parentage, and was born at Schoharie, N.Y., February 8, 1822. He graduated from the Schoharie Academy at the age of fifteen, and for the next thirty years was actively engaged in mercantile pursuits in New York City, Schoharie and Utica. The study of natural history became a fascination for him early in life, and in 1853, he turned his attention especially to insects and rendered valuable aid to Dr. Fitch, who was then making an entomological survey of the State of New York.

Dr. Lintner's first paper upon insects was published in 1862, and six years later he became zoological assistant in the New York State Museum of Natural History. He continued in the service of the State until his death, working as assistant in the Museum for twelve years, and in 1880 receiving the appointment of State Entomologist. This thirty years of continuous, active service in an official capacity, in a useful and limited scientific field, and in a single State, is certainly a remarkable record, and one which speaks volumes of praise for Dr. Lintner.

He richly deserved the honour of the degree of Ph. D. conferred upon him in 1884 by the University of the State of New York. He was also honoured with the presidency of several scientific associations, and his name is enrolled among the members of many entomological and other scientific societies, both in America and in Europe. The publications of Dr. Lintner merit the highest praise and deservedly entitle him to the foremost rank among the economic entomologists of the world. He published more than a thousand miscellaneous articles upon injurious insects, besides his four important " Entomological Contributions " and his twelve reports as State Entomologist ; probably the thirteenth report, for 1897, is in the printer's hands.

These reports are justly entitled to the highest rank among the scientific publications of the great Empire State. They represent the highest ideal or model of what such reports should be, both from a scientific and a practical standpoint. For typographical neatness and scientific accuracy, for the simple, yet elegant and dignified, way in which dry, scientific facts are made interesting and adapted to the understanding of the agriculturist, Dr. Lintner's reports have not been excelled in the world's entomological literature; such indexes as his reports contain are rare in any literature. One is still more impressed with the scientific and literary attainments of Dr. Lintner, when one understands that, practically, he never had any of the modern facilities, such as are found at many of our experiment stations, for studying the habits of insects ; his office was his literary sanctum, laboratory, museum, library and insectary combined.

Dr. Lintner was a man of quiet and dignified manners, always courteous and pleasant to meet in social intercourse. He was ever ready to impart from his vast fund of knowledge ; and being an expressive speaker, ha always commanded the attention of scientific bodies which he was called upon to address. His frequent addresses before horticultural and agricultural societies in his own and in other States, and farmer's meetings of all kinds, were always full of information.

He had recently been granted a well-earned six month's leave of absence, and was spending it in sunny Italy when the death summons came. In Dr. Lintner the agriculturists of New York found one of their best and most helpful friends, and entomologists the world over, a true and sympathetic co-worker. His name well deserves a place in that list of names enshrined in the hearts of every American economic entomologist— Harris, Fitch, Walsh, Le Baron, Riley—and Lintner.

M. V. SLINGERLAND.

BOOK NOTICES.

TWENTY-FIRST REPORT OF OBSERVATIONS ON INJURIOUS INSECTS and Common Farm Pests during the year 1897, with Methods of Prevention and Remedy. By Eleanor A. Ormerod, London : Simpkin, Marshall, Hamilton, Kent & Co., 1898 (1s. 6d., pp. 160.)

We beg to offer our hearty congratulations to Miss Ormerod on the publication of the twenty first of her Annual Reports. Twenty one years is a long period for anyone to carry on a laborious work, but this talented and indefatigable lady has not only accomplished a most valuable and important work, she has done so without any assistance except that of her late lamented sister, and entirely at her own expense. On this side of the Atlantic, Reports of this character are published by the Government of the Province or State to which they belong, but in England no official recognition has been shown, and though the country has undoubtedly been saved hundreds of thousands of pounds by the instructions given in these Reports to the farmers and gardeners of Great Britain, whereby they have been able to intelligently cope with their insect foes and employ the best methods of prevention of their attacks, yet no aid has been afforded her from the public purse—no recognition of the immense value of her work has been vouchsafed by the powers that be. But while officially ignored, Miss Ormerod's name and work are held in the highest honour throughout Great Britain and treated by the press in every department with the utmost respect ; and in many British colonies and several foreign countries her name is widely known and her talents fully recognized.

A single observer, however able and industrious, could not possibly pay attention to all the manifestations of insect injury throughout the British Isles, but Miss Ormerod has by degrees gathered together a corps of observers in every county and district throughout the United Kingdom; and is kept closely informed of all that causes injury or loss to crops or fruit, and to live stock as well. During the past year she received about 3,000 letters on Entomological subjects, and with the aid of a secretary was enabled to attend to them all. She thus conducts at her own charges what ought to be a Division of Entomology in the Department of Agriculture at London.

In the Report before us thirty-six species of insects are dealt with and figured, their ravages described, and methods of prevention and remedy fully given. Several of them are familiar to us on this side of the Atlantic, e. g. Apple Codlin Moth, Cockroaches, *Xyleborus Xylographus,* Mediterranean Flour-Moth (*Ephestia Kuhniella*), etc.

From the care and accuracy which characterize her descriptions and figures, Miss Ormerod's work is of permanent value to economic Entomologists everywhere, and her reports are always received with welcome and gratitude by those who have the good fortune to obtain them. That she may long be spared to carry on her admirable work is the earnest aspiration of her many friends.

C. J. S. B.

OUT DOOR STUDIES: a Reading Book of Nature Study, by James G. Needham ; 1 vol.
    pp. 90. New York, Cincinnati, Chicago : American Book Company.

These are a series of stories of animal life, written in a charmingly interesting way,
and designed to lead on a youthful reader to observe for himself the wonders of nature
that are everywhere open to his view.   It begins with an account of the common wild
Snap-Dragon or " butter and eggs," and tells how the peculiar structure of the flower is
designed for the visits of the bumble-bees who come for the nectar and carry off the
pollen as well.   The next chapters are on Chipmunks ; Galls and their makers ; the
Golden-rod and its visitors and tenants ; Crows and their Doings ; Dragon-Flies which,
as our readers may remember, have been special objects of the author's studies ; Eye-
spots on insects which aid in the protection of their owners ; and Ant-lions.   Any boy or
girl, who takes up the book and dives a little way into its pages, will surely read on with
delight and when the little volume is closed, be anxious to sally forth and see if he (or
she) cannot find some similar marvels of nature and learn their meaning, while admiring
their beauty.

The book is one of a series designed for the use of school-children who are about to
enter the High Schools.   It is beautifully illustrated with about ninety wood-cuts, the
work of Mrs. Needham, the author's wife, and is provided with an index, and a list of
the scientific names of the animals and plants referred to in the text.

                                                                C. J. S. B.

THE PTEROPHORIDÆ OF NORTH AMERICA, by C H. Fernald, A.M., Ph.D., Revised Edition.
    July 30th, 1898. Boston : Wright & Potter Printing Co., 18 Post Office Square,
    1 vol , 8vo, 84 pp., 9 plates.

Any one who has a copy of Professor Fernald's manual of the Crambidæ of North
America will hardly need to be told that this later work is exactly what every student or
collector of the Micro-depidoptera wants, and that the way is now made easy for him
when he wishes to identify his Plume-moths and learn all that is thus far known about
the North American species.   It is characterized by its author's well-known accuracy and
coneiseness of statement, and is a complete monograph of the family as far as this continent is concerned.   It begins with an historical account of the family in the writings of
European Entomologists and the more recent publications in America.   This is followed
by short chapters on the structure, habits, early stages and systematic position of the
Plume-moths.   The body of the work is taken up with descriptions of the genera and
species, including very useful synopses in each case.   Three of the plates illustrate the
external anatomy and the structure of the wings, the remainder depict the genitalia of
the species.   We miss, however, the exquisite coloured plates that so beautifully illustrated the Crambidæ.   We need not say more than that this is a full and entirely
satisfactory work on the Pterophoridæ and that it maintains the high standard of
excellence that we now expect in the author's scientific productions.

                                                                C. J. S. B.

AGRICULTURE, by C. C. James, 200 pp., George N. Morang, publisher, Toronto, 1898.

It has been the lot of few authors to accomplish satisfactorily what in their preface
they state to have been their object as Prof. James has in preparing the 200 page
Manual of Agriculture which has lately been given to the farmers of Canada.   The
author has had special opportunities, which he has made the most of, of learning not only
what was needed by the intelligent farmers of the Dominion, but what was the best way
of presenting this information to them.   Both as Professor of Chemistry at the Ontario
Agricultural College and as Deputy Minister of Agriculture, Prof. James has been
brought into close contact with the leading and rising farmers of Ontario.   The new
Manual will fill a decided want, which is none the less from the fact that this want may
not have been noticed by some until their attention was drawn to it by seeing how well
it has been filled.

The purpose of the book is "to aid the reader in acquiring a knowledge of the *science* of agriculture, as distinct from the *art* of agriculture, that is, a knowledge of the ' why,' rather than a knowledge of the ' how.' The science of agriculture may be said to consist of a mingling of chemistry, geology, botany, entomology, physiology, bacteriology, and other sciences, in as far as they have a bearing upon agriculture. The aim has been to include but the first principles of these various sciences and to show their application to the art of agriculture. . . . An intelligent understanding of the science underlying the art of agriculture will add much interest to what is otherwise hard work, and as a natural consequence, the pleasure of such work may be greatly increased."

Every day the fact is being recognized more and more that the elements of those sciences which underlie all progress in every branch of agriculture *must* be taught in the Public and High Schools of the country. Already simple nature studies and the first steps in chemistry and geology are taught in the schools of Manitoba and Ontario, and these studies have proved to be not only of use and attractive to the students, but a ready means of creating a bond of sympathy between the teacher and his pupils ; more especially has this been the case with those energetic and restless souls too often now called " bad boys " more, perhaps, from lack of understanding or skill in management on the part of the teacher than from a superabundance of real badness on the part of the taught. Boys play truant because they find more to interest them outside the school than at their desks. If therefore the things which appertain to out-of-doors can be brought inside the schoolroom without robbing them of too much of their outside flavor, they will be a sure bait to catch the attention of all bright healthy boys and girls. Their study will arouse interest at once and the habits of concentration, power to observe and compare, and the necessary development of the faculties of exact thought and accurate description will be available for all other branches of study with which the pupil is engaged.

This book may be used as a text-book in High Schools and Public Schools. It would be well indeed for Canada if its use were made compulsory in every school in the land. The great truths laid before the reader are presented in a simple straightforward manner intelligible to all. The subjects are so skilfully arranged and concisely stated that a surprising amount of accurate information is given in this small octavo of 200 pages. The value of this simple knowledge to practical men is not, I believe, overstated when I aver that if all the farmers in Canada would read this little work, as they most certainly should, its appearance would mark an epoch in the history of the Dominion, which would be made manifest to all by an enormous increase in the crops and wealth of the whole country.

The scope of work is shown by the following brief epitome of subjects : Part I. treats of the Plant, its development, structure, food and functions ; Part II , Soil, its nature and treatment ; Part III., Crops of the Field ; Part IV., The Garden, Orchard and Vineyard ; Part V., Live Stock and Dairying ; Part VI., Bees, Birds, Forests, Roads and the Home.

In these different sections the insect and fungous enemies of crops are treated at some length. This little volume is bound in cloth and well got up ; although some of the illustrations are rather roughly executed, it is on the whole most excellent and for the price, 25 cents is a marvel of cheapness.—J. F.

THE WINTER FOOD OF THE CHICKADEE, Bulletin 54, New Hampshire College of Agriculture, by Clarence M. Weed—There is something particularly charming about those confiding little feathered denizens of the woods which brave our cold northern winters and stay to cheer us at a time of the year when there is so little animated life. The Chickadee or Black capped Tit-mouse *(Parus atricapillus)* is at once one of the most cheerful as well as one of the most useful of our common native winter birds. What a bright, busy, happy sight is presented by a flock of these little friends ; for they are all friends these little balls of black satin and grey down, they are far too busy and well employed to waste time in fighting. Satan has a hard time of it in "some mischief finding " for these little fellows to do, for their hands are never idle, as they hurry through the woods, running up or around the trunks of trees or hanging head down-wards from a slender twig, never still for more than an instant, as they peer into every tuft of moss, every crack or cranny in the bark, along the twigs, under the bud scales of deciduous trees or among the leaves of evergreens, talking cheerfully to themselves and each other all the time as they carry out their useful mission in clearing the trees and shrubs of countless insect enemies ; woe to the luckless caterpillar, chrysalis, spider, or beetle which comes within the range of their sharp black eyes. Nothing comes amiss to these insatiable hunters, from the minute, shining black eggs of an aphis to the fat chrys-alis of a Cecropia Emperor Moth ; with deft blows the hard sharp beak soon penetrates the thick silken cocoon and in a very short time the marauder is away looking for another victim. Dr. Clarence Weed publishes in this interesting bulletin the results of some careful investigations which he has carried out as to the winter food of the chick-adee. He shows that more than one half of the food of this bird during the winter months consists of insects, a large portion being in the form of eggs. Vegetation of various sorts made up a little less than a quarter of the food, and two-thirds of this quarter consisted of the buds or bud scales which were believed to have been accidentally eaten along with the eggs of plant-lice. These eggs made up more than one-fifth of the entire food and formed the most remarkable element of the bill of fare. This destruc-tion of myriads of eggs of the plant-lice which infest fruit, shade and forest trees is probably the most important service which the chickadee renders during his winter residence. More than 450 of these eggs are sometimes eaten by one bird in a single day as well as the eggs of many other kinds of our most important insect enemies of the forest, garden and orchard. Dr. Weed figures in his bulletin some twigs of various trees upon which the eggs of insects have been deposited. Among these are represented the egg masses of the tent caterpillars and the Fall Canker-worm, both of which are favourite foods of these useful little birds. In addition to eggs or insects, many caterpillars and other stages in the development of insects are destroyed. One interesting figure shows the winter cases of a small caterpillar, closely hidden behind apple buds ; these are, in all probability, those of the Eye-spotted Bud-moth, sometimes one of the most trouble-some and destructive enemies of the fruit-grower. This bulletin shows much careful work in a field which has been, to a large extent, neglected by entomologists, and Dr. Weed should receive the thanks of all lovers of birds for the proofs which he furnishes of the real benefits we receive from these little favorites. It was pleasing for some people to know and most people to think that these birds were useful, but it is now possible to prove it to all who are willing to learn.—J. F.

SCUDDER'S REVISION OF THE MELANOPLI.

One of the most important works on Entomology which has been issued by an American author in recent years is that entitled a "Revision of the Orthopteran Group Melanopli (Acridiidæ) with Special Reference to North American Forms" by Samuel Hubbard Scudder.* It is more important because it deals with a representative North American group of insects whose members, between April and November, leap from our pathway in profusion whether we stroll through open woodland, sunny meadow, or along the roadside, and yet of whose classification and nomenclature the greatest confusion has heretofore existed. It was only another example showing the truth of the old saying : " that the common things around us are those of which we are most densely ignorant."

True, of one of the members of the group, the "Rocky Mountain Locust," *Melanoplus spretus* (Thos.), more has, perhaps, been written than of any other insect on earth, yet it is but one of 207 of its kind which are described at length by Mr. Scudder. The others are scattered far and wide over the continent of North America and the descriptions of the ninety-two species hitherto rightfully known to science were distributed through an almost equal range of literature. No better evidence of the need of the " Revision " is necessary than to know that after a careful examination of nearly 8,000 specimens, 7,000

*Proc. U.S. Nat. Mus., XX., 1897, No. 1124, pp. 1-421. Plates I.-XXVI.

of which belonged to the single genus Melanoplus, the author has in it reduced forty-seven supposed species to synonyms and has established eighteen new genera and described for the first time 115 species.

With a group whose members are so closely kin as those of the Melanopli it has heretofore been almost an impossibility for the specialist—let alone the tyro—to satisfy his conscience as to the status of a specimen which he might have in hand. The available literature was so scattered and the different authors had seized upon so many different characters as representing what appeared to them the most striking structural features, that the whole mess was worse than a Chinese puzzle. By seizing upon the variations of the abdominal appendages of the male as the most salient features showing specific rank, and by publishing actual drawings of two different views of the male abdomen of each of the 207 species, Mr. Scudder has done much to render possible the ready identification of each species—a task which otherwise would have been very difficult, owing to the size of the group and the close similarity of many of its members. Analytical keys to genera, and to species where the genus is not monotypic are also given, and add much to the value of the work; as does also the full list of localities from which each species has heretofore been taken.

Taking into consideration its size and importance, the defects of the "Revision" are very few. The one thing which the tyro will find most lacking is a glossary of the technical terms. In a work of the kind these are necessarily numerous, and though they may be plain to the author and to specialists, to the beginner they are often extremely confusing. Even a figure of a typical locust with all the parts named would have been a great aid. A tendency to multiply species can here and there be noted, as on p. 138, where *M. bivitattus* is separated from *M. femoratus* only by the color of the hind tibiae, which is an exceedingly variable character.

More might have been added along ecological lines, but this is a work for the future which the student of the group can now take up with renewed energy. For before one can write of a species he must have a name to handle it by; something which in the case of many of the members of this group has heretofore been lacking. Now, by using a little care and accustoming himself to the technical terms, the student can, by the aid of the "Revision," soon bring order out of chaos and label his Melanopli with correctness and despatch. In conclusion, it may be said that any one who will use the work will soon conclude that the aim of the author, "to enlarge and systematize our knowledge of this important group as a basis for future studies," has been well and successfully accomplished.
W. S. B.

A TEXT-BOOK OF ENTOMOLOGY, including the Anatomy, Physiology, Embryology and Metamorphoses of Insects, for use in agricultural and technical schools and colleges, as well as by the working entomologist. By Alpheus S. Packard, M.D., Ph.D. New York: The Macmillan Company, 66 Fifth avenue. 1898. (Price $4.50.)

The book is primarily divided into three parts. Part I. being devoted to morphology and physiology, Part II. to embryology, and Part III. to metamorphoses. Under these divisions Dr. Packard treats his subject as follows: Position of insects in the animal kingdom. Relation of insects to other arthropoda. Insects (hexapoda). The head and its appendages. The thorax and its appendages. The abdomen and its appendages. The armature of insects. The colors of insects. Muscular system. Nervous system. Sensory organs. Digestive canal and its appendages. Glandular and excretory appendages of the digestive canal. Defensive or repugnatorial scent glands. Alluring or scent glands. Organs of circulation. Blood tissue. Respiratory organs. Organs of reproduction. Development of the egg, larva, pupa and imago. Hypermetamorphism. Summary of the facts and suggestions as to the causes of metamorphism.

The volume contains 729 pages, including a carefully prepared index, 654 figures and numerous valuable bibliographical lists. We certainly have nothing in the way of entomological literature, in this country, that will cover the field of development of insects as will this last work of Dr. Packard. Not only the teacher and student, but the educated men and women of the world at large who may desire to know more of the anatomy, physiology and metamorphoses of insects, will find in this work the very aid that is most desired. With this work and some other like Comstock's Manual, any student of ordinary ability can begin at the very foundation of entomology and work his way upward, fully as easily as has heretofore been possible in zoology. The advent of this work certainly marks the trend of entomological studies in America. In future, except in some particular groups, we are to have less species-making and more studies of the development and transformations of those already well known in the adult stage, as well as of their inter-relations with each other and with other organisms about them. We shall not study dried corpses, alone, but life in connection therewith, and the possession of pinned specimens of the adults in our cabinets will only increase our desire to know more of the problems of their existence   F. M. W.

HANDBOOK OF INSECTS INJURIOUS TO ORCHARD AND BUSH FRUIT. By Eleanor A. Ormerod. London : Simpkin, Marshall & Co., Sept., 1898. 8 vo., 286 pp.

The excellent work which has been done for economic entomology by Miss Ormerod, particularly in England, but also in many other parts of the world, is well known to every one. Her valuable annual reports are eagerly looked for every year by all interested in the practical application of the study of insects for the prevention of their injuries to crops. We have just received from this talented authoress another evidence of her unselfish labours for the good of her countrymen. The above named volume is in reality a compendium of the original observations made during the last twenty-one years by Miss Ormerod and her correspondents, together with the latest results and the most approved remedies for the various pests of large and small fruits.

As in all former publications bearing Miss Ormerod's name, the arrangement of the subjects, for convenience of reference, the presswork and the general get-up of the volume, bear the stamp of a most careful and tasteful masterhand. The different fruit crops treated of are : Apple, cherry, currant, gooseberry, medlar, nut, pear, plum, quince, raspberry and strawberry. At the end is a list of the fruit crops infested by insects with the names of the insect infestations ; the subjects are arranged alphabetically ; and after the name of each tree or crop mentioned in the work the names of each of the infestations to which it is liable in England are classified under subordinate headings as Bark, Blossoms, Fruit, Leaves, Shoots, Wood according to the nature of the attack. The insects are given with their scientific and popular name and so far as possible are arranged together as to kinds, as Aphides, Beetles, Moths, etc., with the number of the page of the detailed observation in the volume. In four instances where the pests are causes of much mischief to several kinds of crops, the infestation appears under its own name. These exceptions are Earwig, Red Spider, Root-knot Eelworm and Wasps.

Particular mention must be made of the excellence of the illustrations which seem to be perfect types of what such illustrations should be in works on insects for the use of practical fruitgrowers.   J. F.

THE BUTTERFLY BOOK, a popular guide to a knowledge of the Butterflies of North America, By W. J. Holland, D. D., Chancellor of the Western University of Pennsylvania, etc., Pittsburg, Pa. One vol. 4to., pp. 382· [Price $3.00 postage prepaid. Copies may be procured from the Author, or William Briggs, 29-33 Richmond Street, West, Toronto.]

It is with great pleasure that we announce the publication of this beautiful popular book on the Butterflies of North America. Hitherto the vast number of young people who begin collecting insects have had their enthusiasm sorely chilled by their inability to find names for their specimens and have soon given up the pursuit in despair. Now, there need be no difficulty as far as the butterflies are concerned. In the handsome volumn before us there are no less than forty-eight beautiful colored plates, produced by a new process from photographic representations of specimens from the Author's cabinets and on them are depicted over a thousand butterflies, belonging to 527 species. The colors are remarkably true to nature and a child should have no difficulty in identifying any specimen that he may capture from the plates alone. In the letter press brief de scriptions are given first of the characteristics of the genus, in all its stages, with a wood cut shewing the neuration, and then of each species, setting forth the colours and markings, size, &c., of the butterfly, the early stages where known and the geographical distribution ; references are also given to the works of Edwards, Scudder and other authors, where fuller information can be obtained. As an introduction to the work illustrated chapters describe in a popular and interesting manner, the life-history and anatomy of butterflies, how to capture, prepare and preserve specimens, their classification and the principal books that have been published upon them in North America. Interspersed through the volume are short papers for the most part of an amusing character in which the author varies the monotony of descriptive matter by telling some of his experiences or relating some interesting facts regarding these beautiful creatures. We heartily commend the work to our readers and earnestly hope that it may become widely distributed amongst all lovers of nature throughout North America.   C. J. S. B.

WILLIAM HAGUE HARRINGTON, F.R.S.C.

One of the excellent portraits prefixed to this volume is that of Mr. William Hague Harrington, one of the ablest entomologists in Canada. He was born at Sydney, Cape Breton, on the 19th of April, 1852, and received his early education first at a private school and subsequently at the Sydney Academy, where he distinguished himself by close application in all the lines of study, and particularly in mathematics. In 1870 he removed to Ottawa and on the 30th of November of that year was appointed to a clerkship in the Post Office Department, where he has remained ever since, gradually rising until now he is chief clerk in the money order branch. Mr. Harrington has always been an enthusiastic naturalist and in 1879 he joined with his friend, Dr. James Fletcher, in the formation of the Ottawa Field Naturalists' Club, and has continued to take an active interest in it ever since. During the same year he was elected for the first time a member of the Council of the Entomological Society of Ontario, and has continued to hold some office in it ever since ; in 1884, 5 and 6 and again in 1892 he was its delegate to the Royal Society of Canada ; in 1891 Vice-President and from 1893 to 1895 President of the Society ; for some years past he has also been one of the Editing Committee of the *Canadian Entomologist*.

Beginning with the year 1879, he has been a regular contributor to these Annual Reports. Among his more important and valuable papers may be mentioned those on Elateridæ (1879), Rhyncophora—Weevils (1880), Some Fungi-Eaters (1881), Long-stings, House-flies, Chrysomelidæ (1882), Insects affecting Hickory (1883), Saw-flies (1884), Ants, Wasps and Bees (1885), Insects infesting Maple-trees (1886), The nuptials of Thalessa (1887), Insects affecting willows (1889), Hymenoptera Parasitica (1890), Notes on Japanese insects (1891), Uroceridæ (1893), Notes on Canadian Coleoptera (1894), Winter insects from Swamp-moss (1895) Beetles on Beech (1896), and his Presidential Addresses in 1893 and 4. During all these twenty years he has continually furnished papers of a more technical and scientific character to the pages of the *Canadian Entomologist*, and has described a considerable number of new species of Hymenoptera. His work is so thorough and accurate that it has been awarded the highest praise by those competent to judge.

In 1894 Mr. Harrington was elected a Fellow of the Royal Society of Canada. He is now in the full maturity of his powers, and, if his life be spared, we may feel sure that the coming years will continue to bear fruit and that Entomological Science will be enriched by the outpouring of his accumulated stores of learning, experience and observation.

JOHN DEARNESS.

The other portrait at the beginning of this volume is an excellent likeness of Mr. John Dearness, Inspector of Schools for East Middlesex, President of the Ontario Educational Association, member of the Educational Council for the Province, and from 1895 to 1897 President of the Entomological Society of Ontario. Mr. Dearness was born at Hamilton, Ontario, in 1852, his parents having come to Canada from the Orkney Islands. His early years were spent on a farm near St. Marys, where no doubt he imbibed in his youthful days the love of natural history which he has cherished ever since. His primary education was obtained at the local schools, from which he proceeded to the Provincial Normal School; there he greatly distinguished himself throughout the course and left with the highest honors and certificates. He at once began his professional work as the teacher of a cross-roads log schoolhouse in the country, but was soon promoted to be principal of a village school and then of a town school; after a brief period in a high school he was appointed to the important position of inspector in 1874, having gone through all these gradations of scholastic work in the marvellously short space of three years. He has now been performing the duties of an inspector for nearly quarter of a century, and is also Lecturer on Botany and Zoology in the Western University of Ontario at London. He was one of the editors of the series of "Royal Canadian Readers," and in 1896 was appointed a member of the first Educational Council of this Province.

Though his life has been so fully devoted to educational work, Mr. Dearness has yet found time for the practical study of natural science, especially of mycology, and has applied his leisure hours to the formation of a collection of fungi, which is unsurpassed in Canada, containing as it does a very large number of species new to science. For many years he has taken a warm interest in the Entomological Society of Ontario and since 1892 has held an official position upon its Council as Director, Vice-President and President. His addresses when filling the presidential chair have been published in these Annual Reports and must be familiar to our readers; they treat to a large extent, as might naturally be expected, of the educational value of natural history and the methods by which the study of insects can be successfully introduced into country schools. His scientific writings, however, have consisted for the most part of papers read before the Microscopical and Botanical Sections of the Society and have treated of toadstools and mushrooms rather than of bugs and butterflies. Being of the same age as Mr. Harrington and full of health and vigor, we may form similar expectations of his future work in his chosen fields of both science and education.   C.J.S.B.

AN ACT TO FURTHER IMPROVE THE SAN JOSE SCALE ACT.

Assented to April 1st, 1899.

Her Majesty, by and with the advice and consent of the Legislative Assembly of the Province of Ontario, enacts as follows :   :

1. This Act may be cited as *The San Jose Scale Amendment Act.*   Short title.

2. Section 7 of *The San Jose Scale Act, 1898,* is hereby amended by 61 V. c 33, s. 7
adding the following sub-section : .   amended.

(*a*) If, in the case of an orchard or collection of plants, the inspector finds   Destruction of diseased
scale on plants located in several different parts of the orchard or collection,   plants.
and decides that it is advisable in the public interest to destroy all the plants
in such orchard or in any part or parts thereof and so reports to the Minister,
the Minister may direct that an examination or inspection shall be made by
an additional inspector, and upon their advice in writing he may direct that
all the plants in such orchard or such collection of plants or in such part or
parts thereof shall be destroyed without requiring that every plant in the said
orchard or collection shall be first examined.

3. The owner or proprietor of any nursery shall not send out or permit   Plants to be fumigated before leaving nursery.
any plant to be removed from his nursery without the same being first fumigated by hydrocyanic acid gas in accordance with regulations prescribed by
order of the Lieutenant-Governor-in-Council.

4. No person shall sell or dispose of or offer for sale any plant obtained,   Sale of plants before fumigation prohibited
taken, or sent out from a nursery unless the said plant has previously been
fumigated in accordance with these regulations.

5. In case the inspector finds scale in any nursery and so reports to the   Scale in a nursery—stock not to be removed without leave of Minister.
Minister, the Minister may thereupon inform, by writing, the owner or proprietor or manager of said nursery of the existence of scale in his nursery, and
the owner or proprietor or manager of said nursery shall not thereafter permit
any plant or plants to be removed from the said nursery until he is notified
in writing from the Minister that the inspector has reported to the Minister
that it is safe in the public interest to permit the said nursery stock to be
removed after fumigation.

6. This Act and *The San Jose Scale Act, 1898,* shall be read and construed   Act incorporated with 61 V. c 33
as one Act.

(For the San Jose Scale Act, 1898, see Report of 1897)

REGULATIONS FOR THE FUMIGATION OF NURSERY STOCK.

Toronto, April 7th, 1899.

The following regulations have been prescribed by Order of the Lieutenant-Governor in Council in accordance with the provisions of the *San Jose Scale Amendment Act*, passed April 1st, 1899 :

1. Fumigation must be carried on in a box, room, compartment, or house suitable for the purpose, which must be air-tight and capable of rapid ventilation. The owner or proprietor will notify the Minister as soon as preparation for fumigation is complete. The Minister will thereupon order an inspection of the fumigation appliances. No fumigation under the Act is to be carried on until such inspection has been made and a satisfactory report sent to the Minister.

2. The Inspector, after examining and measuring the box or house, or other compartment in which fumigation is to be carried on, will prescribe the amounts of material to be used for every fumigation, and the instructions as to the same must be carefully followed out. The Inspector may, if thought advisable, supply the material for each fumigation in weighed packages.

3. The fumigation house (which shall include all apparatus or appliances used in the fumigation, such as generators, etc.) is to be subject to the orders of the Minister on the recommendation of the Inspector. Subject to the approval of the Inspector the fumigation house may be on other lots than those on which the nursery stock are growing.

4. The fumigation is to be by hydrocyanic acid gas produced according to the instructions of the Inspector and from such formulas as he prescribes for the purpose.

5. The fumigation is to be continued for a period of not less than forty-five minutes. After the expiration of this time or longer, and when fumigation is complete, the house is to be thoroughly ventilated for fifteen minutes at least.

6. No person is to be allowed to enter the fumigating house until after the ventilation period has expired. Entering before may prove injurious, if not fatal, as the gas is a deadly poison.

7. The fumigation of buds and scions may be done in fumigation boxes of not less than thirty cubic feet capacity, the same to be subject to inspection and approval.

8. Immediately after inspection of the fumigation house, the Inspector will report to the Minister, and the Minister or the Inspector will thereupon give permission in writing for the owner or proprietor to begin fumigation.

9. The owner or proprietor of every nursery will attach to every box and to every package of nursery stock a certificate as follows, and he will furnish every purchaser who so desires a copy of the same.

CERTIFICATE OF FUMIGATION.

This is to certify that this package of nursery stock consisting of...............

. . . .

. . . .

was properly fumigated on the........day of............, 1899, in accordance with the regulations laid down by the Ontario Minister of Agriculture. in accordance with 62nd Victoria, chapter 35.

INDEX.

Lightning Source UK Ltd.
Milton Keynes UK
UKHW010335110119
335176UK00011B/933/P